GREAT EVENTS
FROM
HISTORY II

GREAT EVENTS FROM HISTORY II

Arts and Culture
Series

Volume 2
1922-1937

Edited by
FRANK N. MAGILL

SALEM PRESS

Pasadena, California   Englewood Cliffs, New Jersey

∞ The paper used in these volumes conforms to the
American National Standard for Permanence of Paper
for Printed Library Materials, Z39.48-1984.

Library of Congress Cataloging-in-Publication Data
Great events from history II. Arts and culture series / edited by Frank N. Magill.
    p.   cm.
    Includes bibliographical references and index.
    1. Arts, Modern—20th century. 2. Arts and so-
ciety—History—20th century. I. Magill, Frank Northen,
1907-   . II. Title: Great events from history. 2. Arts
and culture series.

NX456.G72   1993
700′.9′04—dc20
ISBN 0-89356-807-4 (set)   93-28381
ISBN 0-89356-809-0 (volume 2)   CIP

LIST OF EVENTS IN VOLUME II

GREAT EVENTS FROM HISTORY II

GREAT EVENTS
FROM
HISTORY II

ELIOT PUBLISHES *THE WASTE LAND*

Category of event: Literature
Time: 1922
Locale: London, England

T. S. Eliot, in collaboration with fellow American poet and editor Ezra Pound, published a new kind of collage poem composed of fragments from many languages and mythologies

Principal personages:
 T. S. ELIOT (1888-1965), an American poet who moved to London and changed the shape of poetry
 EZRA POUND (1885-1972), a literary activist, poet, and editor who produced the final version of *The Waste Land*

Summary of Event

Between the turn of the century, when Edwardian style dominated English cultural life, and the end of World War I, after millions of young Englishmen had died in the horribly bloody conflicts of no-man's land, a radically new artistic style emerged. Generally known as modernism, this new direction in the arts took its cue from such artists as the Italian Futurists (a group that embraced the new technology) and the French Symbolists (especially Paul Valéry and Jules Laforgue). Modernism also drew inspiration from such sources as the new architecture of Frank Lloyd Wright in America and the new technology as represented by the American entrepreneur Henry Ford.

Skyscrapers were going up in New York, jazz was being played in New Orleans, Chicago, and New York, and Pablo Picasso and Georges Braque were inventing cubism in their Parisian studios. The world was suddenly moving to new rhythms and seeing itself in terms of new imagery. The literary practitioners were among the last to absorb this radically new way of making art, perhaps owing to the innately conservative nature of language itself. Literary change occurred quickly during this period, however, as English writers in particular began to discover the French Symbolists and Asian poetry, especially the haiku of the Japanese. Out of this preoccupation with imagery of the kind favored in much Asian poetry, a literary school known as Imagism emerged in and around London.

The most important Imagist was a young American poet named Ezra Pound, who had taken upon himself the formidable task of changing the whole direction of poetry in the English language. A brilliant linguist and radical thinker, Pound drew upon all his cultural resources, as well as his irrepressible energy, to put the Imagist movement on the center of the literary map. He became the foreign editor for a number of American literary magazines, most importantly *Poetry*, which had been founded in Chicago in 1912. It was at Pound's insistence, for example, that the first American publication of poems by Robert Frost and T. S. Eliot occurred. Had Pound not been on the scene, the literary life of London—and all of the English-speaking world—would have been vastly different.

T. S. Eliot had arrived in London in the summer of 1914 after his attempts to study at Marburg, Germany, had been cut short by the outbreak of World War I. Eliot had already studied languages and philosophy at Harvard University and at the Sorbonne. A remarkably gifted student, Eliot was the scion of a distinguished American family. His grandfather had founded Washington University in St. Louis, Missouri (where Eliot grew up), and the family traced its line all the way back to the *Mayflower*. Eliot had been reading and translating French poetry on his own and had been translating the works of Dante Alighieri and the classical Greek and Roman poets. At that point in his life, though, Eliot imagined himself having a career as a professional philosopher. Poetry was only a sideline, although an important one.

Once in London, Eliot quickly joined a literary circle that included the Bloomsbury Group of Leonard and Virginia Woolf as well as such writers as Stephen Spender, Richard Aldington, Wyndham Lewis, William Butler Yeats, and the ubiquitous Pound. Eliot also fell under the spell of Vivien Haigh-Wood, a vivacious, high-strung, and utterly outspoken young woman who was strikingly different from the socialites and debutantes Eliot had known in Boston and Cambridge.

Eliot married Vivien in 1915, the same year that his first important poem, "The Love Song of J. Alfred Prufrock," appeared in the pages of *Poetry*. Within months of their marriage, Eliot realized that he had made a tragic mistake. Vivien had an affair with the philosopher Bertrand Russell, and her physical condition, aggravated by bouts of neuralgia and painful menstrual cycles, deteriorated steadily. The couple's married life, carried on in a series of cramped and dingy London flats and drafty country cottages, took its toll on both partners. Eliot and his wife were dependent on a whole stable of London specialists, and the young poet was forced to moonlight at various teaching and editorial jobs to supplement his meager salary as a clerk in the Foreign Correspondence Department of Lloyd's Bank. Although some critics have dismissed any claims of autobiographical details in *The Waste Land*, it stretches credibility to assume that Eliot's relationship with Vivien does not account, in some way, for the many frustrating and doomed relationships featured in the poem.

When Eliot began *The Waste Land* in late January or early February of 1921, his own health and that of Vivien were seriously impaired. Besides help from London doctors and a strict dietary regimen, Vivien also had recourse to a French clinic outside Paris. Eliot continued writing during the whole period, although the emerging poem, which he called "He Do the Police in Different Voices," was a sprawling affair with many quotations from the London music halls and off-color snippets from World War I songs. In November, 1921, Eliot's health had deteriorated to the point that he entered a psychiatric clinic in Lausanne, Switzerland, where he gained momentary peace. Whole sections of the poem were completed in Lausanne.

Eliot returned to London in the early months of 1922, and the tragic pattern of his life continued in full force. By this time, he had no idea what to do with the poem, which had grown in length to more than one thousand lines. In sheer desperation, he turned the typescript over to Ezra Pound, who instantly recognized its brilliance— and its purple passages. Pound proceeded to remove all the extraneous material, preserving only those passages where he heard Eliot's distinctive voice—and the passages in which Eliot had borrowed lines or phrases from a foreign text (in Greek, Latin, French, German, or Sanskrit).

Eliot agreed completely with Pound's emendations, dedicated the poem to him, and first published it in the pages of a new literary magazine he was editing, *Criterion*, in October of 1922. In November, the poem made its first American appearance in the pages of *The Dial* magazine, and in December, *The Waste Land* was published as a separate book by Liveright Publishers in New York. Finally, in September, 1923, Hogarth Press, owned by Leonard and Virginia Woolf, brought out a separate English edition of the work.

Impact of Event

T. S. Eliot was certainly conversant with the intrinsic difficulties of his masterwork. In fact, for the Liveright and Hogarth editions, he prepared a special set of scholarly notes to help guide perplexed readers and curious critics. Those notes, by themselves, have accounted for the spilling of oceans of critical ink, as scholars have struggled to offer a coherent theory of this five-part poem numbering 434 lines. It is no exaggeration to say that the shelves of an impressive library could easily be filled with materials about Eliot and *The Waste Land*. Major critics have depended on this work to make their mark in the world of academe, as even a cursory glance at the bibliography of Eliot and *The Waste Land* would suggest. A few notable titles in this connection include such books as F. R. Leavis' *New Bearings in English Poetry* (1932), F. O. Matthiessen's *The Achievement of T. S. Eliot* (1935), Northrop Frye's *T. S. Eliot* (1963), George Williamson's *A Reader's Guide to T. S. Eliot* (1966), and Gover Smith's *T. S. Eliot's Poetry and Plays* (1974) and *The Waste Land* (1984).

The point here is that *The Waste Land* has functioned as a kind of critical benchmark for all modern poetry and for the criticism that poetry engendered. *The Waste Land* simply occupies a unique and privileged place in the landscape of twentieth century poetry. The so-called New Criticism—with its emphases on irony, allusion, and formalism—would be unthinkable without Eliot and *The Waste Land*, the poem that most perfectly justifies and exemplifies the New Criticism's ideals.

Of course, when the poem first appeared, it rocked the literary establishment. Absolutely no one was prepared for the linguistic and thematic complexity of the poem. Its themes of sexual boredom, sterility, loss of faith, and the destruction of civilization, however, appealed instantly to a generation that had seen the virtual bankruptcy of European civilization—and the horrors of World War I. With its collage of bits and pieces on the printed page, the poem spoke eloquently and convincingly about the nature of loss and pain in twentieth century life. College undergraduates memorized the poem, and literary people quoted it constantly, a detail recorded by the novelist Evelyn Waugh in his fictional chronicle of the period, *Brideshead Revisited* (1945).

In America, the poem had a profound and immediate effect on the literary imaginations of the most important writers of the period. F. Scott Fitzgerald's pivotal novel, *The Great Gatsby* (1925), significantly depended upon the presence of a wasteland of ashes that defined and enclosed the metropolis of New York. Like Eliot, Fitzgerald also delineated a world where true love was inevitably frustrated and sexual corruption was commonplace. Other Americans, including the poet Hart Crane, reacted violently against Eliot and tried to write optimistic poetry. In fact, Crane's *The Bridge* (1930) failed precisely because he could not find a myth to justify America, even though he tried valiantly, and, interestingly enough, adopted Eliot's trademark techniques of literary collage and allusion. Eliot did, though, succeed in planting the idea of the long poem in the minds of American poets. Besides Crane's *The Bridge*, *The Waste Land* undoubtedly helped to inspire William Carlos Williams' four-volume epic *Paterson* (1946-1951) and Charles Olson's *The Maximus Poems* (1960).

A long British poem, W. H. Auden's *For the Time Being: A Christmas Oratorio* (1944), with its depiction of a bleak and distorted landscape and its unremittingly ironic posture, also owed something to Eliot's work. This same kind of wasteland, perhaps the dominant archetype of twentieth century literature, provided the backdrop for Samuel Beckett's *Waiting for Godot* (1955). Beckett's famous characters, Vladimir and Estragon, would have been absolutely at home in the zombie-world Eliot created in *The Waste Land*. In like manner, Eliot's vision of London as a place where sexual corruption provided a clue to the larger and more pervasive spiritual breakdowns can be detected rather obviously in a novel such as Martin Amis' *London Fields* (1989), in which love, art, money, and sex are transmuted into a complicated calculus of betrayal.

The Waste Land touched imaginations and sensibilities precisely because its symbolic meaning provided a significant way to encode a world that, largely, had failed to make much sense. There is great irony in the fact that one of the most pessimistic works of the century may have preserved a small measure of the optimism that Eliot's audience desperately needed. Knowledge is indeed power, and *The Waste Land*, for all its darkness, clearly empowered its readers in a way that set it apart from all other poems of the century.

Bibliography

Ackroyd, Peter. *T. S. Eliot: A Life*. New York: Simon & Schuster, 1984. Ackroyd, an award-winning biographer who has written other important biographies of British literary figures, may have done his finest work in this lucid and articulate account of Eliot's life, which reads like a finely crafted novel. Ackroyd is especially good at analyzing Eliot's complex sexual attitudes and his relationships with women, especially Vivien. This biography can be read profitably by specialists or beginners.

Brooker, H. Ralph, and Mary Ann Bentley. *Reading* The Waste Land: *Modernism and the Limits of Interpretation.* Amherst: University of Massachusetts Press, 1990. Aside from the fact that this book is a uniquely successful scholarly collaboration, it offers the reader a part-by-part analysis of the poem—all placed in the context of modernism and its inherent difficulties.

Knoll, Robert E., ed. *Storm over* The Waste Land. Chicago: Scott, Foresman, 1964. Knoll has collected some of the famous articles that damn or praise *The Waste Land.* Knoll's book forces the reader to grapple with the important aesthetic issues raised by the poem, especially the question of its fragmentary structure. Contains notable essays by Delmore Schwartz and Karl Shapiro.

Kenner, Hugh, ed. *T. S. Eliot: A Collection of Critical Essays.* Englewood Cliffs, N.J.: Prentice-Hall, 1962. This collection includes essays by R. P. Blackmur, Allen Tate, William Empson, and Denis Donoghue, but readers will want to focus on F. R. Leavis' "*The Waste Land*" and George Morris' "Marie, Marie, Hold on Tight."

Williamson, George. *A Reader's Guide to T. S. Eliot: A Poem-by-Poem Analysis.* New York: Noonday Press, 1953. With any other poet, one would be tempted to say that a reader's guide would oversimplify the poetry. Yet Eliot's intrinsic difficulty, especially in *The Waste Land*, makes the clarity and common sense of Williamson's book invaluable. Williamson's book is the essential point of departure for any study of the poet.

Daniel L. Guillory

Cross-References
Freud Inaugurates a Fascination with the Unconscious (1899), p. 19; Rilke's *Duino Elegies* Depicts Art as a Transcendent Experience (1911), p. 281; Harriet Monroe Founds *Poetry* Magazine (1912), p. 314; The Imagist Movement Shakes Up Poetry (1912), p. 326; Yeats Publishes *The Wild Swans at Coole* (1917), p. 440; Pound's *The Cantos* Is Published (1917), p. 445; Joyce's *Ulysses* Epitomizes Modernism in Fiction (1922), p. 555; Surrealism Is Born (1924), p. 604; Pound Wins the Bollingen Prize (1949), p. 1443.

THE SOVIET UNION BANS ABSTRACT ART

Category of event: Art
Time: 1922-1934
Locale: Moscow, Union of Soviet Socialist Republics

Initial hopes for a true revolution in art in the new Soviet Union were dashed when the leaders of the Communist Party centralized control of artistic productions and outlawed all forms of art except Socialist Realism

Principal personages:

VLADIMIR ILICH LENIN (1870-1924), the first leader of the Soviet Union, whose conservative tastes in art influenced policies regarding artists and their works

JOSEPH STALIN (1879-1953), the second leader of the Soviet Union, who established Socialist Realism as the only approved form of Soviet art

VLADIMIR TATLIN (1885-1953), the foremost Soviet sculptor to adopt constructivist principles for his art

KAZIMIR MALEVICH (1878-1935), an abstract artist who established the Suprematist school of art shortly before the 1917 Revolution

ANATOLY LUNACHARSKY (1875-1933), the first commissar of education in the Soviet Union, under whose supervision the Department of Fine Arts was established to oversee the production of art in the Soviet Union

WASSILY KANDINSKY (1866-1944), a prominent artist and theoretician who promoted abstract art and directed the Museum of Pictorial Culture in Moscow for several years after the revolution

MARC CHAGALL (1887-1985), an abstract artist who emigrated from the Soviet Union when restrictions began to be imposed on artists

Summary of Event

When, in 1934, the First Congress of the Union of Soviet Writers decreed that Socialist Realism was to be the only acceptable form of artistic expression in the Soviet Union, the final nail was driven into the coffin of Soviet abstract art. The pronouncement was not unexpected, for abstract artists who had been heartened by the promises of new freedom under the Communists had already seen their early hopes dashed by a series of actions that were making it increasingly difficult for them to survive and practice their art in the Soviet Union.

Nevertheless, the declaration was a particularly insidious blow to men such as Vladimir Tatlin, Kazimir Malevich, and Wassily Kandinsky, whose rise to prominence in the decades before the 1934 congress had signaled a true revolution in Russian art. Under their leadership, men and women in what was now the Soviet Union had become part of the larger European artistic community and were advancing the boundaries of artistic expression in a country that had had a history of imposing on its artists long before the Communists had come to power.

During the latter half of the nineteenth century, a group of artists who came to be known as the Wanderers rebelled against the classical style being taught in Russian academies; rejecting both classicism and the new notion of art for art's sake, the Wanderers focused on the folk aspects of Russian life, and embedded in their realistic works a sense of social consciousness. At almost the same time, a group of young Russian artists were discovering the new theories emerging in other European countries. Reacting against both the academies and the Wanderers, these artists brought various forms of abstractionism into the Russian salons and museums. This group reached its zenith in the years immediately before the 1917 Revolution swept the Communists into power. Experimentation became the byword for these artists; Impressionism, cubism, Imagism, Futurism, and Russia's own contributions to the movement—constructivism, under the leadership of Vladimir Tatlin, and Suprematism, under the inspiration of Kazimir Malevich—gained strong footholds in artistic circles.

It was inevitable that the two major forms of artistic expression would come into conflict. There was already bad blood between champions of realistic art and the abstractionists before the 1917 Revolution. The Wanderers, whose popularity waned in the early years of the twentieth century, stressed the importance of content in their works. The various practitioners of abstract art, on the other hand, were interested in the technical possibilities of the various media. For example, constructivist sculptors combined various materials—steel, concrete, wrought iron, even paper—to suggest the variety of human experience that forms the impetus for artistic creation. More attention was paid to form than to substance; meaning was subordinated to the aesthetic experience. In the opinion of more conservative artists, art critics, and (most important) influential Communist leaders, such art had no social conscience.

The 1917 Revolution promised to free art from its capitalist bonds. Communist leaders announced that all forms of artistic expression were to be supported under the new government. Initially, steps were taken to see that this happened. Though he was essentially conservative in his tastes in art, Bolshevik leader Vladimir Ilich Lenin made no overt attempts to control the production of art in the new Soviet Union. On the contrary, Lenin's close associate Anatoly Lunacharsky, the first Soviet commissar of education, appointed important abstract artists to positions of prominence: Kandinsky was named director of the Museum of Pictorial Culture in Moscow, and Malevich and noted painter Marc Chagall were given positions as professors of art.

The euphoria was short-lived, however. By 1921, Kandinsky had resigned his position and had emigrated, expressing frustration at what he saw as meddling by government officials in the handling of commissions and direction of artists' work. Chagall and others were to follow him into self-imposed exile within a few years. By 1922, the proponents of realism had won the sympathy of various influential groups within the Communist hierarchy, especially members of the Soviet military; with their help, realism began to reclaim the position of prominence it had held in the last decades of the nineteenth century. From 1922 forward, the various organizations that had sprung up immediately after the revolution to support a multiplicity of artistic viewpoints found themselves increasingly regulated by the central government.

The death of Lenin and the ascension of Joseph Stalin as the new ruler of the Soviet state signaled the death knell for Soviet abstract art. The last vestiges of real freedom were swept away in 1928, when the government ordered that all artists' organizations be consolidated under a single agency run from Moscow. Few artists held out any hope that this "oversight" agency would permit the freedoms that had become commonplace in the smaller, more specialized groups founded by the artists themselves. Their fears were confirmed in a mandate of the Central Committee of the Communist Party issued on April 23, 1932. Entitled the "Decree on the Reconstruction of Literary and Artistic Organizations," the proclamation dissolved all other organizations previously set up for supporting the arts and centralized control of commissions, sales, and exhibitions under the control of the Party. In effect, this meant that artists already subjected to regulation in housing, studio space, and supplies would be solely dependent on the government for their livelihood.

By this time, it was apparent that the government was interested in supporting only those artists whose work could be readily understood by the masses—in effect, realistic art with a strong socialist message. Named by Stalin himself "Socialist Realism," the new, official art form decreed by the Congress of the Union of Writers in 1934 banned all forms of abstractionism in the arts. Painters, sculptors, writers, and architects found that they would have to conform to the dictates of Party censors or suffer serious consequences for their transgressions.

Impact of Event

The ramifications of the 1934 decree were both immediate and longlasting. During the next several decades, an elaborate apparatus was constructed to control the production of Soviet art, and bureaucrats whose primary interest lay in promoting Party ideals sat in judgment of artists' creations. As historian Joel Carmichael observes, the "indispensable component" of the new artistic program "had to be an absolutely unswerving obedience to the Party"; the result was a "totalitarian homogenizing of culture." The demands that all forms of art have a strong propagandistic quality that could be easily understood by the masses and by Party censors led to uniformity in production. Painting, sculpture, literature, and even architecture became forums for celebrating the worker and the Soviet hero. More often than not, this meant a glorification of the revolutionary leaders, specifically Stalin during his reign and Lenin after Stalin died and was denounced by Nikita Khrushchev.

Artists were forced to conform or suffer the consequences. Several of the most prominent abstractionists had already emigrated before Stalin imposed the monolithic principles of Socialist Realism on the entire creative community. Those who stayed behind either returned to producing works according to the Communist plan or found themselves without supplies for either working or living. Experimentation ceased, and the principles of realism expounded by the Wanderers more than half a century earlier were eagerly embraced by Party officials and reluctantly adopted by those who wished to earn their livelihood as painters, sculptors, or artists in any other medium.

At the same time, contact with the West was discouraged, ostensibly to prohibit decadent influences from cheapening Soviet art. Museum collections were purged of offensive works, and books about abstract art were banned from libraries and art academies. Aspiring artists in the Soviet Union were taught that the function of their work was to serve as a means of conveying a socialist message, and that its ideological content was the primary—in some cases the sole—criterion for judging excellence. With no models to guide them in any direction other than that charted by Socialist Realism, the burgeoning artists of the decades between 1930 and 1970 either passively accepted their role as soldiers in the war against capitalism or groped along blindly to fashion works that challenged the bounds of realism or that ignored the demands of ideology. Striking out in any direction except that charted by the Party, however, often proved dangerous. Artists who did so had their works confiscated and destroyed and were usually blacklisted by government officials who controlled the assignment of commissions; such commissions represented the only guaranteed source of income for Soviet artists, whose works could not be sent abroad without Party approval.

Making matters even worse was the fact that there were no published guidelines for what constituted acceptable art. Only after works were completed could artists gain a review by Party officials, who would then pass judgment on the work's adherence to Socialist Realist principles. What could be considered ideologically sound by one group of bureaucrats might be dismissed as wrongheaded and corruptible by another. As the years passed, artists became more and more conservative in their productions. Any strains of genuine creativity that may have existed in the young men and women who followed in the footsteps of Kandinsky, Malevich, and Tatlin during the reigns of Stalin and his successors were effectively stifled, as art became a tool of the Party in its battle to liberate the masses from bourgeois domination.

Bibliography

Billington, James H. *The Icon and the Axe: An Interpretive History of Russian Culture.* New York: Alfred A. Knopf, 1966. Thoughtful and thoroughly researched examination of the roots of Russian culture, its development under the various Czars, and its demise under the Communists. Explains how Socialist Realism is linked to earlier forms of Soviet artistic and architectural styles.

Carmichael, Joel. *A Cultural History of Russia.* New York: Weybright and Talley, 1968. Examines the culture of Russia from the founding of the nation to the twentieth century. Provides insight into the ways all forms of artistic expression suffered under the control of the Communists, who insisted that art serve the aims of the revolution.

Douglas, Charlotte. *Swans of Other Worlds: Kazimir Malevich and the Origins of Abstraction in Russia.* Ann Arbor: University of Michigan Research Press, 1976.

Analysis of the rise of abstract art in Russia and the initial reaction of Soviet revolutionaries to nonrepresentational works. Outlines the principles upon which such art was created. A useful summary of the movement against which Stalin reacted in demanding a return to realism in all the arts.

James, C. Vaughn. *Soviet Socialist Realism: Origins and Theory.* New York: St. Martin's Press, 1973. Outlines the principles upon which Socialist Realism was founded. Describes the ways art in the Soviet Union was intended to serve both the people and the party. Traces the origins of the movement to Leninist ideology. Contains useful appendices by Lenin and the Communist Central Committee on reforms in the arts necessary to make them compatible with socialist aims.

Medvedev, Roy A. *Let History Judge: The Origins and Consequences of Stalinism.* New York: Alfred A. Knopf, 1972. Study of Communism under the brutal reign of Stalin by a prominent Soviet historian; shows how Stalin's oppressive policies stifled all forms of creativity. Includes a lengthy chapter on the impact of these policies on the arts and sciences; notes how artists were driven to become puppets of the Communist hierarchy or suffer economic and physical hardships.

Salisbury, Harrison E., ed. *The Soviet Union: The Fifty Years.* New York: Harcourt, Brace & World, 1967. Collection of essays reviewing the impact of Communist policies on the Soviet Union. Includes a chapter on the arts, focusing on the deadening influence of official policies that stifled creativity and drove artists into exile or underground.

Valkenier, Elizabeth. *Russian Realist Art: The State and Society.* New York: Columbia University Press, 1989. Studies the influence of the realist tradition in nineteenth century Russia and in the Soviet Union during the twentieth century. Explores the rise of the Wanderers, whose folk style formed the basis of Socialist Realism. Examines the reaction of the abstract schools of art to the Wanderers, the abstractionists' ascendancy during the early decades of the twentieth century, and their demise under Communist oppression.

Laurence W. Mazzeno

Cross-References

The Futurists Issue Their Manifesto (1909), p. 235; Kandinsky Publishes His Views on Abstraction in Art (1912), p. 320; Malevich Introduces Suprematism (1915), p. 413; Socialist Realism Is Mandated in Soviet Literature (1932), p. 908; Stalin Restricts Soviet Composers (1932), p. 914; Shostakovich's *Lady Macbeth of Mtsensk* Is Condemned (1936), p. 1042; Hitler Organizes an Exhibition Denouncing Modern Art (1937), p. 1083; Pasternak's *Doctor Zhivago* Is Published (1957), p. 1747; *The Gulag Archipelago* Exposes Soviet Atrocities (1973), p. 2277.

WALLACE FOUNDS *READER'S DIGEST*

Category of event: Journalism
Time: February, 1922
Locale: New York, New York

Reader's Digest*'s condensed articles, subject matter, optimistic tone, and marketing techniques enabled it to become the world's most widely circulated magazine*

Principal personages:
> DEWITT WALLACE (1889-1981), the founder, owner, editor, and controlling force behind *Reader's Digest* from 1922 until 1973
> LILA BELL ACHESON WALLACE (1889-1984), the wife of DeWitt Wallace, who played a major role in the founding and development of *Reader's Digest*

Summary of Event

In February, 1922, a new pocket-sized magazine appeared published by DeWitt and Lila Wallace. Few could have envisioned that the format, style, and marketing methods of *Reader's Digest* would soon make it the most purchased, the most widely read, and possibly the most influential magazine in the world. By the 1990's, the *Digest* enjoyed a global circulation of twenty-eight million and an estimated readership of more than one hundred million.

The idea of the *Digest* was developed by DeWitt Wallace. The son of a Presbyterian pastor and educator, he was born in 1889. After attending Macalester College in Minnesota and the University of California, Wallace wrote sales-promotion letters for Webb Publishing Company in St. Paul. He then developed and sold a booklet that summarized hundreds of free pamphlets available to farmers. This experience encouraged him to consider creating first an agricultural, then a business, and finally a general digest. World War I intervened, however, and Wallace was wounded while serving with the infantry in France. During a four-month convalescence in an army hospital, he practiced condensing stimulating articles he found in American magazines.

Returning to St. Paul in 1919, Wallace spent six months selecting and compressing articles and produced a trial edition of a digest in early 1920. While other periodicals such as the original *Harper's* and the *Literary Digest* had clipped, pasted, and reprinted, Wallace's proposed magazine added a new ingredient—the skillful abridging of previously published materials. It advertised "thirty-one articles each month from leading magazines—each article of enduring value and interest in condensed and compact form." In addition to the slogan (which changed slightly over the years), this dummy contained all the essential ingredients of subsequent *Digests*: humor, human interest stories, information on health and sex, and practical principles for living, all boiled down for the busy person. At this point, Wallace was willing to give the *Digest* to any publisher who would retain him as an editor, but none showed any interest in his proposed periodical.

In 1921, Wallace married Canadian-born Lila Bell Acheson. A graduate of the University of Oregon, she had taught English in Washington state. When they began dating, she was doing social work around the country for the Young Women's Christian Association (YWCA). That same year, Wallace took a job with the publicity department of Westinghouse in Pittsburgh. After being laid off six months later, he composed a circular for his proposed magazine and solicited provisional subscriptions by writing letters to friends and acquaintances and visiting women's clubs and women's professional groups in Pittsburgh. The Wallaces moved to New York City and rented a basement room under a speakeasy. Using $6300 in assets, they had five thousand copies of their magazine printed.

Most of the characteristics that have made the *Digest* so successful were apparent in the first issue. The magazine was not typographically, editorially, or visually impressive (it had no color or illustrations), and it contained no fiction or advertisements (advertisements were not accepted in the domestic version until 1955). Its sixty-two carefully chosen pages, condensed from such leading general-interest magazines as *Outlook, Good Housekeeping, Scientific American*, and *The Atlantic Monthly*, discussed women, nature, morality, the art of living, self-improvement, and science. Despite its amateur quality, the first issue was well received, and new subscriptions poured in. For twenty-five cents a copy (a price that remained unchanged until 1957), the *Digest* helped busy Americans keep abreast of the flood of news that threatened to overwhelm them in the twentieth century.

Until 1925, when they hired their first editorial assistant, DeWitt and Lila Wallace produced the *Digest* themselves. Lila read magazines and selected articles for use; DeWitt reviewed her choices and did most of the condensations. In the fall of 1922, they moved their operations to Pleasantville, New York, a small town about forty miles north of New York City. They formed the Reader's Digest Association, in which they owned 100% of the stock, assuring their control over the publication, content, and revenue of the magazine. The success of the *Digest* in its early years stemmed from its middlebrow perspective, its choice of varied inspirational, informative, humorous, and practical articles with broad appeal, its provocative titles, and Wallace's ability to shorten articles while preserving their substance and enhancing their readability. Authors of early articles included popular preachers, poets, scientists, humorists, philosophers, best-selling novelists, and crusading journalists.

At first the *Digest* was easily able to obtain permission to reprint articles from other magazines for free, because it seemed to provide valuable publicity and did not compete for advertising. Within a few years, Wallace began to pay modest sums for permission to reprint articles. By the late 1920's, some editors began to consider the *Digest* a parasite that ate into their sales. Wallace was able to convince them, however, that the *Digest* actually stimulated magazine reading, and he entered into agreements with many periodicals that gave him exclusive reprint rights.

Impact of Event

From its small beginning in 1922, *Reader's Digest* rapidly grew to become an extremely profitable enterprise, second in sales and circulation only to the Bible. Like the Bible, the magazine has been translated into many languages and distributed on all continents. Throughout its history, the *Digest* has reflected the social, economic, moral, and literary views of its founders. Their inspirational, hopeful, conservative message has been spread not only through the magazine but also by condensed books, radio programs, films, recordings, and educational projects. The *Digest's* efforts "to inform, inspire, and entertain" have evoked devotion, praise, admiration, envy, and criticism. Its incredible success has inspired the rise of numerous imitators; none, though, has been as well edited as the *Digest* or has threatened its circulation. The impact of the magazine on the publishing world has been immense.

Originally sold only by subscription, the *Digest* grew from circulation of about twenty thousand in 1925 to 216,000 in 1929. Pressure from competitors forced the magazine to begin newsstand marketing that year, and by 1935, circulation had climbed to more than one million. During World War II, the magazine produced special editions for four different war theaters and printed international editions, and sales rose to nearly nine million in 1945. Since the 1960's, the *Digest* has maintained a worldwide circulation of more than eighteen million, has been printed in more than a dozen languages, has been sold in almost all countries, and has been read in one of every four American homes.

The *Digest's* secret of success lies in its choice of articles, its editing process, its format, its guiding philosophy, and its marketing techniques. Essential to the magazine's phenomenal popularity has been its selection of relevant, readable, varied articles that appeal to large audiences. From the beginning, the editors of the *Digest* (who eventually numbered in the hundreds) scoured American (and soon foreign) periodicals, newspapers, and supplements for potential articles. In choosing an article, editors have been guided by the magazine's philosophy of printing only material that is memorable, applicable, constructive, and of lasting interest.

To supplement these reprinted condensations, the *Digest* began using original articles in 1930. Over the years, many of the *Digest's* original articles have attracted sensational attention, perhaps none more so than "And Sudden Death," published in 1935. This grisly account of automobile accidents and fatalities was reprinted in thousands of newspapers and magazines. Judges read it in court and forced traffic violators to copy it by hand. Also provocative have been articles on the Soviet Union, American foreign policy, the relationship between cigarette smoking and cancer, the World Council of Churches, and alleged cures for diseases. In the mid-1930's, Wallace began to commission authors to write pieces for other periodicals that could then be abridged in the *Digest*. By the 1940's, more than half of the magazine's articles originated in this manner.

Digest editors spend many hours on each article to shorten it and clarify its message. Words, sentences, even paragraphs and whole sections that seem unnecessary to a clear exposition of the central thought are deleted, usually reducing articles to about one-fourth of their original length. Many different editors at various levels of authority work on a typical article, continually reappraising, condensing, and refining it.

The format of the *Digest* has contributed greatly to its popularity. Its articles, whether previously published or original, are always brief, clear, and easily read and are often humorous, charming, provocative, and timely. In addition to its articles, the *Digest* has developed many other departments. Its short subjects and jokes began with "Repartee" in 1930. "The Well-Known Human Race," "Quotable Quotes," and "Picturesque Speech" soon followed. Early on, the *Digest* condensed short stories and chapters from books and in 1934 published its first abridgement of a whole book. Since 1933, the magazine has regularly used amusing, varied fillers drawn from life and printed sources. Seeking to provide diversity, balance, and novelty, the *Digest*'s formula includes humor, unforgettable characters, investigations of current affairs, adventure narratives, accounts of medical miracles, consumer reports, and articles on the arts of thinking, loving, and problem managing. As Playsted Wood notes in *Of Lasting Value* (1967), the magazine reduces "baffling complexities to understandable simplicities" and "puts abstract problems into human terms."

From its inception in 1922, the *Digest* has largely reflected the philosophy of its founder. Wallace's tastes, opinions, and preferences have significantly affected the choice and tone of the material the magazine has printed. A political conservative who espoused free-market economics, Wallace stressed the Protestant work ethic and human perfectibility. Expressing his beliefs, the magazine has extolled God, family, neighborliness, country, good works, self-help, and human ingenuity. His unflagging optimism and missionary zeal have been evident in *Digest* appeals to the best in people and in exposés of bureaucratic waste and inefficiency, fraudulent advertising, and dishonest dealing of all kinds.

The tremendous success of the *Digest* has also been a result of its marketing techniques. The magazine's most concerted and effective sales efforts have always been based upon direct-mail promotions. To sell new subscriptions, it has continually relied upon testimonials from both celebrities and ordinary Americans. In its promotions, the *Digest* has used reduced-price offers, free-trial offers, gift subscriptions, and inducements of many kinds, including its summer sweepstakes, which began in 1965. Since 1926, the *Digest* has also employed hundreds of thousands of part-time sales representatives to recruit new customers.

Over the years, the style, methods, and perspective of the *Digest* have often been criticized. Its condensed articles have been ridiculed as one-sided, simplistic, and lacking in subtlety; the magazine has been charged with spoon-feeding lazy readers instead of forcing them to think deeply or debate issues. The method of planting articles in other periodicals for subsequent condensation has been denounced as deceptive. The magazine has been attacked as antilabor, anti-Semitic, and antiblack, as too conservative about everything except excercise, medicine, and sexual activity within marriage. Critics have protested that the *Digest* portrays a rosier, simpler, happier world than most people experience.

In addition to its pioneering efforts in condensation and in creating international versions, the *Digest* also led the way with a Braille edition, a phonograph edition, a special school edition (widely used in the 1940's), radio programs, movies, a program service (which supplied thousands of clubs with topical issues to discuss at their meetings), the *Reader's Digest* Condensed Book Club, how-to books, and specialized encyclopedias.

The *Reader's Digest* was not a totally new concept. *The American Magazine and Historical Chronicle*, founded in 1743, compressed articles printed in leading British periodicals, and *Littell's Living Age* did the same one hundred years later. DeWitt Wallace's innovation was to place considerable content, drawn from many sources, into a tidy, handy package to provide, as he put it, a "service to readers." Millions look to the *Digest* for spiritual guidance, moral direction, and practical advice; hundreds of thousands write to suggest material or to thank the magazine for tips on diet, exercise, and physical and mental health. It is widely quoted and cited by people of varied ages and professions. Countless citizens have been inspired by its articles to improve schools, fight corruption, battle for legislative changes, and eliminate health hazards. Because of its immense circulation, its vast readership, and the implicit trust many place in it, *Reader's Digest* has had an impact on the American popular mind matched perhaps only by the publications of Henry Luce and the productions of Walt Disney.

Bibliography

Bainbridge, John. *Little Wonder: Or, The Reader's Digest and How It Grew.* New York: Reynal & Hitchcock, 1946. Expanded from a 1945 article in *The New Yorker*, the book discusses the history of the *Digest* during its first twenty-three years. Analyzes the magazine's methods, subject matter, and format. This amusing, critical account concludes that the *Digest*'s stupendous success has resulted from its optimism, simplism, dogmatism, and Wallace himself.

Cheever, Benjamin H. "Bad Days in Pleasantville." *The Nation* 250 (May 7, 1990): 628-631. Novelist John Cheever's son laments the change in *Reader's Digest* since 1984, when the original owners died and the organization was taken over by George Grune. Grune slashed worker benefits and gave himself an enormous salary, all in the name of running a profitable business in the savage style of the 1980's.

Rovit, Earl. *Modernism and Three Magazines: An Editorial Revolution. The Sewanee Review* 93 (Fall, 1985): 540-553. A study of Wallace and *Reader's Digest*, Henry Luce and *Time*, and Harold Ross and *The New Yorker*. Rovit argues that all three magazines sprang from a common 1920's impulse that contradicts the notion that the "Lost Generation" writers were emblematic of the period.

Schreiner, Samuel, Jr. *The Condensed World of the Reader's Digest.* New York: Stein & Day, 1977. Written by a former *Digest* editor who labels the magazine's optimism excessive and its style bland. He calls Wallace's running of the magazine paternalistic and criticizes the *Digest*'s planting of articles in other periodicals and its ghostwriting of articles for famous people. At the same time, he praises the *Digest* for its professionalism and commitment to accuracy and the Wallaces for their philanthropic endeavors. Contains many entertaining anecdotes about the magazine.

Wood, Playsted. *Of Lasting Interest: The Story of Reader's Digest.* Rev. ed. Garden City, N.Y.: Doubleday, 1967. An outgrowth of forty articles in *The Christian Science Monitor* written with the full support of the *Digest.* This highly laudatory and colorful account examines many different facets of the magazine, including its founding, original articles, condensed books, editorial research and process, subject matter, international editions, headquarters, advertising, and circulation. Photographs.

Gary Scott Smith

Cross-References

The Christian Science Monitor Is Founded (1908), p. 209; Lippmann Helps to Establish *The New Republic* (1914), p. 385; Ross Founds *The New Yorker* (1925), p. 648; The Book-of-the-Month Club and the Literary Guild Are Founded (1926), p. 686; Luce Launches *Life* Magazine (1936), p. 1031; The Great Books Foundation Is Established (1947), p. 1351.

JOYCE'S *ULYSSES* EPITOMIZES MODERNISM IN FICTION

Category of event: Literature
Time: February 2, 1922
Locale: Paris, France

Criteria of fictional form, orthodoxies of fictional content, and conventions of literary taste were revolutionized by the publication of one of the century's most controversial literary works

Principal personages:
> JAMES JOYCE (1882-1941), an Irish writer whose name is synonymous with modern literary art
> SYLVIA BEACH (1887-1962), the American owner of the Paris bookstore Shakespeare and Company and the publisher of *Ulysses*
> EZRA POUND (1885-1972), an American poet and cultural entrepeneur whose encouragement was crucial to Joyce's career
> HARRIET SHAW WEAVER (1876-1961), an English philanthropist on whose financial and moral support Joyce depended

Summary of Event

Not only does the conception of the twentieth century's most influential work of prose fiction owe a good deal to tales of mythological wanderings—it is based in part on Homer's *Odyssey* (c. 800 B.C.)—but the story of its execution has also acquired semimythological trappings. These too have to do with origins and survival, with wartime dislocations and the travail of exile, with steadfastness and luck.

Such is the status of James Joyce as an embodiment of the artist that it seems almost natural that he should, as he said, have felt attracted to the character of Odysseus while still a schoolboy and that he should have used the title "Ulysses" in the first place for a short story that he planned to add to his collection *Dubliners* (1914). That story drew on the author's experience and memory of his native city and pivoted (as the novel *Ulysses* would if it possessed anything so conventional as a plot) around a cuckold and his unfaithful wife. Morever, because *Ulysses* includes the autobiographical protagonist Stephen Dedalus from Joyce's first novel, *A Portrait of the Artist as a Young Man* (1916), a case can be made that *Ulysses* represents to some degree a thematic coalition and an artistic transcendence of Joyce's early works. The peculiar degree of integrity with which both Joyce's life and writings are invested can make it seem that the whole of his life was a rehearsal for the publication of *Ulysses*. Perhaps something of Joyce's own awareness of this book's status in his life is reflected on his superstitious insistence that *Ulysses* be published on his fortieth birthday.

Bringing the book to publication was an epic feat carried out on various levels by a number of people. Joyce began *Ulysses* in 1914 in Trieste, which was then a city in the Austro-Hungarian Empire, where Joyce was employed as a teacher of English. The onset of World War I, however, required the writer and his family to flee to neutral territory, which brought them to Zurich in Switzerland. It was there that the conception of *Ulysses* matured and that substantial amounts of the manuscript initially took shape. Work on the book was greatly facilitated by the financial support of Harriet Shaw Weaver, an English philanthropist on whose generosity Joyce continued to rely for the rest of his life. Encouragement also came from the sustained attentions of the American poet Ezra Pound, who had already been instrumental in arranging the serialization of *A Portrait of the Artist as a Young Man*; the Zurich *Ulysses* began serialization in *Little Review*.

It is necessary to distinguish between what appeared in *Little Review* and the *Ulysses* published in book form. Part of the drama of the publication of *Ulysses*, and the source of the many controversies surrounding the state and status of the work's various manuscripts and typescripts, arises from the fact that Joyce composed so much of the text when it was in the galley-proof stage. Part of *Ulysses'* notoriety, both in terms of its difficulty and its alleged obscenity, was the result of its serialization, which was eventually discontinued by court order—the first of the work's numerous encounters with the law. In view of its reputation for complexity and poor taste, and in light of Joyce's early history of difficulty with publishers, finding a publisher for *Ulysses* was no easy task, and the decision to issue the work in book form remains notable for its courage and enlightenment.

This decision was taken by Sylvia Beach, who owned and operated a bookstore in Paris named Shakespeare and Company that provided a focus for both the artistic avant-garde and the expatriate literary community. Not a publisher as such, Sylvia Beach showed a good deal of enterprise in ensuring the eventual completion of the text, the location of a printer, and the delivery of the book in an edition of one thousand numbered copies. Delivery was complicated by the fact that the printer was located in Lyons, in central France, and publication was to some extent hampered by the fact that none of the printer's typesetters knew English—though this may have been an advantage, given the work's verbal innovations.

The combination of energy, dedication, good fortune, perseverance, and enterprise, and the somewhat unlikely international community that provided these qualities, make the story of the making of *Ulysses* a peculiarly human one. Such an emphasis is consistent with the work's significance. Composed while Europe was engaged in a war that would have the most profound repercussions for the continent's culture and heritage, Joyce's work represents an alternative set of engagements. These denote an attempt to rehabilitate the European tradition by restructuring a story that is one of its keystones, Homer's *Odyssey*, in such a way as to speak to contemporary civilization. Homer's story has its origin in war, but it much more crucially confronts issues of aftermath and reconstitution. Joyce's adaptation subtly, persistently, and skeptically addresses similar issues.

In addition, the distinctive presence of Joyce himself has an exemplary force in the saga that produced *Ulysses*. Joyce overcame critical neglect, artistic isolation, periods of abject poverty, uncertainty, and ill-health, and his achievement is rather more than the sum of the parts that compose the seven years' effort that went into the work. As though to exemplify the Odyssean qualities of "silence, exile and cunning" with which Joyce's fictional alter ego Stephen Dedalus identified, the author's dedication to his art has become synonymous not only with individual integrity but also with the resources of the imagination in the face of the dislocations of historical reality. Such an example, articulated with rare imaginative freedom and critical intelligence, makes the publication of *Ulysses* a landmark in the development of a distinctively twentieth century sensibility.

Impact of Event

The publication of *Ulysses* in 1922 decisively influenced the conception of what literature might represent and achieve. In that sense, it is a work that is at the heart of the aesthetic revolution that occurred in the West between 1880 and 1930, a revolution that affected every area of artistic endeavor. More for the sake of convenience rather than for reasons of accuracy or clarity, this revolution is known as modernism. Its cultural, historical, and philosophical origins and consequences continue to be analyzed and assessed, and its achievements in literature, painting, and music constitute an ongoing critical challenge.

Ulysses is central to any consideration of what modernism, which is neither a school nor a program, might be thought to signify. The most obvious reason for the work's status is its formal daring. The idea of a piece of fiction being written not only in different styles but also in different forms, and of these differences being both valid and distinctive in their own right as well as, at another level, lending themselves to eventual coordination, was a radical departure from previous conceptions of fiction. Even Ezra Pound, commenting on the work's complex later sequences, remarked brusquely, "New style per chapter not necessary."

Moreover, as though to reinforce the shock of the new that the form of *Ulysses* produced, Joyce also represented scenes from ordinary life that had hitherto been considered beneath the novelist's gaze. These scenes basically deal with the intimacies of personal and conjugal life. So little had such realities been addressed in literature that the scenes in question were responsible for *Ulysses*'s reputation as a salacious production, dangerous to morals and good taste. That view of the work only began to be reconsidered after a U.S. District Court ruled in 1933 that the book was not obscene and could be freely published in the United States, thereby guaranteeing the work access to a wide audience.

While the notorious reputation may have earned *Ulysses* an unexpected audience, it also may have delayed reaction to the book's intellectual achievements. The most obvious of these, consistent with the work's overall daring, is its use of Homeric correspondences. Not only are events in Homer's original adapted—the one-eyed cyclopean giant of the *Odyssey* becomes a monster of ideological single-mindedness in *Ulysses*—but the spirit of the original is recommissioned, however eliptically and despite a marked degree of skepticism. The protagonist Leopold Bloom, as Odysseus, is heroic not because of his extraordinary skills or exotic adventures but because of his persistence, integrity, and openness. Nothing human is alien to Bloom. Thus, in a paradox typical of Joyce's vision, Bloom embodies the largeness of the little man, and his wanderings around Dublin exemplify the presence of universal tropes of experience within what appear to be strictly local and personal circumstances. Joyce, however, has taken care not to patronize or sentimentalize his hero by making him of Jewish ancestry, thereby ensuring, among other things, that he will be perceived as an outsider, detached, vulnerable, and singular. Bloom thus may be perceived as modern man, sustained by nothing more than his own slightly comic doggedness and fragile yet resilient self-respect. In his treatment of the other major characters, Stephen Dedalus and Bloom's wife, Molly, Joyce is equally unsparing— notoriously so in the case of Molly, who is portrayed with a hitherto unheard-of degree of unromanticized earthiness.

One important reason why the Blooms make such an impact is because more of them is made available to readers than is common in novels. Through Joyce's development of the technique of stream of consciousness, the thoughts and thought structures of Leopold and Molly, and also to a lesser degree of Stephen Dedalus, are represented in all their uncensored unpredictability. The unmediated immediacy with which these characters' mental landscapes impinge upon the reader create an impression that *Ulysses* is not so much "about" something but is a discrete entity in its own right. Joyce made of the text a world, and of the world a text. This world is present not merely in the work's superficially forbidding frame of encyclopedic reference but also in the reader's experience of its variety and scope.

Equally radical is Joyce's treatment of time in *Ulysses.* The fictional duration of Homer's original is condensed from ten years to less than twenty-four hours. The substitution of one sequence of waking hours for an epic span implicitly raises questions about the relative nature of the experience and perception of time. These questions receive detailed subtextual attention in the course of the work and also relate to more general cultural shifts introduced by a growing acceptance of the notion of relativity. Joyce's conception of narrative time had a particularly enduring impact on some of the most significant of his literary successors in Europe and America, foremost among whom are William Faulkner, Samuel Beckett, and Claude Simon.

In addition, the condensation of epic time to what might be termed civic time expresses the mundane and constricted nature of the characters' existence. The view in *Ulysses* of fragmented consciousness and humankind in the face of it hapless and impoverished is both acknowledged and redeemed. Despite their various constraints, the characters are not belittled. Against the odds, it seems, they constitute an informal and fundamentally informal polity. As such, and on the understanding that Joyce considered the work to be a comedy, *Ulysses* becomes what Stephen Dedalus termed, in a celebrated phrase, "the uncreated conscience of my race."

Bibliography

Beach, Sylvia. *Shakespeare and Company.* New York: Harcourt, Brace, 1959. An anecdotal autobiography of the original publisher of *Ulysses.* Much of the work is devoted to the author's ownership of the Shakespeare and Company bookstore in Paris and to the literary luminaries who crossed her path there. The material on Joyce is fascinating, and the work as a whole will please the general reader.

Budgen, Frank. *James Joyce and the Making of "Ulysses."* Bloomington: Indiana University Press, 1960. This is a reprint of a work first published in 1933. The author is an English painter who first made Joyce's acquaintance in Zurich when *Ulysses* was in the making. The narrative dwells largely on Joyce's Zurich years, offers many rewarding insights into Joyce's mind, art, and personal circumstances, and is written in an unpretentious, accessible style.

Ellmann, Richard. *James Joyce.* Rev. ed. New York: Oxford University Press, 1982. First published in 1959. The revised edition raises to a further level of excellence a work that is not only the definitive Joyce biography but also a model of modern biographical scholarship. Exhaustive in scope and judiciously sympathetic in tone, it also draws directly on many members of Joyce's family and personal circle.

_____. *Ulysses on the Liffey.* New York: Oxford University Press, 1972. An intellectually elaborate discussion of Joyce's various conceptions of form in *Ulysses.* An overview based on "three propositions" that underwrite *Ulysses* is developed. The study concludes with charts delineating the organization of the book's last six episodes; Joyce's two conceptual schemes for *Ulysses* are reproduced and compared.

French, Marilyn. *The Book As World: James Joyce's Ulysses.* Cambridge, Mass.: Harvard University Press, 1976. A sophisticated academic anatomy of *Ulysses.* The focus is primarily on the proliferation of narrative styles in *Ulysses,* but the wide-ranging discussion deals with much more than stylistic concerns. Of particular interest is the author's sense of *Ulysses's* conception of the reader's role.

Hart, Clive, and David Hayman, eds. *James Joyce's Ulysses.* Berkeley: University of California Press, 1974. Eighteen essays, each by an eminent Joyce scholar and each devoted to one of the eighteen episodes in *Ulysses.* No overall or unified conception of Joyce's work emerges, but a good number of the essays raise issues larger than their immediate occasion.

Kenner, Hugh. *Ulysses.* Rev. ed. Baltimore: Johns Hopkins University Press, 1987. In many ways the most helpful, as well as the most impressive, short study of *Ulysses.* Includes a brief but telling essay on *Ulysses* criticism and an annotated bibliography.

Litz, A. Walton. *The Art of James Joyce: Method and Design in Ulysses and Finnegans Wake.* New York: Oxford University Press, 1961. A sophisticated introduction to some of the textual problems associated with Joyce's masterpieces. In the light of subsequent developments, its study of some of the different versions of *Ulysses* is particularly relevant. Provides fascinating insight into the evolution of an extremely complicated text. Intended for the serious student.

Pound, Ezra. *Pound/Joyce.* Edited by Forest Read. London: Faber, 1968. Collects in one volume both Ezra Pound's numerous essays on Joyce's works, which economically sketch one of the most influential acquaintanceships in the history of modernism, and also the extensive correspondence between the two writers. Many of the letters have a direct bearing on the gestation, progress, and publication of *Ulysses.*

George O'Brien

Cross-References

Freud Inaugurates a Fascination with the Unconscious (1899), p. 19; Jung Publishes *Psychology of the Unconscious* (1912), p. 309; Proust's *Remembrance of Things Past* Is Published (1913), p. 355; Eliot Publishes *The Waste Land* (1922), p. 539; Woolf's *Mrs. Dalloway* Explores Women's Consciousness (1925), p. 637; *The Sound and the Fury* Launches Faulkner's Career (1929), p. 805; Beckett's Trilogy Pushes Against the Frontiers of Fiction (1951), p. 1498.

STRAVINSKY COMPLETES HIS WIND OCTET

Category of event: Music
Time: 1923
Locale: Paris, France

Igor Stravinsky's Octet for Wind Instruments *was one of the most critical compositions that defined a post-World War I musical aesthetic based on objective and emotive elements*

Principal personages:

IGOR STRAVINSKY (1882-1971), a Russian-born composer who was one of the dominant figures of twentieth century art music

SERGEI DIAGHILEV (1872-1929), a Russian impresario who founded the Ballets Russes and commissioned works from Stravinsky

SERGE KOUSSEVITZKY (1874-1951), a Russian-born conductor who commissioned the *Octet for Wind Instruments* and other works from Stravinsky

JEAN COCTEAU (1889-1963), a French writer of uncommon versatility who wrote the text for Stravinsky's opera-oratorio *Oedipus Rex*

ANDRÉ GIDE (1869-1951), a French author who wrote the text for Stravinsky's ballet score *Perséphone*

VERA DE BOSSET (1888-1982), the dedicatee of the wind octet and later Stravinsky's second wife

NADIA BOULANGER (1887-1979), a French musical pedagogue who transmitted Stravinsky's neoclassic ideas to generations of future composers

SAMUEL DUSHKIN (1891-1976), a Polish-born American violinist who collaborated and toured with Stravinsky in the 1930's

Summary of Event

Since the success of his score for the 1910 ballet *The Firebird*, Igor Stravinsky had lived in Paris. The outbreak of World War I in 1914 cut him off from his native Russia, and he took refuge in Switzerland. Compelled to write for reduced instrumental resources rather than the large orchestras he had used for the ballet *The Rite of Spring* (1913) and the opera *The Nightingale* (1914), he experimented with limited scorings, often for unusual instrumental combinations: *The Soldier's Tale* (1918) was scored for violin, string bass, clarinet, bassoon, cornet, trombone, and percussion, and the final scoring for *The Wedding* (1923) called for four pianos and six percussion players to accompany the vocal soloists and chorus.

The Russian Revolution of October, 1917, was to cut Stravinsky off from his native land until 1962. His Russian works done in Switzerland, such as the burlesque *Renard* (1916), featured limited orchestration and use of Russian folktales. Other popular materials in Stravinsky's works of this period are the Spanish *paso doble* (a souvenir of a visit to Spain with Sergei Diaghilev) and ragtime; both appear in *The Soldier's Tale.*

Finally, Stravinsky's aesthetic was changing from an expressive to an objective and astringent one. Denied the expressive resources of the large orchestra for economic reasons, he eschewed this sound in his reaction against the overblown sonorities of older composers such as Gustav Mahler in Austria and Aleksandr Scriabin in Russia. Reducing the number of strings, and finally eliminating them altogether, was one way of getting away from the soaring, lush emotionalism that he particularly detested in Scriabin's music; Stravinsky sought to achieve a more objective sound.

The relatively cool and objective strains of the eighteenth century were a final attraction. During World War I, many composers sought an antidote to the heavily Germanic post-Romantic sound, resulting in such works as Maurice Ravel's *Le Tombeau de Couperin* (1917) and Sergei Prokofiev's *Classical Symphony* (1917), works with piquant modern harmonies but classical orchestration, balance, and restraint. After the war, Diaghilev reorganized his Ballets Russes and commissioned Stravinsky to write a ballet using music purporting to be by the eighteenth century Italian composer Giovanni Battista Pergolesi; Stravinsky did not change the melodies or basses but made subtle modifications to the harmony and scored *Pulcinella* (1920) for classical orchestra.

The strands of Stravinsky's new developments came together for the first time in the *Symphonies of Wind Instruments* of 1920, written as a memorial to Claude Debussy, who had died in 1918. The musical materials are Russian, and the harmonies and counterpoint are reminiscent of *The Rite of Spring*, but the form is very advanced (the German composer Karlheinz Stockhausen took it as a model for his works), and the sonorities, written for the wind section of a large symphony orchestra but without the strings or percussion, are astringent and biting.

With the *Octet for Wind Instruments* of 1923, Stravinsky abandoned Russian musical materials, and the classical ethos of balance and restraint became paramount. The scoring is for flute, clarinet, two bassoons, two trumpets, and two trombones, and each instrument is directed to play solo. This scoring differs from the standard wind octet of the classical period, which consisted of two each of oboes, clarinets, bassoons, and horns.

The work is in three movements. The first movement, "Sinfonia," consists of a slow introduction followed by a fast movement in a modified sonata form; the key center of E-flat major is clearly recognizable. A theme and variations form the second movement; the theme undergoes various transformations, first in a recurring trombone-centered variation, then as a march. After the trombone variation comes a waltz in which the theme is embedded, then a galop (the music used for bareback riders in the circus) as a counterpoint to the theme. The trombone variation returns, followed by a fugato wherein the counterpoint grows increasingly denser and more dissonant; after it thins out, the solo flute plays material similar to that which linked the slow introduction to the allegro moderato of the first movement. This linkage, though, is to a finale that is a homage to Johann Sebastian Bach, in the manner of one of Bach's two-part inventions. This movement is in sonata form, with a very free reprise and a coda that incorporates ragtime elements.

At the work's first performance at the Paris Opéra on October 18, 1923, Stravinsky made his debut as a conductor in the place of Serge Koussevitzky, who had commissioned the work for one of his concerts. Koussevitzky conducted the other two works on the program. Though the published score of the *Octet for Wind Instruments* bears no dedication, Stravinsky privately dedicated it to Vera de Bosset, who became his wife seventeen years later.

In an article written the following year for *The Arts* (January, 1924), Stravinsky stated that his octet was "a musical object" with a form "influenced by the musical matter with which it is composed." He added that the work was "not an 'emotive' work but a musical composition based on objective elements which are sufficient in themselves." The form of his music, he maintained, was derived from counterpoint, and he remarked that his music "has no other aim than to be sufficient in itself . . . the play of the musical elements is the thing." The octet sums up the contrapuntal devices of Bach, the structural ideas of Wolfgang Amadeus Mozart, and elements of musical culture associated with popular entertainments such as the circus.

Impact of Event

The octet determined the future shape of musical neoclassicism. Its atmosphere was one of musical detachment rather than of the intense involvement of such expressionists as Arnold Schoenberg and his pupils. Second, though the name of the movement suggests an imitation of the works of Mozart, in reality neoclassicism embraced nearly all the musically remembered past, principally the works of the composers of the eighteenth century and some early Romantics. Third, elements from popular musical cultures were employed, much as in the eighteenth century. Excluded, however, were the highly emotive musical devices of the late Romantic and post-Romantic composers such as Richard Wagner, Johannes Brahms, Gustav Mahler, and Aleksandr Scriabin. Thus the neoclassicists differed from such composers as Jean Sibelius, Ralph Vaughan Williams, and Carl Nielsen, whose music represented an evolution of the late-Romantic musical tradition.

Stravinsky by now had become fully converted to the neoclassical idiom; his last Russian work of the postwar period, the chamber opera *Mavra* (1922), was a homage to Alexander Pushkin, Mikhail Glinka, and Peter Ilich Tchaikovsky rather than to the "uncultured" folk music of *The Wedding*. After the *Octet for Wind Instruments*, Stravinsky decided to appear as a conductor and pianist, allowing him less time for composition but facilitating the hearing of his music. For this purpose, he wrote the spiky *Concerto for Piano and Wind Instruments* (1924), the *Serenade in A Major* (1925), a 1924 sonata for solo piano, and *Capriccio* (1929), a three-movement piano concerto in all but name, one of his most popular works of the period. The *Concerto for Piano and Wind Instruments* is in the spirit of Bach's rather than Mozart's concertos; Mozart's influence is best seen in the slow movements of the sonata and

Capriccio. Popular elements are evident in the finales of all these works.

The internationalism of neoclassicism is best seen in the largest-scale 1920's work of Stravinsky, the 1927 opera-oratorio *Oedipus Rex* for narrator, soloists, male chorus, and large orchestra. The text, based on Sophocles' drama, was written by Jean Cocteau and then (except for the narrator's summaries) translated into Ciceronian Latin to provide an atmosphere of timelessness. The music is in the Anglo-Italian style of George Frideric Handel's oratorios of the early eighteenth century. Despite the detachment of both librettist and composer from the often-violent plot, the work is highly moving.

An equally monumental (but shorter) counterpart is the *Symphony of Psalms* of 1930, commissioned for the fiftieth anniversary of the Boston Symphony Orchestra by Koussevitzky, its new conductor. The work's texts are portions of psalms from the Latin (Vulgate) Bible. Its form is not that of the conventional symphony, and some of its techniques had been used in Bach's church cantatas. The scoring is for mixed chorus and large orchestra, without violins or violas. Stravinsky had returned to the Orthodox Church in 1926, and the work reflects better than any his newly restored faith.

In 1931, Stravinsky was introduced to the Polish-born American violinist Samuel Dushkin, for whom he wrote a violin concerto and the *Duo Concertant* (1932) for piano and violin for their tours between 1932 and 1934. Their repertoire also included several transcriptions for violin and piano of some of Stravinsky's shorter and more popular pieces. Both the violin concerto and *Duo Concertant* betray some Romantic traits, especially in their slow movements.

The rarely encountered *Perséphone* of 1934 is a ballet with narrator, tenor soloist, mixed and children's choruses, and full orchestra, to a text by André Gide. Though the collaboration with Stravinsky began auspiciously, it did not end thus: Stravinsky came to dislike Gide's verses, whereas Gide did not agree with Stravinsky's idea that musical accentuation should take precedence over poetic scansion or syllabification. The work, one of Stravinsky's most delicately scored compositions, did not receive a satisfactory full-scale production as a ballet until 1961.

Stravinsky did not have any pupils, but he found the French music pedagogue Nadia Boulanger a person who communicated effectively his ideas on music. Her pupils included Aaron Copland, Walter Piston, Virgil Thomson, Sir Lennox Berkeley, Elliott Carter, and Karel Husa.

Though Stravinsky became a French citizen in 1934, thus protecting some of his copyrights, he was not thoroughly accepted as a French composer (he was denied election to the French Academy to succeed Paul Dukas), and he felt the pressure of events leading to World War II. He did not tour foreign countries as frequently, his music was condemned in the Soviet Union as bourgeois formalism and in Nazi Germany as degenerate, and his oldest daughter, mother, and wife died in the late 1930's while Stravinsky himself was suffering from tuberculosis. His music at the time became more practical: The *Concerto for Two Solo Pianos* (1935) was written for him and his son Soulima to play in smaller cities that lacked a professional orchestra, and his 1938 chamber concerto in E-flat known as *Dumbarton Oaks* (from the estate near Washington where Stravinsky's patron commissioned the work) contains very specific markings for the conductor. These two works are among Stravinsky's most accessible neoclassic works, and both show the strong influence of Bach.

Stravinsky began his *Symphony in C Major* in 1938 as a commission for the fiftieth anniversary of the Chicago Symphony Orchestra. Two movements were written in France but interrupted by the composer's trip to the United States, where he was to occupy a chair at Harvard University and deliver the lectures later published as *The Poetics of Music in the Form of Six Lessons* (1947). Stravinsky had been very favorably impressed by the vigor of American musical life, and he welcomed the idea of moving to the United States. The third movement was finished in Cambridge, Massachusetts, the city where he married Vera de Bosset (the marriage endured until the composer's death in 1971); the fourth in Beverly Hills, California. He admitted that he had studied symphonies by Franz Joseph Haydn, Beethoven, and even Tchaikovsky as models. The work is in quite standard symphonic form, but with the instruments often treated in concerto fashion. With this work, one of Stravinsky's masterpieces and a capstone of his neoclassic style, his French period concluded and his American period began.

Bibliography

Asafyev, Boris. *A Book About Stravinsky.* Translated by Richard F. French. Ann Arbor: UMI Research Press, 1982. Completed in 1929, Asafyev's volume is the main study by a Soviet-era musicologist. It contains a perceptive analysis of the octet, but the author deprecates many of Stravinsky's neoclassic works.

Austin, William W. *Music in the Twentieth Century.* New York: W. W. Norton, 1966. A thorough treatment of Stravinsky's neoclassic period within the context of twentieth century music, in a volume that is still the best study of the period.

Dushkin, Samuel. "Working with Stravinsky." In *Igor Stravinsky,* edited by Edwin Corle. Freeport, N.Y.: Books for Libraries Press, 1969. A vivid account of Stravinsky as a musical collaborator. Also contains a firsthand account of Stravinsky's personal and family life during the 1930's.

Stravinsky, Igor. *Stravinsky: An Autobiography.* New York: W. W. Norton, 1962. Originally published in 1936, this volume contains the composer's firsthand account of his work on the octet and other neoclassical compositions during his French years. Unfortunately, the translation is poor.

Stravinsky, Igor, and Robert Craft. *Dialogues and a Diary.* London: Faber and Faber, 1968. When Stravinsky was in his eighties, Robert Craft had him reminisce about his early days and give his current opinions about music. This volume covers the Paris years and the genesis of the octet.

Stravinsky, Vera. *Dearest Bubushkin.* Edited by Robert Craft. New York: Thames and Hudson, 1985. The correspondence of Vera and Igor Stravinsky, with excerpts from Vera's diary from 1922 on. The text is illustrated with numerous photographs.

White, Eric Walter. *Stravinsky: The Composer and His Works.* 2d ed. Berkeley: University of California Press, 1979. The standard English biography of the composer. Includes detailed analyses of his compositions as well as a chronicle of his life.

R. M. Longyear

Cross-References

The Rite of Spring Stuns Audiences (1913), p. 373; "Les Six" Begin Giving Concerts (1917), p. 435; Boulanger Takes Copland as a Student (1921), p. 508; Gide's *The Counterfeiters* Questions Moral Absolutes (1925), p. 620; Stravinsky's *The Rake's Progress* Premieres in Venice (1951), p. 1514.

THE TEN COMMANDMENTS ESTABLISHES SILENT-FILM SPECTACLE

Category of event: Motion pictures
Time: 1923
Locale: The United States

Cecil B. DeMille became Hollywood's preeminent producer-director of silent motion-picture spectacle with the critical and box-office success of The Ten Commandments *in 1923*

Principal personages:

CECIL B. DEMILLE (1881-1959), a celebrated director-producer whose career spanned both the silent and sound motion-picture eras

SAMUEL GOLDWYN (SAMUEL GOLDFISH, 1882-1974), a notable sound-era producer who first entered the movie business in 1913 in partnership with Jesse L. Lasky and DeMille

JESSE L. LASKY (1880-1958), a genial show-business entrepreneur who with DeMille and Goldwyn formed the Jesse L. Lasky Feature Play Company in 1913

JEANIE MACPHERSON (1884-1946), a prominent silent-era screenwriter best known for her highly successful collaborations with DeMille

ADOLPH ZUKOR (1873-1976), one of Hollywood's most influential moguls

Summary of Event

When Cecil B. DeMille's epic *The Ten Commandments* opened in Los Angeles and New York in December, 1923, its enthusiastic reception immediately solidified DeMille's reputation as Hollywood's preeminent showman. Fans, critics, and Hollywood itself, with only few exceptions, were dazzled. Completed at a cost of slightly less than a million and a half dollars, DeMille's silent-era spectacle rang up a box-office take of more than four million dollars. James R. Quirk, the influential editor of *Photoplay* magazine, called it "the best photoplay ever made" and "the greatest theatrical spectacle in history." Hollywood's moguls rejoiced as well, since the film's epochal retelling of the story of Moses leading the Children of Israel out of bondage from Egypt to the Promised Land helped to defuse the efforts of the conservative activists seeking to control the content of films through various forms of censorship.

Produced by the Famous Players-Lasky Corporation and released through its Paramount Pictures distribution arm, *The Ten Commandments* consolidated DeMille's reputation as America's foremost director of movie spectacles. Though esteemed for having codirected Hollywood's first feature-length film, *The Squaw Man* (1914), and for such popular and critically acclaimed productions as *The Cheat* (1915) and *Male and Female* (1919), in 1923 DeMille needed a hit to counter the downward spin of such lackluster releases as *Adam's Rib* (1923), which had received only tepid box-office and critical support. DeMille knew as well as anyone that in Hollywood he was considered only as good as his last picture. With the rousing success of *The Ten Commandments*, DeMille was again atop the short list of bankable and therefore elite Hollywood directors. Also, the epic was the first in a long line of lavish and successful extravaganzas—including his last directorial assignment, a second rendition of *The Ten Commandments* (1956)—that forever would be linked to the name of Cecil B. DeMille.

The Ten Commandments consists of two parts. The first, the spectacle, depicts biblical stories taken from the book of Exodus, including the persecution of the Jews by the Egyptians, the flight of the Israelites through the parted waters of the Red Sea, the giving to Moses of the Ten Commandments, and Moses' defiant breaking of the tablets upon his discovery of the Israelites' worship of the golden calf. The film's second part, a contemporary family melodrama set in San Francisco, centers on the moral conflicts between two brothers, one who is good and keeps the commandments, the other who is bad and breaks them; in essence, the second story is an allegory designed by DeMille and his dependable scenarist Jeanie Macpherson as a warning to modern society to heed God's injunctions. Therefore, when critics and historians refer to *The Ten Commandments* as a spectacle, the subject at hand is the film's sumptuously mounted prologue.

There are several ways of gauging *The Ten Commandments'* larger-than-life dimensions. Though the previously cited cost of making *The Ten Commandments* may not impress a modern reader, in 1923, the film's nearly one-and-one-half-million-dollar budget was staggering, especially since the expense of a typical feature production of the period was about $100,000. Indeed, the film's epic budget, while making for headline-grabbing publicity, exacerbated already strained relations between DeMille and his partners, Adolph Zukor and Jesse L. Lasky, Famous Players-Lasky's president and vice president in charge of production. At one point in the midst of shooting, DeMille, fatigued by the constant carping from New York on such matters as an invoice for $2,500 for a pair of magnificent coal-black horses to draw a chariot, offered to buy the film outright for $1,000,000. DeMille's bold demonstration of faith in his project shocked Zukor and Lasky, who wisely decided to relent. Though each of the New York-based executives sent warm congratulatory telegrams to DeMille upon the film's successful debut, the wedge created by the incessant budgetary wrangling eventually resulted in DeMille's painful resignation from Famous Players-Lasky in 1925.

Budgets aside, what most impressed moviegoers of 1923 and 1924 was the film's on-screen display of spectacle. Though thwarted by the cost-conscious Zukor from shooting on location in Egypt, DeMille bolted the confines of Hollywood for Guadalupe, an arid desert area near Santa Maria in central California, where a construction gang of more than a thousand carpenters, electricians, painters, and landscape gardeners erected a still-amazing facsimile of the ancient Egyptian city of Per-Ramses. As construction progressed, DeMille was commuting to Los Angeles in order to shoot some of the film's interior scenes. Eventually, twenty-five hundred actors and forty-five hundred animals, including two hundred camels, were settled in Camp DeMille, itself a virtual replica of an army camp. For added authenticity, DeMille, in part reflecting the influence of David Belasco, the great theatrical realist with whom he had worked as a young man, hired a contingent of Orthodox Jews to play the Children of Israel.

DeMille's special effects expert, Roy Pomeroy, played a pivotal role by achieving such still-convincing miracles as the parting of the Red Sea, the drowning of the Egyptians, and Moses' reception of the Ten Commandments from the incendiary heavens. Indeed, most film historians have judged Pomeroy's effects of 1923 more convincing than those he created for DeMille's 1956 version of *The Ten Command-ments*. The element of spectacle in the 1923 production was heightened even further by DeMille's decision to shoot parts of the prologue in an early and then experimental version of the Technicolor process (in contrast to the conventional black-and-white treatment given the modern story). Audiences and critics alike were impressed by the enhanced sense of realism.

Impact of Event

The Ten Commandments emphatically confirmed DeMille's reputation as one of Hollywood's most astute judges of public taste. Sensing that the vogue for Jazz Age depictions of fast living had begun to alienate a growing number of Americans—a shift in public attitude hastened by the day's lurid headlines screaming the latest off-screen Hollywood scandals—DeMille devised a narrative-dramatic formula that offered both gaudy titillation and moral rectitude. Given the *The Ten Commandments'* approval from all segments of the public, including the clergy, a high moral tone became a basic thematic component of DeMille's subsequent films. In his condemnations of wrongdoing, however, DeMille felt it dramatically and commercially necessary to portray sin and sexuality with lingering, graphic detail. It was a solution that not only helped to insure DeMille's own future but that of the industry as well. Indeed, when Hollywood was again threatened by censorious pressures in the early days of synchronized sound, DeMille's "have your cake and eat it too" strategy was institutionalized in the canons set forth by the Motion Picture Production Code of 1930.

An extensive press campaign during the production of *The Ten Commandments* kept the director's image before the public. With his drooping pipe, puttees, pistols, riding boots, and silver whistle, DeMille became the public's flesh-and-blood embodiment of the archetypal Hollywood director. DeMille loved the attention and the perks his meticulously choreographed image helped secure. He even appeared in cameo roles, most notably in *Hollywood* (1923) and *Sunset Boulevard* (1950), playing himself. Perhaps most significant, "DeMille" was a name the public knew and responded to with the kind of devotion otherwise given only to stars such as Charlie Chaplin, Mary Pickford, and Douglas Fairbanks.

Another consequence of the success achieved by *The Ten Commandments* was the typecasting of its director as a maestro of the film spectacle. Indeed, DeMille's name remains inextricably linked to the genre, conjuring up images not only of the director's two versions of *The Ten Commandments* but also of a succession of mammoth epics that included *The King of Kings* (1927), *The Sign of the Cross* (1932), *Cleopatra* (1934), *The Crusades* (1935), *The Plainsman* (1937), *The Buccaneer* (1938), *Union Pacific* (1939), *Samson and Delilah* (1949), and *The Greatest Show on Earth* (1952).

In assessing DeMille's overall impact, the director's crucial role as a founding partner of the Jesse L. Lasky Feature Play Company in 1913 should not be forgotten. As the fledgling firm's director-general, it was DeMille who was responsible for deciding to make its first production, *The Squaw Man*, a six-reel feature film. Subsequent features directed and produced by DeMille and employing such well-known personalities as Metropolitan Opera diva Geraldine Farrar and silent-film star Mary Pickford solidified the Lasky Company's leadership in the growing feature-film market. Consequently, DeMille is justly regarded as the individual who deserves greatest credit for establishing Hollywood as the film capital of the world.

DeMille's unique role as a master showman with tremendous ability to anticipate and play to the shifting tastes of the public should also not be discounted. Indeed, his sexual melodramas such as *Old Wives for New* (1918) and *Male and Female* accurately gauged the public's appetite for vicariously sampling the lifestyles of the era's rich and famous, a natural enough manifestation of human curiosity that had been made urgent by the deprivations and sacrifices required by the U.S. involvement in World War I. In the process, DeMille's parade of high fashion, his elevation of bathing to an art form, and his detailed depictions of the rules of etiquette required by high society for getting on in life educated and titillated Americans and influenced their behavior.

Bibliography

Brownlow, Kevin. "Cecil B. DeMille." In *The Parade's Gone By*. New York: Alfred A. Knopf, 1968. Brownlow's incisive assessment of DeMille's silent film career includes telling and balanced quotations from actresses Gloria Swanson, Leatrice Joy, Bessie Love, and Adela Rogers St. Johns, actor Gary Cooper, director William Wellman, producer David O. Selznick, and historian William Everson.

DeMille, Cecil B. *The Autobiography of Cecil B. DeMille*. Edited by Donald Hayne. Englewood Cliffs, N.J.: Prentice-Hall, 1959. A thorough and personal accounting of DeMille's life, times, and career with important insights on the rise of Hollywood, DeMille's switch from theater to motion pictures, and the controversies swirling about his larger-than-life epic films.

Essoe, Gabe, and Raymond Lee. *DeMille: The Man and His Pictures*. New York: Castle Books, 1970. A valuable if flawed source. Includes useful appreciations by Charlton Heston, Henry Wilcoxon, and Elmer Bernstein, an impressive collection of production stills and photos, a filmography, and a listing of DeMille's various honors.

Higham, Charles. *Cecil B. DeMille: A Biography of the Most Successful Film Maker of Them All.* New York: Charles Scribner's Sons, 1973. A lively and indispensable account of DeMille as an initially great director contented, finally, to be a great showman. Higham's penetrating insights are grounded in DeMille's voluminous correspondence and notebooks and extensive interviews with more than two hundred of DeMille's colleagues. Includes a filmography.

Jacobs, Lewis. *The Rise of the American Film: A Critical History.* 1939. Reprint. New York: Teachers College Press, 1968. Jacobs' masterful history includes an incisive and candid essay on DeMille's social-cultural impact and, in Jacobs' view, DeMille's severe limitations as a director.

Koszarski, Richard. "Cecil B. DeMille." In *An Evening's Entertainment: The Age of the Silent Feature Picture, 1915-1928.* New York: Charles Scribner's Sons, 1990. Koszarski provides an incisive overview of DeMille's artistic and cultural importance set against the evolution of the American silent feature film.

Pratt, George C. "Cecil B. DeMille." In *Spellbound in Darkness: A History of the Silent Film.* Rev. ed. Greenwich, Conn.: New York Graphic Society, 1973. Includes Pratt's brief yet trenchant assessment of DeMille's silent-era career as well as reprints of contemporary reviews of several of DeMille's films.

Rotha, Paul. *The Film Till Now: A Survey of World Cinema.* Rev. ed. London: Spring Books, 1967. Rotha's classic 1930 work, one of the first attempts to survey the international film, conveyed the British author's candid assessments of America's most prominent directors, including DeMille.

Zukor, Adolph. *The Public Is Never Wrong: The Autobiography of Adolph Zukor.* Edited by Dale Kramer. London: Cassell, 1954. Zukor's recollections are gentlemanly yet candid and are especially useful in corroborating and expanding on DeMille's pivotal role in the formation and evolving fortunes of Paramount Pictures.

Charles Merrell Berg

Cross-References

The Great Train Robbery Introduces New Editing Techniques (1903), p. 74; Pickford Becomes "America's Sweetheart" (1909), p. 224; Sennett Defines the Slapstick Comedy Genre (1909), p. 230; *The Birth of a Nation* Popularizes New Film Techniques (1915), p. 402; Von Stroheim Films His Silent Masterpiece *Greed* (1924), p. 593; Chaplin Produces His Masterpiece *The Gold Rush* (1925), p. 659; Keaton's *The General* Is Released (1926), p. 691; *The Jazz Singer* Premieres in New York (1927), p. 734; Sound Technology Revolutionizes the Motion-Picture Industry (1928), p. 761.

BESSIE SMITH RECORDS "DOWNHEARTED BLUES"

Category of event: Music
Time: February 15, 1923
Locale: New York, New York

Bessie Smith's modest recording session in 1923 helped her to become the most celebrated blues singer in history

Principal personages:
BESSIE SMITH (1894-1937), a singer who helped make the blues popular in America
MAMIE SMITH (1883-1946), a singer whose 1920 recording "Crazy Blues" proved the commercial potential of the blues
MA RAINEY (1886-1939), an early blues singer who influenced the style adopted by Bessie Smith
CLARENCE WILLIAMS (1898-1965), the jazz pianist who helped to guide Bessie Smith through her first recording session

Summary of Event

Long before her first recording session in 1923, Bessie Smith had sung for audiences in cities throughout the Southeast and Midwest. She began to sing publicly in 1903, when, at age nine, she stood on street corners in her hometown of Chattanooga, Tennessee, and shouted out Baptist hymns she learned from her father, a part-time preacher. In 1912, she joined a traveling vaudeville show in which she first met Ma Rainey, a singer whose powerful, lusty voice influenced the style of singing Smith eventually followed. Moving from city to city appealed to Smith, because Chattanooga had become for her a virtual prison of poverty. There were, however, indignities associated with the traveling show: She was considered too fat, too tall, and too black for featured roles. Smith greatly resented that light-skinned black female performers were given preference. She channeled her hostilities toward positive goals, however; she was determined to succeed.

By 1921, Smith had her own show, and she was considered a star by black audiences. She had an arresting presence on stage that some likened to that of an evangelist, and the presentation of her songs reflected her innermost hurts. She sang the blues as no one had heard them sung before. Her rise to prominence coincided with the recognition by recording companies that there was a market for black music. The OKeh Record Company first recorded a black singer, Mamie Smith, in 1920. Her recording of "Crazy Blues" sold enough copies to convince executives that there was a future for the blues on records. Ma Rainey recorded more than ninety songs in the early 1920's.

Bessie Smith had two auditions with OKeh, but she was turned down each time because her voice was judged too rough to have a general appeal. Black Swan Records, founded by W. C. Handy, also turned her down and chose to promote the less strident singing of Ethel Waters, Smith's principal competitor of the 1920's. Smith's chance finally came when Frank Walker, who produced "race records" for Columbia, decided to give her an opportunity. Walker dispatched pianist Clarence Williams to Philadelphia to bring Smith to New York for a recording session that began on February 15, 1923.

It took two days, under the patient guidance of Williams, for the nervous Smith to record "Downhearted Blues" and "Gulf Coast Blues." Whatever doubts there were about Smith's rough manner, her voice and phrasing proved to be explosive on record. "Downhearted Blues" sold more than 750,000 copies.

After that modest recording session in 1923, Bessie Smith quickly became known as the "Empress of the Blues." By 1924, her record sales passed the two million mark, and she made featured appearances on Milton Stan's black vaudeville circuit. In January, 1925, Smith made what some critics believe to be her best recordings when she teamed for one memorable session with Louis Armstrong, who was then a member of Fletcher Henderson's orchestra. Smith was reluctant to record with Armstrong, but her favorite accompanist, cornetist Joe Smith, was not in New York at the time. As it happened, Smith and Armstrong had an instant rapport, and from this session came the standard version of "St. Louis Blues." In that song and others that she recorded with Armstrong, Smith diverged markedly from a literal reading of the lyrics and, in so doing, created something new and exciting.

As her singing career continued to gain momentum in the second half of the 1920's, though, Smith's personal life collapsed. Wrangling over the distribution of her royalties, excessive drinking, boorish behavior at parties and social gatherings, and an unhappy marriage to a Philadelphia policeman brought her considerable opprobrium and misery. While she blossomed as a professional, such problems remained of secondary importance, but when her career started to slide after 1929, they became open wounds.

The beginning of the end for Smith came from a combination of factors, over some of which she had no control. A failed Broadway show left her depressed, and her appearance in the 1929 movie *St. Louis Blues*, in which she sang the title song, made it clear that she had little talent as an actress. In 1929, the sale of blues records declined, and promoters demanded that Smith and other black stars fill their music with double entendres. With America in the midst of the Great Depression, such efforts did not help sales very much. Also working against Smith in the early 1930's was the expansion of radio and new recording technology. She could not adapt to the new technology, which demanded a softer, more intimate sound that appealed to a nationwide audience listening in its living rooms. It was a way of singing that favored Ethel Waters, Ella Fitzgerald, and Louis Armstrong.

Smith's last great recording session was in 1929, when she recorded "Nobody Knows You When You're Down and Out," "Alexander's Ragtime Band," and "There'll Be a Hot Time in the Old Town Tonight." To each of these songs, Smith imparts an air of hovering tragedy, a reflection of the circumstances in her life at the time.

These recordings reveal her to be as much a jazz singer as a blues singer. "Nobody Knows You When You're Down and Out" became the song with which Smith would be most associated over the years, even more than "St. Louis Blues."

Smith's career went steadily downhill in the 1930's. She no longer received top dollar for her appearances, and her recordings did not sell particularly well. Although her voice remained powerful, numerous comeback efforts between 1933 and 1937 failed. She died in an automobile accident near Clarksdale, Mississippi, while traveling to a singing engagement on September 26, 1937. Stories at the time said she might have lived if she had been admitted to a white hospital that turned her away, but such stories were not accurate.

Impact of Event

More than any other black artist, Bessie Smith opened the door for black musicians to the commercial market. She sang "country blues," as opposed to the "urban blues" of Ma Rainey and Mamie Smith. She sang with a passion, pain, and verve that rang true to black listeners throughout the United States. Her audience appreciated her complete defiance of the white world; she refused to yield to white conventions in her music or in her personal life. There was, as well, a refusal in her singing to blandly surrender to lyrics or melody; therefore, her songs usually bore her personal stamp. It was an attribute that not only endeared her to her faithful followers but also left its mark on other entertainers.

British jazz musician and critic Humphrey Littelton has argued that Smith was one of only three 1920's musicians (Louis Armstrong and Sidney Bechet were the other two) who had the talent and confidence to change the "rhythmic conventions of the day." Smith was able to move away from the legacy of ragtime rhythm by adjusting lyrics (dropping or adding words and syllables) to suit her personal interpretation of a song. Many artists of the 1930's, including some of the highly popular "crooners" of the time, were much influenced by Smith's molding of a lyric to give proper emphasis to a phrase. Louis Armstrong's recording session with Smith in 1925 no doubt also encouraged his departure from standard phrasing.

It is difficult to gauge Smith's influence on other artists in the 1940's and early 1950's. She was not forgotten, but the recorded music of the war and postwar era was scarcely of the same brilliance as that of the 1920's. In the late 1950's, however, the mix of blues and gospel music began to inspire a new era for black artists. Gospel singer Mahalia Jackson, while rejecting Bessie Smith's rather seamy way of life, essentially emulated her stage presence and style of singing to gain considerable popularity.

In addition to Jackson, Dinah Washington and Linda Hopkins were the 1950's singers most obviously in the Bessie Smith mold. Washington studied Smith closely. In many ways, Washington's life, with its poverty, its evangelical roots, and its sorrowful personal problems, paralleled Smith's. Washington, like Smith, had begun by singing hymns; also like Smith, she developed a powerful, expressive, pain-ridden style marked by immaculate phrasing and diction. To hear Washington's version of

"This Bitter Earth" is to experience the same emotional reaction encountered after hearing Smith's "Nobody Knows You When You're Down and Out." It was appropriate that Washington recorded an album entitled *Dinah Washington Sings Bessie Smith* shortly before her death in 1963.

Linda Hopkins proved to be the most thorough student of Bessie Smith's life and the most exacting emulator of her style. In 1936, when Hopkins was only eleven years old, she heard Smith sing in New Orleans; the experience left an indelible impression. One year later, Mahalia Jackson "discovered" Hopkins, and her career as a blues singer ascended. In 1959, Hopkins began to portray Bessie Smith in her performances, and in 1974 she developed a one-woman show in which she played Smith. That show became a musical, *Bessie and Me*, in 1976. More than fifty years after Smith's first recording session in 1923, Hopkins had revived a great interest in her life. In the 1970's, rhythm-and-blues star Aretha Franklin built substantially on the foundation laid by Bessie Smith. To a great extent, Franklin learned of Smith through Hopkins. By helping to introduce the world to modern soul music, Franklin became the most influential female singer since Smith's era of the 1920's.

Bessie Smith's black successors enjoyed something that she never experienced—the enthusiastic approval of and acceptance by white audiences. Ironically, Smith's own recordings, rereleased in 1958 and then reissued in their entirety by Columbia Records in 1970, gained wide popularity and sold more than 500,000 copies. It is not too much to say that the music of Smith and her later counterparts communicated to white listeners the fact that the black experience in the United States was not adequately expressed by the light-hearted sounds of much popular black music.

Bibliography

Albertson, Chris. *Bessie.* New York: Stein & Day, 1972. A solid biography with, perhaps, a little too much emphasis on the rough side of Smith's life, particularly her bisexuality. A good portion of the book is based on interviews with Smith's niece, Ruby Walker. *Bessie* is Albertson's redemption, for in 1970 he wrote the liner notes to Columbia's reissue of Smith's records, and those liner notes (for which Albertson won a Grammy Award) were terribly inaccurate. Many photographs, discography, index.

Feinstein, Elaine. *Bessie Smith.* New York: Viking, 1985. A brief and highly impressionistic look at Smith's life. Feinstein writes little about Smith's music. The author does, however, carefully analyze the controversial events surrounding Smith's death. Suitable only for those who wish an introduction to Smith's life. Photographs, select discography, inadequate bibliography, index.

Jones, LeRoi. *Blues People: The Negro Experience in White America.* New York: William Morrow, 1963. Jones (Amiri Baraka) discusses how blues and jazz evolved in white America. Filled with insights about how blacks survived and how their music flourished in difficult circumstances. Bessie Smith is put in historical context. An interesting and useful study. Index.

Lyttelton, Humphrey. *The Best of Jazz: Basin Street to Harlem.* New York: Taplinger, 1978. An outstanding series of essays on the great names in jazz from the 1920's and 1930's by a well-known British jazz musician and critic. Duke Ellington, Louis Armstrong, Sidney Bechet, and Fletcher Henderson are some of those discussed. Lyttelton's essay on Bessie Smith is essential reading. Select bibliography, discography, index.

Priestley, Brian. *Jazz on Record: A History.* London: Elm Tree Books, 1988. A history of jazz recordings from the 1920's to the 1980's. An impressive undertaking; contains much of interest regarding Bessie Smith. Some of Priestley's comments, however, are a bit arrogant. The record guide is an important feature. Photographs, inadequate bibliography, index.

Ronald K. Huch

Cross-References

Handy Ushers in the Commercial Blues Era (1910's), p. 252; Armstrong First Records with His Hot Five Group (1925), p. 670; Ellington Begins an Influential Engagement at the Cotton Club (1927), p. 739; Billie Holiday Begins Her Recording Career (1933), p. 930; Goodman Begins His *Let's Dance* Broadcasts (1934), p. 968; Mahalia Jackson Begins Her Recording Career (1946), p. 1329.

LUCE FOUNDS *TIME* MAGAZINE

Category of event: Journalism
Time: March 3, 1923
Locale: New York, New York

As the prototype for newsmagazines, Time *developed an approach to journalism and a style that were widely imitated and often criticized*

Principal personages:
HENRY R. LUCE (1898-1967), an entrepreneur and editor who cofounded *Time* and served as the driving force behind Time, Incorporated for forty-four years
BRITON HADDEN (1898-1929), a journalist and editor who cofounded *Time*, developed its style, and directed its policies during its first six years
RAY E. LARSEN (1899-1979), the first circulation manager of *Time*, who played a role second only to Luce's in creating Time, Incorporated

Summary of Event

Appalled by the ignorance of current events displayed by soldiers at their army officers' training school at Camp Jackson in South Carolina in 1918, Yale University sophomores Henry Luce and Briton Hadden first discussed the idea of developing a newsmagazine. As classmates for seven years, Luce and Hadden had worked together (and competed) on the weekly *Record* of the Hotchkiss School, a preparatory school in Lakeville, Connecticut, and on the Yale *Daily News.* Following their graduation from Yale in 1920, Luce studied at the University of Oxford and then worked briefly as a reporter for the *Chicago Daily News*, while Hadden took a similar position with the prestigious *New York World.* In the fall of 1921, both joined the staff of the *Baltimore News.* After working there for only three months, they abruptly resigned in February of 1922 to go to New York City to pursue their dream of developing a new vehicle to inform Americans about major national and international events.

Their creation—*Time* magazine, first issued in March, 1923—became the prototype for other newsmagazines, developed a widely imitated journalistic style, provoked considerable controversy, contributed to establishing a corporation that later published *Fortune, Life,* and *Sports Illustrated*, pioneered in radio broadcasting and film journalism, and significantly influenced American and international opinion. In 1922, these talented but inexperienced twenty-four-year-olds sought simply to produce a weekly magazine that would both report and interpret the news. In this way, it would differ from America's more than two thousand newspapers, from literary periodicals such as *The Atlantic Monthly, Harper's Magazine,* and *Scribner's,* and from magazines such as *Review of Reviews, World's Work,* and *The Literary Digest* (which were basically limited to clippings and quotations from other sources). The pair spent the next eight months, which Luce later described as the hardest period of his life, writing a prospectus, learning how to sell subscriptions, soliciting testimonials, raising money, and trying to devise a new style of writing. Their plan, as explained in their prospectus, was to report all the week's important news in a brief (approximately one hundred articles of four hundred words or less), organized fashion. While their magazine would not have an editorial page and would present competing sides of issues, it would make clear which positions the editors thought were stronger. *Time* would emphasize international events, oppose the increasing interference and rising cost of government, support established manners, and promote new ideas.

After writing their prospectus, Hadden and Luce learned the principles of the mailorder business from William Eaton, the top circulation expert at *World's Work* in New York City, and set out to raise $100,000 as capital for their project. To enhance the creditability of their venture, they secured endorsements from Newton Baker, H. L. Mencken, Bernard Baruch, Yale president James Angell, Franklin Roosevelt, and other prominent people. The money was much more difficult to raise than Hadden and Luce anticipated, primarily because neither of them was good at the task; Luce was reticent, and Hadden was overbearing. Nevertheless, by late 1922 they had collected almost $87,000, largely from Yale alumni and connections, and decided to proceed with their magazine.

The first issue of *Time* appeared March 3, 1923. At twenty-eight pages, it was a thin, unimpressive magazine that sold for the rather high price of fifteen cents. Its cover, as would almost all subsequent ones, featured an individual—Joe Cannon, who at age eighty-six was retiring after twenty-three terms in Congress. The magazine's twenty-two departments, including such titles as "National Affairs," "Foreign News," "Books," "The Theatre," "Cinema," "Education," "Religion," "Law," "Science," "Finance," "Sports," "Crime," and "Milestones," could be read in one hour. "National Affairs," with subsections concerning the presidency, the Congress, the Supreme Court, Prohibition, labor, women, blacks, and radicals, and "Foreign Affairs," with items on fourteen different countries, filled nearly half of the first and subsequent issues. Three other departments—"Imaginary Interviews," "Points with Pride," and "Views with Alarm"—consisted of cryptic comments followed by page numbers designed to encourage a second reading of the issue. As would become standard policy, all articles except one were anonymous. Stephen Vincent Benét reviewed books, and Archibald MacLeish wrote on education; most of the other departments contained writing by classmates from Yale and friends of Hadden and Luce. As the prospectus had envisioned, all subjects were discussed very briefly.

Hadden and Luce had naïvely expected their magazine to be either an overnight sensation or a complete flop. The prevailing reaction to it, however, was apathy. During the next three years, *Time* fought for its life and lost more than $62,000. Despite these financial problems, conflict between Hadden and Luce, and problems with advertising and staff, the circulation (which grew from 18,500 in 1923 to 110,000 in 1926) and influence of *Time* gradually increased.

During the Roaring Twenties, *Time*'s small, inexperienced staff covered the movies of Charlie Chaplin and Douglas Fairbanks, the music of Irving Berlin, the novels of Sinclair Lewis, Ernest Hemingway, Willa Cather, and F. Scott Fitzgerald, the plays of Eugene O'Neill, sports heroes such as Babe Ruth, Bill Tilden, Helen Wills, Bobby Jones, and Jack Dempsey, the Scopes Trial, Prohibition, the growth of big business, the building of skyscrapers, clothing fads, increasing prosperity, and much more.

Impact of Event

Time magazine, and its parent company, Time, Incorporated, have substantially influenced the reporting and understanding of news in the United States and around the world. Its methods and style have been widely copied and frequently criticized; its perspective and its coverage of events have aroused considerable controversy. The success of *Time* led to the publication of other important magazines and to pioneering efforts in radio and cinema presentation of the news.

For its first twenty years, *Time* was primarily a rewrite sheet. In the words of its own authorized history, it was produced "with no more editorial resources than a pile of yesterday's newspapers, some well-thumbed reference books," and the wits of its editors. *Time* provided a superficial but concise summary of the news for those who had no more time or inclination to read; it condensed complex events and complicated issues into bite-sized morsels that could be easily swallowed, if not thoroughly digested. By 1928, when *Time* had become more successful, *Editor and Publisher*, journalism's trade paper, led a concerted attack upon the magazine's reprocessing of news culled from other sources. Nevertheless, *Time* and its imitators continued the practice (declared legal by the Supreme Court in 1918) into the early 1940's, when *Time* finally created its own news sources.

Using the technique of "group journalism," in which reporters, writers, researchers, and editors pooled their knowledge and skills to produce its issues, *Time* developed a lively style that influenced many other magazines. In an effort to get stories off *Time*'s pages and into readers' minds, news was conveyed through the narrative structure, historical background, character development, plot, and suspense characteristic of the short story. Moreover, *Time*'s writers frequently reversed subject and predicate and used alliteration, descriptive adjectives (George Bernard Shaw, for example, was "mocking, mordant, misanthropic"), active verbs, and the middle names of prominent people. The magazine often employed double epithets ("snaggle-toothed," "haystack-haired," "beady-eyed"), tantalizing picture captions, informal snapshots, snappy titles, compound words ("cinemoppet Shirley Temple," "sexational Mae West," "Broadwayfarer"), neologisms, and euphemisms ("great and good friend" for mistress). In *Time*, people did not speak or say things; they croaked, gruffed, sneered, and guffawed. Instead of simply walking, they stalked, strode, and bounced. Shortly after its founding, the magazine initiated a letters column and created its own cast of colorful, irascible, outrageous respondents to irritate and amuse readers. Displaying contempt for stuffed shirts, awe for success, cynicism, egotism, and a Mencken-like irreverence for authority, *Time* was always candid, sometimes rude and disrespectful, and often provocative. After Wolcott Gibbs's parody of "Timestyle" in a now-famous 1936 article in *The New Yorker*, its writers gradually moved toward more conventional English.

Even more controversial than *Time*'s methods of gathering news and its style was its "interpretative reporting." In their original prospectus, Hadden and Luce acknowledged that "complete neutrality on public questions and important news" was "probably as undesirable" as it was "impossible" and that therefore "certain prejudices" might "predetermine their opinions on the news." From its inception, *Time*'s editors sought to slice, condense, flavor, and slant the news to make it more interesting than it was in real life. Over the years, the magazine's selection and packaging of the news, its lavish details, its tone (reverent and laudatory toward its heroes, hardboiled and cynical toward those it disliked), and its use of dramatization have provided a distinctive perspective on events. Many have accused *Time* of being unfair, of twisting the news by exaggeration, selection, and suppression, and of trying to shape the course of events. *Time*'s (and *Fortune*'s) favorable portrayal of Benito Mussolini and Francisco Franco in the 1930's, its negative treatment of Franklin Roosevelt, Harry Truman, and Adlai Stevenson, its strong support of Chiang Kai-shek, and its reporting of the Vietnam War proved especially controversial. From the time of Hadden's death in 1929 until Luce's retirement in 1964, *Time* basically expressed Luce's fervent Protestant, Republican, free-enterprise views and his belief that America had a mission to police, protect, and guide the world. Nevertheless, over the years the magazine has followed no consistent editorial policy or ideological perspective. While espousing many politically conservative positions, *Time* has also supported such liberal causes as the United Nations, the Marshall Plan, the bitter fight against McCarthyism, and the long struggle of black Americans for civil rights.

Time's influence has been tremendous. It has transformed the art and practice of newswriting in America and around the world (more than fifty journals, ranging from Germany's *Der Spiegel* to France's *Express* to Chile's *Hoy*, are based on ideas originated by *Time*) and probably has been more criticized than any other American magazine. Its articles have helped to elect presidents, pass legislation, mold public opinion, and shape foreign policy. The magazine's success led its parent company to found, among other magazines, *Fortune*, a business newsweekly, in 1930, *Life*, a heavily pictorial presentation of news and human interest stories, in 1936, and *Sports Illustrated*, a sophisticated examination of a wide gamut of sports, in 1954. In the late 1920's and 1930's, Time, Incorporated, created several radio programs to publicize its magazine and message. The most significant, *The March of Time*, was performed by live actors supported by a twenty-three-piece studio orchestra. The reenactments of events and impersonations of prominent people first used on the show were soon widely imitated by other radio programs. In the mid-1930's, the corporation began producing a film version of *The March of Time* that combined newsreel, documentary, and dramatic portrayals. Its 257 episodes introduced controversial topics to an international audience estimated at fifteen million, and in 1937, the program won a special Academy Award. Time, Incorporated, has billions of dollars in assets, ranks among America's top five hundred corporations, and each year publishes millions of books and copies of its influential magazines. The founding of *Time* in 1923 has had enormous consequences.

Bibliography

Baughman, James L. *Henry R. Luce and the Rise of the American News Media.* Boston: Twayne, 1987. An essentially favorable biography of Luce that sets its subject in the broader context of twentieth century news media. Explains how his innovative summary and synthesis of the news using a short-story format and visual images changed American journalism. Portrays Luce as a proponent of Republican Party politics and middle-class American values. Bibliography, index.

Busch, Noel F. *Briton Hadden: A Biography of the Co-founder of Time.* New York: Farrar, Straus, 1949. The most thorough account of Hadden's role in creating *Time* and developing its style. Written by Hadden's cousin, who wrote for the magazine in its early years. Very valuable for understanding the origins of *Time.* Told as an American success story, it does little to illuminate Hadden's character.

Elson, Robert T. *Time Inc.: The Intimate History of a Publishing Enterprise, 1923-1941.* New York: Atheneum, 1968. An authorized history of Time, Incorporated, based upon corporate records. Discusses the founding of *Time* and *Life, Time's* approach to journalism and the development of its style, and the personalities of the principal persons involved. Remarkably candid for an official history, it nevertheless portrays Time, Incorporated very favorably. Photographs, index.

_____. *The World of Time, Inc.: The Intimate History of a Publishing Enterprise, 1941-1960.* New York: Atheneum, 1973. Also based upon corporate archives, this volume recounts the history and incredible growth of Time, Incorporated, over a twenty-year period. Easy and enjoyable to read, self-critical, generally positive, and valuable for understanding Luce's thought and life. Photographs, index.

Kobler, John. *Luce: His Time, Life, and Fortune.* Garden City, N.Y.: Doubleday, 1968. A lively and balanced account of Luce's founding of and control over Time, Incorporated, its internal feuds, its influence in foreign affairs, and his skill as a businessman. Written by a senior editor of *The Saturday Evening Post* and first published as a series of articles in that magazine, the book is very readable but lacks coherence. Photographs of key individuals, covers of publications, and cartoons. Bibliography.

Luce, Henry. *The Ideas of Henry Luce.* Edited by John K. Jessup. New York: Atheneum, 1969. A collection of Luce's speeches, article excerpts, and other statements on journalism, politics, law and order, business, art and architecture, Christianity, the New Deal, Communism, China, American presidents, and many other subjects. Useful for understanding Luce's biases, which influenced his publications and provoked much controversy. Includes a brief but insightful biographical introduction.

Swanberg, W. A. *Luce and His Empire: A Biography.* New York: Charles Scribner's

Sons, 1972. Based on substantial research, this polemical biography castigates Luce's motives, commitments, and achievements. Argues primarily that Luce was a megalomaniac who used *Time* and its sister publications to try to shape America's policies. Although engaging and entertaining, the book lacks subtlety and balance, often ignores historical contexts, and frequently presents trivial or repetitious information. Splendid collection of photographs, endnotes, index.

Gary Scott Smith

Cross-References

The Christian Science Monitor Is Founded (1908), p. 209; Lippmann Helps to Establish *The New Republic* (1914), p. 385; Wallace Founds *Reader's Digest* (1922), p. 549; Luce Launches *Life* Magazine (1936), p. 1031; Buckley Founds *National Review* (1955), p. 1683; *60 Minutes* Becomes the First Televised Newsmagazine (1968), p. 2136; *USA Today* Is Launched (1982), p. 2507.

THE FORMATION OF THE BLUE FOUR
ADVANCES ABSTRACT PAINTING

Category of event: Art
Time: 1924
Locale: Europe, the United States, and Mexico

Four leading abstract painters in Germany formed a partnership to promote their work and thereby contributed greatly to the worldwide revolution in modern art

Principal personages:

WASSILY KANDINSKY (1866-1944), one of the Blue Four, a Russian-born painter who is generally regarded as the inventor of nonobjective painting

PAUL KLEE (1879-1940), one of the Blue Four, a Swiss-born painter who contributed humor and originality to abstract painting

LYONEL FEININGER (1871-1956), one of the Blue Four, an American-born cartoonist-turned-painter who taught at the Bauhaus

ALEXEY VON JAWLENSKY (1864-1941), one of the Blue Four, a Russian-born painter who lived in Germany for many years and associated with the Bauhaus artists

EMMY "GALKA" SCHEYER (1889-1945), an art student who founded the Blue Four in 1924 and helped to popularize German avant-garde art in America and Mexico

WALTER GROPIUS (1883-1969), a German architect who founded the Bauhaus School of Design

JSRAEL BER (J. B. NEUMANN, 1887-1961), a New York art dealer who devoted much of his life to popularizing modern German painters in America

Summary of Event

Emmy Scheyer was born in Braunschweig, Germany. As a young student, she discovered the paintings of Russian immigrant Alexey von Jawlensky and was so impressed by the new art form they represented that she decided to devote her life to publicizing his work. Through Jawlensky, she met many other avant-garde painters, including Wassily Kandinsky, Paul Klee, and Lyonel Feininger, who were teaching at the Bauhaus School of Design. Because their art was revolutionary and as yet unpopular, all four men were chronically in need of money.

This was especially true after Germany's defeat in World War I and the devastating inflation that followed. In 1924, Scheyer (who was given the nickname "Galka"—Russian for "black bird"—by Jawlensky) volunteered to promote their paintings in affluent America, famous for its receptivity to new ideas. On March 31, 1924, an agreement was signed designating Scheyer as their American representative. For publicity purposes they christened their group the Blue Four (Die Blaue Vier), a reference to the Blue Rider (Der Blaue Reiter) group of painters who had been inspired and led by the mystical Kandinsky.

In May of 1924, the aggressive, charismatic Scheyer went to New York and began sending out thousands of pamphlets to universities, museums, and art associations, offering them her exhibits and services as a lecturer. In New York, she met and collaborated with J. B. Baumann, another ardent admirer of the new German avant-garde art who eventually became a wealthy Manhattan art dealer.

The first Blue Four exhibition was arranged by Scheyer at the Daniel Gallery, New York, in 1925. Sales were disappointing. Hoping for a better reception in the West, Scheyer traveled to California, lecturing about her artists along the way. For the next three years, she gave lectures and arranged Blue Four exhibitions in San Francisco, Los Angeles, Portland, Oregon, and Spokane, Washington.

Scheyer returned to Europe several times before World War II in order to collect new paintings. In 1929, the Oakland Art Gallery across the bay from San Francisco opened a traveling Blue Four exhibition under the sponsorship of the Western Association of Art Museums. A big show was held in Hollywood at the Braxton Gallery in 1930. In 1931, the prestigious Palace of the Legion of Honor in San Francisco held a Blue Four exhibition under Scheyer's direction. That same year, Scheyer was invited by the famous Mexican artist Diego Rivera to arrange an exhibition at the national library in Mexico City.

By that time, Scheyer was a resident of Hollywood. She became a social celebrity and sold modern German paintings to members of the affluent film colony. The deepening worldwide depression of the 1930's created havoc in the international art market, and Scheyer was forced to earn her living mainly by giving art lessons to children. She never, though, stopped devoting the bulk of her boundless energies to promoting the works of her Blue Four friends.

The American public was slow to accept avant-garde German art, both because the new art was revolutionary in nature and because Germany had only recently been an enemy in World War I. While Americans had become attuned to French Impressionism, they were not ready to accept the radical notions embodied in the new German works. In fact, many critics and connoisseurs regarded the new art as little more than a hoax, calling the works crude, primitive, childish, incompetent, vulgar, or deliberately ugly and offensive.

Yet there were a few who, like Scheyer, immediately understood and responded to what the Blue Four were trying to do. These perceptive individuals, mostly artists themselves, were delighted with the possibility of being liberated from the tradition that held that the artist should copy nature.

An important factor in the appeal of the Blue Four was the rapid development of photography. Just as live performers were being threatened by cinematic photography, painters were being threatened by still photography. Why pay a high price for a painting or drawing when a camera could produce an even better likeness for a much cheaper price?

The artists' defense of painting held that it was the element of human emotion that made the difference between painting and photography, which led to various experiments to capture the essential human emotion while either distorting the subject or doing without a subject altogether.

The Blue Four lasted for only one decade. The group broke up in the face of the growing repression of the Nazi government under Adolf Hitler, who hated what he called "degenerate art" and who favored art that served to promote patriotism, militarism, and totalitarianism. Klee returned to Switzerland in 1933; Kandinsky emigrated to France in 1933 and never returned to Germany. Feininger returned to the United States in 1936. Jawlensky remained in Nazi Germany until his death in 1941, but from 1933 on he was forbidden to exhibit his works.

During its brief lifespan, the Blue Four spread the message—particularly to America—that pictorial art had a potential that exceeded the mere copying of people, places, and things or the creation of attractive pictures to adorn the walls of wealthy patrons. Instead, they demonstrated, art could be used to explore the depths of human consciousness and communicate a vast range of ideas and feelings in a universal language.

Impact of Event

It is hard to overestimate the impact of German expressionist art. It had not only an unmistakable direct influence on oil painting and watercolors but also a far more important influence on the public at large through such things as package designs, newspaper and magazine advertising, textile designs, record covers, book jackets, greeting cards, wallpaper, stage scenery, billboards, posters, comic strips, animated cartoons, and television commercials. The masses have come to accept the concepts of German expressionist art without for the most part realizing where such concepts originated.

In the Walt Disney film *Fantasia*, which was a bold experiment in filmmaking at the time of its release in 1940, there are many examples of the influence of German expressionism to be seen. One of the most striking is the sequence in which abstract shapes of assorted colors are generated and modified to correspond to the music of Johann Sebastian Bach's *Toccata and Fugue in D Minor*. In this instance, the main influence is probably that of Kandinsky.

In the 1930's, when Fred Astaire and Ginger Rogers danced against stylized backdrops representing the skyscrapers of Manhattan or other modernistic settings, most of the members of the motion-picture audience were appreciating artistic concepts first introduced by Feininger, though they would not have recognized him by name. For many years, too, the covers of *The New Yorker* magazine have reflected the influence of all four members of the Blue Four and other German expressionist artists. The most notable example is the work of William Steig. The influence of both Klee and Jawlensky, moreover, is evident in the phenomenally popular comic strip *Peanuts*.

The impact of German expressionists on other painters has also been tremendous.

Visitors to any major art museum are likely to wander through many rooms full of pictures of fat cherubs and portraits of men and women in lace and suddenly to feel as if they have entered a different universe when they find their way into exhibits marked "Modern Art." Even if such viewers do not fully understand abstract painting, they are likely to feel refreshed by the vivid colors and the whole sense of creative liberation represented by such canvases. The influence of such artists as Kandinsky and Klee is unmistakable. So dramatic has been the influence of such artists that many members of the art world have come to regard artists working in the traditional vein with contempt, calling them "illusionists," "illustrators," or, perhaps worst of all, "bourgeois painters."

Such attitudes are clearly unfair to sincere and gifted traditional artists. The impact of German expressionism and related movements has not been an unmitigated good; it has spawned myriad untalented imitators whose main attraction to nonrepresentational art is in being freed from the need to develop technical expertise, the need to work long, hard hours to perfect a piece of art, and the need to have anything in particular to communicate. Many poseurs have capitalized on the sacrifices of true artists such as Kandinsky, Klee, Feininger, and Jawlensky, and some have made substantial money and seen their works displayed in the best museums.

The Blue Four artists and their colleagues had a definite political impact, too. Both the German dictator Adolf Hitler and the Soviet dictator Joseph Stalin hated the new expressionist art; both recognized it for what it was: the proclamation of the freedom of the individual.

Bibliography

Beale, Penny. "J. B. Neumann and the Introduction of Modern German Art to New York, 1923-1933." *Archives of American Art Journal* 29, nos. 1 and 2 (1989): 3-15. An interesting profile of a colorful character who was influential in introducing modern German art to America. Eighty-four endnotes refer to a wide variety of sources. Three other articles in this issue relate directly to artists of the Blue Four.

Joachimides, Christos M., Norman Rosenthal, and Wieland Schmied, eds. *German Art in the Twentieth Century: Painting and Sculpture, 1905-1985.* Munich: Prestel-Verlag, 1985. This big, comprehensive book contains discussions of all aspects of twentieth century German art, including its historical background and its international influence, by many different authorities in the field. Hundreds of full-color and black-and-white illustrations. Kandinsky, Klee, Feininger, and Jawlensky are all discussed and represented with many color reproductions. Contains biographies of all important twentieth century German artists, with bibliographic references for each individual.

Roters, Eberhard. *Painters of the Bauhaus.* New York: Frederick A. Praeger, 1969. A history of Bauhaus painters and art instruction, with considerable attention given to the methods and personalities of Klee, Kandinsky, and Feininger.

Sandback, Amy Baker. "Blue Heights Drive." *Artforum* 28 (March, 1990): 123-127. This is a rare profile of Galka Scheyer, the colorful woman who devoted much of her life to publicizing the Blue Four. Contains photographs of her in her modernistic home in the Hollywood hills, where she entertained such film figures as Charles Laughton, Edward G. Robinson, Greta Garbo, and the Marx Brothers.

Tolstoy, Leo. *What Is Art?* Translated by Almyer Maude. New York: Bobbs-Merrill, 1960. In this neglected masterpiece, one of the world's greatest writers offers a simple definition of art, summarizes the history of aesthetics, and voices a conservative reaction to the modernistic art theories that were emerging at the beginning of the twentieth century.

Whitford, Frank. *Bauhaus.* London: Thames & Hudson, 1984. A history of the most celebrated and influential art school of modern times, with 154 illustrations, mostly photographs of historical interest. Useful for understanding the relationship between Bauhaus ideas about architecture and fine art.

Wolfe, Tom. *The Painted Word.* New York: Farrar, Straus & Giroux, 1975. In this funny, irreverent history of abstract art in the United States one of the leading "New Journalists" illustrates the ways in which the principles behind abstract art have been exploited, abused, and misunderstood.

Bill Delaney

Cross-References

Avant-Garde Artists in Dresden Form Die Brücke (1905), p. 134; Les Fauves Exhibit at the Salon d'Automne (1905), p. 140; Der Blaue Reiter Abandons Representation in Art (1911), p. 275; Kandinsky Publishes His Views on Abstraction in Art (1912), p. 320; Avant-Garde Art in the Armory Show Shocks American Viewers (1913), p. 361; Malevich Introduces Suprematism (1915), p. 413; German Artists Found the Bauhaus (1919), p. 463; The Soviet Union Bans Abstract Art (1922), p. 544; *Abstract Painting in America* Opens in New York (1935), p. 1001; Hitler Organizes an Exhibition Denouncing Modern Art (1937), p. 1083.

MANN'S *THE MAGIC MOUNTAIN* REFLECTS EUROPEAN CRISIS

Category of event: Literature
Time: 1924
Locale: Germany

The debate concerning the condition of the European soul in Thomas Mann's The Magic Mountain reflected the sense of crisis that prevailed in Europe between World Wars I and II

Principal personage:
THOMAS MANN (1875-1955), a major modern novelist and intellectual who was awarded the Nobel Prize in Literature in 1929

Summary of Event

As with any literary text, the significance of Thomas Mann's most powerful novel, *Der Zauberberg* (1924; *The Magic Mountain,* 1927), should first be understood in the context of the author's life and creative output. Mann was born June 6, 1875, in the city of Lübeck to a wealthy merchant family. After the death of his father, the family business was closed, and Mann's mother moved to Munich. Mann worked for a brief time with an insurance company but embarked on a full-time writing career after a short story was published in a prestigious literary magazine. At this time, he became immersed in the writings of the philosophers Arthur Schopenhauer and Friedrich Nietzsche as well as in the music of composer Richard Wagner.

Mann's first literary success was the huge novel *Buddenbrooks: Verfall einer Familie* (1901; *Buddenbrooks,* 1924), the story of four generations of a Lübeck merchant family. The novel begins in 1835 with the founding of the family firm by the hardy Johann Buddenbrooks and ends with the premature death of his great grandson, the young and frail Hanno. In this first novel, Mann established one of his most prominent themes: That spirit, or self-consciousness, is essentially a disease and is inimical to the vitality of existence. In this view, strongly influenced by the ideas of Schopenhauer, the artistic or reflective temperament appears as a perennial outsider, a kind of parasite that sucks the very blood of life. Each succeeding generation of the family becomes more introspective and consequently physically weaker. Mann developed similar themes in his well-known novella *Tonio Kröger* (1903). In *Buddenbrooks,* Mann also employed the technique of the leitmotif, which he adapted from the music of Wagner. A certain phrase or image is associated with a theme or character and is later repeated, with slight variations, to evoke the particular figure or idea. In 1905, Mann married Katja Pringsheim, the daughter of a wealthy Munich family, and they had a total of six children over the ensuing years.

Der Tod in Venedig (1912; *Death in Venice,* 1925) is Mann's most famous novella.

It is the story of the writer Gustav von Aschenbach, a rigid and highly disciplined man who travels to the decaying city of Venice. On the beach, he sees a handsome young Polish boy, Tadzio, and he gradually becomes erotically obsessed with him. Thus begins a slow decline, both physical and moral, and Aschenbach finally dies of the plague when his obsession prohibits him from leaving the city. Mann sounds here again his theme of the artist and intellectual as an outsider, a decadent and diseased individual. The outbreak of World War I saw Mann as a conservative champion of traditional German values. This led him into a bitter conflict with his brother Heinrich, a prominent liberal and democratic author. During the postwar Weimar period, however, Mann became a staunch defender of democracy. His well-known 1929 short story "Mario und der Zauberer" ("Mario and the Magician") was written as a result of his experiences in Benito Mussolini's Italy and is a veiled condemnation of Fascism; ironically, it predicted what would later happen in Adolf Hitler's Germany.

In 1926, Mann began work on an enormous tetralogy of novels devoted to the Joseph story of the Old Testament. He finally completed it in 1943 while in exile. He had left Germany in 1933 for a lecture tour, but his reputation with the Nazi Party was so bad that his children warned him not to return. He stayed for a while in France and Switzerland and then moved to the United States in 1938. He worked on his writing and taught for a time at Princeton University and finally moved to Southern California, home to many prominent German exiles, in 1940. He became an American citizen in 1944. During this time, Mann wrote one of his most ambitious novels, *Doktor Faustus* (1947; *Doctor Faustus*, 1948), the story of the tragic fate of the composer Adrian Leverkühn as narrated by his friend, the bourgeois intellectual Serenus Zeitblom. The novel is a parable of the succumbing of middle-class Germany, with its long tradition of humanism and spiritual values, to the demonic forces of Hitler's racist ideology. As the title suggests, Leverkühn is a Faustian individual who sells his soul to the devil in order to produce a new kind of music. Here, Mann was influenced by the work of Arnold Schoenberg, the modernist composer who also was residing in exile in California. Mann suggested that the romantic German spirit, in its quest for ever-new experiences and its exploration of self-consciousness, had flirted with an abyss of subjectivity and irrationalism that had dangerous consequences. Elements of Nietzsche's biography also figure in the Leverkühn character.

In 1952, Mann moved to Switzerland, where he remained until his death on August 12, 1955. His last novel, *Bekenntnisse des Hochstaplers Felix Krull: Der Memoiren erster Teil* (1954; *Confessions of Felix Krull, Confidance Man: The Early Years*, 1955) again dealt with the theme of the artist, here a con artist who fools himself and the public through a series of poses. Throughout his writings, Mann maintained a sense of ambivalence toward his art, a feeling that he often mediated through a subtle sense of irony.

The plot of *The Magic Mountain* begins in 1907, when the young Hans Castorp from northern Germany goes to the elegant and international tuberculosis sanatorium Berghof in Davos, Switzerland, to visit his ailing cousin. Although he participates in the daily routine of the patients, which involves long periods of rest in the thin Alpine air as well as opulent meals, Castorp is not really ill, and at first he remains merely an observer. He stays, however, for a period of seven years, even after the death of his cousin. His own condition worsens and then improves.

This time becomes a period of education for Castorp, as he is exposed to a variety of experiences, both sensual and intellectual. Indeed, Mann imitates and parodies the nineteenth century genre of the *Bildungsroman*, or novel of education. Castorp falls in love with an elegant and beautiful Russian woman, Clawdia Chauchat, and has a passionate, and at times rather morbid, affair. He reads numerous books on topics ranging from the medical and natural sciences to Freudian psychology and the occult. He goes skiing and almost dies in a snowstorm, during which he has a frightening vision. Above all, he meets two older intellectuals who become his mentors. The first is Settembrini, an Italian humanist who upholds the values of European liberalism and rationalism. The other is Naphta, a dogmatic, formerly Jewish, and charismatic Jesuit priest who speaks for a blind and irrational faith. These two ideologues engage in a battle of minds for the prize of Castorp's intellectual spirit. The contest climaxes in a duel in which the enraged Naphta commits suicide when Settembrini refuses to fire at him.

When Clawdia Chauchat leaves Berghof after their brief affair, Castorp pines away for her. He is both disappointed and impressed when she returns accompanied by her lover, the robust and completely unintellectual businessman Mynheer Peeperkorn, whose unbridled vitality serves as a counterpoint to the sterile intellectuality of Settembrini and Naphta. Here Mann's view of the artist and intellectual as being fundamentally alienated from the vital forces of life is again apparent. Castorp leaves the sanatorium after his seven-year stay, presumably to join the army at the outbreak of the war.

Impact of Event

Mann himself regarded *The Magic Mountain* as a statement about the constitution of the European soul and the intellectual and spiritual impasse it confronted during the first part of the twentieth century. Hans Castorp is to be understood as a kind of Everyman, the average bourgeois European. The Berghof sanatorium, with its international clientele, becomes a microcosm of European society, and with its high altitude, thin air, and febrile atmosphere, it produces a hermetic intensification of all aspects of the individual's sensual and intellectual life.

The dilemma of European intellectuals as posited in Mann's novel can be approached by first examining the horrible vision that Castorp sees during the snowstorm. Initially, he perceives an idyllic landscape, sunny and populated by a seemingly healthy and happy people. In the dark interior of a temple, however, he comes upon a group of ugly and frightening old women who are dismembering a child. Here Mann echoes some of the ideas of Nietzsche concerning the origins of Greek tragic art and culture. Since the Greco-Roman tradition is central to Western culture, he is suggesting that at the heart of the European spirit there is a conflict of light and dark, of an enlightened, civilized, Apollonian world and a Dionysian one of utter barbarism and cruelty. Prior to World War I, Europeans had regarded themselves as a highly cultured and refined people who had produced the likes of William Shakespeare, Voltaire, Leo Tolstoy, and Johann Wolfgang von Goethe. The years 1914 to 1918, however, saw the advent of modern warfare and terrible and unprecedented human destruction. Among European intellectuals, there was a profound sense of shock at the depths to which European culture had sunk. Culture had revealed itself to be nothing more than a thin veneer that masked a mindless, raging beast. A feeling of crisis gradually emerged, in which the powers of the critical intellect and reason were devalued.

Mann gives more in-depth explanation of the dialectical forces that seemed to tear at the European spirit in long conversations between Castorp and his two ideological mentors that take up much of the latter half of the novel. Indeed, much of the novel is taken up by conversation; there is little overt action. Settembrini, the ailing but elegant man from the land in which the Renaissance began, is presented as the champion of the eighteenth century Enlightenment spirit, the dualistic belief that the use of reason can bring about progress and lead humanity out of its spiritual darkness into a more humane world. He stands in the European tradition of rationalistic philosophers such as Gottfried Wilhelm Leibniz, Immanuel Kant, René Descartes, Denis Diderot, and Voltaire. During the course of the Weimar era in the 1920's, Germany became more and more polarized between conflicting political and social ideologies. Settembrini is the spokesman for a liberal democracy in which the educated masses can be trusted to exercise their critical judgment and elect the most suitable representatives. His character echoes the political stance of Mann's brother, the liberal democrat Heinrich.

If Settembrini represents this one cultural and ideological pole of the European scene, then the volatile and cynical Jesuit priest Naphta (whose character Mann modeled, in part, on that of the Marxist literary critic Georg Lukacs) speaks for its opposite. Whereas Settembrini lauds the rationality of the eighteenth century, Naphta praises the Middle Ages, the era of blind (or irrational) faith in forces that are far more powerful than the mere intellect of humankind. When the former speaks of the free exercise of the critical intellect, the latter advocates nonrational belief and a fanatical discipline of the body. Naphta eschews the critical debate of the liberal democrats and urges the extremist rhetoric of the demagogues. His political views touch on those of the radical socialist who sees only violent political change in the terrorist mass movements of ideological zealots.

Mann's *The Magic Mountain* captured the spirit of his age: the dialectical forces of rationalism and irrationalism, intellect and emotion, that seemed to tear at the fabric of the European soul in the years following World War I. In the figures of Settembrini and Naphta, this conflict is presented in the form of ideological debate. It is the great irony of the novel that although Naphta dies, his ideological position would live on in the fanatical yet mesmerizing ravings of Adolf Hitler and in the racist and fascist programs of the Nazis.

Bibliography

Feuerlicht, Ignace. *Thomas Mann.* New York: Twayne, 1968. A thorough critical introduction to the author's life and writings. Recommended for beginning students. Contains notes and bibliography.

Hatfield, Henry, ed. *Thomas Mann: A Collection of Critical Essays.* Englewood Cliffs, N.J.: Prentice-Hall, 1964. A fine collection of academic essays by leading American and European scholars, some of which have been translated from the German. Contains notes and chronology.

Heller, Erich. *The Ironic German: A Study of Thomas Mann.* Boston: Little, Brown, 1958. An early but important study of Mann's major texts and themes by a leading American scholar. Contains notes and bibliography.

Stern, J. P. *Thomas Mann.* New York: Columbia University Press, 1967. A brief but first-rate introduction to Mann's life and major writings. Contains a selected bibliography of Mann's works as well as of important critical texts.

Winston, Richard. *Thomas Mann: The Making of an Artist, 1875-1911.* New York: Alfred A. Knopf, 1981. An excellent biography that focuses on Mann's formative years. Contains notes and bibliography.

Ziolkowski, Theodore. "Thomas Mann: *The Magic Mountain.*" In *Dimensions of the Modern Novel: German Texts and European Contexts.* Princeton, N.J.: Princeton University Press, 1969. A stimulating chapter that situates Mann's novel within the thematic contexts of European fiction. Contains notes and index.

Thomas F. Barry

Cross-References

Rilke's *Duino Elegies* Depicts Art as a Transcendent Experience (1911), p. 281; Proust's *Remembrance of Things Past* Is Published (1913), p. 355; *The Metamorphosis* Anticipates Modern Feelings of Alienation (1915), p. 396; Eliot Publishes *The Waste Land* (1922), p. 539; The New Objectivity Movement Is Introduced (1925), p. 631; Lang Expands the Limits of Filmmaking with *Metropolis* (1927) p. 707.

VON STROHEIM FILMS HIS
SILENT MASTERPIECE *GREED*

Category of event: Motion pictures
Time: 1924
Locale: The United States

Erich von Stroheim probed beneath the surface of life and human behavior to create a triumph of cinematic naturalism

Principal personages:
ERICH VON STROHEIM (1885-1957), a film director who disregarded the economic realities of Hollywood in an artistic quest for authenticity
GIBSON GOWLAND (1872-1951), a British-born character actor who played the male lead in *Greed*
ZASU PITTS (1898-1963), the actress who played the female lead in *Greed*
JEAN HERSHOLT (1886-1956), a Danish-born character actor who played a supporting role in *Greed*

Summary of Event

Erich von Stroheim began production of *Greed*, his film adaptation of Frank Norris' naturalistic 1899 novel *McTeague*, in the spring of 1923. Von Stroheim intended to present Norris' story of avarice and human degradation in authentic detail. Von Stroheim began his film by showing McTeague as a burly young miner at the Big Dipper gold mine in Placer County, California. McTeague, the son of an alcoholic father who dies of delirium tremens in a saloon at the mine, is a giant man with supreme strength and slow wits. He appears to be gentle and good-natured, but the brute within him lies just beneath the surface. McTeague is shown as a victim of circumstance, environment, and heredity, unable to control his own destiny. His mother, an overworked drudge in the camp's kitchen, desperately wants her son to leave the mine to seek a profession. When a traveling dentist stops at the camp, Mother McTeague persuades the dentist to take her son with him as an apprentice.

Several years later, after having learned the basic skills of dentistry, McTeague has opened a dental parlor on Polk Street in San Francisco. McTeague's practice is going well and his life seems comfortable when he meets Marcus Schouler. Marcus is an arrogant, vulgar blowhard who works as an attendant at a nearby dog hospital, but McTeague finds him a likable, colorful character. They soon become good friends. Marcus introduces McTeague to his fiancée, Trina, the shy daughter of German immigrant parents. Trina has a broken tooth, and Marcus has brought her to McTeague to have it fixed. McTeague develops a passion for Trina and finally confesses his love for Trina to Marcus, who, with a false sense of generosity, gives up Trina to his friend. After a few months, McTeague and Trina marry. On the eve of their wedding, Trina, who had previously purchased a lottery ticket for one dollar, learns that she has won $5,000 in the drawing.

The lottery marks the film's descent into tragedy. Marcus feels cheated in having given up the newly rich Trina and, in a moment of anger and self-pity, throws a knife at McTeague. The former friend is now an enemy, and Marcus begins to plot his revenge on the newlyweds. Marcus informs the state medical board that McTeague is practicing without a license, and McTeague is forced to curtail his practice. Trina then becomes a miser, unwilling to spend a cent of her lottery winnings. With the loss of income, the McTeagues slowly sink into poverty. McTeague, once again a victim of circumstance, takes to drinking, while Trina is forced to work as a carver of wooden toys. McTeague begins to act more and more like a brute, and he torments his wife in an unsuccessful attempt to get her money. Eventually, he abandons her. Trina's only comfort (more accurately, her passion) is her money, which she continues to hoard in the form of solid gold coins. Finally, the beast in McTeague rises to full force. He breaks into his wife's room, murders her, and flees with the gold coins.

McTeague, now on the run, briefly returns to his mountain home. Before long, however, he senses pursuit and sets off across the Mojave Desert. At this juncture, Marcus reappears in the film to join the posse in pursuit of McTeague. The posse turns back when the chase reaches Death Valley, but Marcus continues to pursue McTeague on his own. Driven onward by greed, Marcus overtakes McTeague on the salt flats of Death Valley. There, one hundred miles from water and in 130-degree heat, they fight to the death. McTeague manages to kill Marcus but finds himself handcuffed to a corpse. McTeague dies in the desert with the gold coins scattered around him.

Von Stroheim completed production of *Greed* in October of 1923. The shooting had lasted 198 days at a cost of roughly $500,000. Von Stroheim immediately began editing, and on January 12, 1924, he presented a forty-two-reel, nine-and-a-half hour preview to a small group of associates. The studio demanded that further cuts be made, and von Stroheim complied with a twenty-four-reel version. While von Stroheim struggled to cut his film to a marketable length, his parent company (Goldwyn) merged with the Metro Pictures Corporation. Louis B. Mayer took over as head of production, and Irving Thalberg became von Stroheim's new production manager. Both executives foresaw a financial disaster in *Greed*, with its excessive length and pessimistic message, and demanded further cuts. Von Stroheim then sent the film to one of his closest friends, director Rex Ingram, who edited the film to eighteen reels. Von Stroheim took this version of his film to Mayer, who insisted that it be cut to ten reels. Von Stroheim protested that the artistic qualities of the film would be destroyed in the process, but he was powerless to prevent further cutting. Von Stroheim had broken the rules in the pursuit of artistic integrity, and he paid the price. *Greed* was given to an outside "cutter," who gave the film its final editing. The studio first showed this truncated version of the film on December 4, 1924, at William Randolph Hearst's Cosmopolitan Theatre in New York City. The film was shown twice daily and ran for six weeks to mixed reviews. Von Stroheim, who felt his most creative work had been ruined, refused even to look at the final product.

Impact of Event

Erich von Stroheim's *Greed* has become a silent film classic. Von Stroheim was a disciple of the legendary D. W. Griffith and had worked for several years under his tutelage. Von Stroheim's use of close-ups, camera angles, lighting, composition, and symbolism show influences from Griffith. Yet von Stroheim's films in general, and *Greed* in particular, went beyond Griffith's in their stark, realistic analysis and in their attention to authentic detail. Von Stroheim was one of the first directors to struggle with the problem of how to adapt a work of fiction to the screen realistically. Just as Frank Norris had rebelled against the popular fiction of the 1890's, von Stroheim rebelled against the sentimental Hollywood products of the 1920's. Critics attacked both artists for the vulgarity and sordidness of their "realism"; each defended himself as having merely presented life in a truthful manner. Individuals could be good, kind, noble, and idealistic, but they could also be selfish, mean, jealous, and greedy. Their uncompromising portrayal of life and human behavior is more accurately described as "naturalism." Both men believed that heredity and environment controlled human actions and that individuals were merely at the mercy of irresistible natural forces. Both Norris and von Stroheim were concerned about psychological and sociological nuances outside the accepted cultural definition of what should be openly displayed as art.

Von Stroheim relied entirely on actual locations to add force and meaning to the more grotesque aspects of his story. For the scenes that took place in the Placer County mining area, von Stroheim had the Goldwyn Company lease and restore to operation the actual mine described in Norris' novel. When the story shifted to San Francisco, von Stroheim moved shooting there as well. Because the San Francisco earthquake and fire of 1906 had destroyed the seedy Polk Street area described in Norris' novel, von Stroheim had to improvise. He rented a house at the corner of Hayes and Laguna streets, furnished the rooms exactly as Norris had described them, and made the actors actually live in the rooms to get the feel of their surroundings.

Von Stroheim filled each scene with interesting and important details. He believed that objects could be used to create atmosphere and that an emphasis on detail would both enrich the scene and accentuate the dramatic importance of the film. He kept the backgrounds of his scenes in deep focus, so that details were not lost on the viewer and so that contrasting themes and symbols, plots and subplots, could be ironically juxtaposed. Von Stroheim's obsession for realistic detail was also evident in the scenes shot in Death Valley. Von Stroheim rejected the advice of the studio to film the desert scenes on the sand dunes near Los Angeles; instead, he took a film crew consisting of forty-one men and one woman to Death Valley. There, again for the sake of realism and to keep true to the novel, von Stroheim filmed the final scenes in 130-degree heat. He claimed that the combination of intense heat, hellish surroundings, and physical strain gave the film its proper nightmarish conclusion.

In the end, von Stroheim created a film that was ahead of its time but that was a commercial disaster. Studio executives (Mayer and Thalberg), ever conscious of box-office realities, demanded that severe cuts be made to reduce the film's length. They also found the film lacking in star quality. Von Stroheim, unlike most Hollywood directors, rejected the star system then in vogue. Instead, von Stroheim chose his actors primarily from screen comedies. He reasoned that such actors would not be burdened with artificial dramatic mannerisms that would detract from their human qualities. Critics found the film to be unsparingly intense (after severe editing, one dramatic scene appears to follow another almost without respite) and too pessimistic (major and minor characters appear helpless against larger forces). Viewers found the contrast between innocence and degeneracy repellent and the emphasis on the tragic state of human existence too bleak. In short, the film was out of touch with the marketing realities of Hollywood and out of step with the popular culture of the 1920's and 1930's. To the post-World War II generation of film critics and film viewers, though, the film's reception appeared as a failure to confront the ugly side of life and to recognize the directional genius of von Stroheim. More contemporary observers have come to realize the tremendous impact *Greed* has had on the overall development of realism on the screen during the era of sound. Most modern critical viewers marvel at von Stroheim's authenticity, his sophisticated development of character, his innovative production techniques, and his visionary direction.

Bibliography

Curtiss, Thomas Quinn. *Von Stroheim.* New York: Farrar, Straus & Giroux, 1971. This biography, which includes a long chapter on *Greed,* was written by a close friend of von Stroheim and puts the record much as von Stroheim would have wanted it. This volume also includes Idwal Jones's account of the original screening of *Greed.* Jones, the drama critic for the *San Francisco Daily News,* was one of perhaps only a dozen individuals ever to have seen the original, nine-hour-plus version of *Greed.*

Finler, Joel W. *Stroheim.* Berkeley: University of California Press, 1968. A short volume that focuses primarily on *Greed.* Valuable for its comparisons of Norris' novel with von Stroheim's film.

_____, ed. *"Greed": A Film by Erich von Stroheim.* New York: Simon & Schuster, 1972. Contains von Stroheim's original shooting script for *Greed* and includes brief but useful articles from Finler and from Herman G. Weinberg. Also included are valuable recollections concerning the making of *Greed* from actor Jean Hersholt, cameraman William Daniels, and von Stroheim himself.

Koszarski, Richard. *The Man You Loved to Hate: Erich von Stroheim and Hollywood.* New York: Oxford University Press, 1983. The von Stroheim biography that provides perhaps the most useful synthesis on the subject. Includes a long chapter on *Greed.*

Noble, Peter. *Hollywood Scapegoat: The Biography of Erich von Stroheim.* Reprint. New York: Arno Press, 1972. This biography, first published in 1950, was written with the cooperation of von Stroheim. The short chapter on *Greed* is composed largely of excerpts from correspondence between the author and the director. Includes a lengthy appendix that contains a selection of critical essays.

Weinberg, Herman G. *The Complete "Greed."* New York: E. P. Dutton, 1973. Weinberg has attempted to reconstruct the complete *Greed* with the more than four hundred photos that remain from the original production. Scenes cut from the final film are marked, and a description or a fragment of dialogue accompanies each photo. A brief but informative introduction precedes the collection of photographs.

Whittemore, Don, and Philip Alan Cecchettini, eds. *Passport to Hollywood: Film Immigrants.* New York: McGraw-Hill, 1976. An anthology of works about important film directors, including von Stroheim. Describes his career and his major films and includes several articles about the director. No bibliography.

Steven L. Piott

Cross-References

The Birth of a Nation Popularizes New Film Techniques (1915), p. 402; Eisenstein's *Potemkin* Introduces New Film Editing Techniques (1925), p. 615; Gance's *Napoléon* Revolutionizes Filmmaking Techniques (1925), p. 642; Chaplin Produces His Masterpiece *The Gold Rush* (1925), p. 659; Lang Expands the Limits of Filmmaking with *Metropolis* (1927), p. 707; *The Jazz Singer* Premieres in New York (1927), p. 734; Sound Technology Revolutionizes the Motion-Picture Industry (1928), p. 761.

GERSHWIN'S *RHAPSODY IN BLUE* PREMIERES IN NEW YORK

Category of event: Music
Time: February 12, 1924
Locale: New York, New York

George Gershwin's composition and performance of Rhapsody in Blue *combined elements of American popular music with the European classical tradition*

Principal personages:
GEORGE GERSHWIN (JACOB GERSHVIN, 1898-1937), an American composer who produced works for the concert stage and opera that were distinctively American in character
PAUL WHITEMAN (1890-1967), the American bandleader who commissioned Gershwin to write *Rhapsody in Blue*
FERDE GROFÉ (1892-1972), the orchestrator of *Rhapsody in Blue*, who later became a composer in his own right

Summary of Event

While visiting Great Britain with his dance orchestra in 1923, New York bandleader Paul Whiteman began thinking of performing a concert of American popular music in a major concert hall. When a rival bandleader announced similar plans, Whiteman—goaded into action—developed a program to show that popular music had moved from simple dance music to a true art form, and he booked New York City's Aeolian Hall for such a performance on February 12, 1924.

Whiteman had worked with composer George Gershwin in *George White's Scandals of 1922* and had suggested a future collaboration. Gershwin, however, did not learn about his role in Whiteman's upcoming concert until the January 4, 1924, *New York Herald Tribune* announced that he was writing a jazz concerto for the program.

By this time, the twenty-five-year-old Gershwin had acquired a considerable reputation as a writer of Broadway songs, but his composition of a movement for string quartet in 1919 and a one-act "jazz opera" in 1922 indicated greater ambitions. Drawing upon his notebooks, where he found the opening clarinet passage, Gershwin began composition of what he titled *American Rhapsody* on January 7. He later stated that he had no real plan for the piece, but rather only the object of showing that jazz did not need to be written or performed in strict time. While traveling by train to Boston, he developed a structure for the composition, calling it "a sort of musical kaleidoscope of America." After returning to New York, he conceived the middle theme while improvising on a piano at a party.

Gershwin wrote the orchestra accompaniment as a second piano part to be scored by Ferde Grofé, Whiteman's arranger. Apparently completing his composition by

January 29, Gershwin left a blank section for improvisation on which he noted "wait for nod." Grofé's orchestration is dated February 4. Gershwin's brother Ira, meanwhile, suggested a new title, *Rhapsody in Blue.*

Whiteman added nine musicians to his fourteen-member orchestra and held rehearsals for five days at the Palais Royal nightclub, to which he invited critics and writers. During one of these rehearsals, clarinetist Ross Gorman, for a joke, played the opening passage of *Rhapsody in Blue* as a wailing glissando. So taken with the sound, Gershwin asked Gorman to play it that way at the concert.

Despite Whiteman's fears, the hall was filled on February 12. Entitled "An Experiment in Modern Music," the concert began with an address by Whiteman's manager, Hugh Ernst, who stated that the program was educational and was meant to show the development of jazz (an ill-defined term at the time) from discordance to sophistication. An expensive printed program, with notes by Ernst and writer Gilbert Seldes, provided additional information, organizing the concert around such themes as "True Form of Jazz" and "Contrast—Legitimate Scoring vs. Jazzing." The music ranged from "Livery Stable Blues" to "Pomp and Circumstance" and serenades by Victor Herbert.

The audience included luminaries from the New York social and artistic scene as well as people from vaudeville and Tin Pan Alley. After twenty-three sections, however, the crowd had become noticeably restless when George Gershwin walked to the piano to perform *Rhapsody in Blue.* The opening glissando brought everyone to attention; soon they recognized that this loosely constructed Lisztian rhapsody, with its blue-tinged harmonies and jazz-like rhythms, was a truly new sound. At its close they broke into tumultuous applause, calling Gershwin back for several bows.

The critical reaction was mixed, most writers noting both the technical immaturity of the composer and the freshness of his approach. Deems Taylor wrote for the *New York World* that "it was crude, but it hinted at something new, something that has not hitherto been said in music."

Whiteman repeated the concert at Aeolian Hall on March 7 and at Carnegie Hall in April and November, and then took it to Rochester, Pittsburgh, Cleveland, Indianapolis, and St. Louis, after which Gershwin left the program. In June, 1924, Gershwin and Whiteman recorded *Rhapsody in Blue* for the Victor Blue label and sold more than a million copies. Later that same year, T. B. Harms and Company published *Rhapsody in Blue* in sheet music. Grofé reorchestrated the piece for symphony orchestra in 1926 and 1942, the latter being the version most familiar today.

In 1925, the Symphony Society of New York commissioned Gershwin to write a concerto to be performed with the New York Symphony Orchestra in December. Like *Rhapsody in Blue, Concerto in F* did not adhere to textbook formalities and drew upon jazz and popular music, but it had greater structural integrity and was orchestrated by the composer.

Continuing to write hit musicals for the theater, Gershwin also pursued his "serious" composing. 1926 saw his first performance of *Preludes for Piano,* and in 1928 the New York Philharmonic presented his *American in Paris,* an orchestral tone poem. After the relatively unsuccessful *Second Rhapsody* of 1931, Gershwin concentrated on his opera *Porgy and Bess*, a story about poor Southern blacks first performed in 1935. Although criticized for being merely a succession of hit songs, and scorned by many African Americans as a white interpretation of black music and life, the opera survived because of its songs. After a revival in New York in 1942, the opera grew in both popularity and critical reputation. Gershwin, though, died from a brain tumor on July 11, 1937, and did not live to see this success.

Impact of Event

Before *Rhapsody in Blue*, various composers had attempted to draw upon elements of American popular music. Antonin Dvořák's *Symphony No. 9* (1893) reflected the spirituals of the African American, but the more specific influence of commercial popular music appeared in Igor Stravinsky's *Ragtime* (1918) and *Piano Rag-Music* (1919) and Darius Milhaud's *Le Boeuf sur le toit* (1919) and *La Création du monde* (1923). Other works revealing this influence included Erik Satie's *Parade* (1917) and John Alden Carpenter's *Piano Concertino* (1915) and *Krazy Kat* (1921). In the mid-nineteenth century, the American composer and pianist Louis Moreau Gottschalk wrote a number of piano pieces reflecting the musical idioms of the American South. Later, Scott Joplin, the "Ragtime King," used ragtime idioms for some of the songs in his opera *Treemonisha* (1911), and Charles Ives incorporated ragtime elements into his compositions. Yet none of these works gained the attention for combining "jazz" and the European tradition the way that Gershwin's did. The division between classical music and American popular music remained, for the most part, wide.

Paul Whiteman's attempt to lift American popular music to an art form also had its predecessors. In 1914, James Reese Europe's black Clef Club Symphony Orchestra had appeared at Carnegie Hall, and on February 10, 1924, only a few days before the Aeolian Hall concert, bandleader Vincent Lopez held a lecture-concert at the Anderson Art Galleries in New York. The announcement of Lopez's performance had provoked Whiteman into action. At the program, Harvard University professor and composer Edward Burlington Hill discussed the history of jazz, while Lopez's band provided musical illustrations. Although these efforts had relatively little impact, they suggested that the attempt to combine the elite European tradition with American popular culture was more than Whiteman's individual concern. Furthermore, writers such as Gilbert Seldes, the author of *The Seven Lively Arts* (1924), were arguing for the aesthetic validity and importance of American popular culture.

Gershwin's *Rhapsody in Blue* opened the doorway to further experimentation, particularly because of Paul Whiteman's carefully developed publicity campaign for his concert. Furthermore, Henry O. Osgood, one of the music critics who attended the Aeolian Hall program, was inspired to write *So This Is Jazz* (1926), perhaps the first serious examination of the subject.

There now appeared to be a market for compositions drawing upon jazz elements, and "serious" American composers responded. Aaron Copland used jazz idioms in his *Music for the Theater* (1925) and *Concerto for Piano and Orchestra* (1926), as did John Alden Carpenter in his ballet *Skyscrapers* (1926). Other composers incorporated the term "jazz" into the very titles of their works: Louis Gruenberg's *Daniel Jazz* (1923, antedating Gershwin's *Rhapsody*) and *Jazz Suite* (1925), George Antheil's *Jazz Symphony* (1925), Werner Janssen's *Chorale and Fugue in Jazz* (1929), and—changing the terminology slightly—Morton Gould's *Swing Sinfonietta* (1936).

More popularly oriented composers pursued similar goals. Whiteman's arranger Ferde Grofé wrote *The Mississippi Suite* in 1924, drawing upon jazz colors and idioms, and in 1931 made more subtle use of these elements in his famous *Grand Canyon Suite*. Another orchestrator, Robert Russell Bennett, like Gershwin drew upon his experience in musical stage works to write *Charleston Rhapsody* (1926) and *Concerto Grosso* (1932) for jazz band and orchestra. James P. Johnson, the black ragtime and stride piano composer, wrote *Yamekraw: A Rhapsody in Black and White* (1925), which was scored by William Grant Still, who in turn composed *Africa* (1930) and *Afro-American Symphony* (1930).

European composers, some specifically influenced by Gershwin, were also drawn to this American music. Among the more significant efforts were Ernst Krenek's *Jonny spielt auf* (1927), Paul Hindemith's *Neues vom Tage* (1928-1929), Maurice Ravel's *Piano Concerto in D Major for Left Hand* (1931) and *Piano Concerto in G Major* (1931)—both of which have been described as "Gershwinesque"—and Kurt Weill's *Mahagonny Songspiel* (1927) and *Die Dreigroschenoper* (1928). Alban Berg, whom Gershwin met in 1928, included a clarinet glissando in the second song of *Der Wein* (1929) that is clearly reminiscent of *Rhapsody in Blue*'s opening.

Drawn to such elements as syncopation and polyrhythm, the relationship of soloists to accompanying instruments, and special instrumental techniques and sonorities, these composers did not write "jazz;" rather, they produced music in the classical tradition with a distinctively modern sound, one that sometimes reached a wide audience. As Maurice Ravel stated in 1928, "these popular forms are but the materials of construction, and the work of art appears only on mature conception where no detail has been left to chance."

The cross-fertilization of musical worlds popularized by George Gershwin brought recognition to American music and American composers, contributing greatly to the eclecticism of twentieth century "serious" music. When composers draw upon rock music for inspiration, as Leonard Bernstein did in his *Mass* (1971), or when jazz musicians such as Duke Ellington or Dave Brubeck seek to work with classical forms, they are further exploring the path blazed by Gershwin in 1924. Indeed, interest in emphasizing the influence of popular idioms has led to the effort to move beyond the familiar 1942 orchestral arrangement of *Rhapsody in Blue* and restore the jazzier sound of Gershwin's original performance, most notably in 1984 with Maurice Peress' recreation of the entire Aeolian Hall concert.

Bibliography

Alpert, Hollis. *The Life and Times of Porgy and Bess: The Story of an American*

Classic. New York: Alfred A. Knopf, 1990. Examines the development of the opera from its beginnings in DuBose Heywood's novel to performances in 1987. In addition to relating the opera to Gershwin's earlier work, sees the opera's history as a mirror of American social change. Photographs, synopsis of *Porgy and Bess*, bibliography, index.

Ewen, David. *George Gershwin: His Journey to Greatness.* Reprint. Westport, Conn.: Greenwood Press, 1977. A rewritten version of the author's earlier work *George Gershwin: A Journey to Greatness* (1956). Although sometimes inaccurate, the first major biography of Gershwin. Particularly useful for its discussion of the development of Gershwin's reputation. Appendices list Gershwin's works and various stage and motion-picture adaptations and productions. Photographs, index.

Goldberg, Isaac. *George Gershwin: A Study in American Music.* New York: Frederick Ungar, 1931. The first serious examination of Gershwin's music. Useful because of its quotations from contemporaries, particularly reviewers of the Aeolian Hall concert, and its analysis of specific musical examples. Photographs, selected discography with critical discussion, index.

Jablonski, Edward. *Gershwin.* New York: Doubleday, 1987. A popularly written but careful biography that is generally regarded as definitive. Concentrates largely on Gershwin's career and social relationships rather than on probing his mind or music. Includes numerous quotations from those who knew Gershwin. Photographs, bibliography, list of compositions by George and Ira Gershwin, discography, index.

Kendall, Alan. *George Gershwin: A Biography.* New York: Universe Books, 1987. A brief biography containing many quotations from sources. Photographs, catalog of works, index.

Kimball, Robert, and Alfred Simon. *The Gershwins.* New York: Atheneum, 1973. Published for the seventy-fifth anniversary of Gershwin's birth. Contains tributes from family, friends, and admirers. Most significant for memoirs from Gershwin show participants. Photographs, chronology, discography, bibliography.

Rosenberg, Deena. *Fascinating Rhythm: The Collaboration of George and Ira Gershwin.* New York: E. P. Dutton, 1991. Concentrates on Gershwin's songs. Includes excerpts from both music and lyrics. Reference notes, chronology of Gershwin's works. Alphabetical list of Gershwin and Gershwin songs. List of original keys to major songs. Music and lyrics to "The Man I Love," "I Got Rhythm," "A Foggy Day." Photographs, bibliography, discography, index.

Schwartz, Charles. *George Gershwin: A Selective Bibliography.* Detroit: College Music Society, 1974. A more extensive bibliography than appears in other books.

_____. *Gershwin: His Life and Music.* Indianapolis, Ind.: Bobbs-Merrill, 1973. A thorough but sometimes inaccurate discussion of both Gershwin's life and his music. Notable for attention to Gershwin's vanity and self-absorption. Argues for Jewish elements in Gershwin's music. Photographs. Catalog of Gershwin compositions and films based on Gershwin's works. Discography, bibliography, index.

Whiteman, Paul, and Mary Margaret McBride. *Jazz.* Reprint. New York: Arno Press,

1974. Originally published in 1926. Chapter 4 gives Whiteman's own account of the Aeolian Hall concert. Photographs.

Gary Land

Cross-References

Joplin Popularizes the Ragtime Style (1899), p. 13; Handy Ushers in the Commercial Blues Era (1910's), p. 252; Brecht and Weill Collaborate on *Mahagonny Songspiel* (1927), p. 724; Gershwin's *Porgy and Bess* Opens in New York (1935), p. 1016; Agnes de Mille Choreographs *Rodeo* (1942), p. 1234; Graham Debuts *Appalachian Spring* with Copland Score (1944), p. 1284.

SURREALISM IS BORN

Categories of event: Art and literature
Time: October, 1924
Locale: Paris, France

After the publication of André Breton's Manifesto of Surrealism, *avant-garde artists used the new term "surrealism" to define their artistic movement*

Principal personages:
> MAX ERNST (1891-1976), the leading painter among the Surrealists
> ANDRÉ BRETON (1896-1966), the writer and critic who developed the theory of Surrealism
> JOAN MIRÓ (1893-1983), a founding member of the Surrealist group whose paintings emphasized the fantastic
> SALVADOR DALÍ (1904-1989), a painter fascinated by abnormal psychology
> RENÉ MAGRITTE (1898-1967), a painter whose popular art mixed the fantastic and the realistic
> YVES TANGUY (1900-1955), a painter interested in Freudian psychology

Summary of Event

When the young French writer and critic André Breton published his first *Manifeste du surréalisme* (1924; *Manifesto of Surrealism*, 1969) in October, 1924, he did not merely provide a friendly group of writers and artists with a new theory for their new art. He also gave this art its name, and thus fostered the birth of Surrealism. The painters Max Ernst, André Masson, and Joan Miró readily accepted the theories outlined in Breton's manifesto, and so did many of Breton's writer-friends, among whom Louis Aragon, Paul Éluard, and Philippe Soupault were very influential.

As Breton's manifesto defined it, Surrealism sought to break down the boundary between dream and reality and to unite, in one picture or one text, the unconscious and the conscious. "Surrealism is based on the belief in the superior reality of certain forms of associations hitherto neglected, in the omnipotence of dream, in the disinterested play of thought," Breton explained. To capture this new "surreality," Breton and his friends strongly recommended "automatic," instead of premeditated, painting and writing. Surrealist theory thus emphasized a revolution in both the form and content of art.

In the fall of 1924, there existed already a distinctive body of new art for which Breton created his theory. The early works of Max Ernst, for example, exhibit many of the Surrealists' ideas. By inviting the viewer to see an elephant in the form of a huge steel cauldron to which the artist has given legs and tusks, Ernst's painting *The Elephant of the Celebes* (1921) traces how dreams create irrational analogies between different objects. Ernst's depiction of a sky filled with fish shows in action the surrealist principle of "conscious incongruous combination": By placing objects in an impossible context, the picture encourages the viewer to transcend the limits reality imposes on relationships between objects.

Similar in theory, but quite different in its style, Joan Miró's *Catalan Landscape (The Hunter)* (1923-1924) invites a viewer to follow dream logic and see the hills of Catalonia in the painter's mere outline of pencil-thin, wavy lines; the hunter's head can be discovered in a mustachioed, one-eyed triangle at the top left of the picture.

In literature, the field of Breton's own experiments, 1924 saw the publication of two major Surrealist texts. Breton's *Les Pas perdus* (the lost steps) reflects in its antinovelistic form and apparently random content the antirational convictions of its author. In Louis Aragon's *Une Vague de rêves* (a wave of dreams), form and content focus on dreams and "automatic" unmeditated writing.

Though the Surrealists initially defined it, their art had deep roots in earlier experiments with "antiart." Like the Dadaists, they rebelled against artistic tradition and conventional values. Both were committed to experimenting with art. Surrealists, however, wanted art to have meaning and were ready for a theory to give coherence to their divergent goals. Breton's manifesto filled this void. It was only with its publication, then, that Surrealism was truly born as a forceful movement with a clear sense of its artistic identity.

Breton admitted freely that the term "surrealism" was the invention of his deceased friend Guillaume Apollinaire. Breton, however, insisted on his exclusive rights to the new word. Indeed, rival claims to the term literally died out: The three French magazines that used the word independently ceased publication by the spring of 1925. This left only the new review *La Révolution Surréaliste*, of which Breton quickly became the editor. Until 1929, when it was retitled, the journal served as an influential vehicle for disseminating Surrealist literature and theory. Beginning with its first number—the cover of which was graced by an anonymous drawing of a fish bearing the word "SURRÉALISME" on its side—the magazine also carried illustrations by important Surrealists such as Max Ernst and André Masson.

Because of Breton's forceful promotion of their work, more painters felt drawn to the movement, which had originally favored writers and poets. After a one-man show of Masson's work in the Galérie Simon in Paris in 1924, the Surrealists staged their first major collective exhibition in the Galérie Pierre in Paris in 1925.

At the exhibition, a wide audience reviewed works by the founding members of the surrealist group, including Ernst, Masson, Miró, and Man Ray, and by such relative newcomers as Pierre Roy and Jean (Hans) Arp. Also included were works by Pablo Picasso and Paul Klee, who were not strictly Surrealists. Giorgio De Chirico's early work was shown because of its initial influence over Surrealist painters, even though they despised his current art.

A steady stream of exhibitions followed. The acquisition of the Surrealist Gallery, which opened on March 26, 1926, gave Surrealist painting a permanent exhibition space. Increasingly, international artists such as the Spaniard Salvador Dalí and the Belgian René Magritte joined the Surrealists, whose influence spread over Europe, America, and Japan. With Dalí and his fellow Spaniard Luis Buñuel, Surrealists turned to film; Dalí's and Buñuel's *Un Chien andalou* (1928; *An Andalusian Dog*) became the first of several internationally acclaimed Surrealist films. The painters' frequent exhibitions, together with the flourishing review *La Révolution Surréaliste* and the energetic mentorship of Breton, all contributed to the strong and quick growth of Surrealism after its well-tended birth in 1924.

Impact of Event

The energy and creativity of its founders helped to make Surrealism the most influential artistic movement between 1924 and World War II. In the field of the visual arts, the Surrealists' fascination with the unconscious yielded a rather unexpected result. For even though they strove to discard realist modes of representation, they desired to convey the new meaning that their dream-logic gave familiar objects. Consequently, despite techniques that pointed in a different direction, Surrealist painting reemphasized the object, and the idea of meaning, in art.

These divergent artistic aspirations, which would ultimately separate and lead to both abstract expressionism and neorealism, were powerfully unified in such Surrealist paintings as Yves Tanguy's *Genesis* (1926). Tanguy's background openly defies any notion of realist presentation: Painted in virtually the same pastel tones, sky and ground are separated only by a hovering, blue-black fog. In the midst of this dreamscape, however, there grows a distinctly fern-like tree of knowledge, beyond which is a tightrope on which there walks Eve, a naturalistically drawn woman.

To uncover the meaning that Tanguy invests in his objects, one must look at Freudian psychology, which Surrealism greatly helped to popularize. With Sigmund Freud, the Surrealists shared a keen interest in the unconscious and the erotic. Tanguy and other Surrealists readily accepted the sexual connotations Freud saw in everyday objects and incorporated such ideas into their own art. Thus, Eve's passage on the tightrope—a walk into adolescent sexuality—will lead her to a phallic tower of fog, out of which rises an outstretched palm holding a long nail (vagina and phallus); her route continues beneath the vaginal leaves of the tree to its terminus, the top of the phallic obelisk. A green snake and a black triangle complete the Freudian imagery on the fog-infested ground.

Yet while Freud used psychoanalysis to heal patients, the Surrealists were interested in the method alone. At the extreme, Salvador Dalí became fascinated with psychopathology and the sickness of the soul and developed his own branch of Surrealism. The famous melting watches of Dalí's *The Persistence of Memory* (1931) seek to capture the mindframe of the individual paranoiac. His frightening *Soft Construction with Boiled Beans: Premonition of Civil War* (1936) reveals the collective horror of a nation, Spain, which was killing itself in civil war. Here, a violently deformed female torso is split in two, and while one hand squeezes an inflamed breast, a calcified leg presses bulging buttocks against spinal bones.

In the quest for the unconscious, Breton had exhorted the Surrealists to experiment continuously with new techniques. Ironically, the idea of "automatic" writing and painting, which the *Manifesto of Surrealism* had called the key to Surrealism, soon proved a dead end. It was abandoned despite such isolated successes as Miró's *The Gentleman* (1924), the major features of which appeared in the artist's mind at the moment of painting.

Overall, the Surrealists created many techniques that entered the repertoire of contemporary art. Among these lasting inventions are Ernst's collages, which, as in his *The Hundred-Headed Woman* (1929), create strange bird-people out of the cut-out and mixed-up illustrations of nineteenth century novels. Other innovations included Ernst's *frottage* (the rubbing of canvas over natural objects) and *grattage* (the scraping of the canvas). Oscar Dominguez's discovery of "decalcomania" (the spreading of black ink between two sheets of paper), first exhibited in the new Surrealist magazine *Minotaure* in 1936, quickly inspired other Surrealist painters.

Together, the goal of these techniques was to create accidental structures that the artist invests with a subjective meaning. For Masson's *Battle of Fishes* (1927), the artist spread glue randomly on his canvas. After pouring sand on the glue, Masson was left with a sandscape created by accident, which he turned into an ocean floor, the battle zone of his fish. The invitation of the unplanned became an important Surrealist legacy. It directly influenced the action painting of the American Jackson Pollock, who personally observed Max Ernst in the 1940's.

Just as influential were the methods of surrealist painters such as Magritte who painted their objects with often photographic precision but placed them in an impossible context. Magritte's *The Human Condition, I* (1943) offers a view of a window that is partially blocked by a painting, which shows exactly the part of the landscape outside the window that it obscures. Magritte's style, Verism, became widely popular among the pop artists of the 1960's; its appeal even reached the point that Magritte's motifs were used for advertising posters.

Despite its powerful impact, Surrealism was persistently plagued by internal strife. Because Breton looked at the movement as an all-encompassing life-style, he took a personal interest in guarding its purity and expelled many offenders. His continuous development of Surrealist theory is linked to this control over the movement. Breton's discussion of the visual arts, *Le Surrealisme et la peinture* (1928; Surrealism and painting), which appeared in the same year as his novel *Nadja*, was written to refute a rival's idea that there was no Surrealist painting. Similarly, Breton's *Second Manifeste du surréalisme* (1930; *Second Manifesto of Surrealism*, 1969) came on the heels of mass expulsions, including Masson's.

The Surrealists' relationship with the French communists was characterized by the former's tenacious fight for artistic freedom. In *Légitime Défense* (1926; legitimate defense), Breton defended the Surrealists' interest in dreams. Even though he would briefly join the communists—at one point, he renamed his magazine *Le Surréalisme au service de la Révolution* (Surrealism in the service of the revolution), from 1930 on, he knew that Surrealist art remained incompatible with the dogma of Socialist Realism.

Pierre Roy's painting *Rural Electrification* (1930) illustrates this difference. The work's electric poles are relegated to the background, where they are literally dwarfed by four bamboo sticks and small scraps of paper, the artist's childhood toys. By placing the subjective and personal over the communal and objective, Roy provided artists with an alternative to communist art.

After World War II, which caused most Surrealists to flee to America after the Nazis occupied France in 1940, Surrealism, while still productive, lost its initial influence. 1947 brought the last great international Surrealist exhibitions in Chicago and Paris. Yet after the deaths of many Surrealist artists in the 1960's and 1970's, major retrospectives of their works opened in Europe and America. Since then, interest in their art has remained strong, and in 1992, a Magritte retrospective received a warm welcome upon opening in London. Its arrival was eagerly awaited in America, where European Surrealists had flourished late but had left strong traces.

Bibliography

Jean, Marcel, ed. *The Autobiography of Surrealism.* New York: Viking Press, 1980. A valuable companion to Jean's *The History of Surrealist Painting* (1960), this is an anthology of writings by Surrealist painters and writers. Most selections are fine translations of crucial French texts. Richly illustrated with photos of the artists and their works, this volume presents primary texts that shaped surrealist art theory, which the artists took very seriously. Good bibliography.

_____. *The History of Surrealist Painting.* Translated by Simon Watson Taylor. New York: Grove Press, 1960. The definite history of Surrealism up to the date of its publication. Depicts many of the most important Surrealist art works (most in black and white, however) and has photos of the artists themselves. Readable and extremely informative.

Picon, Gaetan. *Surrealists and Surrealism, 1919-1939.* Translated by James Emmons. New York: Rizzoli, 1983. A richly illustrated, oversized book offering a detailed look at the development and growth of Surrealist art. Accessibly written, it discusses many major surrealist art works and celebrates Surrealism's impact on art and artists all over the world. Ten-page chronological survey, bibliography, and a "dictionary-index" with brief entries for each major surrealist artist.

Read, Herbert Edward. *Surrealism.* Reprint. New York: Praeger, 1971. The first serious academic discussion of Surrealism in English, originally published in 1936. Intelligent and informative, written at the height of Surrealism's artistic influence on modern art. Requires some familiarity with art history. Still very valuable for anyone interested in the origins and reception of the Surrealist movement.

Russell, John. *Max Ernst.* New York: Harry N. Abrams, 1967. Perhaps the best comprehensive survey of Ernst's work for the general reader. Drawing on interviews with Ernst, the author accurately recounts Ernst's impact on the birth of Surrealism and his later conflict with Breton. Most of Ernst's major works are reproduced. Chronological survey of Ernst's works, biographical notes, and a useful bibliography.

Schneede, Uwe M. *Surrealism.* Translated by Maria Pelikan. New York: Harry N. Abrams, 1974. Introductory survey aimed at a general audience. Has forty-one discussions of individual surrealist paintings (reproduced in color) and a concise but brief introductory text with black-and-white reproductions. Short chronology (1924-1971) and limited bibliography.

R. C. Lutz

Cross-References

Freud Inaugurates a Fascination with the Unconscious (1899), p. 19; The Dada Movement Emerges at the Cabaret Voltaire (1916), p. 419; Man Ray Creates the Rayograph (1921), p. 513; Buñuel and Dalí Champion Surrealism in *Un Chien andalou* (1928), p. 750; A Dalí Museum Opens in Figueras, Spain (1974), p. 2310.

CRANBROOK ACADEMY BEGINS
A HISTORY OF DESIGN EXCELLENCE

Category of event: Fashion and design
Time: 1925
Locale: Cranbrook, Michigan

Although Cranbrook Academy was founded as a model nineteenth century Arts and Crafts movement educational community, its faculty and students have had a major influence in shaping twentieth century design

Principal personages:
> GEORGE BOOTH (1864-1949), the publisher of *The Detroit News* who founded Cranbrook Academy on his estate outside Detroit, Michigan
> ELIEL SAARINEN (1873-1950), the Finnish architect who acted as president of Cranbrook Academy of Art and designed most of its buildings between 1932 and his death
> EERO SAARINEN (1910-1961), the son of Eliel Saarinen, a student at Cranbrook and an important American architect and designer
> CHARLES EAMES (1907-1978), a student and instructor at Cranbrook who designed significant furniture, architecture, exhibits, and films

Summary of Event

In a style typical of upwardly mobile and upper-class Victorian businessmen, George Booth became something of a patron of the arts after his marriage to Ellen Warren Scripps in 1887 and upon his assumption of a managerial position at *The Detroit Evening News*, the flagship of his father-in-law's publishing empire. Between 1900 and 1920, Booth was actively involved in the promotion of arts and crafts at the local, state, and national levels. His interest in the Arts and Crafts movement of the nineteenth century may be traced to his roots; both his great-grandfather and grandfather had been English coppersmiths.

The importance of the Arts and Crafts movement to the quality of life in his own community was of particular importance to Booth. As the automobile industry in Detroit began to expand and dominate the local economy, Booth felt that he might make real contributions to the city by emphasizing the importance of good design and art education. He was a significant patron of the Detroit Museum of Art, acted as president of the Detroit Society of Arts and Crafts, and helped to found the Detroit School of Design.

By the early 1920's, however, Booth was unsatisfied by the results of his yeoman efforts. He began to consider projects over which he could have a more personal and complete control. Booth spent several years traveling and researching museums and art academies in Europe, and he decided to create his own experimental art-education community on his suburban farm estate, twenty miles from Detroit. In 1924, he asked the Finnish architect Eliel Saarinen, who was a visiting professor at the University of Michigan at the time, to create a master building plan for the site and to act as a consultant for the proposed academy's educational program. The Cranbrook Foundation was organized in 1927, although the Cranbrook Academy of Art, with Saarinen as its first president, was not formally established until 1932.

Booth believed the community's physical plant should be given first priority, and Saarinen immediately began to plan the Cranbrook Academy of Art. Building was dependent on the availability of funding and so took place over a fairly extended period. The first academy building was begun immediately in 1925. Designed by George Booth and J. Robert F. Swanson, it housed an architectural office, library, and museum. The first Arts and Crafts building was finished in 1929. The Academy of Art projects, constructed between 1925 and 1963, include seven studio buildings, seven residences (including the Saarinen House), three dormitories, a foundry, a garage, and a museum and library. The Cranbrook School for Boys was built on the site of the original farm and is made up of twenty-five structures constructed between 1925 and 1979, including several remodeled farm buildings, a hockey rink, and a fire station. The Cranbrook Institute of Science is a complex of five buildings, including a revised version of George Booth's original 1930 design, a planetarium, and a nature center. Kingswood School Cranbrook, for girls, is made up of seven buildings constructed between 1930 and 1973. Brookside School Cranbrook is housed in the meeting house designed by George Booth in 1918 to provide his father with a pulpit. Several additions, a gymnasium, and two residences complete the Brookside facilities. The original estate, including Cranbrook House (designed in 1907 by Albert Kahn to contain Booth's sizable arts and crafts collection and library), a Greek-style theater built in 1915, a greenhouse, and a number of cottages, has also been preserved.

The architectural development of the community was seen as a symbolic and practical emblem of the educational program and goals of the academy. Following the model of the American Academy of Art in Rome, Cranbrook's educational plan was loosely organized. Ideally, there was to be no formal curriculum, and students and scholars would be encouraged to interact informally. Originally, Booth wanted to invite "master artists" to Cranbrook with the understanding that, in addition to working on their own projects, they would contribute to the physical and educational environment of the academy. Residences, studios, and honoraria would be provided, and each "master" would supervise a select group of "fellows," who would also receive payment for work done in cooperation with their teachers. In this spirit, and because costs were high, in 1930 Booth established a gradual self-sufficiency plan for the craft studios.

For Saarinen, this organizational scheme was uncomfortably reminiscent of medieval guilds, and he attempted, not altogether successfully, to guide the school toward a more organic model of the relationship of art and life. Despite a fuzzy theoretical orientation and administrative difficulties (the school did not grant degrees until 1942), beginning in the 1930's, Cranbrook was able to provide a unique educational facility in which students were expected to learn by doing. Personal projects, individual interests, and experimentation were the norm, and the diversity of the professional experiences and backgrounds of both students and faculty made Cranbrook a rich laboratory of design ideas and practices. As a center for advanced study in nine areas—architecture, design, metalwork, photography, sculpture, printmaking, painting, textiles, and ceramics—the Cranbrook Academy of Art has made major contributions to the forms, practice, and production of arts and crafts around the world.

Impact of Event

George Booth founded the Cranbrook Academy in the early 1920's as a utopian community that would focus its energies on returning art and craftsmanship to a primary place in the commercial and industrial arenas of American design. For Booth, the development of social utopia was dependent on aesthetic reform. Booth's ideas for Cranbrook place art and craftsmanship squarely in the center of a number of "reform" movements of importance to American culture: the ideal of the dedicated community that has influenced Americans since the time of the Puritans, the Arts and Crafts movement, which reached its peak in the United States between 1890 and 1910, and later attempts to define an aesthetic that would unite new technologies with moral values and social purposes.

Cranbrook was meant to be a special place, devoted to the integration of labor and leisure, life and art. Contentious British philosophers and artists such as John Ruskin and William Morris argued that industrialization debased both design and production, and, by extension, culture itself; redemption, they claimed, lay in a return to "arts and crafts." In the United States, Arts and Crafts reformers of the nineteenth century were disillusioned with urban society. In response, they attempted to revive handcraftsmanship, to promote simplicity and traditionalism of design and life-style through unification of the applied and fine arts, and to celebrate nativist culture.

Eliel Saarinen, Cranbrook's master planner and guiding hand until his resignation in 1946, embodied both the social and aesthetic components of Booth's vision of reform. Like his contemporary Frank Lloyd Wright, Saarinen was interested in an expansive universe of creative design, from city planning to carpets. His architectural works influenced the stream of modernism that focused on the importance of the environment as a physical and emotional center of meaning. Saarinen's presence as an instructor made Cranbrook a central testing site for early experiments in American modernism, particularly in the decorative arts. By the late 1930's, the interaction of Cranbrook's first generation of European teachers with a second, younger generation of American instructors and students produced works that had a tremendous influence on post-World War II design. Much of the work of Cranbrook students and faculty from the 1920's on reveals how an ideal of the Arts and Crafts movement—the elevation of the applied arts to the level of fine arts—affected the ways modern designers searched for an integration of artistic style and life-style.

Under Saarinen's direction, faculty and students were encouraged to experiment and collaborate. Since there was no established curriculum, national and international competitions often provided the impetus for exploration of new concepts. For example, four designs by Cranbrook students won prizes at the "Organic Design for Home Furnishings Competition" sponsored by the Museum of Modern Art in 1940 and 1941. Charles Eames and Eero Saarinen, both of whom had backgrounds in architecture, collaborated to create a group of chairs, modular storage units, tables, and a sectional sofa that won two first prizes. Benjamin Baldwin and Harry Weese also won prizes in multiple categories of the competition; their most significant entries were for outdoor furniture and lighting fixtures. The competition generated designs that were influential in shaping American furniture between 1950 and 1975 and helped to establish Eames and Saarinen as leaders of American design.

Florence Knoll, a Cranbrook Academy alumna who had attended Kingswood School Cranbrook, made her reputation as an interior designer and entrepreneur. She domesticated the European International Style for American homes and offices and designed elegant hospital, bank, university, and hotel interiors from the 1940's to the 1960's. Along with her husband Hans, in 1951 she formed Knoll Associates, a company that drew on the best talent in Europe and America to design furniture, textiles, and graphics.

The worlds of modern architecture, furniture, and interior design were not the only beneficiaries of the Cranbrook Academy. George Booth's interest in traditional craftsmanship remained a steady influence on study and practice at Cranbrook. Although the Cranbrook Press he founded in 1900 was a short-lived experiment, his efforts on behalf of metalworking, textiles, and ceramics have been central to Cranbrook's continuing importance as an American educational institution. Cranbrook is one of the few U.S. institutions to offer instruction in fine metalworking in an educational environment. Eliel Saarinen was very active in metalworking, and a number of his designs grace the Cranbrook campus. Harry Bertoia revived the metal shop in the late 1930's, first as a student and then as an instructor, and his work there in jewelry, precious and nonprecious metals, and sculpture was a remarkable mixture of technique and technology. After World War II, Richard Thomas began the first teaching department in metalwork at Cranbrook.

Cranbrook's contributions to the crafts of textile and ceramics also began in the 1920's. In the early years, Eliel Saarinen's wife, Loja, established her weaving studio at Cranbrook, and a weaving department and shops soon followed. Many of the carpets, curtains, wall hangings, and decorative textiles for community buildings were produced under Loja Saarinen's supervision. The best known of Cranbrook's textiles students is, no doubt, Jack Lenor Larsen, a practicing weaver whose international corporation is famous for mass-produced fabrics with handwoven characteristics.

Booth intended that ceramics be one of the first arts taught at Cranbrook, although the ceramics department was small and undistinguished until the late 1930's, when Maija Grotell joined the faculty. Under her guidance, the department became a center of individual creative activity at Cranbrook, and Grotell's students have made significant contributions to modern American ceramics.

In attempting to create a community that illustrated the positive relationship between aesthetics and social life, George Booth laid a foundation for the transformation of education and production. Such a spirit has characterized the modernist agenda of the twentieth century and is at the heart of Cranbrook's impact on American design; despite the passage of time and changes in technology, society, and aesthetics, this spirit has continued to influence the work of the graduates, faculty, and students of the Cranbrook Academy of Art.

Bibliography

Becker, Howard. "Arts and Crafts." *American Journal of Sociology* 83 (January, 1978): 862-868. An information-packed introduction to the crafts revival movement by an insightful sociologist of art.

Caplan, Ralph. *The Design of Herman Miller.* New York: Whitney Library of Design, 1976. Charles Eames played a major role in the success of Herman Miller's Zeeland, Michigan, company, which is considered by many to be the premiere producer of modern American furniture. Mediocre illustrations, chatty and informative text.

Clark, Robert Judson, et al. *Design in America: The Cranbrook Vision, 1925-1950.* New York: Harry N. Abrams, 1983. Profuse and beautiful illustrations characterize this excellent volume of essays, which acts as the catalog for an exhibition organized by the Detroit Institute of Fine Arts. Biographies of artists, chronology, notes, and index.

Kaplan, Wendy. *"The Art That Is Life": The Arts and Crafts Movement in America, 1875-1920.* Boston: Little, Brown, 1987. Well-illustrated, articulate catalog, with fine introductory essays written to accompany a Boston Museum of Fine Arts exhibition. Index.

"Nelson, Eames, Gerard, and Propst: The Design Process at Herman Miller." *Design Quarterly* 98 (1975). A special issue of the magazine that discusses the work of four important American designers. Excellent introduction to postwar American design. Well illustrated.

Noyes, Eliot F. *Organic Design in Home Furnishings.* New York: Museum of Modern Art, 1941. Monograph designed to accompany an exhibit. Illustrates various entries and winners. Black-and-white photographs.

J. R. Donath

Cross-References

Hoffmann and Moser Found the Wiener Werkstätte (1903), p. 79; Rietveld Designs the Red-Blue Chair (1918), p. 458; German Artists Found the Bauhaus (1919), p. 463; A Paris Exhibition Defines Art Deco (1925), p. 654; Loewy Pioneers American Industrial Design (1929), p. 777; Wright Founds the Taliesin Fellowship (1932), p. 902; *Arts and Architecture* Magazine Initiates the Case Study Program (1945), p. 1290; Saarinen Designs Kennedy Airport's TWA Terminal (1956), p. 1716.

EISENSTEIN'S *POTEMKIN* INTRODUCES
NEW FILM EDITING TECHNIQUES

Category of event: Motion pictures
Time: 1925
Locale: Union of Soviet Socialist Republics

Sergei Eisenstein created his masterpiece by splicing film shot at many locations, an approach most film directors subsequently adopted

Principal personages:
SERGEI EISENSTEIN (1898-1948), a Soviet film director
ÉDUARD TISSÉ (1897-1961), a cameraman who helped Eisenstein develop several new filming techniques later universally employed by motion-picture directors
VLADIMIR ILICH LENIN (VLADIMIR ILICH ULYANOV, 1870-1924), the leader of the Soviet Union and a proponent of motion pictures as the most effective tool for propaganda
LEV VLADIMIROVICH KULESHOV (1899-1970), a founder of the Russian cinema and Eisenstein's mentor

Summary of Event

After the successful Bolshevik Revolution of 1917, the leaders of the Communist Party (especially Vladimir Lenin) launched a massive propaganda effort to win support for their new government from all segments of Soviet society. Lenin saw motion pictures as potentially the most effective tool not only for gaining public acceptance for Communist rule but also for convincing citizens to make the sacrifices necessary to build a socialist economic system. Accordingly, he authorized the creation of a government bureau to commission the making of "agitprops" (agitational propaganda films) to elicit the desired responses from the public. Lenin's action set in motion a chain of events that eventually led to the production of a motion picture entitled *Bronenosets Potyomkin* (1925; *Potemkin*) that revolutionized the making of motion pictures around the world.

Early in 1925, the Soviet government issued an order that an agitprop commemorating the twentieth anniversary of the unsuccessful revolution of 1905 be produced. To direct the film, government officials chose twenty-six-year-old Sergei Eisenstein, who had already directed several very effective agitprops. Eisenstein, educated as a civil engineer, had joined the Communist Party early and had worked diligently for its success during the revolution. After the revolution, he became interested in theater and joined the Prolitkult Theater (an official government agency, as were all groups involved in the arts). He rapidly became disenchanted with theater because small stages limited his ideas of dramatic productions, and he subsequently turned to the relatively new medium of motion pictures.

After working with Lev Kuleshov (who had been involved in filmmaking since its introduction in czarist Russia) for several years, Eisenstein received permission to direct an agitprop entitled *Stracha* (1925; *Strike*) in 1924 that enjoyed great success. The effectiveness of his first film resulted in his being chosen to direct the commemorative film, tentatively entitled *1905.* The government apparently envisioned a film that would re-create the entire year-long revolt against the czarist government in 1904 and 1905.

Eisenstein, in collaboration with several writers, created a hundred-page script for the film, detailing dozens of events to be filmed at more than thirty locations from Leningrad to the Black Sea. He and his crew began filming in Leningrad on March 31, 1925. When, in August, cloudy weather made filming in Leningrad difficult, Eisenstein and his crew moved to the Black Sea port of Odessa. Even before the move, Eisenstein had concluded that the original script was much too ambitious in scope. When he saw the massive marble steps leading from Odessa down to the seashore, he resolved to discard the film already shot and to concentrate instead on one event to epitomize the entire revolution: the mutiny of the sailors aboard the battleship *Potemkin.*

In making the film, Eisenstein introduced two innovations that have profoundly influenced the making of motion pictures ever since. The first was the use of "typage" for choosing actors. The second was the introduction of montage editing techniques to heighten the emotional impact of the film.

According to Eisenstein's theory of typage, a director should study a character in his script and determine what physical and mental traits might be found in the character's "type." He should then employ a person exhibiting those traits rather than depend on professional actors. The Orthodox priest who figures prominently in *Potemkin* was in reality a gardener whom Eisenstein concluded displayed all the traits usually associated with a priest.

The montage editing techniques Eisenstein perfected for his motion picture undoubtedly became his most important contribution to the evolution of filmmaking. "Montage" refers to the splicing together of segments of film to heighten dramatic effect. One of the most powerful scenes in *Potemkin* occurs during the massacre on the marble steps (arguably the most famous sequence in motion-picture history) when an old woman wearing pince-nez asks the Cossacks to stop the slaughter. Eisenstein shows a closeup of the Cossack swinging his sword, followed by another closeup of the woman with her glasses broken, blood spurting from her eye. The film never shows the sword striking the woman, but because of the placement of the shots, the audience is left in no doubt as to what has happened.

In several scenes, Eisenstein introduced a technique subsequently adopted by many directors called "breaking from real time." In one particular sequence, the audience sees a sailor, disgusted with the food he is forced to eat, break the plate of one of his officers. In real time, this action would have taken only a second. Eisenstein filmed the breaking of the plate from nine different angles, spliced the shots together, and created a four-second sequence with a greatly enhanced effect on the audience.

Finally, Eisenstein also introduced several innovative camera techniques during the making of *Potemkin* that were widely copied by most subsequent filmmakers. In collaboration with cameraman Éduard Tissé, he constructed a camera trolley that enabled a cameraman to descend the Odessa steps with the actors. He ordered another camera to be strapped to the waist of a circus acrobat to capture the movement as the acrobat ran, jumped, and fell down the steps.

The film that ultimately emerged from this tremendous burst of creativity did not entirely please the Communist leadership, although its propaganda effect was undeniable. Outside the Soviet Union, however, motion-picture critics hailed *Potemkin* as a masterpiece.

Impact of Event

When *Potemkin* debuted in Moscow in January, 1926, it stirred immediate controversy in the ranks of the Communist Party and the Soviet artistic community. Many of Eisenstein's rivals in cinematic production accused him of putting art before propaganda. Some of his enemies in the Party hierarchy dismissed the film as a decadent bourgeois documentary. Eisenstein's relationship with the Soviet bureaucracy became strained, and his reputation never fully recovered. Although he continued to direct films in the Soviet Union, the government declined to distribute many of them.

In Western Europe and the United States, *Potemkin* won instant acclaim. American film stars Douglas Fairbanks and Mary Pickford traveled to Moscow in July, 1926, to view the film. Fairbanks, in a widely quoted interview after seeing the film, declared that Eisenstein's film had at last mastered the science of motion. Some months later, Fairbanks, along with German actor Emil Jannings and producer Max Reinhardt, endorsed *Potemkin* as the greatest motion picture made to that time. Fairbanks' praise heightened the anticipation of American audiences when the picture finally premiered in New York City at the Biltmore Theater on December 5, 1926.

Film viewers in the United States were enthusiastic about Eisenstein's film, and American film critics even more so. One critic correctly predicted in *The Christian Science Monitor* that *Potemkin* would make motion-picture history as a model of how films should be made. The National Board of Review of the motion-picture industry chose the film as the best of the year and identified it as a perfect re-creation of a historical event. Ironically, this last bit of praise was totally undeserved. No slaughter of innocents occurred on the Odessa steps in 1905, as depicted in the film's most famous scene; the director fabricated the entire event. The mutiny aboard the *Potemkin* was not an expression of revolutionary ideology as Eisenstein portrayed it but was rather a protest against deplorable conditions. Eisenstein continued a trend that has only rarely been reversed in filmmaking, that of creating history rather than re-creating it.

Potemkin's reception in the West somewhat rejuvenated Eisenstein's standing with Soviet officials. They allowed him to direct the agitprop films *Octyabr* (1927; *Octo-*

ber: Or, Ten Days That Shook the World) and *Generalnaya Linya* (1929; *The Gen-eral Line*), both of which employed many of the techniques pioneered in *Potemkin*. In 1929, Paramount Films brought Eisenstein to Hollywood but ultimately rejected the scripts he submitted for two proposed films, *Sutter's Gold* and *An American Tragedy*. American novelist Upton Sinclair then arranged for Eisenstein to make an epic motion picture about the Mexican revolution, but Soviet officials recalled him to Moscow before he completed the film. An American studio released some of the footage from the Mexican venture as *Thunder Over Mexico* in 1933. This film also employed many of the techniques pioneered in *Potemkin* and, judging from the wide adoption of such techniques by American directors, heavily influenced the evolution of U.S. cinema.

Eisenstein's masterpiece confirmed motion-picture making as a true art form. Although Eisenstein never received the acclaim in the Soviet Union that his work merited, *Potemkin* vindicated Lenin's view of motion pictures as potentially the most effective medium for molding a particular point of view among the masses. The film evokes powerful emotions even among modern viewers: revulsion at the deplorable conditions among the lower classes depicted in the film's scenes; disgust with the arrogant and ruthless officers, czarist officials, and priests; moral outrage at the mas-sacre of civilians on the Odessa steps. Eisenstein achieved this tremendous emo-tional impact through the techniques that continue to dominate the film industry.

Bibliography

Cook, David A. *A History of Narrative Film*. New York: W. W. Norton, 1981. The section of Cook's book dealing with Eisenstein and *Potemkin* identifies the film as an epochal event in motion-picture history. Cook describes Eisenstein's innovative techniques in language understandable by laypersons and locates his film in its proper perspective in world cinema history.

Eisenstein, Sergei M. "The Composition of *Potemkin*." In *The Emergence of Film Art*, edited by Lewis Jacobs. New York: Hopkinson and Blake, 1969. Eisenstein's explanation in his own words of the thought process and chance happenings that resulted in his masterpiece. Invaluable to those who wish to understand *Potemkin*.

_____. *Potemkin*. Translated by Gillon R. Aitken. New York: Simon & Schuster, 1968. The complete script of the film, annotated by Eisenstein himself. Difficult reading, but worthwhile to those who wish in-depth knowledge about the famous film.

Kauffman, Stanley. "*Potemkin*." In *Great Film Directors: A Critical Anthology*, ed-ited by Leo Braudy and Morris Dickstein. New York: Oxford University Press, 1978. Kauffman identifies Eisenstein as perhaps the most important director of his era because of his perfection of montage in *Potemkin*. Contains informative ex-planations of Eisenstein's techniques.

Lawder, Standish D. "Eisenstein and Constructivism." In *Great Film Directors: A Critical Anthology*, edited by Leo Braudy and Morris Dickstein. New York: Ox-ford University Press, 1978. Lawder's article attempts to show that Eisenstein's films, especially *Potemkin*, were heavily influenced by a banned artistic movement in the Soviet Union called constructivism.

Leyda, Jay. *Kino: A History of the Russian and Soviet Film.* London: George Allen & Unwin, 1960. Leyda shows that Eisenstein's genius did not appear out of a vacuum but instead drew heavily on the work of Russian filmmakers who preceded him, especially his mentor, Lev Kuleshov. Leyda also clearly demonstrates the influence that Eisenstein has had on subsequent Soviet directors.

Macdonald, Dwight. "Eisenstein, Pudovkin, and Others." In *The Emergence of Film Art*, edited by Lewis Jacobs. New York: Hopkinson and Blake, 1969. Macdonald portrays Eisenstein as an important member of a trend in Soviet filmmaking, but not as an epochal genius, as some other critics have seen him.

Murray, Edward. *Ten Film Classics: A Re-Viewing.* New York: Frederick Ungar, 1978. Murray maintains that the true greatness of a film should be judged by its ability to communicate with audiences far removed from its original place and time. He concludes that *Potemkin* possesses that rare quality and thus must be considered a true masterpiece of cinematic art.

Nizhny, Vladimir. *Lessons with Eisenstein.* Edited and translated by Ivor Montagu and Jay Leyda. New York: Hill & Wang, 1962. An extremely thorough examination of the innovations that appeared in Eisenstein's films, especially *Potemkin*. Some readers may be put off by the overt Marxist-Leninist philosophy expounded by the author.

Paul Madden

Cross-References

Le Voyage dans la lune Introduces Special Effects (1902), p. 57; *The Great Train Robbery* Introduces New Editing Techniques (1903), p. 74; *The Birth of a Nation* Popularizes New Film Techniques (1915), p. 402; *The Cabinet of Dr. Caligari* Opens in Berlin (1920), p. 486; The Soviet Union Bans Abstract Art (1922), p. 544; Gance's *Napoléon* Revolutionizes Filmmaking Techniques (1925), p. 642; Kuleshov and Pudovkin Introduce Montage to Filmmaking (1927), p. 701; Lang Expands the Limits of Filmmaking with *Metropolis* (1927), p. 707.

GIDE'S *THE COUNTERFEITERS*
QUESTIONS MORAL ABSOLUTES

Category of event: Literature
Time: 1925
Locale: France

*André Gide's questioning of absolutes paralleled doubts on the validity of estab-
lished authorities and reflected the increasing importance of individual conscience
in determining ethics and self-authenticity*

> *Principal personage:*
> ANDRÉ GIDE (1869-1951), a French writer who, in narratives and his
> single novel *The Counterfeiters*, examined the dynamics and conse-
> quences of autonomy

Summary of Event

André Gide's questioning of absolutes reflected the trends and temper of early
twentieth century cultural and intellectual life. As the French celebrated the arrival
of a new century, inventions such as the electric light, the automobile, and film
enriched life; however, France's defeat by Germany in the Franco-Prussian War in
1871 undermined the nation's confidence in traditional beliefs and recognized institutions. For Gide, the ideals and truths that had shaped principles and practices con-
flicted with individual aspirations and differing perspectives. In his works, human
beings confront confusion and crisis.

Gide presented in *Les Faux-monnayeurs* (*The Counterfeiters*, 1927) an anguish
that results from the tensions between the ineffectiveness of authorative
institutions and the significance of individual responsibility. The novel reworks an
incident recorded in 1906. Like the historical counterfeiters on which the story is
based, the characters Léon Ghéridanisol, Georges Molinier, and Philippe Adamanti
pass illegal coins and, although discovered, escape prosecution. Recalling the images of specious currency, they project, along with other characters, appearances
that reflect reality but do not disclose all its aspects. Uncertain and ambiguous, knowledge forms the basis of actions that, derived from illusions, weaken credibility,
induce individualism, and end in conflicts. Nevertheless, personal perspectives determined by relative circumstances can combine to reveal truth. By juxtaposing opposing views, Gide, through the character of Édouard, examines the ambivalence of
illusion and enables the reader to reconcile varying visions into a coherent concept.
Such a privileged position, though, is more apparent than real, and Gide's characters
experience misunderstanding, frustration, disappointment, and dejection.

In the novel, human perception of reality assumes a truth that, ultimately invalid,
controls behavior and influences subsequent artistic and literary representations. Bernard, the illegitimate son of Édouard, the book's narrator, leaves home to seek
freedom and authenticity. By responding to individual impulses, he enjoys indepen-

dence and thereby defeats inner disturbances and social repressions. In replacing his family with other communities, however, Bernard recognizes the contradictions between the incontrovertibility of biological fact and the shifting perceptions of self-identity. Incapable of achieving total detachment, he acknowledges the necessity of participating in society; upon returning home, he attempts to forge the illegitimacy of birthright with the legitimacy of human interaction.

Like Bernard and other characters in the novel, Boris, a schoolboy, suffers an entrapment that fuses fiction and truth, morality and immorality, and autonomy and interdependence. His self-identification proceeds from interaction with others; winning acceptance among his schoolmates requires that he play the dangerous game of Russian roulette, and Boris shoots himself. Man teeters between the futilities of human endeavor and the nothingness of death; however, the certainty of human persistence and pain remains. Like the specious coins that are tangible but worthless, human beings are biologically real but spiritually counterfeit.

Gide develops in his novel themes presented in earlier writings. Like such Symbolist poets as Charles Baudelaire, Arthur Rimbaud, and Stéphane Mallarmé, he reacted initially against the realistic and naturalistic objectivities of Gustave Flaubert and Émile Zola. Through the use of archetypes and myths, he dramatized the contentions between realities of fragmentation and ideals of integration. In Gide's *Les Cahiers d'André Walter* (1891; *The Notebooks of André Walter*, 1968), Angel, or spiritual aspiration, contests for the human soul against Beast, or earthly attractions. Revolt against societal values leads to impotence and, in *Paludes* (1895; *Marshlands*, 1953), to self-destruction. Man is imprisoned in a cosmic game that, in *Le Prométhée mal enchaîné* (1899; *Prometheus Misbound*, 1953), is narratively conveyed as a battle between Zeus's erratic and amoral purposes and Prometheus' resolute and useless yearnings.

When endorsing these views in subsequent works, Gide emphasized ethical implications. His artistry moved from a description of images and self-imaginings to accounts of actions and character portrayals. In shifting from personal confession to fictional narrative, he described the anguish of dilemmas and the ambivalent interpretation of actions. Gidean personages strive to reconcile oppositions through conscious and self-determined acts. Like their Nietzschean and Dostoevskian counterparts, they demonstrate an individualism that attacks and denies moral certainties. Yet the exuberance evolving from questioning and rebellion is transitory and elusive and results in the substitution of one authority for another. Michel in *L'Immoraliste The Immoralist*, 1930) and Lafcadio in *Les Caves du Vatican* (1914; *Lafcadio's Adventures*, 1925), pursue deliverance from moral responsibilities. Michel's defiance of ethical codes and Lafcadio's murder without motive, however, lead respectively to the sadness of solitude and the necessity of human interaction. Through submission to inner impulses, protagonists in *La Porte étroite* (1909; *Strait Is the Gate*, 1924) and *La Symphonie pastorale* (1919; *The Pastoral Symphony*, 1931) reject Protestant ethics, but changes of circumstances rob them of the opportunity to reconcile internal consciousness with external realities. Contradictions persist, and characters experience delusion, displacement, and dejection.

By situating personal perplexities and individual dilemmas within the framework of a social drama, in *The Counterfeiters* Gide adapted previous philosophical and psychological themes to objective reality. Like Flaubert, he entrapped his characters in tangles of amorous relationships. Love requires interpretation and interaction, and personal perceptions deceive but direct destiny, culminating, in Flaubert's work, in Emma Bovary's suicide, and, in *The Counterfeiters*, in Boris' self-destruction. Moreover, Gide, like Marcel Proust, expanded the scope of social realism and, in depicting the dynamics of bourgeois life, described the difficulties of man's search for self-understanding and meaningful values. Moral questions elicited by the Dreyfus affair and World War I compelled thinkers and artists to examine external realities in order to reform society. Like Anatole France and Romain Rolland, Gide attacked social and political practices; however, in constructing numerous credible, interrelated episodes that detail man's futile search for absolutes in a relative, changing world, he universalized the historical and particular. Inner crises characterize a social setting where varying, limited perspectives evolve into the single certainty of despair and death. Authenticity and dignity are based upon absolutes. Yet in questioning authorities and values, Gidean characters become imprisoned by doubt and frustration. As Bernard returns home, the novel concludes at the beginning; and the new story of Caloub Molinier continues the circular narrative of man's disappointments and displacements in a delusionary world.

Impact of Event

In his journal, Gide described *The Counterfeiters* as a failure. His stress upon concision and his abandonment of accepted narrative structures made the book a departure from the engaging novels of Honoré de Balzac, Flaubert, Charles Dickens, and Thomas Hardy. In 1952, one year after Gide's death, the Roman Catholic church prohibited the reading of his works on moral grounds. Nevertheless, this reserved reception of his fiction contrasts with the important impact of his ethical thoughts and novelistic theory on contemporary and subsequent writers. As founding editor of the highly regarded periodical *La Nouvelle Revue française*, moreover, Gide welcomed and advanced innovative and controversial ideas on idealogy and style. *The Counterfeiters* reflected much of his thinking and novelistic practice, and it shaped the direction of attitudes toward later developments in ethics and aesthetics.

Like Gide, proponents of Surrealism and its precursor Dadaism reacted against the values and authorities that had brought about the atrocities of World War I. Dadaism, initiated in Zurich in 1916, denounced arbitrary absolutes that denied individual thought and reduced human worth. A nihilism, expressed in verse by André Breton, Paul Éluard, and Louis Aragon, expressed an empty and disturbing vision of the human situation. Humanity, according to Breton, confronts the conflicts of opposing absolutes; however, through internal images derived from observed realities, humans translate physical phenomena into inner truths that, in Breton's novel *Nadja* (1928), become indicants of external beauty.

Gide did not participate in the Surrealist movement, but his themes of human aspirations, anxieties, exuberance, and futilities reinforced the Surrealist call to reject established values. During the 1930's, the failure of the League of Nations, the economic deprivations of global depression, and the rise of totalitarian governments shattered the illusions of humanity's ability to reform ethics and to attain economic security and social equality within existing orders.

Like Bernard, the characters created by Georges Bernanos contend against falsity; but, instead of enjoying momentary exhilarations, they discover, through moral and physical torments, an inner redemption and spiritual nobility. Gide's skepticism of moral absolutes also assumed the form of revolution in André Malraux's *La Condition humaine* (1933; *Man's Fate*, 1934), in which images of war reflect the need to destroy existing authorities. In Malraux's work, however, unlike in *The Counterfeiters*, a fraternity among the revolutionaries permits an integration of spiritual affiliations.

After the defeat of France in 1940, Jean-Paul Sartre and Albert Camus addressed the validity of absolutes. Sartre saw humans as defined by external realities and inner recognitions; in assuming imposed values, Sartre asserted, humans falsify their true nature and suffer anguish. Rather, Sartre argued, humankind must resist artificial restrictions and assert self-authenticity. Camus, in *L'Étranger* (1942; *The Stranger*, 1946), reaffirms Gide's vision of man who, guided by impulses and checked by absolutes, endures the confusions of absurdity. The hero of Camus' work, Meursault, like Gide's Bernard, finds freedom through rebellion and, in declaring his self-worth, experiences a deliverance.

Stylistically and structurally, *The Counterfeiters* advanced, and foreshadowed later developments in, novelistic techniques. Gide's use of a direct, classical simplicity paralleled styles adopted by François Mauriac, Camus, and T. S. Eliot. The portrayal of diverse characters, moreover, necessitated the use of multiple perspectives. Édouard's journal and comments synthesize views, recalling the scattered but unified perceptions recorded by omniscient narrators in the novels of Marcel Proust or Virginia Woolf. Further, like Roger Martin du Gard, John Galsworthy, and Thomas Mann, Gide presented a social panorama. Yet his emphasis upon individual perspectives also suggests techniques characterizing the French new novel. Michel Butor and Alain Robbe-Grillet, in particular, similarly combined conflicting images that, individually observed, denoted the apparent chaos of existence and the uselessness of human aspirations.

Gide's moral skepticism led to an individualism shared by subsequent thinkers and fiction writers. In assuming a detached, reportorial stance, however, Gide contented himself with describing situations and thereby resisted personal commentary. Through doubts and disappointments, his characters mature in self-understanding and suffer the frustrations of human existence. In fact, by foreshadowing Samuel Beckett's representations of misunderstanding and Jean Genet's dramatizations of meaninglessness, Gide depicted the painful paradox of ideals that inevitably end in misinterpretation, disintegration, and death.

Bibliography

Brée, Germaine. *Gide.* New Brunswick, N.J.: Rutgers University Press, 1963. An enlarged revision of a French study published in 1953, this intelligent, insightful analysis of Gide's works emphasizes novelistic techniques that facilitate the expression of intellectual and ethical themes.

Brennan, Joseph G. *Three Philosophical Novelists: James Joyce, André Gide, Thomas Mann.* New York: Macmillan, 1964. In placing Gide's works within the contexts of Nietzschean and Bergsonian philosophies, this seminal study demonstrates Gide's interpretation of intellectual currents.

Cordle, Thomas. *André Gide.* Boston: Twayne, 1969. A superb reading of Gide's attempts to resolve oppositions that reflect Symbolist expression, Romantic idealism, and realistic objectivity. Includes an annotated bibliography.

Falk, Eugene H. *Types of Thematic Structure: The Nature and Function of Motifs in Gide, Camus, and Sartre.* Chicago: University of Chicago Press, 1967. Although emphasizing a reading of Gide's *The Pastoral Symphony*, Falk elucidates, systematically and rigorously, Gide's uses of plot, characterization, and imagery. Contrasts Gide's themes and techniques with those employed in Camus's *The Stranger* and Sartre's *La Nausée* (1938; *Nausea*, 1949).

Guerard, Albert J. *André Gide.* Cambridge, Mass.: Harvard University Press, 1951. A reading of Gide's works that explores personal tensions between ascetic and amorous impulses, spiritual self-accounts, novelistic techniques, and possible influences. Slightly dated, this intelligent, perceptive study nevertheless provides an indispensable introduction to Gide's works.

Holdheim, W. Wolfgang. *Theory and Practice of the Novel: A Study on André Gide.* Geneva: Droz, 1968. A comprehensive, meticulous study of Gide's novelistic theory and techniques. Holdheim examines Gide's creative works in light of his journal, suggesting parallels between Gide's style and structure with those of earlier novelists.

Hytier, Jean. *André Gide.* Translated by Richard Howard. Garden City, N.Y.: Doubleday, 1962. Originally published as a series of lectures (1938), this first aesthetic survey of Gide's works includes a detailed plot summary of *The Counterfeiters* and interesting insights into the themes of doubt and reform.

Ireland, G. W. *André Gide: A Study of His Creative Writings.* Oxford: Clarendon Press, 1970. Although lacking in defined methodology and single focus, this study contains intelligent, perceptive readings that provide a useful commentary on Gide's works.

Rossi, Vinio. *André Gide: The Evolution of an Aesthetic.* New Brunswick, N.J.: Rutgers University Press, 1967. In tracing Gide's transition from the use of image to the development of narrative, Rossi describes the novelist's artistic growth.

Donald Gilman

Cross-References

Rilke's *Duino Elegies* Depicts Art as a Transcendent Experience (1911), p. 281; Proust's *Remembrance of Things Past* Is Published (1913), p. 355; The Dada Movement Emerges at the Cabaret Voltaire (1916), p. 419; Stravinsky Completes His Wind Octet (1923), p. 561; Surrealism Is Born (1924), p. 604; *The Diary of a Country Priest* Inspires Readers (1936), p. 1026; Sartre's *Being and Nothingness* Expresses Existential Philosophy (1943), p. 1262; The New Novel (*Le Nouveau Roman*) Emerges (1951), p. 1481.

THE GREAT GATSBY CAPTURES THE ESSENCE OF THE ROARING TWENTIES

Category of event: Literature
Time: 1925
Locale: The United States

Although The Great Gatsby *reflected the glitter of the Roaring Twenties, the novel warned of the potential destructiveness of pursuing the American Dream at any cost*

Principal personages:

F. SCOTT FITZGERALD (1896-1940), an American novelist, dramatist, screenwriter, essayist, and short-story writer who captured the essence of the glittering Jazz Age

ZELDA FITZGERALD (1900-1948), F. Scott Fitzgerald's wife, a writer in her own right, a literary adviser to her husband, and a model of the 1920's "flaming youth" who lived for the moment

ERNEST HEMINGWAY (1899-1961), an eminent American writer, a sometime friend, jealous competitor, and critic of Fitzgerald

EDMUND WILSON (1895-1972), a trusted friend, editor, and adviser of Fitzgerald instrumental in reestablishing Fitzgerald's literary reputation in the 1950's

Summary of Event

When Scribner's published *The Great Gatsby* on April 10, 1925, F. Scott Fitzgerald had established himself with a string of impressive money-making stories and had gained some attention from critics who pointed to his occasional flashes of literary genius. He had already published the novels *This Side of Paradise* (1920) and *The Beautiful and Damned* (1922), collections of short stories including *Flappers and Philosophers* (1920) and *Tales of the Jazz Age* (1922), and a play, *The Vegetable: Or, From President to Postman* (1923).

Fitzgerald was successful because he wrote with great gusto about the young post-World War I generation—its bashing of traditional values, its search for wealth, its rebelliousness, and its unorthodox behavior. His stories embodied a high degree of wish fulfillment for readers, pitching them into living vicariously among the smart set of the 1920's, with their wild parties, sporty automobiles, and high-keyed, pleasure-seeking adventures.

Fitzgerald—whether in France, New York, or Hollywood—always used his own personal experiences and observations as the basis for his stories. So it was with *The Great Gatsby*, which presented fictional versions of his painful social rejections, his thwarted loves, his excesses with drink, and his search for success and money. Moreover, his wife, Zelda Fitzgerald, served as the model for Daisy Buchanan in the novel, a quick-silvered beauty representing the unattainable.

For his novel, Fitzgerald drew upon the lavish Long Island parties he had attended, populating his story with a mix of intellectuals, frauds, bootleggers, gangsters, madcap flappers, and sad, naïve young men such as Nick Carraway, the book's narrator. Carraway retrospectively narrates the events of the summer of 1922 that led up to the death of Jay Gatsby. Visiting his distant cousin Daisy Buchanan and her husband, Tom, in West Egg, Long Island, New York, Nick learns that the Buchanans are unhappily married and that Tom is unfaithful and having an affair with plump Myrtle Wilson, the wife of a garage owner.

Through a series of dinner parties, lunches, and drinking sprees, Nick becomes acquainted with the mysterious, wealthy Jay Gatsby, who lives on a nearby estate where he throws fabulous parties for speakeasy society. Nick is alternately repelled and fascinated by Gatsby, a thirty-year-old with adolescent romantic dreams, fictitious upper-class parentage to hide the reality of his impoverished farm background, and bad taste in whatever he buys.

Nick learns that Gatsby is a self-made man. Years before, a poor Gatsby had fallen hard for the dazzling Daisy Buchanan before he went overseas to fight in World War I. Daisy, however, spurned him for arrogant Tom Buchanan, a rich and eligible socialite. Four years later, Gatsby, still pursuing his idealistic love for Daisy, makes a fortune partly from bootlegging liquor, buys a garish mansion across the harbor from the Buchanans, and yearns to reclaim his lost love.

Because Nick is related to Daisy, Gatsby asks Nick to arrange a tea at Nick's house for the purpose of staging a reunion between Gatsby and Daisy. The reunion results in the Buchanans' inviting Gatsby, Nick, and friends to a party at a New York hotel. Events turn ugly when a drunken Tom accuses Gatsby of being a swindler and of trying to steal Daisy. An angry Daisy leaves with Gatsby for the return drive home.

When Tom and Nick return to West Egg, they stop to investigate a fatal accident and discover that Myrtle Wilson (Tom's mistress) has been killed by a hit-and-run driver in a car similar to one owned by Gatsby. Nick learns later that Daisy, not Gatsby, drove the car. Gatsby, though, gallantly offers to shoulder the blame.

Through the connivance of Tom Buchanan, Myrtle Wilson's husband becomes convinced that Gatsby is the cause of his wife's death. A few hours later, an enraged Wilson shoots Gatsby in an act of revenge and then turns the gun on himself. Nick arranges for Gatsby's funeral, but no one comes except for one former guest and Gatsby's father, who believes his son to have been a great man. At the end, Nick breaks off his friendship with the corrupt Buchanans and returns to the Midwest.

The plot outline sounds like material fit for sensational tabloids and pulp magazines. Plots, though, were never the forte of Fitzgerald. What makes *The Great Gatsby* so memorable is Fitzgerald's handling of these melodramatic events.

The critics of the time were generally favorable, praising the spare style of the short (fifty-thousand-word) novel. Commentators were especially impressed by Fitzgerald's compressed details that make scenes blaze with life, his poetic imagery, his framing of complex characters and universal themes in ironic terms, and his use of a sophisticated first-person narrative.

Unhappily, book sales were only modest, and only about twenty-four thousand copies were printed. The book was not reprinted by Fitzgerald's publisher during his lifetime. The reading public seemed put off by the unpleasant characters—each a moral failure—the downbeat ending, and the sophisticated writing techniques so highly praised by critics. Although Fitzgerald made little money from book sales, he did earn close to thirty thousand dollars from stage and film rights.

One result of the lukewarm popular reception of *The Great Gatsby* was that Fitzgerald turned to writing profitable short stories and Hollywood scripts. He faced financial crises caused by the family's expensive living style. Zelda's increasing mental problems required her institutionalization, and Fitzgerald's own increasing alcohol problems, self-doubts, declining health, and inability to write a new novel commensurate with the quality of *The Great Gatsby* made the author's life a troubled one.

Even good friend Ernest Hemingway took Fitzgerald to task for betraying his craft and writing for easy money. The two had been on intimate terms since *The Great Gatsby* appeared, with Fitzgerald—then at the top of his powers—championing the fledgling Hemingway. Over the next few years, they counseled each other, but as Hemingway's star rose and Fitzgerald's declined, the two drifted apart by the 1930's. Hemingway wanted Fitzgerald to discipline his art and to write simply, but Fitzgerald would not.

Impact of Event

The Great Gatsby was the watershed of Fitzgerald's own rise and decline as a writer. Both his career and life paralleled America's fortunes, riding the crest of the prosperity wave of the 1920's and tailing off during the Depression years of the 1930's. Fitzgerald died in obscurity in 1940 as a Hollywood hack writer.

Fitzgerald's novels were largely ignored and unread from the 1930's until the 1950's. Two factors led to the revival of the novelist's reputation: a renewed interest in the personal and artistic tragedy of Fitzgerald himself and an academic interest in the unique way Fitzgerald structured his art.

The interest in Fitzgerald's life and its excesses began with Edmund Wilson, his longtime confidant. Wilson edited *The Crack-Up* (1945), a collection of Fitzgerald's essays, notebooks, and letters revealing the emotional bankruptcy and disillusionments in Fitzgerald's life. The essays not only detailed the extravagant life-style of the Fitzgeralds but also chronicled the devastating effects of the Great Depression on their lives and on his art.

Interest in Fitzgerald's life intensified with the popular success of Budd Schulberg's *The Disenchanted* (1950), a fictionalized account of Fitzgerald's drunken sprees, his fistfights with and insults of friends, and his declining ability to write during his Hollywood years. Arthur Mizener fueled further interest with *The Far Side of Paradise: A Biography of F. Scott Fitzgerald* (1951).

The academic community also helped revive Fitzgerald. The New Criticism, a critical method of scrutinizing the form and texture of literary works, was in vogue during the 1950's, and *The Great Gatsby* was made for such close textual analysis. A spate of academic commentary poured forth, focusing in particular upon Fitzgerald's brilliant handling of the novel's first-person retrospective point of view. Nick Carraway does not merely narrate the tale; he observes, participates, and evaluates. The narrative structure thus allows Fitzgerald to work simultaneously within and without the scenes and to be both immersed immediately in and psychologically distanced from the action. Not since Joseph Conrad had an author been able to pull off such a double-vision feat as Fitzgerald did in *The Great Gatsby*.

In addition, the New Critics wrestled with the ambiguities of Nick Carraway as a reliable narrator and the probability of his moral and ethical development. They disagreed on interpreting the shadowy character of Gatsby: Was he a tragic, noble figure in the Shakespearean sense? Was he a Christlike martyr, an Antichrist figure, or perhaps a knight-errant seeking the grail and idealizing his lady? Or was Gatsby just an unlucky racketeer gunned down in a bizarre twist of fate? In addition, the New Critics charted the complex chronology of the novel, with its sudden shifts of past and present, and traced the imagery clusters found therein, such as the ironic contrasts between the stately mansions of Long Island and the nearby valley of ashes where the poor lived.

A number of critics found the scenes of the valley of ashes in *The Great Gatsby* to be the American counterpart of the British vision in T. S. Eliot's 1922 poem *The Waste Land*. Both authors described intense disillusionments, the results of radical changes in the postwar era. The rich, the middle class, and the lower class were equally portrayed as culturally empty, entrapped in sterile, purposeless lives. Both Fitzgerald and Eliot conceived of the world as coming apart because no moral principle held it together.

The New Critics also scrutinized the novel's use of color images (especially greens), eye and vision cues, careening speedboats and cars, and the changing seasons. They also paid tribute to the animated phrasing and sentence structures used to achieve the novel's rhetorical brilliance and lyric energy.

Later literary criticism focused on Fitzgerald as a social commentator, as the issues and value clashes of the 1920's depicted in the novel were confronted by succeeding generations pursuing the American Dream. Fitzgerald thus was seen as more than a keen-eyed chronicler of the Roaring Twenties; he became a prophet warning oncoming generations of the terrible price to be paid for pursuing illusive dreams.

Besides being a cultural and historical allegory, the novel also presented universal themes of human yearnings. For example, there is the book's class issue, which shows the careless rich victimizing their lessers because of the upper class' empty values. The initiation theme shows a naïve Nick Carraway learning that wealth and power do not necessarily beget happiness; the book's frontier theme implies that the Midwest is morally superior to the corrupt, materialistic East Coast.

In essence, Fitzgerald's *The Great Gatsby* goes beyond capturing the frantic atmosphere of the Roaring Twenties. It is a novel for all ages. Gertrude Stein, writing, ironically, in the early 1930's, when Fitzgerald's reputation was fading, prophesied that "Fitzgerald will be read when many of his well known contemporaries are forgotten." Time has proven Stein's judgment correct.

Bibliography

Bruccoli, Matthew, and Jackson R. Bryer, eds. *F. Scott Fitzgerald in His Own Times: A Miscellany.* Kent, Ohio: Kent State University Press, 1971. A delightful pot-pourri, ranging from early writings of Fitzgerald to his obituary notices. Provides glimpses of his acerbic wit and astute perceptions along with original reviews of *The Great Gatsby.*

Eble, Kenneth E., ed. *F. Scott Fitzgerald: A Collection of Criticism.* New York: McGraw-Hill, 1973. Highly readable commentary by critics who share their insights on the craft and art of Fitzgerald. The essays on *The Great Gatsby* are a must for potential writers.

Lehan, Richard. *The Great Gatsby: The Limits of Wonder.* Boston: Twayne, 1990. Useful historical background about Fitzgerald and the novel, including a chronology of Fitzgerald's life and works. Also provides a series of critical interpretations of the major characters in the novel.

Medlow, James R. *Invented Lives: F. Scott and Zelda Fitzgerald.* Boston: Houghton Mifflin, 1984. Fascinating details of the Fitzgeralds' glamorous lives and their stormy relationships with well-known contemporaries. Basic theme: F. Scott and Zelda actually created their own legend, "acting out their stories in real life." Somewhat moralistic in tone.

Mizener, Arthur. *The Far Side of Paradise.* Boston: Houghton Mifflin, 1951. Chronicles the rise and fall of Fitzgerald as a person and literary artist in dramatic terms. Provides valuable photos of Fitzgerald at various stages of his career and appendices on his method of revision.

Richard Whitworth

Cross-References

Stein Holds Her First Paris Salons (1905), p. 129; Eliot Publishes *The Waste Land* (1922), p. 539; Hemingway's *The Sun Also Rises* Speaks for the Lost Generation (1926), p. 696; *The Sound and the Fury* Launches Faulkner's Career (1929), p. 805; The New Criticism Holds Sway (1940's), p. 1169.

THE NEW OBJECTIVITY MOVEMENT IS INTRODUCED

Category of event: Art
Time: 1925
Locale: Mannheim, Germany

*New Objectivity, an artistic and literary trend in Germany that repudiated ab-
straction, succeeded expressionism in the 1920's and lasted until 1932*

> *Principal personages:*
> OTTO DIX (1891-1969), a painter and graphic artist primarily active in
> Dresden and Düsseldorf who was one of the leading exponents of the
> veristic wing of New Objectivity
> GEORGE GROSZ (1893-1959), a Berlin painter and graphic artist whose
> socially critical pictures exemplified the work of the veristic wing of
> New Objectivity
> MAX BECKMANN (1884-1950), a painter and graphic artist who was in-
> cluded in the movement because his work has some affinities with
> New Objectivity
> GEORG SCHOLZ (1890-1945), a socially committed artist whose work was
> included in the Mannheim exhibition in 1925
> GEORG SCHRIMPF (1889-1938), a painter in the magic realist wing of New
> Objectivity who assimilated neoclassical influences
> ALEXANDER KANOLDT (1891-1939), a painter known mainly for his clearly
> rendered, airless still lifes and landscapes

Summary of Event

In 1923, Gustav Hartlaub, the newly appointed director of the Mannheim Kunst-
halle (museum), planned an exhibition to chart the realistic trend in postwar painting. The exhibition, entitled "New Objectivity" and subtitled "German Painting
Since Expressionism," however, did not take place until 1925. Hartlaub used the
term *Neue Sachlichkeit* ("New Objectivity") to differentiate this style from the subjective and abstract tendencies of expressionism. His aim was to "show those artists
who have remained—or who have once more become—avowedly faithful to positive, tangible reality." Among the artists most fully represented in the 1925 Mannheim exhibition were Otto Dix, George Grosz, Max Beckmann, Alexander Kanoldt,
Georg Scholz, and Georg Schrimpf. In 1925, the art historian Franz Roh also noted
the return to representational painting in an influential book. Roh used the term
"magic realism" to distinguish the new realism from the earlier nineteenth century
style of realism by the artists Hans Thoma and Wilhelm Leibl. For Roh, magic
realism also suggested a connection with French Surrealism and with the work of
the Italian artist Giorgio De Chirico, whose precisely rendered paintings of vacuous

mannequins in ambiguous spatial settings evoked a sense of mystery.

Hartlaub noted that there were two different aspects of the realist trend and divided the movement into two wings. He assigned the artists Dix, Grosz, Beckmann, and Scholz to a socially critical wing that he called "Verism," and the Italianate-inspired German artists such as Alexander Kanoldt and Georg Schrimpf to a neo-classical wing. Although Hartlaub included some of Georg Scholz's work in the verist wing, the artist's work is more often representative of magic realism. The phrases "New Objectivity" and "magic realism" essentially denoted the same thing: After expressionism, artists moved away from abstraction to realism. Although these terms were initially interchangeable, "New Objectivity" became more commonly used.

Both wings of New Objectivity shared some common characteristics. The artists all emphasized visual clarity, sobriety, and unemotional detachment in their work. They concentrated on depicting ordinary people and insignificant scenes from everyday life, which they painted in rigid, tightly compressed compositions. Their preference for static compositions and fidelity to the outlines of objects differed from the dynamic and generalizing manner of the expressionists. Some of the New Objectivity artists did, however, retain expressionistic devices such as distortion, exaggeration of detail, and alteration of reality in their work. The New Objectivity artists, however, eschewed utopian illusions. They scrutinized the cold, hard, often ugly facts of life as Germany struggled to recover from the harsh effects of World War I. During the 1920's, Germans faced economic hardships, runaway inflation, political unrest, uncertainty, and fear; shattered, insecure, corrupt, empty, and banal lives became the subject matter of several leading exponents of the movement, especially Dix, Grosz, and Beckmann.

Dix volunteered for military service during World War I and later became a staunch opponent of war. He became a satirist and exposed the indecencies of postwar life in his paintings and graphics. Motivated by ethical issues, his work was devoted to depictions of people, especially representations of dismembered ex-soldiers, repulsive, greedy prostitutes, and suffering victims. He frequently employed collage-like elements in his paintings to emphasize the fragmented, irrational, inhumane atmosphere of postwar Germany. Dix used these devices in his painting *The Matchseller* (1920), which portrays a mutilated male victim of the war as mere rubbish sitting on an urban street. As the blind, quadriplegic matchseller attempts to sell his wares to people hurrying by, a dog lifts its leg and urinates on him. Much of Dix's work centers on the lack of human values and protests against social injustices.

Grosz volunteered for military service in 1914 before becoming disillusioned with the war and becoming a pacifist. His style was initially influenced by expressionism, and before his association with New Objectivity, he was a member of the most radical, politicized faction of Berlin Dada. In the 1920's, Grosz was frequently charged with blasphemy for his irreverent depictions of German militarism. Harboring a deep hatred for both militarism and bourgeois complacency, he developed a grim, satirical style that portrayed society as morally bankrupt. Grosz unleashed his anger against the social decay in the Weimar Republic and produced numerous images of grisly sex murderers, fat bureaucrats, and power-hungry, duplicitious generals. Many of his paintings, such as *Eclipse of the Sun* (1926), lampoon wealthy, empty-headed bureaucrats conspiring with generals. For Grosz, these despised figures epitomized corruption, power, and cruelty. A consummate social critic, Grosz used his analytic and detached style to develop De Chirico's mannequin figures into dehumanized, mutilated, robot-like representations of people reveling in their own banality. Grosz's precisely rendered painting *Republic Automatons* (1920) depicts faceless, maimed mannequins as symbols of people's lost identities in postwar German society.

Beckmann, along with Dix and Grosz, was perceived to be one of the most important representatives of the verist wing of New Objectivity. Beckmann's work, however, is problematic, and it is difficult to assign his work to a particular style. Although he eschewed abstraction and remained aloof from expressionism, his style had many affinities with the artists of the movement know as Die Brücke (the Bridge), especially the use of distortion and exaggeration of detail. During World War I, Beckmann volunteered for military duty and briefly served as a medical orderly on the front. His horrific war experiences resulted in a nervous breakdown, and he was discharged from the military in 1915. He was permanently affected by the war; his style became transformed, and humanity's inhumanity became the general theme of his work. Beckmann's painting *The Night* (1919) shows a family being robbed and physically violated in their garret by a gang of thugs. In the center of this spatially compressed composition, a woman, naked and splayed, is about to be raped. Beckmann's stark, heavily outlined figures retain the expressionist device of distortion, but the overall somber mood and theme of social injustice anticipates New Objectivity. In this matter-of-fact portrayal of mutilation and physical and mental torture, Beckmann's angular use of line and exaggeration of detail heighten the effect of polar opposites: weak against strong, good against evil. Much of his work centers on the themes of temptation and cruelty, human exploitation and degradation, but Beckmann's view is that goodness does not always triumph over evil. Dix, Grosz, and Beckmann, unlike the members of the magic realist wing of New Objectivity, all shared the common aesthetic of disillusionment.

Scholz, Kanoldt, and Schrimpf were minor artists in comparison to Dix, Grosz, and Beckmann, whose verist works epitomized and dominated New Objectivity. Hartlaub included some of Scholz's work in the veristic wing of the 1925 Mannheim exhibition, but although he painted some socially critical works in the style of Grosz, he is better known for his disquieting still lifes and landscapes that juxtapose industrialized technology with nature or idealized objects from the past. Kanoldt and Schrimpf initially worked in Munich, the center of the magic realist wing of New Objectivity, and they looked toward Italy, not contemporary Germany, for inspiration. They assimilated aspects of De Chirico's metaphysical paintings, which presented a timeless, inanimate, yet disquieting world, into their own clearly rendered, tightly ordered compositions. The magic realists created gentle, neoclassic images of simple, monumental forms that were smoothly painted and carefully modeled.

Their rigid reconstructions of reality were far removed from the concerns of the veristic wing of New Objectivity.

Impact of Event

When Adolf Hitler came to power in the early 1930's, the New Objectivity movement quickly dissipated. By 1933, Hitler initiated cultural purges to cleanse the nation of modernism. Museums and galleries were emptied of offending examples of modern art. Hitler outlawed modernism and imposed an official style, a realistic naturalism; Dix, Grosz, Beckmann, Scholz, Schrimpf, and Kanoldt were forbidden to paint, and their works were defamed. For the next twelve years, Nazi art policy dominated the arts in Germany, and illusionistic painting prevailed there. After World War II, German artists who survived the war and Nazi defamation resumed their work. At first, illusionistic painting still prevailed after the war, but gradually abstract art and semi-abstract painting became popular in Germany.

The impact of New Objectivity remained chiefly a German phenomenon. In the 1960's, a new group of German artists known as critical realists merged the stylistic characteristic of New Objectivity with the formal elements of pop art and Socialist Realism in an attempt to revive the critical social commentary of Dix and Grosz. In the late 1970's, a group of German artists sharing some unified stylistic affinities exhibited together in a Berlin show focusing on "ugly realism"; artists featured in the exhibit included Salomé (Wolfgang Cilarz), Helmut Middendorf, Rainer Fetting, and Bernd Zimmer. Their raw, abrasive images of sexual and political brutality are a stylistic and thematic mixture of the verist wing of New Objectivity and the brashness of American pop art. Yet unlike the New Objectivity artists, who primarily depicted social outcasts (prostitutes, beggars, mutilated individuals) as the victims of society, these Berlin artists demonstrate in their work their conviction that everyone is a political victim in modern society.

Bibliography

Barton, Brigid S. *Otto Dix and Die Neue Sachlichkeit, 1918-1925.* Ann Arbor, Mich.: UMI Research Press, 1981. One of the few good studies in English on Dix. Provides an excellent overview of the artist and discusses his role in the emergence of the New Objectivity movement. Well researched and thoroughly documented. Recommended for students of Dix and New Objectivity. Contains good bibliography and numerous reproductions of Dix's work.

Beckmann, Max. *Max Beckmann: Retrospective.* Edited by Carla Schultz-Hoffmann and Judith C. Weiss. Munich: Prestel-Verlag, 1984. A compilation of essays providing a solid overview of Beckmann's work, style, and career. Unfortunately does not discuss his role in the New Objectivity movement. Profusely illustrated with excellent color reproductions of the artist's paintings and numerous examples of his graphics. Good bibliography. Recommended for students of Beckmann.

Eberle, Matthias. *World War I and the Weimar Artists: Dix, Grosz, Beckmann, Schlemmer.* Translated by John Gabriel. New Haven, Conn.: Yale University Press, 1985.

Small book discussing the work and biographical backgrounds of four artists whose styles were fundamentally formed by their experiences during World War I. Specifically focuses on how these artists, other than Schlemmer, were actively involved in political events that they assimilated into their art. Useful source for the general public and students.

Grosz, George. *George Grosz: An Autobiography.* Translated by Nora Hodges. New York: Macmillan, 1983. The artist's lively and provocative account of his life in the 1920's as well as of the art of the period. Presents a fusion of Grosz's art and politics during the Weimar Republic. Contains numerous illustrations, including thirty-seven reproductions of Grosz's major artworks.

Hayward Gallery. *Neue Sachlichkeit and German Realism in the Twenties.* Translated by David Britt and John Whitford. London: Arts Council of Great Britain, 1978. Contains two excellent essays defining and examining this artistic phenomenon during the Weimar Republic. Discusses both New Objectivity painters and photographers. One of the best sources in English on the topic. Highly recommended for students. Includes biographical annotations, a good bibliography, and many reproductions.

Joachimides, Christos M., Norman Rosenthal, and Wieland Schmied, eds. *German Art in the Twentieth Century: Painting and Sculpture, 1905-1985.* Munich: Prestel Verlag, 1985. Presents a broad survey of German art with a compilation of excellent essays, including two on Dix and Beckmann. Profusely illustrated with numerous color reproductions and an extensive, useful bibliography. Contains short biographical annotations on the major German artists. Recommended for both students and the general reader.

Laqueur, Walter. *Weimar: A Cultural History, 1918-1933.* New York: G. P. Putnam's Sons, 1974. An insightful survey of Weimar culture that explores the rise and decline of the avant-garde in Germany. Highly readable and interesting. Contains some photographs and a few illustrations of artists' works. Good bibliography.

Lewis, Beth Irwin. *George Grosz: Art and Politics in the Weimar Republic.* Madison: University of Wisconsin Press, 1971. In-depth study of Grosz examining his relationship between art and politics. Provides an excellent understanding of the artist as well as insight into the Weimar Republic. Many black-and-white illustrations of the artist's line drawings. Highly recommended for students of Grosz and the New Objectivity movement.

McGreevy, Linda F. *The Life and Works of Otto Dix: German Critical Realist.* Ann Arbor, Mich.: UMI Research Press, 1981. Scholarly endeavor that focuses on Dix as a social critic by examining his graphic work of the 1920's. Only one chapter on Dix's work and his role in New Objectivity in Germany. Some black-and-white reproductions and an extensive bibliography. Good source for Dix's biographical background.

Schrader, Bärbel, and Jürgen Schebera. *The Golden Twenties: Art and Literature in the Weimar Republic.* Translated by Katherin Vanovitch. New Haven, Conn.: Yale University Press, 1990. A good, broad survey of Weimar culture. The authors examine the opera, street entertainment, popular music, films, literature, art, and architecture to demonstrate that the Weimar Republic's cultural life was as troubled as its politics. Numerous photographs and illustrations.

Carmen Stonge

Cross-References

Avant-Garde Artists in Dresden Form Die Brücke (1905), p. 134; Les Fauves Exhibit at the Salon d'Automne (1905), p. 140; Kandinsky Publishes His Views on Abstraction in Art (1912), p. 320; The Dada Movement Emerges at the Cabaret Voltaire (1916), p. 419; Mann's *The Magic Mountain* Reflects European Crisis (1924), p. 588; Surrealism Is Born (1924), p. 604; Brecht and Weill Collaborate on *Mahagonny Songspiel* (1927), p. 724; Hitler Organizes an Exhibition Denouncing Modern Art (1937), p. 1083.

WOOLF'S *MRS. DALLOWAY* EXPLORES
WOMEN'S CONSCIOUSNESS

Category of event: Literature
Time: 1925
Locale: London, England

Virginia Woolf, already recognized as having made a stylistic break with the past, made a powerful statement about how women perceive themselves and society in her 1925 novel Mrs. Dalloway

Principal personages:
VIRGINIA WOOLF (1882-1941), a novelist who quite consciously worked toward the development of the modern style and who was often concerned with commenting on the conditions of women
LEONARD S. WOOLF (1880-1969), Virginia Woolf's husband and a vital support for her during her periodic spells of emotional instability
GEORGE DUCKWORTH (1869-1934), Virginia Woolf's half brother, whose sexual abuse of her as a child was a powerful influence in her views about women and the way they were treated
VANESSA BELL (1879-1961), Virginia Woolf's sister, who was a strong lifelong support for and influence on her sister

Summary of Event

Virginia Woolf was born into a family noted for its literary achievements. Her father, Leslie Stephen, is best known as the editor of the *Dictionary of National Biography*, the standard against which biographical dictionaries have long been measured. The Stephens have often been cited as the model Victorian family, with the loving if gruff father and the doting mother providing a supportive home environment. The appearance of such a family situation was almost entirely a façade. Leslie Stephen not only disassociated himself from the problems of his children (his parental concern was mostly expressed in letters to his wife) but also demanded an exaggerated level of attention for himself.

Virginia's mother was Leslie's second wife, Julia (née Jackson) Duckworth. They were married March 26, 1878, and had between them five children from their former marriages. They were to have four of their own, of which Virginia was the third. By the time Virginia was old enough to be aware of her surroundings, Laura, Leslie's daughter from his first marriage, had been confined to a separate section of the house because of her emotional problems. Although Laura may have been of less than normal intelligence, it appears that her real crime was willfulness—completely unacceptable in a Victorian daughter and to be curbed by virtually any level of force needed. Laura's fate was a powerful message about the importance of conformity for the other daughters in the Stephen family.

Worse emotional traumas were to follow. Virginia's half sister Stella Duckworth was not protected from the exuberant courtship of J. W. "Jack" Hills, and although the young woman was certainly frightened and possibly raped, Hills was not excluded from the house. No child could feel protected. Further, after the death of Julia Stephen in 1895, Stella was forced into the role of wife and mother and was expected to run the house and tend to the needs of Leslie and the children. There are hints, though no hard evidence, that her wifely functions included sex with her stepfather. She eventually married Hills in 1887 only to die of peritonitis shortly after returning from her honeymoon. It is quite possible that her illness was the result of an injury occurring during sexual intercourse.

Nor were Leslie and Julia's own children safe and secure. Both Virginia and her elder sister Vanessa were sexually abused by their half brothers George and Herbert Duckworth. In an autobiographical fragment, Virginia recalls the first incident: She was about six, and George Duckworth put her up on a shelf outside the family's dining room and felt her genitalia. The abuse expanded in nature and continued through her teenage years. It is not surprising, then, that Virginia never found much pleasure in heterosexual activity or that she suffered from bouts of depression throughout her life. During her teenage years, these resulted in periods of reduced activity and reductions—which she resented bitterly—in the already limited education the daughter of a Victorian was allowed.

After the death of Leslie Stephen early in 1904, the Stephen children were left to fend for themselves. They eventually settled in the Bloomsbury section of London, where a literary circle formed around the family. This loose association, often called the Bloomsbury Group, included Clive Bell (eventually Vanessa's husband), Lytton Strachey, E. M. Forster, and Saxon Sydney-Turner. Bloomsbury, which came to include a number of other intellectuals such as Roger Fry and John Maynard Keynes, was known for a bohemian life-style and sexual freedom. It was as part of this group that Virginia began to write—she needed money—and met her husband, Leonard Woolf, who had spent a number of years as a colonial administrator in India. The wedding occurred in 1912.

Virginia Woolf's first novel, *The Voyage Out*, did not appear until 1915. Although she had already begun to make a name for herself as a critic and reviewer, the tension of waiting for reviews and the desire for success took an emotional toll. Her husband, who had not been prepared for the intensity of his bride's emotional storms, got the necessary medical help and saw that she had several months of rest until she recovered her equilibrium. This sort of breakdown, though not always as serious, accompanied the publication of most of her novels. Clarissa Dalloway, the protagonist of Woolf's 1925 novel, makes a brief appearance in *The Voyage Out*.

The success of her first book started Woolf on a career as a novelist. She began to develop a new style of novel that rejected the past, which she saw as represented by the works of Arnold Bennett, John Galsworthy, and H. G. Wells. Her novels were about everyday life, but they added layer after layer of symbolism and meaning. She wrote *Mr. Bennett and Mrs. Brown* (1924) to set forth her ideas about what fiction should be.

Meanwhile, in 1922 she had decided to write two books at the same time—a novel and a book of criticism. These became *The Common Reader: First Series* (1925) and *Mrs. Dalloway.* She hoped that this approach would help ameliorate the emotional disturbance that publishing a novel produced. Her expectation of critical comment about *Jacob's Room* (1922) had caused her significant difficulty. Although the projects were not connected, her reading of Greek classics for an essay entitled "Not Knowing Greek"—she resented the lack of education for girls—clearly influenced the psychological symbolism in *Mrs. Dalloway.*

The character Clarissa Dalloway has been associated with Kitty Maxse, whose death in a fall in 1922 Woolf attributed to suicide. Woolf intended to write of the realities of English life: "I want to give life and death, sanity and insanity; I want to criticise the social system and to show it at work, at its most intense." As is always the case in Virginia Woolf's fiction, many symbols and meanings can be found in *Mrs. Dalloway*, but one theme in the book is Clarissa Dalloway's effort to give her life meaning.

Impact of Event

Mrs. Dalloway was met with significant critical approval when it was published. Although the book was not as widely regarded as a work of genius as *To the Lighthouse* (1927) and especially *A Room of One's Own* (1929) would later be, it left few serious critics with doubt that Virginia Woolf was a major figure in modern literature. It was also, for a serious novel, a popular success as measured by sales. It further marked, perhaps coincidentally, the beginning of one of the longest periods of stability and happiness in Woolf's life.

Superficially, the novel is the story of a day in Clarissa Dalloway's life. She is planning one of her famous parties—giving parties is her only talent—and preparations bring her into contact with a number of friends and acquaintances. The unexpected arrival of an old flame, Peter Walsh, brings some complications and memories of youth. Woolf is brilliant in her ability to weave past and present into a seamless picture. Other than Mrs. Dalloway and her friends, the only significant character is Septimus Warren Smith, a shell-shocked World War I veteran who is slipping into madness because of what he describes as an inability to feel, though his plight might be better described as feeling too much and too intensely. Smith's friend Evans was killed at the end of the war, and in confusion and pain Smith married in search of comfort and support. He is unable to satisfy his wife's demands for love and children, he is haunted by visions of Evans, and he feels guilt for being alive when his friend is dead. Ultimately, Smith kills himself.

On first reading, there might seem to be little comment about feminism in the novel. Clarissa, however, has found a way to escape some of the limitations placed on women in her society. In her parties, she brings together people from a variety of walks of life, even across class lines. Clarissa's parties are experiments in communication, much as Virginia Woolf's novels were for her. Clarissa has a consciousness of the potential for a unity in life in which divisions created by gender, class, and wealth disappear.

Freedom, as far as Woolf was concerned, came from successfully coping with the barriers one faced and from finding a vision such as Clarissa Dalloway's. Miss Kilman, the teacher of Clarissa's daughter, is the novel's representative modern woman. She has a profession and much integrity—she lost her standing by refusing to condemn German friends as monsters during the war. Her consciousness of facts and logic leaves her, however, narrow and unfulfilled. Unlike Clarissa, she has no sense of transcendence. She is unhappy and unloved. Clearly, Woolf did not see the triumph of women as simply a matter of moving into the sphere that in the 1920's was still regarded as that of the male; women could and had to be more than that.

Regrettably, but hardly surprisingly given her experiences, Woolf's male characters do not fare particularly well. With one exception, they are inept at life and love. Richard Dalloway, Clarissa's husband, upon hearing that Peter Walsh has returned, resolves to take his wife some flowers and tell her that he loves her. He manages only the flowers. Walsh, who has had trouble with women all his life, is so governed by his passions that, although he follows a pretty girl around the city, he can never bring himself to approach her; he must be satisfied with his fantasies. The only admirable male character, Septimus Smith, is mad. He has a sense of transcendence, but unlike Clarissa, who remembers with longing the time another woman kissed her on the lips, he cannot cope with his homoerotic feelings. Ultimately, only Clarissa—who does not regret her almost total lack of education or her lack of productive employment and who has only the gift of party-giving—has a sense of completeness.

It is easy to see in Virginia Woolf's background the elements of life portrayed in *Mrs. Dalloway*. The sexual abuse had to leave her with a jaundiced view of men and heterosexual activity and must have produced feelings much like those described by Septimus. Woolf, unmoved by heterosexuality, found lesbian relations more fulfilling. Just as she was writing *Mrs. Dalloway*, she was developing a relationship with Vita Sackville-West that seems to have been the most sexually fulfilling of her life. Woolf never escaped the traumas of her childhood, and if, like Clarissa, she knew transcendence, like Septimus, she found it hurt too much to survive. In 1941, Virginia Woolf put a stone in her pocket and walked into the River Ouse to drown.

Bibliography

Bell, Quentin. *Virginia Woolf: A Biography.* New York: Harcourt Brace Jovanovich, 1972. Written by Woolf's nephew, this book is filled with facts, some probably known only to the family. Bell, though, tends to dismiss the traumas of childhood as of little importance. An important source, but should not be used without consulting the work of Louise DeSalvo.

Bloom, Harold, ed. *Clarissa Dalloway.* New York: Chelsea House, 1990. A collection of critical writings focused on the character of Clarissa Dalloway. Brings together a variety of critical comment from seven decades.

DeSalvo, Louise. *Virginia Woolf: The Impact of Childhood Sexual Abuse on Her Life and Work.* Boston: Beacon Press, 1989. Although DeSalvo depends on inference and comparison of Woolf's comments about her life and problems with those of women who have chosen to speak openly of their experience of sexual abuse, there is a powerful and convincing logic to this book. No student of Woolf or her fiction can reasonably avoid reading DeSalvo.

Kelley, Alice van Buren. *The Novels of Virginia Woolf: Fact and Vision.* Chicago: University of Chicago Press, 1973. This book, including a chapter about *Mrs. Dalloway,* focuses on Woolf's recurrent theme of transcendence versus logic as a defining characteristic of personality. A well-written work of criticism that provides important insights into Woolf's understanding of consciousness.

Woolf, Virginia. *Mrs. Dalloway.* New York: Harcourt Brace, 1925. In the study of a writer's ideas, there is no substitute for the original work. Anyone interested in the topic should start with *Mrs. Dalloway.*

——————. *Three Guineas.* New York: Harcourt, Brace & World, 1938. This work, written less than three years before the author's suicide, is a statement of her views and anger about the mistreatment of women. A sense of it may be gotten from one of the working titles: "On Being Despised." A useful book for anyone seeking to understand Woolf's ideas about women and life.

Fred R. van Hartesveldt

Cross-References

Jung Publishes *Psychology of the Unconscious* (1912), p. 309; Cather's *My Ántonia* Promotes Regional Literature (1918), p. 452; Eliot Publishes *The Waste Land* (1922), p. 539; Joyce's *Ulysses* Epitomizes Modernism in Fiction (1922), p. 555; Hemingway's *The Sun Also Rises* Speaks for the Lost Generation (1926), p. 696; Plath's *The Colossus* Voices Women's Experience (1960), p. 1850.

GANCE'S *NAPOLÉON* REVOLUTIONIZES FILMMAKING TECHNIQUES

Category of event: Motion pictures
Time: 1925-1927
Locale: France

Filmmaker Abel Gance revolutionized the epic motion picture and expanded the horizons of world cinema by employing new techniques for his innovative treatment of the French national hero Napoleon Bonaparte

Principal personages:

ABEL GANCE (1889-1981), a pioneering French filmmaker who created dazzling spectacles of cinema during the 1920's, utilizing new techniques of editing and cinematography and inventing the concept later called Cinerama

ANDRÉ DEBRIE (1891-1967), an inventor and manufacturer of film equipment Gance used for the panoramic sequences of *Napoléon*

LÉONCE-HENRY BUREL (1892-), Gance's main cameraman, who worked on both *Napoléon* and its later revision, *Bonaparte et la Révolution* (1971)

RICCIOTTO CANUDO (1879-1923), a champion of avant-garde artists who influenced Gance's ideas about the potential of the cinema

ÉLIE FAURE (1873-1937), an art critic and historian who impressed Gance with his vision of the cinema as a unifying, collective art form that could create "visual symphonies"

JEAN EPSTEIN (1897-1953), a leading avant-garde filmmaker whose ideas and inventive visual techniques influenced Gance

KEVIN BROWNLOW (1938-), an archivist, historian, and film editor who worked with Gance to reconstruct and restore *Napoléon* to an approximation of its original length

Summary of Event

By the early 1920's, Abel Gance had made twenty-three films, including *J'Accuse!* (1919) and *La Roue* (1923), and had established himself as France's most innovative avant-garde filmmaker, particularly in his rapid editing technique and camera movement in the melodrama *La Roue*. By 1923, he had started the screenplay for his monumental French epic *Napoléon*, a project that would take four years to complete. Gance completed the script in 1925, originally intending to make six massive films to capture the epic sweep of the emperor's life. Each film was intended to run about ninety minutes, but in June, 1925, Gance's major financier for the series withdrew his support. Eventually, Gance found new backers, but they were willing to fund only the first film of the series, which Gance then expanded to include as much of the original project as possible.

What Gance produced became a monument of the silent cinema and surely one of the most impressive and innovative biographical features ever made. The completed version, which premiered at the Paris Opera House on April 7, 1927, was epic in scope and length and traced Napoleon's life from his childhood in Corsica through the turmoil of the French Revolution and the Reign of Terror, and concluding with Napoleon's Italian campaign and his rise to power. The film was released about the time the new technology of talking pictures came into prominence and fell into obscurity during the sound period. Thanks to the dedicated efforts of Kevin Brownlow, who collected whatever materials he could locate, the film was eventually restored during the 1970's and 1980's, partly under Gance's supervision, to a version that ran to nearly six hours.

The achievement of the film is partly a matter of technical innovation but is mainly a consequence of Gance's personal vision of what the cinema might become. Gance's ideas in this regard were influenced by a number of artists and intellectuals with whom he was associated, particularly the journalist and editor Ricciotto Canudo. Other artists in this circle included the novelist Blaise Cendrars, who would eventually write more than twenty books, the filmmaker Jean Epstein, and the art critic and historian Élie Faure, who influenced Gance's belief in the power of the cinema as a collective and unifying art. Canudo and the others helped to shape Gance's belief that the primary function of the cinema was to create dazzling spectacles, "cathedrals of light," that would surprise, stun, and elevate the consciousness of the spectator as no other art form could do. In *Napoléon*, Gance attempted to put those notions to the test; his challenge was to find technicians who could help him to realize the vision.

A key talent who assisted Gance in expanding the horizons of the cinema was the inventor André Debrie, who, over his lifetime, personally patented nearly fifty cinema-related inventions, including the Parvo camera, the Matipo printer, an ultra-high-speed camera developed during the mid-1920's, and, perhaps most important for the achievement of *Napoléon*, the means of interlocking three synchronized cameras to create a panoramic triple-screen projection through the use of three projectors. The approach was both creative and innovative, permitting a cinema spectacle unlike any ever seen before, but it was also complicated and expensive, since specially equipped theaters were needed to demonstrate the effect. The Gance-Debrie creation was in fact a precursor of what was later called Cinerama, but it represented the invention of a technology that proved to be ahead of its time. Sound was the novelty of choice at the time Gance's film was released.

Most of Gance's film, apart from location footage shot at Nice, Toulon, and Corsica, was made at the Billancourt Studio outside Paris. Gance recruited an army of technicians for the project, including seven cameramen, led by Léonce-Henry Burel and Jules Kruger, and six gifted assistant directors: Alexandre Volkoff, Victor Tourjansky, Henry Krauss, Henri Andréani, Marius Nalpas, and Anatole Litvak.

According to the French critic Léon Moussinac, Gance's original ideas "enlarged the resources of cinematography," and the release of *Napoléon* marked a significant date "in the history of the technological development of the cinema." Gance's assistant director Alexandre Volkoff later remembered Gance as being obssessed by the idea of "surpassing himself and all others."

Gance was determined to liberate the camera in ways that had never been tried before with a demonstration of visual pyrotechnics that would astonish the viewer. A sequence concerning the young hero's time at school experimented with camera movement for subjective effect. Gance, for example, instructed cameraman Jules Kruger to use a camera strapped to his chest, enabling the cameraman to run into the action of a snowball fight in which the young Napoleon marshals his forces to win the day. Kruger also mounted the camera on a sled that could be pushed into the fray. In a later sequence that begins with Napoleon's escape from Corsica in a small boat, the camera was mounted on the boat to capture the turbulence at sea. In the chase to the sea, it was mounted on horseback. Intercut with Napoleon's escape at sea are dramatized scenes of turmoil at the Convention Hall in Paris as the revolution takes a violent turn. Here, Gance mounted the camera on a pendulum that could be swung down and over the crowd.

The film became famous for its multiplication, manipulation, and orchestration of images. Gance had already experimented effectively with the use of rapid montage for emotional effect in *La Roue*; in *Napoléon*, Gance carried this sort of experimentation to new levels of achievement. In places, the editing is so rapid that the effect is nearly subliminal. In addition to using this highly subjective montage technique, Gance experimented with layered, superimposed images, piling one image on top of another with up to sixteen overlays. Gance later remarked in Nelly Kaplan's documentary film *Abel Gance: Yesterday and Tomorrow* (1964) that, since no single viewer could sort out all the images of a single, multilayered frame, no two people would "see" exactly the same action when viewing these overlays. Gance also experimented with a split-screen technique that divided the screen into four panels, then into six, then into nine, and superimposed full-frame images over the split screen. Used to show the young Napoleon engaged in a pillow fight, the technique created a perfect emblem of boyhood frenzy.

The film's most impressive innovation, though, was its use of the triple-screen effect (in the drastically cut version of the film that was originally released in America, however, the effect was largely lost). The triple-screen projection is sometimes used to create a panoramic effect as Napoleon moves his army into Italy; at other times, three separate images are projected, the center screen carrying the main action and the outside screens framing it with ancillary action. In a final burst of patriotism, the three screens are tinted to present the image of the French tricolor flag over images of Napoleon at the height of his authority. The conclusion of *Napoléon* has not been surpassed in visual effect by any other film.

Impact of Event

There are few films in the history of cinema that have had quite the impact of *Napoléon*. D. W. Griffith's *The Birth of a Nation* (1915) first served to make the cinema an art form to be taken seriously. Gance's achievements came a few years after Griffith's epic landmark and a few years before Sergei Eisenstein's ground-breaking work in the Soviet Union. Gance's vision was perhaps even larger than Griffith's (the two men did meet in the early 1920's in New York); Gance's intellectual sophistication surpassed Griffith's, and his film techniques tended to advance rather than duplicate those of the American master. In the Soviet Union, Eisenstein had studied Gance's earlier montage techniques, which influenced Eisenstein's montage work in *Strike* (1925) and *Potemkin* (1925), paying close attention to what Gance had achieved in *La Roue*. When *Napoléon* was released in 1927, however, it served to demonstrate as no other film had done the full potential of a thoroughly cinematic spectacle. When it was rediscovered and revived fifty years later, *Napoléon* still had the power to astonish spectators in London, Paris, Washington, and New York. Cinema historians invariably would mention the film as an important technological landmark, but the original film was eclipsed by the novelty of sound and was unseen for decades.

It is surprising, however, that *Napoléon*, despite its achievements, was destined to lay dormant for more than half a century and become a nearly lost and forgotten masterpiece. This was partly a consequence of economics and popular taste. Gance's film made demands on audiences because of its length, and it was also costly to mount properly in theaters, which had to be specially equipped to handle its triple-screen spectacle. The film also tended to be overlooked because of the craze for talking pictures.

Gance, though, was also a pioneer in developing sound film technology in France. In 1929, Gance patented his Perspective Sound technique, and he directed the first French talking feature, *La Fin du Monde* (1931). In 1934, he completed a shortened, synchronized sound version of his masterpiece entitled *Napoléon Bonaparte*. In later life, he would return repeatedly to the Napoleon project, reworking its content and its technology. In 1956, he developed an experimental program called "Magirama," which used sequences from his earlier films. Gance's Magirama spectacle in Paris paralleled the Cinemascope craze in the United States and was intended to demonstrate the potential of what Gance called "Polyvision."

In his later years, Gance set about remaking *Napoléon* in collaboration with film-maker Claude Lelouch. The result of their work was released in 1972 under the title *Bonaparte et la Révolution* and was grandly billed as "the masterpiece of master-pieces, the greatest film of the history of the cinema, four hours and thirty-five minutes in length, forty-five years in the making." In fact, however, the Gance-Lelouch version is inferior in every way to the original masterpiece of 1927, which was being quietly restored by the British historian, archivist, and filmmaker Kevin Brownlow, who had devoted a lifetime to restoring *Napoléon* to an approximation of its original length.

In 1973, the Brownlow reconstruction, running to nearly five hours, was screened with the triple-screen triptych finale at the American Film Institute Theater in Washington, D.C., but the Brownlow reconstruction was blocked from wider distribution because of the Gance-Lelouch remake. Six years later, an expanded Brownlow version was screened at the Telluride Film Festival in Colorado in August of 1979. Gance himself, more than ninety years old and in failing health, flew to Colorado to accept an award for his achievements on August 31. The film was also screened the next year at the London Film Festival of 1980 at the Empire Cinema, accompanied by music arranged by Carl Davis and played by a forty-three-piece orchestra. By that point, it had also been screened at the Pacific Film Archive and at the Walker Arts Center in Minneapolis.

In the United States, Francis Ford Coppola joined forces with film distributor Robert A. Harris to organize a *Napoléon* revival at Radio City Music Hall in New York. The film was well presented, accompanied by the sixty-piece American Symphony Orchestra under the baton of Maestro Carmine Coppola, who composed more than three and a half hours of original music for the premiere on January 23, 1981. Because of union regulations and financial considerations, the film was compromised, since the Radio City presentation was not to exceed four hours in running time. Among purists, this abridgement of the Coppola version raised questions about exactly whose *Napoléon* was being shown.

Despite Coppola's shortening of the film, the Radio City premiere was a huge critical and financial success, playing to a packed house of six thousand people. The original screenings set for January 23 through January 25 quickly sold out, and additional performances were extended during the following weeks. The showing was the first premiere of a silent film in New York City in more than fifty years and was treated as an unusual, spectacular, and newsworthy event. It was covered by network television news shows, by *Time* and *Newsweek* magazines, and by major newspapers in cities as distant as Toronto and Washington.

Napoléon was destined to become the media event of the year. The film then went on a national tour, playing other major American cities from coast to coast. The immediate impact of the film was that other talents imitated its inventions and technology. The ultimate impact was to come fifty years after its original release, as *Napoléon* became recognized as the ultimate demonstration of the power and the achievement of the silent cinema.

Bibliography

Abel, Richard. *The French Cinema: The First Wave, 1915-1929.* Princeton, N.J.: Princeton University Press, 1984. In this meticulously researched survey of French silent cinema, Abel covers Gance's career through the period and includes a substantial twenty-page treatment of *Napoléon.*

Ballard, Bambi, ed. *Napoleon.* Translated by Moya Hassan. London: Faber, 1990. The script of the film, started in 1923, has been painstakingly edited to indicate scenes cut from extant prints of the film. Includes Gance's comments to spectators written upon the film's release in 1927, a listing of cast and credits, and an introduction by Kevin Brownlow.

Brownlow, Kevin. *Napoleon: Abel Gance's Classic Film.* New York: Alfred A. Knopf,

1983. This is the definitive treatment of Gance's film, written by the filmmaker and archivist responsible for its later reconstruction and revival, in collaboration with Gance himself. This book, following the *Napoléon* revival of the 1980's, expands Brownlow's earlier published research on the film and includes an expanded synopsis, cast, and credits. Thorough and invaluable.

_____. *The Parade's Gone By . . . .* New York: Alfred A. Knopf, 1968. A beautifully produced book on the silent cinema dedicated to Gance. Offers a substantial chapter on *Napoléon* based upon interviews with Gance and other research culled from French sources. Brownlow writes from the perspective of an informed enthusiast and collector who went on to become a filmmaker and cinema historian. This is the best brief introduction to the film.

King, Norman. *Abel Gance: A Politics of Spectacle.* London: BFI, 1984. Follows the response of left-wing critics who objected to the film's alleged "fascistic representation of Bonaparte as restorer of order in the midst of chaos." The book intends "to reinsert the political" into its discussion of Gance's aesthetic and finds a polarity between "progressive form" and "reactionary content." A filmography is included.

_____. "History and Actuality: Abel Gance's *Napoléon vu par Abel Gance.*" In *French Film: Texts and Contexts,* edited by Susan Hayward and Ginette Vincendeau. London: Routledge and Kegan Paul, 1990. Aptly calls *Napoléon* a "filmic *chanson de geste*" and asserts that it is a film "of and for its own time." King admits that the film is innovative but also authoritarian. His interest is still on the "proto-fascism" he finds in the picture, rather than on its innovative techniques.

Kramer, Steven Philip, and James Michael Welsh. *Abel Gance.* Boston: Twayne, 1978. The first book-length study of Gance's life and career published in English. Includes a twenty-five-page chapter on *Napoléon.* Attempts to place Gance in his cultural context (Chapter 2: "The Birth of the Seventh Art"). Begins with a chronology and ends with a selected bibliography and filmography. Also reprints an original interview with Gance ("Film as Incantation").

James M. Welsh

Cross-References

The Birth of a Nation Popularizes New Film Techniques (1915), p. 402; Von Stroheim Films His Silent Masterpiece *Greed* (1924), p. 593; Eisenstein's *Potemkin* Introduces New Film Editing Techniques (1925), p. 615; Kuleshov and Pudovkin Introduce Montage to Filmmaking (1927), p. 701; Lang Expands the Limits of Filmmaking with *Metropolis* (1927), p. 707; Warhol's *The Chelsea Girls* Becomes a Commercial Success (1966), p. 2053.

ROSS FOUNDS *THE NEW YORKER*

Category of event: Journalism
Time: February 21, 1925
Locale: New York, New York

The New Yorker *set standards of style for other literary magazines, helped to advance the careers of many significant American authors, and powerfully affected American literature in the twentieth century*

Principal personages:

HAROLD ROSS (1892-1951), a journalist who founded *The New Yorker* in 1925 and edited the magazine until his death in 1951

JANE GRANT (1895-1972), a journalist who was married to Harold Ross from 1920 to 1929 and played a major role in the founding of the magazine

PETER ARNO (CURTIS ARNOUX PETERS, JR., 1904-1968), a cartoonist whose drawings contributed significantly to the early success of *The New Yorker*

E. B. WHITE (1899-1985), an outstanding essayist who was the primary writer of the "Talk of the Town" and "News and Comments" sections of the magazine during its first decade

JAMES THURBER (1894-1961), a longtime member of the editorial staff and a humorist who provided hundreds of articles and cartoons for *The New Yorker* during its formative years

S. J. PERELMAN (1904-1979), a humorist and cartoonist who contributed lampoons of advertising, films, and romantic fiction to *The New Yorker*

KATHARINE SERGEANT WHITE (1892-1977), a journalist who, as literary editor and then as managing editor, did much to establish the standards and style of the magazine

Summary of Event

On February 21, 1925, a new magazine of reporting, humor, fiction, and criticism hit the newstands of New York. Originally unimpressive, *The New Yorker* seemed destined to be stillborn. Few could have guessed that it would soon attract a large, sophisticated readership, publish the work of America's most talented authors, and significantly influence the nation's literary standards and tastes.

The eventual success of *The New Yorker* was in large part the result of its founder and first editor, Harold Ross. Ross, who was born in 1892 in Aspen, Colorado, at age seven moved with his parents to Salt Lake City. After quitting high school to take a job with the *Salt Lake City Tribune*, Ross worked with newspapers in Sacramento, Atlanta, Panama City, New Orleans, and San Francisco. During World War I, he edited *Stars and Stripes*, a newspaper published in Paris for American servicemen.

After the war ended, Ross successively edited three different magazines in New York City: *Home Sector* (a stateside version of *Stars and Stripes*), the house organ of the American Legion, and the humor magazine *Judge*. In 1920, Ross married journalist Jane Grant. During the early 1920's, they frequently discussed ideas for various kinds of new magazines.

The publication of *Yank Talk*, a collection of jokes from *Stars and Stripes*, had provided the Rosses with twenty-five thousand dollars to invest in a new magazine. Believing that such a venture would require at least fifty thousand dollars, Harold Ross appealed to Raoul Fleischmann, the heir to a yeast and baking fortune whom Ross knew from their mutual association with the Algonquin Round Table, a group of prominent New York literati. Arguing that the older humor magazines attempted to reach too broad an audience, Ross proposed to create a magazine for a sophisticated and educated urban elite, primarily in New York City. Looking for a creative outlet, Fleischmann agreed to help finance the project, an investment that by 1928 grew to more than $500,000.

Ross's prospectus explained that the magazine would be "a reflection in word and picture of metropolitan life" that would not appeal to "the old lady in Dubuque." To be characterized by "wit and satire," *The New Yorker* would be "entertaining and informative." The magazine would cover contemporary events, people of interest, amusements, and arts. It would include reviews of books, films, and plays, prose and verse, editorials, caricatures, sketches, cartoons, and humorous drawings. Ross planned to employ the best features of earlier "smart" magazines such as *Smart Set* and *Vanity Fair* and of the humor weeklies, but he resolved to avoid their weaknesses, such as stale jokes and dreary visual formats.

While this prospectus was an accurate description of what *The New Yorker* would soon become, the issues produced during the first year were not of high quality. Fifteen thousand readers paid fifteen cents a copy to read the original issue, which appeared on February 21, 1925. Its thirty-six pages included six pages of ads, two pages of short news items about life in New York, brief analyses of music, books, and films, a profile of an opera impresario, sketches, satirical drawings, and cartoons. By April of 1925, the magazine's circulation had dropped to eight thousand an issue, and the enterprise was losing eight thousand dollars a week. Some ridiculed the magazine; most simply ignored it. Contrary to Ross's expectations, his friends from the Algonquin Round Table initially provided little material, and Ross, who could not write original copy, struggled to attract publishable work and to develop a winning formula. He scoured the city for talent, placing notices on bulletin boards, examining other publications, and calling everyone he knew. In May, Ross, Fleischmann, and two advisers met at the Princeton Club. Discouraged by the magazine's lack of success and his financial losses, Fleischmann almost decided to pull the plug on the venture, but at the last moment he relented.

By the fall of 1925, advertising revenues had increased slightly, but the magazine's existence was still precarious. An article entitled "Why We Go to Cabarets," by Ellin Mackay, appeared in the November 28, 1925, issue and helped *The New Yorker* turn the corner. Although the article was poorly written, its thesis was rather shocking: New York debutantes went to cabarets to meet men who interested them because the men they met at high-society functions were boring. Discussed by *The New York Times*, the article stirred considerable controversy and brought *The New Yorker* to the attention of the Park Avenue set. By the end of 1925, both the advertising revenues and circulation of the magazine had risen substantially. Although *The New Yorker* did not earn a profit until 1928, its survival had been assured.

While hundreds of artists, writers, and editors passed through the magazine's editorial offices during its early years, several individuals played key roles. The art work, primarily because of the direction of Rea Irvin and the drawings of Peter Arno, was superior to the writing of the magazine. The most important writers to join *The New Yorker* in its formative period were E. B. White and James Thurber. Through his clear, precise, graceful prose, White helped to establish the style of the magazine, and he wrote two of its major departments. Thurber's comic writing and his cartoons (filled with strange dogs, amused seals, frustrated men, and predatory women) set a new standard for magazine humor. As a literary editor and then as managing editor, Katharine Sergeant White did much to promote staff harmony and to produce a well-written magazine.

Impact of Event

The New Yorker emerged after 1930 as the nation's leading magazine of literature, humor, and cultural analysis. Its refined, literate style of writing was widely applauded, admired, and imitated. Many prominent American authors and artists furthered their careers through the magazine's pages. It elevated the character of American humor, developed a new approach to magazine biography, and followed high standards of investigative reporting. The style of *The New Yorker* has been especially evident in its compelling short stories and beautifully polished essays. In all these ways, it significantly influenced American journalism.

The success of *The New Yorker* stemmed primarily from Harold Ross's outstanding editorial ability and leadership. Ross did not seem to possess either the background or the personality needed to create or direct an urbane, witty, sophisticated literary magazine intended for New York's upper crust. Lacking formal education, ignorant about many important facts, an explosive man who frequently lost his temper and used profanity, he was arrogant, aloof, tactless, and rude. Moreover, Ross could not write copy, but he shaped the character of *The New Yorker*, established its basic policies and principles, assembled a talented team of writers, artists, and contributors, guided it through its formative years, and meticulously edited it for twenty-seven years.

Ross also continually experimented with the magazine's format until he found the best blend of layout, fiction, commentary, reviews, and art. The centerpiece of the magazine became its regular departments, especially "Goings on About Town," a thorough guide to the city's sports, films, shows, concerts, museums, and nightclubs, "On and Off the Avenue," a shopper's guide, and "The Talk of the Town," a collection of narratives, anecdotes, essays, and quips. Profiles have also been an important aspect of *The New Yorker*. These biographical sketches of industrial leaders, writers, actors, politicians, and other interesting personalities have featured people as diverse as Nicholas Murray Butler, W. C. Fields, Henry Luce, Cecil B. De Mille, Jimmy Walker, and Carl Sandburg.

Another of Ross's contributions was his recognition that the best way to attract advertisement was to have a well-defined audience that could be easily targeted. Over the years, *The New Yorker* gained large revenues from advertising and pioneered in advertising craftsmanship. Its advertisements have often been read with as much care and pleasure as its commentaries and articles.

In addition, Ross's painstaking editorial method helped to produce *The New Yorker*'s lucid, suave, informative, humorous prose style. He meticulously edited all the contents of each issue, demanding factual accuracy and complete clarity. Ross's passion for precision led him to organize a checking system that closely examined all facts printed in the magazine. Often his notes, complaints, questions, and directions were as long as the printer's galleys themselves. William Shawn, his successor, who served as editor of the magazine from 1952 until 1987, has written that Ross's queries "influenced writers and other editors, set technical and literary standards, established a canon of taste, and laid the basis for a tradition of good writing." Ross's editorial style was somewhat overbearing, but he knew how to sift wheat from chaff, and he did give way when the others were better informed than he was.

Many of America's best writers, humorists, and artists have worked for *The New Yorker*. Among the literary greats who have written for the publication are Sherwood Anderson, James Baldwin, Rachel Carson, John Cheever, F. Scott Fitzgerald, Ernest Hemingway, Lewis Mumford, Irwin Shaw, John Updike, Rebecca West, and Edmund Wilson. Truman Capote, John O'Hara, and J. D. Salinger have each had more than one hundred pieces published in the magazine. By the 1930's, most of America's leading humorists were contributing to *The New Yorker*, including Ring Lardner, Robert Benchley, Ogden Nash, Dorothy Parker, Frank Sullivan, Clarence Day, and H. L. Mencken. The magazine also originated the one-line cartoon. Drawn by such artists as Gardner Rea, Gluyas Williams, Helen Hokinson, Whitey Darrow, Jr., and Charles Addams, these witty cartoons have focused on business, the sexes, politics, and the pretentions of the upper middle class.

Since the mid-1930's, *The New Yorker* has been, in the words of George Douglas, "the quintessential American smart magazine, the one against which, today, all the others are judged." Skillful editing, careful planning, and graceful writing have combined to make *The New Yorker* instructive, amusing, and entertaining. In 1985, the Fleischmann family, which had owned *The New Yorker* since its inception, sold it to the Newhouse media empire, but the magazine continued to serve as the nation's leading arbiter of literary taste. College students throughout the country are taught to emulate its style; aspiring writers look to it for inspiration. In Douglas' words, the magazine "has enjoyed a long and enviable history and an enduring popularity and mystique that are probably unequaled among American magazines."

Bibliography

Bryan, J., III. *Merry Gentlemen (and One Lady)*. New York: Atheneum, 1985. Humorous profiles of fourteen writers who were connected in one way or another with the Algonquin Round Table and with *The New Yorker* in its early years. Among those profiled in Bryan's memoir are Robert Benchley, Finis Farr, Dorothy Parker, and S. J. Perelman.

Douglas, George H. *The Smart Magazines*. Hamden, Conn.: Archon Books, 1991. An analysis of various magazines of literature, culture, and humor, including *Vanity Fair*, *Smart Set*, *Life*, and *Judge*. The best short account of the early history of *The New Yorker*; describes the context in which the magazine arose, matured, and achieved greatness and the personality, style, and contribution of both the magazine and its founder.

Gill, Brendan. *Here at the New Yorker*. New York: Random House, 1975. An illuminating account of the magazine by a writer who by 1975 had spent almost forty years on its staff. This insider's view of colleagues, artists, and contributors discusses their idiosyncrasies and their attitudes about fame, literature, money, and one another. Filled with funny stories, the book compares and contrasts the long running regimes of the magazine's two most influential editors, Harold Ross and William Shawn.

Grant, Jane. *Ross, "The New Yorker," and Me*. New York: Reynal, 1968. An account of the lives of Harold Ross and the author, who was married to Ross, from 1919 until 1951. The book concentrates more on New York literati and the flavor of the 1920's than it does on Ross's editorship of *The New Yorker*.

Kramer, Dale. *Ross and "The New Yorker."* Garden City, N.Y.: Doubleday, 1951. Although not well organized, this is the best single source about Ross's founding and editing of the magazine. A detailed and at times entertaining account of the history and policies of *The New Yorker*, filled with amusing anecdotes and interesting facts.

Mahon, Gigi. *The Last Days of "The New Yorker."* New York: McGraw-Hill, 1988. An account of events leading to the sale of the magazine to S. I. Newhouse in 1985. Mahon concludes that the sale represented the triumph of business interests over editorial integrity. While most of the book focuses on the 1980's, it does briefly describe the magazine's founding and early days.

Thurber, James. *The Years with Ross*. Boston: Little, Brown, 1959. Based upon his own memory, letters, and contributions from colleagues, Thurber, long associated with *The New Yorker* as a writer, cartoonist, and staff member, produces a personal account of Ross's character and editorial style and discusses the tensions and feuds between Ross and his staff. This highly anecdotal account of episodes in Ross's life is both admiring and critical.

Gary Scott Smith

Cross-References

The Christian Science Monitor Is Founded (1908), p. 209; Lippmann Helps to Establish *The New Republic* (1914), p. 385; Wallace Founds *Reader's Digest* (1922), p. 549; *The Great Gatsby* Captures the Essence of the Roaring Twenties (1925), p. 626; Young Readers Embrace *The Catcher in the Rye* (1951), p. 1493.

A PARIS EXHIBITION DEFINES ART DECO

Categories of event: Architecture; fashion and design
Time: May-June, 1925
Locale: Paris, France

Paris hosted a large invitational applied arts exhibition seeking the best in contemporary design at which designers came to terms with modernism

> *Principal personages:*
> CHARLES PLUMET (1861-1928), the chief architect for the 1925 fair and designer of the Crafts Court
> LOUIS BONNIER (1856-1946), the chief landscape designer for the fair site
> PIERRE PATOUT (1879-1965), an architect who designed the Porte de la Concorde, a sumptuous model home, and, with André Ventre, the twin pavilions for Sèvres, the porcelain manufacturer
> JACQUES ÉMILE RUHLMANN (1879-1933), a gifted cabinetmaker who created numerous items for the interior of the Pavilion of a Rich Collector, also called the Ruhlmann Townhouse
> LOUIS SÜE (1875-1968), a designer
> ANDRÉ MARE (1885-1932), a designer, partner of Süe

Summary of Event

Art Deco was a major decorative arts style of the 1920's that survived in altered forms through the 1930's and into the early 1940's. During those decades, it also was called *moderne* or Art Moderne. It was in part a compromised modern style, but its association with the modern style caused much confusion in the reassessments made at the end of the twentieth century. The now nearly universal term "Art Deco" did not appear until the late 1960's, when a revival of interest in 1920's and 1930's interior design and decorative arts occurred. That revival gained tremendous momentum for at least the next twenty years. The term "Art Deco" is derived from the invitational exhibition of decorative and industrial arts hosted in Paris, France, in 1925. The goal of the style was to adapt design to the needs of mass production. Items thus incorporated straight lines instead of curves and symmetry rather than asymmetry, as forms of this type were easier to produce with machines. Art Deco also attempted to incorporate manufactured, rather than natural, materials.

The Exposition Internationale des Arts Décoratifs et Industriels Modernes occupied the same central Parisian site as the World's Fair of 1900, a fair that introduced Art Nouveau to an international audience. The area of the Esplanade des Invalides was smaller than the area used twenty-five years earlier, reflecting the major focus upon just the decorative arts. The Grand Palais, immediately adjacent, was serviceable and quickly was transformed for display use.

Approximately seventy-five pavilions and other structures graced the grounds. As in past fairs, most were intended to be temporary. Individual pavilions were composed of wood frames covered with plaster, a style similar to the so-called "staff architecture" of the "White City" of the World's Columbian Exhibition in Chicago in 1893. Temporary construction or not, the exterior surfaces of the pliable structures seemed to encourage widespread decorative relief sculpture, often a hallmark of Art Deco design. Otherwise, all the pavilions respected established ordinances for low heights and gardenlike settings, taking care to utilize existing trees. Altogether there were about 130 buildings and thirteen entrances, four of which were major, in addition to a good number of intervening gardens and fountains.

Architecturally speaking, the fair buildings ranged from neoclassical constraints to bold cubist experimentation and novelties. Said to be among the best designs were the pavilions of the department stores Au Printemps, Au Bon Marche, Grands Magasins du Louvre, and Galéries Lafayette. Collectively they embodied grandiosity, with faceted planes, rich decorative surfaces, and prominent use of metal and glass. To author Martin Battersby, the best-designed structure was the Pavilion (townhouse) of a Rich Collector, by architect Pierre Patout. This closely resembled a home Patout had produced for Jacques Émile Ruhlmann, a gifted furniture designer in the Art Deco style. In turn, Ruhlmann and his design team were responsible for most of the interior design and contents of Patout's pavilion.

Regardless of building styles, building interiors received the most attention, as they promoted changes in contemporary life-styles and sought to showcase the best of the new decorative arts. Redesigned family spaces included living rooms, dining rooms, specialized bedrooms for gentlemen and ladies, libraries, tea rooms, smoking rooms, and the study, in addition to accommodations for live plants and flowers in volume. The decorative appointments for those rooms suggested high ideals, as unrestricted patronage was the rule. That resulted in items of high craftsmanship but occasionally of dubious practicality. For example, furniture was generally sumptuous and surface-oriented, with a preference for rare and imported woods. It was often large or exhibition-oriented, even pompous and overly finished. When less hybrid in style, however, it was civilized, striking, and comfortable. Legs on Art Deco furniture at this fair were often tapered or minimized by a platform for a chair or chaise, adding a sense of importance. Key designers in 1925 included Ruhlmann, Louis Süe and André Mare, André Groult, and Pierre Chareau.

Lighting in contemporary interiors was more scientific, at least in theory, than it was at the 1900 Paris World's Fair. Illumination was more logical than the Tiffany lamps used twenty-five years earlier. Indirect lighting diffused and softened electric lighting, which had become affordable. Table lamps and chandeliers, however, often incorporated the French passion for exotic materials, forms, and surface treatment.

The Paris fair of 1925 was a study in contrasts, contradictions, and crosscurrents. Rising architect Le Corbusier (Charles-Édouard Jeanneret) observed that the fair was a turning point away from antiques and handcraft toward machined solutions, as well as an expression of a keen interest in newness and experimentation. Caught in the middle of this flux was a major ornamental design style, Art Deco.

Impact of Event

Europe seemed to be more affected by the decorative arts of the 1925 Paris fair than by its architecture. The exhibition focused almost exclusively upon applied art, and the exhibitors almost all were Europeans.

Careers were launched immediately for some designers, while the reputations of others were solidified. The furniture design partnership of Süe and Mare, critically successful at the fair, continued in a firm called the French Art Company until it was purchased in the late 1920's by the Maison Fontaine. The exposure of Süe and Mare at the 1925 exhibition surely helped them land major commissions for the luxury-class cabins of the steamship *Paris* and decorative schemes for the grand salon of the ocean liner *Île de France.*

The success of Süe and Mare, whose workshop was relatively large, was repeated by smaller design studios, although Art Deco furniture was popularized by aggressive Parisian department stores more than by designers' showrooms or the annual salons. For example, the Grands Magasins du Louvre produced designs for a wide variety of household items in the Art Deco style without extravagant decoration, manufactured them, and subsequently introduced a large public to an affordable range of Art Deco items.

In the fields of art glass and utilitarian glass, René Lalique's fortunes following the 1925 exhibition are legendary. By 1900, he was the leading Art Nouveau jewelry designer in Europe and could have rested comfortably on that reputation and retired. Instead, he embarked upon a serious exploration of both art and production glass and mastered them by the 1925 exhibition. By then, he was well past sixty years of age. Within a few years of the fair, his production had become exceptionally varied. His company was prolific, producing items ranging from ashtrays to clock cases, from decanters to perfume vaporizers. Lalique became the leading Art Deco glass designer of the 1920's and 1930's. His firm survived the German occupation of World War II and was perpetuated by a son and grandson. To the examples of Süe and Mare and of Lalique can be added dozens more in the media of metalwork, graphic design, sculpture, ceramics, textiles, painting, and silver.

The designers of Art Deco responded to changes in life and society, which both had become more urban and faster paced. Products reflecting this new life, including automobiles, cigarette cases, cocktail shakers, radios, electric lamps, and posters, were created in Art Deco style. In addition, those items were produced in newer ways, often by adding new materials or experimental combinations of existing ones. Likewise, themes and imagery reflecting a changing society were explored well into the 1930's in the media of sculpture, glass, painting, and lighting. These themes included flight, the emancipation of women, the machine, modern art movements, non-Western cultures, dance, and jazz.

The 1925 Paris fair was influential in introducing Art Deco to a broad public. One wish or dream of the fair organizers, however, was not realized. The 1925 Paris fair showcased both decorative and industrial arts, as the full title of the exhibition stated. Its organizers hoped that artists, designers, manufacturers, and capitalists would collaborate in the design, production, and marketing of domestic items of high design but realistic prices. The hoped-for collaboration saw few projects by the fair's opening or even after it closed, as manufacturers generally were wary of expensive-sounding proposals of doubtful financial success.

Collaboration did occur between designers and teams of designers for complete interiors, both at the fair and elsewhere, but that was a different development. The creation of a more affordable or popular Art Deco occurred primarily in the United States, with its much larger middle class and its advanced marketing, advertising, and capitalist potential.

Thousands of visitors from the United States traveled to the 1925 exhibition. Many may have wanted to visit an American pavilion, but there was none. President Herbert Hoover had declined the invitation to have America represented. Among the throngs of Americans in attendance, there were members of numerous professional design organizations who made detailed reports of the pavilions and their contents for respective design groups back home.

These reports translated into a major impact upon architecture and design in America for the next fifteen years. Within a year of the 1925 Paris fair, selections from it toured the United States, on view at the Metropolitan Museum of Art in New York City and at other major sites. Two years later, the fashionable New York City store Lord and Taylor hosted an exhibition of furniture by Jacques Émile Ruhlmann and Francis Jourdain. Their strain of Art Deco design, combining a respectful classicism with ornamentally elegant surfaces, found favor in America as something both old and contemporary.

That kind of thinking encouraged the rise of a major architectural style, American Art Deco. The result was a compromised modernism. It was both decorative and functional, new but not shocking, and it appealed to corporate image-makers and real estate developers who were somewhat frightened by the international style of modernism.

Art Deco architecture was the most noticeable impact in America of the 1925 Paris exhibition. The movement primarily was surface-oriented, with design motifs or relief sculpture at the cresting and at the base of buildings and their lobbies. New York City has the largest number of Art Deco buildings, including the highly emblematic and even spectacular Chrysler Building by William Van Alen, the Empire State Building by the firm of Shreves, Lamb, and Harmon, and the Fuller Building by A. Stewart Walker and Leon Gillette.

World War II interrupted the Art Deco episode in architecture and the decorative arts. People seemed ready to forget it during the 1950's, but from the 1970's onward an amazing revival occurred. Museum-quality decorative arts items began to fetch tremendous prices in galleries devoted to Art Deco and at auction. Many major Art Deco buildings have been restored, and four hundred or so "Tropical Deco" buildings have survived in Miami. They are protected as the largest architectural historic district in America, and many have been renovated and restored. Postmodern architecture of the 1980's and 1990's, reflecting a hunger for ornamentation and inclusion of past styles, has incorporated aspects of Art Deco, as have the fine-art media of painting and sculpture.

Bibliography

Arwas, Victor. *Art Deco*. New York: Harry N. Abrams, 1980. The standard recent introduction to Art Deco in its original European setting, its sources, and its major designers and their seminal works. A twenty-three-page chapter is devoted to the 1925 exposition, with special emphasis upon pavilions and their contents' designers.

Bouillon, Jean-Paul. *Art Deco, 1903-1940*. Translated by Michael Heron. New York: Rizzoli International Publications, 1989. Tracks avant-garde design and ornament from 1900 to the eve of World War II. A subtheme of sumptuous materials and anthropomorphic decorative motifs versus taut abstract patterns weaves through the chapters. Perceptive relationships are presented between major art movements and corresponding developments in interior design and decorative art.

Duncan, Alastair. *American Art Deco*. New York: Harry N. Abrams, 1986. Architecture, interiors, and decorative arts created in the United States by both European immigrants and American-born designers are presented and discussed. Two formative international design tendencies are stressed: the German-Austrian emphasis on logic, geometry, and function applicable to mass production, and the colorful, ornamental, and playful French tendencies.

Hillier, Bevis. *The World of Art Deco*. New York: E. P. Dutton, 1971. Responding to a late 1960's interest in Art Deco, this Minneapolis Institute of Arts exhibition catalog documents one of the largest Art Deco shows since the 1925 Paris exhibition.

McClinton, Katherine M. *Art Deco, A Guide for Collectors*. New York: C. N. Potter, 1972. An important publication written by a knowledgeable professional who visited the 1925 exposition. McClinton's preface and first two chapters, "Collecting Art Deco" and "What Is Art Deco?" offer helpful descriptions of major emblematic features of the style.

Morgan, Sarah. *Art Deco: The European Style*. Greenwich, Conn.: Dorset Press and Brompton Books, 1990. A general study prepared for collectors and connoisseurs of the style. A dutiful account of the 1925 Paris exhibition is followed by fourteen chapters showcasing major divisions of decorative arts.

Tom Dewey II

Cross-References

Hoffmann and Moser Found the Wiener Werkstätte (1903), p. 79; Hoffmann Designs the Palais Stoclet (1905), p. 124; The Deutscher Werkbund Combats Conservative Architecture (1907), p. 181; The Futurists Issue Their Manifesto (1909), p. 235; *De Stijl* Advocates Mondrian's Neoplasticism (1917), p. 429; Rietveld Designs the Red-Blue Chair (1918), p. 458; German Artists Found the Bauhaus (1919), p. 463; Expo 67 Presents Innovative Architectural Concepts (1967), p. 2081.

CHAPLIN PRODUCES HIS MASTERPIECE
THE GOLD RUSH

Category of event: Motion pictures
Time: June 26, 1925
Locale: The United States

With its characteristic combination of humor and pathos, The Gold Rush *would become a landmark film in both Chaplin's career and the history of motion-picture comedy*

Principal personages:

CHARLES CHAPLIN (1889-1977), a comedian and filmmaker whose famous "Tramp" character became a Hollywood icon

GEORGIA HALE (1906-   ), a young actress who appeared as Chaplin's love interest in *The Gold Rush*

ROLAND H. TOTHEROH (1890-1964), a motion-picture cameraman whose long association with Chaplin included *The Gold Rush*

MACK SWAIN (1876-1935), a burly character actor who appeared in the film as the Tramp's prospecting partner

LITA GREY CHAPLIN (1908-   ), a teenage actress whose marriage to and divorce from Chaplin caused a scandal

Summary of Event

Charlie Chaplin's place in film history was already assured long before the release of *The Gold Rush* in 1925. Within two years of his film debut in the 1914 two-reel comedy *Making a Living* (1914), Chaplin had become the most popular performer in motion pictures. His "Little Tramp" character was an internationally recognized figure, well on its way to becoming a cinematic icon so powerful that it remains one of the few images capable by itself of evoking the idea of Hollywood moviemaking.

Chaplin's career had begun while he was still a child. Abandoned by his father, who died when Chaplin was twelve, and with his mother often a patient in mental asylums, Chaplin, along with his older brother Sydney, was forced to make his own way in the world from the age of nine. He gained experience as an actor, dancer, and comedian on England's music-hall stages, finally joining the popular Fred Karno Company—which also included a young Stan Laurel—in 1908.

At the close of an American tour by the group in 1913, Chaplin chose to remain in the United States to embark on a career in motion pictures. Under contract to the Keystone Film Company, he made thirty-five comedy shorts during the next year; his Tramp character appeared for the first time in his second film, *Kid Auto Races in Venice* (1914). Chaplin described the character's creation in his 1964 autobiography:

> I thought I would dress in baggy pants, big shoes, a cane and a derby hat. . . . I added a small mustache. . . . the moment I was dressed, the clothes and the make-up made me

feel the person he was. I began to know him, and by the time I walked onto the stage he was fully born.

Before the year was through, Chaplin was directing as well as starring in his films, and he had already begun to achieve a remarkable degree of popularity among moviegoers across the country. The character of the Tramp—down on his luck but always resourceful, agile, and quick-witted—struck a chord with audiences and soon emerged as a creation of such complexity and durability that Chaplin would continue to develop and refine him for more than two decades. After leaving Keystone for the Essanay Studios, Chaplin began to explore the character's potential in more depth, experimenting for the first time in *The Tramp* (1915) with the combination of comedy and pathos that would become his trademark. The film ends with the Tramp losing the girl he loves and setting off down the road alone, his back to the camera.

The introduction of pathos into Chaplin's films gave the Tramp a vulnerability that marked him as more than merely a comic figure, and it won for Chaplin a measure of artistic respect beyond that already accorded him as a comedian. In films such as *The Vagabond* (1916), *The Immigrant* (1917), and *A Dog's Life* (1918), Chaplin demonstrates a style of comic filmmaking that combines both slapstick and subtlety while at the same time incorporating a potent measure of heartfelt human emotion. Chaplin's decision to allow his essentially comic character to experience pain, loss, and disappointment—and to end some of his films on that note—is almost unique in the annals of film comedy. That he did so at a time when the medium was still in its infancy is especially remarkable.

In 1920, Chaplin released his first feature-length film featuring the Tramp. *The Kid* costarred Jackie Coogan as the abandoned boy the Tramp adopts and nearly loses, and the film demonstrated Chaplin's ability to sustain his character's appeal in a format longer than the short comedies in which he had previously appeared. The film was a great success, and although Chaplin would make two more short films and one four-reel comedy in the years that followed, *The Kid* marked the beginning of his career as a feature filmmaker.

In 1924, Chaplin began work on *The Gold Rush*. Inspired by his interest in the tragedy of the Donner Party, a group of settlers who resorted to cannibalism while snowbound in the Sierras, the film is the story of the Tramp's adventures as a gold prospector in turn-of-the-century Alaska: his run-ins with the villainous Black Larson (Tom Murray), his near-starvation in a snowbound cabin with his partner, Big Jim (Henry Bergman), and his love for Georgia (Georgia Hale), a beautiful dancehall girl. The film contains two of Chaplin's best-known comic scenes: his attempts to cook and eat his boot and the famous "Oceana Roll" sequence, in which he manipulates a pair of rolls on forks as if they are dancing feet. *The Gold Rush* also features scenes of great poignancy, particularly the sequence in which the Tramp waits forlornly for Georgia and her friends to arrive for a dinner he has prepared—an invitation she has forgotten.

Chaplin always worked slowly on features, and *The Gold Rush* was a year and a half in the making. The period would prove to be a tumultuous one in Chaplin's life. His original costar was to be a fifteen-year-old girl named Lita Grey, who had appeared briefly in two earlier Chaplin films. By the fall of 1924, however, Lita was expecting Chaplin's child, and their subsequent marriage—and divorce two years later—was the source of a scandal that haunted Chaplin for many years to come. Lita was replaced in the film by Georgia Hale, and shooting resumed in early 1925.

The Gold Rush opened to tremendous critical acclaim, with *The New York Times* terming it "the outstanding gem of all Chaplin's pictures" and the *New York Daily News* calling it "the funniest and saddest of all comedies." The film is a masterpiece of silent comedy, drawing on all of Chaplin's skills in pantomime, comic timing, and the careful construction of sight gags. Its story is tailor-made for the Tramp's particular blend of plucky resourcefulness and vulnerability, and Chaplin succeeds behind the camera in telling an engaging story that brilliantly showcases his talents onscreen.

After *The Gold Rush*, Chaplin devoted himself exclusively to feature-length productions. He would make only eight more films during the next fifty years, with *City Lights* (1931) and *Modern Times* (1936) joining *The Gold Rush* in the ranks of his acclaimed masterpieces, and *The Circus* (1928) winning for its creator a special Oscar at the first Academy Awards ceremony in 1929.

Impact of Event

Comedy has been an important component of theater since its earliest incarnation, with Aristophanes' work surviving into the modern age alongside that of Euripides and Aeschylus. The strong link between theater and film, therefore, led quite naturally to a position of similar importance for comedy in the medium of film. That early films were silent made them particularly well suited to visual comedy, in which a minimum of dialogue is needed to convey the story; as the medium grew in popularity, its comedians quickly emerged as favorites with moviegoing audiences. Founded in 1912, the Keystone Company produced one split-reel comedy a week and introduced Mabel Normand, Roscoe "Fatty" Arbuckle, director Mack Sennett and his Bathing Beauties, and the Keystone Kops to the screen. When Chaplin joined their ranks two years later, the studio had already established itself as a leading force in Hollywood by tapping into the universal language of laughter and adapting it to the new technology of film.

Chaplin's training in the acrobatic style of English music-hall comedy had prepared him well for the physical nature of silent film comedy. The early shorts produced by the Keystone company relied primarily on sight gags and actors' talent for comic pantomime. Chaplin excelled at the physical agility needed for such routines, and his skill at mimicry and wordless self-expression remains unsurpassed. The specific nature of silent comedy would also lend itself brilliantly to the deadpan comedy of Buster Keaton and the boyish enthusiasm of Harold Lloyd, both of whom successfully tailored their talent for physical comedy to the requirements of the screen.

One of those requirements arose from the camera's ability to bring a viewer closer to the action taking place than is possible for a theater audience. That factor, coupled with the exaggerated size that figures projected on a screen assume, made it necessary for film comedians to master subtle gestures and expressions in addition to slapstick. The best silent comedians soon learned that a laugh could be achieved not only through a pratfall or a well-aimed pie but also with a raised eyebrow or deadpan stare. Chaplin, Keaton, and Lloyd all excelled at combining slapstick with subtlety, but only Chaplin used this skill to move his screen persona into the realm of pathos. With his expressive dark eyes and mobile face, the Tramp could evoke sorrow as readily as humor with a shrug or a glance.

Chaplin's extraordinary combination of popular and critical acclaim made him the yardstick against which other comedians were measured, often to their detriment. So great was Chaplin's fame during the years of silent comedy that he in many ways unfairly overshadowed the work of his contemporaries. Indeed, both Buster Keaton and Harold Lloyd have grown in critical stature in the years since their best work was done. Keaton, in particular, has achieved well-deserved cult status among silent comedy aficionados—a welcome development that does not detract from Chaplin's own mastery of the field, but rather enhances the field itself by recognizing the depth of talent it contained. The era that produced *The Gold Rush* also produced such comic masterpieces as Keaton's *The Navigator* (1924) and *The General* (1927) and Lloyd's *Safety Last* (1923) and *The Freshman* (1925).

Ironically, however, the release of these films marked not only the pinnacle of silent film comedy but also the beginning of the end of the silent era. In 1927, two years after *The Gold Rush*—and the same year as *The General*—*The Jazz Singer* introduced sound to motion pictures and changed the medium forever. Chaplin resisted the change longer than his contemporaries; *City Lights*, released in 1931, contains sound effects but no spoken dialogue, while *Modern Times* (1936) confines its spoken lines to a character using a loudspeaker and a nonsense song sung by the Tramp near the film's close. Despite these few concessions, both remain silent films in spirit.

Although the introduction of sound changed filmmaking irrevocably, the techniques perfected by Chaplin and his contemporaries continued to influence film comedy. The screwball comedies of the 1930's and the films of Preston Sturges in the 1940's effectively combined physical comedy with witty dialogue. In films such as *Bringing Up Baby* (1938) and *The Lady Eve* (1941), slapstick is an integral part of the humor, and actors such as Cary Grant, Katharine Hepburn, Henry Fonda, and Barbara Stanwyck rely on the same pratfalls and elaborate sight gags that were the highlights of silent comedies. During the 1950's and 1960's, French director Jacques Tati drew heavily on the silent comedy tradition in such films as *Les Vacances de Monsieur Hulot* (*Mr. Hulot's Holiday*, 1953) and *Playtime* (1968), in which he created a screen persona who rarely spoke in films that relied almost entirely on visual humor.

The work of Mel Brooks and Woody Allen also owes a debt to Chaplin and silent comedy. Allen's earlier films, in particular, combine verbal and physical humor and feature central characters who are outsiders and hapless "little guys" thrust into situations larger than themselves. Brooks's films have long made use of slapstick humor, a debt he acknowledged in the film *Silent Movie* (1976), which contains only one word of dialogue. Indeed, physical comedy in any visual medium, whether it be film, television, or live theater, continues to draw on the brilliant comic technique of Chaplin and his contemporaries.

Yet Chaplin's contribution to motion pictures does not end with comedy. In his hands, comedy was transformed into art at a time when the relatively new medium of film was struggling to gain credibility as more than simple entertainment. Chaplin's role in achieving this was recognized by the Academy of Motion Picture Arts and Sciences in the special Oscar he received in 1971. The award was presented to the eighty-three-year-old Chaplin for "the incalculable effect he has had in making motion pictures the art form of the century."

Bibliography

Brownlow, Kevin. *The Parade's Gone By.* Berkeley: University of California Press, 1968. One of the best books available on the history of silent film. Thoughtfully conceived and exceptionally well written and researched, the book offers an engrossing look at Hollywood's early years, drawing extensively on interviews that bring the material to life. A highly recommended source for anyone with an interest in film history.

Chaplin, Charles. *My Autobiography.* New York: Simon & Schuster, 1964. Chaplin's life and career in his own words. The early portions of the book are its finest, as Chaplin recalls in vivid detail his harrowing, Dickensian childhood in the slums of Victorian London. Also interesting for its behind-the-scenes reminiscences on his life and films and the perspective it offers on Chaplin's assessment of his own work.

Huff, Theodore. *Charlie Chaplin.* New York: Henry Schuman, 1951. The first, and for many years the only, in-depth study of Chaplin and his work. Contains the first complete (up to that time) Chaplin filmography. The book is weakest where Chaplin's autobiography is at its best—his childhood years—devoting only five pages to the first twenty-four years of Chaplin's life.

McCabe, John. *Charlie Chaplin.* Garden City, N.Y.: Doubleday, 1978. A thorough, well-researched biography containing an extensive bibliography and a filmography with credits. McCabe, who has also written on Laurel and Hardy, draws on his many interviews with Stan Laurel for unique insights into Chaplin's career. Informative and well-written.

McCaffrey, Donald W., ed. *Focus on Chaplin.* Englewood Cliffs, N.J.: Prentice-Hall, 1971. An excellent compilation of essays and reviews of Chaplin's work. Contributors include George Jean Nathan, Louis Delluc, Gerald Mast, Walter Kerr, Winston Churchill, and Chaplin himself. The book also contains scenario extracts from three of Chaplin's films, *Shoulder Arms* (1918), *The Kid*, and *Modern Times*

McDonald, Gerald D., Michael Conway, and Mark Ricci, eds. *The Films of Charlie*

Chaplin. New York: Cadillac Publishing, 1965. Two brief introductory essays followed by a chronological listing of all of Chaplin's films except *The Countess from Hong Kong* (1967). Each entry contains credits, a plot synopsis, photographs, and excerpted reviews of the film in question. A useful reference, although the credits do not include character names.

Manvell, Roger. *Chaplin.* Boston: Little, Brown, 1974. A well-written, well-researched biography. Manvell offers an absorbing and highly readable account of Chaplin's life and work, and the book remains one of the better entries in the vast array of literature on the comedian. Contains a limited bibliography and suggestions for further reading.

Mast, Gerald. *A Short History of the Movies.* Indianapolis, Ind.: Bobbs-Merrill, 1976. One of the best comprehensive overviews of film history, the book as a whole offers a context within which to place Chaplin's work. In addition to a general outline of Chaplin's career, Mast also devotes a chapter to a comparison of *The Gold Rush* and Keaton's *The General.* A valuable addition to any film library.

Robinson, David. *Chaplin: His Life and Art.* New York: McGraw-Hill, 1985. The best and most comprehensive examination of Chaplin's life and work to date. Vividly written, exhaustively researched, and thoroughly annotated, the book offers not only a detailed retelling of Chaplin's life but also a look at his work that includes numerous interviews with colleagues and contemporaries. Contains a useful chronology of the major events in Chaplin's life, appendices chronicling his early theatrical career, scenarios from three Keystone shorts, an excellent filmography, and a "who's who" of people who figured prominently in Chaplin's life and career.

Janet Lorenz

Cross-References

Sennett Defines the Slapstick Comedy Genre (1909), p. 230; *The Birth of a Nation* Popularizes New Film Techniques (1915), p. 402; Keaton's *The General* Is Released (1926), p. 691; Sound Technology Revolutionizes the Motion-Picture Industry (1928), p. 761; The First Academy Awards Honor Film Achievement (1929), p. 799; The Classic Screwball Comedy Reaches Its Height in Popularity (1934), p. 951; Allen's *Annie Hall* Captures Complexities of 1970's Life (1977), p. 2381.

BAKER DANCES IN *LA REVUE NÈGRE*

Category of event: Dance
Time: October-December, 1925
Locale: Paris, France

The Parisian café society was spellbound by exotic dancer Josephine Baker, who would soon change how Europe viewed modern dance

    Principal personages:

        JOSEPHINE BAKER (1906-1975), an American dancer who became a symbol of expressive, exotic performing in Europe during the 1920's

        ANDRE DAVEN, the director of the Théâtre des Champs-Élysées during the showing of *La Revue nègre*

        ROLF DE MARE (1888-1964), the manager of the Théâtre des Champs-Élysées during the showing of *La Revue nègre*

        PAUL COLIN (1892-1985), an amateur painter responsible for designing the cover of the program and the poster for *La Revue nègre*

        CAROLINE DUDLEY, the chief organizer in New York City of the black song-and-dance show that sailed to Paris to perform at the Théâtre des Champs-Élysées

        JACQUES CHARLES, a producer at the Moulin Rouge who helped with the production of *La Revue nègre*

Summary of Event

By the age of nineteen, Josephine Baker had risen from her poverty-stricken background at her East St. Louis home to the endless possibilities of New York City show business. In 1921, she first made her name known in Noble Sissle and Eubie Blake's show *Shuffle Along.* She later appeared in their show *Chocolate Dandies* Both of these all-black Broadway shows are remembered as helping to introduce black entertainment to the stages of New York City. The clownlike, comical style of Baker helped to get her noticed during rehearsals and auditions. Baker appeared in these productions only briefly, as a dancer or a "walk-on." Her well-known "ragamuffin period" was labeled as such because of her popular cross-eyed and knees-turned-in dance position that eventually helped her break into entertainment. Baker was by no means appearing on stage because of her dancing ability or beautiful body. On the contrary, Baker was perceived as an ugly tomboy, clad in big shoes and tattered clothes.

In the summer of 1925, show coordinator Caroline Dudley organized a black song-and-dance troupe at the request of a French theater director, Andre Daven. If anything would help save the Théâtre des Champs-Élysées from hard economic postwar times, it would be a real African-American show. The theater was very large for such a small production, but the directors hoped to move the show into smaller dance halls later. Baker was one of the twenty-four musicians, singers, and dancers to travel across the Atlantic Ocean and perform in what is one of the best-known American productions of the 1920's, *La Revue nègre*, or the Black Revue.

Baker arrived in Paris dumbfounded and ready to return to America immediately after the show was completed. Her attitude would soon change. *La Revue nègre* was developed to give the European audience an idea of how black America danced. When the opening night of *La Revue nègre* finally came, Paris was caught by surprise. A popular comment from the audience was that the show had the most black people they had ever seen on stage at one time. To the Parisian café society, the popular class of people involved in the city life of downtown Paris, this was a part of the world they knew little about.

Before *La Revue nègre* was ready for its preview showing at the Théâtre des Champs-Élysées, director Andre Daven and producer Rolf de Mare had to make significant changes to the format and content of the show, which had been presented in Britain and across Europe as *Blackbirds*. They thought the show was too noisy, too long, inelegant, and not black enough. Jacques Charles, a producer of the well-known Moulin Rouge, rearranged the dancers and put more focus on Baker. She was given the spotlight in one particularly exotic dance, the "Danse sauvage." This dance was placed strategically at the end of the show to create a shocking finale. Baker and her partner appeared in bare skin and feathers, and they raced around the stage to upbeat African music. Baker's part in the "Danse sauvage" was the foundation of her exotic dance period. What is interesting to note is that Baker was not originally scheduled to star in the show. When Maud de Forrest, the original lead singer, could no longer handle the pressure of performing in *La Revue nègre*, she was dismissed from the show. Thus, Baker took her place as the leading lady, and a star was born.

When the show was ready for opening night, journalists and celebrities were given an exclusive preview showing. An enormous amount of publicity appeared in the French tabloids and newspapers. What mattered was not whether the reviews were good or bad, but that the show had become the most talked-about production in Paris. Almost immediately after opening night, Baker became a well-known success. Surrounded by handsome men, publicity people, and artists, her impression of Paris quickly changed, and she became accustomed to the European life-style. France would soon become her new home, and she became part of France's growing obsession with black entertainment.

An artist by the name of Paul Colin was partly responsible for Baker's fame in *La Revue nègre*. Colin was called in to draw the publicity program cover and poster. As the posters covered walls throughout Paris, positive reviews continued to flourish, and more and more Parisians came to see the show. *La Revue nègre* had created a celebrity and proved to Paris that black was beautiful. Artists soon drowned Baker with requests to photograph or paint her in the nude. She was at first too modest but soon realized that nude portrayals were going to become common.

Although Baker was said not to have liked *La Revue nègre*, she would not have become a dance celebrity without it. Colin's posters made her recognizable long before the public knew her by name. *La Revue nègre* played for three months, October to December of 1925. As the directors of the Théâtre des Champs-Élysées had predicted, *La Revue nègre* was able to continue its run by moving into smaller theaters. The show traveled from Paris to Brussels, and then to the Nelson Theatre in Berlin. Although it was not a long-running show, by the end of 1925 it had made Baker one of the most famous dancers in Europe.

The fame Baker received from *La Revue nègre* was only a fraction of what was to come. In 1926, she was asked to join productions of the Folies-Bergère, a major tourist attraction in the Paris theater district. In 1927, she performed at the Folies-Bergère with two live cheetahs, wearing nothing but a girdle made of imitation bananas. Her performances included singing as well as dancing, but her dancing is what made her famous. She performed all over the world in various shows, then eventually went on a solo world tour. Baker visited America on her tours and, in later years, said that she thought of it once again as her home. With the stamina of a twenty-year-old, Baker performed into the final days of her life, appearing in *Josephine*, a show commemorating her fifty years in show business, five days before she died.

Impact of Event

When *La Revue nègre* opened at the Théâtre des Champs-Élysées, the French had no idea what impact Baker would have on the history of dance. European audiences were enchanted immediately when Baker stepped out on stage and became a beautiful, flowing piece of art. Because there was so little known about African dance, Baker became even more of a celebrated creature. When she danced, her unproportioned body became unexplainably beautiful and perfect, moving in ways no one knew were possible. Baker danced so exotically that the audience was mesmerized just by watching her move. She was said to have been on the verge of being obscene.

From Baker and *La Revue nègre*, European society gained a knowledge and understanding of a dance culture that was previously all but unknown to it. Credit for this discovery must be given not only to Charles, Daven, de Mare, and the other show organizers, but to Baker and her unique talent. Her dance was not regarded immediately as artistically valuable. On the opening night of *La Revue nègre*, Baker was pleased to hear what she thought were whistles of approval coming from the audience. She soon found out that whistling in Paris meant rejection and dislike. Baker was in disbelief. In the weeks after opening night, the whistling was drowned by chants of "Josephine," yelling for more wonderful dance. Parties were thrown for the singers and dancers night after night.

Many different events illustrate how African dance was regarded after the popularity of *La Revue nègre*. According to the average Parisian audience member, black dancers were instinctive and incapable of discipline. When on stage, they were thought of as indecent, primitive, and savage. Because Baker's dance moves were so unconventional and so different from those of Caucasian dancers, it was easy to understand why these thoughts were prevalent. *La Revue nègre* came to symbolize postwar modernism, bringing to Europe the spirit of Americanized Africa. The dance culture was left refreshed and more dynamic, with unconventional forms more accepted. Baker helped introduce popular American dances to Europe, including the Charleston and the Black Bottom. Her dancing also helped to popularize the jazz music that accompanied it. Critic Andre Levinson wrote about jazz, "The music is born from the dance and what a dance!"

La Revue nègre certainly left an impression on Jacques-Émile Blanche, a renowned French portrait painter. He had been searching for a "manifestation of the modern spirit" in the Art Deco Show but found it instead in *La Revue nègre*. This led other people to look at the show in that manner. The numerous reviews became Baker's texts for learning the French language. Whether good or bad, the critiques of *La Revue nègre* educated Baker and the public. One critic compared the dance movements in the show to St. Vitus' Dance, a nervous disorder that makes the body tremble. Another labeled Baker as a "Black Venus."

A particularly harsh critic of Baker was distinguished dance critic Andre Levinson. He referred at first to black dance as primitive and prehuman, saying that black dancers turned their bodies into percussion instruments. Although somewhat condescending, he gave *La Revue nègre* a favorable review and later was persuaded of the validity of black dance and jazz music. Librettist and playwright Robert de Flers referred to *La Revue nègre* as "the most direct assault ever perpetrated against French taste." It is difficult to assess these vastly different opinions of Baker and the show. Unfortunately, there are no film recordings of *La Revue nègre*, only photographs and stories told by Baker's friends and family.

The impact Baker had on the European culture was strong. Restaurateurs and club owners named their establishments after her. Fashion designers followed the advice of Baker and eventually designed dresses in her name, such as Robe Josephine. Baker's style became an institution in French society.

Ironically, Baker was not received as well when she returned to the United States to appear in *Ziegfeld Follies of 1936*. It would be fifteen years before she would return to her native country again. Baker joined the French Women's Air Force at the outbreak of World War II and later joined the French Resistance, earning the Croix de Guerre with Palm among other decorations. When she did return to the United States in 1951, she refused to appear in clubs that did not allow black patrons. Her stand convinced the Copa City Club in Miami, Florida, to change its discriminatory policies, and other clubs began to follow the trend.

Baker died on April 12, 1975, in Paris. Her funeral was publicized on a national level. Starting at the church of the Madeleine, the procession went by theaters at which she had performed. Eulogies recognized her civil and military achievements as well as her artistic ability. Baker is remembered as one of the most famous female performers, responsible in large part for bringing new dance forms to Europe, beginning with her performance in *La Revue nègre*.

Bibliography

Baker, Josephine, and Jo Boullion. *Josephine*. Translated by Mariana Fitzpatrick.

New York: Harper & Row, 1977. Biography written by Baker and her former husband, with many interviews with her associates. Because of Boullion's relationship to Baker, the information is very accurate. Baker reveals personal thoughts and stories that do not appear in other biographies. Portions of the book tend to include Boullion excessively, but the reader can overlook these excerpts. Good index and small section of photographs.

Hammond, Bryan. *Josephine Baker.* London: Jonathan Cape, 1988. Complete photographic biography of Baker's performing life. Extraordinary photographs of Baker on stage, at home, and in various publicity pieces. Complete discography and index. The text is very brief, but this book adds visually to other biographies of Baker's life.

Haney, Lynn. *Naked at the Feast: A Biography of Josephine Baker.* New York: Dodd, Mead, 1981. A good basic reference concerning Baker's dance career. Haney is thorough and accurate in her accounts of which theaters, directors, and other celebrities were involved at each stage of Baker's performing life. A large part of the book is devoted to Baker's problems with her husbands and children.

Rose, Phyllis. *Jazz Cleopatra.* New York: Vintage Books, 1989. Excellent biography in a story format. The book is separated into three sections, of which the first, covering 1925 and 1926, is the most complete. Only one chapter on *La Revue nègre*, but the "Danse sauvage" is covered extensively. Numerous photographs show all the diverse stages Baker went through.

Wiser, William. "Josephine Baker, 1906-1975." In *The Great Good Place: American Expatriate Women in Paris.* New York: W. W. Norton, 1991. Wiser offers a succinct but lively account of the dancer's life. He paints a picture of a 1920's Paris so jaded that almost nothing could shock it—except Baker's energetic seminude dancing.

David Francis

Cross-References

Duncan Interprets Chopin in Her Russian Debut (1904), p. 113; Stein Holds Her First Paris Salons (1905), p. 129; Artists Find Inspiration in African Tribal Art (1906), p. 156; *L'Après-midi d'un faune* Causes an Uproar (1912), p. 332; Ellington Begins an Influential Engagement at the Cotton Club (1927), p. 739.

ARMSTRONG FIRST RECORDS
WITH HIS HOT FIVE GROUP

Category of event: Music
Time: November, 1925
Locale: Chicago, Illinois

Louis Armstrong's Hot Five recording sessions between 1925 and 1928 led to recognition of Armstrong as the father of modern jazz music

Principal personages:

LOUIS ARMSTRONG (1898?-1971), the most influential jazz musician in the history of American music

LIL ARMSTRONG (1898-1971), the original pianist in the Hot Five group and Louis Armstrong's second wife

FLETCHER HENDERSON (1897-1952), the leader of the most important jazz band in the 1920's

BESSIE SMITH (1894?-1937), the "Empress of the Blues," who recorded with Armstrong in 1925

EARL HINES (1903-1983), the famed jazz pianist who, in 1928, recorded "Weather Bird" with Armstrong

KING OLIVER (1885-1938), a New Orleans trumpet player and bandleader who gave Armstrong early guidance

Summary of Event

On November 12, 1925, Louis Armstrong and his Hot Five band recorded three songs for OKeh records in Chicago. These were the first of more than fifty records made by the group that changed the course of jazz music. Besides Armstrong, the original Hot Five included Johnny Dodds (clarinet), Kid Ory (trombone), Lil Harden Armstrong (piano), and Johnny St. Cyr (banjo). Except for one or two isolated public appearances, these musicians performed together only in the OKeh studios. From 1925 to 1928, the Hot Five, also known by a variety of other names during this period, recorded on twenty-two occasions; those sessions reflect a musical growth that has caused music critics to conclude that the Hot Five, and especially Armstrong, had a major influence on the evolution of twentieth century American popular music.

Armstrong had established himself as a popular showman and musician prior to the Chicago recording session in 1925. He performed as a soloist in cabarets, as an accompanist for other jazz musicians, and in various jazz bands. Audiences already knew him as the "World's Greatest Trumpet Player," and they came by the hundreds to hear him. Reared in New Orleans from his birth (most probably in 1898, and not on July 4 as legend has it) until he left in 1922, Armstrong naturally adopted the loose ensemble style of music common in that city.

Between 1922, when he first arrived in Chicago, and 1925, Armstrong was a member of Joe "King" Oliver's band and also a member of Fletcher Henderson's East Coast-based jazz band. Oliver established a dominant relationship with Armstrong, and, while Armstrong did not learn much about the cornet from Oliver, he did learn something about responsibility. Henderson's band was easily the best jazz band of the early 1920's, and Armstrong profited from his years (1922-1924) in Henderson's group. During these years, Armstrong gradually broke away from the New Orleans ensemble style. When not playing with a band, he made public appearances that emphasized his singular virtuosity with the horn.

In some ways, the Hot Five recordings, especially the early ones, were a return for Armstrong to the more relaxed New Orleans music. Armstrong and others in the Hot Five group viewed the Chicago recording sessions as a holiday in their rigorous schedule of performances. Many critics argue that this informal attitude is what made the sessions so successful. The composition of Armstrong's group changed frequently between 1925 and 1928, and with each change, Armstrong advanced his improvisation without disrupting the casual New Orleans rhythm. The group's recording of "Potato Head Blues" in 1927 is generally considered a breakthrough for Armstrong and for jazz music in general. In the song, Armstrong improvised two solos that set a standard for future musicians. Earlier, in 1925, he had revealed his potential for improvisation in a remarkable recording session with the great blues singer Bessie Smith.

By the time he left Chicago in 1929, Armstrong was just short of star status. His recordings brought him thousands of new followers, and his personal appearances attracted both musicians and the general public. Near the end of the Hot Five sessions in 1928, Armstrong began to sing regularly on the recordings, and singing gradually became a more important part of Armstrong's music. He began by singing in a tenor voice similar to the "crooners" of his time, but he soon developed the gravelly, rasping style for which he was famous.

The Depression years were rough for Armstrong. His record sales and bookings declined, his second marriage ended, and he was arrested for smoking marijuana in California. Things soon turned around for him, though, and he extended his horizons as a popular and commercial performer in the 1930's and 1940's. He began to tour Europe on a regular basis, and he acquired a hard-driving, well-connected agent, Joe Glaser, who demanded that he smile as broadly as possible and use facial expressions to endear himself to audiences. Some black musicians and critics objected to this "jolly darky" routine, but most who knew Armstrong agreed that his onstage antics were merely extensions of his joyous personality. He was now often referred to as "Satchmo," an appellation of uncertain origins.

As his commercial star ascended, Armstrong's cornet playing declined. A recording contract with Decca in 1935 required him to play and sing innocuous popular songs, songs that were suitable for radio listeners in the comfort of their living rooms. The big bands were all the rage, and Armstrong fell into line by leading a number of mediocre groups during this era. There was also a serious problem with Armstrong's lips. Throughout his career, he suffered from split lips, which forced him to rest for long periods of time. The scar tissue hampered his ability to play with clarity. His singing, however, was not affected. One of his 1930's songs, "A Kiss to Build a Dream On," clearly demonstrates his brilliant application of jazz phrasing to an otherwise ordinary lyric.

Armstrong reached the peak of his popularity in the 1950's and 1960's. Although he had been almost completely deserted by jazz enthusiasts, the general public responded to his many film appearances and to his singing. His hit records included "Blueberry Hill," "Mack the Knife," and "Hello, Dolly!" The latter song was such a smash that it became number one on the charts in May, 1964. It also led to a much-heralded appearance in the movie by the same name and to many television bookings. This success marked the penultimate moment in Armstrong's show-business career. Shortly thereafter, his health began to fail, and he died on July 7, 1971. Armstrong had fulfilled the promise of the Hot Five sessions, but not quite in the way jazz musicians had expected, or would have preferred.

Impact of Event

James Lincoln Collier, Armstrong's best biographer, has written that Armstrong "struck the first two generations of jazz musicians with the force of a sledgehammer." This is not an exaggeration. Most jazz writers and musicians without hesitation cite Armstrong as the father of modern jazz or as the "Bach of Jazz." He was truly a creator, for there was almost no musician who influenced him. He learned something from King Oliver, but what he learned was related more to presentation than to the music itself. Armstrong displayed technical and imaginative talent that astounded and inspired Roy Eldridge, Dizzy Gillespie, Benny Goodman, Humphrey Lyttelton, and a legion of other jazz musicians. The clarity of Armstrong's horn, his sharp attacks, and his ability to play effectively in the highest register startled those who heard him for the first time in the 1920's. His imagination appeared boundless in those early days; he could create melodies of grace and power almost instantly. The most cherished of Armstrong's attributes, however, and the one that had the greatest impact on future musicians, was his ability to lift all around him, musicians and audiences alike, by the sheer joy and energy he brought to his music. He taught American musicians how to "swing," how to give even simple music verve and excitement. It certainly helped if one had the virtuosity possessed by Armstrong, but lesser musicians could at least emulate his enthusiasm.

The Hot Five recordings, particularly "Potato Head Blues" and "Weather Bird," convinced musicians to be more independent and to eschew jazz orchestras, in which they sat in sections and played notes, for the delight of improvisation, the opportunity to soar. Armstrong had, in effect, given all musicians the opportunity to use their creative talent to the fullest. Whether a musician played the clarinet, the piano, the bass, or the cornet, Armstrong was the model. His 1928 recording of "Weather Bird" (which he and King Oliver wrote in 1923) with pianist Earl Hines was so spectacularly successful that such collaborations became standard for jazz musicians from that time onward.

Although Armstrong's major contribution was to the future of jazz, Armstrong's influence can also be traced in rhythm and blues, rock and roll, country music, and all forms of popular singing. Even when he ceased to produce great creative music after the early 1930's, his impact persisted. The Beatles, Collier points out, played as an "extra" for a jazz band in England that emulated the Hot Five numbers. Jimmie Rodgers, one of the original country singers, had Armstrong as an accompanist on his recording of "Blue Yodel No. 9," and Rodgers' singing always had a jazz flavor. Bing Crosby, a regular for Armstrong's Chicago appearances, undoubtedly profited from observing Armstrong's impeccable understanding of lyrics. Crosby once said he learned to swing from watching Armstrong.

No summary of Armstrong's impact can be complete without some mention of his effect on those who listened to his recordings, watched him in movies, or saw him in person. There was the Armstrong who influenced musicians, and there was the Armstrong who taught the general public how to enjoy the music. While his impact was greatest with black audiences early in his career, in the later years, most in his audiences were white. White crowds found joy in his very appearance on stage, but not all the reasons for this were positive. As the Civil Rights movement in the United States intensified in the 1960's, many blacks found Armstrong's wide smile, rolling eyes, and general mugging increasingly grating. To some, he seemed to be pushing the happy-go-lucky image a little far. Many whites, though, found comfort in Armstrong, especially in an era of racial stress. By his rise from abject poverty and rejection to the heights of success, he seemed to prove that the American Dream did apply to blacks. In a time of growing anger and strident demands, Armstrong continued to play and sing and look happy. He was marvelous reassurance, and the popularity of his 1964 hit record "Hello, Dolly!" said as much about the political and social circumstances in the United States as it did about Armstrong's singing.

The reaction to Armstrong was the same throughout the world. When he first appeared on screen in the 1969 film *Hello, Dolly!*, the huge gathering in a London cinema burst into sustained cheering and applause. This response was not so much for Armstrong's great musical contributions since the Hot Five days, but rather a recognition of the warmth that emanated from his horn, his voice, and his entire being.

Bibliography

Collier, James Lincoln. *Louis Armstrong: An American Genius.* New York: Oxford University Press, 1983. A superb biography filled with insights. Very strong on all phases of Armstrong's life and music. Even Collier's occasional inconsistencies are enlightening. Highest possible recommendation for casual and serious students of Armstrong. Notes, photographs, discography, index.

Jones, LeRoi. *Blues People: Negro Music in White America.* New York: William

Morrow, 1963. Jones (Amiri Baraka) discusses how blues and jazz evolved in white America. The parts of the book in which Jones focuses on Armstrong are especially valuable. Generally an important and useful study. Index.

Jones, Max, and John Chilton. *The Louis Armstrong Story, 1900-1971.* Boston: Little, Brown, 1971. Written by two British critics, this biography was rushed into print shortly after Armstrong's death. It is anecdotal and filled with reminiscences. Authors try to revive interest in Armstrong's big-band phase, but without much success. Inadequate index.

Lyttelton, Humphrey. *The Best of Jazz: Basin Street to Harlem.* New York: Taplinger, 1978. An excellent series of essays on the great names in jazz history by a well-known British jazz musician. Bessie Smith, Duke Ellington, Fletcher Henderson, and Bix Beiderbecke are some of those discussed. Two essays dealing with Armstrong contain explanations for his musical influence. Strongly recommended. Select bibliography, discography, index.

Priestley, Brian. *Jazz on Record: A History.* London: Elm Tree Books, 1988. A history of jazz recordings from the 1920's to the 1980's. An impressive achievement, but Priestley's condescending judgments can be irritating. The record guide is an important feature. Photographs, slight bibliography, index.

Ronald K. Huch

Cross-References

Joplin Popularizes the Ragtime Style (1899), p. 13; Handy Ushers in the Commercial Blues Era (1910's), p. 252; Bessie Smith Records "Downhearted Blues" (1923), p. 572; Gershwin's *Rhapsody in Blue* Premieres in New York (1924), p. 598; Ellington Begins an Influential Engagement at the Cotton Club (1927), p. 739; Billie Holiday Begins Her Recording Career (1933), p. 930; Goodman Begins His *Let's Dance* Broadcasts (1934), p. 968; Parker's Playing Epitomizes Bebop (1946), p. 1318; Davis' *Birth of the Cool* Recordings Spawn 1950's Cool Jazz (1949), p. 1438; Wynton Marsalis Revives Acoustic Jazz (1980's), p. 2454.

WSM LAUNCHES *THE GRAND OLE OPRY*

Category of event: Music
Time: November 28, 1925
Locale: Nashville, Tennessee

With the start of its barn dance show, soon to be known as The Grand Ole Opry, *WSM brought country music to millions and helped to build Nashville into a major recording center*

Principal personages:

GEORGE D. HAY (1895-1968), the first master of ceremonies for the Opry and source of its name and initial success

UNCLE JIMMY THOMPSON (1848-1931), a seventy-seven-year-old fiddler who was the first performer on the WSM barn dance

UNCLE DAVE MACON (1870-1952), an early Opry favorite who played the banjo and sang

ROY ACUFF (1903-1992), the first singing star on the Opry, who brought an intense East Tennessee vocal style to the program

Summary of Event

On November 28, 1925, WSM, a Nashville, Tennessee, radio station barely a month old, launched a music show that would help to revolutionize America's taste, mold a huge industry, and stimulate a sleepy Southern city to become a national center for the recording of popular music. WSM had hired nationally famous radio announcer George D. Hay as program director; Hay had been successful on radio in Memphis and with WLS Chicago's *The National Barn Dance* old-time music program, which had been inaugurated in 1924. Lured to Nashville, Hay wanted to set up a show similar to the WLS affair so that WSM, broadcast throughout the South, could tap the region's rich tradition of folksong.

Hay did not have to look far for talent for that first night. The Nashville region itself was rich in performers of old-time and folk music: fiddlers, banjo players, harmonica players, and an assortment of string bands made up of part-time musicians eager to be heard over the airwaves, though they were paid nothing.

Hay seized upon a seventy-seven-year-old champion fiddler named Uncle Jimmy Thompson. After setting Thompson down before a single microphone, Hay let him play some of the hundreds of tunes he knew for two hours. The response was swift; phone calls and telegrams poured in, and Uncle Jimmy was back the next week. By December, Hay had decided to expand the program with more old-time and folk musicians. *The National Barn Dance* had already been successful with this kind of music, although it favored some pop music in the mix. Other radio stations, such as WSB in Atlanta, had experimented with broadcasting old-time tunes and had succeeded. Old-time music—also to be called "hillbilly" and, later, "country" music—

had first drawn the attention of record executives in 1923 and now was selling well in rural areas. New radio stations (the first had opened only in 1920) were eager to give their audiences what they liked.

Although Hay wanted to develop a full-scale show with all kinds of performers, many executives at WSM remained skeptical. The National Life and Accident Insurance Company, which owned the station, had sophisticated leaders who largely did not know this kind of music, and an insurance company putting down roots in the "Athens of the South" could hardly afford to appear too backwoodsy. After all, Nashville had an upper class that was proud of the city's historic origins and of its many schools, colleges, churches, and financial institutions. Indeed, even late into the twentieth century, the city's social and cultural leaders remained aloof from, and often disdainful of, its most famous product—country music.

Hay persisted, however, and the response continued to grow. People even came to the studio, in the fifth floor of the majestic stone building that housed National Life, to gaze at the performers through the glass window. Nothing succeeds like success; even the skeptics reconsidered. By 1928, National Life decided that by offering low-cost insurance policies to the rural poor and by having its salesmen introduce themselves as from the station that broadcast *The Grand Ole Opry*, they had a gold mine.

In 1925 and 1926, though, Hay still had a long way to go before the show would achieve an identity and workable format. By early 1926, with the program still known as *The WSM Barn Dance*, Hay started to add the variety of performers with which *The National Barn Dance* had succeeded. The talent was easy to find locally. Next to Uncle Jimmy Thompson in popularity were Uncle Dave Macon and the harmonica player Deford Bailey. Although Thompson died in 1931, Bailey stayed on until the late 1930's, and Macon remained a favorite until his death in 1952.

Hay started to format the show into fifteen- and thirty-minute segments, and the show was expanded from two hours to three and, later, four hours each Saturday night. The curious crowds who flocked to the building were soon better accommodated in a larger studio. Soon the show would have to respond to the crowds by moving to several theaters in Nashville, where the program would be done as a remote broadcast. The show moved to its most famous home, the downtown Ryman Auditorium, around 1941. There it generally hosted crowds of several thousand until its move to Opryland in 1974.

In 1927, the station hooked up with the new National Broadcasting Company (NBC) radio network. On Saturday nights immediately before the barn dance show, WSM carried a program of classical and grand opera music from New York. On one such Saturday, George Hay got a bright idea for a catchy name for the barn dance. Since the listeners had heard an hour of grand opera music, now they could hear music of the "Grand Ole Opry." The name stuck.

In the early years and on into the 1930's, *The National Barn Dance* from Chicago dominated the barn-dance formats. Starting in 1924, it held the edge until the late 1930's, when *The Grand Ole Opry* caught and surpassed it. Several explanations for the Opry's eventual leadership have been suggested. Certainly, Hay's ability to spot talent in a region rich in it was one factor in the show's success. Chicago did not have so rich a talent pool of folk musicians in the area; in addition, *The National Barn Dance* tended to mix more pop music into its format than the Opry did. Yet with stars such as Gene Autry, *The National Barn Dance* gave the Opry stiff competition in the early 1930's.

Impact of Event

During the Depression, *The Grand Ole Opry* changed from its initial studio-bound format to a combination radio and live-audience entertainment variety show. Show-business values began to alter things. Hay costumed his performers for visual excitement; pseudo-rustic wear became a norm. Rustic comedians were added to provide visual humor suited to the watching crowds. An artists' bureau was instituted to help Opry acts tour the region and to travel into other regions where the clear-channel WSM could reach. WSM expanded from 1,000 to 50,000 watts in 1932, giving it an enormous reach across most of the country.

The greatest change in the Opry's direction, though, was the shift to a singing star system. Roy Acuff's arrival as an Opry member in 1938 signaled the change dramatically. With his intense and piercing East Tennessee mountain voice, Acuff quickly took over as the Opry's greatest favorite. His repertoire of love songs, old ballads, and hymns was delivered with great emotion and sincerity. Still performing on the Opry as he neared ninety, Acuff became known as the "king of country music." He was joined in 1939 by another seminal figure, Bill Monroe from Kentucky. Monroe also sang with great intensity and, like Acuff, wrote songs and arranged old folk-songs. In addition, he was an accomplished mandolin player, and he developed a style of hard-driven string-band music later to be called bluegrass. With bands such as Pee Wee King's Western-flavored group also added to the Opry, a new era opened.

By the time of World War II, recordings began to dominate performers' careers. Nashville became a recording and publishing center in its own right, in large part because of *The Grand Ole Opry*'s contingent of singers, musicians, and support personnel. In the late 1940's and into the 1950's, Nashville became the center of the growing country music industry.

With the arrival of Texan Ernest Tubb on the Opry in 1943, another historic shift occurred. Tubb became the leading exponent of "honky-tonk," or hard country, music. Songs of failed love and marriages, adultery, divorce, and hard times soon became the norm for country music. Tubb's use of an electric lead guitar in his band—and his later use of a steel guitar with prominent string bass and drums—set the pattern for modern country music.

When Hank Williams joined the Opry in 1949, the show in a sense reached its artistic peak. This enormously talented singer and songwriter was only a member of the Opry until late 1952, and he died at the age of thirty in January, 1953, but his legacy of songs still haunts country music. No one has ever rivaled his intense style, inspired by Acuff and Tubb but influenced by his rural roots in the pine woods of south Alabama.

After Williams' death, the Opry took on honky-tonk singers who began to put the older styles in the shadows. Rock and roll offered a threat, too. By the early 1960's, the Opry started to feel the pinch, and audiences declined. With the new interstates and touring buses, stars could make more money touring than by playing the Opry, with its minimum pay scale and its rule that performers appear twenty-six Saturday nights in a year. Those performers who could succeed on the basis of record sales, concert dates, and syndicated country shows on television either quit the Opry after a short membership or found they could bypass it entirely.

New female superstars such as Loretta Lynn and Dolly Parton were members for a time in the 1960's and 1970's, but the field had grown so large and diverse that the Opry simply ceased being the "only show in town." Furthermore, the recording studios in Nashville met the challenge of rock and roll by developing the "Nashville Sound," which reached out toward pop music audiences with smooth choral and string arrangements and by eschewing fiddles and steel guitars. It was a manufactured sound, and the Opry as a live show could hardly duplicate it. Located in the increasingly archaic Ryman, the Opry had to move to more modern and technically sophisticated quarters.

In 1974, the program moved to the Opryland complex twenty miles outside downtown Nashville. The new Opry House was a marvel of modern entertainment technology, and its location on the same site as the Opryland theme park gave the show access to tourists who might have avoided the old downtown location of the show in an increasingly seedy area of Nashville. In one sense, the Opry had indeed gone "uptown" to the suburbs.

It took awhile for it all to come together. In the 1980's, though, *The Grand Ole Opry* witnessed a rebirth. Young, fresh performers, male and female, managed by the early 1990's to put country music on the popular music charts in an unprecedented way. The Opry was quick to make many of these singers cast members.

Perhaps just as significant in the revitalization of the Opry was the formation of The Nashville Network (TNN) cable television station in 1983. Located on the grounds of Opryland, the network broadcasts a half-hour of the Saturday night Opry show live and features Opry stars on its other live shows. TNN and the Opry showcase live country music in a new manner in which traditional live and recorded music can interact under the imperatives of changed channels of communication.

Bibliography

Daniel, Wayne W. *Pickin' on Peachtree: A History of Country Music in Atlanta, Georgia.* Urbana: University of Illinois Press, 1990. A good introduction to country radio and its relation to local talent and tradition.

Evans, James F. *Prairie Farmer and WLS: The Burridge D. Butler Years.* Urbana: University of Illinois Press, 1969. Another study of the context for barn-dance shows. Explains the commercial and business aspects well. Coverage of *The National Barn Dance* as well of its different focus when compared with the Opry.

Hagan, Chet. *Grand Ole Opry.* New York: Henry Holt, 1989. A full history of the show, generously illustrated with informative captions. The best history.

Malone, Bill C. *Country Music, U.S.A.* Rev. ed. Austin: University of Texas Press, 1985. The definitive history of the subject. Puts the barn-dance shows in context succinctly and accurately. Few but telling illustrations. Full bibliography with essays. Full indexes.

Malone, Bill C., and Judith McCulloh, eds. *Stars of Country Music.* Urbana: University of Illinois Press, 1975. Essays on early country music pioneers. Several key Opry members have individual essays. Bibliographies included; full index.

Wolfe, Charles K. *The Grand Ole Opry: The Early Years, 1925-35.* London: Old Time Music, 1975. More than one hundred pages of text, illustrations, and documents that thoroughly explore the subject. Wolfe is a meticulous scholar who has delved into sources not used by more popular histories.

Frederick E. Danker

Cross-References

Handy Ushers in the Commercial Blues Era (1910's), p. 252; The Art of Radio Develops from Early Broadcast Experience (1920's), p. 469; Rodgers Cuts His First Record for RCA Victor (1927), p. 729; Guthrie's Populist Songs Reflect the Depression-Era United States (1930's), p. 810; Radio Programming Dominates Home Leisure (1930's), p. 828; Bill Monroe and the Blue Grass Boys Define Bluegrass Music (1939), p. 1121; Hank Williams Performs on *The Grand Ole Opry* (1949), p. 1415; Presley Becomes a Rock-and-Roll Sensation (1956), p. 1705; *Wanted: The Outlaws* Revitalizes Country Music (1976), p. 2365.

BERG'S *WOZZECK* PREMIERES IN BERLIN

Category of event: Music
Time: December 14, 1925
Locale: Berlin, Germany

Alban Berg's opera Wozzeck *demonstrated that it was possible to write an effective opera that utilized both a modern story and nontraditional compositional techniques*

Principal personages:
ALBAN BERG (1885-1935), an Austrian composer whose *Wozzeck* was the first atonal opera
ARNOLD SCHOENBERG (1874-1951), an Austrian-born American composer of atonal music who was Berg's musical mentor
GEORG BÜCHNER (1813-1837), the German dramatist who wrote the play on which Berg's opera was based

Summary of Event

The beginning of the twentieth century was a time of tremendous upheaval in politics, science, technology, philosophy, and the arts. The first two decades of the century would see, among many dramatic events, the horrifying carnage of World War I; the fall of the Russian czars and the birth of the Soviet Union; Albert Einstein's development of the special theory of relativity, which would change the way humanity viewed the universe; and the work of Sigmund Freud, which would change the way humanity viewed itself.

In the arts, the work of such masters as Wassily Kandinsky, Pablo Picasso, Igor Stravinsky, Kazimir Malevich, Franz Kafka, and Sergei Diaghilev was challenging artistic traditions. Not even Vienna, a city that had long been known both as a center of the arts and as a bastion of conservatism, was immune to the changes sweeping the world. Indeed, it was a brilliant, self-taught Viennese composer, Arnold Schoenberg, who would develop a compositional approach that would change music forever.

Schoenberg's primary contribution to composition was his championship of atonality, a compositional style that does not adhere to a single musical key, or tonal center. (The commonly used term "atonality" implies the rejection of tonality, but Schoenberg actually preferred the term "pantonality," which implies the acceptance of all tonalities.) Ultimately, Schoenberg developed the "twelve-tone system," also called "serialism," which involved using all twelve tones of the chromatic scale (that is, all the notes in the Western system of music) in a single predetermined order as the basis for composition.

It is ironic that, although Schoenberg was the architect of a new style of composition, his compositions in that style would never be as artistically successful as those of his two greatest students, the Viennese composers Anton von Webern and Alban

Berg. Both Webern and Berg developed their remarkable musical gifts rapidly under the stern tutelage of Schoenberg, who was intolerant of those who did not agree with him in all things. To his credit, however, he insisted from the very beginning that his pupils express their own personalities in their music, and their later achievements testify to his ability as a teacher.

In spite of the ability of Schoenberg, Webern, and Berg, the infrequent performances of their works in Vienna met with little success; in fact, whenever their works were performed, they met with furious reactions from conservative musicians, critics, and listeners who could not understand or appreciate what they were doing musically. It was not until 1925, when Berg's opera *Wozzeck* premiered, that an atonal work met with a significant measure of acceptance and success.

On May 5, 1914, Berg attended the premiere in Vienna of *Woyzeck*, a play written in 1836 by Georg Büchner, a German dramatist who had died in 1837. (Because Büchner's manuscript was extremely difficult to decipher, the name *Woyzeck* was misread by the compiler of Büchner's collected works, and the play was first published as *Wozzeck*, the title that Berg gave to his opera.) In spite of the fact that the play had been written more than seventy years earlier, its undiluted, bitter realism had a powerful effect on the audiences of Berg's time.

Woyzeck, which was based on an actual event, tells the story of a soldier who is destroyed by his times and by his station in life. Taunted by his superior officer and victimized by a sadistic doctor who pays him a small amount of money to adhere to a series of extreme and unhealthy diets, Woyzeck, the protagonist, drifts farther and farther into madness. Ultimately, he murders his mistress, Marie, after she is seduced by a drum major, and drowns while trying to wash off the blood in which he imagines he is inundated. The unrelenting horror of the story and the work's condemnation of an unjust society were a tonic to audiences who were accustomed to stylized, genteel works. Berg was overwhelmed by the power of the play, and he determined at once to use it as the basis for an opera.

Although he was ultimately rejected as unfit for active military duty because of his chronic asthma and general poor health, Berg was called into military service in 1914, when World War I broke out, and it was not until 1922 that he completed *Wozzeck*. Berg not only wrote the music but also composed the libretto, which was quite faithful to Büchner's play.

Berg took the twenty-six scenes in Büchner's play and reduced them to fifteen. He was able to use much of the material in the deleted scenes in the scenes that he retained. In that way, he was able to use most of Büchner's material without producing a dramatic structure that would have been too long to function as an effective opera. The final form of *Wozzeck* consisted of three acts of five scenes each.

Although *Wozzeck* is an atonal work, Berg was extremely conscious of tradition—particularly the musical tradition of his beloved Vienna—and it is characteristic of Berg's approach to composition that he used traditional musical structures as vehicles for his extremely modern music. In addition, Berg sometimes used atonality in ways that suggested tonality, which occasionally led Schoenberg to criticize him but which also enabled him to combine the best aspects of tonality and atonality in a way that Schoenberg himself was never able to achieve.

Wozzeck was not performed immediately after Berg completed it, but one of Berg's friends suggested that Berg take selections from the opera and create a concert cycle that could be performed more easily than could the entire opera. Berg did so, and on June 15, 1924, the *Wozzeck* cycle was performed at a festival in Frankfurt, Germany. Berg was pleased with the performance, and the cycle became the hit of the festival. Meanwhile, Berg had asked a pianist he knew to play the score of the opera for Erich Kleiber, who was the conductor of the Berlin State Opera. Kleiber was impressed by the work, and he is reported to have said: "It's settled! I am going to do the opera in Berlin, even if it costs me my job!"

Kleiber's willingness to perform the opera was a stroke of luck for Berg, particularly because Kleiber made every effort to ensure that the work would be exhaustively rehearsed and well performed. In fact, the rehearsal schedule consisted of an unheard-of thirty-four full orchestral rehearsals and fourteen ensemble rehearsals—far more rehearsals than are customary for even the longest and most complicated works.

When *Wozzeck* received its premiere performance on December 14, 1925, it became an immediate sensation. Although, as everyone had expected, some critics attacked the exceedingly modern opera in the most virulent way, many critics recognized the work for the tremendous achievement that it was. In spite of its unusual compositional techniques, *Wozzeck* won over audiences and critics with its emotional power and with the effective way in which the music not only reflected but also enhanced the physical and psychological action of the play. Subsequent performances of the opera in Prague and Leningrad were also extremely successful, although they, too, were marked by attacks on the modern style of *Wozzeck*. With the success of his atonal opera, Berg achieved international renown.

Impact of Event

It is remarkable that Berg broke completely with the traditional approach to opera—both dramatically, in his choice of story, and musically, in his use of atonality—and still produced an effective dramatic work that has been accepted as part of the operatic tradition. *Wozzeck* is regularly performed as part of the operatic repertoire, in spite of its avant-garde nature, and it is one of the few twentieth century operas that are regularly performed. It is interesting to note that other modern operas, such as Schoenberg's *Moses und Aron* (begun in 1930 but never completed), are rarely staged. Berg's *Wozzeck* is simply a particularly effective work that has found favor with musicians, audiences, and critics alike.

Structurally, *Wozzeck* is unlike any opera that preceded it. After Berg had settled on the dramatic structure of his work—three acts of five scenes each—he sought out particular musical forms that he believed would best express the essence of each scene. He found the forms he needed in the traditional forms of music, but the forms he chose were not, traditionally, part of opera.

The first act of *Wozzeck* consists of five scenes that introduce the opera's primary characters and indicate the kind of relationship that Wozzeck has with each of them. Berg selected musical forms that would serve those functions for each scene: a suite (a form made up of a number of separate movements), a rhapsody (a kind of fantasy), a military march and a lullaby, a passacaglia (a baroque form in a triple, or waltz, meter), and an andante affetuoso (a slow form played warmly, or affectionately).

The second act is, strangely enough, cast in the form of a symphony in five movements. The first scene is in the classic sonata form, the second scene consists of a fantasia (fantasy) and fugue (a form in which a theme is played at different times by different instruments), the third scene is a largo (slow) movement, the fourth scene is a scherzo (a fast, rhythmic movement), and the fifth scene utilizes a rondo (a strictly organized form often used to end symphonies).

The third act is made up of five inventions, which consist of creative explorations of counterpoint (counterpoint consists of multiple melodic lines played simultaneously). These five are an invention on a melodic theme, an invention on a note, an invention on a rhythm, an invention on a chord, and an invention on a movement in eighth notes. It is interesting that, between the fourth and fifth inventions in this atonal piece, Berg inserted an orchestral interlude that is an invention on a tonality.

It should also be mentioned that Berg provided, in all three acts, connecting music that heightened the drama of the opera and united the individual scenes into a coherent whole. Berg also ended all three acts on the same chord, thereby enhancing the unity of the three acts.

The structure of the opera has been emphasized both to demonstrate its complexity and to emphasize the care that Berg took in selecting the forms that he thought would best express the nature of the action that took place in each scene. The danger of using such a complex structure is that it is difficult to write moving music in so many forms. In the hands of a lesser artist, this structure might have been nothing more than a fascinating exercise. The fact that the complex and unusual musical structure of the opera is not apparent when *Wozzeck* is performed but is instead seamlessly merged with the dramatic action is evidence of Berg's tremendous talent and skill.

It is even more significant that the music of *Wozzeck* explores the psychological aspect of the action that takes place on the stage. The music not only supports the action that takes place but also extends the range of meaning of that action. It is the combined effect of the drama and the music that gives the opera its undeniable power. At a time when Sigmund Freud was becoming famous for opening up the field of psychology, Berg—like Freud a Viennese—scored an unprecedented success for atonal music by demonstrating the power of music to explore the psychological realm of operatic drama.

Berg was, to some extent, gratified by the success of *Wozzeck*, particularly because it earned for him a measure of respect throughout the world that was never extended to him in his native Vienna. He was never quite comfortable with the acclaim, however, because he doubted the good judgment of the listening public. In fact, he wondered at times whether he had failed in composing *Wozzeck*, whether he had unconsciously pandered to the public in his most accepted work.

Berg summed up his achievement in the following words:

> What I do consider my particular accomplishment is this. No one in the audience, no matter how aware he may be of the musical forms contained in the framework of the opera, of the precision and logic with which it has been worked out, no one, from the moment the curtain parts until it closes for the last time, pays any attention to the various fugues, inventions, suites, sonata movements, variations about which so much has been written. No one pays heed to anything but the vast social implications of the work which by far transcend the personal destiny of Wozzeck. This, I believe, is my achievement.

Berg went on to compose another superb opera, *Lulu* (1937), which used the twelve-tone system devised by Schoenberg, and a violin concerto that is one of the most beautiful works composed in the twentieth century. Berg's primary goal was to create music of great beauty, and he demonstrated conclusively that atonality could be used to achieve that goal.

Bibliography

Carner, Mosco. *Alban Berg: The Man and the Work*. London: Duckworth, 1975. An excellent examination of Berg's life and music. Perhaps the best place to begin a study of Berg.

Jarman, Douglas. *Alban Berg: "Wozzeck."* Cambridge, England: Cambridge University Press, 1989. An in-depth analysis of Berg's first opera that includes background information about Büchner and his play *Woyzeck*, musical analysis, information about the opera's premiere and subsequent performances, reviews both favorable and unfavorable, and writings by Berg himself.

Perle, George. *Wozzeck*. Vol. 1 in *The Operas of Alban Berg*. Berkeley: University of California Press, 1980. An excellent, detailed study that includes much background information. Also, however, contains careful musical analysis that will be over the heads of readers who are unschooled in music.

Redlich, H. F. *Alban Berg: The Man and His Music*. New York: Abelard-Schuman, 1957. A fine volume that is divided into four parts. The first discusses "The Second Viennese School" and "The Problem of Tonality." The second examines Berg's music in detail, and the third consists of a brief biography of Berg. The fourth is a section of appendices that includes Berg's lecture on *Wozzeck* and Schoenberg's brief reminiscences of Berg.

Reich, Willi. *Alban Berg*. Reprint. New York: Vienna House, 1974. An insightful biographical and musical study that is all the more interesting for having been written by a man who knew Berg well. Personal reminiscences and insights make this book extremely useful.

Shawn Woodyard

Cross-References

Schoenberg Breaks with Tonality (1908), p. 193; Webern's *Six Pieces for Large Orchestra* Premieres in Vienna (1913), p. 367; Schoenberg Develops His Twelve-Tone System (1921), p. 528; Berg's *Lulu* Opens in Zurich (1937), p. 1078; Boulez's *Le Marteau sans maître* Premieres in Baden-Baden (1955), p. 1656.

THE BOOK-OF-THE-MONTH CLUB AND THE LITERARY GUILD ARE FOUNDED

Category of event: Literature
Time: 1926
Locale: New York, New York

The success of the Book-of-the-Month Club and the Literary Guild revolutionized the publishing, sales, and reading of books in the United States

Principal personages:
HARRY SCHERMAN (1887-1969), the moving force behind the founding and success of the Book-of-the-Month Club (BOMC)
MAXWELL SACKHEIM (1890-1982), a cofounder of the BOMC
ROBERT K. HAAS (1890?-1964), a founding partner of the BOMC and its first president
HENRY SEIDEL CANBY (1878-1961), the founder and editor of the *Saturday Review of Literature* and the first chair of the BOMC board of judges
SAMUEL CRAIG (1874-1960), the man responsible for launching the Literary Guild of America
HAROLD K. GUINZBURG (1900-1961), Craig's partner in founding the Literary Guild
NELSON DOUBLEDAY (1889-1949), a publishing magnate who purchased the Literary Guild in 1934

Summary of Event

The modern book club emerged in the United States during the 1920's because of a complex of supporting conditions. Prosperity was one; another was a shortening of the work week that gave at least some segments of the population more leisure time. Even more important was the dramatic increase in the size of the reading public resulting from the rapid expansion of high school and college enrollments. The simultaneous growth in the number of titles published annually meant that would-be readers needed, or at least wanted, guidance to select the best books available.

The father of the modern book club, Harry Scherman, was born in 1887 in Montreal, Canada. When he was two, the family moved to Philadelphia. After his laborer father abandoned the family, his mother had to struggle to keep the family going. While still in high school, Scherman began to do free-lance writing for local newspapers. After briefly attending the University of Pennsylvania, he became in 1907 a reporter for a New York City weekly. In 1912, he left to devote himself full-time to free-lance work in journalism and advertising. In 1913, he joined the newly established advertising agency of Ruthrauff and Ryan, writing copy for direct-mail sales. The following year, he was hired by the direct-mail department of the J. Walter Thompson advertising agency.

In 1916, Scherman joined with the brothers Charles and Albert Boni in launching a series of low-priced reprints of the classics to be known as the Little Leather Library. Later, the Bonis sold their interest to Scherman and Maxwell Sackheim, an advertising copywriter who had worked at the Thompson agency with Scherman. When sales through retail stores began to fall off, Scherman and Sackheim decided to shift the focus of their sales efforts to mail order. Recognizing that the key to a successful mail-order business was finding a repeat-sale gimmick, they borrowed from the magazine-subscription business the idea of a Book-of-the-Week Club to provide subscribers with a classic each week for five dollars a year. The Book-of-the-Week Club faltered until Robert K. Haas, who had been working for the mail-order division of J. Walter Thompson, joined the operation. His aggressive promotional efforts boosted sales of the Little Leather Library to 48 million copies by 1925.

Foreseeing saturation of the market for the classics, Scherman reasoned that if millions of Americans could be persuaded to buy classics through the mail, they could be persuaded to buy current books the same way. The upshot was the organization of the Book-of-the-Month Club (BOMC) in February, 1926, with capital of $40,000. Haas put up half this amount and was made president of the corporation; Scherman and Sackheim each put up a quarter of the amount. Subscribers would agree to buy one new book per month for a year, at full retail price plus postage. The most important innovation was the formation of a selection committee, or board of judges, to guide customers in choosing from the multitude of titles coming out. The board was promised a free hand in selecting the "book of the month" without any interference from management; the only limitation was that the price could be no higher than three dollars. Board members would write comments upon the selection for a monthly newsletter called the *Book-of-the-Month Club News* and would choose a list of alternatives for which subscribers could exchange the monthly selection if, after its receipt, they found that book not to their liking.

As a contemporary reader aptly observed, the BOMC's board of judges "carried the stamp of culture without being too frighteningly highbrow." Its first chairman, and most influential member until his retirement in 1955, was the founder and editor of the *Saturday Review of Literature*, Henry Seidel Canby. The others making up the five-person board were two popular novelists, Dorothy Canfield Fisher and Christopher Morley, along with two of the country's most famous and respected journalists, Heywood Broun and William Allen White. The BOMC promised to deliver, conveniently and with certainty, the important current books that a knowledgable person would choose if given the time. The BOMC's advertising simultaneously underlined the social benefits that subscribers would gain by staying up to date with the latest in the world of culture. The approach brought almost immediate success. The BOMC's first selection, Sylvia Townsend Warner's *Lolly Willowes*, was sent out to 4,750 members in April, 1926. By the end of the year, membership had climbed to more than forty-six thousand.

In 1928, Sackheim sold his quarter interest in the BOMC to Scherman for $150,000 and left publishing to become vice president of a Cleveland-based wire and fence company. In 1931, Haas left to study economics at Columbia University, but he would later return to publishing as a partner in the Random House firm. Scherman took over as president of the BOMC, retaining that position until moving to chairman in 1950. He was succeeded as president by a longtime associate, Meredith Wood. Although the BOMC went public with its stock in 1946, Scherman and members of his family continued to hold a majority of the shares. The board of judges had similar continuity. Although Broun died in 1939, he was not immediately replaced. Only after White died in 1944 were the novelist John P. Marquand and literary critic and anthologizer Clifton Fadiman named to fill the two openings. Later replacements included drama critic John Mason Brown and Columbia University classics professor Gilbert Highet.

The club's major competitor, the Literary Guild, was founded the same year as the BOMC as the brainchild of Samuel Craig. Craig would later claim that he had first drawn up the plan for the Literary Guild in 1922 but had failed to attract the requisite capital. Heartened by reports about the success of the German book guilds that had been established after World War I to distribute low-priced reprints of the classics, Craig revived his plan, linked up with the cofounder of Viking Press, Harold K. Guinzburg, and incorporated in late 1926 as the Literary Guild of America. Like Scherman, Craig arranged for a jury of experts to make selections. The jury's chairman was the respected literary critic Carl Van Doren; the other members were the novelist Zona Gale, the poet Elinor Wylie, and the drama critic Joseph Wood Krutch. University of Wisconsin president Glenn Frank and popular historian Hendrik Willem Van Loon were soon added. Like BOMC subscribers, Literary Guild subscribers would receive twelve books a year; the difference was that the cost would be only eighteen dollars (later raised to twenty-one dollars) a year, including delivery.

The Literary Guild's first selection—sent out in March, 1927—was Heywood Broun and Margaret Leech's debunking biography of Anthony Comstock. What did most to publicize the Literary Guild, however, was its June, 1927, selection of *Trader Horn*, which went on to become one of the best-sellers of 1927 and 1928. The Guild's membership reached more than forty-one thousand by the time of its twelfth selection. By then, Craig had left because of a dispute over policy, leaving Guinzburg in full charge. Learning that its members were attracted more by the low price of its books than by the jury method of selection, the Literary Guild began in the summer of 1929 to deemphasize the jury-selection aspect in its advertising. That same year, Nelson Doubleday, the president of Doubleday, Doran and Company, bought a forty-nine percent interest in the Literary Guild. In 1934, he bought the rest of the stock. He began to screen publishers' submissions for the jury; three years later, the Literary Guild abandoned the jury method of selection. Under Doubleday's management, the Literary Guild would specialize in the mass marketing of light, escapist fiction to nonbookish customers.

Impact of Event

The pressure of competition—first from the Literary Guild, then from new, low-priced publishers' lines spawned by the Depression—led the BOMC to adopt changes in the late 1920's and the 1930's that became standard policy for book clubs. The subscription contract was modified to require the purchase of only four books a year. The exchange policy was replaced with the practice of allowing subscribers to refuse a selection or order an alternate selection in advance of the shipping date. A free book was offered as a premium to attract new members. A "book dividend" plan gave a free book to members who purchased four books a year. First occasionally, then more regularly, the price of selections was cut below list. The BOMC had started out purchasing regular-edition copies of its selections from publishers at a discount. To cut its costs, the BOMC instituted in 1930 the practice of giving publishers a flat payment for the plates to run off its own editions of books. The savings were so large that in mid-1945, the BOMC would give away seventy-five cents in free books for every dollar taken in.

The formula was so successful that the BOMC continued to grow despite the Depression. Its most rapid expansion occurred during and immediately after World War II, with membership reaching almost 900,000 by 1946. The typical BOMC member was a relatively well-off, youngish college graduate. Appealing to what appeared a less sophisticated audience, the Literary Guild came to pass the BOMC in membership. In 1946, the two organizations combined distributed in paid copies, dividends, and bonuses approximately seventy-five million books, or one book for every two Americans. At first, most booksellers and even many publishers angrily accused the clubs of unfair competition. Publishers, however, could not resist the large sale guarantees offered by the clubs. Even booksellers came to accept that selection by a major book club boosted a title's sales through retail stores.

Intellectuals and devotees of the avant-garde have accused book clubs of hostility to experimentation, of standardizing taste at the middlebrow level and thereby undermining, rather than promoting, cultural values. These complaints were exaggerated, at least in regard to the BOMC. While the BOMC judges made their share of mistakes, their selections included works by the leading writers of the time—including Nobel Prize winners Sinclair Lewis, John Galsworthy, Thomas Mann, George Bernard Shaw, Pearl Buck, Ernest Hemingway, and Eugene O'Neill. At the same time, the BOMC came more and more to offer to its readers works on important current issues, biographies, and history. In 1948, the BOMC made a deal with the Metropolitan Museum of Art to distribute the museum's sets of full-color miniature reproductions of great works of art. By 1956, the club had distributed more than five million sets. In 1958, the BOMC arranged with RCA Victor to launch the RCA Victor Society of Great Music "to help serious lovers of music build up a fine record library."

The success of the BOMC and the Literary Guild immediately attracted a host of imitators. Some—such as the short-lived Book League of America launched by Literary Guild founder Samuel Craig in 1928—aspired to compete with the big two for the general reader. The more lasting imitators, though, were geared to a specialized niche in the market. One of the most successful was the Religious Book

Club, founded in 1927. The following year saw the beginning of Doubleday's Crime Club. There was even a Limited Editions Club to distribute deluxe reprints of classics. In the years following World War II, the number of book clubs proliferated at an accelerated pace to appeal to an ever-larger array of tastes, interests, and occupational specialties. By the 1970's, there would be more than a hundred book club companies, many operating several different clubs. Total membership was estimated at more than seven million.

Bibliography

Lee, Charles. *The Hidden Public: The Story of the Book-of-the-Month Club.* Garden City, N.Y.: Doubleday, 1958. An admiring account written with BOMC cooperation, but indispensable because of its information about the club's inner operations and finances.

Madison, Charles A. *Book Publishing in America.* New York: McGraw-Hill, 1966. A handy brief survey that deals only sketchily with the book clubs but that shows the larger context of the commercialization of literature.

Radway, Janice. "The Scandal of the Middlebrow: The Book-of-the-Month Club, Class Fracture, and Cultural Authority." *South Atlantic Quarterly* 89 (Fall, 1990): 703-736. An illuminating examination of the attacks on the BOMC for its middlebrowism.

Rubin, Joan Shelley. *The Making of Middlebrow Culture.* Chapel Hill: University of North Carolina Press, 1992. Explores the role of the BOMC in shaping American culture. Includes excellent analyses of the themes featured in BOMC advertising and the values of the BOMC judges.

Tebbel, John. *A History of Book Publishing in the United States.* 4 vols. New York: R. R. Bowker, 1972-1981. Much information not readily available elsewhere, but also a nearly unreadable mass of ill-digested facts. The treatment of the book clubs is in volumes 3 and 4.

John Braeman

Cross-References

Wallace Founds *Reader's Digest* (1922), p. 549; Luce Founds *Time* Magazine (1923), p. 577; Ross Founds *The New Yorker* (1925), p. 648; Luce Launches *Life* Magazine (1936), p. 1031; The Great Books Foundation Is Established (1947), p. 1351.

KEATON'S *THE GENERAL* IS RELEASED

Category of event: Motion pictures
Time: 1926
Locale: The United States

At the apogee of an arc of creativity that produced ten films between 1923 and 1928, Buster Keaton directed and acted the principal role in the great silent comedy The General

Principal personages:
BUSTER KEATON (1895-1966), a master of physical comedy and an innovative genius whose achievements in silent film rank with those of Charlie Chaplin and Harold Lloyd
JOSEPH M. SCHENCK (1878-1961), a film producer who supported Keaton and gave him the creative freedom to thrive

Summary of Event

Although Buster Keaton's career as a filmmaker began with a kind of apprenticeship to Roscoe "Fatty" Arbuckle in 1917 and continued into the 1960's, the work Keaton did as an actor and director in the mid-1920's is at the core of his achievement as a film artist. Beginning with the moderately amusing *The Three Ages* in 1923, Keaton made a series of silent comedies that demonstrated the range of possibility of the medium. *Our Hospitality* (1923), *Sherlock Jr.* (1924), *The Navigator* (1924), *Seven Chances* (1925), *Go West* (1925), *Battling Butler* (1926), and *The General* (1926) are the heart of a body of work (including *College* in 1927 and *Steamboat Bill Jr.* in 1928) that exhibits a style, philosophy, and technical proficiency achieved by only the greatest masters in any area of artistic achievement. When Keaton began work on *The General*, he had developed his skills as a director and actor in his previous films and was at a peak of energy and enthusiasm; he was also in his prime as an athlete. In addition, his relationship with his brother-in-law, producer Joseph Schenck, enabled him to work on a scale equal to his ambitions, and the striking authenticity of the period settings and decor of *The General* reflect Keaton's access to a production budget sufficient to his needs.

Schenck had formed a connection with the recently established United Artists distributing organization, a company designed to release the independently produced films of such notables as Charlie Chaplin, D. W. Griffith, and Douglas Fairbanks, and Schenk became the company's president in 1926. The organization needed films to release, and Schenck made a commitment to Keaton to distribute his next film, guaranteeing Keaton the kind of lavish budget to which Chaplin and Fairbanks were accustomed. Keaton had completed *Battling Butler* and was considering other projects when the writer Clyde Bruckman showed him a book entitled *The Great Locomotive Chase* (1868) by William Pittenger, an eyewitness account of a Civil War incident in which a small squad of Union raiders operating behind Confederate lines tried to steal a steam locomotive. The narrative had no comic qualities, but Bruckman knew the comic potential of any kind of chase, and Keaton was captivated by the idea of re-creating the appearance of the Civil War era. He was also intrigued by the chance to place a man in conjunction with a gigantic piece of machinery, one of Keaton's basic comic preoccupations. He asked Bruckman to be his assistant director and told him that he planned to spare no pains to make the film seem authentic.

Keaton and Bruckman originally intended to stage the film on its original location along the Alabama-Tennessee border, but they found no suitable railroad track left in the region and were refused permission to use the original locomotive, which was in a Chattanooga museum. Keaton then decided to make his film in Oregon, since, he later recalled, "the whole state is honey-combed with narrow-gauge railways for all the lumber mills." Keaton's chief technical assistant, Fred Gabourie, found sufficient rolling equipment to provide three locomotives and many freight cars. Keaton hired five hundred men from the Oregon National Guard to play soldiers, and seventeen railway carloads of equipment were shipped from Los Angeles. The crew was housed in tourist cars rented from the Union Pacific railroad, and the film was shot during June and July of 1926. Typically, Keaton was directly in charge of almost every aspect of the production. "Now this was my own story, my own continuity," he later commented. "I directed it, I cut it and titled it. So actually it was a pet."

Pittenger's original story was told from the Union point of view, but Keaton knew that, to make a comedy, he had to make the main character a sympathetic underdog. Keaton remarked that "You can always make villains out of the Northerners, but you cannot make a villain out of the South." His story was centered on an engineer named Johnnie Gray—an almost generic name for an American Southerner—who tries to enlist when war breaks out but is turned down, since his skills are needed to operate trains during the conflict. In the midst of typical comic confusion, his prospective bride, Annabelle Lee—whose name echoes Edgar Allan Poe's poetic vision of romantic innocence—rejects him as a coward. Gray is then involved in the double task of trying to win her back and to recapture his engine, the *General*, after Union spies seize them both. The first half of the picture involves Gray's pursuit of the Union troops on another locomotive, the *Texas*; in a symmetrical turn, the second half depicts Gray and Annabelle fleeing from the Union forces on the *General* while the *Texas* gives chase. The visual climax of the film occurs when the Union commander orders the *Texas* to cross a burning bridge to prevent Gray's escape. The bridge does not support the locomotive, and in one of the most expensive single takes to that point in film history (Schenck estimated the cost at forty-two thousand dollars), the locomotive falls into the river below, sending steam and debris across the screen. This stunning and still-effective moment is given a dramatic emphasis by Keaton's cut to the stunned expression on the face of the commander. The film moves from beginning to end with almost no breaks in time and uses only fifty subtitles, primarily in the earlier parts of the narrative; most eight-reel silent features used more than three hundred. Keaton was very pleased with his work, and he discussed the film enthusiastically for the rest of his life.

Impact of Event

In 1977, the American Film Institute asked its members to submit lists of the fifty greatest films produced in the United States. Only five films from the silent era were chosen—D. W. Griffith's *Intolerance* (1916) and *The Birth of a Nation* (1915), Charlie Chaplin's *The Gold Rush* (1925) and *City Lights* (1931), and Keaton's *The General.* Yet acclaim for Keaton's achievement was hardly immediate. The film was released in Christmas week in Los Angeles and then put into general release in February, 1928. Initial critical response was almost uniformly negative. Of the eleven New York newspapers that reviewed the film, eight were actively hostile, and only the *Brooklyn Daily Eagle* critic Martin Dickstein acknowledged Keaton's accomplishment. Even he felt it necessary to point out that the film would not seem funny for "lots of people," and *The New York Times'* critic Mordaunt Hall found it "by no means as good as Mr. Keaton's previous efforts." Another reviewer judged it "the least funny thing Keaton has ever done," and still another called it "a pretty trite and stodgy piece of screenfare" and observed that the audience responded with "occasionally a laugh, and occasionally a yawn."

Such an assessment of viewer reaction was generally accurate, since the film grossed $474,264, more than $300,000 less than the receipts for *Battling Butler.* The basic production costs of *The General* had exceeded $400,000, and United Artists took a considerable loss, since 1920's films did not become profitable until receipts totaled about twice the production cost. Keaton never publicly acknowledged his disappointment or even admitted that the film lost money, but he knew the figures and was under some pressure to succeed financially with his next effort. His creative freedom was curtailed by the experience, and Schenck essentially was responsible for the decision to make *College*, a film that resembled Harold Lloyd's very successful *The Freshman*, one of the most popular films of 1925. For the first time since *The Saphead* (1920), Keaton was not listed as director or codirector, and the words "Supervised by Harry Brand" on the credits meant that there was someone present to watch the budget during production.

When Keaton signed a contract with Metro-Goldwyn-Mayer (MGM) in 1928, a proviso to the agreement indicated that although Keaton would "be consulted as to story and direction," the decision of the producer would be final. This effectively ended the brief era in which Keaton made some of the finest comic films in motion-picture history. Yet while Keaton's career continued on a downward curve through the next three decades, reaching a nadir of sorts with cameo appearances in American International films such as *How to Stuff a Wild Bikini* (1965), his reputation gradually began to move in an opposite direction. In 1953, *The General* was selected to share a place of honor with Chaplin's new film *Limelight* (1952) at the coronation of Elizabeth II of England. When the Museum of Modern Art in New York presented an exhibition of United Artists films, *The General* was the only film that had to be shown more than once because of demand for tickets. By the 1960's, serious full-length academic studies of Keaton were appearing, especially in Europe. The turning point in the appreciation of Keaton's work can be traced to a famous essay by James Agee in the September 5, 1949, issue of *Life*. In the essay, "Comedy's Greatest Era," Agee discussed Keaton, Lloyd, Chaplin, and Harry Langdon. Although Agee devoted only a few pages to Keaton's work, his perceptions were so accurate and his prose so compelling and lucid that no one who read the article could look at a Keaton film without being struck by the truth of Agee's observations.

What Agee understood and described was that Keaton's finest films were not only great comic statements but also great filmmaking and, perhaps more crucially, great American art. The striking authenticity of *The General*'s sets, props, costumes, and milieu were as instrumental as Mathew Brady's photographs in projecting a sense of reality about the Civil War. Keaton's rare combination of almost Lincolnesque nobility, daunting handsomeness, and appealing friendliness is at the heart of his visual conception of Johnnie Gray, the underdog hero of *The General*. Gray's struggle to serve his country, win the hand of the woman he loves, overcome the forces of darkness, and amuse the audience is so engrossing that it is hard to understand how contemporary audiences in Keaton's time were not captivated. As some critics have observed, though, the film was so rich—such a mixture of comedy, adventure, suspense, and serious commentary about war—that its fusion of categories overwhelmed an audience unprepared by anything they had seen previously. Keaton had to instruct the filmgoers of the 1920's in the art of vision, and *The General* was part of a process that formed the film-literate public capable of appreciating Keaton's masterpiece.

The General displays Keaton's endless invention, his ability to link comic bits in a remarkably tight structure, his extraordinary capabilities as a physical performer, his feeling for the fascination and perplexity men and women experience in the presence of gigantic machines, his sensitivity to such cultural values as decency, modesty, resoluteness, quick wit, and courage, and ultimately, the generosity of spirit and humane qualities that are the essence of comic art. Because Keaton worked in celluloid rather than print or canvas, his accomplishments were undervalued at the time of their creation. In time, though, his genius was recognized, and his place among the giants of film history is secure.

Bibliography

Benayoun, Robert. *The Look of Buster Keaton*. Translated by Randall Conrad. New York: St. Martin's Press, 1982. An oversized glossy book. Benayoun combines somewhat esoteric, theoretical analysis with a wonderful collection of stills from Keaton films. An excellent filmography with a biographical outline complements the text.

Blesh, Rudi. *Keaton*. New York: Collier Books, 1966. An affectionate biography by one of Keaton's friends, including considerable inside information, anecdotes, and some critical analysis.

Dardis, Tom. *Keaton: The Man Who Wouldn't Lie Down*. New York: Charles Scribner's Sons, 1979. A good complement to the Blesh biography, written from a more distant perspective and utilizing additional information and interviews with some of Keaton's contemporaries. Includes a detailed filmography and some illustrative photography.

Mast, Gerald, and Marshall Cohen. *Film Theory and Criticism.* New York: Oxford University Press, 1974. Includes James Agee's landmark essay on film comedians, "Comedy's Greatest Era."

Moews, Daniel. *Keaton: The Silent Features Close Up.* Berkeley: University of California Press, 1977. Contains a lucid, extremely detailed analytical chapter on *The General* as well as a useful survey of Keaton scholarship.

Robinson, David. *Buster Keaton.* Bloomington: University of Indiana Press, 1969. A solid critical introduction to Keaton's films. Occasionally obtuse on aspects of American society, though, perhaps because of Robinson's British background.

Rubinstein, Elliot. *Filmguide to* The General. Bloomington: University of Indiana Press, 1973. Rubinstein attempts to be descriptive as well as explanatory while concentrating on the qualities that made Keaton a screen presence and a cinematic genius.

Leon Lewis

Cross-References

Sennett Defines the Slapstick Comedy Genre (1909), p. 230; *The Birth of a Nation* Popularizes New Film Techniques (1915), p. 402; Chaplin Produces His Masterpiece *The Gold Rush* (1925), p. 659; The Classic Screwball Comedy Reaches Its Height in Popularity (1934), p. 951.

HEMINGWAY'S *THE SUN ALSO RISES* SPEAKS
FOR THE LOST GENERATION

Category of event: Literature
Time: October 22, 1926
Locale: New York, New York, and Paris, France

The novel changed forever when Ernest Hemingway evoked the lives of disillusioned Lost Generation expatriates in a novel of brilliant dialogue and understated style

Principal personages:

ERNEST HEMINGWAY (1899-1961), an American journalist turned avant-garde author who captured life in expatriate Paris and Spain in a revolutionary prose style

GERTRUDE STEIN (1874-1946), an avant-garde author and hostess of a literary salon in Paris who influenced Hemingway's writing and provided an epigraph for his novel

F. SCOTT FITZGERALD (1896-1940), a best-selling author who touted Hemingway's work to mainstream publishers and whose work influenced *The Sun Also Rises*

MAXWELL PERKINS (1884-1947), an editor for the Scribner's publishing house, who recognized Hemingway's unique talents

Summary of Event

By October of 1925, Ernest Hemingway was identified as a rising literary star with the publication of his unified short-story collection *In Our Time*. Hemingway's collection alternated autobiographically derived stories of the Michigan woods and war-torn Europe with miniature pieces that seemed the distillation of prose fiction under the influence of the principles of the Imagist poets, who preached attention to the moment of perception and the presentation of poetic images in a minimum of words. The collection's title was taken from a line in the Book of Common Prayer: "Oh Lord, give us peace in our time." It was an impressive beginning to Hemingway's career as a popular but artistic writer, yet cementing his reputation required that he write in that most commercial but also most difficult of forms, the novel.

This would not be so easy. Hemingway had begun his literary efforts by burlesquing the sports fiction of Ring Lardner for his high school newspaper and had moved on to work as a cub reporter for the *Kansas City Star*. After being seriously wounded during a stint with the American Red Cross Ambulance Corps on the Italian front during World War I, he had written fiction unsuccessfully and then turned to journalism, becoming a foreign correspondent for the *Toronto Star* by the age of twenty-three. In the atmosphere of literary Paris, he had continued his efforts in fiction, internalizing the influences of such American literary expatriates as Gertrude Stein and Ezra Pound as well as of British novelists James Joyce and Ford Madox Ford. Yet his pieces seemed more like sketches than stories to many editors to whom he submitted them at the time, despite the fact that he was working with Stein's emphasis on psychological insight and the economy of language urged by the Imagist Pound. The subtlety of his achievements began to be realized in *In Our Time*, which also owed a considerable debt to American regionalist Sherwood Anderson's *Winesburg, Ohio* (1919).

Vacation trips from Paris to the religious and bullfighting fiesta in Pamplona, in the Basque Navarre region of northern Spain, provided the setting (and some of the characters) for *The Sun Also Rises*, which Hemingway began writing on or about his twenty-sixth birthday, July 21, 1925. For his participating narrator, he was indebted to the example of F. Scott Fitzgerald, whose classic short novel *The Great Gatsby* had appeared on April 10 of that year. He also would be indebted to Fitzgerald for his influential new editor, Maxwell Perkins of Scribner's, who at Fitzgerald's insistence lured Hemingway away from the publisher of *In Our Time*, Horace Liveright. Both Perkins and Fitzgerald would contribute valuable advice on the polishing of *The Sun Also Rises*. In particular, Fitzgerald counseled against a rambling, discursive introduction that attempted to explain rather than directly to present the characters and their situation; Perkins curbed Hemingway's satiric tendencies.

Like Fitzgerald's Nick Carraway, the narrator of *The Great Gatsby*, Hemingway's journalist-narrator Jake Barnes was a fairly ordinary person out of place among the fast-living set in which he traveled. Jake's sensational war wound (he has had his genitals shot away) and his thus doomed love affair with the alcoholic Lady Brett Ashley helped to assure the novel's notoriety and popular success, as did the sensational aspects of Brett's successive sexual alliances with a Jewish-American novelist, a bankrupt Scottish war veteran, and a young Spanish matador, affairs that Jake Barnes witnesses and sometimes abets. That many of these characters were based upon real people from Paris' colony of literary expatriates increased interest in what some critics saw as a story of meaningless drinking and fornication. An epigraph to the novel taken from Gertrude Stein, "You are all a lost generation," seemed to sum up the meaninglessness of it all. The epigraph certainly did name the rising young writers of the 1920's; they became known as the Lost Generation, wounded forever.

Still, the work struck a chord with readers who had experienced the war or its aftermath. It was for a time a campus fad in the United States, with young men adopting Jake Barnes's stoic persona, if not his sexual incapacity, the young women copying Brett Ashley's brilliant, tense conversation.

More important, attentive readers and critics recognized that there was more to the novel than a crude summary might indicate. It was not a popular potboiler but a literary work of art. Read perceptively, it was in many ways like a prose version of T. S. Eliot's resonant long poem *The Waste Land* (1922). In Eliot's modernist poem, meaning is sought in an exploration of civilization and history, both of the East and the West. Similarly, *The Sun Also Rises* is a quest for meaning in which the novel's main characters leave behind the modern world, broken by the world war, to travel to a seemingly more innocent, rural Spain. To these pilgrims, such sports as fishing and bullfighting marked a return to pre-Christian rituals of control and unity with the natural world. A parallel control is seen in Hemingway's prose style, in which dialogue is precisely rendered and in which description is designed not only to set a scene but also to evoke an emotional response on the part of the reader.

A major theme of the novel involves "knowing the values." At first, this seems merely a matter of knowing how much things cost. As the novel progresses, however, it becomes clear that the characters ultimately may be judged by how well they know real values, values that might have some hope of enduring even in a modern world in which all traditional, received values have lost their force. Such a view of the novel balances the Stein epigraph with the novel's second epigraph, taken from the Book of Ecclesiastes, which emphasizes the cyclical renewal of the Earth's promise: "One generation passeth away, and another generation cometh; but the earth abideth forever . . . The sun also ariseth . . ."

Impact of Event

The Sun Also Rises launched Hemingway's subsequent career as novelist, short-story writer, journalist, and public personage. That career took him to fame as the author of such American literary classics as *A Farewell to Arms* (1929), "The Snows of Kilimanjaro" (1936), "The Short Happy Life of Francis Macomber" (1936), *For Whom the Bell Tolls* (1940), and *The Old Man and the Sea* (1952). As a public figure, he was often somewhat misidentified as a macho man: World War I veteran, big-game hunter and deep-sea fisherman, amateur boxer, war correspondent in the Spanish Civil War and World War II, connoisseur of fine food and drink, world traveler. He was all these things, but unlike the reputation that sometimes seemed to imprison him personally as he grew older, his fiction often made clear the psychic cost of such roles to twentieth century man.

His protagonists, including Jake Barnes, usually are vulnerable men, wounded psychically if not physically. Their plight is often seen as existential in nature, a matter of discovering how to live day to day when conventional structures of meaning have lost their power to compel belief. They also are usually American innocents meeting the far from innocent world and finding they have lost the ability to return to the innocent America in which they were nurtured. Yet, over time, Hemingway continues to chart his heroes' search for meaning. Jake Barnes finds it in work. The hero of *A Farewell to Arms*, a World War I deserter, places all his belief in the woman he loves—and loses her, ending the novel wandering the streets alone. The protagonist of *For Whom the Bell Tolls* begins as a loner, a saboteur in the Spanish Civil War, yet finds by novel's end that "no man is an island" and sacrifices himself in the cause of humanity. Santiago, the impoverished Cuban fisherman of *The Old Man and the Sea*, suffers months without a catch yet survives his greatest defeat with dignity and optimism. In Hemingway's work, some meaning finally is found.

In addition to describing the modern dilemma, Hemingway influenced and reshaped Americans' way of writing. Hemingway's skill in dialogue and narration (for which he admitted a debt to Mark Twain's 1884 *The Adventures of Huckleberry Finn*) and his artistic integrity made him a hero and model to American writers, ranging from Dorothy Parker to Norman Mailer, who wished to tell the truth without hiding behind conventional literary devices and values. Hemingway's apparently simple sentences and clarity of style influenced writers for magazines as apparently diverse as *The New Yorker* and the pulps; hard-boiled detective fiction owes him a considerable debt for its manner and subject matter. The Beat Generation writers of the 1950's who went "on the road" in America and abroad in a sense were following in the footsteps of Jake Barnes and his friends. Indeed, Hemingway's influence on modern writers, particularly in style, is so ingrained and nearly ubiquitous as to seem invisible, save to literary scholars comparing the mainstream writing that went before and that followed his work. His emphasis on the value of the ordinary person and ordinary experiences—a part of a line of influence passing through Mark Twain and Gertrude Stein—continues to have its effect as well.

Bibliography

Baker, Carlos. *Ernest Hemingway: A Life Story.* New York: Charles Scribner's Sons, 1969. The standard full-length biography of Hemingway and still the best introduction to Hemingway's life.

Bruccoli, Matthew J. *Scott and Ernest: The Fitzgerald/Hemingway Friendship.* Carbondale: Southern Illinois University Press, 1978. Pays primary attention to the personal aspects of the famous friendship, but also discusses Hemingway's literary debts to Fitzgerald, who read and commented upon *The Sun Also Rises* before publication. Long quotations from a number of the authors' letters to each other are included.

Griffin, Peter. *Less Than a Treason: Hemingway in Paris.* New York: Oxford University Press, 1990. Less a biography than an imaginative re-creation of Hemingway's life in Paris, this book evokes the spirit of creation in the 1920's. Its weakness is in sometimes blurring the distinction between Hemingway's life and his writings.

Hemingway, Ernest. *A Moveable Feast.* New York: Scribner's, 1964. Published posthumously, this highly fictionalized memoir of the life of Hemingway as a young artist in 1920's Paris makes clear the dedication that he felt to his art. It accounts of his relationships with Gertrude Stein, F. Scott Fitzgerald, and others are best taken with a grain of salt so far as the facts are concerned, but they cannot be overlooked for their emotional resonances.

The Hemingway Review 6, no. 1 (Fall, 1986). A special issue devoted to *The Sun Also Rises* that includes articles addressing questions of religion, the treatment of women, and bullfighting in a reader's understanding of the novel. Also gives accounts of the novel's composition, Hemingway's use of language, and the reactions of a more traditional writer, Western novelist Owen Wister, to the book's subject matter.

Reynolds, Michael S. *Hemingway: The Paris Years.* New York: Basil Blackwell, 1989. A meticulous re-creation of Hemingway and his life in Europe during the composition of *In Our Time* and *The Sun Also Rises.* Includes detailed maps and chronology.

_____. *"The Sun Also Rises": A Novel of the Twenties.* Boston: Twayne, 1989. An evaluation and close reading of the novel in the context of its time. Particularly good at explaining how to avoid common misreadings of Hemingway's book and in explaining many of the subtleties involved in coming to a full understanding of the novel.

Sarason, Bertram. *Hemingway and the Sun Set.* Washington, D.C.: NCR Microcard Editions, 1972. Sarason's study is a good guide to *The Sun Also Rises* as *roman à clef.* Discusses the novel's many sources among the real people of Paris whose characteristics Hemingway adapted in constructing his fictional characters.

Svoboda, Frederic. *Hemingway and "The Sun Also Rises": The Crafting of a Style.* Lawrence: University Press of Kansas, 1983. Analyzes the composition of Hemingway's novel and the development of his prose style through the examination of its manuscript drafts and revisions. A number of facsimiles of manuscript pages are included, as is the text of the first chapters cut from the novel at Fitzgerald's urging.

Wagner-Martin, Linda, ed. *New Essays on "The Sun Also Rises."* Cambridge: Cambridge University Press, 1987. A useful collection of much recent commentary, which has tended to discount the macho Hemingway reputation in favor of discovering what of his work will stand rigorous literary scrutiny.

Frederic Svoboda

Cross-References

Stein Holds Her First Paris Salons (1905), p. 129; The Imagist Movement Shakes Up Poetry (1912), p. 326; Eliot Publishes *The Waste Land* (1922), p. 539; Joyce's *Ulysses* Epitomizes Modernism in Fiction (1922), p. 555; *The Great Gatsby* Captures the Essence of the Roaring Twenties (1925), p. 626; *The Maltese Falcon* Introduces the Hard-Boiled Detective Novel (1929), p. 793; *The Sound and the Fury* Launches Faulkner's Career (1929), p. 805.

KULESHOV AND PUDOVKIN INTRODUCE MONTAGE TO FILMMAKING

Category of event: Motion pictures
Time: 1927
Locale: Moscow, Union of Soviet Socialist Republics

Lev Kuleshov and his pupil Vsevolod Pudovkin through their experimental work, theoretical writings, and films by 1927 brought Soviet cinema to a high level of achievement

Principal personages:

LEV VLADIMIROVICH KULESHOV (1899-1970), an influential film theoretician and director, the acclaimed father of Soviet cinema

VSEVOLOD ILLARIONOVICH PUDOVKIN (1893-1953), an actor, director, and film theoretician, a true virtuoso whose films and writings continue to inspire

SERGEI EISENSTEIN (1898-1948), an extraordinary director and film theoretician whose creative and literary work ranks among the finest achievements in world cinema

DZIGA VERTOV (DENIS KAUFMAN, 1896-1954), the pioneer innovator of Soviet newsreel and documentary film, who believed true film-art showed life as it really was

VLADIMIR ILICH LENIN (VLADIMIR ILICH ULYANOV, 1870-1924), a Russian revolutionary leader and first Soviet premier, who encouraged the rapid growth of cinema for political and educational purposes

Summary of Event

By 1927, the tenth anniversary of the Bolshevik Revolution, Soviet cinema had reached the pinnacle of international success. Filmmakers formulated their basic doctrines and theories, guiding the young film industry with the support and approval of the government. Cinema, thus encouraged, developed as a singular art form, with its own principles and aesthetics, different from other art. Filmmakers rose to the challenge by creating films both politically pleasing and invigorated with artistic dynamism.

Ten years earlier, in March, 1917, the czar was replaced by a provisional government headed by Aleksandr Kerensky. The government moved to abolish film censorship and even permitted production of anticzarist pictures. In October of that same year, the Bolsheviks, headed by Vladimir Ilich Lenin, overthrew the government, and the Soviet era began. Lenin was acutely aware of the importance of cinema in spreading the development of Communism and consolidating his power among the vast population. He declared, "Of all the arts for us the cinema is the most important." He created a formula that came to be known as "Lenin's proportion," which established a ratio of entertainment movies to such educational movies as travelogues, studies of cultures, and anticapitalist statements that could be played at Soviet cinemas.

Although Lenin had in mind a cinema specializing in agitation and propaganda, two individuals emerged who changed the projected course of Soviet cinema. The first was Dziga Vertov, now hailed as the father of Soviet newsreel and documentary film. Born Denis Kaufman (brother of noted filmmakers Boris and Mikhail Kaufman), he took the name of Dziga Vertov, which in Russian means "spinning top," a reference to the action of winding film. His success came through clever editing and camera manipulation. Vertov gathered together and inspired a number of documentarists who believed life should be filmed as it really is, not staged with a narrative format. The group called itself Kinoki ("cinema eyes"). They believed fictional films were unimportant, opium for the masses.

The other seminal individual in Soviet motion pictures was Lev Kuleshov. Heavily influenced and inspired by American film-editing techniques, particularly the work of D. W. Griffith, Kuleshov realized that film was a plastic art form that could be manipulated by a filmmaker. He used experiments to prove that film must be edited and constructed frame by frame. Taking Griffith's epic 1916 masterpiece *Intolerance*, with its four interlocking stories, he completely re-edited the footage into very different combinations.

In one of Kuleshov's best-known film experiments, two people—a man and a woman in two separate shots—are seen walking in different districts of Moscow. In a third shot, they meet, shake hands, and look off in the distance as the man points. The fourth shot shows the American White House followed by the final shot, the couple climbing the steps of a famous Moscow cathedral. Through five different shots taken at different times and places, Kuleshov created a cinematic illusion of spatial and temporal unity. In another example, he photographed various parts of different women, then cut the film in such a way as to synthesize a new entity. Perhaps his most famous experiment involved using the expressionless face of matinee idol Ivan Mozhukin. Kuleshov intercut it with shots of a bowl of borscht, a dead woman in a coffin, and a girl playing with a toy bear. In each case, the audience raved about the power of Mozhukin's acting. He was pensive in the first, sorrowful in the second, and smiling in the third.

Kuleshov, through such experiments, slowly formulated the concept that became known as the "Kuleshov effect." Kuleshov argued that a film shot has two values: its own photographic image of reality, and what it acquires when spliced next to another shot. To Kuleshov, editing, or "montage," was the key to cinema, because it subordinated time and space and could also be used symbolically on a nonliteral level.

Kuleshov gathered into his workshop some of Soviet cinema's brightest filmmakers: Sergei Eisenstein, Boris Barnet, Mikhail Kalatzov, and Yakov Protazanov. The brilliant Eisenstein, in particular, although he studied only briefly with Kuleshov (and also worked briefly with Vertov), launched a remarkable film career based on montage. Kuleshov's special disciple, however, and the one most associated and influenced by his work, was Vsevolod Pudovkin, who collaborated with his teacher on a number of experimental film projects. Pudovkin was six years older than his professor and had originally studied to be a chemist. His primary goal was to become an actor, but Kuleshov expected his students to learn all aspects of cinema. Pudovkin was an eager pupil and quickly assimilated Kuleshov's important concepts. He was particularly fascinated by the way a film performance could be manipulated via skillful editing.

Pudovkin's scientific training and his dramatic visual sense prompted him to become a director. He gained experience working on Kuleshov's films before embarking on his own. Pudovkin created three silent masterpieces of the 1920's, *Mother* (1926), *The End of St. Petersburg* (1927), and *The Heir to Ghengis Khan* (1928). His appeal in all three was directly to the audience's emotions, and he kept his story lines simple and powerful, in contrast to his fellow filmmaker Eisenstein, whose work seemed detached and intellectual. Kuleshov remained proud of both his pupils and found much to admire in their creative work.

Impact of Event

In 1926, Kuleshov abandoned his workshop to become involved with a project that became his most important film, *By the Law*. The film was adapted from a short story by Jack London entitled "The Unexpected" and was made on one of the smallest budgets in Soviet cinema history. It was set in a one-room cabin in a desolate part of the Yukon. The story line concerns justice and how two people must try, condemn, and execute a third person who murdered their friends. *By the Law* is economical and polished in style; artistically, it implies social criticism. Kuleshov cleverly used montage to create a remarkable film that achieved international success when released in December of that year.

The same year, Pudovkin was emerging as a self-confident artist and began the first of his three revolutionary films, *Mother*, based on a Maxim Gorky novel that takes place during the 1905 revolution. The story is about a poor peasant woman married to a brutal drunkard, and their son. Father and son come to blows over differing political views, and the father is killed. The mother naïvely betrays her son to the authorities, and he is sentenced in a rigged trial. Mother helps him to escape jail, and later both unite and are killed at a workers' demonstration held on May Day. Pudovkin edited the film brilliantly, creating breathtaking montage effects; the film always stays in touch with the human drama unfolding underneath the great moments of history.

Pudovkin also found time in 1926 to write two books on filmmaking that helped to clarify the Kuleshov-Pudovkin concept of montage. He restated Kuleshov's basic premise that films are not "shot" but are artistically "built" from separate strips. Both artists discovered that individual film clips become part of a larger form with intrinsic structural unity and effectiveness. Pudovkin stated that the key process was actually one of a cognitive "linkage" of frames. In his films, he intercut images in exciting new ways, arranging them on a metaphysical as well as narrative level, clearly showing his indebtedness to Kuleshov. Pudovkin stressed the story, keeping it simple and clear; his attitude was personal and emotional. He used fluid narrative editing and used shock montage effects sparingly. His handling of actors was brilliant, and his films are memorable for their performances. He excelled in using montage to contrast the horrible brutality of wars with the idealism that fuels them.

By 1927, both Kuleshov and Pudovkin, through their experiments, writings, and films employing the principle of montage, had had a decided impact on Soviet and world cinema. Their editorial concepts opened up the artistic possibilities of film. Filmmakers could now manipulate what the audience experienced, enabling them to elicit certain emotions, associations, and thoughts. Kuleshov and Pudovkin not only demonstrated theoretically their concepts of montage but also created masterpieces of early Soviet cinema.

In 1927, Pudovkin made the film that won him an international reputation, *The End of St. Petersburg*, which had the distinction of being the first Soviet film to play in New York City at Broadway's largest theater, the Roxy. Through the eyes of a peasant, the film shows the historic events that rocked Russia from 1912 to 1917, when it was transformed from czarist to Soviet rule. Pudovkin graphically showed how his hero radically changes from a bumbling youth to a mature man aware of his country's suffering. The director intercut the hysteria of the czarist stock-market exchange with the hysteria found on the battlefield. When the peasant enters Leningrad, he is viewed from above the building, as though he is an ant, but by picture's end, the camera is on the ground looking up at him. One breathtaking sequence shows a midlevel bureaucrat in an elevator with a tycoon promising a great promotion. As the elevator rises, the light changes, and the toady's smile grows as he rises to the top; the scene stands as a brilliant testament to the montage theories of Kuleshov and Pudovkin.

By the end of 1927, the first decade of the Soviet Union was over. There was much to celebrate in the film industry. Soviet filmmakers, inspired by Kuleshov, were producing exciting and celebrated films. Montage was being employed in new and innovative ways. Important theoretical developments in the cinema had been established and encouraged because they played an important role in promoting the revolution. The aim was to build a glorious Communist future. Pudovkin wrote that when "the old and familiar artistic methods crumbled and collapsed. . . . Lev Kuleshov forced us to acquire visual taste and taught us the ABC of montage."

The honeymoon of state and art would not last. Joseph Stalin had assumed complete power after Lenin's death, and by the end of 1927, he was moving to consolidate his hold over the Communist Party. Stalin grew increasingly suspicious of criticism, particularly from the cinema, which was forced to eschew artistic concerns and was pressured into creating pictures for the working classes. No wonder, then, that both Kuleshov and Pudovkin would never again achieve their original critical success and even, along with Eisenstein, fall into political disfavor. Yet during the mid-1920's they created a vital cinematic language that invigorated the screen and made the Soviet cinema the envy of the world.

Bibliography

Birkos, Alexander S. *Soviet Cinema: Directors and Films.* Hamden, Conn.: Archon Books, 1976. Study is divided into two comprehensive and alphabetized sections focusing on Soviet cinema from 1918 to 1975. The first part examines the creative lives of the important directors; part two concerns the important films released during the period. Encyclopedic approach, with a good short introduction to the subject.

Dickinson, Thorold, and Catherine De La Roche. *Soviet Cinema.* New York: Arno Press, 1972. A short study pairing two essays by different critics, one on silent film and the other on sound. Illustrated with many photographs.

Feldman, Seth R. *Evolution of Style in the Early Work of Dziga Vertov.* New York: Arno Press, 1975. Dissertation on Vertov's pioneering work and his important place in Soviet cinema. Examines political, historic, and aesthetic concerns as they relate to Vertov's theories.

Kuleshov, Lev. *Kuleshov on Film: Writings by Lev Kuleshov.* Edited and translated by Ronald Levaco. Berkeley: University of California Press, 1974. Kuleshov's essays reveal him to be cinema's first aesthetic theorist. Levaco, through his essay selection, translation, and editing of Kuleshov's writings, has transformed Kuleshov from a shadowy figure to a director with a unique place in Soviet cinema.

Leyda, Jay. *Kino: A History of the Russian and Soviet Film.* London: Allen & Unwin, 1960. Classic study of Russian/Soviet cinema that gives a marvelous overview, beginning with the screening of films in 1896 through the revolution, the great achievements in the 1920's, the repressive Stalinist era and the resurgence following Stalin's death.

Pudovkin, V. I. *Film Technique and Film Acting.* Translated by Ivor Montagu. London: Vision Press, 1954. Pudovkin's two studies on cinema are as important as any of his films and are considered classics both by filmmakers and scholars. He openly acknowledges Kuleshov as his mentor.

Schnitzer, Luda, Jean Schnitzer, and Marcel Martin, eds. *Cinema in Revolution: The Heroic Era of the Soviet Film.* New York: Da Capo Press, 1973. Excellent collection of twelve essays by the leading Soviet filmmakers, including Kuleshov, Vertov, Eisenstein, Pudovkin, and Alexander Dovzhenko.

Taylor, Richard. *Film Propaganda: Soviet Russia and Nazi Germany.* New York: Barnes & Noble, 1979. Study demonstrates the significance of propaganda in twentieth century politics and the controlled way cinema has been used. Less useful than other studies, the book offers a limited look at Soviet film achievement.

Vertov, Dziga. *Kino-Eye: The Writings of Dziga Vertov.* Edited by Annette Michelson. Berkeley: University of California Press, 1984. Valuable collection of Vertov's work, gathered from his articles, public addresses, notebooks, diaries, creative projects, and proposals. Good introductory section by the editor, who includes Vertov's filmography.

Vorontsov, Iu, and Igor Rachuk. *The Phenomenon of the Soviet Cinema.* Translated by Doris Bradbury. Moscow: Progress Publishers, 1980. Politically correct Soviet interpretation of cinema from its origins through the 1970's. Includes chapters on Soviet audiences, films shown abroad, and a good alphabetized filmography to close the work.

Terry Theodore

Cross-References

Le Voyage dans la lune Introduces Special Effects (1902), p. 57; *The Great Train Robbery* Introduces New Editing Techniques (1903), p. 74; *The Birth of a Nation* Popularizes New Film Techniques (1915), p. 402; *The Cabinet of Dr. Caligari* Opens in Berlin (1920), p. 486; Eisenstein's *Potemkin* Introduces New Film Editing Techniques (1925), p. 615; Gance's *Napoléon* Revolutionizes Filmmaking Techniques (1925), p. 642; Buñuel and Dalí Champion Surrealism in *Un Chien andalou* (1928), p. 750.

LANG EXPANDS THE LIMITS OF FILMMAKING WITH *METROPOLIS*

Category of event: Motion pictures
Time: 1927
Locale: Berlin, Germany

Fritz Lang's Metropolis *used boldly innovative cinematic techniques to tell a story that blended futuristic science fiction with nineteenth century melodrama and prophetic social criticism*

Principal personages:

FRITZ LANG (1890-1976), an Austrian filmmaker who developed a visually dynamic cinematic style while exploring humanity's compulsions

THEA VON HARBAU (1888-1954), a novelist and screenwriter whom Lang married in 1922 and who collaborated with Lang on a number of films

KARL FREUND (1890-1969), the cinematographer who helped create the elaborate and innovative visual style of *Metropolis*

GÜNTHER RITTAU (1893-1971), the assistant cinematographer for *Metropolis*

EUGEN SCHÜFFTAN (1893-1977), the special photographic effects artist for *Metropolis* who invented his "Schüfftan Process" for the film

OTTO HUNTE (1881-1949?), the head set designer for *Metropolis*

Summary of Event

In 1924, Fritz Lang journeyed from Germany to the United States with the intention of touring American film studios in New York and Hollywood. Lang had already achieved critical acclaim as an innovative filmmaker with such films as the spy thriller *Dr. Mabuse der Spieler* (1922; *Dr. Mabuse the Gambler*) and the lavish, two-part *Die Nibelungen* (1924), a retelling of the Siegfried legend. Upon reaching New York, Lang was immediately struck by the city's glittering skyline of concrete, glass, and neon, a sight responsible for the germ of an idea for a new film. Lang envisioned a futuristic world where machines and efficiency were worshiped and where human compassion and sacrifice were things of the ancient past. When he returned to Germany, Lang discussed this basic concept with his wife, screenwriter and novelist Thea von Harbau, who turned the idea into a novel.

Over the next two years, Lang labored to bring his vision of the world in the year 2000 to the screen. Because of his earlier successes, Universium Film, Germany's premier film studio, agreed to finance the project. Two years later, the studio was nearly bankrupt, largely because of Lang's project. Lang shot nearly two million feet of film during a shooting schedule consisting of three hundred ten days and sixty nights. He employed a cast of more than thirty-five thousand, built elaborate full-scale sets and intricate miniatures, developed innovative special-effects techniques, and spent close to two million dollars, making his film the most expensive European production up to that time. The result was a dazzling, sixteen-reel extravaganza, cut down to nine reels for its American premiere. The film was described in a contemporary review as "an extraordinary motion picture, in some ways the most extraordinary ever made," and in another review by American film critic and playwright Robert E. Sherwood as "too much scenery, too many people, too much plot and too many platitudinous ideas."

Like Sherwood, many who first saw *Metropolis* were overwhelmed by its scope, its amazing visual richness, and its strange blending of the ultramodern and the mystically medieval. Many were awed by the film's innovative special effects, which showed masses of humans scurrying through towering landscapes made up of thousands of Art Deco and gothic skyscrapers and monstrous, steam-belching machines. Although contemporary reviewers praised the film for its dazzling look and innovative cinematic techniques, they also condemned its story as a confusing mishmash of politics, social commentary, Christian symbolism, and futuristic prophecy. Although the film was a commercial success, it never made enough money to save the studio that financed it.

Over the years, the film suffered more re-editings, further muddling its already confusing story line. It was not until 1984, when music producer Giorgio Moroder put together a restored version of the film based on all existing film fragments and using key stills to fill in gaps in the story line, that the public was finally able to experience *Metropolis* as Lang and his collaborators had first envisioned it. Although the restored version is still missing footage, Moroder's version clarifies the story line, making the film a much more strongly cohesive blending of astounding imagery and thought-provoking storytelling.

The film itself deals with the story of a mastermind builder, Fredersen, who has designed and now lords over his glittering city, Metropolis. He and his elite followers live in luxury far above ground while the workers who built and run the machines that power the city slave below, living in drab communal structures underground. The workers who man the machines move in piston-like formation, as if being exposed to the giant machines for so long has turned them too into soulless automatons. When Fredersen's son, Fredor, encounters the spiritual leader of the workers, Maria, he begins to question the reasons for maintaining the brutal division between the slave workers and the decadent elite. Fredor eventually joins the ranks of the workers and falls in love with Maria, who believes Fredor can help act as a mediator—as the heart needed to mend the rift between the head that designed Metropolis and the hands that built it. When Fredersen learns of Maria's existence and her powerful influence over the workers, however, he persuades a mad inventor, Rotwang, to fashion the likeness of Maria onto one of Rotwang's inventions, a robot, so that Fredersen can use the Maria robot to keep the workers in line. After Rotwang kidnaps Maria and empowers his robot with her likeness, the false Maria develops an evil mind of its own and leads the workers on a rampage that destroys the city. The film's climax has Fredor and Rotwang battling for the real Maria on the top of a gothic cathedral, as Fredersen and the workers watch horrified from below amid the wreckage of the city. In the end, Rotwang falls to his death, and Fredor acts as the city's heart, joining its head and hands to presumably build a more compassionate future.

Impact of Event

Even in its restored version, the story line of *Metropolis* is handled far too melodramatically and is marred by overacting, principally by Gustave Frölich, who played the Christlike mediator Fredor. What has endured and has continued to awe everyone who has seen the film, however, is its overwhelmingly dazzling imagery. Lang, who studied architecture, art, and painting before becoming a filmmaker, confessed many times to his strong preference for using visual imagery to express his personal philosophical insights. In all of his films, and most especially in *Metropolis*, Lang uses the visual to express his ideas regarding the conflict that exists between man's divine and demonic sides. The entire film is an amazing, swirling dance of opposites, of humans acting as machines and machines acting as humans, of scientists using advanced technology and black magic to create a robotic thing that represents a perverted image of perfection, of gorgeously glittering superstructures powered by ugly, massive, soul-killing machines. In one amazing scene, the machines transform into a likeness of the cannibal god Moloch, which begins to devour the workers who march willingly into its gaping mouth.

Lang, who had been the first choice to direct another visually innovative landmark German film, *Das Kabinett des Dr. Caligari* (1919; *The Cabinet of Dr. Caligari*), used that film's creative yet cinematically static set designs as a model for the *Metropolis* sets, but he then went far beyond the look of the earlier film by combining moody, expressionistic lighting with fluid camera movements. The most dynamic example of this innovative combination of lighting and camera movement occurs in the scene in which the real Maria is stalked by the scientist Rotwang through underground catacombs. As Rotwang pursues Maria, he uses a strong beam of light from his electric torch to "capture" her, propelling her forward through the catacombs with his light and at one point letting the beam crawl up her body like a snake. In other scenes depicting the city's awesome, intricate skyline, complete with towering skyscrapers, flashing neon lights, scurrying masses of people, and quaint flying machines circling above the structures, Lang and his special-effects master, Eugene Schüfftan, pioneered the "Schüfftan Process" of using two cameras to simultaneously depict live-action figures cavorting through miniature sets. Still another innovative touch was Lang's use of the robot in the scene showing Rotwang empowering his creation with the likeness of Maria. Although the concept of the robot had been created earlier, Lang took the concept to a most elaborate extreme, using dynamic lighting, electrical effects, and expressive staging to overpower the viewer.

At the time the film was made, Lang was interested in mysticism, and he wanted to play up the contrast between the world of soulless technological efficiency and the mysterious world of spirits and powers from beyond. Although he ultimately toned down this aspect of the film, he still managed to include an amazing scene of statues representing the seven deadly sins coming alive and dancing around a cathedral, while the false Maria dances provocatively amid a leering group of rich admirers and a delirious Fredor twists in bed, gripped by vivid, decadent dreams. In another scene, Lang sought to parallel the fate of Metropolis with the fate of the Tower of Babel, and to do so he created an intricate miniature tower and surrounded it with thousands of worker-extras, who struggle to build the decadent structure and finally rebel against the tower's spiritually bankrupt architects. Such scenes, elaborately (and expensively) staged, visually dynamic, cinematically innovative, yet at the same time expressing the filmmaker's personal view of the world, made *Metropolis* an enduring classic and an inspiration for a legion of filmmakers who followed. Such big-budget film spectaculars as Stanley Kubrick's *2001: A Space Odyssey* (1968), George Lucas' *Star Wars* trilogy (1977, 1980, 1983), Francis Ford Coppola's *Apocalypse Now* (1979), Steven Spielberg's *Close Encounters of the Third Kind* (1977) and *E.T.: The Extraterrestrial* (1982), Ridley Scott's *Blade Runner* (1982), and James Cameron's *Terminator 2: Judgment Day* (1991) all owe a debt to *Metropolis* and to Lang's megalomaniacal attention to detail, innovative cinematic techniques, and personal, dynamic vision. Although Lang would go on to create several more film masterpieces expressing his ideas on the spiritual and moral conflicts within each individual, it is *Metropolis* that remains the most spectacular example of his personal vision of the soul of man.

Bibliography

Armour, Robert A. *Fritz Lang*. Boston: Twayne, 1978. An overview of Lang's life, the factors that influenced his unique vision of the world, and the films he wrote and directed. Thoroughly researched, the book contains detailed descriptions of Lang's complete film output.

Bogdanovich, Peter. *Fritz Lang in America*. London: Studio Vista, 1968. Although primarily about Lang's American film period, the book also includes information about his early German period, with many comments about the making of *Metropolis*. The book is in interview form and vividly captures Lang's opinionated and humorous character.

Eisner, Lotte. *Fritz Lang*. Translated by Gertrud Mander. New York: Oxford University Press, 1976. Eisner, a respected film critic and personal friend of Lang, gives a detailed analysis of Lang's entire film career, with many insightful comments by Lang himself. The book also contains a fragmented autobiography left uncompleted by Lang.

Jenkins, Stephen, ed. *Fritz Lang: The Image and the Look*. London: British Film Institute, 1981. A collection of essays written by film authorities on various aspects of Lang's approach to filmmaking, including analyses of his cinematic themes and his methods of expressing his personal views with visual imagery.

Jensen, Paul M. *The Cinema of Fritz Lang*. New York: A. S. Barnes, 1969. A concise overview of Lang's life, with a film-by-film examination of his artistic output. Includes photographs from each production.

Ott, Frederick. *The Films of Fritz Lang.* Secaucus, N.J.: Citadel Press, 1979. A profusely illustrated book with a long, detailed biographical introduction examining Lang's life and influences. Also contains plot synopses of each film, some of Lang's own set and scene drawings, and insightful information on Lang's film output.

Jim Kline

Cross-References

Le Voyage dans la lune Introduces Special Effects (1902), p. 57; *The Cabinet of Dr. Caligari* Opens in Berlin (1920), p. 486; Eisenstein's *Potemkin* Introduces New Film Editing Techniques (1925), p. 615; Gance's *Napoléon* Revolutionizes Filmmaking Techniques (1925), p. 642; Kubrick Becomes a Film-Industry Leader (1964), p. 1989; The *Star Wars* Trilogy Redefines Special Effects (1977), p. 2391; Scott's *Blade Runner* Is a Visual Masterpiece (1982), p. 2486; *E.T.: The Extraterrestrial* Breaks Box-Office Records (1982), p. 2491.

THE BRITISH BROADCASTING CORPORATION IS CHARTERED

Category of event: Television and radio
Time: January 1, 1927
Locale: London, England

The British Broadcasting Corporation (BBC), a public rather than private institution, set the world's standards for quality production in radio and television

Principal personages:
JOHN REITH (1889-1971), the first director general of the BBC and one of the most influential Britons of the twentieth century
STANLEY BALDWIN (1867-1947), the British prime minister when the BBC was chartered
GODFREY ISAACS (?-1925), the managing director of the Marconi Wireless Telegraph Company and a leading business spokesman for radio
PETER ECKERSLEY (1892-1963), the chief engineer of the BBC from 1923 to 1929
JOSEPH ALBERT PEASE, LORD GAINFORD (1860-1943), the first chairman of the BBC

Summary of Event

After several years of evolution and development, the British Broadcasting Company, Limited, a private company, was rechartered in late 1926 as the British Broadcasting Corporation (BBC). On January 1, 1927, the new entity officially came into being. The new BBC, however, was not a radical departure from what had previously existed. Rather, the new public corporation was a logical outcome of various social, cultural, institutional, and political developments established long before the founding of the private company in 1922.

The development of the transmission of sound by "wireless" broadcasting instead of through telegraphic wire methods began in the nineteenth century. Numerous scientists and inventors, particularly Guglielmo Marconi, provided the theory and the technology. Electronic wave transmission also coincided with other fundamental changes in media communication. In Great Britain, Alfred Harmsworth (later Lord Northcliffe) revolutionized print journalism with his *Daily Mail*, a development paralleled by the accomplishments of Joseph Pulitzer and William Randolph Hearst in the United States, and motion pictures started to affect society as early as the 1890's. Even the possibility of television was predicted before the end of the century. Wireless development was not unique.

World War I added to the interest and application of wireless technology. When the war ended in 1918, however, the wireless, or radio, was still primarily an amateur activity. In Great Britain, the Post Office had been given responsibility for transmitting telegrams in 1869 and for licensing various wireless stations in 1904. Unlike in the United States, where government involvement was initially minimal, in the United Kingdom the British government played a larger role in influencing the direction and content of radio broadcasting. The leading British radio company was the Marconi Wireless Telegraph Company, headed by its managing director, Godfrey Isaacs, who was not alone in seeing the possibilities inherent in radio. On June 15, 1920, Lord Northcliffe's *Daily Mail* sponsored a radio concert by the famous singer Dame Nellie Melba, and the concert was heard all over Europe. Nothing in radio history had so captured the public's attention.

The Marconi Company was the largest but not the only private radio company in Great Britain. In many quarters, however, there was a fear of excessive competition and chaotic rivalry, and in May, 1922, the Post Office took the lead in bringing together the Marconi Company and the other wireless companies in an attempt to bring order and comprehensiveness to radio service in Great Britain. The Marconi Company probably could have provided adequate service itself, but both its business rivals and most politicians, fearful of a private monopoly, were opposed to such a development. On the other hand, Post Office officials were reluctant to assume day-to-day operational control of the new technology. The result, after long negotiations, was the establishment of the British Broadcasting Company, Limited, in October, 1922. The new company represented two potentially conflicting aspects of radio broadcasting; the interests of private business were essentially economic, but it was also argued that there was a broader public interest that had to be served. The company's shares were owned by the British manufacturers of wireless equipment. No advertising would be accepted as a means of financing radio; instead, a small fee would be collected by the Post Office from individuals having wireless receivers, or radios. Half of such fees would then be given to the company.

There were issues other than advertising that had to be resolved. The newspaper proprietors feared the wireless as a news competitor; thus, initially, the BBC was forbidden to have its own news service. Also, despite discussion of a second broadcasting company during the negotiations, the decision in 1922 was to give the British Broadcasting Company a monopoly. Finally, there was a concern that the BBC might present shows that were too controversial, particularly in regard to political, social and economic issues such as birth control and socialism.

The first chairman of the BBC was Joseph Albert Pease, Lord Gainford, who remained on the BBC's board until 1932. The key figure in the years that followed was John Charles Walsham Reith, a Scotsman who had been injured and disfigured in the war; Reith had had business experience, but he had not worked in radio. Nevertheless, in late 1922 he applied for the position of the BBC's general manager and was accepted. By the following November, he had become managing director, and by the end of 1923, he was the recognized head of the BBC. Reith, whose father was a Presbyterian minister, believed that the function of the BBC should be primarily to educate rather than to entertain the public. In his official capacity, he gave the BBC both the substance and image of quality and public service, a reputation that continued long after he left the BBC.

The company grew rapidly. When the BBC was founded, it had only four employees; by December, 1923, the staff numbered almost four hundred. By the end of 1923, there were more than half a million privately owned receiver sets, and a year later the number had increased to more than a million. Such growth would doubtless have occurred even if Reith had not been the driving force of the BBC, but it was Reith more than anyone else who transformed the private company operating through a Post Office license into a public corporation. Of course, he was not the only figure committed to the public possibilities of the wireless, but it was his vision and leadership that led the way. In May, 1925, Great Britain's postmaster general announced the appointment of a committee to examine the status of the BBC. Chaired by Lord Crawford, the committee ultimately accepted Reith's argument that broadcasting must be for public service and should not merely be the province of private business interests. In Reith's opinion, the British Broadcasting Company was a threat to the fulfillment of what the wireless could and should accomplish for the betterment of society. The Post Office had already arrived at a similar conclusion. In July, 1926, the postmaster general accepted the recommendations of the Crawford Committee and announced that a public corporation, the British Broadcasting Corporation, established by royal charter, would supersede the private British Broadcasting Company. In spite of dire predictions of socialism, bureaucracy, and monopoly, on January 1, 1927, the era of the British Broadcasting Corporation officially began.

Impact of Event

The first chairman of the newly constituted BBC was Lord Clarendon, whose selection did not meet with Reith's approval; he preferred Gainford. Reith was given a knighthood and named director-general. The corporation was chartered for ten years, and the chairman and the other four governors, including Gainford, served five-year terms. During Reith's reign, his influence was paramount; he generally got his way with the chairman and the other governors, and it was his vision of the BBC that continued to govern the direction of radio broadcasting in Great Britain.

Wireless in the United Kingdom had been strongly influenced by the development of radio in the United States in the years after World War I. In 1919, the private Radio Corporation of America (RCA) was created under the leadership of David Sarnoff. A competitor, Westinghouse, led the way in regular broadcasting beginning in 1921. By 1924, there were more than five hundred radio stations in the United States, and in spite of opposition to the practice, the American stations accepted advertising. British observers, including Godfrey Isaacs and Frank James Brown, an assistant secretary at the Post Office, although impressed by the business acuity of the American radio industry, predicted chaos in Great Britain if the same unregulated growth transpired. There was also agreement that advertising had no place on British radio. Monopoly rather than competition and licensing fees instead of advertising had been adopted when the British Broadcasting Company was founded in 1922, and the policy continued after the British Broadcasting Corporation began operation in 1927.

Because licensing fees were paid through the Post Office, the British government retained its ultimate hold on the BBC. Governmental oversight of, and possible interference with, radio broadcasts thus always existed.

The early restrictions upon discussing controversial issues on the radio and upon the BBC's having its own news service were only gradually relaxed. Reith attempted to have the BBC provide live coverage of parliamentary debates, but he was rebuffed by the politicians of the day. The company did, however, broadcast a speech by King George V in April, 1924, that was heard by ten million people. Reith's emphasis upon public service saw him establish a number of advisory committees on religion, music, and education in order to give the proper tone and substance to radio programs. When newspaper publishers threatened to charge the BBC a fee for printing program announcements, Reith established *Radio Times*, which provided information on programs and developments. Founded in 1923, by the end of 1927 *Radio Times* was selling more than a million copies an issue; by the eve of World War II in 1939, it had a circulation of three million. By 1935, 98 percent of the British population had access to the programs of the BBC.

One of the challenges for the BBC both before and after the creation of the public corporation in 1927 was the difficulty of being relevant and significant while it was required to remain noncontroversial. Reith hoped to have political issues seriously discussed on the radio by major politicians, but most only very reluctantly made use of the new technology. The 1920's leaders of both the Liberal and Labour parties, David Lloyd George and Ramsay MacDonald, were failures in the use of radio. The most successful politician to use the wireless in the 1920's was Stanley Baldwin, prime minister in 1923 and then again from 1924 to 1929. Baldwin's relaxed and conversational style in his 1924 campaign address anticipated the "fireside chats" of U.S. president Franklin D. Roosevelt in the 1930's. Baldwin was also the central figure in the most severe challenge to the BBC's educative objectivity during the interwar years. In May, 1926, a general strike broke out in Great Britain, and the subsequent walkout by most British union workers seemed to some to threaten both representative government and the capitalist economic system. Winston Churchill, Baldwin's chancellor of the exchequer, wished the BBC to become a mouthpiece for the government, but Reith refused, arguing that the BBC should remain objective in its reporting of events. A number of leading politicians spoke on the radio during the days of the strike, but none more effectively than Baldwin, whose calming words were widely credited with keeping the strike both peaceful and short. Years later, during World War II, Churchill's own oratory, often carried on the BBC, inspired Great Britain and the world against the evils of Nazism.

Reith and the BBC's attempt to uplift, to educate, and to be objective was generally, but not universally, approved. Churchill was not the only dissenter from Reith's approach to broadcasting. From the founding of the company through the establishment of the corporation and beyond, many listeners desired more entertainment and less education, more popular and dance music and less classical music, more humor and less serious discussion. Some objected to the domination of the BBC by London, demanding more programs reflecting the various regions of Great Britain. Although compromises were made and more entertainment programs were presented, the belief and practice that the BBC should level society up rather than down predominated. Both speech and dress standards were imposed upon announcers, who were not identifiable personalities, as in American radio, but simply gentlemen of culture. The BBC's standard speaking style, sometimes called "BBC English," perhaps did help break down some of the regional and class divisions among the British. Announcers were required to wear formal dress, including dinner jackets, when speaking over the radio. Moral uplift was even carried over to the private lives of BBC employees; Peter Eckersley, an important radio figure even before the company was founded in 1922 and the BBC's chief engineer from 1923 until 1929, was forced to resign because of his involvement in a divorce.

Nevertheless, the path established by the early founders of the BBC continued even after Reith's own resignation in 1938. Pure entertainment was secondary to education and societal improvement, quality was paramount, and the primary goal remained public service. The BBC retained its monopoly position in British broadcasting until long after World War II ended, still financed by licensing fees rather than through advertising. The precedents set during the early radio era were carried over when the BBC began television transmission in 1936. The monument created in the 1920's by Reith and others continued to cast its influential shadow over Great Britain and the world decades later.

Bibliography

Boyle, Andrew. *Only the Wind Will Listen.* London: Hutchinson, 1972. The best biography of John Reith; reflects the author's own conversations with Reith toward the end of the latter's life. Indispensable to any study of Reith and the BBC.

Briggs, Asa. *The BBC: The First Fifty Years.* New York: Oxford University Press, 1985. The writer, author of numerous works on British society, is the major historian of British broadcasting. This is an excellent one-volume summary of the BBC.

_____. *The Birth of Broadcasting.* Vol. 1 in *The History of Broadcasting in the United Kingdom.* London: Oxford University Press, 1961. Carries the story of the BBC to its transformation into a public corporation in 1927.

Middlemas, Keith, and John Barnes. *Baldwin: A Biography.* New York: Macmillan, 1970. The most satisfactory study of Baldwin and his times. Includes an excellent discussion of the General Strike and gives insights into why Baldwin was such a successful radio performer.

Taylor, A. J. P. *English History, 1914-1945.* Vol. 15 in *The Oxford History of England.* New York: Oxford University Press, 1965. A brilliant study of the two world wars and the years between in England. Always provocative, Taylor is not an admirer of Reith's BBC, and his criticisms are worth noting.

Eugene Larson

Cross-References

The Art of Radio Develops from Early Broadcast Experience (1920's), p. 469; WSM Launches *The Grand Ole Opry* (1925), p. 675; The *Amos 'n' Andy* Radio Show Goes on the Air (1928), p. 755; Radio Programming Dominates Home Leisure (1930's), p. 828; Welles Broadcasts *The War of the Worlds* (1938), p. 1103; NBC Launches American Television at the World's Fair (1939), p. 1143; *The Forsyte Saga* Is a Hit on Public Television (1969), p. 2168.

MONET'S *WATER LILIES* ARE SHOWN AT THE MUSÉE DE L'ORANGERIE

Category of event: Art
Time: May 17, 1927
Locale: Musée de l'Orangerie des Tuileries, Paris, France

Depicting the water lilies of his residence at Giverny, the canvases of painter Claude Monet, forerunner of the Impressionist movement, were unveiled to the public five months after his death

Principal personages:
> CLAUDE MONET (1840-1926), a French painter, forerunner of the Impressionist movement
> EUGÈNE BOUDIN (1824-1898), a French landscape artist and seaside painter who influenced Monet at the start of Monet's career
> GEORGES CLEMENCEAU (1841-1929), a French statesman who championed Monet's importance to French art and supported him in old age
> WASSILY KANDINSKY (1866-1944), the originator of abstract art, which was a direct outgrowth of Monet's influence

Summary of Event

The patriarch of Impressionism, Claude Monet, who pioneered techniques of converting observations of the effects of light and cloud clusters on textured foliage and water into lyrical brushwork, did not live to see his transient, iridescent images hung in the two specially designed galleries on the ground floor of the Musée de l'Orangerie set aside to honor his artistic vision. Five months after his death, the focal point of the exhibit—his *Décorations des Nymphéas*, the ephemeral, liquid impressions of the water lilies in the pond on the grounds of his rural home near Vernon, northwest of Paris—drew record crowds of admirers. Unaccustomed to contemporary scenes depicted under the dappled, shimmering luminosity of light and indistinct leafy patterns reflected in shallow water, patrons of the arts absorbed the rich, evocative canvases and lauded the painter as one of the world's most creative and innovative artists.

The oldest son of a wealthy, iron-willed wholesaler, Monet, who was drawn to the subtleties of color and light during long hours spent on the shore at the seaport of Le Havre, began drawing in childhood. He incurred the displeasure of his father yet persevered in the development of his talent. Influenced by the work of Johan Jongkind and his mentor, Eugène Boudin, he chose Paris as the place to study. At the age of nineteen, surrounded by other young rebels defying the stuffy, proprietary conventions of academic art, he joined the admiring coterie that formed around Édouard Manet and Edgar Degas. Along with his peers, Monet rejected the emphasis on religious and historical representations and established a working relationship with the outdoors, where he studied the optic phenomena that allow the eye to separate segments of objects into patches of light.

Under the influence of photography, which was still in its infancy, Monet duplicated lifelike moments in ordinary life by breaking down each scene into a free-form chiaroscuro of light and component hues, thereby freeing perception from traditional limitations. Working from a floating deck near Argenteuil, he concentrated on riverside activities along the Seine and re-created typical scenes of strollers and boaters eating, drinking, and enjoying the outdoors. Later, through travels to the Riviera, Rouen, Normandy, Venice, Norway, and London, he expanded his repertoire to a variety of subjects, most of which emphasized the interplay of sky and water.

The first public acclaim for Monet's canvases came in 1874, at what came to be known as the First Impressionist Exhibition. This was a decade after Manet's humiliation by protests against his *Déjeuner sur l'herbe* (1863, luncheon on the grass), capped by the Emperor Napoleon III's description of the work as offensive to public sensibilities. Reacting with similar vitriol to Monet's departure from the static guidelines of the École des Beaux-Arts, scoffing critics, preferring the hard outlines of realistic art, evolved the pejorative term "Impressionism" to refer to the softer, less well-defined images in his work. The term came from the title of Monet's *Impression: Sunrise* (1872). The term indicated the rise of an avant-garde approach to perception, centering on the elusive optical effects of shifting flecks of light on outdoor settings. Applying a matrix of short, precise brushstrokes, Monet utilized bright colors to emulate natural scenes, often painting sequential groupings representing the same object viewed at different times of day and under varying weather conditions. The best of Monet's serial works depict haystacks, poplar trees, the Gare Saint-Lazare, and the stone façade of Rouen Cathedral.

In contrast to the vibrant, cheery subject matter of his paintings, Monet survived a somber period of poverty and public disparagement, during which his wife and chief model, Camille, the mother of his two sons, suffered from tuberculosis. Married in 1879 to Alice Raingo Hoschedé, the widow of his agent, after his first wife's death, he entered a more promising era as public response to his innovations began to mellow. As his prospects improved, Alice, an uplifting companion, helped establish local and familial ties, which provided a necessary emotional support for his endeavors.

Moving in 1883 from oppressive rented quarters in Poissy, the Monets settled at Giverny in the Seine Valley near the Epte River. Monet expanded the original grounds, the Clos Normand, to include a fern-edged pond, overhanging willows, footpaths, wisteria trellises, clumps of bamboo, and a gently arched Oriental bridge. To expedite his work, he erected a photographic lab, a garage, and the first of three studios. After the death of his wife in 1911 and his son Jean's death three years later, he grew more reclusive and intensified his work. For the remaining years of his life, he battled double cataracts and underwent two eye operations that were only marginally successful.

Still attuned to his earlier philosophies despite impaired vision, Monet concentrated his remaining artistic output on the lilies rising from the waters behind the flowerbeds and produced his massive *Water Lily* cycle, which the French government commissioned in 1914. To accommodate his oversized canvases, he built a larger studio and immersed himself in the beauties of his garden. Blanche Hoschedé, his widowed stepdaughter, tended the house and kept him company. Painting primarily from memory as his eyesight deteriorated, he retreated in despair and grew discouraged with his works; he reworked some and burned others.

By 1920, critics drawn to Monet's unique style agreed with Georges Clemenceau's support for a permanent collection at the Hôtel Biron and initiated a more thorough study of his technique and point of view. Plagued by increasing bouts of depression and exhaustion, Monet lost heart with his work yet continued painting. On April 12, 1922, pressed by Clemenceau for a formal agreement, Monet signed papers donating *Water Lilies* to France. The notarized statement pledged two salons in the Orangerie, where nineteen panels would be arranged in an oval. Monet did most of the work on these panels during World War I but continued to rework them. On his death in 1926, Monet was attended by Clemenceau, his longtime friend and supporter. The *Water Lilies* cycle at the Orangerie was dedicated on May 17, 1927.

Impact of Event

A profound influence on the field of art, Monet's unrestrained experimentation with chromatic abstraction led to an irrevocable break with the old order, which had been dominated by gallery critics. Most significant of his influence was the emergence of abstract art, a direct outgrowth of his limpid reflecting pools, which distorted the shapes of objects and allowed the imagination full play in viewing hard realities. Applying intense study of the complex relationship between light and object, Monet's followers evolved their own reality, which often required a leap of faith from the viewing public. Splinter movements associated with Impressionism included pointillism, the use of minute, controlled points of color to create images. Pointillist works often are unclear when viewed up close and take shape only when viewed at a distance. Pointillism is exemplified in Georges Seurat's *Un Dimanche d'eté à la Grande Jatte* (1884-1886, Sunday afternoon on the island of La Grande Jatte). Moving in the opposite direction, Vincent van Gogh's swirling, emotional, distorted expressionism, as represented in *The Starry Night* (1889), brought an ecstasy to the canvas never before seen in European art. Similarly, Paul Gauguin's Symbolist canvases—among them *Where Do We Come from? What Are We? Where Are We Going* (1897-1898), and *The Yellow Christ* (1889)—evolved from his sojourn in Tahiti and shocked European sensibilities with his frank assessment of island settings, nude Polynesians, and a juxtaposition of Christian and pagan religious symbols.

During this same era, Auguste Renoir and Paul Cézanne returned to a closer identity with solid form. Renoir, one of Impressionism's most skilled craftsmen, extended Monet's use of patchy light with a pearly glow exuding a harmony and beneficence on his graceful subjects. In his best-loved paintings, he imparts a mature, dignified beauty to middle-class Europeans engaged in lighthearted pastimes.

An even greater departure from realism, the Fauvism of Henry Matisse, Maurice Vlaminck, Raoul Dufy, and André Derain, carried Impressionism into the realm of flat planes of exotic colors. Likewise, the cubism of Georges Braque and Pablo Picasso took similar liberties with geometric forms, often viewing subjects simultaneously from several blended points of view by breaking the whole into planes and cubes. The resulting geometric treatments created greater demands on a bewildered viewing public, which was, on first exposure, repulsed by both artistic styles.

Delving deeper into the elements of perception, Russian painter Wassily Kandinsky, influenced by a viewing of Monet's haystack paintings early in his career, wrote an incisive theoretical commentary, *Concerning the Spiritual in Art, and Painting in Particular* (1912). Kandinsky's paintings, energized by swirls of color, demonstrated an intensity of geometric interest similar to the abstractions of the cubists. His disciples Paul Klee, Franz Marc, and August Macke formed Der Blaue Reiter group, which exhibited at the German Bauhaus until the Bauhaus was suppressed by Nazis in 1933.

Still viable and influential a century later, Monet's art, with its free splashes of color and emphasis on ordinary activities, undergirded a burst of enthusiasm from publishers, who met the public's demand for art with affordable photographic reproductions, prints, and art books. Completely trouncing the tyranny of elitism, followers of Monet created a market for galleries, museums, and open-air markets.

To the average patron of the arts, the post-Monet era proved baffling, as artists including painters, musicians, dancers, sculptors, writers, and architects moved further away from finite, hard-edged objectivity toward the dreamy, indistinct Impressionism of Monet's water lilies. The presentation of Monet's artistry unleashed a drive for self-expression, experimentation, and rebellion against the values inherent in the Edwardian era. Some artists, particularly Picasso, abandoned controlled brush strokes for dots, swirls, and dollops of paint on canvas. Sculptors used found objects such as gears, and tangles of wire to create free-form art, sometimes creating a pictorial collage which was a textural blend of painting and sculpture.

Minimalism, a direct outgrowth of Impressionism that sprouted in the 1950's, saw painting develop into colorful geometric shapes—circles, squares, chevrons, nested boxes, and grids—on oversized canvases. Like Monet, the minimalists often serialized their work, concentrating on a single theme, often producing diptychs and triptychs that critics labeled "systematic." Huge, austere sculptures, equally pared down to modular shapes, appeared in public plazas, courtyards, and modern galleries such as New York's Guggenheim Museum.

Offshoots of minimalism produced a burst of energy in optical art and pop art, as demonstrated by the intensity of Andy Warhol's experimental canvases, including his notorious Campbell's Soup cans and Brillo boxes. Likewise, poets, dramatists, and novelists strove for the focus and freedom of the Impressionists by shutting out needless detail and concentrating on the stream of consciousness of a single character, as with the speakers in William Faulkner's *As I Lay Dying* (1930) and the absurdist dramas of Eugène Ionesco, Edward Albee, Harold Pinter, Jean Genet, and

Samuel Beckett, whose *Waiting for Godot* (1952) served as the highwater mark of Surrealist drama. Equally unfettered were the atonal musical compositions of Charles Ives and Paul Hindemith, the daring twelve-tone works of Arnold Schoenberg, the whimsical, unpredictable tunes of Erik Satie, and the modern dance forms of Martha Graham.

Another important adjunct to Monet's twentieth century audience was the restoration of his deteriorating house and garden, which he willed to his second son, Michel. Underwritten by the Académie des Beaux-Arts, the project, begun in 1966, reestablished the public's admiration for Impressionism by providing a spot of natural beauty for recreation and relaxation. An inviting outdoor retreat and museum, Monet's Giverny ranks as one of France's most beloved tourist attractions. Its popularity inspired a review of turn-of-the-century art at a Metropolitan Museum of Art exhibit entitled *Monet's Years at Giverny: Beyond Impressionism*, featuring eighty-one of his canvases dating from 1883 to 1926.

Bibliography

Burchell, S. C. *The Age of Progress*. The Great Ages of Man Series. New York: Time-Life Books, 1966. A compelling overview of the guiding philosophy that steered nineteenth century artists into new realms, particularly in art, music, and literature. Covers the era that gave birth to Monet and his fellow Impressionists.

Clay, Jean. *Impressionism*. New York: Putnam, 1973. A well-organized text, with an essay on prices, concise essays about each author, and bibliography but no index.

Herbert, Robert L. *Impressionism: Art, Leisure, and Parisian Society*. New Haven, Conn.: Yale University Press, 1988. A grand, complete study of Impressionism, including ample color plates, a list of the museums in which each painting is hung, notes, lengthy bibliography, and index.

Kemp, Gerald van der. *A Visit to Giverny*. Translated by Bronia Fuchs. Versailles, France: Éditions d'Art Lyc, 1980. A useful paperback guide to Monet's home, this volume contrasts photographs of the original residence and grounds with later paintings and pictures after the estate's restoration. Backed by sufficient fact and commentary, this eighty-page pamphlet provides a detailed grounding in Monet's Giverny period.

Monet, Claude. *Monet's Years at Giverny: Beyond Impressionism*. New York: Metropolitan Museum of Art, 1978. A lavish picture book of Monet's art, featuring photographs of the artist in his studio and country home, a chronology, incisive essays about his work and influence, and a selected bibliography. On first examination, this work appears to be a standard coffee-table book; closer examination proves its use to the student and art historian.

Picon, Gäeton. "Impressionism." In *Modern Painting: From 1800 to the Present*. New York: Newsweek Books, 1974. A respectable guide for the general reader. This work contains a satisfying balance of text and illustration to define art philosophy of the late nineteenth century. Especially helpful are writings by the principal artists (including an interview with Claude Monet concerning his early training), as well as a detailed chronology, and a thorough index.

Time-Life Books. *Seven Centuries of Art.* New York: Author, 1970. A useful overview of art history, setting Impressionism within its time frame, with brief commentary about its offshoots. Although too fleeting and shallow for the scholar, this explicit work provides an appropriate beginning for students.

Mary Ellen Snodgrass

Cross-References

Avant-Garde Artists in Dresden Form Die Brücke (1905), p. 134; Les Fauves Exhibit at the Salon d'Automne (1905), p. 140; Artists Find Inspiration in African Tribal Art (1906), p. 156; The Salon d'Automne Rejects Braque's Cubist Works (1908), p. 204; Kandinsky Publishes His Views on Abstraction in Art (1912), p. 320; Avant-Garde Art in the Armory Show Shocks American Viewers (1913), p. 361; The Formation of the Blue Four Advances Abstract Painting (1924), p. 583; Surrealism Is Born (1924), p. 604; The Musée d'Orsay Opens (1986), p. 2588; Van Gogh's *Irises* Sells for $53.9 Million (1987), p. 2603.

BRECHT AND WEILL COLLABORATE
ON *MAHAGONNY SONGSPIEL*

Categories of event: Music and theater
Time: July 17, 1927
Locale: Baden-Baden, Germany

Bertolt Brecht and Kurt Weill collaborated in the first manifestation of "epic theater" in the Mahagonny Songspiel; *their use of* Gebrauchsmusik *in* Rise and Fall of the City of Mahagonny *and in* The Threepenny Opera *introduced "cheap" music into opera and theater*

Principal personages:

BERTOLT BRECHT (1898-1956), a German playwright who wrote the texts for the *Mahagonny Songspiel, The Threepenny Opera*, and *Rise and Fall of the City of Mahagonny*

KURT WEILL (1900-1950), a German composer who collaborated with Brecht on the *Mahagonny Songspiel* and introduced the use of popular music within serious compositions

LOTTE LENYA (KAROLINE BLAMAUER, 1898-1981), Weill's wife, a singer and star of *The Threepenny Opera* and *Rise and Fall of the City of Mahagonny*

PAUL HINDEMITH (1895-1963), a German composer who launched an annual festival of new music in Baden-Baden and introduced the concept of *Gebrauchsmusik*

FERRUCCIO BUSONI (1866-1924), an Italian composer and teacher of music composition who influenced Weill's first musical success

Impact of Event

The meeting in 1927 between the avant-garde composer Kurt Weill and the revolutionary playwright Bertolt Brecht and their ensuing collaboration was significant for the development of both their careers. When Weill heard a radio production of Brecht's *A Man's a Man* (1926), he responded with a highly complementary review and subsequently asked Brecht whether he could use some of Brecht's poems for a song cycle he was preparing for the festival of new music in Baden-Baden. Brecht was interested in Weill's ideas about "gestic" music since they corresponded to attempts he was making to popularize drama through the use of popular culture motifs from cinema and the cabaret. According to Weill, gestic music, a concept that also relates to Paul Hindemith's notion of *Gebrauchsmusik*, or functional music, instead of processing the text for purely musical ends focuses on the manner through which the words of a song communicate the gest, or social attitude, through rhythmic means, including pauses. The object was to extend the communicative quality of music in order to make social statements. Composers such as Weill sought corresponding texts with simplicity of diction and clarity of sense. Similarly, Brecht was attempting to strip drama of figurative language in order to bring out the "epic," or communicative nature, of his texts. He did this by concentrating on the message rather than the subtext in order to foreground the social rather than the psychological situations of his plays.

Brecht and Weill were not alone at this time in considering the traditional theater and opera to be out of step with an egalitarian modern society, for these were notions central to *Neue Sachlichkeit*, or New Objectivity, in the arts. In particular, Hindemith was influential in exploring applied music. He and the composers in his group rejected the purely aesthetic explorations of atonality represented by Arnold Schoenberg and others. The new music was to project an ease of execution and accessibility to the unsophisticated ear. For that reason, Hindemith and Weill, as well as composers such as Igor Stravinsky and "Les Six," established a kinship with the dynamic rhythms and unsnobbish popular appeal of jazz and cabaret songs. From the outset, Brecht's songs, initially with simple tunes of his own, were central to his attempts to popularize theater. At the same time, Weill, one of the most prominent of Ferruccio Busoni's students, was the first German composer of any consequence to show an interest in setting texts by contemporary German writers such as Iwan Goll, Georg Kaiser, and ultimately Brecht. For that reason, the collaboration between Brecht and Weill was particularly fruitful. It gave both the opportunity to explore similar concerns regarding the relationship between popular culture and the arts.

Weill and Brecht's collaboration began with the *Mahagonny Songspiel*, sometimes known as *The Little Mahagonny*, which consisted of six songs with orchestral interludes, lasting about forty-five minutes in all. Brecht and Weill chose the English word "song" as part of the title as an obvious gesture to disassociate it from the German word *Lied*, which to them seemed to relate too strongly to the classical *Lieder* tradition. The *Mahagonny Songspiel* was produced at the Deutsche Kammermusik festival in Baden-Baden on July 17, 1927. The work can be described as a chamber opera that thematically represents the degeneration of life in a mythical American city and is set to music with a jazzy accent. Caspar Nehar, Brecht's scenic designer, produced a series of sketches for the setting with themes relating to the greed and corruption of capitalism in the symbolic American city of Mahagonny, with a location kept intentionally vague in order to project the allegorical universality of social conditions. In addition, a small boxing ring, as a metaphor for the fighting inherent in capitalistic competition, became the platform for the performance. Weill requested that his wife, Lotte Lenya, sing the leading role. Her obviously untrained, gravelly voice, with its grotesque mispronunciations of the English words of the "Alabama Song," symbolized the rejection on the part of the Brecht/Weill duo of the accepted standards of high culture. In addition, Weill, having caught Brecht's eagerness to twit the pretensions of high culture, made good musical capital out of the glottal catch between "Ma" and "hagonny," imbuing the setting of the six poems with a musical accompaniment that brought out its comic quality and an aggressive provocative edge as well.

The audience reaction was divided: There was booing, whistling, cheering, and stomping. The singers participated by pulling out whistles from their pockets. Later that evening in the bars throughout town, however, everyone seemed to be singing lyrics from the opera. *The Little Mahagonny* brought Weill popular success and also projected him into a striking new area of emphasis on "song," a development that was to endure for the remainder of his career, both in his collaboration with Brecht and also later in his Broadway musicals.

Impact of Event

The immediate consequence of the attention that both Weill and Brecht received in Baden-Baden was the continuation of their collaboration in *The Threepenny Opera* (1928), *Happy End* (1929), *Rise and Fall of the City of Mahagonny* (1929), the ballet *The Seven Deadly Sins* (1933), and songs for a revival of *A Man's a Man*. In particular, *The Threepenny Opera* became the rage of the season and immediately was translated into many languages, bringing Weill a reputation in the United States even before he arrived in 1935. The text for *The Threepenny Opera* was based on the eighteenth century play by John Gay called *The Beggar's Opera*. Its plot concerns Macheath, a thief of thieves, who marries Polly, daughter of his fellow crook, the entrepreneur Peachum. Peachum plans his arrest, and though Macheath flees, he is caught through the treachery of Jenny and other whores. He is sentenced to be executed but is reprieved in a deliberately artificial happy ending. Brecht's text was cobbled together quickly from a translation of Gay's work, and Weill composed the music virtually overnight. *The Threepenny Opera* opened in the Theater am Schiffbauerdamm in Berlin on August 31, 1928. Lenya had one of the leading roles, that of the whore Jenny, and once again Weill's score infected the public. The audience would barely allow the song "Mack the Knife" to finish before demanding an encore. Theatergoers left humming and whistling such tunes as the "Cannon Song" and "Mack the Knife." It is no exaggeration to say that the play swept across Europe. Within its first year, it was performed more than forty-two hundred times. In addition, it was recorded by seven companies. Overnight, Weill was transformed from a serious composer to a commercial success.

A year after the premiere of *The Threepenny Opera*, its producer, hoping to capitalize on its phenomenal success, persuaded Brecht and Weill to write another play with songs. *Happy End*, which opened in Berlin in September of 1929, did not, however, justify its title and was both a critical and a popular flop. Brecht was later to repudiate writing it, but several of Weill's songs, in particular "Surabaya-Johnny," belong to the general repertory of famous Weill songs. At the same time, Brecht and Weill continued working on the full-length opera *Rise and Fall of the City of Mahagonny*, first produced in Leipzig in March of 1930, then in Berlin in December of 1931, with Lenya once again singing the leading role. The political content of that opera became a source of conflict between Brecht and Weill. Brecht saw the opera as a parable of capitalism and wanted members of the cast to sing and march about the stage carrying placards as Mahagonny goes up in flames. Weill became less interested in the political view and saw the opera as a parable of greed. With the rise of

Nazism, the opera was met with resistance from the public, though critics noted Weill's musical accomplishment of blending the teachings of Busoni with his popularized version of jazz.

In addition to his collaboration with Brecht, Weill also composed songs, choral numbers, and instrumental movements for Georg Kaiser's *Silbersee*, which unfortunately opened as Adolf Hitler became chancellor of Germany in January of 1933. Immediately after the burning of the Reichstag, Brecht emigrated to Prague, and performances of Weill's music were prohibited until 1945. In addition, since both Weill and Lenya were Jewish, they left Germany in March of 1933, escaping across the border to France.

Upon his arrival in America in September of 1935, Weill began his second career, composing for Broadway. Although his compositions were not generally known by the American public, his work was known to a number of important musicians and theater directors, and he soon was presented with a number of projects. One of the first was *Knickerbocker Holiday*, based on Washington Irving's book, which met with considerable success when it opened in October of 1938. It was not until *Lady in the Dark* (1941), however, that Weill achieved his first Broadway hit. After its premiere on January 23, 1941, the show ran for two seasons. In 1944, Paramount bought the rights to make its film version, starring Ginger Rogers and Ray Milland. *One Touch of Venus*, Weill's greatest Broadway success, followed, opening on October 7, 1943. Another popular hit was the folk opera *Street Scene*, composed in 1946.

In his adjustment to Broadway, Weill abandoned the bold and disillusioned bitterness of his musical style from *Mahagonny Songspiel* and *The Threepenny Opera* in favor of sophisticated love songs, barbershop ballads, and mock patriotic songs. Contemporary critics point out that Weill's contributions to American music are as significant as those of his European period, because in this transition he consciously attempted to create an indigenous American operatic tradition based on the classic American themes. The impact of Weill's popularization of serious composition is apparent in the many versions of "Mack the Knife" by popular singers and the recording of the "Alabama Song" by the Doors. At the same time, serious interpretations of Weill's music continue. *Rise and Fall of the City of Mahagonny* belongs to the repertoire of the Metropolitan Opera, and opera singer Teresa Stratas has recorded his collected songs.

Bibliography

Brecht, Bertolt. *Brecht on Theatre.* Edited and translated by John Willet. New York: Hill & Wang, 1964. Contains the only comprehensive collection of Brecht's writings on theater. Significant essays for the understanding of the Brecht/Weill collaboration include "The Modern Theatre Is the Epic Theatre," "The Literarization of the Theatre" (notes to *The Threepenny Opera*), "On the Use of Music in Epic Theatre," and "On Gestic Music." Photographs and index.

Jarman, Douglas. *Kurt Weill: An Illustrated Biography.* Bloomington: Indiana University Press, 1982. Provides a two-part discussion focusing on Weill's life and analysis of his musical style. Jarman assesses Weill's early instrumental and vocal music, the music that characterizes his collaboration with Brecht, and the American period of his popular Broadway productions. A well-researched, balanced, and informative text. Numerous photographs, chronological list of works, discography, bibliography, notes, and index included.

Kowalke, Kim. *Kurt Weill in Europe.* Ann Arbor, Mich.: UMI Research Press, 1979. A scholarly analysis of Weill's career. Kowalke provides a context for the development of Weill's musical style, acknowledging the influence of his teacher Ferruccio Busoni and the relevance of his period of experimentation. The text is illustrated by examples from Weill's scores and is clearly directed to the reader with a strong background in musicology. Includes appendix with catalog of Weill's compositions (1900-1935) and annotated translations of Weill's essays. Notes, bibliography, and index.

_____, ed. *A New Orpheus: Essays on Kurt Weill.* New Haven, Conn.: Yale University Press, 1986. Kowalke provides a wide range of essays by Weill scholars covering the full spectrum of his musical career. A number of the essays focus on Weill's collaboration with Brecht in creating "epic opera," while others focus on Weill in America and his influence on the Broadway musical. A chronology of Weill's life and works, index, and illustrations are included.

Sanders, Ronald. *The Days Grow Short: The Life and Music of Kurt Weill.* New York: Holt, Rinehart and Winston, 1980. A comprehensive, easily accessible biography and analysis of Weill's musical career. Sanders skillfully interweaves biographical information and relates the effects of Weill's personality on his individual musical style. Includes source notes, list of Weill's principal composition, discography, and illustrations.

Willett, John. *The Theatre of Bertolt Brecht.* New York: New Directions, 1959. Willett provides a short chronology and brief analysis of Brecht's plays. A discussion follows of eight aspects of Brecht's theatrical style, including subject matter, use of language, theatrical influences, music, theatrical practice, theory, and politics. The discussion on music is of particular interest to the Brecht/Weill collaboration. An invaluable, concise introduction to Brecht's work. Bibliography, index, and illustrations provided.

Christine Kiebuzinska

Cross-References

Busoni's *Sketch for a New Aesthetic of Music* Is Published (1907), p. 166; Schoenberg Breaks with Tonality (1908), p. 193; Webern's *Six Pieces for Large Orchestra* Premieres in Vienna (1913), p. 367; *The Rite of Spring* Stuns Audiences (1913), p. 373; "Les Six" Begin Giving Concerts (1917), p. 435; The New Objectivity Movement Is Introduced (1925), p. 631; Berg's *Wozzeck* Premieres in Berlin (1925), p. 680; Hindemith Advances Ideas of Music for Use and for Amateurs (1930's), p. 816; Berg's *Lulu* Opens in Zurich (1937), p. 1078; Brecht Founds the Berliner Ensemble (1949), p. 1410.

RODGERS CUTS HIS FIRST RECORD FOR RCA VICTOR

Category of event: Music
Time: August 4, 1927
Locale: Bristol, Tennessee

Commercial country music was in its infancy when Jimmie Rodgers cut his first record for RCA Victor; he would soon become famous and influential in country and blues music

Principal personages:
JIMMIE RODGERS (1897-1933), a singer, guitarist, and composer whose music and "blue yodeling" have enjoyed lasting fame
RALPH S. PEER (1892-1960), a pioneer of the recording industry who discovered Rodgers and became his principal manager

Summary of Event

In the early 1920's, the recording industry became interested in the rural market and therefore in rural music and performers, particularly in the American South. "Old-time music" and "mountain music" were two of the terms often used to describe what the industry wanted, and the phrase "hillbilly music" was also coined at the time. In addition, there was a new interest in rural blues as performed by African Americans.

One of the pioneers in recording such music was Ralph S. Peer, at one time with OKeh Records but by 1927 under contract with the RCA Victor company. (It was Peer who first applied the term "hillbilly" to white country tunes.) A staunch believer in field expeditions, he set out to find and record new talent from among performers already known in their native locales. In July, 1927, Peer brought his wife, two engineers, and some new electrical recording equipment to Bristol, Tennessee. He already knew, or knew of, some of the people whom he would record, but he also welcomed walk-in performers. One of them was James Charles Rodgers.

Jimmie Rodgers was born on September 9, 1897, in Pine Springs, near Meridian, Mississippi, the son of Aaron and Eliza Rodgers. Like his father, Rodgers became a railroad worker—he would one day be billed as the "Singing Brakeman"—but from childhood on he was fascinated by show business, and he managed to combine some professional musical performances with his railroading and other jobs. By 1925, however, ill health ruled out further railroad work; Rodgers had been suffering from tuberculosis for some time, and so he committed himself entirely to the entertainment industry. He worked in vaudeville, performed dance music, and, briefly, worked for a radio show, poverty always dogging his steps, especially since he now had a small family to support.

He had already become connected with a small string band, renamed the Jimmie Rodgers Entertainers, when he heard about Ralph Peer's expedition to Bristol. The

Entertainers auditioned for Peer, but the band broke up the night before their recording date. The band members' musical styles and personalities had never matched very well, and Rodgers had earlier announced his intention to leave the band, so a quarrel arose over whether they should keep the name "Jimmie Rodgers Entertainers" for recording purposes. As a result, the other band members recorded for Peer under their original name, the Tenneva Ramblers, while Rodgers showed up alone with only his guitar. It was a fortuitous development, one apparently encouraged by Peer himself. Thus it was that Rodgers cut his first record for RCA Victor on August 4, 1927.

By that time, he had absorbed influences from so many sources that it is difficult to trace them and equally difficult to categorize the result. He had been singing and playing guitar, banjo, and other instruments in a number of styles. Sometimes he sang popular music, sometimes African American blues—fragments of which he remembered from railroad and vaudeville days—and sometimes he did "old-time" sentimental tunes. He also yodeled. This was nothing new; there had long been Swiss-style and other yodeling, and even the new, commercial country music field had at least a nodding acquaintance with that genre. Rodgers' yodeling, though, was something special; it was "blue yodeling," a type unique at that time to Rodgers himself, incorporated into his white man's version of the blues.

Which of these types of music would Rodgers choose for his recording debut? Peer was anxious to record something new in the way of country music, new in the sense that it would catch the public's attention, but also new in the sense that it could be copyrighted. Yet Rodgers apparently did not feel that his blue yodeling was ready for recording; moreover, Peer was insisting on "hillbilly," or something like hillbilly—whatever that was. Rodgers may also have wanted to prove that he could sing any sort of music. In any case, he chose an old song he had reworked called "The Soldier's Sweetheart," a ballad about a World War I soldier (as Rodgers' version would have it) who died in battle, leaving his sweetheart to live a single life forever in his memory. These sentimental lyrics were put to an old Irish melody, "Where the River Shannon Flows," but the final product was new enough for copyright purposes.

The second cut was another old song, a lullaby called "Sleep, Baby, Sleep." Rodgers' version included some of his soon-to-be-famous yodeling, fine work, although it, and the whole performance, seem a bit loud for a lullaby. Still, his voice in song and yodel had a loving sound that was appropriate. Although Rodgers had apparently intended the first cut to be his showpiece, "Sleep, Baby, Sleep" has been preferred by many over the years. Peer was somewhat disappointed that "Sleep, Baby, Sleep" was uncopyrightable, but Rodgers simply did not have much else ready to go. Yet both songs were good enough to lead to later recording sessions and instant fame in 1928.

Impact of Event

The Bristol sessions are justly famous in the history of country music, not only because of Jimmie Rodgers but also for the other talented performers who recorded there, especially the Carter Family. Yet the importance of those sessions could scarcely have been imagined at the time. In Rodgers' case, many months would pass before his recordings caught on with the public. It was his first blue yodel, "T for Texas," that made him a star upon its release in 1928. There would be thirteen blue yodels in all, plus other songs that featured yodeling and bluesy lyrics or tunes.

Before long, Rodgers was hard-pressed for new material, and he accepted songs from various sources, in particular from his sister-in-law, Elsie McWilliams. True to his heritage, he recorded in many different styles. In addition to the blues, with their often somewhat bawdy lyrics, he composed or accepted sentimental songs, songs of unrequited love, prison songs, quasi-cowboy songs, lullabies, a pseudo-Hawaiian tune, novelty songs, and even some semiautobiographical songs such as "T.B. Blues." Often he recorded alone with his guitar, often with side men, and sometimes with jazz orchestras; Louis Armstrong joined him on "Blue Yodel No. 9." He also did some comedy skits with the Carter Family. One type of music he hardly touched was gospel, in contrast to the practice of most hillbilly musicians such as the Carters; Rodgers was not a religious man.

Much of this product has been regarded as outstanding. Most of the blue yodels were stunningly good, as were many of his other recordings, such as "Waiting for a Train." On the other hand, a number of his records were flawed, either because he had run out of good material or because he gave indifferent performances. Some of these sides were released, it seems, only because Rodgers' death prevented the recording of better material. Much of what he produced must have sounded trite even then, such as his recording of "Desert Blues," which features a tuba. Yet trite lyrics and "cornball" productions in most cases simply added to his music's charm. If one sets out to produce a novelty tune such as "Desert Blues," why not go all the way and use a tuba? As for performance problems, Rodgers had scant musical training, and sometimes his guitar work was, to put it gently, unorthodox. Again, though, the primitive nature of some of his singing and playing made him all the more authentic-sounding and therefore appealing. Rather than merely rising above his limitations, he carried them with him, making his unorthodox style part of his greatness.

When considering the impact of his work, one must first note the lasting fame of his recordings. Although Rodgers' sales declined in the final year or so of his career, this was not a reflection of his true worth. Rather, it was a reflection of the deepening Depression of the early 1930's, which cut into sales everywhere, and also a reflection of his own declining health. Rodgers died in New York City on May 26, 1933, shortly after exhausting himself in his final recording session. Yet his records continued to sell. Of his career total of some 110 sides, twenty-five were released after his death. Many of his songs were later reissued on 78 and 45 RPM, and the entire corpus of Rodgers' work was rereleased on albums in the 1950's and early 1960's; a complete edition appeared in Japan in 1973. On November 3, 1961, Rodgers was installed as the first member of the new Country Music Hall of Fame.

His influence on country music in the short run is obvious. Many artists of the

1930's copied his style of singing and yodeling; new songs were written in his manner; and many of his own songs were performed by other artists in the 1930's and after. "Mule Skinner Blues," for instance, has been sung by Bill Monroe and Dolly Parton; "In the Jailhouse Now" is another example. One of the later giants of country music, Hank Snow, named his son after Rodgers. In the longer term, much of what Rodgers did has not remained standard. Few modern country artists have continued the practice of recording with only an acoustic guitar for accompaniment, and the records he made with jazz orchestras did not set much of a precedent. Few white country artists have continued to sing the blues in his style since World War II, and fewer still have carried his yodeling tradition into the postwar era.

Rodgers' brief career raised a number of unanswered questions: Would much of what he made famous have caught on even without his help? "Cowboy" music, for example, predated Rodgers' career and probably did not require his work to guarantee its subsequent popularity. To what extent did he inspire young artists? To what extent did he make country music acceptable to urbanites? Though such questions are perhaps unanswerable, Rodgers clearly deserves the title "father of country music."

Bibliography

Malone, Bill C. *Country Music U.S.A.: A Fifty-Year History.* Austin: University of Texas Press, 1968. Scholarly and well written, this book has become a classic in the field. Contains a chapter on Jimmie Rodgers.

Paris, Mike, and Chris Comber. *Jimmie the Kid.* London: Eddison Press, 1977. The first full-length study; contains a detailed discography. Superseded by Nolan Porterfield's book.

Porterfield, Nolan. *Jimmie Rodgers: The Life and Times of America's Blue Yodeler.* Urbana: University of Illinois Press, 1979. Based to a very large extent on original sources and interviews, balanced in interpretation, this is the indispensable book on Rodgers' life and music.

Rodgers, Carrie Cecil Williamson. *Jimmie Rodgers' Life Story (Complete).* Nashville, Tenn. Ernest Tubb Publications, 1935. A personal and somewhat romantic account by Rodgers' widow, this book is nevertheless valuable for its insights and anecdotes.

Sanjek, Russell. *American Popular Music and Its Business: The First Four Hundred Years.* Vol. 3, *From 1900 to 1984.* New York: Oxford University Press, 1988. Lengthy, scholarly, and fact-filled, this book has many references to both Rodgers and Peer.

Karl G. Larew

Cross-References

Joplin Popularizes the Ragtime Style (1899), p. 13; Handy Ushers in the Commercial Blues Era (1910's), p. 252; Bessie Smith Records "Downhearted Blues" (1923), p. 572; Armstrong First Records with His Hot Five Group (1925), p. 670; WSM

Launches *The Grand Ole Opry* (1925), p. 675; Guthrie's Populist Songs Reflect the Depression-Era United States (1930's), p. 810; Bill Monroe and the Blue Grass Boys Define Bluegrass Music (1939), p. 1121; Hank Williams Performs on *The Grand Ole Opry* (1949), p. 1415; Presley Becomes a Rock-and-Roll Sensation (1956), p. 1705; *Wanted: The Outlaws* Revitalizes Country Music (1976), p. 2365.

THE JAZZ SINGER PREMIERES IN NEW YORK

Category of event: Motion pictures
Time: October 6, 1927
Locale: New York, New York

Though primarily a silent film, The Jazz Singer *was the first feature-length film to include audible music and dialogue as integral parts*

Principal personages:

AL JOLSON (ASA YOELSON, 1886-1950), the star of *The Jazz Singer*

GEORGE JESSEL (1898-1981), the star of the Broadway production of *The Jazz Singer* and original choice for the screen role

HARRY WARNER (1881-1958), one of the Warner brothers who produced and owned screen rights for *The Jazz Singer*

JACK WARNER (1892-1978), a producer and owner of screen rights for *The Jazz Singer*

SAM WARNER (1888-1927), a producer and owner of screen rights for *The Jazz Singer*

MAY MCAVOY (1901-1984), the costar and love interest for Jolson's character

EUGÉNIE BESSERER (1870-1934), the costar who played the mother of Jolson's character

WARNER OLAND (1880-1938), a Hollywood character actor who played the role of Jolson's father in the film

Summary of Event

In retrospect, Al Jolson could be seen as a natural choice for the starring role in *The Jazz Singer.* By the mid-1920's, when Warner Bros. developed the idea of producing a feature-length film that would include sound, Jolson had established himself as a star. Born in Lithuania in 1886, Asa Yoelson was the fifth child of Rabbi Moses Yoelson. In the early 1890's, Rabbi Yoelson emigrated to Washington, D.C., and became the cantor for a small synagogue. Shortly after, the rest of the family arrived.

When Asa was eight years old, he arrived home from school, alone, and witnessed his mother's death. It was an event that affected young Asa profoundly, one that never completely left his mind. In later years, when singer Al Jolson dropped to one knee and sang "Mammy," the tears were real.

Rejecting his father's Orthodox Jewish customs, Asa and his older brother, Hirsch, Americanized their names to Harry and Al Joelson and began touring in vaudeville. Al's rise was nothing less than meteoric; by 1911 he had become one of the strongest attractions on the Broadway stage. His style of singing was a mixture of popular melodies and jazz. Jolson often improvised his routines and monologues within the context of his performances, sometimes whistling chorus songs. Much of this style would be incorporated into *The Jazz Singer.*

Jolson was not the original choice for the starring role in the film. The film was based on a short story called "The Day of Atonement," written by Samson Raphaelson. Ironically mirroring much of Jolson's career, the story describes the life of a young Jewish boy who rejects much of his Orthodox heritage. The boy becomes an entertainer. In the end, however, he returns to the synagogue to sing for the Kol Nidre service, which represents the holiest night of the Jewish year.

Jolson met with Raphaelson in 1922 to discuss the possibility of making the story into a play. Jolson had in mind a lavish musical, which was against the interests of the author. The two parted company, but Jolson continued his interest in the project.

In 1925, Albert Lewis and Max Gordon purchased the option on the play. Originally titled *Prayboy*, it was renamed *The Jazz Singer* and starred George Jessel. The play premiered on July 9, 1925, in Stamford, Connecticut. It opened on Broadway that fall, running for the full season. During 1926 and 1927, the play toured the country, eventually amassing some three hundred performances.

In April, 1926, Warner Bros. signed an agreement with Western Electric to form a new company, the Vitaphone Corporation, with the intended purpose of recording both popular artists and scores for films. Both Jessel and Jolson were among the entertainers signed to appear in these shorts. In September, 1926, Jolson was filmed singing several songs and delivering a monologue. While speaking with Sam Warner, Jolson, never an introvert, expressed his interest in a film version of *The Jazz Singer.*

The original choice for the lead in the film was George Jessel, but both Jack and Sam Warner seem to have preferred Jolson. Jessel's film contract, however, did not include provisions for "talkies." Jessel held out for additional money, and the Warners signed Jolson for the role. This transaction was to create bitterness between the actors for the rest of their lives.

Shooting of the film was carried out between July and September of 1927. The cast was solid. In addition to Jolson, it included Warner Oland, who later starred in the Charlie Chan series, Eugénie Besserer, and May McAvoy, all established stars. Included in a bit part was William Demarest, who later played Jolson's mentor in the 1946 film biography *The Jolson Story.* Demarest was best known to television audiences for his later role on *My Three Sons.* A young Myrna Loy also appeared as an extra.

The Jazz Singer was not what one would call a "talkie." It was primarily a silent film, with songs and some dialogue recorded. The first sound scene was recorded on August 16, 1927. Jolson's character, Jakie Rabinowitz/Jack Robin, has just sung "Dirty Hands, Dirty Face" to a dance-hall crowd. The first spoken words, typical of Jolson's style and ad-libbed for the picture, follow: "Wait a minute! Wait a minute! You ain't heard nothing yet." He then proceeds to sing, dance, and whistle his way through the next song, "Toot, Toot, Tootsie." The first scene in which singing is audible occurs earlier, when Bobby Gordon, playing the young Jakie, croons to a saloon crowd.

During a later scene, Jack Robin, now a success in show business, returns for a visit to his mother. Following a rendition of "Blue Skies," Jolson proceeded to ad lib a touching scene with his mother: "If I'm a success in this show, we're gonna move from here. . . ." Eugénie Besserer, obviously surprised by Jolson's routine, could only murmur, "Oh, no." Jolson continues to ad lib the scene until the father appears, shouting "Stop!"

The film version of *The Jazz Singer* premiered on October 6, 1927, opening at the Warner Theatre in New York City. It attracted a large crowd, including Jolson himself. At the film's conclusion, applause and cheers from the crowd brought Jolson to the stage.

Although not an artistic triumph, *The Jazz Singer* was nevertheless a success. Eventually, it was shown all over the world, generating a profit of three and a half million dollars. The talking era had begun.

Impact of Event

The release of a "talkie" had an immediate and profound impact on the film industry. The public posture of the industry was "business as usual." *The Jazz Singer* was described as a novelty, and "talkies" as a curiosity in which the public would eventually lose interest. Reviewers generally favored the film and praised Jolson's acting. Few associated any revolutionary potential with the use of sound. In fact, it was noted by the reviewer for *The New York Times* that the sound was not even well coordinated. The sound level of songs or dialogue appeared to be the same regardless of how far away from the camera the actors stood. Privately, however, assessments were much more realistic. The owners of the studios had not become rich by rejecting innovations. It was clear that films with sound represented the future of the industry.

The owners acted accordingly. Studios were altered, literally changing overnight. Film studios were wired for sound; silent film projects either were altered to include sound sequences or were simply terminated. The Warner Bros. studio, in the forefront of sound technology, was among the first to reap the rewards. Warner Bros. had been close to bankruptcy when it filmed *The Jazz Singer*. Its second musical, *The Singing Fool* (1928), was an even greater commercial success. Warner Bros. released its first all-talking film, *Lights of New York*, in 1928. By the end of 1929, the studio began showing profits. Not the least of its assets was its contract with Al Jolson. Warner Bros. had emerged as a giant in the movie industry.

The Vitaphone system, developed and utilized by the Vitaphone Corporation in these early sound films, was itself short-lived. The principle of the system involved recording sound on a disk which was played along with the film. During the course of projection, it was not unusual for the film and disk to lose their synchronization. In fact, it was this problem that plagued an earlier sound experiment carried out by Warner Bros. with a 1926 film entitled *Don Juan*, starring John Barrymore and Mary Astor. A film score was recorded on disk by the New York Philharmonic, but because of frequent loss of synchrony, many theaters refused to use a sound system.

The film remained, for all intents and purposes, a "silent."

Alternative means of recording sound were developed. Two systems in particular proved successful: a variable-area sound track and a variable-density sound track. Developed by Fox studios (Movietone), both procedures worked according to similar principles. A sound pattern, or track, was recorded along the edge of the film. During projection, a photoelectric cell converted the pattern to electrical impulses, which were transmitted as sound waves from a loudspeaker. The use of a sound track eliminated the problem of synchronization. By 1931, the Vitaphone system was abandoned.

Ironically, the use of sound in films had an immediate regressive effect. The movie camera had become increasingly mobile, often being mounted on cars or trains. With a sound system, however, the actors had to remain in close proximity to the microphone. This was readily demonstrated in the first all-talkie movie, *Lights of New York*. The vacuum-tube microphones functioned in only one direction. The actors therefore tended to congregate around tables or objects, rather than exhibiting normal motions. It was several years before the effective use of microphones on a "boom" eliminated the problem.

The impact of sound was also seen on the actors and actresses themselves. In some cases, the poor projection or quality of a voice was sufficient to end a movie career. Silent actor John Gilbert proved a victim of this problem. Clara Bow's thick New York accent seemed incongruous with her charming beauty. Fair or not, the effect was significant.

The use of spoken dialogue also ended an era of international films. Most people would not attend films in which dialogue, central to a plot, was spoken in a foreign language. It would be several decades before the use of dubbing or subtitles became common in foreign films.

The advent of "talkies" had a tremendous effect on the career of Al Jolson. Although he was a veteran of decades of touring on the stage, his appearance in *The Jazz Singer* made Jolson's voice and style accessible to a much larger audience. His next film, *The Singing Fool*, was even more profitable for the studio, yet in a sense Jolson's career peaked with the release of *The Jazz Singer*. The impact of Jolson's presence could not be felt within the confines of a film. Further, the plots of his films became increasingly predictable. For a time, the studios placed him in lavish musicals, but Jolson's personality did not lend itself to film. He enjoyed a comeback in the late 1940's with the release of two film biographies. In 1950, Jolson became the first Hollywood star to visit Korea to entertain troops. The strain proved too much, and he died from a heart attack soon after his return, on October 23, 1950.

The Jazz Singer was primarily a silent film, and subtitles remained the primary means of communication with the viewing audience. It was not the first "talkie"; the short film *Don Juan* could more appropriately lay claim to that honor. As the first feature-length film to incorporate sound, however, *The Jazz Singer* represented a watershed: the beginning of the sound era.

Bibliography

Freedland, Michael. *Jolson.* New York: Stein & Day, 1972. An entertaining, concise biography of Jolson. It represents the first major biography of the entertainer. In places it is short on detail, but it is still a first-rate story. Included are standard photographs of Jolson.

Geduld, Harry. *The Birth of the Talkies.* Bloomington: Indiana University Press, 1975. An excellent source for following the development of sound in films. Highlights the role of pioneers who developed sound technology.

Goldman, Herbert G. *Jolson: The Legend Comes to Life.* New York: Oxford University Press, 1988. The classic biography of Jolson. Well written and detailed. Included are numerous photographs from all aspects of Jolson's life. Includes an extensive listing of Jolson's appearances on stage, in films, and on records.

Lyman, Darryl. *Great Jews on Stage and Screen.* Middle Village, N.Y.: Jonathan David, 1987. Included is a section on Al Jolson that provides an overview of the entertainer's career. A description of *The Jazz Singer* is included in the biography. Not detailed by any means, but a good summary.

Shipman, David. *The Story of Cinema.* New York: St. Martin's Press, 1982. The book is well written, with an appropriate amount of detail for use as a reference. Included is a chapter on the history and development of sound films. Also included are numerous photographs.

Richard Adler

Cross-References

Sound Technology Revolutionizes the Motion-Picture Industry (1928), p. 761; The First Academy Awards Honor Film Achievement (1929), p. 799; Hollywood Enters Its Golden Age (1930's), p. 822; Berkeley's *42nd Street* Revolutionizes Film Musicals (1933), p. 925; The Hollywood Studio System Is Transformed (1946), p. 1307.

ELLINGTON BEGINS AN INFLUENTIAL ENGAGEMENT AT THE COTTON CLUB

Category of event: Music
Time: December 4, 1927
Locale: New York, New York

Duke Ellington began a three-year engagement at Harlem's Cotton Club that launched his career as the most important composer-arranger-leader in jazz history

Principal personages:

DUKE ELLINGTON (1899-1974), a pianist, composer, arranger, and bandleader who elevated music for dance bands to a respectable art form

JAMES "BUBBER" MILEY (1903-1932), a trumpeter for Ellington's band

JOSEPH "TRICKY SAM" NANTON (1904-1946), a trombonist for Ellington's band

IRVING MILLS (1894-1985), a song publisher and promoter who guided Ellington's career during his first crucial years as a leader

JOHNNY HODGES (1906-1970), an alto saxophonist who joined Ellington at the Cotton Club and became the band's most important soloist

Summary of Event

With Louis Armstrong and Charlie Parker, Edward Kennedy "Duke" Ellington is one of the greatest figures in jazz and twentieth century American music. His importance rests on his achievements as a composer, orchestrator, and pianist-leader of the remarkable orchestra he headed for almost half a century. When he and his band made their debut at New York City's Cotton Club in 1927, Ellington was still a musician with a modest if growing reputation. He already had acquired the nickname that reflected his suave good looks and courtly manner when he emerged as the leader of a small black cooperative dance band that had moved to New York City from Washington, D.C., in 1923.

Ellington's debut at the Cotton Club on December 4, 1927, is now recognized as one of the most important openings in jazz history even though the unprepared band's first few performances there were unimpressive. The band soon mastered the demanding fifteen-act program and also played for dancing and radio broadcast. It quickly became a major attraction in itself, as Ellington used the opportunity to transform his dance-show band into a collaborative vehicle for superior artistic expression.

The Cotton Club was one of the best-known and most successful of more than a dozen Harlem establishments that catered exclusively or mainly to a white clientele. Ellington's white manager, Irving Mills, had arranged for the job at the club. Its success was based mainly on its exotic and relatively sophisticated ambience, the quality of its all-black entertainment, and the sale of illegal alcohol. The elaborate shows, which usually featured comedians, dancers, vocalists, a chorus line, and the house band, were staged by experienced Broadway showpeople with original music by Jimmy McHugh.

The engagement at the Cotton Club enabled Ellington to build and consolidate his all-star band. It also spurred him to create a body of distinctive compositions and orchestral arrangements that drew on the African-American tradition and expanded and elevated the vocabulary of jazz. Many of the club's acts appealed to white fantasies of exotic and primitive Africa, and the muted brass growls that the Ellington band had developed were labeled and marketed as "jungle style." Compositions such as "Echoes of the Jungle" served a functional purpose at the Cotton Club; they also transcended that context and, together with other original works, made an impact when heard on records and radio.

Nationwide radio broadcasts from the Cotton Club on the fledgling Columbia Broadcasting System (CBS) network made Ellington's name and music familiar to millions. Records by Duke Ellington and His Famous Cotton Club Orchestra sold widely and were heard in Europe, where Ellington became a celebrity before his first visit there in 1933. In 1929, Mills arranged for Ellington to lead his band in Florenz Ziegfeld's theater production of George Gershwin's *Show Girl*. The band performed with Maurice Chevalier, then traveled to Hollywood to make the film *Check and Double Check* (1930). Ellington was included in a group of important African Americans invited to the White House in 1931.

In addition to writing arrangements in the jungle style, Ellington mastered the sectional formula developed by Fletcher Henderson for his own much-admired orchestra. Henderson's model became the basis for many big-band arrangers. Ellington frequently departed from the formula, mixing instrumental voices from across the trumpet, trombone, and reed sections to produce unique and sometimes haunting blends, as in the muted trumpet, muted trombone, and clarinet sound of "Mood Indigo" (1930).

Ellington often borrowed or developed the ideas of his musicians in creating music for his band. The frequent use of unwritten "head arrangements," which gradually evolved as suggestions were incorporated, contributed to the collaborative expression of the band but sometimes made the question of authorship difficult, even though the organizing intelligence was clearly Ellington's. In his more formal and personal arrangements, Ellington sometimes used sound in much the same way as the pointillists used paint. His impressionistic compositions, skillful use of dissonance, and unusual textures led to comparisons with such modern European composers as Claude Debussy, Frederick Delius, and Maurice Ravel, of whom Ellington probably had little knowledge. In his career of more than fifty years, Ellington wrote approximately twelve hundred compositions of an amazing variety, including simple blues, popular hit songs, dance tunes, showcases for individual musicians, short orchestral pieces, extended works designed mainly for concerts, film music, television themes, ballet and opera scores, and religious music for his "sacred concerts." Ellington's abiding inspiration was the black American community and its culture, which he sought to portray in compositions such as "Black Beauty," *Black, Brown, and Beige,* "Harlem Airshaft," and "My People."

One of Ellington's greatest achievements was the creation of an orchestra unrivaled for its stability, longevity, and number of influential musicians who stayed within its ranks for prolonged periods. Throughout his life Ellington was in an almost constant state of exploration, reevaluation, and development; his music is so various that it defies classification. He kept the band together, sometimes at great personal expense, because he needed to hear his compositions and arrangements played on the instrument for which they were intended: his orchestra.

Impact of Event

The Ellington orchestra's success was in part a result of the talent of its individual members, many of whom became models for thousands of other artists. Johnny Hodges was one of the preeminent alto saxophonists in jazz, influencing almost all who came after him, even tenor saxophonists such as bandmate Ben Webster and modernist John Coltrane. Harry Carney, who was with the band from 1927 until Ellington's death in 1974, is known as the father of the baritone saxophone, which he established as an important ensemble and solo voice. Trumpeter James "Bubber" Miley and trombonist Joe Nanton developed the plunger-mute techniques on their respective instruments that created the "jungle sounds" that were an important characteristic of the Ellington orchestral style. These expressive techniques sprang from the roots of the jazz instrumental tradition and subsequently were used by brass players everywhere. Miley's successor with Ellington, Charles "Cootie" Williams, became an influence in his own right, as did trombonist Lawrence Brown, trumpeter Clark Terry, and saxophonist Ben Webster. In his short life, Jimmy Blanton established the path followed by most jazz bass players since 1940. Ellington himself was a competent if not outstanding pianist who began by playing mainly in the "stride" style that had developed out of ragtime. He also developed an effective accompaniment style and ways of voicing chords that are widely imitated. Imitations of Ellington's influence can be heard in the work of the modernist pianist/composer Thelonious Monk, who made a piano-trio recording of Ellington compositions.

Ellington's appeal to jazz musicians has transcended periods and styles and proved timeless; there are few who have not acknowledged his influence in one way or another. Ellington's life and musical interests spanned the first seventy-five years of jazz history. He recorded and sounded comfortable with the greatest artists of every period, including Louis Armstrong, Coleman Hawkins, Dizzy Gillespie, Charles Mingus, and John Coltrane.

Because they seem so quintessentially to belong to his orchestra, Ellington's longer compositions are seldom heard performed except on his own recordings. They are demonstrations that the American dance band can be an extremely flexible vehicle, both for popular entertainment and for high artistic expression. Although the Ellington spirit and influence permeate big-band music, few arrangers (aside from his collaborator and musical alter ego, Billy Strayhorn) have been able to duplicate El lington's unique orchestral sound. The bands of Charlie Barnet and Woody Herman at times provided rough approximations, aided by the fact that both leaders were saxophonists in the style of Johnny Hodges. The persistence of Ellington's influence as a composer and orchestrator can be heard in the modern works of Charles Mingus, Gil Evans, and Oliver Nelson.

Ellington's compositions have been played by groups large and small since the 1930's, and his legacy is perhaps most alive in the thirty or so short compositions that are still part of the working repertoire of most jazz musicians around the world. Melodies such as "Satin Doll," "In a Mellow Tone," "Solitude," and "In a Sentimental Mood"—works on a par with those of Cole Porter, George Gershwin, and Irvin Berlin—can be heard wherever jazz is played. Ellington's compositions have been recorded thousands of times by musicians ranging from traditionalists to the avant-garde and have been reinterpreted as they have been discovered by each succeeding generation.

In his many tours abroad, some under the aegis of the United States government, Ellington took his music and the American ideals of individuality and freedom of expression within a cooperative group context to thousands of people. In addition to his influence on musicians and leaders such as Ted Heath of Britain and Francy Boland of Belgium, Ellington absorbed and later (often with Strayhorn) transformed foreign musical influences in such works as *Far East Suite, Virgin Islands Suite*, and *Latin American Suite.*

Wynton Marsalis, one of the most impressive and influential musicians to appear in the 1980's, has stated that "Duke Ellington is what jazz is, he is the greatest jazz musician . . . because he addressed most comprehensively what jazz music actually is . . . the fundamentals of group improvisation, vocalization, and a swinging optimism." Marsalis has devoted much of his considerable talent to educating young musicians in the value of Ellington's music and in performing his works with the Lincoln Center Jazz Orchestra, as on the recording *Portraits by Ellington.*

Ellington's musical achievement elevated jazz as an African-American art form and brought increased acceptance and respect to its practitioners. His personal sophistication and dignity made him an important representative of the black community. Ellington's hundreds of honors and awards, including many honorary doctorates, also served to acknowledge the contributions of black people to American society and culture. On the occasion of his seventieth birthday, a celebration was held at the White House at which President Richard Nixon presented Ellington with the highest civilian award of the United States, the Presidential Medal of Freedom.

During the height of big-band popularity in the 1930's and early 1940's, Ellington's band was not as commercially successful as many white bands, but his organization was often the standard against which other bands were measured, especially by musicians. Through courage, hard work, and artistry, Ellington was able to sustain his band after all but a handful of others had disappeared. When Ellington died in 1974, the leadership of his still-functioning band was taken up by his son Mercer, who continued to present his father's music to the world into the 1990's.

Bibliography

Collier, James Lincoln. *Duke Ellington.* New York: Oxford University Press, 1987. A well-written scholarly biography of Ellington that sets his work within its historical, social, and musical context. Examines the importance and role of Ellington's musicians, both as instrumentalists and as contributors to compositions generally ascribed to their leader. This standard and sometimes controversial study includes musical analysis, photographs, a discographical note, and an index.

Dance, Stanley. *The World of Duke Ellington.* New York: Charles Scribner's Sons, 1970. A group of articles, interviews, memorabilia, sketches of musicians, and diary entries written mainly in the 1960's by the author, a longtime Ellington associate and observer. The whole adds up to a fascinating picture of the personalities and interrelationships of many of the most important members of the Ellington musical family. Photographs, a selective discography, an index, and a chronology from 1899 to 1970 highlighting the major events in Ellington's life, band personnel changes, important compositions, and performances.

Ellington, Edward Kennedy. *Music Is My Mistress.* Garden City, N.Y.: Doubleday, 1973. Ellington's autobiography is a large book that reflects his lively and at times eccentric mind, his sophistication, and his ironic sense of humor. A potpourri including straight memoir, flights of imagination, sketches of more than one hundred musicians and other associates, anecdotes, religious meditations, poems, prose poems, a libretto, and journals of various foreign tours. Rich in personal commentary but of uneven literary quality, Ellington's love of life and passion for music are revealed, but, as always, he guards his privacy and the essential man remains elusive. Photographs, lists of honors and awards, compositions by year of copyright, and a bibliography, but no index.

Ellington, Mercer, with Stanley Dance. *Duke Ellington in Person: An Intimate Memoir.* New York: Da Capo Press, 1978. Written after Ellington's death to supplement the autobiography and the Dance book above. Reveals the darker side of Ellington's personality, his love-hate relationship with his son, his amorous liaisons, and his professional and artistic struggles. Photographs, added copyright and discographic information, and an index.

Haskins, James. *The Cotton Club.* New York: Random House, 1977. The story of the nightclub that, between 1923 and 1940, brought Broadway-type entertainment to Harlem, although for white audiences only. The club introduced and served as a showplace for many of America's greatest black artists. Despite some inaccuracies, a good introduction to an important chapter in entertainment history. Photographs, notes, and a bibliography.

Schuller, Gunther. "Duke Ellington, Master Composer." In *The Swing Era: The Development of Jazz, 1930-1945.* New York: Oxford University Press, 1989. Studies Ellington's music into the 1940's. Successfully combines historical detail with a systematic analysis of the music in terms best understood by trained musicians. Many transcribed musical illustrations, a select discography, glossaries, and indexes.

_____. "The Ellington Style: Its Origins and Early Development." In *Early Jazz: Its Roots and Musical Development.* New York: Oxford University Press, 1968. Examines Ellington's music as recorded from 1926 through the Cotton Club period to 1931.

Douglas Rollins

Cross-References

Joplin Popularizes the Ragtime Style (1899), p. 13; Handy Ushers in the Commercial Blues Era (1910's), p. 252; Bessie Smith Records "Downhearted Blues" (1923), p. 572; Armstrong First Records with His Hot Five Group (1925), p. 670; Billie Holiday Begins Her Recording Career (1933), p. 930; Goodman Begins His *Let's Dance* Broadcasts (1934), p. 968; Parker's Playing Epitomizes Bebop (1946), p. 1318; Davis' *Birth of the Cool* Recordings Spawn 1950's Cool Jazz (1949), p. 1438; Wynton Marsalis Revives Acoustic Jazz (1980's), p. 2454.

SHOW BOAT INTRODUCES
AMERICAN MUSICAL THEATER

Categories of event: Theater and music
Time: December 27, 1927
Locale: New York, New York

Show Boat *was the first major musical production to have a strong, plotted story line*

Principal personages:
JEROME KERN (1885-1945), a composer who worked with European operettas and modern musicals
OSCAR HAMMERSTEIN II (1895-1960), a librettist who, with different partners, created several groundbreaking works in musical theater
EDNA FERBER (1887-1968), the Pulitzer Prize-winning author who wrote the novel *Show Boat*
FLORENZ ZIEGFELD (1869-1932), the impresario who produced *Show Boat*

Summary of Event

By 1927, Jerome Kern, Oscar Hammerstein II, and Florenz Ziegfeld already had made significant contributions to the world of musical theater. Ziegfeld was known primarily as an impresario whose yearly editions of Ziegfeld Follies introduced New York audiences to such performing talents as Fanny Brice and Bert Williams and such writing talents as Irving Berlin and the team of Richard Rodgers and Lorenz Hart. The Ziegfeld Follies were revues that featured skits, stand-up comedy, specialty acts, individual songs, and many beautiful women. Ziegfeld had made the decision to branch out into the more conventional musical comedy. He also had decided, in 1927, to open a new theater that bore his name; it was built on Sixth Avenue and Fifty-Third Street. He promised Kern and Hammerstein that their new musical would be the first production in the new theater.

Hammerstein and Kern, along with Otto Harbach, had written an earlier musical for Ziegfeld. *Sunny,* produced in 1925, featured Marilyn Miller. Hammerstein came from a theatrical family. His grandfather was an opera impresario, his father ran a vaudeville house, and his uncle produced shows on Broadway. Hammerstein had studied law at Columbia University but was soon drawn into theater. With Harbach, he teamed on the book and lyrics (the libretto) for several musicals with a variety of composers. Kern was impressed with his work on *Sunny* and approached him to create the libretto for *Show Boat.*

Turning *Show Boat* into a musical was Kern's idea. This was not the first time Kern was involved in groundbreaking musical theater. In 1915, Kern, along with librettist Guy Bolton, wrote a musical called *Nobody Home.* This was the first of a series of musicals that have become known as the Princess Theater shows. The name came from the theater where the shows were first performed. In an era of operetta with the libretto serving as a showcase for songs and set pieces by featured comics, usually in the setting of a lush European fantasy, the Princess Theater shows were marked by smaller productions (usually two sets), smaller casts (eight chorus members or fewer), and smaller orchestras (ten instruments or fewer).

Although the physical production of the Princess Theater shows might have been smaller, the ambitions and talents involved were quite large. The Princess Theater shows used American situations, and the songs and comedy grew out of these situations. Other musicals in the series included *Very Good Eddie* (1915), *Oh, Boy!* (1917), and *Oh, Lady! Lady!!* (1918). The last two had the added feature of the British wit of P. G. Wodehouse.

Work on *Show Boat* began during the intermission of another Kern musical, *Criss Cross* (1926). Kern had read the 1926 novel by Edna Ferber and was determined to meet her to discuss its musical possibilities. Kern approached his friend, Alexander Woollcott, to ask for an introduction. Conveniently, Ferber was Woollcott's guest that evening at the theater. In the lobby, during intermission, Kern broached his idea to the novelist. Ferber was no stranger to the theater. She had written a play with George S. Kaufman. In fact, it was a casual comment from Kaufman that sparked the idea for the novel *Show Boat*. When the novel was published, it quickly became a best-seller. This only added to Ferber's fame, as she had won the Pulitzer Prize in 1925 for her novel *So Big*.

The idea of turning *Show Boat* into a musical at first did not appeal to Ferber. Her experience with musicals had been shows such as *Criss Cross* that featured comic routines, tap dancing, and lines of chorus girls. Kern had a different vision and was able to convince the novelist that *Show Boat* would not be a conventional musical comedy but rather a musical play.

Having won her consent, Kern approached Hammerstein to write the libretto and Ziegfeld to produce the show. Kern and Hammerstein went to work, secure with the promise from Ziegfeld that *Show Boat* would open the new Ziegfeld Theater. What they did not know was that Ziegfeld had made the same commitment to Guy Bolton and Harry Tierney, who were writing *Rio Rita*. On February 2, 1927, the theater was ready and so was *Rio Rita*. Ziegfeld was a man of business and opened his theater with a likely hit. Allowing *Rio Rita* to open the Ziegfeld Theater removed any sense of time pressure on Kern and Hammerstein to finish *Show Boat*, allowing them to fine-tune their work and to introduce innovations.

Show Boat tried out in Washington, D.C., in November of 1927. The show was too long, but the audience responded well. Kern and Hammerstein continued to refine their work. The production then moved to Philadelphia, where refinements continued. On December 27, 1927, *Show Boat* opened at the Ziegfeld Theater in New York City. Though the show was still long, the response from the critics and the audience was very positive. *Show Boat* ran for two years in New York, went on a national tour, returned to New York for another run, opened a production in London, generated three film versions, and became the first Broadway musical to be part of the repertory of the New York City Opera.

Impact of Event

When *Show Boat* opened in 1927, the musical theater was divided between revues such as Ziegfeld's Follies and George White's Scandals, European operettas, and American musical comedies such as the Princess Theater shows. Although these musical comedies represented a distinct departure in style and subject matter from the operetta, the music and comedy were the focus. This often meant that character-driven plots were sacrificed for comic situations and catchy tunes.

It would be misleading to suggest that one show, even *Show Boat*, could change all that. Such is not the nature of art. *Show Boat* did, however, point the way for such artists as Richard Rodgers and Stephen Sondheim. This happened because of the promise Jerome Kern made to Edna Ferber. Instead of using the outline of Ferber's novel as a skeleton for songs and comic routines, Kern and Hammerstein were concerned with telling the story.

This was an ambitious task. *Show Boat* tells the story of Magnolia Hawkes, the daughter of Cap'n Andy, proprietor of the Cotton Blossom, a show boat. Magnolia meets and falls in love with Gaylord Ravenal, a suave riverboat gambler. They marry and have a daughter named Kim. Ravenal leaves his wife and child. Another performer with the Cotton Blossom company, Julie, is found to be a mulatto, and, since she is married to a Caucasian, she is charged with miscegenation and forced to leave the show boat. She later turns up as an alcoholic saloon singer in Chicago. Magnolia and Kim also are in Chicago during the World's Fair, and they have a brief reunion with Ravenal. *Show Boat* is a sprawling tale that covers several decades and locales. Alcoholism, racism, and broken families are some of the issues that drive the plot. This was not the usual material for musical comedy.

Show Boat demonstrated that, if handled with skill and taste, such issues could be material for musical theater. *Carousel* (1945) by Rodgers and Hammerstein dealt with spousal abuse and dysfunctional families. *South Pacific* (1949) by the same team uses interracial marriage as a key element. Alan Jay Lerner and Frederick Loewe told the story of King Arthur in *Camelot* (1960); several adulterous affairs are central to that story. Kern and Hammerstein first demonstrated that the American musical could deal with serious issues, breaking the ground for these later shows.

Serious issues alone did not make *Show Boat* great. The source material, though successful as a novel, did not guarantee a successful musical. Kern and Hammerstein had to combine their experience, their talents, and their ideas for innovation to create *Show Boat*. Many of the songs they wrote have become standards. The score includes "Only Make Believe," "Why Do I Love You?," and "Can't Help Lovin' Dat Man of Mine." Each of these shows Kern's considerable melodic gifts. They also demonstrate Hammerstein's unique lyrical turn with love songs. Instead of writing the commonplace "I love you," Hammerstein suggested that the characters "make believe" they love each other.

There is a love song in *Show Boat* with lyrics not written by Hammerstein. The song "Bill," sung by Julie, was written by Kern and P. G. Wodehouse. It was intended for *Oh, Lady! Lady!!* but had been cut. When Helen Morgan was cast as

Julie, Kern thought that the song "Bill" would lend itself perfectly to Morgan's trademark of sitting on a piano to sing a torch song. Hammerstein was given credit so often for this song that he took pains to include a program note giving due praise to Wodehouse.

Another song, "Ol' Man River," also had a lasting effect on the musical theater. With such a sprawling story to tell, Hammerstein thought it necessary to use a song to tie the work together. Using a slowed down, inverted version of the Cotton Blossom theme, Hammerstein fashioned a ballad of pain, despair, and some hope based on the unceasing flow of the Mississippi River that binds all these lives together. Oddly enough, this song, which is the theme of the show, is sung by Joe, a relatively minor character.

The idea of a concept or theme tying a musical together has been used in some of the most enduring productions. *Fiddler on the Roof* (1964) uses the idea of tradition, both in the family and in society, as the theme that ties the plot together. Stephen Sondheim, a protégé of Hammerstein, wrote a musical, *Company* (1970), that all but dispenses with plot and relies heavily on the themes of marriage and New York City to unite the production. *Company* is often called the first "concept" musical. Summer theaters and opera companies make sure that *Show Boat* itself, in so many ways a pioneering show, endures.

Bibliography

Engei, Lehman. *The American Musical Theater.* New York: Macmillan, 1975. The obvious source for any serious study of the musical theater. Engel uses his experience as a conductor and theorist to evaluate trends in musical theater history. A chapter titled "Breakaway" includes Engel's analysis and opinions of *Show Boat.* He writes not to worship Kern and Hammerstein but to evaluate them. Contains several useful appendices.

Ewen, David. *The World of Jerome Kern.* New York: Henry Holt, 1960. Highly readable, this is a library biography for the lay person. Kern is clearly the hero, so scholars should be wary of a lack of objectivity. The anecdotes and direct quotes from Kern on *Show Boat* are valuable, but information on his work with Hammerstein is sketchy. The pictures do little good for research.

Green, Stanley. *The World of Musical Comedy.* New York: Grosset & Dunlap, 1962. One of the first major histories of the musical. Green chose to treat his subject with a cross between chronology and studies of the writers. The section on Kern is very good, with valuable notes on getting *Show Boat* to the stage.

Kislan, Richard. *The Musical.* Englewood Cliffs, N.J.: Prentice-Hall, 1980. A textbook for a general course in musical theater. It includes a brief but thorough history, and a study of the various crafts and artists in the musical theater. Features a chapter on Kern and goes into some depth on Ziegfeld and the Princess Theater. The pictures are very good.

Smith, Cecil, and Glenn Litton. *Musical Comedy in America.* New York: Theatre Arts Books, 1981. An excellent overall history of the musical theater. The pictures are adequate, and the text is thorough and literate. Smith and Litton go beyond the expected chronology and discuss technique. Smith, who wrote the earlier part, is particularly good at creating a sense of what the theater was like at the time.

William B. Kennedy

Cross-References

Cohan's *Little Johnny Jones* Premieres (1904), p. 108; Gershwin's *Porgy and Bess* Opens in New York (1935), p. 1016; *Oklahoma!* Opens on Broadway (1943), p. 1256; Porter Creates an Integrated Score for *Kiss Me, Kate* (1948), p. 1404; Bernstein Joins Symphonic and Jazz Elements in *West Side Story* (1957), p. 1731; *The Sound of Music* Captivates Audiences (1965), p. 2033.

BUÑUEL AND DALÍ CHAMPION SURREALISM
IN *UN CHIEN ANDALOU*

Category of event: Motion pictures
Time: 1928
Locale: Paris, France

The Surrealist film Un Chien andalou *launched the career of Luis Buñuel and gave him a vehicle for expressing his deeply felt indignation at the moral failures of church and society*

Principal personages:
LUIS BUÑUEL (1900-1983), a Spanish filmmaker/moralist whose films used Surrealist concepts, irony, and postmodern blurring of opposites such as good and evil
SALVADOR DALÍ (1904-1989), a Spanish Surrealist painter who collaborated with Buñuel on two films
ANDRÉ BRETON (1896-1966), a former Dadaist who became the founder of the Surrealist movement in Paris in the 1920's

Summary of Event

The intellectual movement that dominated the careers of both Luis Buñuel and Salvador Dalí and that drove them to produce *Un Chien andalou* (1928, an Andalusian dog) was Surrealism. Along with Dadaism and expressionism, it was a revolt against representational art.

Led by founder André Breton, the Surrealist movement had its first exhibition in Paris in 1925. Surrealists believed that the contents of the unconscious mind were as real as was the concrete world; therefore, artistic rules that governed merely the physical world, such as those of perspective, were not sufficient as an expression of reality. Surrealist art attempted to depict objects in incongruous juxtapositions, as they might occur in a dream.

Dalí and Buñuel met in 1920 at the University of Madrid. Dalí called his friends a "strident and revolutionary group." The first one-man exhibition of his paintings came in 1925 in Barcelona. Dalí held Jean-Auguste-Dominique Ingres and Jacques-Louis David, realist painters from the nineteenth century, in high esteem. In arguing for tradition and classical form, Dalí shocked his Spanish contemporaries, most of whom were absorbed in the Postimpressionist rejection of academic rules and traditions. Dalí's Surrealism would permit him his realism, but with unrelated objects depicted in dreamlike, infinitely receding landscapes. In 1927, he dedicated to Buñuel an essay suggesting that film could promote a new way of seeing.

After an apprenticeship from 1925 to 1928 at Jean Epstein's Académie du Cinéma in Paris, Buñuel joined Dalí in making a Surrealist film. The script was written in three days, and filming was completed in less than two weeks. The short film *Un*

Chien andalou was shown to Breton and other Paris Surrealists, who enthusiastically received it and accepted the pair into their ranks.

Dalí described the aim of the film as jolting viewers. He and Buñuel wanted to make a film that "would carry . . . the audience back to the secret depths of adolescence, to the sources of dreams, destiny, and the secret of life and death, a work that would scratch away at all received ideas." Buñuel wrote that in working out the plot, every idea of a rational, aesthetic, or other preoccupation with technical matters was rejected as irrelevant. He described the aim of the film as producing instinctive reactions of attraction and repulsion. Despite the fact that both artists insisted that nothing in the film symbolizes anything, *Un Chien andalou* has been interpreted as having various meanings.

Analysts agree that the opening sequence of the twenty-minute film, in which a razor slices a human eye, was intended as a typical, if horrifying, Surrealist attack upon the viewer's (and the world's) complacency in the midst of worldwide atrocities. What follows is a series of intentionally unrelated scenes that has been called "a catalogue of Freudian metaphors."

A male bicyclist, dressed as a nurse and thus sexually ambiguous, arrives at a woman's apartment. To recordings of Argentine tangos alternating with Richard Wagner's *Liebestod* from *Tristan and Isolde*, the script calls for a close-up of a hand full of crawling ants. This dissolves into a close-up of the hairy armpit of a woman who is sunbathing and then to a close-up of the spines of a sea urchin.

From the window, the two observe a girl being run over in the street. This sexually excites the cyclist. The woman allows his fondling but then becomes frigid. Protecting herself with a tennis racket, she too manifests a certain androgyny. Desperately trying to reach her, the man must drag two grand pianos, on which are dead and putrefying donkeys, and two priests. This grotesque comic relief may symbolize, as one critic suggested, "the dead weight of a decaying society chaining the free expression of man's desire."

A more assertive man, the alter ego of the bicyclist, enters. The bicyclist shoots him dead, possibly symbolizing the murder of the man he might have been. Later, the woman is walking on a beach with another man, possibly another alter ego. He appears mature and confident but still unhappy. At the end, they are seen buried up to their chests in sand and being eaten alive by swarms of insects. The scene is enigmatically titled "In the Spring."

Buñuel and Dalí's collaboration ended during work on the 1930 Surrealist masterpiece *L'Âge d'or*, Buñuel's first feature-length film at 63 minutes. Dalí called that film a caricature of his ideas. Perhaps Buñuel was too strident in his assault on religion and conventional morality as constraints on human freedom. This frontal attack, first signaled in *Un Chien andalou* and powerfully extended in this film, caused *L'Âge d'or* to be banned widely.

A documentary-like prologue shows two scorpions killing a rat. Scenes follow in Surrealist juxtaposition. Prosperous colonists arrive on an island. They recall Spain's voyages of discovery and Christianization. In a famous sequence, four lavishly attired bishops turn into skeletons. Next, a couple making love in public are arrested by scandalized society. The colonists then dedicate a stone to their new colony. A small pile of soft cement on the stone looks like excrement.

Polite socialites at a party barely notice an ox cart filled with drunken peasants crossing the hall, a kitchen fire, and a murder, but they are horrified at an insult and a slap in their midst. Later, at a concert, they seem oblivious to the passionate groping of the reunited lovers and unmoved by the surging crescendos of the *Liebestod*. Finally, in a sadistic orgy in a medieval castle, a duke is depicted as Christ and a cross is decorated with the heads of religiously exploited women. Buñuel's message appears to be that respectability requires society to repress its sexuality and spontaneity. A culture that does this is not alive but a fossil (the bishop/skeletons). Not only does institutional religion not serve, but it is harmful and degrading.

Impact of Event

Buñuel's next silent film had to be funded privately, but his 1932 documentary *Las Hurdes* ranks among the best ever made. Miserable in a Spanish region hostile to life in any form, the people of Las Hurdes eat only potatoes and beans, and they incestuously produce retarded children. In school, barefooted, ragged children are taught bourgeois values. Here documentary becomes editorial, indicting a morality that ignores human degradation, surrealistically juxtaposing peasant hovels and ornate churches and surveying the people's animal existence against the inspiring strains of Brahms's Fourth Symphony.

From 1932 to 1959, Buñuel learned to moderate his fervor, making sound films in the United States, France, Spain, and Mexico. His seventeen Mexican films, previously dismissed as commercial, have been found to be rich in veiled satire on the hypocrisy of conventional morality.

The period saw his 1950 masterpiece, *Los Olvidados* (*The Young and the Damned*). Pedro, refused love by his prostitute mother, is taught to steal by Jaibo. In a Surrealist dream sequence, Pedro appeals for love, and his mother responds erotically. Jaibo comes out from under the bed. Reality and dreams are skillfully and inextricably confused. Pedro is murdered by Jaibo and, ironically, the mother becomes the lover of her son's killer.

Buñuel's pessimism was even more pronounced in *Nazarin* (1959) and *Viridiana* (1961). Both won prizes at the Cannes film festival; both are criticisms of the church, whose most sincere ministers do more harm than good in the world. The priest Nazarin symbolizes Christ's return being rejected in the modern world. *Viridiana*, Buñuel's first film shot in Spain in thirty years, was banned for its criticism of Francisco Franco. A religious novice, Viridiana unintentionally destroys those who helped her and is nearly raped by blind and poor beggars she has helped. Values are reversed as the ungrateful poor destroy her house and eat everything, in a parody of the Last Supper. She renounces her vocation.

In 1962, Buñuel produced *El Angel exterminador* (*The Exterminating Angel*), a Surrealist masterpiece. The elegant guests at a dinner party find that, unaccountably, they cannot leave the dining room. Somehow they must adapt to their curious situation. An older man dies and frustrated lovers commit suicide. The bodies are stuffed in one closet while another closet serves as a bathroom. The prisoners engage in a variety of superstitious rituals and vices. Finally extricated, on Sunday they appear at church. Again they find themselves unable to leave.

Diary of a Chambermaid (1964) was a commentary on the social changes in France after World War I. The chambermaid Celestine openly despises her Royalist employers. Their neighbor is an insulting republican who pitches his garbage into their yard. Their gamekeeper is a fascist triumphantly demonstrating in the streets of Paris for the moral rebirth of France, but he brutally rapes and murders a child and gets away with it. Celestine marries the old republican but cruelly turns him into her servant. Buñuel again provides a coldly dispassionate, even documentary, view of decadent class privilege, gross injustice, the failure of idealism, and the reversal of values.

In 1965 came *Simon of the Desert.* A fifth century hermit, Simon Stylites, spent his life atop a sixty-foot column. Buñuel shows him preaching, healing, and overcoming sometimes bizarre temptations. Later, conveyed to twentieth century New York City, he learns that for all of his virtue and self-negation, people have remained morally unchanged. In his own time he was significant, but in the modern age he has no lasting impact.

In *Belle de Jour* (1967), Buñuel so smoothly moved between fantasy or dreams and actuality that the audience often cannot tell them apart. His Surrealist message is that both realms are equally real. In *The Milky Way* (1969), Buñuel again assaulted the church. The title refers to the pilgrimage to the Spanish shrine of Santiago Campostella. The film is an allegorical journey through church history. Along the way, ordinary people discuss important theological mysteries. Nearing the shrine, two vagrant pilgrims are diverted from their quest by a prostitute. Here, as in *Simon of the Desert*, the imposing doctrines of the church appear sterile and irrelevant.

Buñuel's Surrealism overturns conventional values. Evil triumphs over good and often results from the good intentions of the innocent, who themselves become compromised. Opposites, even good and evil, do not exist but are fictions of the conscious mind. Physical beauty is no better than ugliness. Buñuel's camera sees "objects and men without blinking at deformity and without winking at a superior viewer." Poor and deformed people do not generate pity, since he depicts them as vicious and greedy.

Buñuel's audiences, conditioned to seeing morality triumph, are left bothered by the apparent moral ambiguity of a filmmaker who has been called one of the great moralists of the twentieth century. Henry Miller, who considered Buñuel a genius, wrote in 1932 that Buñuel portrays "the lunacy of civilization, the record of man's achievement after ten thousand years of refinement." In achieving this goal, however, Buñuel falsified the Surrealist denial of intentionality. After he had reached the age of seventy, he produced a series of films—*Tristana* (1970), *The Discreet Charm of the Bourgeoisie* (1972), and *Cet obscur objet du desir* (1977)—that are among the greatest masterpieces of Surrealism in any medium. Buñuel's influence probably has been less over the films of other directors than over audiences and film critics, who gradually have come to better understand his art, insights, and bite.

Bibliography

Ades, Dawn. *Dalí and Surrealism.* New York: Harper and Row, 1982. A fine biography with special reference to Dalí's attachment to the Surrealist movement and chapters on his role in Surrealist cinema.

Durgnat, Raymond. *Luis Buñuel.* Berkeley: University of California Press, 1967. An excellent filmography (twenty-six films are treated from a moderate Marxist view), copiously illustrated with stills of key scenes.

Higginbotham, Virginia. *Luis Buñuel.* Boston: Twayne, 1979. An excellent but modestly illustrated introductory biography and filmography of Buñuel.

Lippard, Lucy R., ed. *Surrealists on Art.* Englewood Cliffs, N.J.: Prentice-Hall, 1970. The article entitled "Luis Buñuel and Salvador Dali" consists of a translation of the actual screenplay of *Un Chien andalou.* This should be read as the primary source for interpreting the pioneer Surrealist film.

Nadeau, Maurice. *The History of Surrealism.* Translated by Richard Howard. New York: Macmillan, 1965. An extremely detailed history of Surrealism in literature, art, and film. It contains translations of André Breton's three "Surrealist Manifestos" and other documents of the movement.

Read, Herbert. "Introduction." In *Surrealism.* New York: Praeger, 1971. A sophisticated but clearly written definition of every nuance of Surrealism, using historical, artistic, and Freudian points of departure; with illustrations.

Schillaci, Peter P. "Luis Buñuel and the Death of God." In *Three European Directors,* edited by James M. Wall. Grand Rapids, Mich.: William B. Eerdmans, 1973. A highly recommended interpretation of Buñuel, rich in insights into the director's mind and vivid descriptions of his major films.

Daniel C. Scavone

Cross-References

Freud Inaugurates a Fascination with the Unconscious (1899), p. 19; The Dada Movement Emerges at the Cabaret Voltaire (1916), p. 419; *The Cabinet of Dr. Caligari* Opens in Berlin (1920), p. 486; Surrealism Is Born (1924), p. 604; Renoir Marks the High Point of Prewar Filmmaking (1937), p. 1073; A Dalí Museum Opens in Figueras, Spain (1974), p. 2310.

THE *AMOS 'N' ANDY* RADIO SHOW GOES ON THE AIR

Category of event: Television and radio
Time: March 19, 1928
Locale: Chicago, Illinois

Amos 'n' Andy, *a pioneer of radio network comedy shows, greatly influenced the direction of national commercial radio and became a controversial yet integral part of American popular culture*

> *Principal personages:*
> CHARLES CORRELL (1890-1972), a cocreator of *Amos 'n' Andy* as well as one of the show's writers and principal actors
> FREEMAN FISHER GOSDEN (1899-1982), a cocreator of *Amos 'n' Andy* and one of the show's chief writers and actors
> WALTER WHITE (1893-1955), a leader of the National Association for the Advancement of Colored People (NAACP) and opponent of *Amos 'n' Andy*

Summary of Event

At ten o'clock on the evening of March 19, 1928, radio station WMAQ, broadcasting from its studio in Chicago's Merchandise Mart, aired the first episode of the *Amos 'n' Andy* comedy series, primarily for Chicago area listeners but also for a number of smaller stations elsewhere by means of recordings. The show immediately proved to be successful and was quickly bought by the National Broadcasting Company's (NBC) Blue Network. NBC began broadcasting the show nationwide beginning on August 19, 1929.

Thereafter, *Amos 'n' Andy* was destined to become a radio legend. Its share of the radio audience has probably never been equaled by any other serial broadcast. It became a national mania. Estimates made between 1931 and 1932 placed the fifteen-minute show's audience at forty million, or one-third of the American population. Officials of all ranks, including presidents, made it known that they were listeners; work schedules were altered so that employers and their employees could tune in; and national conventions and local gatherings alike characteristically interrupted their proceedings so that followers among the attendees would not miss a single episode. Although the show's character and content increasingly provoked racial controversy, especially after the television adaptation began airing in 1951, its audience appeal was nearly universal, cutting across political, sectional, social, ethnic, and color lines. By the time *Amos 'n' Andy* left the air on November 20, 1960, after 4,090 broadcasts, it had become an integral part of American popular culture as well as an abiding reminder of unresolved conflicts in national life.

Amos 'n' Andy was the creation of Freeman Fisher Gosden and Charles Correll. They not only conceived the comedy but through most of the show's history wrote each of its scripts themselves and, unrehearsed, furnished the voices of its principal characters. Both men had Southern backgrounds. Gosden was born in Richmond, Virginia, the son of a man who had served with the famed Confederate raider Colonel John Singleton Mosby. He was reared with African Americans as members of his household. Correll, though born the son of a skilled stonemason and construction foreman in Peoria, Illinois, also shared a strong Southern heritage through his maternal grandmother. Both men pursued careers as performers, chiefly in minstrel shows and blackface comedy—entertainment traditions that predated the Civil War—before and after joining Joe Bren's Chicago theatrical company, where they met. Gosden and Correll's Southern antecedents and their blackface comedy careers were vital to the creation of *Amos 'n' Andy*, for its featured characters, as well as nearly all others, were black.

Amos 'n' Andy sprang from an earlier comedy broadcast, *Sam 'n' Henry*, that also was the brainchild of Gosden and Correll. Aired initially on January 12, 1926, by the *Chicago Tribune*'s station, WGN, *Sam 'n' Henry* was radio's first serialized situation comedy. Its name derived from its two main characters, two African Americans who left Birmingham, Alabama, for Chicago. Like millions of real black migrants, they had joined what historians have since labeled the Great Migration to Northern cities that began in the 1920's, seeking opportunity denied them in the South. Because WGN owned *Sam 'n' Henry*, Gosden and Correll were obliged to change the show's name to *Amos 'n' Andy* when, after 586 episodes of *Sam 'n' Henry*, their services were purchased by station WMAQ and NBC in 1928. Other changes were minor. Instead of having left Birmingham, for example, Amos Jones and Andy Brown had left Atlanta for Chicago's increasingly black, and generally poor, South Side.

Although their speech was identifiably a Southern black dialect, replete with mispronunciations and other linguistic distortions, the characters of the *Amos 'n' Andy* show depended less for appeal on their blackness—and the humor attending their speech—than they did on their manifest humanity. Amos was recognizably a decent, hardworking, amiable, and lovable, if uneducated, poor man surviving in a depression-ridden and altogether strange urban environment, thus resembling millions of his fellow Americans of all colors. Ostensibly more intelligent than Amos, Andy was pretentious, pompous, lazy, equally uneducated, and invariably engaged in using and abusing his long-suffering companion as the two tried their hands at enterprise, running their hand-to-mouth Fresh-Air Taxicab Company. In dramatic contrast to this pair, the real villain (such as anyone was) was the Kingfish (George Stevens), who slyly and crookedly presided over a fraternal lodge known as the Mystic Knights of the Sea and continually sought to exploit everyone. The show's characters, in short, were not intended overtly to be racially demeaning. Rather, they reflected Gosden and Correll's prior show-business experience with and mastery of a plausible black dialect. Otherwise, their characters and story lines could equally well have been applied (as they were by other writers and performers) to immigrant Poles, Italians, or Germans, or for that matter to any befuddled and unlettered country bumpkins. Similar stories and characters were common in earlier American comedy and vaudeville productions and in other comedy shows during the early days of radio. Gosden and Correll's version put the elements together in a way that the public particularly enjoyed, and after two decades of effectively uncontroverted success, *Amos 'n' Andy* became a part of national folklore and an identifiable contribution to American culture.

Impact of Event

Amid the initial chaos of radio's early development, with more than six hundred stations vying for both audiences and sponsors, and without guidelines or precedents to indicate to broadcasters what either group wanted, the *Amos 'n' Andy* show was, in many significant ways, a pioneering experiment. As much as any other single nontechnical factor, the show was responsible for the explosive success of commercial radio. The broad human appeal of Amos, Andy, and Gosden and Correll's other characters, along with the common denominator of the easily understood troubles they encountered, drew audiences of unimagined magnitude. Sponsors previously had been reluctant to trust the repute of their products to the relatively untried advertising forum of radio. After noting Pepsodent's ballooning sales, attributable in part to its sponsorship of *Amos 'n' Andy*, they scrambled to identify themselves with any of the host of subsequent radio comedies and dramas that the show helped spawn.

The Great Depression virtually mandated that entertainment be provided at low cost, preferably within the home. Sales of radio sets increased by geometric leaps, as they provided virtually unlimited free entertainment after the initial purchase of a set. With a mass market beckoning, cheaper radios (the earlier models had been expensive console sets) were soon on the market. By 1933, one authority estimated that three-fourths of all radio sales were inexpensive table models that cost between twelve and twenty dollars. *Amos 'n' Andy* was a major contributor to this aberrant prosperity for an industry.

Amos 'n' Andy provided powerful impetus to the success of commercial radio, and also, in less quantifiable but doubtless equally significant ways, steadied the morale of millions of its listeners by supplying nightly laughter in the face of adversities. The plight of the show's principals was easy to identify with. The common sense and down-home candor of the two struggling urban African Americans cut through the welter of official nostrums, pontifications, predictions, exhortations, and superficial idealism about the state of the economy, the stock market, unemployment, and the trials of disadvantaged rural folk seeking a living in an urban environment. Even their additions to America's vernacular were unpretentious, to the point, and funny. The show offered bits of wisdom, as in this speech by Andy to the Mystic Knights of the Sea: "I might talk about de repression an' good times bein' around de corneh, soon as I check up wid somebody an' find out whut corneh 'tis." Although Amos and Andy sometimes voiced dour expectations about the length and seriousness of the Depression, they, as marginal entrepreneurs, exuded optimism and by implication reaffirmed the cult of individual success and the work ethic—for which

President Herbert Hoover and President Franklin D. Roosevelt thanked the show's creators.

Although *Amos 'n' Andy*'s immense audience was drawn from all classes and races, there were black protests against the show almost from its inception. Theresa Kennedy of St. Louis was among the first to voice complaints publicly. She admitted that she and her black neighbors were entertained by *Amos 'n' Andy* and that the show's characterizations were true to life. On the other hand, she complained that the obvious ignorance and shiftlessness of many of its characters gave a false impression of African Americans. Black newspapers during the early years of the show were divided, a majority praising it enthusiastically, as did most of the black organizations contacted by Gosden and Correll. A few were ambivalent about the show or were frankly hostile. A Chicago bishop, W. J. Walls, fell into the former category, while editor Robert L. Vann of the *Pittsburgh Courier* from the show's start denounced Gosden and Correll's "exploitation" of certain types of American blacks for their own gain, with a result of undermining black self-respect. In support of his position, Vann claimed to have 740,000 signatures on petitions against the show by the fall of 1931. Some black trade unionists and business organizations likewise protested that Amos, Andy, and their cohorts reflected adversely upon the integrity of African-American enterprise.

Over ensuing years, divisions within black communities over the show mirrored varying degrees of African-American security, self-respect, and personal identity. Concerns over long-standing racial injustices and a resurgent national Civil Rights movement came to the fore in national life during later years of the show. *Amos 'n' Andy* was launched as a television comedy in 1951, its major roles being played by black actors. Leaders of the National Association for the Advancement of Colored People (NAACP), some of whom, like Roy Wilkins, had earlier either enjoyed the radio show or had tolerated it, became more vigorously opposed to it, in company with some white liberals. During Walter White's tenure as executive secretary of the NAACP, strenuous efforts were made first to alter the show's characters and content, then to abolish it as a continuing harm to African Americans and a caricature of their race. No one ever accused Gosden or Correll, however, of stooping to pointed racial language, and many critics conceded that the race of the show's characters was largely incidental to their unfolding stories.

The radio show left the air in 1960. The television version was broadcast in first-run episodes from 1951 to 1953, then rerun widely on local stations. The television show remained popular in reruns and even was sold to broadcasters in Kenya and Western Nigeria. After an official of Kenya's government announced that the program would be banned in his country, controversy over the show reemerged. The program was withdrawn from sale in 1966. Gosden and Correll also created an animated television show with animal characters, titled *Calvin and the Colonel*. That show aired in 1961 and 1962. The animal characters had origins in the Deep South but had migrated to a large Northern city; the show had obvious similarities to *Amos 'n' Andy* but avoided racial controversies through use of animated animal characters.

Amos 'n' Andy left legacies of several types. It is remembered as the most popular radio serial of its time, and as such was important in the development of radio as an entertainment medium. It was a pioneering effort in the emergence of serialized stories that were broadcast, both on radio and on television. More important, it indicated the effects that entertainment presentations could have on the popular consciousness and showed that art and entertainment often reflected reality and could point out existing problems and conflicts. The controversy about racial presentations endured past the end of *Amos 'n' Andy*, and creators of shows learned to evaluate the plots and characters of their shows carefully to avoid obvious insults or slurs against any group. This contributed to what some observers have called the relatively homogenized entertainment fare of the late twentieth century.

Bibliography

Barnouw, Erik. *A Tower in Babel: To 1933.* Vol. 1 in *A History of Broadcasting in the United States.* New York: Oxford University Press, 1966. The finest history of its kind. Comprehensive, authoritative, detailed, and well written. Gives great credit to *Amos 'n' Andy* for launching successful commercial radio. The author is more critical of the show's racial content than many other analysts. Seventeen pages of fine photos and documents. Superb bibliography, detailed chronology, appendix of relevant laws, and index.

Douglas, George H. *The Early Days of Radio Broadcasting.* Jefferson, N.C.: McFarland, 1987. Good chapter-length summary of *Amos 'n' Andy*'s influence, as well as useful background and context. Splendid bibliography, adequate notes, excellent index, and twenty pages of photos.

Ely, Melvin Patrick. *The Adventures of Amos 'n' Andy: A Social History of an American Phenomenon.* New York: Free Press, 1991. The definitive study of the show, its context, and its influences. Detailed and scholarly, but well written and intended for lay readers as well as specialists. Several chapters deal with the show's racial content, problems of race, and racial opposition. Good notes, useful bibliographical essay, and index.

Harmon, Jim. *The Great Radio Comedians.* Garden City, N.Y.: Doubleday, 1970. A breezy, knowledgeable survey of forty prominent radio comedies, including *Amos 'n' Andy.* The book's value lies in dealing with the content of these shows, rather than, as is true of other studies on radio, on their place in the radio industry or history. Allows comparison of Gosden and Correll's comedy with those of other writers. Twenty-five excellent photos, many of them collective portraits of radio stars. Ably researched with humorous excerpts that afford the reader a feel for these comedies. No notes or bibliography, but a detailed index.

Wertheim, Arthur Frank. *Radio Comedy.* New York: Oxford University Press, 1979. Authoritatively traces the evolution of radio comedy (*Sam 'n' Henry* and *Amos 'n' Andy* included) and its impact on American values and society through the Great Depression and World War II. It also ties the content and character of comedy shows to traditional vernacular humor manifested earlier in vaudeville and stage comedy, highlighting radio comedy's innovations. Scholarly and detailed but easily read. Fifteen pages of excellent photos. Many funny quotations from shows' script humor. Ample primary and secondary source notes for each chapter replace bibliography. Useful index.

Clifton K. Yearley

Cross-References

The Art of Radio Develops from Early Broadcast Experience (1920's), p. 469; WSM Launches *The Grand Ole Opry* (1925), p. 675; The British Broadcasting Corporation Is Chartered (1927), p. 712; Radio Programming Dominates Home Leisure (1930's), p. 828; NBC Launches American Television at the World's Fair (1939), p. 1143.

SOUND TECHNOLOGY REVOLUTIONIZES THE MOTION-PICTURE INDUSTRY

Category of event: Motion pictures
Time: May 11, 1928
Locale: The United States

Hollywood's major film studios signed an agreement with the American Telephone & Telegraph corporation (AT&T) to use AT&T technology to produce films with sound, leading to an explosion in the popularity of motion pictures

Principal personages:

HARRY WARNER (1881-1958), the head of Warner Bros., the motion-picture company that pioneered the use of sound in films

ALBERT WARNER (1884-1967), the second-in-command at Warner Bros.

SAM WARNER (1887-1927), the Warner brother who found the necessary technology to pioneer talkies but who died before sound films transformed the film industry

WILLIAM FOX (1879-1952), the head of the Fox Film Corporation, the motion-picture company that followed Warner Bros. in pioneering sound technology

Summary of Event

When Hollywood's major studios agreed in May, 1928, to incorporate sound into their films, the decision transformed the American film industry almost overnight. Attendance doubled; new talent poured into Hollywood; "talkies" became the rage around the world. The introduction of sound to the movies created America's favorite midcentury leisure-time activity.

The production of the first sound films required several stages of innovation. First, scientists had to develop apparatus to record and synchronize sounds and images, complete with a quality and tone that would permit the resulting product to be shown before large audiences. Moreover, companies had to learn how to market sound films to the public, knowing the inherent risk in trying to sell something many critics said would not work. Finally, the major film companies had to decide to accept the new technology and to substitute it for the standardized silent film.

Such a transformation took place between 1926 and 1930. The silent-film era ended; Hollywood switched completely to the making of talkies. In 1925, silent filmmaking stood as the standard; a mere five years later, Hollywood produced only films with sound. The speed of the transition surprised almost everyone. Within the space of half a decade, formerly perplexing technical problems were resolved, marketing and distribution strategies were reworked, soundproof studios were constructed, and fifteen thousand theaters were wired for sound. Since Hollywood so dominated the film business throughout the world, foreign film industries were forced to follow suit, and by 1935, sound films had become the world standard.

The transformation to sound films did not begin in Hollywood. It took one of the world's largest corporations, American Telephone & Telegraph (AT&T), to overcome the frustrating technological problems involved. During the silent era, mammoth picture palaces used seventy-five-piece orchestras to provide live sound for silent films. Every two-hundred-seat neighborhood house had a hardworking piano player plunking out a musical accompaniment. Inventors, though, had long sought to develop a mechanical sound system to supply needed music and even dialogue. In the early years of the twentieth century, single inventors (including Thomas Alva Edison) failed to link phonograph technology to the silent movie; they could not solve the problem of synchronizing sounds from a speaker with film of speaking actors.

During the 1910's, AT&T's scientists, working in a corporate unit that would later become known as Bell Labs, perfected an electronic sound-on-disk recording and reproducing system in order to test AT&T's then-new long-distance telephone network. As a spin-off of this telephone research, AT&T scientists invented the first true loudspeaker and sound amplifier. Combining these inventions with film technology produced a system that could record and project clear, vibrant sounds to audiences even in huge picture palaces.

In 1922, AT&T had begun trying to sell its new sound technology. Despite AT&T's formidable technical reputation and financial muscle, however, the barons of the American film industry, fully cognizant of the multitude of embarrassing failures of talkies a decade earlier, passed when initially offered the new AT&T equipment.

A minor Hollywood company, Warner Bros., took up the challenge. The brothers Warner (led by the eldest, Harry, who was assisted by his younger brothers Albert and Sam) had come a long way from their nickelodeon days in Ohio, but their company was still tiny in comparison to giants such as Famous Players-Lasky, then Hollywood's largest company. Warner Bros. sought a means by which to grow, and so in 1924, the brothers expanded into more expensive feature-film production, added offices for worldwide distribution, and bought a chain of picture palaces.

During this phase of corporate growth, Sam Warner learned of AT&T's inventions. He was immediately smitten, but he somehow had to trick the head of the family, Harry, into approving a deal. Harry saw a demonstration, and soon the brothers were working up a strategy to use sound to further build up their company. The Warner brothers decided to make sound films of vaudeville acts and offer them as novelties to exhibitors along with Warner Bros. feature-length (still silent) films. The Warner sales pitch stressed that these vaudeville sound shorts could substitute for the then-omnipresent stage shows offered by picture palaces. Thus, the very first talkies were conceived as short recordings of the acts of top musical, comic, and variety talent.

In September, 1925, Warner Bros. set in motion its strategy of using vaudeville shorts to innovate sound films. It took a year to work out the technical problems, but by August, 1926, Warner Bros. was ready to premiere the marvel it called "Vitaphone." The premiere held that August allowed audiences to see and hear operatic favorites sung on film by such stars as Metropolitan Opera tenor Giovanni Martinelli. The presentation of the silent film *Don Juan* (1926), with music on a sound track replacing the usual live orchestra, followed.

As Warner Bros. developed more silent feature films with orchestral music on disk and more sound vaudeville shorts, the Warner brothers quickly realized that the public preferred recordings of popular musical acts to recordings of opera stars. Al Jolson and Elsie Janis, two of the biggest names in the pop music business during the 1920's, became the first stars of Vitaphone vaudeville shorts.

Warner Bros. soon began to insert vaudeville numbers into its features, beginning with Al Jolson in *The Jazz Singer*, which premiered in October, 1927. The enormous success of *The Jazz Singer* forced rival studios to take notice of the new sound technology.

During 1927 and the early part of 1928, Warner Bros. had only one competitor, the Fox Film Corporation, in the production of sound films. Fox had adapted a version of AT&T's pioneering technology to make newsreels with sound. Like the brothers Warner, William Fox did not see a future for feature-length talkies, but he reasoned that the public might prefer newsreels with sound to current silent offerings.

William Fox never made a better business decision in his career. Fox Film engineers labored to integrate sound with accepted newsreel techniques. On the final day of April, 1927, five months before the opening of *The Jazz Singer*, Fox Film presented its first sound newsreels. Less than a month later, Fox stumbled across the publicity coup of the decade when it tendered the only sound footage of the takeoff and triumphant return of Charles Lindbergh.

The enormous popularity of Lindbergh's hop across the Atlantic undoubtedly contributed heavily to Fox's success with sound newsreels. Fox newsreel cameramen soon spread to all parts of the globe in search of stories "with a voice." Theater owners queued up to wire their houses simply to be able to show Fox Movietone newsreels. To fans of the day, Movietone newsreels offered as much an attraction as any feature-length film.

The major film companies, led by Paramount, did not want to be left behind. For more than a year, a committee of experts from Paramount, Metro-Goldwyn-Mayer (MGM), First National, and United Artists met secretly to study their options. They examined AT&T's sound film technology and drew up plans to anticipate all attendant problems. After nearly six months of haggling over terms, on May 11, 1928, at AT&T's headquarters in Manhattan, these four major companies signed up with AT&T, and the rush to make talkies was on.

Impact of Event

Once the necessary contracts were signed, the diffusion of sound proceeded logically. First, Paramount, MGM, and the other major studios came out with "scored features," existing silent films with recorded music added. Theater owners immediately let go resident orchestras, freeing funds to help pay for the necessary wiring.

Musicians' unions protested, but by 1930, only a handful of theaters in America's largest cities still maintained a house orchestra and organist. By January, 1929, less than a year after Paramount, MGM, First National, and United Artists had signed their original contracts, the majors began to distribute "one-hundred percent talking" features, and the silent film became a thing of the past.

The widespread adoption of sound took place within the space of two years; the major Hollywood companies had too much at stake to procrastinate. Few unanticipated difficulties arose. Within the framework of the Academy of Motion Picture Arts and Sciences, the major studios cooperated to resolve any remaining problems as quickly as possible.

In short, the big studios continued to prosper. Smaller producers—save for pioneering Warner Bros. and Fox—could not afford the transition and either went out of business or were taken over by larger concerns.

The Hollywood studios went on a building boom, doubling studio space in less than two years. Several companies reopened studios near New York City to accommodate Broadway stage talent unwilling to trek to California. Paramount's Long Island City complex, a simple commute across the East River, was the largest. The greatest construction, however, came in California, as the modern studios came to life as filmmaking centers.

Fox had adapted a version of AT&T's pioneering technology that recorded sound on a film itself. Warner's original sound-on-disk system proved ever more cumbersome, and by 1930, sound on film would become the industry standard.

Theaters owned by Hollywood companies received their sound film installations first; smaller, independently owned houses had to sign up and wait, sometimes for more than a year. The major Hollywood companies could hardly keep track of the millions they were making. Warner Bros. and Fox moved to the top of the industry, and a new major company, Radio-Keith-Orpheum (RKO), was formed. In a rush to compete with AT&T, the Radio Corporation of America (RCA) developed its own version of sound on film, but RCA could not convince the major Hollywood companies to use its product, the "Photophone." To make the best of this situation, RCA founder and president David Sarnoff turned to a friend, financier Joseph P. Kennedy, the patriarch of the Kennedy political family. At the time, the elder Kennedy owned a small Hollywood studio, the Film Booking Office (FBO). During the last six months of 1928, Sarnoff and Kennedy merged RCA's sound equipment with the FBO studio and added the theaters from the Keith-Albee-Orpheum vaudeville theater empire to create RKO.

The public's infatuation with talkies set off the greatest rush to the box office in American history. At its peak in the months before the Great Depression, on average, every person over the age of six in the United States went to the movies once a week. Profits for the major Hollywood companies soared.

Mergers and takeovers became the order of the day. By 1930, there were but five major studios in Hollywood (Paramount, Loew's/MGM, Warner Bros., Fox, and RKO) and three minor studios (Columbia, Universal, and United Artists). Unlike their larger cousins, the minor studios owned no theaters. The coming of sound had set in place a corporate structure that would define the studio era of the 1930's and 1940's—the Golden Age of Hollywood.

By controlling picture palaces in all of America's downtowns, the major studios took in three-quarters of the average box-office take. Naturally, they granted their own theaters first-run privileges for top films, and only then permitted smaller, independently owned theaters (found, by and large, outside America's downtowns, and in thousands of small towns) to scramble for remaining bookings, sometimes months, or even years, after a film's premiere. The major studios' regulation of the distribution and exhibition of films provided them with the power base from which they dominated American filmmaking for the next three decades.

Bibliography

Balio, Tino, ed. *The American Film Industry*. Rev. ed. Madison: University of Wisconsin Press, 1985. Offers a series of articles analyzing the history and development of the American film industry, including the coming of sound. Aimed at a scholarly audience, although most of the articles are clear and well written.

Geduld, Harry M. *The Birth of the Talkies*. Bloomington: Indiana University Press, 1975. A history of the coming of sound to the cinema. Analyzes the transition through the discussion of key figures from Thomas Alva Edison to Al Jolson.

Kindem, Gorham, ed. *The American Movie Industry*. Carbondale: Southern Illinois University Press, 1982. A series of articles analyzing the history and development of American film industry, including the coming of sound. Although this is a scholarly tome, the articles are clearly written.

Mast, Gerald, ed. *The Movies in Our Midst*. Chicago: University of Chicago Press, 1982. A social history of the American cinema; generally readable and lively. Mast provides useful introductions and a comprehensive bibliography.

Walker, Alexander. *The Shattered Silents*. New York: William Morrow, 1979. A survey of the history of the coming of sound, based primarily upon a close reading of the trade paper *Variety*. Little on the technology or industrial transformations. Often unclear and disjointed in organization, but some of the material from *Variety* is fascinating to read.

Weis, Elisabeth, and John Belton, eds. *Film Sound: Theory and Practice*. New York: Columbia University Press, 1985. Offers a collection of articles about the place of sound in the cinema. The first two articles in this collection deal with the transition to sound. A first-rate introduction.

Douglas Gomery

Cross-References

The Jazz Singer Premieres in New York (1927), p. 734; The First Academy Awards Honor Film Achievement (1929), p. 799; Hollywood Enters Its Golden Age (1930's), p. 822; *Little Caesar, Public Enemy,* and *Scarface* Launch the Gangster-Film Genre

(1930), p. 839; Berkeley's *42nd Street* Revolutionizes Film Musicals (1933), p. 925; The Classic Screwball Comedy Reaches Its Height in Popularity (1934), p. 951; *Top Hat* Establishes the Astaire-Rogers Dance Team (1935), p. 984; The Hollywood Studio System Is Transformed (1946), p. 1307.

ALL QUIET ON THE WESTERN FRONT STRESSES THE FUTILITY OF WAR

Category of event: Literature
Time: 1929
Locale: Berlin, Germany

Written by a participant in World War I, All Quiet on the Western Front, *with its vivid descriptions of the horror and waste of armed conflict as well as of the humanity and comradeship of the combatants, became a powerful antiwar statement*

Principal personages:

ERICH MARIA REMARQUE (ERICH PAUL REMARK, 1898-1970), the flamboyant German-born author whose first successful novel, *All Quiet on the Western Front*, stirred up great controversy

JOSEPH GOEBBELS (1897-1945), a leader of the Nazi Party in Germany who spearheaded the attack on Remarque and his book

CYRILL SOSCHKA, an official of the publishing company responsible for getting the novel in print

JUTTA ILSE ZAMBONA (1901-   ), the author's wife during the years when his novel was published and he first became the target of persecution

Summary of Event

In August, 1914, after the longest period of uninterrupted peace in European history up to that time (forty-three years), Germany plunged the world into war. Four years of slaughter brought unheard-of human and material loss. Of all the nations involved, Germany, with 1.8 million dead, suffered the greatest number of casualties.

After the war's end, two general currents of thought emerged in German life and literature. The first promoted militaristic, belligerent, authoritarian beliefs. The second, profoundly pacifistic, denounced militarism and war.

A full decade after World War I ended, Erich Maria Remarque, who was destined to become a leading figure of pacifism, published an influential, controversial, and successful novel about trench warfare, written from a German perspective. *Im Westen nichts Neues* (1929; *All Quiet on the Western Front*) is semiautobiographical, recounting many of the author's experiences as a World War I infantryman.

Although christened Erich Paul Remark in 1898, the author changed his name over the years, first substituting his mother's middle name for his own a year after her death in 1917. In 1920, he published a novel so poorly received that the embarrassment caused him to adopt his great-grandfather's spelling of the family name.

In 1916, when Remarque was an eighteen-year-old student at a teacher's college, he was drafted; he received military training at the Westerberg barracks in Osnabrück (the "Klosterberg" of *All Quiet on the Western Front*). In June, 1917, he was assigned to a trench unit near the Western Front and was devastated when a friend whom he had rescued on the battlefield died of head wounds (an incident reflected in the death of the character named Stanislaus Katczinsky in the novel). After another daring rescue, Remarque himself was severely injured by grenade splinters and spent almost a year recuperating.

The war changed Remarque forever. He gained an appreciation for the value and fragility of life, saw the futility and destructiveness of war, and became disillusioned with patriotism and the glorification of battle. Against the background of the horrors of combat, civilian life seemed trivial. These attitudes and beliefs were translated into the messages of *All Quiet on the Western Front.*

For the next few years following the war (amid shortages, inflation, unemployment, and extremist politics), Remarque had a difficult time, as did many. He ridiculed the war, wandered from job to job, married, became a regular in Berlin society, and finally took a job as an associate editor of a sports magazine. In 1927, Remarque began to publish a number of pieces that reflected his love of cars and motor racing. During the latter part of that year, over a six-week period, *All Quiet on the Western Front* was written. The manuscript, however, remained in Remarque's desk for six months before he submitted it for publication.

At first, publishers were not interested. Finally, Cyrill Soschka, manager of the production department of Ullstein Publishers, read the book and believed that it would be successful. In fact, Soschka threatened to establish his own firm just to publish Remarque's novel if no one else would.

The new war novel was first serialized in a German newspaper owned by Ullstein, *Vossische Zeitung,* between November 10 and December 9, 1928. The novel appeared in book form in January, 1929, and was translated into English that same year. The overnight success of the book astonished everyone, including Remarque himself, and irrevocably altered the course of his life. The theretofore unknown journalist became a wealthy, world-famous author.

Remarque claimed that he had not set out to write a best-seller but had written instead to rid himself of the bleak moods that he and his friends were still experiencing as a result of the war. He said that the shadow of war had continued to hang over them, especially when they tried to shut their minds to it. Thus, as a kind of cathartic enterprise, the novel tells the story of a generation of young men who were destroyed by World War I—even if they survived the fighting. Remarque narrates the tale through the main character, Paul Bäumer.

Though the book was instantly popular, it generated such tremendous controversy in some circles that Remarque was accused of writing solely to shock and to sell. Others believed the book was nothing more than sentimentalism or pacifistic drivel.

Ignoring it as a work of literature, the Nazis regarded the book as an insult to and an attack on the greatness of the Germany they wanted to control. Remarque's ideas were antithetical to the Nazis' ideology and intended course of action. To the Nazis, the novel seemed to symbolize the beliefs of men who had stabbed Germany in the back by conceding defeat in a war the Nazis claimed their country should have won.

The Nazis tried to undermine Remarque's popularity by spreading rumors about his credibility, claiming that he was, among other things, a French Jew (apparently the worst combination of traits the Nazis could imagine) or an old man who had never seen battle. Leading the attack was Joseph Goebbels, the Nazi Party's chief propagandist.

In 1931, Remarque published a sequel to *All Quiet on the Western Front* based on his and his friends' experiences after they returned from the front. Entitled *Der Weg zurück* (*The Road Back*, 1931), it further angered the Nazis.

During this period, the author and his first wife, a young actress named Jutta Ilse Zambona, lived in Berlin. After Nazi persecution forced Remarque to leave in 1931, the couple was divorced in 1932. (They did remarry, but were divorced for good in 1951.) Remarque emigrated to Switzerland, bought a villa at Porto Ronco on Lake Maggiore, and began filling it with valuable antiques; he also spent a great deal of time in France and America, both before and after World War II.

Remarque's fame spread as he pursued a glamorous life-style. He hobnobbed with Hollywood stars and American authors, enjoyed fine food and expensive clothes, received awards and honors, became an American citizen, married another actress (Paulette Goddard), and even acted in *A Time to Love and a Time to Die* (1958), the film version of one of his novels. Through it all, he continued to write, producing eleven novels altogether. Each was written in German but simultaneously translated and published in English, and each developed themes first introduced in *All Quiet on the Western Front.*

Impact of Event

The significance of *All Quiet on the Western Front* lies, first, in the influence it had on European and American thought, and, second, in the reaction it generated among the new Nazi leaders of Germany. The novel deeply moved people on both sides of the Atlantic. It was (and is) a powerful condemnation of war. It touched the hearts and minds of readers, not so much by its literary quality as by the force of its conviction that war is unmitigated waste—a conviction that grew out of Remarque's witnessing horrible suffering.

In America, for example, magazine and newspaper reviews immediately hailed Remarque's work as an updated version of Stephen Crane's *The Red Badge of Courage* (1895). *All Quiet on the Western Front* taught its readers that World War I was one of the most terrible catastrophes of all time—worse, even, than the American Civil War in which Crane's work had been set. At best, World War I reduced the lives of its participants to the level of simple survival. At worst, the war reduced human beings to the level of animals.

Though some decried the book's scenes as horrible, it was precisely the graphic realism that made the novel sell. In the first year of publication, German readers alone bought more than one million copies. British, French, and American audiences purchased many hundreds of thousands more. By 1932, the book had been translated into twenty-nine languages. The edition in Afrikaans inspired a flood of "war diaries" about the second Boer War.

The new war novel also made an important impact on the world when it was made into an American motion picture. One of the first sound pictures, the film, starring Lew Ayres and Lew Wolheim, became a classic. In 1930, however, the film was banned by the Nazis in Berlin, and the event signaled the start of the intense persecution directed at Remarque.

Remarque was not the only member of his family to suffer at the hands of the Nazis. *All Quiet on the Western Front* had so poisoned the Nazis against anyone or anything associated with Remarque that in 1943, the author's younger sister, Elfriede Scholz, was beheaded for spreading subversive propaganda. Reference was made to Remarque during his sister's trial, and Remarque himself acknowledged that the mere fact that Scholz was his sister had something to do with the verdict.

Twenty-five years after the death of Elfriede Scholz a street on the outskirts of Osnabrück was named after her. In 1971, one year after the author died, authorities of Osnabrück named a section of road along the town walls the Erich Maria Remarque Ring.

In 1933, when the Nazis had taken full control of Germany, both *All Quiet on the Western Front* and its sequel, *The Road Back*, were burned by the new regime in the notorious book-burning ceremony in Berlin. (Even before that episode, they had been placed on the Nazi index of prohibited literature.)

The two novels continued to arouse the ire of totalitarian regimes in the twentieth century; Remarque's works were banned by the Soviet Union and other Eastern Bloc nations in 1949. Soviet authorities feared that the antiwar sentiments of the books might adversely affect Communist youth. Though the Eastern Bloc countries removed the ban on the books in 1962, Remarque's works were still seen as a powerful argument against those who preached that unquestioned service to the state was the highest aim in life.

Latent disapproval of *All Quiet on the Western Front* by some in Germany finally manifested itself after Remarque's death in 1970. The weekly journal *Der Spiegel* published an obituary that managed to omit any mention of Remarque as ever having written a profoundly influential World War I novel.

Nevertheless, the public had not forgotten Remarque's work. By the time of his death, millions of copies of *All Quiet on the Western Front* had been sold; many more were sold following his death. The continuing widespread popularity of the novel testifies to the timelessness of its message, and the book has continued to exert a powerful impact on attitudes about the horror and futility of war.

Bibliography

Barker, Christine R., and R. W. Last. *Erich Maria Remarque*. London: Oswald Wolff, 1979. A thorough yet concise history of the man and his work. Places his novels in historical context and devotes special attention to Remarque's first major success.

Fussell, Paul. *The Great War and Modern Memory*. New York: Oxford University Press, 1977. This prize-winning book explores the literary sources and means by which the British experience on the Western Front has been remembered. Contains only a few explicit references to Remarque's work, but helps the reader to place it in the context of the whole literary culture that centered on World War I and to compare the experiences of different nationalities in the trenches.

Owen, C. R. *Erich Maria Remarque: A Critical Bio-Bibliography.* Amsterdam: Rodopi, 1984. Provides an informative biography, arranged chronologically into chapters, each with accompanying annotated bibliography of books and articles about Remarque and all of his published writings. The bibliography is the most complete assembled anywhere. Most titles are in German, but the annotations are in English. An essential tool for scholarly research.

Schwarz, Wilhelm J. *War and the Mind of Germany.* Frankfurt: Peter Lang, 1975. A collection of five short scholarly essays, three of which discuss the life and work of Remarque. Comparisons are made between Remarque's World War I novel and the writings of German authors Ernst Junger and Theodor Plievier. Another essay discusses Remarque's World War II novels.

Wagener, Hans. *Understanding Erich Maria Remarque.* Columbia: University of South Carolina Press, 1991. A useful introduction to Remarque's works. Contains analysis of Remarque's major works, a chronology of his life, and an annotated bibliography.

Andrew C. Skinner

Cross-References

Proust's *Remembrance of Things Past* Is Published (1913), p. 355; Hašek's *The Good Soldier Švejk* Reflects Postwar Disillusionment (1921), p. 523; Mann's *The Magic Mountain* Reflects European Crisis (1924), p. 588; Hemingway's *The Sun Also Rises* Speaks for the Lost Generation (1926), p. 696; *The Sound and the Fury* Launches Faulkner's Career (1929), p. 805; Huxley's *Brave New World* Reflects Fears About the Future (1932), p. 896; Mailer Publishes *The Naked and the Dead* (1948), p. 1373; *Catch-22* Illustrates Antiwar Sentiment (1961), p. 1866; *Dog Soldiers* Portrays Vietnam in Fiction (1974), p. 2315.

HALLELUJAH IS THE FIRST
IMPORTANT BLACK MUSICAL

Category of event: Motion pictures
Time: 1929
Locale: Metro-Goldwyn-Mayer studios, Culver City, California

King Vidor sacrificed salary to direct the first serious all-black musical, success-fully blending music and drama to depict Southern farm life and its tragedies

Principal personages:
> KING VIDOR (1894-1982), a film director who became famous for films about the problems of the common man
> DANIEL L. HAYNES (1894-1954), a black Broadway actor and minister who played Zeke, the hero of *Hallelujah*
> NINA MAE MCKINNEY (1913-1967), a black Broadway chorus girl who played Chick, the woman who almost destroys Zeke

Summary of Event

Warner Bros.' 1927 release of *The Jazz Singer* brought silent films to an end, but some studio heads believed sound to be a fad. Metro-Goldwyn-Mayer (MGM) did not release a sound film until 1928; its first musical was *Broadway Melody* of 1929, a backstage musical full of young women in abbreviated costumes. The studio intended to follow this musical with similar money-winners, and it turned down King Vidor's proposal of an all-black musical tragedy set among impoverished farmers.

By then, however, Vidor had achieved a considerable reputation. A Galveston, Texas, native who as a boy had taught himself film techniques by watching silents, Vidor had come to California in 1915 and had taken every studio job he could get in order to learn his profession. He made his reputation with *The Turn in the Road* (1919); it was characteristic of Vidor that he convinced a group of physicians to back the film, which had a Christian Science theme. The film showed a man's search for his personal truths, a theme that was to dominate Vidor's films.

D. W. Griffith's films taught Vidor the relationship of films to musical forms, and from Roberty Flaherty's *Nanook of the North* (1922) he learned the dramatic value of everyday experience. His two most important silent films foreshadow *Hallelujah* in evidencing both interests. In *The Big Parade* (1925), starring John Gilbert, he showed a common soldier, neither a hero nor a coward. In *The Crowd* (1928), Vidor showed a common office worker whose struggles were everyman's: marriage, parenthood, dead-end work, unemployment, the loss of a child, alcoholism, and periods of happiness. Vidor's most spectacular use of music was in the background for *The Big Parade.* He conceptualized this film in terms of musical movements, pacing off the troops' steps with a metronome and speeding up the beat as tension mounted.

As troops marched toward the battlefront and death, the musical score ceased, and the soldiers moved only to the cadence of an ominous bass drum. Although critics attacked Vidor's use of music in *Hallelujah* as a racist depiction of black music and attacked the hero's sordid story and emotionalism, these themes were in fact set in Vidor's work before he came to *Hallelujah*. In the film, Vidor's hero, Zeke, is searching for his true life. He is caught between two women who represent the two extremes of his own psychological needs. Music represents this conflict. Gospel songs and traditional spirituals are associated with the order and family harmony of Zeke's family's farm; syncopated jazz represents the world that tempts him. (Until the end of his life, Vidor was disturbed by the studio's insistence on adding such elements as two Irving Berlin songs, "At the End of the Road" and "Swanee Shuffle," that gave the film a Tin Pan Alley air he wanted to avoid.)

Vidor's was not the first all-black musical. Earlier in 1929, Fox (later Twentieth Century-Fox) released *Hearts in Dixie*, which featured the talented actor Clarence Muse and provided the first major role for comedian Stepin Fetchit. *Hearts in Dixie*, though, focused on the happy-go-lucky life of a fictional plantation. Later in 1929, *St. Louis Blues*, released by Warner Bros., provided singer Bessie Smith her only film role, but the film was not feature-length, running only seventeen minutes.

Vidor took a more serious risk. He wanted to treat his black hero as seriously as he had treated the white soldier in *The Big Parade* and the white office worker in *The Crowd*. Vidor's operational problems were staggering, with sound techniques still in their infancy, and MGM refused to make the film until Vidor donated the money due him under his MGM contract to the production.

For his cast, Vidor went to Chicago, New York, and Memphis, visiting black churches to hire his singers. For Zeke, he first wanted Paul Robeson, who was unavailable. Instead, he hired Daniel Haynes, the understudy for Jules Bledsoe, who sang "Ol' Man River" in the 1927 Broadway production of *Show Boat*. Nina Mae McKinney was hired from the chorus of a Broadway show. Three child musicians were hired when Vidor saw them dancing for quarters in a Memphis hotel. Vidor approached Harry Gray, who had been born into slavery, to play the father of the family. Musician Victoria Spivey played Missy Rose; William Fountaine played the gambler Hot Shot, and Fannie Bell McKnight was cast as the mother. All were relatively unknown.

The mood of *Hallelujah* was as somber as that of *The Crowd*. Zeke, the eldest son of a hardworking farm family, goes to town with his brother and is fascinated by Chick (McKinney), who plays a tempting Eve. He is cheated by Hot Shot; in a brawl, he accidentally shoots his brother. In atonement, he becomes a preacher, but, still fascinated by Chick, he leaves the ministry. Vidor explicitly shows his religious fervor to be an unsuccessful attempt to sublimate a sexual drive that finally conquers him. Zeke and Chick flee. Zeke ultimately kills her lover, Hot Shot, and she dies in a symbolic fall. Zeke serves time in prison, then returns to the order and stability of his father's farm, where Missy Rose, the good girl, waits for him. They return to harvesting the earth and to the cycles of the seasons.

Impact of Event

By the end of Vidor's long life, the significance of *Hallelujah* was recognized, but its immediate reception was mixed. As Vidor recalled, the film may never have shown a profit. For the actors and actresses in the film, it was virtually a dead end, and no one at the time understood that Vidor had created a new film genre. His technical accomplishment, however, was immediately apparent.

Vidor shot the film on location near Memphis, Tennessee, and in Arkansas. Sound equipment, large and difficult to move, did not arrive, so much of the film was shot as a silent and then matched with sound tracks recorded in Hollywood, a feat so difficult that it literally drove one film cutter to a nervous breakdown.

For the scenes shot as silents, Vidor used impressionistic special effects. Perhaps the most dramatic scene shows Zeke chasing Hot Shot through a swamp. In his autobiographical *A Tree Is a Tree* (1953), Vidor recalled that, "When someone stepped on a broken branch, we made it sound as if bones were breaking," and that when Hot Shot drew his foot from the sticky mud, "we made the vacuum sound strong enough to pull him down into hell." Recording a group of dock workers, Vidor for the first time used synchronous sound recording in the studio. The final print had flaws, but remarkable effects were readily evident.

Controversy, however, arose about the film's content. Although accused of racism, Vidor was unquestionably sincere; he had not intended to portray the black race as a whole but simply to show the harsh lives of the black people he had known in Galveston, where his father's lumber company had employed mostly black men and where he was taken to witness river baptisms. While reviews in the white East Coast press were generally favorable, the black press reacted against the gambling and emotionalism of the black characters depicted in the film.

Controversy even surrounded the film's showing. In New York, the film was given dual premieres, one at the Lafayette Theater in Harlem and one downtown. Black journalists were indignant, assuming this meant that white audiences were willing to see blacks on film but were unwilling to sit next to them in audiences. In Chicago, two major theaters, the Balaban and Katz, refused to book the film for fear the black audiences would drive off white patrons. Vidor had to visit Chicago, show the film to critics, and wait for the positive reviews. Once these appeared, it was possible to convince a small independent theater to book the film. Its success at that theater forced major Chicago theaters to show it. In an attempt to get Southern bookings, Vidor talked a Jacksonville, Florida, theater owner into booking the film by promising him a personal check for one thousand dollars if *Hallelujah* did not bring in more profit than whatever was currently showing. It did, and the man booked it into his theaters, but there were few other Southern showings. Even in Paris, where black entertainers had received a warmer welcome than in the United States, the film's showings were restricted. In a 1932 essay in *Le Crapouillot*, Pierre Bost recalled, perhaps with some exaggeration, that he could see the film only in the early hours of the morning and in a cellar, although it was the talk of the city.

The minor actors of *Hallelujah* are virtually lost in time. Of the stars, Nina Mc-

Kinney was signed to an MGM contract, but there were few roles for black women. Her portrait of Chick, however, is said to have created the figure of the feisty vamp later acted by such stars as Dorothy Dandridge and Jean Harlow. McKinney is said to have dubbed Harlow's songs in *Reckless* (1935). She appeared in a number of major studio films and in films made by independent black companies; in England, she appeared opposite Paul Robeson in Alexander Korda's *Sanders of the River* (1935). Her final film appearance was in *Pinky* (1949). There were also few roles for black men in American films after *Hallelujah*. Daniel Haynes played in Marc Connelly's *The Green Pastures* (1930) for five years on Broadway and for almost two thousand performances on tour; he played the major figure of De Lawd in a later revival. Haynes also played secondary roles in a number of films and achieved a distinguished career as pastor of New York churches.

Vidor went on to make a series of distinguished films. *Street Scene* (1931) and *Our Daily Bread* (1934) were in many ways reminiscent of his earlier films, with their emphasis on the overlooked dramas of everyday life. Other Vidor films included *Billy the Kid* (1930), *Stella Dallas* (1937), *The Citadel* (1938), *Northwest Passage* (1940), *Duel in the Sun* (1947), *The Fountainhead* (1949), *Ruby Gentry* (1952), and the Italian-American production of *War and Peace* (1956). He directed the "Over the Rainbow" scene and other Kansas scenes for *The Wizard of Oz* (1939) when director Victor Fleming was called away. In 1979, he received a special Oscar for career achievement.

By that time, he was, among other things, recognized to have been the originator of the American folk musical film, a genre that tends to be set in a mythic American past and to focus upon domestic and traditional values. The genre's peculiar synthesis of these elements can be traced to the stage performance of *Show Boat*, which opened on Broadway in 1927, but it was in *Hallelujah* that it came to first fruition in film. After *Hallelujah* were to come such folk musicals as *Cabin in the Sky* (1942), *Meet Me in St. Louis* (1944), and *The Harvey Girls* (1946) and the film versions of *Oklahoma!* (1955) and *Carousel* (1956), but Vidor's seriousness of tone and fervor of purpose in *Hallelujah* were to distinguish it from all the rest.

Bibliography

Altman, Rick. "The Folk Musical." In *The American Film Musical*. Bloomington: Indiana University Press, 1989. Despite Altman's tendency toward unnecessary scholarly jargon, this chapter, which contains a lengthy analysis of *Hallelujah*, is essential reading for anyone interested in the folk musical form and its development.

Bogle, Donald. *Toms, Coons, Mulattoes, Mamas, and Bucks: An Interpretative History of Blacks in American Films*. New York: Viking, 1973. This is by far the most important book on black films and stereotypes. It contains a lengthy and moderately sympathetic analysis of *Hallelujah* and a discussion of McKinney's influence on the figure of the vamp in film.

Dowd, Nancy, and David Shepard. *King Vidor*. Metuchen, N.J.: Scarecrow Press,

1988. This lengthy interview is essential reading not only for anyone interested in Vidor and *Hallelujah* but also for students of silent and early sound films. There is little repetition of material from the Vidor works cited below.

Mordden, Ethan. *The Hollywood Musical.* New York: St. Martin's Press, 1981. Mordden's readable, witty, and opinionated book contains several pages about *Hallelujah* and in general remains the best starting place for students of film musicals.

Vidor, King. *King Vidor on Film Making.* New York: David McKay, 1972. This book is of the least interest of the three Vidor studies cited here. The work lacks coherent organization and ranges from such topics as the importance of directors to film festivals and how cameras work. Much repetition of anecdotes from Vidor's autobiography, but anything by Vidor is worth reading.

_____. *A Tree Is a Tree.* New York: Harcourt, Brace, 1953. Vidor's autobiography is extremely readable, offering fascinating insights into how the founders of film learned their trade by trial and error. This is a professional, rather than personal, autobiography, with much about direction of silent films. Includes filmography from 1918 to 1952.

Betty Richardson

Cross-References

The Jazz Singer Premieres in New York (1927), p. 734; Sound Technology Revolutionizes the Motion-Picture Industry (1928), p. 761; Berkeley's *42nd Street* Revolutionizes Film Musicals (1933), p. 925; Lubitsch's *The Merry Widow* Opens New Vistas for Film Musicals (1934), p. 941; The Classic *The Wizard of Oz* Opens (1939), p. 1109; Marian Anderson Is Barred from Constitution Hall (1939), p. 1126; *Stormy Weather* Offers New Film Roles to African Americans (1940's), p. 1159; *I Spy* Debuts to Controversy (1965), p. 2044; *The Wiz* Brings African-American Talent to Broadway (1975), p. 2334; *The Jeffersons* Signals Success of Black Situation Comedies (1975), p. 2339.

LOEWY PIONEERS AMERICAN INDUSTRIAL DESIGN

Category of event: Fashion and design
Time: 1929
Locale: New York, New York

With his redesign of the Gestetner duplicating machine in 1929, Raymond Loewy became a pioneer in the new profession of industrial product design in the United States

Principal personages:

RAYMOND LOEWY (1893-1986), one of the moving forces in the professionalization of industrial product design in the United States

SIGMUND GESTETNER (1898-1956), the British manufacturer of a stencil-duplicating machine whose redesign in 1929 was Loewy's first important commission

WALTER DORWIN TEAGUE (1883-1960), one of the founders of the industrial design profession in the United States

NORMAN BEL GEDDES (1893-1958), a theatrical stage designer turned industrial designer whose 1932 book *Horizons* did much to popularize the style known as "streamlining"

HENRY DREYFUSS (1904-1972), a leading innovator in industrial product design

WILLIAM T. SNAITH (1908-1974), a longtime associate of Loewy who was in charge of the firm's work in retail store design and planning

Summary of Event

Raymond Fernand Loewy was born in Paris, France, on November 5, 1893, into an economically secure family. From childhood, he was fascinated with train locomotives and automobiles. While still a schoolboy, he invented a prizewinning model airplane powered by an elastic band. He studied engineering and, during World War I, served in the French army, rising from private to captain. In 1919, after finishing his engineering degree, he left France for New York City, where he became a free-lance illustrator for fashion magazines and a window designer for stores.

In 1929, Loewy launched his own design firm. His first major commission was from Sigmund Gestetner, the head of a British company that manufactured stencil-duplicating machines. Loewy recalled that Gestetner came one day unexpectedly to his apartment after having read a promotional card that Loewy had written about how improving product appearance would boost sales. Gestetner reportedly insisted that the redesign of the machine would have to be done in three days, before he returned to England. Loewy agreed to do the job for two thousand dollars if Gestetner liked the result, or five hundred dollars if he did not. Loewy's solution was brilliant in its simplicity. He covered the machine in clay, reshaped the clay into a shell that concealed all the mechanical parts except for the operating controls, and mounted the whole thing upon a cabinet-like base to get rid of its protruding legs. Gestetner was so pleased that he would keep the Loewy design in production for forty years.

Despite his success with Gestetner, Loewy had a difficult time traveling around the country trying to sell his services to manufacturers during the Great Depression. The turning point came in 1934, when he introduced three landmark designs—the GG-1 diesel locomotive for the Pennsylvania Railroad, the Hupmobile automobile for the Hupp Automobile Company, and the remodeled Coldspot refrigerator for Sears, Roebuck and Company. The GG-1 locomotive marked the beginning of a long and productive relationship between Loewy and the Pennsylvania Railroad—including his design of the S-1 steam locomotive (1938) and (with University of Pennsylvania architect Paul Cret) the interior of a train for the Pennsylvania Railroad (1938). The whale-like deck shapes of the ferryboat *Princess Anne* that he designed for the Pennsylvania Railroad's affiliate, the Virginia Ferry Company, was so admired that commissions from other shipping lines followed. Perhaps most important, the spectacular increase in the sales of the new Coldspot refrigerator impressed upon businessmen the importance of design as a sales tool.

Those successes led to the rapid growth of the firm. By 1938, Loewy had eighteen designers working for him; by 1941, there were fifty-six. During the firm's peak years, from 1947 through the mid-1960's, there were more than 150 regular employees, with more temporarily added for special projects. When the firm was reorganized in 1944 under the name Raymond Loewy Associates, Loewy made five key associates partners with a share in the profits. The business remained wholly owned by Loewy, however, and all the finished designs were signed with his name, regardless of who had done the work.

In its early years, the firm had three divisions—transportation, product design, and packaging. Later, a corporate identity division was added. What became the largest and most profitable division, though, was the firm's Department of Architecture and Interior Design, established in 1937 under William T. Snaith (and renamed in 1944 the Department of Specialized Architecture) to handle the design and planning of retail stores. In his autobiography, Loewy recalled that "a whole new world opened up for my design organization the first day we convinced a client that a store was an implement for merchandising and not a building raised around a series of pushcarts."

The New York World's Fair of 1939 and 1940 transformed Loewy from a designer for corporate America into a household name. His commissions for the fair included the design of the House of Jewels, the Railroad Building, and, most important, the focal exhibit for the fair's "Transportation Zone," the Chrysler Motors Building. His imaginative animated diorama for the Chrysler Motors Building, entitled "Rocketport," depicted the possibilities of space travel and became one of the fair's most popular attractions.

Other major commissions included Loewy's 1941 design of a new red-and-white package for Lucky Strike cigarettes, a corporate identity program for the International Harvester Company, and work for the Greyhound Bus Company that culminated in the 1954 creation of the Greyhound Scenicruiser bus. Loewy's most visible role during the post-World War II years was his work for the Studebaker automobile company. The three Loewy-designed Studebaker cars—the 1947 Champion, the 1953 Starliner, and the 1962 Avanti sports car—were praised at the time, and have been even more admired since, for their innovative, compact lines.

Impact of Event

Interest in industrial product design first appeared in Europe, climaxing in the 1925 Paris Exposition Internationale des Arts Décoratifs et Industriels Modernes. Yet industrial design emerged as a profession first in the United States, because the rise of a consumer culture occurred earlier in America than in Europe. The major impetus was the pressure during the 1920's to mass-market consumer durables such as automobiles, sewing machines, refrigerators, radios, and other electric appliances. At the suggestion of their advertising agencies, manufacturers began to give more attention to the appearance of their products. No single event did more to alert businessmen to the importance of style than Henry Ford's decision in 1927 to meet the competition from General Motors by replacing the Ford Model T automobile with the new Model A. The Great Depression reinforced the attraction to product design as a merchandising tool.

Loewy became popularly identified as the founder of the new profession of industrial design. That identification was not fully accurate; he had contemporaries who were equally important. The oldest of the group was Walter Dorwin Teague. Born in 1883 in Decatur, Illinois, Teague had a successful career as an advertising illustrator before he began his second career as an industrial designer by creating, around 1930, several cameras for Eastman Kodak. He would count among his clients such other corporate giants as the Ford Motor Company, Texaco, and DuPont. Another Midwesterner (from small-town Michigan), Norman Bel Geddes—born the same year as Loewy—moved from advertising illustration to theater stage design before going on to industrial design. His 1932 book *Horizons* did much to popularize what became known as "streamlining," and his "Futurama" exhibit for the General Motors Building at the New York World's Fair pictured a utopian future built around the automobile and the high-speed highway. The fourth of the founders of American industrial design, Henry Dreyfuss, born in New York City in 1904, moved from theatrical design to industrial design in the late 1920's. His most famous designs were Bell Telephone's standard desk telephone (1937) and the Grand Central Railroad's Twentieth-Century Limited train (1938).

Loewy, though, did make a major—perhaps crucial—contribution to the establishment of the new discipline. A total of approximately five hundred designers worked for Loewy; many would go on to set up their own offices. In 1944, Loewy was one of the organizers of what became the Industrial Designer Society of America. In 1946, he was president of the group and was responsible for drawing up a code of professional ethics for its members. Loewy probably did more than any other person to sell industrial design through a genius for self-promotion that seized every opportunity for media exposure.

Loewy did not share the technocratic utopianism of Teague or Geddes, who envisaged industrial design transforming the world. His major criteria for a successful design were simplicity, convenience, economy, durability, and ease of maintenance and repair. Yet he was as interested in an aesthetically pleasing result as he was with the product's utilitarian functioning. Once, when asked why he had included a particular detail in one of his designs, he bluntly replied, "Because I liked it that way." His artistic creed was: "Good design keeps the user happy, the manufacturer in the black and the aesthete unoffended." Most important, he had what one of his partners termed "an unerring vulgar taste"—"vulgar" in the literal sense of appealing to large numbers of people.

In broad terms, Loewy's work belongs to the style known as "streamlining." The key to streamlining was the separation of the outer shell of a product from its internal mechanism. That outer shell typically had a smooth and flowing surface with rounded edges. Streamlining owed much to aerodynamics—the science of eliminating the friction of air resistance to a moving vehicle. Aerodynamics researchers concluded that the teardrop was the ideal shape for a moving vehicle. Industrial designers in the 1930's extended the teardrop shape from its use in locomotives and automobiles to use in stationary objects. Psychologists have hypothesized that the popularity of streamlining lay in its appeal to the 1930's yearning to overcome the Depression's frictions.

In the post-World War II years, Loewy consciously adapted to the "planned obsolescence" approach of the corporate world. His most popular designs of the time were conceived with the potential for minor future changes in the basic model. When critics complained about the practice of annual model changes, Loewy replied pragmatically, "There is no curve so beautiful as a rising sales graph."

Perhaps Loewy's most important long-term impact upon the American environment came from his collaboration with William T. Snaith in transforming retail merchandising. The Loewy-Snaith team was responsible for the first suburban branch store of a major downtown retailer, the Lord & Taylor branch at Manhasset on Long Island, outside New York City, which opened in the spring of 1941. The firm's 1945 Lucky store in San Leandro, California, became the model for the post-World War II grocery supermarket; its new building for the Foley Brothers store in Houston, Texas, in 1947 revolutionized conventional department store operations by rearranging selling and stock areas in accord with a profit-per-square-foot calculus.

In 1956, Loewy withdrew from active management of the firm, Snaith taking over as managing partner and, from 1961, as president of the successor business, Raymond Loewy/William Snaith, Incorporated. When Loewy died on July 14, 1986, he was the last of the pioneer generation of American industrial designers.

Bibliography
Bush, Donald J. *The Streamlined Decade.* New York: George Braziller, 1975. Excel-

lent survey of the application of streamlining during the 1930's to locomotives, automobiles, ships, airplanes, household appliances, and even buildings. Extensively illustrated.

Loewy, Raymond. *Industrial Design.* Woodstock, N.Y.: Overlook Press, 1979. Includes an introductory chapter, "My Life in Design," in which Loewy answers questions from an interviewer. The bulk of the volume is a collection of photographs and drawings of designs, with Loewy's accompanying explanatory commentary.

_____. *Never Leave Well Enough Alone.* New York: Simon & Schuster, 1951. Loewy's autobiography remains the fullest available account of his career. Entertainingly written and highly readable. The 1951 French version appeared, appropriately, under the title *La Laideur se vend mal* ("ugliness sells badly").

Meikle, Jeffrey B. *Twentieth Century Limited: Industrial Design in America, 1925-1939.* Philadelphia: Temple University Press, 1979. The fullest account of the formative years in the professionalization of industrial design. Focuses upon Loewy, Walter Teague, Norman Bel Geddes, and Henry Dreyfuss, with illuminating analyses of the concepts and values shaping their work.

Pulos, Arthur J. *The American Design Adventure, 1940-1975.* Cambridge, Mass.: MIT Press, 1988. Carries on Pulos' history of American industrial design from where the first book left off, with the same first-rate results.

_____. *American Design Ethic: A History of Industrial Design.* Cambridge, Mass.: MIT Press, 1983. A pathbreaking and indispensable survey of American product design from the colonial period through the 1930's. The last third of the text deals with the 1920's on, when Loewy played a major role. Extensive illustrations; fine bibliography.

Schönberger, Angela, ed. *Raymond Loewy: Pioneer of American Industrial Design.* Translated by Ian Robson and Eileen Martin. Munich: Prestel, 1990. This byproduct of a major exhibition honoring Loewy includes excellent contributions on his work and its place in the history of industrial design. Extensively illustrated. Includes a bibliography listing contemporary commentary upon Loewy's work and relevant secondary works.

John Braeman

Cross-References

Hoffmann and Moser Found the Wiener Werkstätte (1903), p. 79; Behrens Designs the AEG Turbine Factory (1909), p. 219; Rietveld Designs the Red-Blue Chair (1918), p. 458; German Artists Found the Bauhaus (1919), p. 463; Cranbrook Academy Begins a History of Design Excellence (1925), p. 610; A Paris Exhibition Defines Art Deco (1925), p. 654; Dreyfuss Designs the Bell "300" Telephone (1937), p. 1057.

NEW YORK'S MUSEUM OF MODERN ART IS FOUNDED

Category of event: Art
Time: 1929
Locale: New York, New York

Alfred Barr's scholarship and passion, backed by Rockefeller money and prestige, put previously despised radical art at the center of American culture

Principal personages:
ALFRED H. BARR, JR. (1902-1981), a young art historian intensely concerned with explaining and justifying post-1900 art to the public
ABBY ALDRICH ROCKEFELLER (1874-1948), an heiress, philanthropist, and collector of modern and folk art
CONGER GOODYEAR (1877-1964), a wealthy industrialist and collector of modern art with ties to the American museum world
PAUL SACHS (1878-1965), a professor of art history at Harvard University, adviser to the Museum of Modern Art's founders, and Barr's mentor

Summary of Event

Americans were first exposed to radical art, from Postimpressionism to cubism to expressionism, at the famous independent exhibition held in New York's Sixty-ninth Street Armory in 1913 (the "Armory Show"). The new styles were appreciated only by a few independent collectors, however, and American artists who adopted them had next to no support. In the 1920's, American museums and the American rich collected European Old Master art as a counterweight of "culture" to the disturbing forces that were transforming American society. European art after Impressionism was almost impossible to find, and only a few zealots collected the most innovative work being done in Europe. Even Vincent van Gogh and Pablo Picasso were dismissed as frauds or madmen.

The idea for the Museum of Modern Art (MOMA) came from three women who collected Postimpressionist art and who wished to spread appreciation for it in America. Abby Aldrich Rockefeller, the wife of John D. Rockefeller, Jr., was concerned that interest in art after 1880 was entirely private in America and that her children's generation would have no chance to experience an art appropriate to its own time. Lizzie P. Bliss, the heiress of a textile fortune, had been guided to modern art by Arthur B. Davies, one of the organizers of the Armory Show. Mary Sullivan was a former design teacher and a collector of work by such avant-garde figurative artists as Picasso, van Gogh, Paul Cézanne, and Georges Braque. The women knew that in Europe, such state-run museums as the Tate Gallery in London and the Luxembourg in Paris showed advanced art of the recent past and the present, from which the best works might be chosen for official government collections. The position of modern art in America, they believed would be much more secure if such a museum existed in the United States to give modern art the imprimatur of accepted taste.

Rockefeller, Bliss, and Sullivan began to discuss backing a museum devoted to such art in the winter of 1928-1929. They would loan the museum art until its director could set a firm course and begin a collection. In May, 1929, they asked Conger Goodyear to chair a committee to establish the museum. Goodyear had recently been forced out of the presidency of the Albright Gallery in Buffalo because he had spent five thousand dollars of the museum's money on a Picasso. He quickly assembled a panel of art patrons and historians. In June, on the advice of committee member Paul Sachs, the backers approached Sachs's former Harvard student Alfred H. Barr, Jr., to direct the museum.

Barr was the most brilliant and impassioned of the museum professionals whom Sachs steered toward modern art. The son of a Presbyterian minister, Barr studied art history at Princeton University and Harvard University. He was one of the first American historians to visit the Bauhaus in Germany and the Soviet Union's art academies. Believing in a liberal, forward-looking idea of historical evolution, he was convinced that the greatest radical art of his day was as inevitable an expression of the modern world as the Gothic cathedral had been of the Middle Ages.

Paul Sachs made Barr view modernism in the art historian's usual terms of value: connoisseurship, the description of how particular artists made their works beautiful, and the evolutionary idea that styles were created along a time line of direct influences. This view put Barr in line with the conservative, art-appreciation outlook of Rockefeller and her friends. Barr, though, loved much more radical art than Sachs did and was willing to look for examples of the creative spirit outside painting (in architecture, product design, and films). He became convinced that his real mission was to make modernism popular among tomorrow's millionaire art buyers—the students Barr taught at Harvard and at Wellesley College. Only in that way could modernism get its full due as a cultural expression.

Barr's ambition of making modernism popular matched Rockefeller's, Bliss's, and Sullivan's hope that their own tastes could be shared with the public. Despite Barr's youth and scholarly unworldliness, Rockefeller accepted him as the new museum's director in July, 1929. His first exhibition for the museum, "Cézanne, Gauguin, Seurat, and van Gogh," was made up of paintings loaned by the founders and other supporters. None of the shown work was abstract—indeed, all the artists had died before the emergence of cubism—and it was already being collected by Francophiles in the American upper class. The work displayed, however, broke sharply with Old Master definitions of art prevalent in America. While conservative by Barr's standards, the display of work by "the founders of modern painting" would be a springboard from which he could launch shows of the more demanding art that followed them. The museum's exhibitions would be a class in the development of modernism.

When the Museum of Modern Art opened in rented space in a New York office building on November 8, 1929, it marked a milestone in respectability for avant-garde art. Forty-seven thousand people visited the exhibition during its month on display. Newspapers and art journals announced that the paintings shown had "converted" antimodernists by their beauty. The social exclusiveness of the museum's backers reassured viewers that a taste for the modern was an acceptable thing. Most important, the works of artists whose place in art history was beyond question but who had been kept from American audiences by museums' reactionary attitudes were finally presented to a starved public.

Impact of Event

Barr and Rockefeller's new museum quickly developed along the lines both had hoped. Barr went to Europe and convinced museums, collectors, and artists to lend to the institution. He mounted shows of increasing scope and artistic daringness, notably "Vincent van Gogh" (1935), "Cubism and Abstract Art," "Fantastic Art, Dada, and Surrealism" (both 1936), and "Picasso: Forty Years of His Art" (1939). Lizzie Bliss's bequest of her collection and other trustee gifts in 1931 made possible Rockefeller's ambition to build a permanent public collection of the work she loved best. At the same time, Barr mounted shows devoted to, and began collections of, aspects of art in genres other than painting. These included modern architecture (1932), industrial design (1934), classic films (1935), and photography (1940). The museum moved into its own building in 1934 and acquired a new, radically modern headquarters on former Rockefeller property in 1939.

Barr intended his museum to be a teaching institution first and foremost. The erudite catalogs that accompanied his shows explained how the radical works on display had developed naturally from the art that had preceded them. Even a form as incomprehensible as abstraction had a pedigree, and its artists were as accountable to the connoisseur's taste as any Old Master. Such an approach reassured viewers without making the art itself any less revolutionary. Barr's personal charisma attracted young, well-placed academics and art lovers, including Philip Johnson, Edward Warburg, Dorothy Miller, and Beaumont Newhall, to the museum's staff. The publicity department's handling of exhibitions of van Gogh's paintings and of James McNeill Whistler's "Mother" added to the museum's reputation for shocking, brilliant innovation.

Because of the high social status of MOMA's backers, affiliation with the museum could be a strategy of social advancement. A taste for avant-garde art became fashionable in New York, and MOMA's shows of modern architecture and design changed the upper class's idea of what its homes were supposed to look like. Barr himself was instrumental in helping the radical German architects Walter Gropius and Ludwig Mies van der Rohe find teaching posts in America after Adolf Hitler came to power. By the 1940's, for MOMA's audience, radical style became what Barr believed modern art itself was: a sign of liberal (but not destructive) historical progress.

The museum's impact on artists themselves, and thus on the nature of art, was more ambiguous. American painters were offended that the first show had featured French art. Barr himself always tried to show American work, but he was constrained by the trustees' preferences and by his own feeling that the future lay with

European abstraction. Barr's art-history background itself, which made him judge art based on stylistic development and formal beauty, tended to discourage him from looking at art as a means of social change. The uproar that occurred when the museum showed politically radical murals in 1932 (some pillorying MOMA's own backers as capitalist oppressors) made it act more cautiously. Moreover, the institution could always be faulted for conservatism when it showed potentially subversive art, such as Soviet films or Bauhaus product designs, as works of beauty without regard to their social import.

The new audience for modernism created by MOMA led to new dealerships and galleries for avant-garde art, a development that exposed American painters to new inspiration and gave them more outlets for their works. The museum's importance in the art world, however, led to fears that MOMA, its backers, and the dealers were colluding to push certain styles on the art market. MOMA, after all, set itself up as the halfway house where modern art would be judged for its lasting merit and consequently its sale value. While doing so, MOMA was often dependent on the personal purchases of the trustees, who were building up the museum's small permanent collection. Accordingly, American artists of all stylistic persuasions distrusted the museum as much as they learned from it.

Alfred Barr's museum was transformed by the success he brought to it. By 1939, he had created a complex bureaucracy of scholars, publicists, and business administrators. Barr's painstaking scholarship (which put him behind schedule and over budget) and roving interest in all the modern arts came to be seen as a hindrance to the museum's mission and stability, and in 1943, Barr was removed as director of the institution. After an interim period, he was given the new, less powerful post of director of collections. While his influence on MOMA's taste remained great, his idea of a free-ranging educational museum was slowed by institutional realities.

Although the Museum of Modern Art became a museum in the more conventional sense, conserving the aesthetic values of a particular institution, its example forced other museums to take contemporary art seriously. New York's Metropolitan Museum itself began buying newer art (some from MOMA's overstock) and eventually joined the bidding war for new talent that hit museums after World War II. The scholarship of Barr and his MOMA staff showed historians and curators how to write about radical art responsibly. The great role that museums came to play in the creation of art would not have been possible without the Museum of Modern Art.

Bibliography

Barr, Alfred. *Defining Modern Art.* Edited by Irving Sandler and Amy Newman. New York: Harry N. Abrams, 1978. A collection of Barr's catalog prefaces and other Museum of Modern Art publications. Together, they make a laconic, somewhat repetitive argument for the historical inevitability and aesthetic merit of most branches of modern art. Chronology, index.

Chase, Mary Ellen. *Abby Aldrich Rockefeller.* New York: Macmillan, 1950. Biography of the woman who led the effort to create the Museum of Modern Art. Respectful and conventional treatment that discusses the museum in the context of Rockefeller's philanthropy and love of art. Index.

Lynes, Russell. *Good Old Modern: An Intimate Portrait of the Museum of Modern Art.* New York: Atheneum, 1973. The best account of the museum up to 1970. A discursive style makes chronology hard to follow, but solidly based on research, interviews, and personal contacts. No annotation, however. Emphasizes social status as an aspect of the museum's appeal. Chronology of museum exhibitions, index.

Marquis, Alice Goldfarb. *Alfred H. Barr, Jr.: Missionary for the Modern.* Chicago: Contemporary Books, 1989. Accounts for Barr's devotion to modernism and traces his relations with museum backers and staff more fully than Lynes's account. Otherwise, follows Lynes's interpretation closely. Overworks the idea that Barr followed in his father's footsteps as a kind of preacher. Endnotes, index.

Meyer, Karl E. *The Art Museum: Power, Money, Ethics.* New York: William Morrow, 1979. A report for the Twentieth Century Fund. Dated as investigative reporting and with little treatment of art collected by American museums, but valuable background on the kind of institutional pressures faced by MOMA in its maturing years. Bibliography, index.

M. David Samson

Cross-References

Avant-Garde Art in the Armory Show Shocks American Viewers (1913), p. 361; The Formation of the Blue Four Advances Abstract Painting (1924), p. 583; The Whitney Museum Is Inaugurated in New York (1931), p. 885; *Abstract Painting in America* Opens in New York (1935), p. 1001; Peggy Guggenheim's Gallery Promotes New American Art (1942), p. 1239.

THE BEDBUG AND THE BATHHOUSE EXEMPLIFY REVOLUTIONARY THEATER

Category of event: Theater
Time: 1929-1930
Locale: Moscow, Union of Soviet Socialist Republics

Vladimir Mayakovsky created a theater of spectacle in The Bedbug *and* The Bathhouse, *which laid down the principles for revolutionary theater but were banned by Soviet authorities*

Principal personages:
VLADIMIR MAYAKOVSKY (1893-1930), a playwright and poet who promoted a theater of mass spectacle using satirical propaganda
VSEVOLOD MEYERHOLD (1874-1940), a famous director who staged innovative productions of *The Bedbug* and *The Bathhouse*
ALEXANDER RODCHENKO (1891-1956), an artist and designer who created the futuristic sets for *The Bedbug*
DMITRI SHOSTAKOVICH (1906-1975), an experimental composer who wrote the score for *The Bedbug*

Summary of Event

Vladimir Mayakovsky had won accolades from Vladimir Lenin and had become the foremost poet of the Russian Revolution, but after the revolution, aspects of Western capitalism had been introduced into the Soviet Union under the New Economic Program (NEP). This plan fell into disfavor, and Lenin's successor, Joseph Stalin, began to introduce his plan for industrializing the Soviet Union. As postrevolutionary society began to set up rigid guidelines for all forms of culture, Mayakovsky came under attack from the Soviet authorities charged with overseeing the artistic community, who advocated Socialist Realism as the proper form for theater. Socialist Realism promoted a theater that reflected realistic situations and emphasized psychologically rounded characters. Mayakovsky was opposed to this movement, and he joined forces with antirealist director Vsevolod Meyerhold to produce two theatrical spectacles: *Klop* (1929; *The Bedbug*, 1931) and *Banya* (1930; *The Bathhouse*, 1963). On December 28, 1928, Mayakovsky read *The Bedbug* in the Meyerhold Theater. Meyerhold felt that the play would not only hold a special place in Soviet theater but also would become part of the repertoire of world theater.

The Bedbug, which opened at the Meyerhold Theater on February 13, 1929, satirizes those Communist backsliders who had reverted to the crude and vulgar lifestyles of the bourgeois. Prisypkin, a worker with callouses on his hands and a union card in his pocket, is seduced into guzzling vodka, playing sentimental songs, dancing the foxtrot, and following other reactionary bourgeois pursuits. Changing his name to Pierre Skripkin and jilting his proletariat girlfriend Zoya Berezkina, Prisypkin marries Elsevira Renaissance, a grotesque sex symbol with affected French mannerisms. Their wedding at the Renaissance beauty salon is a mixture of maudlin sentimentality, conspicuous consumption, and all-out drunken debauchery, ending in a brawl and a fire that reduces the beauty salon and everyone in it to ashes.

Prisypkin's unscathed body, buried under the ice, is discovered in the futuristic world of 1979. The power structure in this highly organized, completely sanitized society resurrects Prisypkin, only to find that he infects their society with such bad habits as drinking vodka, engaging in modern dances, and falling in love. Finally, he is captured and put in a zoo. In desperation, Prisypkin urges the audience to join him, but his plea is dismissed as an attack of lunacy.

Mayakovsky's use of grotesque characters to satirize socialist evils set up the theater of lampooning and burlesque as a model for democratic theater. In Oleg Bayan, the effete, self-indulgent poet who teaches Prisypkin how to wiggle his behind correctly and scratch his back discreetly, Mayakovsky caricatures reactionary poets. The tawdry decor of the Renaissance beauty salon created a dismal picture of life under the New Economic Policy. No less dismal was Mayakovsky's futuristic world. It is a sterile, automated world with mechanical voting arms, mass meetings, and elaborate cleansing paraphernalia. Even worse, it is an emotionless world where love is defined as a pathological condition. Mayakovsky even had to assure the authorities that his play was not a satire on the socialist future.

The production of *The Bedbug* was a true theater spectacle. In Meyerhold's production, actors marched through the audience hawking bras and ran in all directions when the police came. Three artists who called themselves Kukrynisky designed the first half. Using clothes from Soviet shops, they designed a pop art decor with various kinds of kitsch items. The actor playing Prisypkin walked in broad strides, swaying his pot belly and bulging rear. Prisypkin came across as a thick-lipped, slit-eyed, pigeon-toed grunter and screecher. The wedding scene consisted of grotesque pantomimes and slapstick antics in which characters beat each other with fish. The futuristic scenes were designed by Alexander Rodchenko, who used large utilitarian objects, modern glass-like structures (including a glass bell-like prison for Prisypkin), and poster-like costumes in rose and light blue to add to the futuristic tone. Scientists were dressed in sterile white garb, and their scenes were bathed in a white glow. Dmitri Shostakovitch wrote an original score for the production. For the wedding scene, he took a foxtrot theme and built it into a cacaphonous fantasia. Bells, flashing lights, and motion-picture screens all added to the overall effect of the production. Mayakovsky had created a futuristic spectacle for the masses. Mayakovsky's critics, though, attacked the play for creating poster-like caricatures without psychological depth. They found that his attack on bourgeois socialists allowed him to pick an easy target and to avoid criticizing more menacing enemies of socialism.

In *The Bathhouse*, Mayakovsky and Meyerhold fought back and again created a futuristic spectacle. From the start, the play created controversy. First, Mayakovsky was unable to get the script approved by censors without making changes. When he finally got approval, he was attacked in the press before the play opened. Vladimir Ermilov, an important member of the Russian Association of Proletarian Writers, criticized Mayakovsky for his exaggerated art. Ermilov's criticism was reprinted in *Pravda* on March 9, 1930. When the play opened on March 16, Mayakovsky attacked Ermilov in one of the banners in the theater. Ermilov demanded that the banner be removed, and Mayakovsky complied.

The Bathhouse is a vicious attack on Soviet bureaucracy. Pobedonosikov, a paper-shuffling, cliché-mouthing, indifferent bureaucrat surrounded by bootlickers and incompetents, is too busy to deal with the problems of ordinary people. So when Chudakov, an inventor, gets caught in red tape and bureaucratic shuffles while trying to get a patent for his time machine, he sneaks the machine into Pobedonosikov's apartment. The machine is accidentally triggered into action, producing the Phosphorescent Woman, a Communist prototype from the year 2030. She paints a picture of a glorious Communist future and promises to take all qualified Communists there. Only Pobedonosikov and his cohorts are left behind, because they are "not needed for communism."

In *The Bathhouse*, Mayakovsky again attacks the theater of his day. In a Pirandello-like third act, Pobedonosikov becomes a character watching a play about himself. He complains that he has been presented in a bad light and that the caricature of him is unnatural and not lifelike. He and his cohorts demand a drama of "poeticized reality." In this clever piece of metatheater, Mayakovsky attacked the realistic school of the Moscow Art Theater as well as the Russian ballet theater, which tried to poeticize life. He also reduced the objects of his satire to grotesque types, broke with fourth-wall realism, and tried to jar his audience into action. Again, he wanted to create a theater of spectacle so that he could "transform the boards of the stage into a rostrum."

The Bathhouse, however, was Mayakovsky's theatrical downfall. It not only flopped, closing after three performances, but also outraged Mayakovsky's enemies, who accused him of writing abstract dramas for coterie audiences and of failing to create heroic workers who would overcome the bureaucracy. Shortly after the failure of *The Bathhouse*, on April 14, 1930, Mayakovsky shot himself. In his suicide note, he expressed his regret at having given in to the critic Ermilov.

Impact of Event

Mayakovsky's plays were banned in the Soviet Union, and their impact was not immediately felt. Mayakovsky, though, set the tone for revolutionary theater not only in Russia but also throughout the West. Mayakovsky broke with bourgeois realism to fight for a democratic art that would allow the free word of the creative personality to be "written on the walls, fences, and streets of our cities." He eschewed notions of absolute value and eternal beauty and created a theater for the masses—a theater that produced poetic and scenic devices that were based on their ability to propagandize. Mayakovsky, along with Meyerhold, wanted to create utopian art "which would not only pose the problems of today but would project decades into the future." Mayakovsky also tried to move theater away from dreary slice-of-life realism. Realizing that the stage was "only one third of the auditorium," Mayakovsky brought the action of drama into the auditorium. Instead of creating believable characters hidden behind a proscenium arch and seen against a background of decorative scenery, he created grotesque figures—slapstick clowns bouncing across constructivist sets composed of ropes, grids, and platforms. Mayakovsky turned the stage into a soapbox and used satire to effect political change.

As Stalinist repression started to ease off, the time was right for the return of Mayakovsky to the Soviet theater. In December, 1953, Victor Pluchek, a disciple of Meyerhold, successfully produced *The Bathhouse* at the Moscow Theater of Satire. Pluchek followed this production with *The Bedbug* and other Mayakovsky plays, and he toured Mayakovsky's plays from Leningrad to the Urals. By 1958, the Theater of Satire had performed *The Bathhouse* two hundred times and *The Bedbug* five hundred times. In 1957, the Theater of Satire took first prize at the All Union Festival of Drama for its productions of Mayakovsky's plays. Soon, Mayakovsky's works were being produced throughout the Soviet Union and its satellite countries.

In the 1960's, Mayakovsky's brand of theatricalism returned to the Soviet theater. Dissident playwright Andrei Remezov's *Yest-li zhizn na Marse?* (1961; is there life on Mars?) begins with spectators who come to witness life on Mars. The Martian society is an antiutopian world reminiscent of the futuristic automatons in *The Bedbug*. Robot-like characters live in a nightmarish world where one government minister has to look up the word "principle" because he does not know its meaning. Remezov's play falls directly in line with Mayakovsky's brand of fantastic satire.

Basing his views partially on Mayakovsky, writer Andrei Sinyavsky called for the end of Socialist Realism and wanted a "phantasmagoric art" in which writers could "teach us to be truthful with the aid of the absurd and the fantastic." Yuri Lyubimov took up the banner of Mayakovsky and Meyerhold. Serving as the director of the Taganka Theater from 1964 to 1984, he rebelled against the sterile realism of the Moscow Art Theater. Like Mayakovsky, he tried to create a theater of imagination and metaphor. His productions were epic and carnivalesque. He combined the sublime and the ridiculous and mixed social commentary with theatrical art. He even did a production based on Mayakovsky's poetry.

Mayakovsky's influence soon began to be felt in revolutionary theater outside the Soviet Union. Italian theater artist Dario Fo was especially influenced by Mayakovsky. Fo's leftist dramas combine mime, circus antics, and brutal satire in an attempt to arouse the working class. Fo's *L'operaio conosce trecento parole, il padrone mille: Per questo lui è il padrone* (1969; *The Worker Knows Three Hundred Words, the Boss Knows a Thousand: That's Why He's the Boss,* 1983) is a mixture of the fantastic and the grotesque. The play features a self-important bureaucrat styled right out of *The Bathhouse* and has Mayakovsky's girlfriend present a futuristic ballet incorporating Mayakovsky's own techniques of mime and dance to convey a political message. Mayakovsky is seen, like Fo himself, as a man outside of the Party, playing directly to the people.

In the 1960's, the Mayakovsky/Meyerhold brand of theatricalism became prevalent in American avant-garde theater. Politically oriented theater groups such as the Living Theatre and the Performance Group used visible lighting, performed with house lights on, and featured acrobatics, clowning, and choral chants. They made extensive use of mime and extended the action of the drama into the audience. In dramas such as *Frankenstein* (1965), the Living Theatre presented futuristic spectacles on raised platforms. In *Prometheus* (1978), Julien Beck, the founder of the Living Theatre, like Fo, introduced Mayakovsky as a character. In *Prometheus*, a scene from a Mayakovsky play is enacted in gymnastic style before Mayakovsky commits suicide.

Many of the radical popular theaters arising in the 1960's, such as the San Francisco Mime Troupe, employed Mayakovsky's methods. They appealed directly to working people, played in noise-filled rooms and open areas, used clowning and popular music, encouraged contact with the audience, and tried to raise political awareness through satire. Like Mayakovsky, these groups used satire not to amuse but to arouse anger. Their dramas, like his, do not offer a comic resolution but leave an open ending or produce a fantastic resolution. Though his effect was somewhat delayed, Mayakovsky helped to set down the techniques that would become the framework for revolutionary theater in the 1960's and 1970's. Many of these techniques have now been incorporated into mainstream theater.

Bibliography

Brown, Edward J. *Mayakovsky: A Poet in the Revolution.* Princeton, N.J.: Princeton University Press, 1973. The first major critical biography of Mayakovsky in English. The book shows a close connection between Mayakovsky's life and his works. It provides close readings of Mayakovsky's major and minor works and even focuses on his didactic verse.

Shklovsky, Viktor. *Mayakovsky and His Circle.* Edited and translated by Lily Feiler. New York: Dodd, Mead, 1972. A tribute to Mayakovsky by a close associate and intimate friend. The book covers not only the relationship between Shklovsky and Mayakovsky but also focuses on the other figures in the Futurist movement in Russia. Although it promotes Shklovsky's formalist bias, it is a good firsthand account of Mayakovsky's development as a poet as well as a history of the artistic revolutions in Russia from 1910 to 1930.

Terras, Victor. *Vladimir Mayakovsky.* Boston: Twayne, 1983. An excellent critical introduction to Mayakovsky. The book provides a clear, well-organized biographical sketch of Mayakovsky's life followed by a close analysis of Mayakovsky's major works. Terras defines critical terms, traces the history of artistic movements, and provides a clear critical assessment of Mayakovsky's works.

Woroszylski, Wiktor. *The Life of Mayakovsky.* Translated by Boleslav Taborski. New York: Orion Press, 1970. A translation of a 1966 work by a Polish poet. The book is an encyclopedic compendium of documentary sources on Mayakovsky's life and work. It is a good reference work for someone looking for primary source material, but it does not present a clear perspective for the reader who is unfamiliar with Mayakovsky's work.

Paul Rosefeldt

Cross-References

Stanislavsky Helps to Establish the Moscow Art Theater (1897), p. 1; The Soviet Union Bans Abstract Art (1922), p. 544; Socialist Realism Is Mandated in Soviet Literature (1932), p. 908; Stalin Restricts Soviet Composers (1932), p. 914; Shostakovich's *Lady Macbeth of Mtsensk* Is Condemned (1936), p. 1042.

THE MALTESE FALCON INTRODUCES THE HARD-BOILED DETECTIVE NOVEL

Category of event: Literature
Time: 1929-1930
Locale: The United States

Dashiell Hammett's masterpiece of hard-boiled detective fiction established a distinctively American alternative to the classic British mystery and raised the genre to the level of literature

Principal personages:
DASHIELL HAMMETT (1894-1961), a former Pinkerton's detective who brought a new realism and psychological complexity to the field of detective fiction
LILLIAN HELLMAN (1905-1984), a playwright, screenwriter, and essayist who was Hammett's closest companion for the last three decades of his life

Summary of Event

Dashiell Hammett brought a new realism to detective fiction and introduced the tough, cynical private eye into American popular mythology. His best-known work, *The Maltese Falcon*, was first published in five serial installments from September, 1929, to January, 1930, with publication in book form in February, 1930. The book was an immediate popular success and was reprinted seven times the first year. Critics were equally impressed, acclaiming the book as an important novel and not simply another mystery story. Three film versions were made in the next decade; in the third, the John Huston film of 1941, Humphrey Bogart crystallized the image of Sam Spade for American audiences.

Hammett left school at the age of fourteen, and he held several different jobs for short periods of time until 1915, when he became an operative for the Pinkerton National Detective Agency. His experience with Pinkerton provided him with the background for the writing of his realistic detective fiction. When pulmonary tuberculosis ended his career as a detective in 1921, Hammett began publishing short fiction in *Black Mask*, the pulp magazine that would publish his first four novels in serial form. The appearance of his first two novels, *Red Harvest* and *The Dain Curse*, in book form in 1929 made him a successful writer, and the next two, *The Maltese Falcon* and *The Glass Key* (1931), made him internationally famous. It was then, at the height of his fame, that he met Lillian Hellman, with whom he had a close relationship until his death.

Hellman was near the beginning of her distinguished career as a writer, which would be aided considerably by Hammett's expertise as an editor and critic; Hammett, though, would publish only one more novel, *The Thin Man*, in 1934. Though he stopped writing, he still received royalties from his books and from a series of sixteen popular films, three weekly radio shows, and a daily comic strip based on his characters and stories. In 1954, his income from these various sources was more than eighty thousand dollars, an enormous sum for the time and an indication of how popular his work had become. The reasons that Hammett suddenly stopped writing are unknown, but speculation has centered on his involvement in left-wing politics, a dangerous commitment given the national temper of that time. In 1951, Hammett received a six-month sentence in federal prison for refusing to answer questions about a civil rights group. As a result, he was branded a Communist, his books went out of print, his radio shows were taken off the air, and his income was attached by the Internal Revenue Service. In a word, he was blacklisted, and the year before his death his reported income was thirty dollars. Ironically, Hammett, as a veteran of two wars, was buried as a hero in Arlington National Cemetery.

Red Harvest, Hammett's first novel, is now generally regarded as one of his best, though also one of his darkest and most violent. The corruption that permeates the book eventually contaminates even the nameless protagonist, the Continental Op (an operative for the Continental Detective Agency). Hammett creates suspense by developing a technique of severely restricted first-person narration to tell the story; the reader sees and hears only as much as the Op does, and knows far less, as the protagonist seldom reveals his thoughts. At the book's close, most of the major characters have been murdered, and the ending suggests that things will continue relatively unchanged; corruption is the norm, not the aberration. Many critics have found early evidence of Hammett's Marxist views in this implicit critique of capitalist society. After a second Op novel, *The Dain Curse*, Hammett turned to a rigorously objective third-person narration for *The Maltese Falcon* and *The Glass Key*, describing details of gesture and expression from the outside, as from a camera-eye point of view, but never revealing characters' thoughts or motives. This shift removes even the few traces of interpretation that had been provided by the taciturn Op and makes the analysis of the character of the detective himself a central concern. The question that readers of *The Maltese Falcon* must resolve is not Who committed the crime? but What sort of man is Sam Spade?

The story begins when a woman hires Spade and his partner, Miles Archer, to follow a man named Floyd Thursby. Archer and Thursby are both murdered that night, and the woman, Brigid O'Shaughnessy, turns out to be involved in a plot to steal a priceless jeweled statue of a falcon; Thursby is revealed to have been her accomplice. Other parties pursuing the falcon include Joel Cairo, one of the first homosexual characters portrayed in an American novel, and Caspar Gutman, the "Fat Man" who is the mastermind behind the quest. Unlike Hammett's first two novels, *The Maltese Falcon* contains little violence; the emphasis is on Spade's gradual uncovering of the complex relations among the various criminals and on the efforts of the criminals and police to determine Spade's own motives and intentions. Hammett's objective narration limits the reader's own knowledge to the same set of lies and half-truths that the characters must sift through.

In the novel's dramatic conclusion, Spade turns Brigid O'Shaughnessy, who has become his lover, over to the police as Archer's murderer. The reasoning that leads Spade to solve the crime is based upon clues available from the start, suggesting that he may have known of her guilt all along. The question remains open as to whether he has really fallen in love but is forced by his rigid personal code of ethics to turn her in or whether he has been cold-bloodedly manipulating her throughout in order to solve the case. Both hypotheses may be partially true, and ultimately the mystery of the novel resides more in understanding the character of the protagonist than in resolving the plot. As Ross Macdonald put it, "Hammett was the first American writer to use the detective-story for the purposes of a major novelist." This interest in exploring character is extended in Hammett's fourth novel, *The Glass Key*, which is as much a psychological novel as a mystery. Hammett's fifth and final novel, *The Thin Man*, is unique in its light comic tone, which fitted it for popular adaptation in a series of films. The centerpiece of the book is the relationship between the worldly and jaded detective Nick Charles and his young and enthusiastic wife, Nora. The Charles's happy marriage, one of the few depicted in modern fiction, is clearly based on the relationship between Hammett and Lillian Hellman, to whom the book is dedicated.

Impact of Event

Before Hammett laid the foundation of the modern realistic detective novel, virtually all detective fiction had been designed on the pattern established by Edgar Allan Poe in three short stories written between 1841 and 1844: "The Murders in the Rue Morgue," "The Mystery of Marie Roget," and "The Purloined Letter." The basic ingredients of the formula were simple: a brilliant but eccentric amateur detective, his loyal but somewhat pedestrian companion and chronicler, an even more pedestrian police force, and a bizarre crime. The solution of the mystery called for a complex series of logical deductions drawn by the scientific detective on the basis of an equally complex series of subtle clues. These clues were generally available to the detective's companion, who was also the narrator, and through him to the reader, who would derive interest and pleasure from the attempt to beat the detective to the solution. The canonical popular version of this classical tradition of the mystery as a puzzle to be solved is of course the British writer Arthur Conan Doyle's Sherlock Holmes series, the success of which paved the way for similar work by other British writers such as Agatha Christie. Though this classical model was invented by the American Poe and practiced by several American mystery writers, its popularity with British writers has led to its being labeled the English school, in opposition to a more realistic type of mystery being written in the 1920's by a small group of American writers.

Hammett proved to be the master of the new kind of detective story written in reaction against the English model. Raymond Chandler made the point that "Hammett gave murder back to the kind of people that commit it for reasons, not just to provide a corpse; and with the means at hand, not hand-wrought dueling pistols, curare and tropical fish." Rather than serving as the vehicle for a bewildering set of clues and an often implausible solution, the realistic story of detection emphasized characterization, action, and rapid-fire and colloquial dialogue—as opposed to the often flat characters, slow pace, and stilted set speeches of the classical school. The essentials of the realistic model are found complete in Hammett's earliest work, almost from the first of his thirty-five stories featuring the Continental Op, just as the entire classical formula was complete in Poe's earliest stories.

Hammett's familiarity with the classical paradigm is established in the seventy-three reviews of detective novels he wrote for the *Saturday Review of Literature* and the *New York Evening Post* between 1927 and 1930, and his rejection of it is thorough. He specifically contrasted his theory of the detective with that of Doyle in describing Sam Spade: "For your private detective does not . . . want to be an erudite solver of riddles in the Sherlock Holmes manner; he wants to be a hard and shifty fellow, able to take care of himself in any situation, able to get the best of anybody he comes in contact with, whether criminal, innocent by-stander, or client." Hammett underscored the difference in methods in a 1924 short story, "The Tenth Clew," which parodies the classical detective plot with a set of nine bewildering clues, including a victim missing his left shoe and collar buttons, a mysterious list of names, a bizarre murder weapon (the victim was beaten to death with a typewriter), and so on. The solution, of course, the "tenth clue," is to ignore all nine of the earlier clues and to use standard methods such as the surveillance of suspects to find the killer.

Just as the detective is different in Hammett, so are the crimes and criminals. The world of the traditional mystery is one of regularity disrupted temporarily by the aberrant event of the crime. Once the detective solves the crime through the application of reason, normalcy is restored. The worldview implicit in this plot was comforting for a largely middle-class English readership at the turn of the century, but remote from the experience of the generation of American readers who had just survived World War I. The world of the hard-boiled detective, as conceived by an author who had been through the horrors of that war, is one in which criminal behavior is the norm rather than the exception. There are usually several crimes and several criminals, and the society is not an orderly one temporarily disrupted but a deeply corrupt one that will not be redeemed after the particular set of crimes being investigated is solved.

Raymond Chandler observed that Dashiell Hammett "took murder out of the Venetian vase and dropped it into the alley." The two main ingredients of his breakthrough are the creation of the hard-boiled detective, a ruthless and often violent man who is bound only by his own rigid and private code of ethics, and the perfection of an almost entirely objective narrative style, restricted to terse descriptions and crisp, idiomatic dialogue, revealing the characters' thoughts and emotions only between the lines. Hammett's objective technique laid the foundations for similar stylistic experiments by Ernest Hemingway and, later, the French New Novelists of the 1950's. Moreover, his creation of the hard-boiled detective provided the inspiration for his most noteworthy successors in the mystery field, Raymond Chandler and Ross Macdonald, and introduced the tough, cynical private eye into American popular mythology.

Bibliography

Chandler, Raymond. "The Simple Art of Murder." *Atlantic Monthly* 174 (December, 1944): 53-59. An important essay by one of Hammett's most distinguished successors, analyzing Hammett's decisive role in the development of detective fiction.

Dooley, Dennis. *Dashiell Hammett.* New York: Frederick Ungar, 1984. A survey of Hammett's work for the general reader. Considers some of the better-known short fiction in more detail than usual. Bibliography, index.

Gregory, Sinda. *Private Investigations: The Novels of Dashiell Hammett.* Carbondale: Southern Illinois University Press, 1985. A full-length study of the major novels, insightful in close readings of individual passages but breaking little new interpretive ground. Bibliography, index.

Johnson, Diane. *Dashiell Hammett: A Life.* New York: Random House, 1983. Includes valuable material, but somewhat impressionistic and subjective in places, attributing minutely detailed thoughts and emotions to Hammett and others. Selective bibliography, index, photographs.

Layman, Richard. *Shadow Man: The Life of Dashiell Hammett.* New York: Harcourt Brace Jovanovich, 1981. The most scholarly and reliable of Hammett biographies, objective, readable, and carefully researched and documented. The one indispensable book on Hammett. Contains the full text of the testimony that sent him to prison. Thorough index, bibliography, photographs.

Marling, William. *Dashiell Hammett.* Boston: Twayne, 1983. A concise and well-informed survey, combining a biographical framework with a unified overview of Hammett's short fiction and novels. Lightly annotated bibliography, index.

Nolan, William F. *Dashiell Hammett: A Casebook.* Santa Barbara, Calif.: McNally & Loftin, 1969. The first book-length study of Hammett's life and work, now somewhat dated. Has an extensive listing of Hammett's work in various fields, including newspapers and radio. Bibliography, index.

_____. *Hammett: A Life at the Edge.* New York: Congdon & Weed, 1983. A thorough research job, but often subjective and personal, offering detailed interpretations of the information covered rather than letting the data speak for itself. Selective bibliography, index, photographs.

Symons, Julian. *Dashiell Hammett.* San Diego: Harcourt Brace Jovanovich, 1985. A general survey of Hammett's life and work aimed at a popular audience. Excellent photographs. Bibliography, index.

Wolfe, Peter. *Beams Falling: The Art of Dashiell Hammett.* Bowling Green, Ohio: Bowling Green University Popular Press, 1980. Close critical analyses of Hammett's novels and short fiction. Some valuable information, though the readings are not always convincing.

William Nelles

Cross-References

The Mysterious Affair at Styles Introduces Hercule Poirot (1920), p. 496; Hemingway's *The Sun Also Rises* Speaks for the Lost Generation (1926), p. 696; *Little Caesar, Public Enemy,* and *Scarface* Launch the Gangster-Film Genre (1930), p. 839; The Sherlock Holmes Film Series Begins (1939), p. 1131; *The Maltese Falcon* Establishes a New Style for Crime Films (1941), p. 1223; Blacklisting Seriously Depletes Hollywood's Talent Pool (1947), p. 1340; The New Novel (*Le Nouveau Roman*) Emerges (1951), p. 1481; *Dragnet* Is the First Widely Popular Police Show (1951), p. 1531; *The Mousetrap* Begins a Record-Breaking Run (1952), p. 1551.

THE FIRST ACADEMY AWARDS
HONOR FILM ACHIEVEMENT

Category of event: Motion pictures
Time: May 16, 1929
Locale: Hollywood, California

The first Academy Awards celebration was an anticlimactic if gala affair, since the winners in the twelve categories had been announced three months earlier

Principal personages:

DOUGLAS FAIRBANKS, SR. (DOUGLAS ULMAN, 1883-1939), a swashbuckling screen hero and dynamic moral force in Hollywood, the founding president of the Academy of Motion Picture Arts and Sciences

LOUIS B. MAYER (1885-1957), a powerful studio boss who provided inspiration and guiding genius to the Academy

CONRAD NAGEL (1897-1970), a leading man who helped found the Academy and served as an early president

FRED NIBLO (FEDERICO NOBILE, 1874-1948), a popular director specializing in action/adventure films, instrumental in promoting the Academy

FRED BEETSON (1879-1953), an important producer who was influential in bringing creative artists together to form the Academy

WILLIAM C. DEMILLE (1878-1955), a respected writer, producer, and director, an articulate founding member of the Academy

Summary of Event

On May 16, 1929, the first Academy Awards presentation was held, in the Blossom Room at the Roosevelt Hollywood Hotel in Hollywood, California. From a simple banquet affair, the tribute has grown to gigantic proportions. The annual Academy Awards, sponsored by the Academy of Motion Picture Arts and Sciences, has become an important international event. Millions of people worldwide watch the televised event each spring. To many, the Academy Award, or Oscar, symbolizes the highest achievement in film and is seen as the film industry's most important award.

The presentation of awards for artistic merit was largely an afterthought by the founding members of the Academy. The originally stated goals of the Academy, published in 1927, were mostly idealistic and self-serving. The Academy planned to take aggressive action in meeting outside attacks that were unjust and to promote harmony and solidarity among the membership and among the different branches, reconciling internal differences that might exist or arise. It intended to further the welfare and protect the honor and good repute of the profession and to encourage the improvement and advancement of the arts and sciences of the profession, through exchange of constructive ideas and by awards of merit for distinctive achievements.

The Academy thus intended to do for the motion picture profession what other national and international bodies had done for other arts and sciences and industries.

To better understand the background and beginnings of the first Academy Awards ceremony, it is necessary to examine the formation of the Academy. Its genesis, by all accounts, occurred in early January, 1927. Louis B. Mayer, powerful studio boss of Metro-Goldwyn-Mayer (MGM), invited four of his studio personnel to a Sunday dinner. They were Conrad Nagel, Fred Niblo, Fred Beetson, and William C. deMille. Mayer wanted to form an organization that could speak for the film industry, arbitrate labor disputes, help solve technological problems, and police screen content. The five men planned a dinner to be attended by representatives of the creative branches who might join the organization. On January 11, at the Ambassador Hotel in Los Angeles, thirty-six people heard the proposals and enthusiastically supported the idea. The International (this word was later dropped) Academy of Motion Picture Arts and Sciences was formed. Douglas Fairbanks, Sr., was named as president, Fred Niblo as vice-president, M. C. Levee as treasurer, and Frank Woods as secretary.

On May 4, 1927, the Academy was granted a charter by the state of California as a nonprofit corporation. One week later, an organizational banquet took place at the Biltmore Hotel in Los Angeles, with more than three hundred guests in attendance. Speaking to the gathered assembly, Fairbanks convinced 231 of them to join and pay $100 for membership.

In his comments, Fairbanks mentioned that the new organization would bestow certain awards of merit for distinctive achievement. Days later, a Committee for the Awards of Merit was formed. The following year, in July, 1928, the awards committee developed a voting system. Each member of the Academy would cast one vote in his or her branch. Nominees for awards would be selected from films released in the Los Angeles area between April 1, 1927, and July 31, 1928. The deadline for selection was set as August 15, 1928. A board of judges would tabulate the results, determine the top ten nominees, and narrow the field to three contestants. Lastly, the Central Board of Judges, comprising five individuals representing each of the five divisions of the Academy—producers, actors, directors, writers, and technicians—would select the winners in twelve achievement categories.

The winners of the first awards were selected at an Academy gathering on Friday, February 15, 1929, six months after the submission deadline. The press and the winners quickly were notified. Three months later, the awards were officially presented at a glittering black-tie dinner dance. Chairman of the evening William C. deMille welcomed the assembled guests and introduced Fairbanks, who then explained the voting rules, suggested that acceptance speeches be kept short, and called up the winners to receive their trophies.

The first Academy Awards could be given for a single achievement, multiple achievements, or a body of work. Twenty additional certificates of honorable mention were given to runners-up. The winners that first evening were as follows: most outstanding production, *Wings* (1927); most unique or artistic production, *Sunrise* (1927);

achievement by an actor, Emil Jannings; achievement by an actress, Janet Gaynor; achievement in dramatic directing, Frank Borzage; achievement in comedy directing, Lewis Milestone; achievement in cinematography, Charles Rosher and Karl Struss; achievement in art directing, William Cameron Menzies; achievement in engineering effects, Roy Pomeroy; achievement in original story writing, Ben Hecht; achievement in writing adaptation, Benjamin Glazer; and achievement in title writing, Joseph Farnham. The categories were revised the following year. Awards for most artistic or unique production and achievement in engineering effects were dropped. The dramatic and comedy directing awards were combined, as were those for achievement in original story writing, writing adaptation, and title writing.

Award winners each received a statuette slightly more than a foot high. It had been designed by Cedric Gibbons, art director at MGM, and sculpted by George Stanley. The same model of statuette was given in subsequent years. The gold-plated figure is of a knight holding a crusader's sword, standing on a reel of film. The statuette got its nickname of Oscar in the 1930's, following a comment by a secretary that the figure reminded her of her uncle Oscar.

Special Academy Awards were also presented to Charles Chaplin for his work acting in, writing, producing, and directing *The Circus* (1928) and to Warner Bros. for producing *The Jazz Singer* (1927). Only Jannings and Chaplin were not present to accept their statuettes. Speeches by Hollywood celebrities including Mary Pickford, Louis B. Mayer, Cecil B. DeMille, and others followed the awards. Entertainer Al Jolson, star of the just-honored *The Jazz Singer*, brought the festivities to a close. The first Academy Awards presentation was a quiet success.

Impact of Event

None of the founding members of the Academy could have foreseen the impact the first Academy Awards would have not only on the Hollywood community but also on the world. The awards, at the beginning, were a secondary consideration. Concern about the myriad changes taking place within the motion picture industry was the main reason for formation of the Academy. Without realizing it, the first Academy members established one of the oldest, and certainly the most-coveted, prizes in cinema. The tradition begun in 1929 continued uninterrupted.

During the 1920's, a series of technological and cultural breakthroughs occurred, particularly in the area of mass communication. The second Academy Awards ceremony thus took on greater importance to the media. There was full newspaper coverage, and Los Angeles radio station KNX broadcast the entire event. The Academy Awards had arrived as a media event and would never again have the intimacy of the first presentation. Over the years, especially after the awards ceremony began to be televised in 1953, the audience has grown to more than one billion viewers worldwide.

Hollywood's financial success led to calls by spiritual leaders and government figures to control the film industry unless it could police itself. The founding of the Academy was meant to do that. Further, the Academy Awards were to be used to promote the organization and deflect public criticism by focusing on and showcasing Hollywood's past achievements.

The task the Academy faced from the beginning was formidable. Hollywood was moving slowly from its adolescence to maturity in the 1920's, and from silent to sound pictures. The first Academy Awards nominated only silent films as best picture, but within two years only sound pictures were considered. Technological changes were not the only problem. Hollywood had to come to grips with the various trade unions. By the end of 1926, a Studio Basic Agreement was signed by six of the major studios and the basic trade unions. Attempts to unionize performers and writers failed. A little over a month after signing the Studio Basic Agreement, Mayer launched his campaign to form the Academy. Its first order of business, after incorporating, was to mediate a labor dispute concerning the West Coast studios and their financial backers in New York. This function of the Academy caused considerable turmoil, because many members viewed Academy activities as favoring the studio. This dispute almost led to the demise of the organization through a mass defection of its members in the 1930's. Realizing its increasing unpopularity and the lack of an enforcement mechanism, the Academy rigorously reshuffled itself and stopped interfering. The organization also removed another source of controversy in 1936 by having the prestigious accounting firm of Price Waterhouse and Company supervise and tabulate, in secrecy, the results of Academy Awards balloting. The company continued in this role in succeeding years.

The Academy today performs many services in addition to the Oscar ceremonies. From the beginning, it sponsored lectures and seminars in the latest film technology and published various magazines and directories. The two best known are the *Annual Index to Motion Picture Credits* and *Academy Players Directory*. Ever mindful of its origins, the Academy also serves as a watchdog to contain unfavorable publicity and promotes public relations efforts to create goodwill. The Academy also has been concerned about the film industry's product and promotes efforts to preserve and restore old pictures.

Over time, the award ceremony and its importance changed. The number of nominees for each regular merit award became standardized to five, and nominations were for single achievements. In the second year of the awards, the twelve merit awards were reduced to seven. As of 1992, there were twenty-three. In addition to the annual merit awards, the following awards are given at the annual ceremony: the Scientific or Technical Achievement Awards; the Irving G. Thalberg Award, "to a creative producer whose body of work reflects a consistently high quality of motion picture productions"; the Jean Hersholt Humanitarian Award, "to an individual in the motion picture industry whose humanitarian efforts have brought credit to the industry"; the Gordon E. Sawyer Award, "to an individual in the motion picture industry whose technological contributions have brought credit to the industry"; and honorary awards "for outstanding achievements not strictly within the other categories, for exceptionally distinguished service in the making of the motion pictures or for outstanding service to the Academy."

From its humble origins in 1929, the reputation of the Academy Awards had surpassed that of other awards given in other fields, such as the Emmy, the Tony, and the Grammy. An Oscar is considered to be a higher level of recognition than are awards bestowed by critics and trade associations. Internationally, the Oscar is considered to be the most important film prize, surpassing prizes offered by other countries. It is accepted universally as cinema's most prestigious award.

Bibliography

Bergan, Ronald, Graham Fuller, and David Malcolm. *Academy Award Winners.* New York: Crescent Books, 1986. Year-by-year account of the Oscar winners and losers, written in a comprehensive yet readable style. Profusely illustrated.

Brown, Peter H., and Jim Pinkston. *Oscar Dearest: Six Decades of Scandal, Politics, and Greed Behind Hollywood's Academy Awards, 1927-1986.* New York: Perennial Library, 1987. Inside and readable account of the prize, the performers, and the passion that make up the annual Oscar-night ritual. Chapters are arranged by topics, such as "Winners and Losers" and "Oscar Curse." Must-read appendix and annotated bibliography.

Levy, Emanuel. *And the Winner Is . . . . : The History and Politics of the Oscar Award.* New York: Ungar, 1987. Excellent study dealing less with winners and losers than with the preeminence of the Academy Award, its meaning, the nomination system, the voting process, and the place occupied by the Oscar in American culture.

Likeness, George C. *The Oscar People: From "Wings" to "My Fair Lady."* Mendota, Ill.: Wayside Press, 1965. Good introductory work. Detailed biographies of performers as well as film summaries give an in-depth look at Oscar winners. Includes chapters on the supporting players and craftsmen.

Osborne, Robert A. *Sixty Years of the Oscar.* New York: Abbeville Press, 1989. Fascinating and well-researched study of the Academy and the Academy Awards. Six chapters, each devoted to a different decade. Concludes with an interesting index on Oscar facts and records. Lavishly illustrated.

Pickard, Roy. *Hollywood Gold: The Award Winning Movies.* New York: Taplinger, 1977. Alphabetical listing of all Oscar-winning films to 1977, with year of victory, other Oscars won, plot description, and artists who created it. Appendix lists winners each year in some of the most interesting categories.

Shale, Richard. *Academy Awards: An Ungar Reference Index.* New York: Frederick Ungar, 1978. An excellent fact book about the Academy and its origins, purpose, and activities. Details the first fifty years of films by various categories and features a short introduction, useful appendices, select bibliography, and index. The study is well organized.

Wiley, Mason, and Damien Bona. *Inside Oscar: The Unofficial History of the Academy Awards.* Edited by Gail McColl. New York: Ballantine Books, 1986. Gossipy look at the Academy on a yearly basis from 1927 to 1985. The authors weave together short vignettes and quotations from participants and winners in various categories, concluding with a list of winning films. Provides a fascinating glimpse into the Oscar ceremonies.

Terry Theodore

Cross-References

Pickford Becomes "America's Sweetheart" (1909), p. 224; *The Ten Commandments* Establishes Silent-Film Spectacle (1923), p. 567; Chaplin Produces His Masterpiece *The Gold Rush* (1925), p. 659; *The Jazz Singer* Premieres in New York (1927), p. 734; Sound Technology Revolutionizes the Motion-Picture Industry (1928), p. 761; Hollywood Enters Its Golden Age (1930's), p. 822; Temple Receives a Special Academy Award (1935), p. 1011; *Gone with the Wind* Premieres (1939), p. 1154; The Hollywood Studio System Is Transformed (1946), p. 1307.

THE SOUND AND THE FURY
LAUNCHES FAULKNER'S CAREER

Category of event: Literature
Time: October 7, 1929
Locale: New York, New York

Though not widely appreciated at the time of its publication, The Sound and the Fury *was Faulkner's breakthrough novel, launching both his own career and modernist fiction in the United States*

Principal personages:
WILLIAM FAULKNER (1897-1962), a Nobel Prize-winning fiction writer
BEN WASSON (1899-1982), Faulkner's literary agent and friend
HARRISON SMITH (1888-1971), a partner in Cape and Smith Publishers who wished to publish *The Sound and the Fury*

Summary of Event

In 1928, when he completed *The Sound and the Fury*, William Faulkner was a struggling, relatively unsuccessful writer working at odd jobs in Oxford, Mississippi, his hometown. Though his first novels, *Soldier's Pay* (1926) and *Mosquitoes* (1927) had been well received in literary circles, they had not sold well, and Faulkner was unable to support himself by writing as he wished to do. Publishers continued to reject his short stories and what he believed his best novel, *Flags in the Dust*, the manuscript title for what became *Sartoris* (1929). *Flags in the Dust* was finally published uncut in 1973.

Faulkner repeated in interviews that he composed *The Sound and the Fury* in a mood of despair. Doubting that he would have a successful publishing career, he felt freed to write what was closest to his heart in the way that seemed best to him. He often said this novel was his favorite, calling it his "most splendid failure." In the book, he tried to capture those things that were most important to him personally, culturally, and artistically. In a 1933 introduction to the novel, Faulkner indicated that being able to write without the objects of publishing and selling led to his discovering what became fundamental to him in storytelling and led to his thinking himself worthy to be among the writers he considered great:

[T]he writing of it as it now stands taught me both how to write and how to read, and even more: It taught me what I had already read, because on completing it I discovered, in a series of repercussions like summer thunder, the Flauberts and Conrads and Turgenievs which as much as ten years before I had consumed whole and without assimilating at all, as a moth or a goat might.

When *The Sound and the Fury* was completed, Faulkner was complexly involved with two publishers, Horace Liveright and Harcourt Brace. Harrison Smith was an editor for Harcourt Brace and, as Faulkner's friend, had offered the manuscript to his publisher, who was bringing out *Sartoris*. Harcourt Brace, though, showed little interest in this strange, almost incomprehensible book. Though there are hints in Faulkner's earlier work of what he would do in *The Sound and the Fury*, it breaks decisively with the readability of his previous novels. *Sartoris* was the first novel to make full use of Yoknapatawpha County, a fictional version of northwest Mississippi, the "postage stamp of native soil" that became the setting of Faulkner's great series of novels. *The Sound and the Fury*, set in Jefferson, a fictionalized Oxford, Mississippi, presents a composite portrait of a decayed aristocratic family in the latter stages of its destruction, of a Southern culture in the painful throes of transition from the Victorian era to the modern age, and of an American society undergoing a parallel, if more diffused, transition. What makes the novel seem unreadable is the unusual mode of representation that most visibly identifies Faulkner as a modernist writer.

The novel developed as series of experiments to capture in a moving way the reaction of the family of Caddy Compson, a daughter, sister, and mother who makes a modern woman's choices at the turn of the century. Caddy struggles to liberate herself from family and male domination. In doing so, she removes herself from a family so heavily dependent upon her that the suffering proves unbearable. Her pregnancy leads to a forced marriage that ends in divorce. Unable to make her way easily, she abandons her daughter to her family's care. Faulkner finally chose to tell the story mainly from the points of view of Caddy's brothers, who feel abandoned and betrayed by her. Benjy is retarded, his mental growth arrested before he learns speech. His section of "narration" opens the novel, plunging the reader into perceptions of a character who cannot make judgments, who can feel but who cannot comprehend or explain the loss of the one person who has mothered him. Nearly as difficult to read as Benjy's section, the next part shows brother Quentin's activities and thoughts on the day he commits suicide. Quentin is a sensitive and disturbed young man who finds that the values he wants to use to order his world and keep Caddy with him—values inherited from his family—repeatedly betray him into paradox and helplessness. The third section presents the internal monologue of Jason, a violently angry materialist who believes his sister's divorce has ruined his chances for wealth and power. The final section tells about Dilsey, the black servant who becomes mother to the family after Caddy departs. This section and Jason's give indirect expression to the point of view of Caddy's daughter, also named Quentin, who has been abandoned to a painful life in the suffering and vindictive family.

Though the story is readable with patience and considerable rereading, it clearly was not, in 1929, the sort of novel to be accepted easily by a commercial publisher. Harcourt Brace was glad to be able to turn it over to Cape and Smith. Upon the book's publication, the initial reviews were very positive, especially among academics and intellectuals. During the two decades after its publication, there was a fairly steady trickle of highly laudatory reviews identifying *The Sound and the Fury* as a great novel. During this period, Faulkner produced the series of novels that extended his literary experimentation and his presentation of Yoknapatawpha County as a microcosm of the modern world. Among the great novels of this period are *As I Lay Dying* (1930), *Light in August* (1932), *Absalom, Absalom!* (1936), and *Go Down, Moses and Other Stories* (1942). This series, which begins with *The Sound and the Fury*, constitutes the accomplishment for which Faulkner was awarded the 1949 Nobel Prize in Literature.

Impact of Event

The immediate impact of the publication of *The Sound and the Fury* is difficult to measure. For the general reading public, the novel was not accessible and thus not widely read; the book sold fewer than two thousand copies in the first two years after it appeared. Sales were not helped by the stock market crash that occurred two weeks after publication and the Great Depression that followed. For general readers, the more significant event was the 1931 publication of *Sanctuary*, with its treatment of the sensational subjects of flappers, rape, and gangsters. *Sanctuary* tended to define the general view of Faulkner until after his Nobel Prize, bringing him the notoriety that allowed him to earn a living writing Hollywood screenplays.

The more important immediate impacts were on Faulkner's own conception of his writing career and on the literary and artistic intelligentsia who became his admirers and who followed his career. These readers tended to assure that Faulkner's works would continue to be published, that he would receive prizes and honors, that he would be translated, especially into French, and that he would be studied and read in colleges and universities. In this way, his literary reputation was sustained until a complex series of events, beginning perhaps with Malcolm Cowley's publication of *The Viking Portable Faulkner* (1946) and the Nobel Prize, established Faulkner as a world author.

Faulkner's career can be seen as one flowering of the literary tradition of modernism. Modernism may be defined as the Western world's attempt to create a culture viable in the face of almost universal disbelief in traditional Christianity among intellectuals and a parallel secular, commercial materialism in popular culture. Faulkner's novels embody many of the problems and conflicts that result from this attempt to re-create culture in an age of religious doubt. That he was aware of himself as involved in this project is clear in his Nobel Prize acceptance speech, in which he affirms that humanity as a whole possesses a soul, as evidenced by the human capacity for love, compassion, sacrifice, endurance, and other "universal truths of the heart." He also asserts that literature is among the activities that can fill some of the former roles of religion, by lifting people's hearts and by reminding them about the soul's needs and yearnings, so that "the poet's voice . . . can be one of the props, the pillars" to help humanity "endure and prevail."

Modernism appears in almost every aspect of *The Sound and the Fury*. The worldview of *The Sound and the Fury* echoes, sometimes in direct paraphrase, T. S. Eliot's *The Waste Land* (1922), with its vision of the modern West as a spiritual desert. Faulkner follows Henry James, Joseph Conrad, and James Joyce in the use of complex subjective points of view and stream-of-consciousness techniques to render the sense of being imprisoned in a culture no longer able to believe in an objective reality that possesses absolute truth. Faulkner's main answer to this sense of isolation is his belief in the community of humanity that he sees in the struggles of the human heart for communion and love. The central theme of the novel is loss, and though it centers on family breakup as a cause of loss, larger causes of the family's disintegration are shown in the shift from the Old South, with its emphasis on traditional, Christian values, to a New South, with an emphasis on secular and commercial values. The novel's attitude toward this shift is ambivalent; much of good and evil is lost, and much is gained. A meaningful and moral life is not easy in either world. In worldview, technique, and theme, Faulkner illustrates a modernist point of view, bringing to completion in American fiction the influences of his great precursors and contemporaries in Europe, including Joyce and Marcel Proust.

The influence of *The Sound and the Fury* and of Faulkner's whole career pervades modern culture, not only in the English-speaking world but also in Europe, Japan, and Latin America. Like Mark Twain, Willa Cather, and other important U.S. writers, Faulkner made a microcosm of his home region and wrote to a world audience from that base. Thus, he helped to inspire writers such as Richard Wright, Ralph Ellison, and Flannery O'Connor. Jean-Paul Sartre was among the European writers to express admiration for Faulkner. Among American writers in Spanish, Gabriel García Márquez is only one of many to name Faulkner as an important influence. The continued study of Faulkner in colleges helps to prepare readers for difficult modernist and postmodernist fiction and helps them to develop the intellectual and emotional tools for understanding and dealing with the complexity of contemporary Western culture.

Bibliography

Bassett, John Earl. *William Faulkner: An Annotated Checklist of Criticism.* New York: David Lewis, 1972. Arranged by subject and then chronologically within subjects, this is an excellent tool for surveying published responses to Faulkner's work and career. In about twenty pages, one can read brief summaries of and quotations from most of what was written about *The Sound and the Fury* from 1929 to 1971.

_____. *William Faulkner: An Annotated Checklist of Recent Criticism.* Kent, Ohio: Kent State University Press, 1983. Supplements Bassett's earlier volume.

Bleikasten, André. *The Most Splendid Failure: Faulkner's* The Sound and the Fury. Bloomington: Indiana University Press, 1976. This provocative study of the novel examines Faulkner's writing before *The Sound and the Fury* and studies each character and each section of the novel in detail, offering structuralist and psychoanalytic interpretations of Caddy, Benjy, Quentin, Jason, and Dilsey. Includes bibliography and index.

_____, ed. *William Faulkner's* The Sound and the Fury: *A Critical Casebook.* New York: Garland, 1982. Bleikasten gathers selections from Faulkner's own commentary on the novel and adds eight interpretive essays on subjects such as Faulkner's composition process and the structure of the novel. Special emphasis on recent literary theory. Includes bibliography.

Blotner, Joseph. *Faulkner: A Biography.* New York: Random House, 1974. A massive two-volume official biography providing the most detailed account of Faulkner's life and works. Blotner is somewhat reticent about the less savory aspects of Faulkner's life, presenting the facts but not interpreting them, out of deference to Faulkner's family. Contains many photographs, a chronology of Faulkner's life, a genealogical chart, and a detailed index.

Kinney, Arthur, ed. *Critical Essays on William Faulkner: The Compson Family.* Boston: G. K. Hall, 1982. Contains twenty-three critical essays, selections from early reviews, and related materials by Faulkner, as well as Kinney's introduction. Dealing with all of Faulkner's fiction about the Compson family, this volume sheds light on *The Sound and the Fury* from several interesting directions.

Matthews, John T. *"The Sound and the Fury": Faulkner and the Lost Cause.* Boston: Twayne, 1991. A solid and useful interpretation for those familiar with the novel. Includes a brief presentation of the literary and historical context followed by careful studies of the main characters, the setting, the technical aspects of the novel, and the various commentaries, including the appendix, that Faulkner constructed for the book. Also includes an annotated bibliography and an index.

Minter, David. *William Faulkner: His Life and Work.* Baltimore, Md.: The Johns Hopkins University Press, 1980. Much shorter than Blotner's biography. A good choice for general readers wishing to examine how Faulkner's life is reflected in his work, especially his major novels. The analyses of the novels are especially good. No photographs, but includes a genealogy, a chronology, a map of Yoknapatawpha County, and an index.

Terry Heller

Cross-References

Henry James's *The Ambassadors* Is Published (1903), p. 96; Proust's *Remembrance of Things Past* Is Published (1913), p. 355; Cather's *My Ántonia* Promotes Regional Literature (1918), p. 452; Eliot Publishes *The Waste Land* (1922), p. 539; Joyce's *Ulysses* Epitomizes Modernism in Fiction (1922), p. 555; *The Great Gatsby* Captures the Essence of the Roaring Twenties (1925), p. 626; Hemingway's *The Sun Also Rises* Speaks for the Lost Generation (1926), p. 696; Ellison's *Invisible Man* Is Published (1952), p. 1541; O'Connor's *A Good Man Is Hard to Find* Is Published (1955), p. 1645; García Márquez's *One Hundred Years of Solitude* Is Published (1967), p. 2086.

GUTHRIE'S POPULIST SONGS REFLECT THE DEPRESSION-ERA UNITED STATES

Category of event: Music
Time: The 1930's
Locale: The United States

An authentic frontier balladeer, Woody Guthrie expanded the appeal of traditional American folk music by writing protest songs about poverty and social injustice

Principal personages:

WOODY GUTHRIE (1912-1967), a folk balladeer, writer, and poet of social protest

LEADBELLY (HUDDIE LEDBETTER, 1888-1949), a friend of Guthrie and a great folksinger and composer

PETE SEEGER (1919-   ), a friend of Guthrie and an influential protest singer and composer

MARJORIE GUTHRIE (1917-1983), Guthrie's second wife, a devoted collector of his manuscripts, letters, and memorabilia

WILL GEER (1902-1978), a radical friend of Guthrie, an itinerant folksinger and actor

ALAN LOMAX (1915-   ), a superb Library of Congress folklorist and recorder of Guthrie and other folksingers

GILBERT "CISCO" HOUSTON (1918-1961), a singing partner of Guthrie and the closest of his friends

Summary of Event

Before the Great Depression, the diverse regions composing the American South lagged far behind the rest of the United States in nearly every regard. From the close of the Civil War through Reconstruction and into the 1950's, the South remained, distinctively and overwhelmingly, rural. Its economy was tied to a few staples, principally cotton, tobacco, corn, and sugar beets. Farms tended to be small and tenant-run; worse, they were enmeshed in the perpetual indebtedness characterizing the sharecrop and crop-lien systems. Labor was cheap and drew subsistence wages. Unions were considered anathema. Internal racial relations steadily, if legally, deteriorated after the close of the nineteenth century, and Southerners remained under the dominance of a conservative Democratic Party. The South's generally decrepit educational institutions were only one manifestation of its backward social structure. President Franklin Roosevelt's declaration that one-third of 1930's America was ill-clothed, ill-housed, and ill-fed perfectly described the American South—which, Roosevelt added, constituted the nation's number-one economic problem. Such was the South of Okemah, Oklahoma, where Woodrow Wilson "Woody" Guthrie was born, and of Pampa, Texas, where he was reared.

Guthrie's upbringing, like his region, was sad. His mother steadily declined under the inroads of Huntington's chorea, an incurable inherited degenerative disease that would eventually claim Woody and others of his family. His father, though at times on the make as a small-town political worthy, seldom managed to match his luck and competencies with his dreams. It appears likely that Woody's mother set fire to and killed Woody's sister and later attempted the same thing with her husband. The family lived poorly, at times being thrown individually or collectively on the sufferance of relatives. Woody wandered away from all of them as soon as he could.

A small, wiry man with fine features and a distinguishing mop of unruly hair, Guthrie was humorous, optimistic, gregarious, generous, infectiously engaging, and immensely talented. He was an omnivorous reader with wide-ranging interests. He was also a self-taught cartoonist, versifier, poet, cornball humorist, and explosively undisciplined writer. He had an amazingly eclectic bent, heedlessly putting his own words to tunes written by others, notably those of famed hymnists and of the great Virginia folksinging Carter Family. Unlike his later friends Huddie "Leadbelly" Ledbetter and the musically well-trained Pete Seeger, Guthrie was a mediocre guitarist. His nasal voice was untrained except by experience. Although he married three times and had many children, he was lovingly lazy, feckless, adulterous, frequently drunken, and an irresponsible family man. He was the quintessential free spirit—the "ramblin' man" of song and story.

From his early days in Pampa, Guthrie's real family were the marginally employed and the dispossessed: oil-field roughnecks and roustabouts, Okies—southwestern farmers of the nation's "Dust Bowl" who were evicted from their lands and who migrated to California by the tens of thousands—railroad tramps, hoboes, dockers, seamen, the remaining Wobblies, "reds," migratory workers, and unskilled laborers. It was for audiences of these people that he began singing and songwriting with hillbilly bands in Texas and thereafter on radio and in public appearances from Los Angeles to New York City. He sought to give the beleaguered masses relief and to shore up their dignity and sense of purpose. It was through their appreciation of him that he persistently sought a place in the public domain, using his untrained but authentic folk voice to carry his populist messages.

Guthrie first gained prominence with his "old-time hill-country songs" on Los Angeles' KFVD radio in 1936 before an audience largely composed of Dust Bowl migrants. He augmented his reputation when he moved to New York City—in the 1930's the nation's radical capital—joining union, Communist, and Popular Front political causes and accepting welcome as a folk hero. There, in 1940, he began writing his Columbia River and Grand Coulee Dam songs—"Roll on Columbia," "Pastures of Plenty," "Jack Hammer John," "Hard Traveling," and, in a different context, "So Long, It's Been Good to Know You," "Those Oklahoma Hills," and "This Land Is Your Land." Typically, Guthrie attempted to use his music as a vehicle in the class struggle. While Guthrie was in New York, Pete Seeger persuaded him to join the Almanac Singers, whose political purposes appeared identical to Guthrie's and with whom he wrote and sang many more songs.

Thanks to the genius of folklorist Alan Lomax (later a close friend), Guthrie was interviewed and recorded for the Library of Congress on March 21, 22, and 27, 1940. In the recordings, he presented his landmark protest songs, among them "Tom Joad," "Dust Can't Kill Me," "I Ain't Got No Home," "Talking Dust Bowl," "Do Re Mi," "Blowin' Down This Road," and "Dust Pneumonia Blues." Meantime, he continued writing and singing union songs at picket lines, rallies, and fund-raisers. His compositions included prolabor songs such as "Union Maid" and "The Ladies' Auxiliary" and others equally political in nature such as "The Philadelphia Lawyer."

Guthrie, fully at home with the American proletariat and already a folk hero by the close of the 1930's, believed that the oppressed, individually and collectively, had both the right and the responsibility to sing their protests in the face of injustice. Unlike some intellectuals and academicians of his day, he was a populist by tradition and a communist of a sort by experience. He was a utopian, largely uninterested in accumulating money and even less interested in power or political position for himself. Rather, Guthrie used his heartfelt folk renditions to ensure himself a place in the public memory. It was fame that he sought—and managed to achieve.

Impact of Event

Philosophically, Guthrie identified the spirit and content of his songs and writings with those of Robert Burns, Walt Whitman, and Alexander Pushkin (just as he identified his politics with those of Jesus, Abraham Lincoln, Andrew Jackson, and Karl Marx), all of whom spread their messages by speaking, writing, and rhyming in the vernacular. Yet the immediate tradition upon which Guthrie drew—and which he would elaborate and help to expand—was nourished by his Southern environment. Protest songs were commonplace in the repertoires of Southern blues and country (or "hillbilly") singers, as well as among some of the region's gospel singers, by the 1920's.

Union-organizing efforts among Southern laborers and tenant farmers, successions of strikes in the Piedmont textile towns, and lockouts, strikes, and open warfare between capital and labor in the Eastern Kentucky and Cumberland coalfields from the late 1920's through the mid-1930's yielded substantial crops of revolutionary lyrics. These were partly inspired and augmented by the Communist-led National Miners' Union, National Textile Workers' Union, and Southern Tenant Farmers' Union, but they also grew from the almost endless erosions of hard times. Songs written by a young Gastonia, North Carolina, mother and textile worker, Ella May Wiggins, who was murdered in 1929 by antiunion thugs, not only lifted the morale of her fellow workers but also advertised their cause. Similarly, in Kentucky's coal-mining Harlan County, Florence Reece's "Which Side Are You On?," aimed at brutal company-paid deputy sheriffs, became one of labor's most beloved ballads. Elsewhere in Kentucky, similar anticapitalist balladeers sprang forth, including Aunt Molly Jackson ("I Am a Union Woman"), Sara Ogan ("I Hate the Capitalist System"), and Jim Garland ("I Don't Want Your Millions Mister"). Scores of other Southern protest singers and their songs have been described by such folklorist-historians as R. Serge Denisoff, John Greenway, Archie Green, and Lawrence Gellert.

Guthrie's reputation and influence surmounted them all by the close of the 1930's. Ironically, too, like his fellow Southern protesters, his songs and character became as well known in Northern liberal circles as they were generally throughout the South. In New York, particularly, Guthrie became a rallying point for other expatriate Southern musicians such as Lee Hays, Sonny Terry, Josh White, Brownie McGhee, Aunt Molly Jackson, Sis Cunningham, and the inimitable Leadbelly; many of these performers sang or appeared with the Almanac Singers or with Seeger's legendary folk band the Weavers. Within a national context, however, even in the 1930's, Guthrie and his fellow protest singers enjoyed only limited visibility, and the significance of their music went largely unnoticed.

Yet Guthrie's songs and social messages directly influenced many country singers and songwriters in the 1930's and 1940's, and many of these musicians won national celebrity during the protests of civil rights advocates, college and university students, feminists, and peace activists during the late 1950's and the 1960's. Among the most prominent was Seeger, a responsible, cultivated, musically trained and disciplined Harvard University dropout who not only worked closely with Guthrie—and re-garded him as a mentor—but also continued Guthrie's commitment to folk protest songs as weapons against social injustice. With the commercialization of folk music in the late 1950's and the 1960's, the Guthrie cult that Seeger stimulated placed Seeger himself in the forefront of the urban folk-music revival. Other Guthrie disci-ples who gained prominence just before and immediately after Guthrie's death were his devoted imitator Ramblin' Jack Elliot and Guthrie's dear friend Cisco Houston.

Guthrie's work began to receive renewed attention in the late 1950's, when such folk-oriented bands as the Kingston Trio attained national prominence. Soon, popu-lar folk groups including the Limelighters, the Chad Mitchell Trio, the Brothers Four, and Peter, Paul, and Mary, in company with solo artists such as Joan Baez, Tom Paxton, Odetta, and Judy Collins, were playing and recording Guthrie material and giving added currency to his work.

It was Robert Zimmerman, a fanatical devotee of Guthrie's music, who, as Bob Dylan, caught the wave of radical folk music in the early 1960's and carried Guth-rie's style to new aesthetic and popular heights. Much of the best of the material on his first album, *Bob Dylan*, both in substance and style is classic Guthrie. Although the immensely creative and productive Dylan subsequently moved through at least half a dozen stylistic phases, it was in the person of a Guthrie-style balladeer that he became a popular national folk-protest phenomenon. In so doing, he ensured the longevity of Guthrie's strain of music in the nation's popular culture.

Bibliography

Denisoff, R. Serge. *Great Day Coming: Folk Music and the American Left.* Urbana: University of Illinois Press, 1971. An excellent discussion of Southern protest sing-ers, including Guthrie, their connections with Northern radicals, and the effects of this affiliation on the development of urban folk music. Clearly written, and the best and broadest work on the subject. Notes, good bibliography, and index. First-rate.

Guthrie, Woody. *Born to Win.* Edited by Robert Shelton. New York: Macmillan, 1965. A collection of Guthrie's essays, poems, notes, lyrics, and letters. Conveys the spirit of a man whose often sad life might have made him a loser, but did not. Even with editing, he is a bright and accomplished figure, full of insightful observations on himself, his world, and his objectives. The book is filled with Guthrie's wonderfully humorous, sometimes biting, cartoons and sketches, as well as with verses, lyrics, and rhymes. There are no reader aids, but it would hardly have reflected Guthrie's life accurately to have included them. Understandable that these words inspired Dylan.

Hampton, Wayne. *Guerilla Minstrels.* Knoxville: University of Tennessee Press, 1986. A fine study of the protest tradition through analysis of four individuals: Joe Hill, John Lennon, Guthrie, and Dylan. Engagingly written. While sympathetic to each of these protest singers, the author maintains critical objectivity. Very informative on Guthrie-Dylan linkages. There are a few photos, page notes, a splendid select bibliography for each singer, discographies, and an excellent double-columned index. Essential reading.

Klein, Joe. *Woody Guthrie: A Life.* New York: Alfred A. Knopf, 1980. An important nonacademic study of Guthrie's character rather than an analysis of his music or its impact. A comprehensive, easy to read, matter-of-fact, and objective biography. Among the several biographies of Guthrie, this is in many ways the best. Many photos, annotated chapter notes in place of bibliography, and excellent double-columned index. Must reading.

Malone, Bill C. *Southern Music, American Music.* Lexington: University Press of Kentucky, 1979. A well-written, scholarly survey of the subject. Excellent for placing Guthrie in a broad context, and more important for underlining the powerful influences of varieties of Southern music upon the national musical culture. No illustrations, but an outstanding bibliographical essay, and a useful index. A very informative work.

Marsh, Dave, and Harold Leventhal, eds. *Pastures of Plenty: A Self-Portrait, Woody Guthrie.* New York: HarperCollins, 1990. Aside from explanatory introductions and acknowledgments, this is a posthumous editing of Guthrie's scrapbooks and other personal sources that recapitulates Guthrie's life in his own words. Thus, perhaps with more discipline than Guthrie could have managed, it is an intimate chronological view of his life until illness overwhelmed him in 1952. Though something of Guthrie's engaging vigor is lacking, he still shines through. Essential, informative, enjoyable. No notes, bibliography, or index; brief appendix. Many photos and Guthrie's wonderful cartoons and sketches.

Clifton K. Yearley

Cross-References

Handy Ushers in the Commercial Blues Era (1910's), p. 252; Bessie Smith Records "Downhearted Blues" (1923), p. 572; WSM Launches *The Grand Ole Opry* (1925), p. 675; Rodgers Cuts His First Record for RCA Victor (1927), p. 729; Bill Monroe and the Blue Grass Boys Define Bluegrass Music (1939), p. 1121; Hank Williams Performs on *The Grand Ole Opry* (1949), p. 1415; Dylan Performs with Electric Instruments (1965), p. 2038.

HINDEMITH ADVANCES IDEAS OF MUSIC FOR USE AND FOR AMATEURS

Category of event: Music
Time: The 1930's
Locale: Germany

Paul Hindemith emphasized a new trend toward music as a social activity through his concepts of Gebrauchsmusik *(music for use) and* Hausmusik *(music to be performed at home)*

Principal personages:

PAUL HINDEMITH (1895-1963), the principal German composer of the twentieth century

ARNOLD SCHOENBERG (1874-1951), an Austrian-born composer whose system of serial music was the opposite of Hindemith's tonal aesthetic

IGOR STRAVINSKY (1882-1971), a Russian-born composer whose neoclassic work produced between 1920 and 1951 paralleled and rivaled Hindemith's musical output

CARL ORFF (1895-1982), a German composer whose *Schulwerk* represents the peak of educational *Gebrauchsmusik*

MATTHIAS GRÜNEWALD (MATTHIAS GOTHARDT, c. 1475-1528), a German painter whose career was the inspiration for Hindemith's finest opera

WILHELM FURTWÄNGLER (1886-1954), a German conductor whose advocacy of Hindemith's music was condemned by the Nazis

Summary of Event

Paul Hindemith began his composing career as an expressionist, exploring musical territory opened up by Arnold Schoenberg and Béla Bartók. His setting of Oskar Kokoschka's *Mörder, Hoffnung der Frauen* (1919) is an example of his use of dissonance with an extremely shocking text.

Hindemith's early creative years coincided with the Weimar Republic that governed Germany in the wake of World War I, after Kaiser Wilhelm II abdicated in defeat and was replaced by a democratic regime. The culture of the Weimar Republic was the first self-consciously modern one and saw striking advances in literature, drama, art, architecture, and film as well as in music. Though the republic's early years were characterized by foreign occupation, strikes, attempted putsches (including one by Adolf Hitler in 1923), and drastic inflation, Germany after 1924 settled into a period of stability and economic growth that was abruptly terminated by the Great Depression that began in 1929. The high levels of support for the arts were curtailed by the economic stringencies, which also resulted in the polarization of Germany between Nazis and Communists. When Hitler was voted into power early in 1933, the Weimar Republic was over, and many of its leading figures emigrated.

Beginning in 1922 and for most of the remainder of the decade, Hindemith associated with a movement known as "New Objectivity" (Neue Sachlichkeit), a repudiation of both Romanticism and expressionism. In literature, New Objectivists sought to be detached and unemotionally matter-of-fact and to focus on objective reality and ordinary people. The movement's music renounced the nineteenth century past by being unemotional and concentrating on everyday life. Elements of popular music and even jazz were included in New Objectivist music, but such elements were treated with satire and parody.

Hindemith's piano suite of 1922 clearly shows elements of both expressionism and New Objectivity. The harmonic texture is extremely dissonant, but the individual movements have parodistic subtitles: The opening march is a circus, not a military march, and is treated parodically. Such popular dances as the shimmy and the Boston (a kind of waltz) and even ragtime are included in the suite. The ragtime movement bears directions that tell the performer to forget skills learned in piano lessons and to treat the piano as an interesting kind of percussion instrument.

The opera *Neues vom Tage*, which Hindemith completed in 1929, is an excellent example of New Objectivity. The opera, which focuses on the marital problems of a couple, includes offices, a hotel room, a jail cell, and a nightclub in its stage settings and contains many elements of popular music, which are often used in a parodic style. The opera mocks the legal system, bureaucracy, the commercialization of daily life, and the power of the news media, especially tabloid journalism. Musical effects include a chorus of typists, an operatic aria sung in a bathtub, and a cabaret revue featuring a chorus line.

Hindemith's rise in the 1920's was meteoric. He developed a style that, in its spare lines and linear writing, can be compared to the contemporaneous architecture of the German Bauhaus school. In 1927, he was appointed professor of composition at the Berlin Staatliche Hochschule für Musik despite his lack of formal academic training and his activity as a practical musician, writing music for his own performances (he was one of the world's foremost violists) as well as concertos and solo pieces for others. He received prestigious commissions, including one to produce concert music for the fiftieth anniversary of the Boston Symphony in 1930. He felt, though, that much modern music was becoming too isolated from its audience; in 1929, he wrote an article in which he stated that the old music public was dying out and that a new one would have to be created. Here lay the roots of a musical philosophy called, for want of a better name, *Gebrauchsmusik*, or "music for use."

The term itself derived from the work of musical historians who wrote about the dance suite of the early seventeenth century; these scholars made distinctions between music written to accompany actual dancing and dance-like music written for artistic performances. In its strictest sense, *Gebrauchsmusik* has no independent value in itself but serves a special use, especially for radio or film, and is the opposite of art or concert music. Hindemith was later to repudiate this term, saying that it sounded as ugly in German as it did in English. His goal, rather, was the creation of community music (*Gemeinschaftsmusik*), with the idea that the young public he was striving to educate should be making music themselves rather than listening to compositions in a concert hall or on records.

Hindemith's model in this effort was *Hausmusik*, works of music from the fifteenth through the eighteenth centuries that were written for performances in the home. Examples are the *Glogauer Liederbuch*, a set of vocal and instrumental pieces by mostly unnamed composers written in the late fifteenth century, and various collections of ensemble pieces by German composers of the sixteenth and seventeenth centuries. Franz Joseph Haydn's early string quartets, for example, were written for mostly amateur performers.

A good example of Hindemith's community music is the *Plöner Musiktag* (day of music at Plon), written in 1932 for a daylong music festival at a boarding school that culminated in a concert in which all the students were participants. Another notable work is the children's operetta *Wir bauen eine Stadt* (we build a city), written, as Hindemith explained, for the instruction and practice of children rather than for the entertainment of adult observers. In both works, the style is simple without being naïve, dissonances are employed sparingly, and the children are treated with respect; as Hindemith explained, there should be some difficulties to be solved by the performers, even if they are children.

At the same time, Hindemith was changing his musical style. Characteristic of much Weimar culture during the early 1930's was an artistic conservatism marked by the use of older forms and structures; Hindemith followed this trend by reviving older musical forms, such as the sonata, the fugue, and the passacaglia (a repeated melodic pattern in the bass over which new and increasingly elaborate designs are contrived).

Impact of Event

When the Nazi Party took power in Germany in the 1930's, the party's leaders stressed the need for community—but in a restricted, ethnic, and racist sense that was unlike the universal community Hindemith had in mind for his music. When the Nazis attacked Hindemith's music as degenerate, it was for the music of his New Objectivity period, his parodies of marches, and his association with Jewish musicians such as Kurt Weill and Otto Klemperer. Nazi propaganda minister Joseph Goebbels attacked *Neues vom Tage* as obscene and sensational.

Hindemith's major work of these years was his opera *Mathis der Maler* (1934), based on the life and career of the medieval painter Matthias Grünewald. The concert symphony taken from the opera, one of Hindemith's most enduring compositions, reveals the basic features of his mature musical style: finely arched melodies harmonized by sturdy chords in a carefully arranged system of tension and release; energetic rhythms; dramatic climaxes reinforced with powerful chords; and the idea of a musical continuity from the Middle Ages to the present emphasized by the use of musical techniques and even quotations from earlier periods.

Mathis der Maler received its long-delayed premiere under the conductor Wilhelm Furtwängler in 1938. Furtwängler had championed Hindemith's music; he had conducted the premiere of the symphony drawn from the opera in 1934 and had gotten in trouble with the Nazis for doing so. Hindemith had been given an extended leave of absence from the Berlin Hochschule, during which he toured and even advised the Turkish government on music education. He visited the United States for the first time in 1937, and he gladly accepted a position on the faculty at Yale University in 1940.

At Yale, he taught theory and composition for thirteen years and also organized and directed the Collegium Musicum, a group organized to perform early music from the Middle Ages through the time of Johann Sebastian Bach. A strict teacher who granted only twelve graduate degrees in composition during this period, he influenced a number of musicians and, despite a heavy teaching load, continued to compose.

His attitude toward community music and music for use revealed itself in a variety of ways. Foremost are the sonatas he wrote for virtually every instrument, not only those with a substantial repertoire but also those, such as the English horn, tuba, double bass, trombone, or viola, for which there were few worthwhile compositions. His trumpet sonata particularly set the standard for all subsequent extended compositions for the instrument. Despite their difficult and sometimes thickly written piano parts, these sonatas remain Hindemith's most frequently performed compositions.

Second are his orchestral showpieces, beginning with the 1930 concert music written for the Boston Symphony. Among the most popular of his orchestral works are his *Symphonic Metamorphoses of Themes by Carl Maria von Weber* (1943), arrangements of piano pieces originally intended as a ballet. His numerous concertos for various instruments are scored counterparts to his sonatas. His Symphony in B-flat, written in 1951 for the United States Army band, set a high standard for concert-band literature.

Hindemith's most American work, the *Requiem: For Those We Love* of 1946, is a setting for soloists, chorus, and orchestra of Walt Whitman's poem "When Lilacs Last in the Dooryard Bloom'd." Whitman's poem was written as an elegy for Abraham Lincoln and the dead of the Civil War; Hindemith regarded it as a fitting text for his work, which was written to commemorate Franklin Roosevelt and the dead of World War II. The piece was composed for performance by a high-quality amateur chorus and professional orchestra, but the work has been done by many university music schools.

Finally, Hindemith codified his musical ideas and techniques in a series of treatises. His *Unterweisung im Tonsatz* (1937-1939; *The Craft of Musical Composition*, 1941) consists of a theoretical explanation followed by various exercises in part writing. In his book *A Composer's World: Horizons and Limitations* (1952), originally lectures delivered at Harvard University, Hindemith stated his musical philosophy for the general reader, reaffirmed the importance of tonality (which he compared with gravity and artistic perspective) and the continuity of musical tradition, and proclaimed the moral imperative of music, arguing that it is a form of communication between author and listener. Practical music, he claimed, should be the basis of musical instruction (he expected his composition students in Berlin to learn the instruments for which they were writing). Though he favored open admission to schools of music instruction, he believed that such a policy should be complemented by a well-functioning weeding system to remove the presumptious and the untalented. His enthusiasm for community music did not wane; he felt that composers should write music that amateurs could play and sing.

Hindemith's musical style was so individual that he could not develop a school of composers. His idea of educational music was effectively continued by Carl Orff, whose *Schulwerk* was written for children to perform and featured drums and tuned percussion as the principal instruments. Orff's methods were brought to North America early in the 1960's and have since become a favored way of introducing children to music.

Hindemith resigned from Yale in 1953 to accept an appointment at the University of Zürich, from which he retired two years later. He had been actively teaching for more than twenty-five years and wanted to devote himself to conducting. His interests had also turned to vocal music; his last composition, finished two months before his death, was a setting of the Mass written for a virtuoso choir. An octet Hindemith wrote in 1958 is an excellent illustration of his post-American style, combining lyricism with humor, Baroque contrapuntal techniques with old-fashioned dances such as the waltz, polka, and galop. Igor Stravinsky's and Hindemith's octets can very well serve as the framing works for a neoclassical style in twentieth century music.

Bibliography

Austin, William. *Music in the Twentieth Century.* New York: W. W. Norton, 1966. The chapter on Hindemith is the best capsule introduction to his music and musical philosophy in English.

Cook, Susan C. *Opera for a New Republic.* Ann Arbor: UMI Research Press, 1988. A study of German opera during the 1920's, with much emphasis on works by Hindemith. The author also includes chapters on New Objectivity and on the effect of jazz on European music.

Hindemith, Paul. *A Composer's World: Horizons and Limitations.* Cambridge, Mass.: Harvard University Press, 1952. Based on the series of lectures that Hindemith gave at Harvard during the 1949-1950 academic year. Hindemith states his musical philosophy for the general reader and emphasizes his moral and ethical view of the art.

Hinton, Stephen. *The Idea of Gebrauchsmusik.* New York: Garland, 1989. Very useful for the origins and cultural background of the concept of *Gebrauchsmusik*, although the musical information is directed toward specialists.

Laqueur, Walter. *Weimar: A Cultural History, 1918-1933.* New York: G. P. Putnam's Sons, 1974. The best study in English of the Weimar Republic in Germany and its variegated cultural life. Both art and entertainment music are discussed.

Noss, Luther. *Paul Hindemith in the United States.* Urbana: University of Illinois

Press, 1989. Describes the composer's life and activities in the United States, mostly between 1937 and 1953, with a postlude on his later years.

R. M. Longyear

Cross-References

Schoenberg Breaks with Tonality (1908), p. 193; German Artists Found the Bauhaus (1919), p. 463; Schoenberg Develops His Twelve-Tone System (1921), p. 528; Stravinsky Completes His Wind Octet (1923), p. 561; Brecht and Weill Collaborate on *Mahagonny Songspiel* (1927), p. 724; Hitler Organizes an Exhibition Denouncing Modern Art (1937), p. 1083.

HOLLYWOOD ENTERS ITS GOLDEN AGE

Category of event: Motion pictures
Time: The 1930's
Locale: Hollywood, California

The motion-picture studios employed new technologies in sound, color, and special effects and cultivated the images of major stars to make Hollywood the entertainment capital of the nation

Principal personages:

FRANK CAPRA (1897-1991), the creative director who managed to overcome small budgets at Columbia studios

CLAUDETTE COLBERT (CLAUDETTE LILY CHAUCHOIN, 1905-   ), an articulate actress who often played sophisticated characters

CLARK GABLE (1901-1960), the rugged son of an Ohio oil-field worker who translated toughness into screen stardom

GRETA GARBO (GRETA LOUISA GUSTAFSSON, 1905-1990), a Swedish actress who achieved legendary stardom in Hollywood silents and then excelled in sound films

CHICO MARX (1886-1961), the eldest of the Marx Brothers, who spoke one-liners in a heavy Italian accent

GROUCHO MARX (1890-1977), the leader of the Marx Brothers, whose fake mustache, big cigar, and rapid patter set their comedic tone

HARPO MARX (1888-1964), the Marx Brothers' nonspeaking, harp-playing, woman-chasing specialist in visual puns

ZEPPO MARX (1901-1979), the singer and straight man for the Marx Brothers

LOUIS B. MAYER (1885-1957), the autocratic studio boss of both Gable and Garbo at Metro-Goldwyn-Mayer

Summary of Event

In the same decade that a massive depression wracked the world's economy, the film industry of the United States enjoyed its golden age. The Hollywood studios brought forth technical innovations that captivated audiences at the same time that stars such as Clark Gable, Greta Garbo, and the Marx Brothers achieved a public following that was the envy of political and business leaders.

The introduction of sound to motion pictures was one of the most revolutionary changes in the history of the film industry, and, like most revolutions, it was accompanied by uncertainty, confusion and excitement. The Warner Bros. studio was pleased by the enthusiastic response to the 1927 premier of *The Jazz Singer*, the first full-length film with sound, but the technology of "talking movies" remained experimental for several years. In *The Jazz Singer*, vaudevillian Al Jolson was shown speaking and singing a few words through the use of a recorded disc system that was synchronized with his image on the screen. This disc system and its rivals had their flaws; silent screen stars faced the challenge of speaking into equipment that was often unmerciful to the human voice. By the early 1930's, however, this technology had improved considerably, and sound was recorded on a track that was part of the film itself. By 1932, nearly all Hollywood productions were "all talking"; the era of the silent screen had passed.

While improved sound systems became common in motion pictures during the decade, high-quality special effects were rare. *King Kong* (1933), therefore, was a remarkable film. An adventure tale in which a greedy entrepreneur captured a giant ape became a vehicle for the creative genius of a team of directors and technicians. The real stars were neither human nor ape; the film's miniature animal figures, made from latex rubber over metal skeletons, the huge mechanized face and upper torso of the ape, and the painstaking stop-motion and rear-projection photography instead stole the show. Radio-Keith-Orpheum (RKO) directors Merian Cooper and Ernest Schoesdack turned to Willis O'Brien for special effects and Marcel Delgado for the construction of the animated models. In addition to the giant ape, dinosaurs inhabited the screen and held audiences in awe with displays of prehistoric combat.

The use of color also reached a critical phase in the 1930's. The Technicolor Corporation devised a system of color photography and projection as early as 1915, but its complexity and expense held back commercial exploitation. The Technicolor system evolved into the "three-strip" process, in which chemical treatment added color to the film. In 1935, director Rouben Mamoulian's *Becky Sharp* appeared in vibrant—perhaps overdone—color. By 1939, this problem had disappeared, and producer David O. Selznick and director Victor Fleming brought *Gone with the Wind* to the screen with an improved Technicolor process.

The attraction of Hollywood films went far beyond innovations in technology. The most powerful phenomenon, stardom, was also the most nebulous. Film stars had national and even international status that rivaled that of political and business leaders of the day. Although numerous stars had large and devoted followings, two stood out: the tall, dark, mustachioed Clark Gable and the svelte, blond, stunning Greta Garbo. Both achieved acclaim at Metro-Goldwyn-Mayer (MGM), where performers had to submit to the rules and expectations of powerful studio bosses. Yet both projected qualities into their screen appearances that went beyond what executives and directors could control. Gable's and Garbo's individual films came to mean less than did their personal appeal to the mass audience.

Gable and Garbo manifested different qualities on the screen. Gable was the rough, sometimes brash American male who generally had his way with women and with life. Garbo was often the victim of circumstances, the fallen woman or the self-sacrificing lover who somehow suffered through her anguish with subdued resolve. His image was that of the pragmatic, bullish, determined American hero, while hers was that of the disdainful, worldly cosmopolitan. Fan magazines and gossip columnists relished tidbits of information from their private lives but seldom grasped their personal responses to stardom. Gable was surprised and even amused by his celebrity, but Garbo, whose reclusive nature created an air of mystery, rarely revealed her inner feelings.

The Marx Brothers achieved another type of stardom as they cavorted through a series of uproarious, chaotic comedies. Their quick minds and lack of inhibition pushed comedy beyond traditional boundaries. Veterans of vaudeville and the stage who broke into films when sound allowed for the spoken joke, Groucho, Chico, Harpo, and Zeppo used the new medium to improvise and improve upon old tricks. Double entendres, painful puns, manic chases, and risible pantomimes conveyed their sometimes whimsical, often cynical views of institutions ranging from real estate brokerage to university administrations to the national government. Their wild antics matched spoken humor with visual comedy in a balance suited for talking pictures.

The launching of new technologies and the luster of the stars helped the Hollywood studios weather the storms of the Depression. MGM, Warner Bros., and RKO led the way, but Fox, Paramount, Universal, Columbia, and United Artists also survived the nation's worst economic crisis. Established as the world's center of commercial film production, Hollywood became a major contributor to popular culture, an occasional contributor to high culture, and a dynamic, if unsteady, force in the nation's economy.

Impact of Event

The aggressive bosses of Hollywood engaged in a frantic scramble for profits, but some of their films were successful not only at the box office but also in the collective judgment of film critics and historians. Admittedly, most films were moderately entertaining escapism: musicals, B-Westerns, and soap operas. A few studio productions, though, transcended commercialism to reach the rarefied heights of artistic achievement or social and political commentary.

Frank Capra, a young, relatively unknown director for financially embattled Columbia, emerged in the 1930's as one of Hollywood's major filmmakers. Working with a small budget and barely a month to complete shooting, Capra brought together Claudette Colbert and Clark Gable (on loan from MGM to Columbia as punishment for standing up to MGM boss Louis B. Mayer) to form one of the screen's most electric duos in 1934's *It Happened One Night.* Colbert played a New York socialite opposite Gable's pushy journalist. At first on the trail of a news story about the idle rich, Gable took a personal interest in Colbert and, after some brisk exchanges in risque situations, the two forgot their class differences to become enamored of each other. This unlikely matching of a daughter of the social elite and a hard working journalist bridged the barriers of status and, in the Depression, represented an unorthodox reconciliation between haves and have-nots. This prototypical "screwball comedy" set a much-imitated formula and made Capra an influential director.

Gable and Colbert had broken the barriers between great wealth and middling income, but such differences were not always so gracefully overcome. In the early

1930's, Warner Bros. released a series of gangster films in which the protagonists were hard-bitten, violent products of urban mean streets. Edward G. Robinson's "Rico" was gunned down at the end of 1931's *Little Caesar*, but he left an unforgettable impression as to how an aggressive, unscrupulous individual could grab wealth and power, at least for a short time. A reflection of the headlines in the daily press, *Little Caesar, The Public Enemy* (1931), with James Cagney, and Paul Muni's evocation of Chicago's Al Capone in *Scarface* (1932) remain as a lasting legacy of a turbulent era in which criminal activity took on disturbing proportions.

Social structure and cultural values were unstable in many films of the 1930's, but only rarely did studio executives allow their motion pictures to slash respected institutions to the core. Yet the Marx Brothers did just that. In five films made for Paramount between 1929 and 1933, they called into question the rationality and legitimacy of some of the basic components of American national life. Sometimes viewed at the superficial level of slapstick comedy, these films had an ideological angle. *The Cocoanuts* (1929) ridiculed the Florida real-estate industry at a time when the country was beginning to skid into the Depression. The culmination of their anarchistic comedy was *Duck Soup* (1933), which portrayed political leaders as demagogues, government as their pernicious plaything, and war as a result of scoundrel-dominated diplomacy.

The biting humor of the Marx Brothers was at times too much for 1930's film audiences, who often sought relief from the bleak reality of Depression life. Audiences found escape in films of glamour and excitement that featured stars who approximated a kind of royalty in the public mind. Although the lustre of her image faded over the years after her unexpected retirement in 1941, Garbo's presence in motion pictures went far beyond sex appeal and skillful acting to reveal a persona that held fascination for the public. She combined an air of sophistication with a tinge of sadness at lost opportunities; in many of her films, Garbo did not live happily every after. *Anna Christie* (1930), *Anna Karenina* (1935) and *Camille* (1937) defined the image of this reclusive and enigmatic star. Entangled in a contract with MGM's autocratic Louis B. Mayer, Garbo played redundant roles for the sake of the box office. Only in *Ninotchka* (1939), a comedic tour de force that starred Garbo as a bland, low-key Soviet agent whose personal liberation offered commentary on the pretensions of ideological purity, was Garbo able to break loose from such typecasting. Ironically, the adoring public that found escape in her films ensured her entrapment in roles that limited her development as an actress.

While Garbo's magnetism stemmed from her aloofness and subtlety, Clark Gable built his star image by projecting an aggressive directness. He and Garbo costarred in *Susan Lenox*, a 1931 MGM production for Mayer. Garbo, the fallen woman, pursued engineer Gable as her last hope for the good life. Many female fans, too, pursued Gable throughout the decade. His work in *It Happened One Night* confirmed his position at the top of Hollywood's list of stars, and *Gone with the Wind* gave him the quintessential male role of the decade as the charming Rhett Butler, a cool realist who used his wits to survive the Civil War but who never found happiness with the mercurial Scarlett O'Hara. His parting thrust at her—"Quite frankly, my dear, I don't give a damn"—remains one of the best-known lines in film history. Unlike Garbo, Gable remained active in films all of his life, but the roots of his public persona and much of his film legacy is contained in his work of the 1930's.

In the 1930's, Hollywood enticed an agglomeration of ambition, money, and talent to California that, through hard work, luck, and creativity, produced a golden age in motion pictures. The studios combined new technologies of sound, color, and special effects with legendary stars to produce films of immense commercial appeal and, in a few cases, lasting cultural value.

Bibliography

Bergman, Andrew. *We're in the Money: Depression America and Its Films.* New York: New York University Press, 1971. General overview of film and society in the 1930's, with brief but insightful discussions of the Marx Brothers, women's roles in film, and Frank Capra's contributions to the screwball comedy and political dramas.

Capra, Frank. *The Name Above the Title.* New York: Macmillan, 1971. Lengthy, detailed, unusually frank autobiography that covers Capra's life, from his beginnings among Sicilian peasantry through his ascension to the top of Hollywood's motion-picture elite in the 1930's to his decline after World War II. Fast-paced writing, with numerous quotations from reviews.

Dooley, Roger. *From Scarface to Scarlett: American Films in the 1930's.* New York: Harcourt Brace Jovanovich, 1981. Discusses a wide selection of films, organized in thematic sections. For example, "Continental Style" places Garbo and several of her films in the context of Hollywood's image of European history and culture.

Gabler, Neal. *An Empire of Their Own: How the Jews Invented Hollywood.* New York: Crown, 1988. Interesting biographical sketches of studio executives. The author is more sympathetic to Louis B. Mayer than are most students of the era.

Gronowicz, Antoni. *Garbo: Her Story.* New York: Simon & Schuster, 1990. Fascinating but controversial perspective on Garbo's life, ostensibly from Garbo's point of view. Too valuable to ignore in any study of her career, but readers should use with awareness of its subjectivity. Richard Schickel's afterword is a model of carefully considered judgment on the strengths and weaknesses of Garbo's work in Hollywood.

Higham, Charles. *The Art of the American Cinema.* Garden City, N.Y.: Doubleday, 1974. Emphasizes the efforts of major directors of the 1930's. Skillfully analyzes the often-competing stresses of commercial entertainment and artistic standards.

Maland, Charles J. *Frank Capra.* Boston: Twayne, 1980. Carefully written scholarly assessment of Capra's work, with emphasis on *It Happened One Night.*

Marx, Groucho. *Groucho and Me.* New York: Bernard Geis, 1959. Rambling, autobiographical reminiscence replete with anecdotes, wisecracks, and some valuable observations on the Marx Brothers' rise from vaudeville to Hollywood stardom.

Tornabene, Lyn. *Long Live the King: A Biography of Clark Gable.* New York: Putnam, 1976. Traces Gable's rise to stardom, with more attention to his personal life than to his screen performances. Emphasizes the insecurities of stardom, Gable's combative personality, and his troubled relationship with Louis B. Mayer.

Weales, Gerald. *Canned Goods as Caviar: American Film Comedy of the 1930's.* Chicago: University of Chicago Press, 1985. A critical analysis of a dozen comedies, including a challenging critique of *Duck Soup.*

John A. Britton

Cross-References

The Jazz Singer Premieres in New York (1927), p. 734; Sound Technology Revolutionizes the Motion-Picture Industry (1928), p. 761; The First Academy Awards Honor Film Achievement (1929), p. 799; The Studio System Dominates Hollywood Filmmaking (1930's), p. 833; The Classic *The Wizard of Oz* Opens (1939), p. 1109; Ford Defines the Western in *Stagecoach* (1939), p. 1115; *Gone with the Wind* Premieres (1939), p. 1154; Welles's *Citizen Kane* Breaks with Traditional Filmmaking (1941), p. 1200; *Casablanca* Marks the Artistic Apex of 1940's War-Themed Films (1942), p. 1245; The Hollywood Studio System Is Transformed (1946), p. 1307.

RADIO PROGRAMMING DOMINATES HOME LEISURE

Category of event: Television and radio
Time: The 1930's and the 1940's
Locale: The United States

For two "golden" decades, radio broadcasts of music, comedy, drama, news, and sports pervaded Americans' daily lives

Principal personages:
FRANKLIN D. ROOSEVELT (1882-1945), the first U.S. president to use radio effectively
RUDY VALLEE (1901-1986), a singer, impresario of radio's first popular variety show
FRED ALLEN (JOHN FLORENCE SULLIVAN, 1894-1956), an early radio star with his own show
GEORGE BURNS (NATHAN BIRNBAUM, 1896-   ), a leading comedian, along with his wife, Gracie Allen
EDDIE CANTOR (EDWARD ISRAEL ISKOWITZ, 1892-1964), an enduring star of his own scheduled comedy show
JACK BENNY (BENJAMIN KUBELSKY, 1894-1974), a top popular comedian and star of his own show
WALTER WINCHELL (1897-1972), a popular, staccato-voiced newsman
KATE SMITH (1909-1986), one of radio's most beloved singers
BOB HOPE (1903-   ), a comedian with a fast delivery
BING CROSBY (1904-1977), a popular singer

Summary of Event

The inauguration of radio networking and broadcasting after 1926 and the increasing sale of air time for advertisements by the close of the 1920's further opened the door for the radio industry's exploration of entertainments capable of attracting and holding mass audiences. The remarkable profits earned from such efforts were a powerful underpinning to radio's phenomenally successful insertion of its messages, programs, and personalities into American life. Radio held sway as the reigning entertainment medium until the 1950's, when its regency was in some respects usurped by the dissemination and public embrace of television.

The "Golden Age" of radio was a result of outside events as much as it was a bonus from the scramble for profits. The onslaught of the Great Depression, the most massive peacetime crisis in American history, forced the leisure of tens of millions of ordinary folk, through economic necessity, back into the home. The manifestations of the Depression, including unemployment, debt, evaporating profits, a collapse of effective government, folk migrations, labor strife, and, by the late

1930's, the awareness of a distintegrating international order and of impending war, created a popular hunger for morale boosting, optimism, diversion, escapism, and a sense of brotherhood and belonging. Confirmation of the extent to which radio met these wants and needs came in many ways. Social workers noted in the mid-1930's that needy families surrendered nearly all of their possessions when necessary but insisted on retaining their radios, and President Franklin D. Roosevelt, the first chief executive to use radio effectively, tried to encourage optimism and weld the nation together, beginning in March, 1933, with his series of broadcast "fireside chats."

The vastness of radio's potential audience was revealed by the reception of Free-man Gosden and Charles Correll's series *Amos 'n' Andy*, eventually a claimant to having been the most popular show ever presented by any of the media. Lesser, but still substantial, success attended broadcast of *The Rudy Vallee Show*. Crooner Vallee, the host, established a format for variety shows and introduced dozens of vaudeville's greatest talents, including Eddie Cantor, Alice Faye, Milton Berle, Joe Penner, Bob Burns, and Bing Crosby, among others who were soon to host their own shows.

Programming hours were filled quickly. Morning broadcasts continued, as they had in the 1920's, with "wake-up" shows and home, health, and happiness presentations aimed primarily at female audiences. Morning shows sometimes were augmented with livestock prices in rural areas. "Soap operas," so named because soap companies were early sponsors, appeared by 1932. Some of these had been "evening light" romances of the late 1920's, including *The Smith Family*, *The Rise of the Goldbergs*, and *True Story Hour*. To these were added *Ma Perkins*, *The Romance of Helen Trent*, and *Myrt and Marge*, all serials that aired for years and had audiences so caught up that some newspapers printed synopses of each day's adventures so that listeners forced to miss a show could keep up. More serious, novel, and educational were the spontaneous interviews of notable personalities offered eventually by *The Mary Margaret McBride Show* on the Columbia Broadcasting System (CBS).

Early afternoons posed difficulties for network broadcasters, who aired a few soap operas during those hours. A number of what proved to be long-running "kids' shows" successfully blocked out late afternoons. WOR-New York's *Uncle Don*, one of the most beloved of these shows, featured original stories, personal announcements, words of caution and advice, and piano tunes and songs. Other shows that became household favorites were *The Singing Story Lady*, *Let's Pretend*, and, especially for school-age boys, *Jack Armstrong*, the *All-American Boy*. For younger children, there were numerous "uncle and aunt" broadcasts such as WLS-Chicago's *Lullaby Twins*. Also important but hardly central to network broadcasting were educational shows such as conductor Walter Damrosch's *Music Appreciation Hour*, a precursor of Leonard Bernstein's later, similar, and justly famed television music series for children that reportedly reached millions of schoolchildren.

By the mid-1930's, the evening hours had become "prime time." Sponsors discovered the large potential audiences available during these hours and competed for these audiences with shows featuring constellations of stars, many of whom survived as household names into the television era. Radio's stellar personalities, such as Eddie Cantor, Fred Allen, Ed Wynn, Edgar Bergen (and Charlie McCarthy), Bing Crosby, George Burns and Gracie Allen, Jim and Marion Jordan (*Fibber McGee and Molly*), Will Rogers, Major Edward Bowes, Fanny Brice, Bob Hope, and Al Jolson, often accompanied by almost equally notable announcers and bandleaders, preempted Americans' prime leisure time with their own buoyant styles of music, wisecracks, nonsense, silliness, humor, and wit. Radio personalities became the intimates of nearly every family in the country, with popularity matching that of Hollywood's film stars.

Although serious drama played a modest role in the broadcast day and was almost nonexistent in prime time, a niche for it was carved out after the mid-1930's. Writers, poets, and dramatists such as Archibald MacLeish, Arthur Miller, Norman Rosten, Norman Corwin, Arch Obler, and Orson Welles, in company with notable actors such as John Houseman, Agnes Moorehead, Maurice Evans, John Barrymore, and Welles, created stirring dramas. Welles became famous for his terrifying production of H. G. Wells's *The War of the Worlds* in 1938. Another niche was found for news, despite a dearth of sponsors and low ratings. News programs gained popularity after the mid-1930's, as dictatorial regimes in Europe and Asia dismantled the peace. American listeners wanted current news of these events. CBS's William Paley pioneered radio news, building a superior cadre of newsmen, among them Edward R. Murrow, William Shirer, David Schoenbrun, Richard Hottelet, and, a bit later, Charles Collingwood and Howard K. Smith. Several of them would gain fame as news reporters in their own right.

Impact of Event

During the 1930's, radio network broadcasting dominated the leisure and preempted the daily attention of Americans as no other communications medium ever had. Its myriad sounds, music, and voices, heard in homes, factories, shops, and cars, became an integral part of the daily environment. Franklin D. Roosevelt, along with lesser politicians, embraced radio as a prime instrument of communication. New York's Mayor Fiorello La Guardia read the comics to his constituents; demagogues such as Huey Long and Father Charles Coughlin used radio's power to broadcast their values. Leaders in all types of fields, including the arts, politics, education, and religion, were dazzled by radio's possibilities and dismayed by its purported abuses.

The pervasive influences of radio on daily life during the 1930's were measurable in a narrow sense; audience samplings produced estimates of programs' comparative popularity. The radio industry's influence on the business world could be measured by profits, which almost invariably were high. Such losses as occurred usually were on a smaller scale, pertaining to specific sponsorships, shows, or stations.

Radio's more massive and profound influences, though certain, remain less precisely calculable. One of these, ephemeral as it may have been, was to provide, to those who were the actual or prospective economic casualties of the Great Depression, solace, diversion, escape, and the perceived companionship of a vast audible support group. Radio thus helped keep a healthy edge on national morale and made valuable contributions to a sense of national unity, a fact upon which political, business, and military leaders were able to capitalize.

Leaders from all fields, but particularly politicians, quickly discovered that radio had the dual capacity to exalt and enhance them, as it did with Roosevelt and Winston Churchill, or to leave the public disenchanted, as it did with the twangings of President Calvin Coolidge and the nervous deliveries of President Herbert Hoover. For more ordinary folk, the medium, by virtue of announcers and performers whose American English was soon divested of regionalisms and dialects, set new standards of clarity for speech, a judgment already being made by educators by the mid-1930's. Coast-to-coast broadcasting, while doing little to banish dialects within their home territories, further eroded the country's historic localism and sectionalism, something that the automobile and films were also accomplishing along other lines. Americans were becoming aware of wider worlds through exposure via film and radio, and they could more readily travel to those worlds with automobiles. Radio reinforced the power of the spoken word. It likewise introduced a measure of intimacy matched neither in its availability nor in its pervasiveness by any other medium. Radio invited performers directly into listeners' homes and lives, and radio listeners worldwide learned to be entertained by outsiders on a daily basis rather than finding pastimes that were more active and in their own communities.

Radio helped create a unified national culture in the United States. This was particularly true for music. Radio could introduce new music and songs to the nation as a whole. Jazz and "race music" became available to the general public in the 1930's through radio. Presentations of jazz musicians, most of them black, as well as the songs of black singers, such as the legendary Bessie Smith, were still confined largely to the clubs in large cities or to controlled recordings and sales by record companies. Radio, far more than did the more timid movies, changed that, making jazz respectable and giving it a wider audience. The same effect occurred with transmission of traditional country music. Because of the immediacy of radio, with programming decisions made on a daily basis, innovations can be disseminated far more swiftly and flexibly than in other media. Although radio created a national culture, it also allowed cultural elements to spread more quickly from local roots.

Before the close of the 1930's, radio broadcasts had become one of the most formidable informal educational forces in American life. Speech, manners, acceptable forms of humor, and opinions on virtually every topic were all changed because of the uniquely intimate medium of broadcast radio. The accessibility of educational programs, popular culture, discussions of personal problems, and, increasingly by the end of the decade, floods of hard information on an unprecedented scale about the state of the country and the world helped move Americans into a more urbane, cosmopolitan, and sophisticated state.

Bibliography

Barnouw, Erik. *The Golden Web: 1933 to 1953*. Vol. 2 in *A History of Broadcasting in the United States*. New York: Oxford University Press, 1968. Barnouw's trilogy is, overall, the most comprehensive and authoritative scholarly history of its subject. The second volume is clearly written, spare, and fascinating on the 1930's, covering network battles as well as shows and radio personalities. Plenty of photos, splendid bibliography, and extensive index.

Buxton, Frank, and Bill Owen. *Radio's Golden Age: The Programs and the Personalities*. Ansonia Station, N.Y.: Easton Valley Press, 1966. The authors concentrate on anecdotes, glimpses of early transitions of vaudevillians to radio, shows, and personalities. For popular audiences. Knowledgeably written as an insider's book. Some photos and a brief note on sources.

Douglas, George H. *The Early Days of Radio Broadcasting*. Jefferson, N.C.: McFarland, 1987. Excellent on the start of networking; the rise of announcers, news, and sportscasting; and the filling in of the broadcast day. An admiring and sympathetic though not uncritical view of the subjects. Many photos, brief chapter notes, excellent bibliography, and extensive index.

Ely, Melvin Patrick. *The Adventures of Amos 'n' Andy: A Social History of an American Phenomenon*. New York: Free Press, 1991. A scholarly yet easily read detailed account of the radio show that was at one time the nation's most popular. Discusses its racial content and impact. Many photos, excellent chapter notes and "Word on Sources," and a fine index. Probably the definitive study of the show.

Harmon, Jim. *The Great Radio Comedians*. Garden City, N.Y.: Doubleday, 1970. An insider's view of 1930's comedians. The author has interesting insights and anecdotes that make this book informally informative.

Wertheim, Arthur Frank. *Radio Comedy*. Oxford, England: Oxford University Press, 1979. Wonderful on the "Golden Age," authoritative, and written with obvious joy. Interesting chapters on the war years and on radio comics' sometimes sad transition to television. Good chapter notes compensate for lack of a bibliography. Many photos and an excellent index. Essential for serious readers.

Clifton K. Yearley

Cross-References

The Art of Radio Develops from Early Broadcast Experience (1920's), p. 469; WSM Launches *The Grand Ole Opry* (1925), p. 675; The British Broadcasting Corporation Is Chartered (1927), p. 712; The *Amos 'n' Andy* Radio Show Goes on the Air (1928), p. 755; Goodman Begins His *Let's Dance* Broadcasts (1934), p. 968; Welles Broadcasts *The War of the Worlds* (1938), p. 1103.

THE STUDIO SYSTEM DOMINATES HOLLYWOOD FILMMAKING

Category of event: Motion pictures
Time: The 1930's and the 1940's
Locale: Hollywood, California

Motion-picture production changed profoundly during the Great Depression and World War II, as studio executives exercised control over much of the creative process of filmmaking

> *Principal personages:*
> FRANK CAPRA (1897-1991), a director whose "screwball" comedies captured critical and popular acclaim
> CARL LAEMMLE (1867-1939), the founder and patriarch of Universal Studios
> CECIL B. DeMILLE (1881-1959), a producer-director whose career lasted from the 1910's to the 1950's
> LOUIS B. MAYER (1885-1957), the hard-driving, eccentric head of Metro-Goldwyn-Mayer during the studio's "golden age"
> IRVING G. THALBERG (1899-1936), a brilliant young executive at Metro-Goldwyn-Mayer from 1923 until his premature death
> JACK L. WARNER (1892-1978), the youngest of the Warner brothers and head of Warner Bros. studio management

Summary of Event

Motion-picture fans often fail to appreciate that Hollywood film production began as a form of private enterprise. Vigorously competitive since the early years of the twentieth century, the companies that made Hollywood famous were locked in an intense competition during the Depression-ridden 1930's and the war-torn 1940's. These trying times witnessed the emergence of the studio system, consisting of five major corporations—Metro-Goldwyn-Mayer (MGM), Paramount, Radio-Keith-Orpheum (RKO), Warner Bros., and Twentieth Century-Fox—and three smaller organizations—Universal, Columbia, and United Artists. Studio executives consolidated their operations through "vertical integration," which gave them control of the entire process from film production to exhibition in theaters. These eight studios accounted for ninety-five percent of U.S. film rentals by the late 1930's. Internal centralization of studio operations meant that executives often personally supervised actual film production. For many screenwriters, directors, and performers, this extension of executive authority was an intrusion into the creative process. For management, it was a necessary means to reduce costs and increase production. In spite of this and other conflicts, the studio system left a lasting imprint on American popular culture.

Not only did the studios confront rivals in Hollywood, they also faced other challenges, such as the growth of modern home entertainment with the rise of radio in the 1930's and the advent of television in the 1940's. The catastrophe of the period, however, was the Great Depression. By 1932, national unemployment was at least twenty-five percent. Public attendance at movie theaters declined sharply from 1930 to 1933, and studio profits plummeted. The prosperity of the 1920's had encouraged heavy investments in new theaters, sound equipment for talking pictures, and new studios. In the 1930's, Hollywood staggered under the burden of these debts and became increasingly dependent on New York bankers.

MGM rode out the Depression with the least difficulty, but the reasons for its success are difficult to pinpoint. The paternalistic, flamboyant studio boss Louis B. Mayer was certainly no model of efficient management. One obvious MGM strength, however, was the brief but brilliant tenure of executive producer Irving Thalberg, whose sickly physique contained a dynamo of energy. He pushed the studio while he drove himself to an early death. Thalberg supervised production, from the hiring of screenwriters to the final editing of the film. At a time when other studios cut their budgets, MGM maintained an expensive payroll. The results were impressive, and the studio provided audiences with relief from the doldrums of the Depression through its popular, lavish productions.

In contrast to MGM, both Paramount and RKO stumbled through the 1930's in financial disarray. Paramount's legendary chief, Adolph Zukor, lost control of his company's finances as box-office receipts declined. Banks and investment companies removed Zukor as Paramount slipped into bankruptcy. An extensive housecleaning followed. Paramount survived under new management, with a trimmed-down structure that could support only a few major productions each year. RKO fared little better. Frequent changes in management and a few box-office successes such as 1933's *King Kong* were not enough to solve basic financial weaknesses. In the 1940's, both Paramount and RKO continued to struggle and were backed by increasingly skeptical investors.

Warner Bros. was closest to MGM's profit levels. Jack Warner, a somewhat heavy-handed version of Irving Thalberg, assumed control of studio operations and intervened at various stages of production. Unlike Thalberg, who was concerned with quality, Warner pressed for quick, efficient production. He held down costs to the point of personally switching off lights in studio bathrooms. Though Warner was the subject of surreptitious humor among writers, directors, and actors, his notorious cost-control methods seemed to work. The studio clung to a respectable prosperity in the 1930's.

Twentieth Century-Fox gambled on new sound equipment and a large theater chain in the late 1920's, but the studio's timing was disastrous. Studio head William Fox borrowed heavily just before the initial shocks of the Depression hit. Rights to the Fox sound system became entangled in a legal battle, and the payments on the studio's immense debt overwhelmed its income. Corporate restructuring removed Fox, and the studio survived on a narrow margin.

The "little three" of the Hollywood studios also experienced rough times. Universal was an industry leader in the 1920's under Carl Laemmle, but he was forced to sell his interests in 1936. Like Columbia and United Artists, Universal struggled through the Depression. All three small studios enjoyed momentary box-office successes with the work of certain directors or stars, but the general trends were reduced income and corporate retrenchment.

World War II provided relief from financial troubles, but only temporarily. Hollywood turned out a series of morale-boosting films that pleased politicians in Washington, bankers in New York, and theater audiences across the country. The basic problems, however, were uncertain income and rising production costs. Shortages of lumber made set construction more expensive. Technicians, writers, and performers commanded higher salaries. The most devastating blow, however, came from the courts in the Paramount case (1940-1949). Federal judges ordered Paramount to sell its theater chain on the grounds that control of both production and exhibition facilities constituted unfair competition against local theaters. This decision eventually changed the structure of the film industry. Pressed by the expansion of television and rising costs, the studios faced a dim future.

Impact of Event

Economic problems shifted the artistic force behind motion pictures from the individual director—the focus of film production before 1930—to the studios themselves and to the producers and directors entrusted with the task of converting budgets directly to screen images. Each studio emphasized certain popular themes to find formulas for success at the box office. Although restricted budgets, tight schedules, and intrusive bosses generally suffocated the creative impulses in filmmaking, some strong-willed producers and directors managed to achieve high quality productions. Studio heads, whether the autocratic Louis B. Mayer or short-term executives chosen by East Coast bankers, were quick to identify themselves and their corporations with the style and success of producers and directors who could attract large audiences and occasionally please the critics.

Two of the most solvent studios offered a striking contrast in the types of films that brought them profits. MGM used elegance and glamor to provide audiences with escapism, while Warner Bros. turned to films of social and political relevance. Hyperkinetic Irving Thalberg left his personal imprint on many of MGM's expensive productions, including the South Seas saga *Mutiny on the Bounty* (1935) and the Victorian romance *The Barretts of Wimpole Street* (1934). After Thalberg's death in 1936, MGM continued to attract large audiences. Director Victor Fleming worked with independent producer David O. Selznick on 1939's immensely popular *Gone with the Wind.* The studio shared in the profits, and in 1944, MGM purchased sole rights to the long-term money-maker.

Warner Bros. did not attempt to match MGM's grandeur, but Jack Warner used his limited resources well. Organized in 1923 by four brothers who were outcasts in Hollywood's movie-mogul society, the studio took a large risk on sound films in the 1920's and vaulted to the forefront in the 1930's. Warner Bros. pushed directors for fast-paced, low-cost productions. Mervyn LeRoy responded by pioneering the gangster film; he directed a strong performance from Edward G. Robinson in the title role of *Little Caesar* in 1930 and then worked with Paul Muni as the victim of a corrupt judicial system in the powerful *I Am a Fugitive from a Chain Gang* (1932). William Wellman directed James Cagney to stardom in *Public Enemy*, the gangster film of 1931. John Huston's 1941 version of *The Maltese Falcon* created a grim world of ambiguity and betrayal, and his *Treasure of the Sierra Madre* (1948) dramatized moral degeneration through greed. World War II elicited the studio's patriotism, as reflected in *Casablanca* (1942), a potent combination of romance, character study, and propaganda. Warner Bros.' production methods were exemplified in *Casablanca*, as director Michael Curtiz made the most of inexpensive sets and screenwriters completed the sharp, literate script while the film was being shot.

Hard-pressed RKO had a remarkable string of much-admired films. *King Kong* astounded audiences with its innovative special effects, and in 1937 the studio began to distribute the inventive products of cartoon genius Walt Disney, bringing adults and children alike into theaters. Orson Welles's *Citizen Kane* (1940) was a powerful and controversial film but drew small audiences. Val Lewton produced eleven low-budget, highly impressive horror classics led by *Cat People* (1942). Producer Adrian Scott, director Edward Dmytryk, and screenwriter John Paxton collaborated on *Murder, My Sweet* (1944), a dark, moody detective story punctuated by witty dialogue adapted from Raymond Chandler's novel. This film and the work of Welles and Lewton were typical of RKO's stylish, literate productions that, somehow, never solved the company's financial woes.

Paramount and Twentieth Century-Fox also floundered financially but, thanks to skillful directors, both studios produced some superior films. Veteran producer-director Cecil B. DeMille brought out a series of historical dramas, including *Cleopatra* (1934) and *Union Pacific* (1939). Billy Wilder directed and cowrote two taut stories about contemporary life: *Double Indemnity* (1944) featured murder, and *Lost Weekend* (1945) took a somber look at alcoholism. Twentieth Century-Fox survived with help from John Ford's 1940 film version of John Steinbeck's 1939 novel *The Grapes of Wrath*, which was perhaps the epitome of topicality as it sympathetically portrayed the migration of a dispossessed farm family from Oklahoma to California. The commercial mainstay of Fox, however, was child star Shirley Temple, who acted, sang, and danced her way through a series of box-office hits.

Carl Laemmle turned over Universal to his twenty-one-year-old son, Carl, Jr., in 1929. The younger Laemmle supervised the production of *All Quiet on the Western Front* (1930), a provocative antiwar film, and then innovated in the horror genre with Bela Lugosi's *Dracula* (1931) and Boris Karloff's *Frankenstein* (1931). These creative thrusts, though, fell victim to bad timing. Audiences were too small in the Depression years, and Universal soon faced a fiscal crisis. The Laemmles sold their interest in the studio, which worked its way back to solvency through B-pictures, serials, and the popularity of teen star Deanna Durbin. By the 1940's, Universal had achieved a modest prosperity.

The two remaining minor studios relied heavily on talented directors. Frank Capra carried Columbia with films of social and political relevance, including *It Happened One Night* (1934), in which romance overcame class barriers, and highly charged populist films, including *Meet John Doe* (1941). Robert Rossen's 1949 exposé of the perils of demagoguery, *All the King's Men*, marked Columbia's return to solvency. United Artists turned to the legendary Charlie Chaplin, who poked fun at industrial society in *Modern Times* (1936) and ridiculed authoritarian leaders in *The Great Dictator* (1940). John Ford brought maturity to the Western in his popular United Artists release *Stagecoach* (1939).

The legacy of this colorful, turbulent era contains major contradictions. The period's forceful, profit-seeking executives undercut the creative process but left an impressive list of popular, critically acclaimed films including *The Grapes of Wrath*, *Casablanca*, and *Gone with the Wind*. The drive to boost profits, however, ultimately failed. The growth of television, rising production costs, and adverse court decisions meant the decline and ultimate demise of the studio system in the 1950's and 1960's. The Hollywood film industry, for all its power, notoriety, and many contributions to American popular culture, had a short life span.

Bibliography

Bergman, Andrew. *We're in the Money: Depression America and Its Films.* New York: New York University Press, 1971. Brief, interpretive study of the connection between films and society in the 1930's. Especially interesting on gangster and "shyster" lawyer films of the early part of the decade.

Dick, Bernard. *The Star-Spangled Screen: The American World War II Film.* Lexington: University Press of Kentucky, 1985. Wide-ranging analysis that includes film content and historical accuracy.

Dooley, Roger. *From Scarface to Scarlett: American Films in the 1930's.* New York: Harcourt Brace Jovanovich, 1981. Extensive coverage of Hollywood films, organized by thematic chapters. Useful for thematic discussions and as a reference on individual films.

Gabler, Neal. *An Empire of Their Own: How the Jews Invented Hollywood.* New York: Anchor, 1988. Social history enlivened by biographical portraits of the generation of studio executives who led the motion-picture industry through the 1930's and 1940's. Concentrates on Laemmle, Mayer, Jack and Harry Warner, Fox, Zukor, and Cohn.

Kindem, Gorham, ed. *The American Movie Industry: The Business of Motion Pictures.* Carbondale: Southern Illinois University Press, 1982. Eighteen specialized studies on business aspects of film, including the rise of the studio system and competition with television.

Koppes, Clayton R., and Gregory D. Black. *Hollywood Goes to War: How Politics, Profits, and Propaganda Shaped World War II Movies.* New York: Free Press, 1987. Carefully researched account of the film industry and its relations with the government and the war effort in general. Concentrates on the Office of War Information and its influence on the propagandistic content of Hollywood's World War II films.

McElvaine, Robert. *The Great Depression.* New York: Times Books, 1984. A social, economic, and political history of the United States in the 1930's that focuses on the causes and consequences of the Depression. McElvaine sees Hollywood films as a reflection of culture and values of the era, especially the public's ambivalence toward individualism and collectivism.

Sklar, Robert. *Movie-Made America.* New York: Vintage Books, 1975. Historical survey that connects trends in Hollywood motion pictures with broad economic and social forces. Chapters 10 through 17 cover the 1930's and 1940's and contain much useful information on the rise and fall of the studio system.

Stanley, Robert. *The Celluloid Empire.* New York: Hastings House, 1978. Readable study on the business side of the film industry. Succinct analysis of the eight studios that dominated Hollywood from the Depression to the end of the 1940's.

John A. Britton

Cross-References

Hollywood Enters Its Golden Age (1930's), p. 822; *Little Caesar, Public Enemy,* and *Scarface* Launch the Gangster-Film Genre (1930), p. 839; Karloff and Lugosi Become Kings of Horror (1931), p. 863; The Classic Screwball Comedy Reaches Its Height in Popularity (1934), p. 951; The Classic *The Wizard of Oz* Opens (1939), p. 1109; Ford Defines the Western in *Stagecoach* (1939), p. 1115; *Gone with the Wind* Premieres (1939), p. 1154; *The Maltese Falcon* Establishes a New Style for Crime Films (1941), p. 1223; The Hollywood Studio System Is Transformed (1946), p. 1307.

LITTLE CAESAR, PUBLIC ENEMY, AND *SCARFACE* LAUNCH THE GANGSTER-FILM GENRE

Category of event: Motion pictures
Time: 1930-1932
Locale: The United States

Emerging out of the depths of the Depression, the gangster film revealed much about America's frustrations and proved one of the most popular and resilient of film genres

Principal personages:

EDWARD G. ROBINSON (1893-1973), the actor who played Rico in *Little Caesar*, creating the first powerful gangster persona

WILLIAM WELLMAN (1896-1975), the director of *Public Enemy*, probably the best-crafted of the early 1930's gangster movies

JAMES CAGNEY (1899-1986), a unknown actor whose portrayal of Tommy Powers in *Public Enemy* helped to make the film a hit and secured him a place among Hollywood's top stars

HOWARD HAWKS (1896-1977), the director of the popular and controversial *Scarface*

PAUL MUNI (MUNI WEISENFREUND, 1895-1967), an actor whose flamboyant acting made memorable the role of Tony, the protagonist of *Scarface*

Summary of Event

The period from 1930 through 1932 was Hollywood's time of the gangster. Caught in a widening Depression, the American people were disillusioned and angry. The national dream of economic opportunity had become a nightmare, and society's institutions, especially President Herbert Hoover's federal government, seemed unable to do anything except utter hollow, optimistic nostrums. The film industry, itself suffering from sagging attendance, discovered that tapping this mounting public discontent would bring people back to the theaters. In addition to normal escapist fare, the studios began offering productions dealing with corrupt politicians and businessmen, shady lawyers, dishonest journalists, and women driven to prostitution by economic necessity. These pictures showing the United States in a bleak, unsavory light were popular, but the film type that most caught the public's interest and offered the deepest insights into the troubled national psyche was the gangster film. There had been few gangster films before the Depression; now they would proliferate, and the screen mobster, especially as he appeared in *Little Caesar* (1930), *Public Enemy* (1931), and *Scarface* (1932), would offer himself as a new, disturbing hero.

Little Caesar, made by Warner Bros. in late 1930, broke the ground. It is a simple tale of a small-time hoodlum, Rico (played by Edward G. Robinson), who joins a mob and quickly gains power by being tougher, more relentless and more ferocious than anyone else. Eventually, he becomes the second most important boss in the city. Rico is extremely ruthless, although ultimately not ruthless enough. He falls because he cannot bring himself to kill an old friend who wants to leave the mob. Rico stays his hand, the friend betrays him to the authorities, and Rico's organization crumbles. Alone, on the run, he is finally gunned down by the police in an unfair fight. The police kill Rico, yet they really have little to do with his actual destruction. His doom stems from his going soft over friendship.

Little Caesar was an instant hit. The film is not particularly well made or plotted; its effectiveness comes from its violent action and the character of Rico as realized by Robinson. Rico is a compelling figure who, despite his murderous nature, emerges as a somewhat sympathetic protagonist.

Rico's prime ambition is to get ahead, to make something of himself. He wants wealth and control; even more, he desires status. He seeks to be somebody. He is a Horatio Alger of the Depression era, one who a few decades before might have aspired to be a robber baron. Totally devoted to his ambition and rather puritanical in his personal behavior, he does not drink, involve himself with the easy women of the underworld, or do anything else that he thinks might distract him from his goals. For most of the film, Rico is successful. Through Rico, *Little Caesar* suggests that, given the shambles of American society, crime is perhaps the only way left to secure at least some of the American Dream.

Warner Bros. quickly followed up *Little Caesar* with *Public Enemy* in 1931. Made by veteran director William Wellman, the new picture surpassed *Little Caesar* in its realism, its complexity of story, and its indictment of American society. *Public Enemy* chronicles the career of Tommy Powers, a young man from a poor working-class district who savors the high life-style of the wealthy mobster. Tommy, played with ebullient energy by James Cagney, takes up crime as a boy and then, with brutal efficiency, moves up the ranks of organized crime. He, too, is a Horatio Alger; though he never obtains as much control or status as Rico, he has more fun. Powers likes alcohol, partying, and blondes. Tommy is witty and engaging and, despite the fact that he also shoots people, he is presented as a hero. In this film, those who have honest jobs and play by the legal rules fail. If you want to win, *Public Enemy* seems to say, be like Tommy Powers.

Tommy enjoys his life immensely; nevertheless, he too will die, murdered by rival hoodlums while lying helpless, recovering from wounds. The gangsters of these films meet violent ends; Hollywood was unwilling to risk the wrath of censors by letting screen criminals off completely. Significantly, though, the film gangster's death usually does not illustrate a crime-does-not-pay moral or occur in order that justice be upheld. Rarely does a protagonist's demise have much to do with the nature of his crimes. He succumbs because of a personal weakness—in Rico's case, affection for an old buddy—or, like Tommy, from power struggles within the underworld. In facing death, the film gangster is often given stature and nobility; he becomes a tragic hero.

The gangster films' primary focus, however, is on these men's lives, not their deaths, and their lives are sagas of achievement. In the midst of economic chaos and spiritual malaise, they make money in adventurous ways and enjoy great material comfort. They are common men, men of the city, men often of immigrant roots. In other words, they are men with whom millions can identify. They advance by their own talents and without hypocrisy. In a society in which the stock-market crash had revealed many business, professional, and political leaders as frauds, the screen gangsters do not cover up what they are. Although they break the law, the law as presented in these films is either corrupt or irrelevant. In *Little Caesar,* the top criminal in the city, the only man more powerful than Rico, is clearly an established member of the upper-class governing elite. There are no courts, and police, when they appear, are ineffectual at best. The police may show up at the end of a film to kill the gangster, as they do in *Little Caesar*; however, such endings are usually tagged-on resolutions that have little to do with the logic of the films' plots. By the time the police appear, the protagonist is already finished. In *Public Enemy,* neither law nor government exists. The society belongs to those who will seize control.

Box-office triumphs, *Little Caesar* and *Public Enemy* generated a host of similar films. From *Little Caesar's* release through 1932, the industry released dozens of gangster films. Americans wanted to see gangster pictures; the individualistic criminal as a culture hero and the savage portrayal of American society struck responsive chords. There were other reasons, too, for the outlaw's fascination. Gangsters were part of the daily scene, not simply creations of Hollywood's imagination. Every major city had its colorful mobsters, and their contemporary notoriety must have enhanced the genre's attraction. Moreover, Prohibition still existed. Gangsters provided alcohol for the average citizen, and many Americans were willing to accept them as long as they only killed one another and kept the booze flowing. The gangster films, by the nature of their subject matter, also included a good deal of sex and violence, which have always been popular with audiences. During the Depression, they seemed especially popular as escapist elements.

While the gangster film helped to revive Hollywood's fortunes, there were many in society who were outraged by the new genre. Religious and other groups that sought to monitor community standards complained loudly about the films' level of sex and violence, glorification of the criminal, and disparaging view of law and order. Killing off the mobsters did not satisfy them. As protests mounted, independent producer Howard Hughes released *Scarface.*

Directed by Howard Hawks, who, like Wellman, was an established filmmaker, *Scarface* purportedly deals with Al Capone, the best-known gangster in 1930's America. Capone, whose nickname was "Scarface," supposedly was the model for Tony Calmonte, the film's protagonist. Actually, there is little of Capone's career or personality portrayed in the film. Capone was an ugly, bestial, thug of a man. Tony Calmonte, as played by Paul Muni, is good-looking, somewhat boyish, and occasionally naïve. Hardly a brute, although certainly murderous, Tony is almost a composite of Rico and Tommy. Determined to get to the top and merciless in his methods, Tony does take over the city. As he does so, however, he indulges himself with women and spends his ill-gotten gains along the way. Muni's Calmonte is a man with a gun in his hand and a twinkle in his eye, a likable killer.

Although the film's story is the familiar one of a hood's progress, Hawks' direction makes *Scarface* special. Hawks utilizes a fast pace, goes well beyond the normal gangster film in both body count and sexual suggestiveness, and wraps the whole film with an absorbing, impressionistic visual style. Tony, of course, dies at the end; he is one of those with a weakness. Hawks, though, makes Tony's flaw singularly different: Tony has incestuous feelings for his sister. When he discovers his best friend has gone off with his sister, he kills him. The sister informs on Tony, and the police, who have spent the film doing little besides occasionally bemoaning their powerlessness, show up at the end to kill Tony. It takes large numbers of them, and a huge shootout scene, to get Tony Calmonte, who goes down with almost operatic grandeur.

Impact of Event

Scarface would be the last of the seminal gangster films of the 1930's. By 1933, the cycle was ending. The election of Franklin Delano Roosevelt was a major factor; as Roosevelt's New Deal took hold, people felt that the government was finally doing something to help them. The angry national mood that had sustained the gangster films' appeal diminished considerably. Roosevelt also ended Prohibition, eliminating any need for most people to feel grateful to organized crime. Most important, outcries against films depicting America as sick, films with too much sex and killing—especially mobster films—became deafening. Church and civic groups threatened boycotts, censors raged at state and local levels, and possible federal intervention loomed. Hollywood panicked. After *Scarface*'s release in mid-1932, the studios began curtailing gangster production and moving to a self-censoring system to maintain control of their films. Theoretically, Hollywood had regulated itself since the 1920's, but the program was feeble. In 1933 and 1934, the studios accepted a tougher production code that was to keep sex, excessive violence, severe disrespect for society, and glorification of such nasty people as gangsters out of films for decades.

The new code at first kept the mobster off the screen, but soon he began a slow comeback. He had been so popular, had made the studios so much money, that they were loathe to part with him. By 1935, Hollywood decided to make gangster films again, although with differences. There would be less violence and no sex. The moral message of the film must be clear: Crime does not pay. Government and the law, particularly the federal government in the person of the Federal Bureau of Investigation (FBI) agent, or "G-man"—and not the criminals—must be presented as admirable.

With these changes, the gangster returned. His hard edge gone, he was no longer the gutsy protagonist making his way in lawless world. The spirits of Rico, Tommy Powers, and Tony Calmonte, however, were hard to lay. As the years went by, the gangster subtly and incrementally took control of films. While law-and-order themes prevailed through World War II, the screen gangster emerged increasingly as a more potent, attractive character, and in postwar America, he once more came into his own. The code atrophied, and the crime film again became popular at the box office. Many of the same themes of the early 1930's reappeared: sex, violence, a corrupt, lawless society, and the mobster as success story. Shaken by such issues as the Vietnam War, Watergate, urban problems, and economic stagnation, America remained troubled, and the film gangster continued to serve as a representative of people disillusioned by the distance between the American Dream and its actuality. Many of the numerous *film noir* pictures of the late 1940's and the 1950's, as well as films of later decades such as *The Godfather* (1972) and its sequels, *GoodFellas* (1990), and *Bugsy* (1991), are heirs of the early 1930's, and their protagonists are often similar to those of *Little Caesar, Public Enemy*, and *Scarface.*

Bibliography

Bergman, Andrew. *We're in the Money: Depression America and Its Films.* New York: New York University Press, 1971. An excellent study of the Depression through its films. Bergman provides an analysis of the gangster genre and also looks at other film types that reveal discontent with American society. The book is fairly short and contains an index and a most helpful bibliography.

Clarens, Carlos. *Crime Movies: From Griffith to "The Godfather" and Beyond.* New York: W. W. Norton, 1980. A comprehensive history of the crime film. Clarens writes for both the film buff and the serious cinema scholar. He examines most of the major crime films, and his discussion of the gangster genre is full and insightful. Fully illustrated, with more than three hundred pages of text, index, and bibliography.

Mast, Gerald. *Howard Hawks, Storyteller.* New York: Oxford University Press, 1982. A biography and also a study of Hawks' films. A valuable source for anyone who wishes to learn more about the making of *Scarface* and its different layers of meaning. Full bibliography, filmography, and index.

Roffman, Peter, and Jim Purdy. *The Hollywood Social Problem Film: Madness, Despair, and Politics from the Depression to the Fifties.* Bloomington: Indiana University Press, 1981. A study of the social-problem film from the Depression to the 1950's. Contains an important, if brief, discussion of the gangster film and looks at other pivotal Depression films. Most of the book deals with the 1930's. Index, select bibliography, and filmography.

Warshow, Robert. *The Immediate Experience: Movies, Comics, Theatre, and Other Aspects of Popular Culture.* Garden City, N.Y.: Doubleday, 1962. Warshow's book is a series of essays on popular culture. One of these essays, "The Gangster as Tragic Hero," is generally considered one of the most important and original analyses of the meaning of the early gangster films.

Clarke Wilhelm

Cross-References

The Maltese Falcon Introduces the Hard-Boiled Detective Novel (1929), p. 793; Hollywood Enters Its Golden Age (1930's), p. 822; Hitchcock Becomes England's Foremost Director (1934), p. 946; The Sherlock Holmes Film Series Begins (1939), p. 1131; *The Maltese Falcon* Establishes a New Style for Crime Films (1941), p. 1223; The Hollywood Studio System Is Transformed (1946), p. 1307; *Dragnet* Is the First Widely Popular Police Show (1951), p. 1531.

VON STERNBERG MAKES DIETRICH A SUPERSTAR

Category of event: Motion pictures
Time: 1930-1935
Locale: Hollywood, California

In a series of seven films from 1930 to 1935, the Austrian-born director Josef von Sternberg created a hauntingly ambiguous myth of womanhood, using Marlene Dietrich as Galatea to his Pygmalion

Principal personages:
> JOSEF VON STERNBERG (1894-1969), a film director, cameraman, and superb technician who perceived film as an aesthetic, not a narrative, experience
> MARLENE DIETRICH (1901-1992), a film star and theater performer extraordinaire who made seven films with von Sternberg
> TRAVIS BANTON (1894-?), a costume designer at Paramount who carried von Sternberg's ideas to completion to give Dietrich an iconic power
> LEE GARMES (1898-1978), a director of photography who shot the first three of Dietrich's American films

Summary of Event

In the fall of 1929, Josef von Sternberg was in Germany to film *Der blaue Engel* (1930; *The Blue Angel*). His involvement in this project, which was under the aegis of the famous *Universarium Film* studios in Berlin, derived from his earlier collaboration in the United States with the famous German actor Emil Jannings. He had directed Jannings in the 1928 film *The Last Command*, and Jannings was sufficiently impressed to ask for von Sternberg to direct the first German sound film to be made for Universarium with Eric Pommer as producer. Von Sternberg agreed, since his career was on the slide in Hollywood; as usual, though, he insisted on having complete control of the project. Complete control extended to the selection of the female lead to play opposite Jannings. Both Jannings and Pommer supported the casting of either Trude Hesterberg or Lucie Mannheim for the part, but von Sternberg had a specific idea of character, and neither of those women fit his idea. The woman he wanted was someone akin to the woman who comes to the poet in Percy Bysshe Shelley's *Alastor* as he sleeps. She is the vision of his own soul, her voice speaking "knowledge and truth and virtue." Von Sternberg found this woman in Marlene Dietrich.

Dietrich became for von Sternberg a summation of the Romantic beauty, the fatal woman whose effect on men is simultaneously liberating and imprisoning. Richly complex, this woman exists as metaphor of the male desire forever frustrated; yet she also represents the woman as Other, as necessarily lonely because the world cannot accommodate such independence and erotic power. She is a fetish, the object of the male gaze and the objectification of his desire. Even Dietrich's name "Marlene"—a contraction of her given names Maria Magdalene—indicates her ambiguity. In his memoir, *Fun in a Chinese Laundry* (1965), von Sternberg indicated his interest in this fatal woman, especially in her decadent, late nineteenth century form, when he notes that the specifications for the woman he wanted for his film "had been drawn up by Felicien Rops," a Belgian artist who was popular in the late 1880's. In Rops's work, the woman is polymorphously erotic; in her, innocence and experience come together. While attending the theater one night, von Sternberg found the woman he had imagined.

Marlene Dietrich, it seems, was reluctant to play the character, Lola-Lola; she thought she was not attractive enough for the part. Indeed, she was, in the words of Herman Weinberg, a "plump, pretty dumpling," and she conducted herself lethargically at the first interview she had with the film's director. Von Sternberg, however, persevered, and soon "she behaved as if she were there as my servant. . . . Not the slightest resistance was offered to my domination of her performance." In her autobiography, *Marlene* (1989), Dietrich substantiated this, noting that von Sternberg set out to "Pygmalionize" her; she credited him with having "breathed life into this nothingness. . . . I was nothing but pliable material on the infinitely rich palette of his ideas and imaginative faculties."

Before *The Blue Angel* was released in the United States, American audiences saw Dietrich in *Morocco* (1930). For that film, she had shed thirty pounds, and her face had begun to take on a mysteriously contoured look, as von Sternberg's camera and lighting played over it with effective shadows. As she had in *The Blue Angel*, Dietrich played a cabaret singer. This time, she is Amy Jolly, a woman with a past who has traveled to Morocco, the end of the line for her, it seems. Two men seek her affections, the rangy legionnaire Tom Brown (Gary Cooper) and the suave and wealthy Frenchman LeBessiere (Adolphe Menjou). The plot is simple, even melodramatic: Offered wealth and security by LeBressiere, Amy Jolly turns her back on community and follows her soldier into the desert. More important than the melodramatic plot is the play of light and shadow on the screen and the ambiguous sexuality of Dietrich. In her first appearance in the cabaret, she wears a man's top hat and tails; in one famous scene, she leans over to plant a kiss on the lips of a giggling girl in the audience.

Dietrich and von Sternberg followed *Morocco* with a spy thriller, *Dishonored* (1931), in which Dietrich plays a prostitute-turned-spy known as "X-27." The story is von Sternberg's. As Amy Jolly sacrificed a life of leisure and comfort for her man, so too does X-27 sacrifice her life for her lover, Lieutenant Kranau (Victor McLaglen). In this film, von Sternberg extends the range of Dietrich's character portrayal and her costumes. Lee Garmes photographs her to look like Greta Garbo, like a country maid, and like the Dietrich who would become legendary. Travis Banton arrays her in all sorts of costumes. The film reaches its high point as X-27 faces the firing squad. She takes a blindfold from the young officer who offers it to her, wipes a tear from his eye, then adjusts her makeup and straightens her stockings. Before the sound of the guns, von Sternberg cuts quickly to a close-up of X-27's enigmatic smile. America's Depression-era audiences loved it.

Von Sternberg, though, felt that further collaboration would be harmful to both himself and his star. Dietrich disagreed. She refused to work with another director, and Paramount brought the two of them together for *Shanghai Express* (1932). The opening of this film is remarkable for von Sternberg's masterful re-creation of Peking, the claustrophobia of its streets echoed in the claustrophobia of train compartments and corridors. Again, Dietrich appears as a woman of questionable behavior. She is Shanghai Lily: "It took more than one man to change my name to Shanghai Lily," she tells Donald Harvey (Clive Brook). Unlike Lola-Lola but like the characters in her American films with von Sternberg, the Dietrich character in *Shanghai Express* may be fallen, but she is not without honor and loyalty. She appears ready to sacrifice herself for her lover, although here von Sternberg is less forthright than in the earlier films. Perhaps more than any other of the von Sternberg-Dietrich films, *Shanghai Express* captures the mysterious beauty of Dietrich. Lee Garmes won an Oscar for the film's cinematography, and both the film itself and its director received nominations.

As much as von Sternberg's visual style captures the viewer, especially as it affects the appearance of Dietrich, his use of sound is equally significant. Unlike many in Hollywood who feared the coming of sound to the film industry, von Sternberg welcomed it as another element in the aesthetic effect of film. He avoided the use of background music; instead, he incorporated natural sound into the filmic effect. For example, in *Morocco* he uses no music; instead, the drums of the legionnaires punctuate the action and intensify the emotional effect of the scene in which Amy hears them approach and realizes she must seek out her true lover. In *The Blue Angel*, sound articulates place: The classroom, the cabaret, the dressing room. The guns that fire to execute X-27 in *Dishonoured* reverberate in the airplane hanger von Sternberg used to film the sequence. In *Shanghai Express*, the actors speak in monotone to complement the sound of the train. Similarly, the thudding tempo of Dietrich's "Hot Voodoo" number in *Blonde Venus* (1932) accentuates the soap-opera emotionalism of the story.

Blonde Venus is generally taken to be the most autobiographical of von Sternberg's films with Dietrich. Once again, however, the surface is the thing to catch the eye and interest of the audience. The film shimmers with light right from the opening sequence, in which Dietrich bathes nude in a glitteringly bright forest lake. The subtleties of light and shade are once again a cue to the film's interest in style, and the conventional ending with Dietrich—the film's Venus—returning to her son and husband is a perfunctory addition. Von Sternberg's great strength is to present on film both reality and the fantasy world lying deep within his audience. Much of the play with light and shade and enclosed space evokes a dream world, but not the dream world of Hollywood musicals or comedies. Von Sternberg's dream world is the dream world of the unconscious. He was fascinated with mental aberration, the depths of desire, anxiety, fear, and the urge to violence.

All of this comes together in a baroque manner in the penultimate film von Sternberg made with Dietrich, *The Scarlet Empress* (1934). Ostensibly the story of Catherine the Great of Russia, *The Scarlet Empress* shows von Sternberg at his most excessive: Camera angles, sets, costumes, cutting, and other film techniques draw attention to themselves in every frame. Much of the film offers a shot-by-shot rhythm of frames that alternate between light and dark. The sets are large-scale; gargoyles and grotesque sculptures leer at the viewer from the screen. Dietrich herself is nearly lost in furs or amid sculptures, candles, fog, or smoke. Von Sternberg called the film "a relentless excursion into style."

After *The Scarlet Empress*, one film remained in the pair's collaboration; von Sternberg had done all he could with his Galatea. He would complete only seven films in the next thirty-five years of his life. For her part, Dietrich was also ready to move on. An intelligent and gifted actor and performer, she would have a brilliant career in film and on stage. First, though, the two consummated their artistic relationship with *The Devil Is a Woman* (1935). Once again the costumes are varied and chic. Parades, festivals, confetti, and balloons decorate the screen. Aluminum paint was sprayed on dresses and backgrounds to give von Sternberg complete control over light. The film is a fitting conclusion to the years of collaboration between von Sternberg and Dietrich. She called the film their "crowning achievement" and "the most beautiful film that was ever made."

Impact of Event

It is easy to see the influence of von Sternberg's silent gangster film *Underworld* (1927); what is less clear is the influence of the seven films he made with Marlene Dietrich. Indeed, these films are strange genre pieces. Later films continued to exploit these familiar genres: the Foreign Legion film, the spy thriller, the journey through dangerous territory, the domestic tragedy, the historical romance. No one else who made such films, though, dismissed plot with such insistence as von Sternberg. Luis Buñuel comes to mind as a director who likes to use formula plots for ideological purposes, but his art is more directly social than von Sternberg's. For von Sternberg, emotion was style. Perhaps the closest parallel of the time was Busby Berkeley, whose 1930 musicals dispense with plot in order to present a choreography of camera, costume, and design.

Von Sternberg's high-key lighting shows up in many films of the 1930's, including Rouben Mamoulian's *Song of Songs* (1933), with Dietrich, John Ford's *Mary, Queen of Scots* (1936), with Katherine Hepburn, and Howard Hawks's *Barbary Coast* (1935), with Miriam Hopkins. In the 1940's, his lighting effects were used in such Michael Curtiz films as *Casablanca* (1942), with Ingrid Bergman, and *Mildred Pierce* (1945), with Joan Crawford; in Hitchcock's *Notorious* (1946), with Bergman; and in Orson Welles's *The Lady from Shanghai* (1948), with Rita Hayworth. Bob Fosse's *Cabaret* (1972), with Liza Minnelli, also echoes the costumes and ambience of *The Blue Angel.* On a more technical level, von Sternberg's tendency to avoid cutting within scenes, his use of lighting and angles to create mood, and his use of natural sound anticipated the work of Michelangelo Antonioni.

Finally, the woman fashioned by von Sternberg continued to serve Dietrich well in many roles, from Frank Borzage's *Desire* (1936) to Billy Wilder's *Witness for the Prosecution* (1957). Many echoes of her beauty appear on the screen, from Joan Crawford to Anouk Aimee.

Bibliography

Baxter, John. *The Cinema of Josef von Sternberg.* New York: A. S. Barnes, 1971. Provides cogent readings of all von Sternberg's films. Shows how the stylish aspects of the films make sense thematically. Good appreciation of von Sternberg's technique: use of sound, light, cross-cutting, wipes, tracking shots, and so on. Nicely points out the irony of von Sternberg's obsession: The woman he fashioned becomes his undoing. Select bibliography and fairly accurate filmography.

Baxter, Peter, ed. *Sternberg.* London: British Film Institute, 1980. A collection of seventeen articles dating from 1930 to 1980. Includes the famous essay by Aeneas MacKenzie, "Leonardo of the Lenses," and essays by Rudolph Arnheim, Siegfried Kracauer, Barry Salt, and von Sternberg himself. The essay on *Morocco* by the editorial staff of *Cahiers du Cinema* offers a detailed analysis of the film's social milieu.

Dietrich, Marlene. *Marlene.* Translated by Salvator Attanasio. New York: Grove Press, 1989. Covers much of the same ground as von Sternberg's *Fun in a Chinese Laundry.* Dietrich's admiration for von Sternberg is unbounded. She has perceptive things to say about lighting and camera work. Opinionated, idiosyncratic, and delightfully candid, even if Dietrich's memory fails at times.

Nichols, Bill. *Ideology and the Image.* Bloomington: Indiana University Press, 1981. Chapter 4 presents a detailed semiotic analysis of *Blonde Venus.* Short sections examine "Sternberg and the Critics," "Editing," "Lighting," "Decor," "Clothing," and "Performance." The analysis is helped by the strategic use of still photographs. Nichols' thesis is that the film's visual style deals not with pleasure but with "the control of pleasure."

Sarris, Andrew. *The Films of Josef von Sternberg.* Garden City, N.Y.: Doubleday, 1966. A short, readable survey of von Sternberg's films. Sarris is a perceptive viewer of actors, and he has much to say regarding Dietrich's performances in each film. He also accepts von Sternberg's evaluation of himself as a poet. For Sarris, these films are dream poems to be appreciated for their visual delights.

Spoto, Donald. *Falling in Love Again: Marlene Dietrich.* Boston: Little, Brown, 1985. The title indicates Spoto's affection for his subject. He gives a brief and useful survey of the years of collaboration between von Sternberg and Dietrich. No index or filmography, but many exquisite photographs.

Von Sternberg, Josef. *Fun in a Chinese Laundry.* New York: Collier, 1965. Meandering, eccentric, and fascinating account of the author's life and theory of filmmaking. Not always accurate, but always provocative. With regard to Dietrich, he notes: "I gave her nothing that she did not already have." He makes clear his interest in film as a two-dimensional canvas on which he paints his images.

Weinberg, Herman G. *Josef von Sternberg: A Critical Study.* New York: E. P. Dutton, 1967. The work of an idolator; however, the book is useful because it contains an interview with von Sternberg, a few excerpts from his correspondence, passages from the shooting scripts of *Shanghai Express* and *The Saga of Anatahan* (1953), a good selection of early reviews of von Sternberg's work. Filmography and bibliography.

Roderick McGillis

Cross-References

The Cabinet of Dr. Caligari Opens in Berlin (1920), p. 486; Von Stroheim Films His Silent Masterpiece *Greed* (1924), p. 593; Sound Technology Revolutionizes the Motion-Picture Industry (1928), p. 761; Hollywood Enters Its Golden Age (1930's), p. 822; Berkeley's *42nd Street* Revolutionizes Film Musicals (1933), p. 925; Lubitsch's *The Merry Widow* Opens New Vistas for Film Musicals (1934), p. 941; *Top Hat* Establishes the Astaire-Rogers Dance Team (1935), p. 984.

CRANE PUBLISHES *THE BRIDGE*

Category of event: Literature
Time: February, 1930
Locale: New York, New York

This dauntingly ambitious and difficult modernist poem was characteristic of its times in Crane's effort to see modern urban America in mythological terms

Principal personages:
    HART CRANE (1899-1932), a poet born in Garrettsville, Ohio, who made a major contribution to American modernist poetics before his suicide in 1932
    T. S. ELIOT (1888-1965), a modernist poet who wrote *The Waste Land* (1922) and other poems
    JAMES JOYCE (1882-1941), a leading Irish novelist whose major works include *Ulysses* (1922) and *Finnegans Wake* (1939)
    WALT WHITMAN (1819-1892), the epic poet of nineteenth century America whose most famous work is the long poem "Song of Myself" (1855)

Summary of Event

Hart Crane began work on his long poem *The Bridge* in 1923. He conceived this epic work as a rejoinder to the pessimism and sense of apocalyptic decline expressed in T. S. Eliot's epochal poem *The Waste Land*, which had been published in 1922. Though Crane much admired Eliot, he felt *The Waste Land*, with its representation of the sterility of civilization after World War I, had not done justice to the energy and excitement of the modern urban and industrial era. Hence Crane began, slowly and methodically, to put together an idiomatically American synthesis of the twentieth century machine age.

Crane's work on the poem through the 1920's was fitful and was interrupted by bouts of alcoholism, depression, and foreign travel, as well as by numerous homosexual affairs. His most productive period came in 1926, the year that also saw the publication of *White Buildings*, a collection of his shorter lyric pieces. During the late 1920's, Crane's epic endeavor attracted the private sponsorship of Otto H. Kahn, a wealthy banker, and it was Kahn's support that helped Crane to complete the poem. *The Bridge* finally appeared in a special edition printed by the Black Sun Press in February, 1930, before being published in America by Liveright in April of the same year.

The Bridge is made up of nine sections. It starts with an introductory "Proem: To Brooklyn Bridge," set in 1920's Manhattan, which hails Brooklyn Bridge as modern-day deity mysteriously empowered to "lend a myth" to the capitalist affairs of Wall

Street. This is followed by "Ave Maria," which features Christopher Columbus in mid-Atlantic narrating the story of his discovery of America as he returns home to Spain. Section 2 of *The Bridge* is entitled "Powhatan's Daughter" and encompasses five distinct shorter poems that recount the history of Native American life. With section 3, "Cutty Sark," the reader returns to a saloon in lower Manhattan, where old sailors recall their seafaring adventures; section 4, "Cape Hatteras," then focuses upon epic exploits of the air, notably the aviation experiments conducted in 1903 by Wilbur and Orville Wright off the coast of North Carolina. Section 5, "Three Songs," again brings the reader back to the world of twentieth century New York; one of the section's three shorter poems, "National Winter Garden," takes its title from a burlesque theater in Greenwich Village that Crane used to frequent. Section 6, "Quaker Hill," proceeds to cast a jaundiced eye at golf courses in suburban Connecticut. Section 7, "The Tunnel," describes an infernal and nightmarish subway ride from Manhattan to Flatbush, passing under the East River and so beneath the Brooklyn Bridge; the final section, "Atlantis," circles back to the poem's first image of the deified bridge, a construction now found to be illuminated with an intense mythological splendor.

No simple narrative description of *The Bridge*, however, can capture the full extent of Crane's artistic ambitions in this work. He aspired to invent an aesthetic design of multiple interlocking strands, so as to bring to light—and into an idealistic harmony—suppressed analogies between different geographical areas and historical eras in American life. Crane's goal was indeed to evoke a series of conceptual bridges: the railway bridging the American continent, the Wright brothers' bridging of land and air, bridges between the white man and the Indian, between childhood and adulthood, between fifteenth century Christopher Columbus and twentieth century Columbus Circle in New York City. Thus, each section of *The Bridge* anticipates and echoes all the other sections. As Crane himself said in a 1926 letter, his poetic technique can be seen as "symphonic in including the convergence of all the strands" introduced separately within the narrative structure of the poem.

On one level, then, Crane was reinventing the kind of mythic version of America that Walt Whitman had promulgated during the nineteenth century. Indeed, Crane explicitly pays tribute to Whitman in "Cape Hatteras," saluting the great "Saunterer" as a pioneer who sought to impose a mythic form upon the most unpromising and inchoate American materials. Crane's own style, though, should be understood as Whitman crossed with Eliot and James Joyce, for Crane believed Whitman's language of bluff, colloquial Romanticism to be no longer adequate to address the complexities and dislocations of modern life. Instead, Crane, like Eliot and Joyce, used a dense and complicated mixture of verbal allusion and wordplay to convey his sense of the fragmented and radically unstable landscape of technological society. Crane was very interested in the first installments of Joyce's *Finnegans Wake* (1939)—then known as "Work in Progress"—which were being published during the late 1920's in the Parisian magazine *transition*, and Joyce's elaboration of punning as a narrative principle in that work was something Crane also chose to pursue, working with the idea of the pun as a bridge between disparate meanings.

Crane himself visited Paris in 1929 while putting the final touches to *The Bridge*. At the time, the French capital was home not only to Joyce but also to the Surrealist movement in art and literature, and throughout his career, Crane was conversant with the self-reflexive strategies of Surrealists such as Marcel Duchamp and Man Ray, whose perception of art as an ingenious but ultimately nihilistic game also came to influence certain aspects of the American poet's work. *The Bridge*, in fact, is shot through with moments of black humor in which its visionary idyll seems knowingly to collapse into self-parodic or burlesque forms. There is in Crane's poem an element of deliberate buffoonery, a dark self-mockery that does not altogether cancel the poem's mythological idealism but that holds it in an ambiguous suspension. It was not by chance that Crane fixed upon the image of a suspension bridge to convey his sense of how mythological transformation might (or might not) operate within the hardheaded business world of Manhattan.

Impact of Event

Immediate reaction to publication of *The Bridge* was disappointing. Crane's poem finally appeared only a few months after the Wall Street crash, and the literary climate of the early 1930's was no longer favorable to the poem's dense and cryptic style of high modernism. *The Bridge* materialized at the moment when American writing was developing methods of journalistic realism that had more direct social and political relevance to the Great Depression era; within that context, Crane's ornate rhetoric appeared uncomfortably inward-looking and self-indulgent. Even intellectuals such as Allen Tate and Yvor Winters, who had both encouraged Crane when he was writing the poem, were lukewarm in their response to the final product. In part, this happened because Crane's idiosyncratic brand of hyperbolic wordplay did not conform to any definition of "myth" sanctioned by the classical learning Tate and Winters admired. Crane was depressed at these responses, but he spent time in Mexico on a Guggenheim Fellowship during 1931 and 1932, and he began to plan another epic poem, this time centered on Hernán Cortés' conquest of Mexico. He completed only a few fragments of this work, however; gray-haired and exhausted by his emotional traumas and intellectual travails, Crane took his own life on April 27, 1932, by jumping into the Caribbean Sea from the SS *Orizaba* as he was returning home from Mexico to New York.

The most obvious long-term effect of *The Bridge* was its validation of American urban life as a fit subject for poetry. As Crane wrote in his "Modern Poetry," his intention was to ensure that the environment of the machine could form "as spontaneous a terminology of poetic reference as the bucolic world of pasture, plow, and barn." The Beat poets of the 1950's were to build upon this idea of a visionary quality implicit within everyday urban life, as was another Manhattan poet of that period, Frank O'Hara. In fact, *The Bridge* helped to redress a long-standing imbalance in the American poetic tradition, which up until Crane's time had been weighted heavily toward the rural and pastoral mode.

For thirty years after Crane's death, however, the most common reaction to *The Bridge* was that the poem represented a heroic but ultimately pathetic failure. It was held to be a frustrated attempt to invent a grandiose myth of America, a myth that could not be sustained either by the mundane, lapsed environment of the twentieth century or by the erratic lyric gifts at Crane's disposal. Philip Horton's 1937 biography of Crane characterized the poet as a lost romantic soul, helping to reinforce this image of noble self-immolation, which lasted for more than a quarter of a century. During the 1950's, for example, Allen Ginsberg in several poems invoked Crane as a doomed victim of corporate America, a homosexual iconoclast and visionary whose genius had been crushed by the impersonal weight of the nation's unfeeling commercial culture. Robert Lowell's poem "Words for Hart Crane," published in his 1959 collection *Life Studies*, paints a similar picture of Crane as a tortured *poète maudite*, "the Shelley of my age." At this time, the legend of Crane's short and robustious life was still overshadowing the legacy of his poetic achievement, and it was not until the 1960's that critics began paying more attention to the intricacies and achievements of Crane's texts themselves.

Gradually, though, the aesthetic impact of *The Bridge* began to be felt. A spate of fine close readings during the 1960's and 1970's was supported by the publication of John Unterecker's massive biography, *Voyager: A Life of Hart Crane* in 1969. Since that time, interest in Crane's work has continued to grow. In the 1980's, a new generation of critics such as Lee Edelman and Thomas E. Yingling wrote of Crane as having developed a radical style of gay poetics, an elliptical series of rhetorical tropes that in failing to acquiesce to the orthodox conventions of language could be seen as mirroring Crane's own ambivalent stance toward the dominant ideologies of American society. It is also significant that postmodernist writers of long poems such as Richard Howard and Alfred Corn have acknowledged a greater debt to Crane than to the "concrete" poets of mid-century such as Charles Olson. Whereas Olson's style of clear-eyed realism could be seen as antithetical to Crane's thrusting rhetoric, Corn's narrative poem *Notes from a Child of Paradise* (1984) conjoins epic and mock-epic in a way very reminiscent of Crane's edgy tone in *The Bridge*. Corn has also written an admiring critical essay on *The Bridge*, and these two long poems also resemble each other in their uneasy juxtaposition of public concerns with private identities, their teasing affiliation between objective myth and subjective romance, and their knowing interrogation of how precisely one side of this equation depends upon the other.

For many years, *The Bridge* was seen as something of a white elephant in American literary history: an ambitious and impressive event, but also a strange, puzzling, and ultimately perturbing one. Yet what in the 1930's was generally perceived as a weakness—Crane's refusal to adopt any standard intellectual formula for his mythic endeavor—has in many later critics' eyes been revealed as an unexpected source of strength. Because the poet enjoyed an oblique relationship with the aesthetic conventions of American modernism, *The Bridge* has managed subsequently to keep its distance from the various large-scale theories about a misplaced mythopoeic idealism that is sometimes said to constitute the "failure of modernism." Crane was never emotionally or intellectually wedded to utopian ideals in the manner of T. S. Eliot or Ezra Pound; rather, the ubiquitous element of mythic gamesmanship in *The Bridge* distinguishes it as a work touched more by the Surrealist mode. From this perspective, the poem's quirky humor and self-mocking wordplay lend it an elusive quality that the more solemn epic works of Eliot and Pound tend to lack. With its wry mixture of romanticism and subversive comedy, its delicate balance between sentimentalism and irony, *The Bridge* is a poem that continues to offer challenges and surprises to the reader.

Bibliography

Corn, Alfred. *The Metamorphoses of Metaphor: Essays in Poetry and Fiction.* New York: Viking Press, 1987. Considers the final section of *The Bridge* in relation to Crane's revision of utopian legends. Notes connections with Dante Alighieri and T. S. Eliot. Of special interest in the light of artistic parallels between *The Bridge* and Corn's own poetry.

Crane, Hart. *The Poems.* Edited by Marc Simon. New York: Liveright, 1968. The most complete edition of Crane's poetry. Includes *The Bridge* and all other published works, plus unpublished poems, incomplete works, and fragments.

Crane, Hart. *Letters, 1916-1932.* Edited by Brom Weber. Berkeley: University of California Press, 1965. The best single collection of Crane's letters to his friends, relatives, and publishers. Helpful for getting a sense of the range of Crane's interests. Marred by some editorial bowdlerizing.

Edelman, Lee. *Transmemberment of Song: Hart Crane's Anatomies of Rhetoric and Desire.* Stanford, Calif.: Stanford University Press, 1987. A general discussion of stylistic issues in Crane's work, followed by close attention to particular poems, including *The Bridge.* Especially perceptive in its psychoanalytical readings of Crane's poetry.

Giles, Paul. *Hart Crane: The Contexts of "The Bridge."* Cambridge, England: Cambridge University Press, 1986. Relates *The Bridge* to a series of historical and conceptual contexts, such as relativity, capitalism, burlesque theater, and European Surrealism. Places *The Bridge* within a particular historical framework, showing links between Crane's work and that of his artistic contemporaries.

Unterecker, John. *Voyager: A Life of Hart Crane.* New York: Farrar, Straus & Giroux, 1969. The lengthiest and most complete biography. Unterecker's method was to include anything that might possibly be of significance. Hence, the book is difficult to read from cover to cover, but indispensable for tracing particular aspects of Crane's life. Judicious use of the index is advised.

Yingling, Thomas E. *Hart Crane and the Homosexual Text: New Thresholds, New Anatomies.* Chicago: University of Chicago Press, 1990. Concentrates upon the development of Crane's poetic style in terms of a specifically homosexual aesthetic. Sees some of the alleged obscurity in Crane's work as connected with a general reluctance on the part of critics to engage with Crane's radical subject matter. Many perceptive readings, though—like many a reworked doctoral thesis—somewhat narrow in its approach.

Paul Giles

Cross-References

Harriet Monroe Founds *Poetry* Magazine (1912), p. 314; The Imagist Movement Shakes Up Poetry (1912), p. 326; Pound's *Cantos* Is Published (1917), p. 445; Eliot Publishes *The Waste Land* (1922), p. 539; Joyce's *Ulysses* Epitomizes Modernism in Fiction (1922), p. 555; Surrealism Is Born (1924), p. 604; *The Great Gatsby* Captures the Essence of the Roaring Twenties (1925), p. 626.

POEMS ESTABLISHES AUDEN AS A GENERATIONAL SPOKESMAN

Category of event: Literature
Time: September, 1930
Locale: London, England

The publication of W. H. Auden's Poems *in 1930 immediately established him as the spokesman for the interwar generation in Great Britain*

Principal personages:

W. H. AUDEN (1907-1973), an English poet and critic who was from a young age the acknowledged leader of a literary generation

T. S. ELIOT (1888-1965), a renowned poet and essayist who, as poetry editor for a London publisher, was responsible for seeing Auden into print

CHRISTOPHER ISHERWOOD (1904-1986), a close friend of Auden and the leading prose writer of the group claiming him as leader

CECIL DAY LEWIS (1904-1972), an Irish-born poet and early associate of Auden

LOUIS MACNEICE (1907-1963), an Anglo-Irish poet closely associated with Auden

STEPHEN SPENDER (1909-   ), a London-born poet and early promoter of Auden's poetry

Summary of Event

The University of Oxford in the late 1920's was a breeding ground for poets. When Wystan Hugh Auden entered Christ Church College in 1925, he soon met John Betjeman, Cecil Day Lewis, and Rex Warner, all of whom would make their marks as poets—and all of whom were impressed by the intelligence and talent of this eighteen-year-old from York. Subsequently, Auden and Day Lewis jointly edited the 1927 edition of *Oxford Poetry.* A year after Auden entered, Louis MacNeice enrolled at Merton College; though he and Auden were not close friends at Oxford, the two would be viewed as confederates a few years later.

Also in 1927, Auden submitted his first book of poems to Faber & Gwyer (later Faber and Faber), the London publisher whose poetry editor, T. S. Eliot, had leaped into prominence a decade before with the publication of his *Prufrock and Other Observations* (1917) and had attained the status of a major modern poet with *The Waste Land* (1922). Eliot rejected the book but, as Auden judged, offered encouragement.

Following his graduation in 1928, Auden issued a book of poems that was privately printed by another Oxford friend, Stephen Spender, then an undergraduate at University College. Thereafter, Auden left England to spend a year in Berlin, where he continued to read and write and incidentally witnessed the profound German unrest of the time. Violence between Communists and the police erupted on May Day, 1929, not far from where Auden lived. "All this time was anxiety at night,/ Shooting and barricade in street," he wrote. Both the violence and the anxiety would become characteristic Auden themes. Returning to England two months later, Auden found employment in London as a tutor; the following year, he secured a position teaching English and French in a private boys' school in Scotland. Around this time, Faber accepted for publication Auden's *Poems* (1930), a totally different collection from the 1927 submission, though containing some poems from the 1928 effort.

By 1930, the errors of the World War I settlement were becoming obvious. A worldwide economic depression had set in, and communism, fascism, and Nazism were becoming household words. It was a time when young artists and intellectuals could hardly have escaped preoccupation with social and governmental ills, and Auden's early poetry, despite its obscurity, ushered in a period in which young poets expressed the bitterness and frustration of a failed economic order and—as became increasingly clearer—a failed peace.

According to Spender, Auden did not think of himself as the leader of a movement or as a public figure. In his poetry, he was trying to apply the techniques he had learned from such older poets as Eliot and William Butler Yeats to the composition of poems that spoke to a generation embittered by the economic breakdown, by the drift toward dictatorial regimes in some European countries, and by the complicity of free nations. A number of the poetic movements of recent generations, such as French Symbolism, "art for art's sake," and Imagism, had produced a private poetry of interest mainly to sophisticated coteries; Auden and his companions—particularly Spender, Day Lewis, and MacNeice—wanted to bring poetry within the orbit of people distressed by the political and social evils of the time.

Insofar as Auden and his contemporaries had a literary hero, it was Eliot; despite the older poet's bold new voice, however, he seemed too conservative to be a model. The year of Auden's first commercially published book was also the year of *Ash Wednesday* (1930), the first of Eliot's religious poems signaling his growing Church of England sympathies. While Auden saw that wasteland imagery effectively symbolized aspects of the modern world, Eliot seemed too detached, too much a part of the older generation that had inflicted that world on those in the new century. To Eliot, the modern city was "unreal"; to Auden (in a poem that came to be called "Family Ghosts"), it was "assaulted." *The Waste Land* is populated by merchants, habitués of pubs, and bored lovers; Auden's 1930 poems are populated by spies, secret agents, and vengeful proletarians. Eliot had heaped scorn upon decadents; Auden now warned against enemies.

The 1930 volume contained thirty-nine poems bearing roman numerals rather than titles, a feature that encouraged readers to regard them collectively as a kind of sequence rather than as an assortment from which one might pick and choose favorites. The first lines of the poems often projected urgency, even alarm: "Control of the passes was, he saw, the key" (VIII), "Consider this and in our time" (XXX),

"Get there if you can and see the land you once were proud to own" (XXXI), "Doom is dark and deeper than any sea-dingle" (XXXVII). Auden's voice differed distinctly from any heard before in English poetry.

Impact of Event

It would be a mistake to assume that Auden's book, despite its publisher, made a large impact on the literary establishment of 1930. *The Times Literary Supplement* found the poems "eccentric," and *The Listener* professed an inability to understand them at all. The favorable reviews came from Auden's Oxford friends Spender, Mac-Neice, and Day Lewis, more or less obscure young men who would, in time, be recognized as among the most important writers of their generation.

The impact on young activists in England, however, was immediate and profound. They took such lines as "Get there if you can and see the land you once were proud to own" as signifying the necessity of transforming a failed society. Auden had articulated in *Poems* what such activists had been feeling all along. Some joined the New Party, formed by a few Parliamentary dissidents in February of 1931 in opposition to the Labour Party, which had had little success in dealing with the massive unemployment caused by the 1929 stock market crash. Later that year, *Action*, a weekly radical newspaper, began publication. Auden did not contribute to the paper, but his friend Christopher Isherwood did. Hopes of engineering change by political means faded, however, when the New Party, some of whose spokesmen clearly frightened voters with assorted fascist and communist sentiments, won no seats in the general election of October, 1931.

The young people motivated by Auden were attempting not just political but also social reform. Formal education, seen as denying students the chance of developing free personalities, came under attack. Young radicals scorned marriage as an unnatural and immoral institution; they urged sexual freedom, including homosexual and bisexual relationships.

Auden's second book, *The Orators*, issued by Faber in 1932, created more of a stir in the literary establishment. Almost impossible to describe, the book is a mélange: hortatory prose, poems, diagrams, journal entries. The first part, heavily indebted to the thought of the recently deceased D. H. Lawrence, consists of four diverse "orations" united by a theme Auden referred to as "the failure of the romantic conception of personality." The second part, which critics found most interesting, expresses the plans of a dedicated but mentally disordered revolutionary leader. The third part consists of six odes that dramatize, ambiguously and often parodically, the sentiment for a leader who can "save" England.

As often happens with the second book of a previously neglected author, the new work drew attention back to the earlier one. Although few critics professed any great understanding of Auden's poetry, they agreed on the brilliance with which he had caught the perspective of his generation. He spoke for an embittered, confused, and worried generation with no settled views but with a sense of the need for action to remedy a civilization sinking deeper into a mire. Faith in democracy, capitalism, and traditional religion were all fast waning; the most committed people were either communists or fascists. Neither the obscurity of the book nor the apparent incoherence of its author's philosophy were regarded as flaws.

Not only did reviewers for *Criterion* and *The Times Literary Supplement* praise the book, but influential men of letters on both sides of the Atlantic also took notice. Edmund Wilson began advising his literary friends to read *The Orators, Poems,* and Auden's 1933 play *The Dance of Death.* The influential editor of *Scrutiny,* F. R. Leavis, chose to attack Auden's work, a sure sign of his growing importance. In retrospect, much of the criticism both pro and con looks imperceptive or even irrelevant, but it made Auden a very famous man while still in his mid-twenties.

Auden was essentially a private man much more interested in doing his own work than in leading a movement, but by force of his intellectual interests he was leading one anyway. No other poet could match his command of Freudian psychology, Marxist political theory, and general scientific knowledge. His formidable poetic vocabulary and the exceptionally wide range of his allusions confounded efforts to interpret individual poems, but collectively, they communicated an indelible impression of a poet fully engaged with the world and society of his time. Isherwood pointed out in 1937 that when Auden contemplated a ruin, it was not that of an ancient abbey such as Sir Walter Scott, William Wordsworth, or even Eliot might celebrate, but of an abandoned factory or mill. Auden's poetry accommodated subject matter outside the ken of other poets.

Many of the young Auden enthusiasts rushed off to support the Republican cause in the Spanish Civil War against General Francisco Franco, and some lost their lives there. Auden himself went to Spain for a few weeks early in 1937, presumably with the intention of driving an ambulance. He attributed the fact of his finding little to do there to his having failed to join the Communist Party.

When, later that year, Auden accepted the King's Medal for Poetry for his 1936 collection of poems *Look, Stranger!,* some of his support among young radicals fell away, but his general readership had increased greatly. Also in 1937, Geoffrey Grigson devoted one issue of his *New Verse* (which had been featuring Auden's poetry since its inception in 1932) entirely to articles about him.

An assessment of the impact of Auden's early poetry must take into account its effect on the poet. A comparison of Edward Mendelson's edition of *Collected Poems* (1976), including only those poems that Auden wished to preserve, and the same editor's *The English Auden: Poems, Essays, and Dramatic Writings, 1927-1939* (1977) demonstrates how many early poems Auden later rejected, including some of the incendiary ones that had excited his early champions. Whether dissatisfied with these poems or afraid that they distorted the body of his work by implying a Marxist outlook to which he never committed himself (although he was for a time in the 1930's taken up enthusiastically by Marxist critics), Auden did much throughout the 1930's to modify the impression that his poems of the late 1920's and very early 1930's had made on the reading public.

Finally, in a celebrated 1939 poem, Auden repudiated a conviction which, rightly or wrongly, both friendly and unfriendly critics had widely attributed to him. "In Memory of W. B. Yeats," following within weeks of the death of the great Irish poet, asserts that "poetry makes nothing happen." His point was not that poetry has no effect on people—quite the contrary—but that poetry is a celebration of its subject matter and of language itself. It is not propaganda, not a blueprint for a program.

Like Eliot before him, Auden turned religious, disappointing followers who, for the most part, continued to admire him immensely. He continued to write forcefully for more than three decades, but by 1940 he seemed less the leader of a poetic generation than the imposing individual he had always been.

Bibliography

Auden, W. H. *The English Auden: Poems, Essays, and Dramatic Writings, 1927-1939.* Edited by Edward Mendelson. New York: Random House, 1977. The works that established Auden in their complete and original versions as edited by Auden's literary executor. Mendelson meticulously re-creates a body of work some of which Auden, from the perspective of his maturity, sought to suppress.

Carpenter, Humphrey. *W. H. Auden: A Biography.* Boston: Houghton Mifflin, 1981. A comprehensive and extensively documented life of the poet. Carpenter has done a thorough job of tracing reviews of, and reactions to, Auden's early poems. Chiefly a chronological narrative, this book features considerable information about Auden's literary friends as well as many photographs of them. Contains a good bibliography of primary sources.

Hynes, Samuel. *The Auden Generation: Literature and Politics in England in the 1930's.* New York: Viking Press, 1976. In contrast to the Spender and Symons books, Hynes's is scrupulously scholarly and nonpartisan, with a firm and balanced sense of historical context. Hynes also illuminates the often neglected subject of the influences of Auden's contemporaries on his own development.

Spears, Monroe K., ed. *Auden: A Collection of Critical Essays.* Englewood Cliffs, N.J.: Prentice-Hall, 1964. Contains a number of excellent essays, including Christopher Isherwood's "Some Notes on Auden's Early Poetry" and G. S. Fraser's "The Career of W. H. Auden." Isherwood's essay, originally printed in Geoffrey Grigson's 1937 Auden issue of *New Verse*, represents the best in 1930's criticism of Auden.

Spender, Stephen. *The Thirties and After: Poetry, Politics, People, 1933-1970.* New York: Random House, 1978. A collection of Spender's essays, including reminiscences of Auden and Louis MacNeice as well as somewhat edited versions of the author's early pronouncements on the relationship between poetry and revolutionary thought and on his espousal of communism. The final essay is the memorial address he delivered at Oxford in 1973.

Symons, Julian. *The Thirties: A Dream Novel Revolved.* London: The Cresset Press, 1960. Symons quotes from a variety of literary and journalistic sources, many of them leftist, and comments on them to convey a sense of the intellectual, social, and political background of a decade in which he himself was young, leftist, and thoroughly imbued with Auden's poetry. Symons deftly evokes the period with well-chosen photographs of social, artistic, and theatrical subjects.

Robert P. Ellis

Cross-References

Rilke's *Duino Elegies* Depicts Art as a Transcendent Experience (1911), p. 281; Harriet Monroe Founds *Poetry* Magazine (1912), p. 314; The Imagist Movement Shakes Up Poetry (1912), p. 326; Yeats Publishes *The Wild Swans at Coole* (1917), p. 440; Pound's *Cantos* Is Published (1917), p. 445; Eliot Publishes *The Waste Land* (1922), p. 539; Crane Publishes *The Bridge* (1930), p. 851.

KARLOFF AND LUGOSI BECOME KINGS OF HORROR

Category of event: Motion pictures
Time: 1931
Locale: Hollywood, California

Bela Lugosi in Dracula *and Boris Karloff in* Frankenstein *created the archetypes for the two most famous monsters in the horror-film genre*

Principal personages:
BORIS KARLOFF (WILLIAM HENRY PRATT, 1887-1969), a British-born actor whose portrayals of monsters, fiends, and other ghoulish characters made him the premiere horror-film star of the 1930's
BELA LUGOSI (BÉLA BLASKO, 1882-1956), a Hungarian-born actor who became an overnight sensation as the star of the 1931 film *Dracula*
JAMES WHALE (1896-1957), a Hollywood director who directed Karloff in the 1931 film *Frankenstein*
TOD BROWNING (1882-1962), a Hollywood director who directed Lugosi in *Dracula*

Summary of Event

No two performers have been more associated with a motion-picture genre than Boris Karloff and Bela Lugosi. Lugosi's chilling portrayal of the vampire in *Dracula* and Karloff's sensational incarnation as the monster in *Frankenstein* left Hollywood with a legacy of definitive performances that established a standard for horror films to come.

Dracula and *Frankenstein*, both released in 1931, were the first horror films produced by Universal Studios. The horror-film genre, though, dates back to the beginnings of cinema and to the works of such directors as Georges Méliès and Thomas Edison. Edison produced an extraordinary one-reel version of *Frankenstein* in 1910, the first attempt to transfer Mary Shelley's novel to film. Universal's horror hits of the 1930's and 1940's, however, remain the classics of the genre. The enduring popularity of horror films is to a great extent a result of the performances of Lugosi and Karloff in these early productions.

In 1930, Universal bought the film rights to a play based on the 1897 novel *Dracula* by Bram Stoker; the play had had a successful run on Broadway in 1927. The play, written by Hamilton Deane, starred the Hungarian-born actor Bela Lugosi. Lugosi had fled his homeland in 1919 after a period of political unrest there and had made his way to New York, where he joined the Hungarian community and began working in Hungarian-language theater productions.

The director of *Dracula*, Tod Browning, had a talent for creating films about the macabre. His direction of Lon Chaney, a master of grotesque disguises, resulted in several notable melodramas in the 1920's, including *The Unholy Three* (1925), *The*

Big City (1928), and *West of Zanzibar* (1928). Originally, Universal had chosen the play as a vehicle for Chaney; when Chaney died of cancer in 1930, Browning considered several other actors for the lead in *Dracula*. Lugosi, who had not yet mastered English, badly wanted the part and was finally hired perhaps because he had successfully played the role on Broadway.

The tremendous impact the film had on audiences was in part due to Lugosi's exotic and mysterious presence. His halting command of English, his long black cape, and his refined manners created a stir among women, some of whom actually fainted during showings of the film. In the credits, however, Lugosi was merely listed along with the other players.

In the film, Lugosi plays the part of Count Dracula, a 500-year-old vampire whose thirst for human blood cannot be quenched. As the undying vampire constantly in search of new victims, he moves from his castle in Transylvania to the ruins of an abbey in England. While attending an opera one evening, he meets two young women from polite society. Using his cultivated charm and mysterious gaze, he begins stalking them, apparently with the aim of turning them into vampires also, but a famous vampire killer, Dr. Van Helsing (Edward Van Sloan) comes to the rescue. After some psychic struggle between the two, Van Helsing tracks Dracula to his coffin lair and drives a stake through his heart, thus breaking the spell.

Because *Dracula* was being filmed during the Depression, when Universal operated under rather severe budget restraints, every effort was made to save money. In one scene, Universal even used footage cannibalized from one of its other films. Most of the $400,000 it cost to make *Dracula* went into the fantastic sets of Dracula's castle; Lugosi was paid a mere thirty-five hundred dollars for his performance.

Universal was at first unsure of the impact *Dracula* would have on the public. Fearing that the film might be rejected as too horrible or disgusting, the studio had its publicity department advertise the film as "the story of the strangest passion the world has ever known."

Dracula was released on Valentine's Day, 1931, and was an instant success. The popularity of the film owed as much to Lugosi's sinister charisma as to Tod Browning's direction and the magnificent sets. The role of Count Dracula was Lugosi's greatest success, and he became permanently typecast as a player of vampires, monsters, and fiends. His "Count Dracula" was copyrighted by Universal, and virtually all subsequent movie vampires were modeled after him in name or in style.

So successful was *Dracula* that Universal immediately set out to make another horror film. Choosing the right material was a challenge; however, Mary Wollstonecraft Shelley's Gothic novel *Frankenstein: Or, The Modern Prometheus* (1817) was considered a likely follow-up to *Dracula*. While an early treatment was prepared by writer-director Robert Florey, the studio finally gave the picture to director James Whale.

Whale, a theatrically trained director, selected Boris Karloff, an established character player in Hollywood films, to test for the part of the monster. Karloff saw the role as a dramatic challenge and had Jack Pierce, Universal's greatest makeup artist, design the monster's image for his audition. When Whale saw the result, he immediately gave the part to Karloff. Oddly enough, the part of the monster had originally been offered to Lugosi. Lugosi, who was not interested in a nonspeaking part and who did not like having to wear the heavy makeup, turned down the role.

As adapted for film, *Frankenstein* is the story of a slightly mad scientist, Dr. Frankenstein (Colin Clive), who attempts to create a living man by stitching together parts of cadavers. His final and most important step in the process is to find a suitable brain. Frankenstein's assistant, Fritz (Dwight Frye), a half-witted hunchback, mistakenly brings his master a criminal brain rather than a normal one. After being subjected to electrical current from bolts of lightning, the monster comes alive. Though Frankenstein is thrilled at the success of his work, the monster is so hideous that he is kept hidden from view in a dungeon-like cell. After being tortured by Fritz and finally escaping, the monster accidentally kills a child and is pursued by an angry mob of villagers. Dr. Frankenstein joins the mob in search of the monster. During the night, the monster grabs his creator and seeks refuge in an old windmill. The villagers finally surround the windmill and set fire to it, apparently killing the monster in the process.

Jack Pierce's artistry transformed Karloff into a truly horrible creature, with hinged skull, electrodes protruding from his neck, and a stiff-legged, lurching walk. So fearful were studio managers that Karloff would terrify audiences that a prologue was added to warn the audiences that the film was capable of frightening and shocking them.

On December 6, 1931, *Frankenstein* premiered in Santa Barbara, California. The film created a huge sensation. Karloff, who was not even invited to the premiere, became an overnight horror superstar. In choosing Karloff to play the monster, James Whale had made a brilliant choice. Karloff, who had served a lengthy apprenticeship both on the stage and in films, gave the monster a sympathetic quality. Though the character had no dialogue, Karloff was able to convey a wide range of emotions, from childlike innocence to terrified bewilderment. The poignant performance confirmed Karloff's ability as a first-rate actor.

Impact of Event

Not only are *Frankenstein* and *Dracula* the most famous of the Universal horror films of the 1930's and 1940's, but they also influenced the development of the entire genre. One of the most significant results of the success of the films has been the enduring popularity of Bela Lugosi and Boris Karloff. Both men were highly regarded actors who had already established their careers well before becoming involved in horror films. Because of their definitive performances, though, Lugosi and Karloff became typecast in the horror genre. For better or worse, their names have become forever linked in the minds of the public to films that evoke fear and terror.

Frankenstein was quickly followed by *Murders in the Rue Morgue*, which was released in 1932. Based on the short story by Edgar Allan Poe (but drastically altered), the film starred Lugosi as Dr. Mirakle. This odd and disappointing melodrama is notable mainly for the presence of Lugosi as the mad scientist intent on proving his bizarre theory of evolution.

Two other Universal films of 1932, *The Old Dark House* and *The Mummy*, starred Karloff. In the first film, Karloff's performance was both brief and undistinguished. A much better film is *The Mummy*, which was directed by Karl Freund and starred Boris Karloff in the dual roles of Imhotep, a mummy, and the resurrected Egyptian high priest Ardeth Bey. Karloff plays Ardeth Bey with an articulate charm and sense of style that resulted in one of his finest performances. *The Mummy*, noted for its excellent script, cast, and direction, is also famous for the incredible makeup by Jack Pierce. A unique and intelligent horror film, *The Mummy* spawned such lookalike films as *The Mummy's Hand* (1940) and *The Mummy's Tomb* (1942) and maintains a place alongside Universal's two great horror films of 1931. Universal followed *The Mummy* with *Secret of the Blue Room* (1933) and *The Invisible Man* (1933). *The Invisible Man*, directed by James Whale and starring Claude Rains, was adapted from the novel by H. G. Wells. Because of the innovative special effects devised to convey the illusion of invisibility, *The Invisible Man* is considered a unique film in Hollywood history.

Lugosi and Karloff made their first joint appearance in a Universal film in *The Black Cat* (1934). Based loosely on a story by Poe, the film is a catalog of depravity, with various episodes of sadism, torture, mutilation, and murder acted out in a loosely woven tapestry of melodramatic sensationalism.

In the film, arch-enemies Dr. Vitus Wedergast (Lugosi) and Hjalmar Poelzig (Karloff) go at each other almost immediately upon reuniting in Poelzig's mountaintop home. Wedergast accuses Poelzig of having killed his wife while Wedergast served time as a prisoner of war. In the years since their last meeting, Poelzig has been conducting monstrous experiments involving the preservation of the dead bodies of beautiful women. When Poelzig shows Wedergast the preserved body of his wife, Wedergast goes berserk, unleashing the forces of murder and mayhem that result in the death of both protagonists. Although *The Black Cat* was recut extensively prior to its release in order to placate studio chiefs who felt the film was too grisly, it remains a fascinating and bizarre horror film.

Lugosi and Karloff were to be paired again in the 1930's in another Universal adaptation of a Poe tale, *The Raven* (1935). Karloff was to re-create his role as the monster in two *Frankenstein* sequels, *The Bride of Frankenstein* (1935) and *Son of Frankenstein* (1939), which also featured Lugosi. Among the other memorable films of those years are *Dracula's Daughter* (1936), *The Wolf Man* (1941), and *The Mummy's Tomb*. The studio even successfully rereleased *Frankenstein* and *Dracula* on a double bill in 1938.

While Lugosi was perhaps as talented an actor as Karloff, he did not select his roles carefully, and he went on to make a number of forgettable, even embarrassing, films. In later years, marital and health problems took their toll, and by the mid-1950's he was broke and addicted to drugs. He died practically destitute in 1956. Karloff, though also typecast as a horror-film star, had a busy and varied career in other areas of show business, including television and the stage. In 1941, he achieved critical success in the Broadway production of *Arsenic and Old Lace.* His gentle nature and quiet refinement were in stark contrast to the fiendishness of the ghouls he played in films.

Although fans still turned out to see the latest Universal tales of horror, by the end of the 1930's, many of the studio's films were mere remakes that exploited earlier films. The result was that each new title seemed to parody the horror genre. Though they were far from perfect, *Dracula* and *Frankenstein* are considered minor master-pieces by horror fans. Despite the fact that the films have since lost much of their power to frighten, the monsters created by Lugosi and Karloff have remained the definitive horror performances.

Bibliography

Bojarski, Richard. *The Complete Films of Bela Lugosi.* New York: Citadel Press, 1980. All Lugosi's film appearances are listed, including his earliest films made in Hungary and Germany. Carol Borland, who played the female vampire Luna alongside Lugosi in *Mark of the Vampire* (1935) contributes a wonderful introduc-tion. A brief biography precedes the catalog of films. Many rare photographs throughout, plus a chronology of Lugosi's stage career.

Brunas, Michael, John Brunas, and Tom Weaver. *Universal Horrors: The Studio's Classic Films, 1931-1946.* Jefferson, N.C.: McFarland, 1990. A critical examination of horror films produced by Universal in the 1930's and 1940's on a year-by-year, picture-by-picture basis. The authors' insightful commentary is presented with a nice touch of humor. Includes photographs and three detailed appendices.

Lindsay, Cynthia. *Dear Boris.* New York: Alfred A. Knopf, 1975. An intimate, very readable biography of Boris Karloff by a longtime friend. Carefully explores Kar-loff's early years in England and his moves first to Canada and then to the United States. Contains numerous quotes by Karloff as well as excerpts from letters by such Karloff friends as Vincent Price and Ronald Reagan. Includes photographs, family tree, and filmography.

Nollen, Scott Allen. *Boris Karloff: A Critical Account of His Screen, Stage, Radio, Television, and Recording Work.* Jefferson, N.C.: McFarland, 1991. A scholarly historical and critical analysis of Karloff's body of work. Reprints a 1969 assess-ment of Karloff's artistic contributions by Ray Bradbury. Well organized and doc-umented throughout; includes a filmography, a list of television and radio perfor-mances, and an extensive bibliography.

Underwood, Peter. *Karloff: The Life of Boris Karloff.* New York: Drake, 1972. Biog-raphy that effectively recalls Karloff's struggle to become an actor, first on the stage and then in films. Offers detailed, anecdotal account of the making of *Frank-enstein.* Photographs, selected bibliography, discography, and filmography.

Francis Poole

Cross-References

Le Voyage dans la lune Introduces Special Effects (1902), p. 57; *The Cabinet of Dr. Caligari* Opens in Berlin (1920), p. 486; Hitchcock Becomes England's Foremost Director (1934), p. 946; *Psycho* Becomes Hitchcock's Most Famous Film (1960), p. 1855; Scott's *Blade Runner* Is a Visual Masterpiece (1982), p. 2486.

LE CORBUSIER'S VILLA SAVOYE REDEFINES ARCHITECTURE

Category of event: Architecture
Time: 1931
Locale: Poissy-sur-Seine, near Paris, France

Architect Le Corbusier used a weekend house to demonstrate that functionalist rules for architecture could produce a new style and a great work of art

Principal personages:
> LE CORBUSIER (CHARLES-ÉDOUARD JEANNERET, 1887-1965), a Swiss-born French architect, planner, design propagandist, and primary figure in the radical architecture movement of the 1920's
> PIERRE JEANNERET (1896-1968), an engineer and cousin of Le Corbusier, the principal design partner in his major works from 1921 to 1940
> M. and MME PIERRE SAVOYE, a wealthy Parisian couple who commissioned Le Corbusier to design a weekend house for them near Paris

Summary of Event

The Savoye house, "Les Heures Claires," is the most beautiful, rigorous, and subtle building designed during the tumultuous developing years of modern architecture, 1919-1930. When the building's architect, Le Corbusier, undertook its design in 1928, he had been the leading spokesman for the modern movement in architecture for the past five years. His aphorism "a house is a machine for living," published in his 1923 book *Vers une architecture* (*Towards a New Architecture*, 1927), articulated the beliefs of many radical architects in the decade after World War I. Architecture, Le Corbusier declared, could be a living art only if architects ceased to copy past artistic styles and worked toward a simple expression of functional needs. The bare white walls and relentlessly regular streets in Le Corbusier's drawings of as-yet-unbuilt designs, and his praise of automobiles, steamships, and mass-produced cheap goods, gave him a reputation as a farsighted but extreme propagandist for functionalism. Because of the broad scope of his proposals, he was much better known as a theorist of urban planning than as an architect.

In 1928, Le Corbusier's office was busy with several large-scale commissions, including a hostel for Swiss students in Paris and a government office complex in Moscow. He had built a few low-budget houses around Paris for artists and patrons. In the fall of that year, Madame Savoye, whom Le Corbusier later described as without preconceptions for or against modernism, asked him to design a three-bedroom weekend villa on some twelve acres above the Seine valley. The building budget—some 350,000 francs—was far greater than any of his previous house budgets.

The house was to be built on a gently domed hill in the middle of a field. As presented in October, 1928, the plans for the project called for a square reinforced-concrete dwelling unit with four long strip windows, lifted a story above ground level on twenty-five slim concrete pillars (*pilotis*). Within the open ground-floor space was a driveway curved around a glass-walled entry chamber. On the top floor was another curved-wall space enclosing Mme Savoye's bedroom. When this project was rejected as too expensive (758,000 francs), Le Corbusier did a second, less elegant proposal in November, 1928; thereafter, though, he fought to return to the layout of the first concept. Optimistic budget estimates and the elimination of the top-floor bedroom (its curved wall remained as a roof-garden screen) led the Savoyes to approve the project in December, 1928, at a budget of 487,000 francs. Construction began in April, 1929. The Savoyes moved into the villa in the spring of 1931, but Le Corbusier began featuring the house in his writings and lectures as early as October, 1929. For the architect, it represented the culmination of all his work and theories to date.

The Villa Savoye's design owed much less to the Savoyes' specific requirements than to the "Five Points of a New Architecture" Le Corbusier and Pierre Jeanneret had formulated in 1926. These "points" were a list of functional requirements for buildings in the Machine Age city that would become a universal stylistic vocabulary for architecture. The first point called for the elevation of the building on concrete posts, separating man-made buildings from the landscape and making the space under them accessible to nature and human circulation. The second point called for the creation of roof gardens, replacing the light, air, and greenery eliminated by a building by making them part of the building itself. The third point concerned the "open plan," the separation of load-bearing pillars (concrete or steel) from walls that were to act only as screens—a requirement of structural honesty. The fourth point, the strip window, was intended to give the interior uniform light and the outside a sense of horizontal repose. The fifth, the "free facade"—the construction of the outside wall as a thin screen, not a bearing wall—would allow building fronts to be composed for aesthetic effect. The sense of overlapping thin walls, punctuated by windows and cutouts, would create an abstract, cubist aesthetic for the building.

The Villa Savoye fulfills all five points masterfully in a complex yet integrated whole. The principle of the "open plan" separates the structural *pilotis* from the enclosure, made of taut, thin concrete walls finished in smooth white stucco. Resting on its white *pilotis*, the house rises from its field as the image of abstract reason in harmony with nature. The "open plan" also turns practical circulation into dramas of spatial experience—first as one drives up to and under the house by car, then as one climbs the interior ramp or the adjacent spiral staircase from the entry to the free-form living floor. This floor wraps around an open terrace, from which another ramp climbs to the steamship-funnel-like roof screen. The terrace represents the principle of the roof garden inserted into the mass of the building. The ribbon windows are uniform on all four sides, even where they cut through the wall that encloses the terrace. The house thus combines symmetry and repose with an exciting intermingling of closed and open spaces.

The Villa Savoye was a "machine" for beauty and harmony with nature. Le Corbusier declared that the Savoyes, "who will have come here because this countryside was beautiful . . . will contemplate it, preserved intact, from the height of their suspended garden or from the four sides of the long window. Their domestic life will be inserted into a Virgilian dream."

Impact of Event

Le Corbusier himself saw the Villa Savoye as the climax of his ideas of the 1920's, but not as a new starting point. His designs soon began to change radically. The house's critical success, however, forced reconsideration of the nature of Le Corbusier's achievement and provided justification on several levels for adopting his methods.

For critics, the house disproved the common estimation of Le Corbusier as an art-hating functionalist who could conceive utopian cities but not real buildings. In reality, as the Villa Savoye proved, Le Corbusier saw architecture as an art before anything else. The white, rectilinear style in which he worked symbolized for him the marble classical architecture of the Mediterranean world, the exotic stucco architecture of the Arabs, and the vision-transforming planes of cubist painting. (The architect was himself a painter; he called his orderly version of cubism "Purism.") Functionalism was only the twentieth century's means toward architecture's eternal purpose: to give walls and space vivid emotional impact.

The Villa Savoye realized this purpose in a new, abstract way. In its geometric purity, it could be read as a contemporary version of the perfect harmony of the classical temple or the Renaissance country mansions of Andrea Palladio. The interplay of wall screens, solid geometrical shapes, and half-hidden open spaces gave the house an abstractness unknown to classical architecture, as did the way in which functional elements became part of the composition. Modernity and technology, in Le Corbusier's hands, could call up the whole past history of the architectural art without ceasing to be the tools of "the machine for living."

The Villa Savoye's aesthetic success seemed to bear out the inevitability of the "Five Points of a New Architecture." With the very limited repertory of the "points"— white free-standing walls, exposed supports, ribbon windows, unornamented right-angle forms, flat roofs Le Corbusier had created a structure that seemed to meet all possible requirements of modern building, practical, urbanistic, ideological, and aesthetic. Younger architects who had come to doubt the usefulness of classic and Gothic Revival styles took Le Corbusier at his word and declared that his manner was a perfected style—in fact, the only possible style. This was the argument made by the Museum of Modern Art (MOMA) in New York in its seminal "International Style" exhibition of 1932, which showed the work of Le Corbusier and others in order to prove that such a new style existed. The argument was taken up by such architects as Wallace Harrison and Edward Durrell Stone in America, Bertold Lubetkin and the Tecton Group in England, and Oscar Niemeyer in Brazil. Despite angry disclaimers by modernists with different approaches such as Frank Lloyd Wright, the "white box" style canonized in the Villa Savoye came to seem mandatory for contemporary architecture.

The Villa Savoye also proved that functionalist beliefs did not necessarily lead to low-budget, utilitarian decisions in design. A sensitive artist could transform a type or program—in this case, the modern house—into a personal, unique work. That Le Corbusier had transformed functionalism into art was a crucial point in the arguments over modernism in the period from 1928 to 1931. His own earlier writings had given the (mistaken) impression that he saw modern architecture as a cheap form of social planning, not an aesthetic discipline. The idea that functionalism could be the means of building a new visual and social world economically had been even more strongly advanced by Walter Gropius, the founder of the Bauhaus design school in Germany, and by German municipal housing architects. To such designers at the beginning of the Depression, preoccupation with art in preference to society seemed blinkered, willfully individualist, and reactionary. By putting art, in the form of the Villa Savoye, before social reform, Le Corbusier seemed to be breaking with this position.

Supporters of the modernist aesthetic who feared that social planning would replace artistic judgment in a social revolution were relieved to see that the greatest practitioner of the modern style was not a revolutionary. This sense of relief was essential to MOMA's encouragement of the Villa Savoye's style and helped lead to the adoption of Le Corbusier's manner (and that of the equally art-conscious German modernist Ludwig Mies van der Rohe) as the style of the corporate establishment after World War II. The power of Le Corbusier's earlier urban-renewal arguments, however, made his approach equally acceptable to the architects of government housing projects during and after the Depression. After World War II, urban-renewal architects tended to confuse his arguments with those of Gropius.

By the time "Les Heures Claires" was completed in 1931, Le Corbusier himself had begun to transform the elements of the "five points," especially the *piloti*, box, and free wall, into heavier and more earthbound terms. His Swiss Pavilion in Paris (1931) used massive concrete *pilotis* with sculptural shapes and stone facings on the hostel block. The De Mandrot house of the same year rested on the ground, not on posts, and used fieldstone and rough plywood. Having proved in the Villa Savoye that machine-like abstract geometry could be used to make great buildings, Le Corbusier began to explore organic shapes and materials toward the same end. It would be some two decades before his followers took up this path themselves, and still longer before architects and critics realized that his ideal had been the freedom of the artist, not the necessity of machine functionalism.

Bibliography

Benton, Tim. "The Villa Savoye and the Architect's Practice." In *Le Corbusier*, edited by H. Allen Brooks. Princeton, N.J.: Princeton University Press, 1987. Traces how Le Corbusier developed the Villa Savoye's design, using the architect's preliminary drawings and his lectures about the house. Discussions of budget and the clients' complaints illuminate the practical problems of Le Corbusier's art. Placing illustrations at the essay's end makes it difficult to follow descriptions of the drawings. Index.

—————————. *The Villas of Le Corbusier, 1920-1930.* New Haven, Conn.: Yale University Press, 1987. A chronological catalog that describes the circumstances, characteristics, and importance of all the architect's house designs before 1930. Little discussion of nonresidential work of the same years, and the account is less easy to follow than Benton's essay in the Brooks anthology. Full list of surviving architectural drawings of buildings discussed. No index.

Blake, Peter. *The Master Builders: Le Corbusier, Mies van der Rohe, Frank Lloyd Wright.* Rev. ed. New York: W. W. Norton, 1976. An accessible and entertaining account of Le Corbusier's life and principles. Somewhat dated; chapters written during the subject's life were not revised after his death, and the book reflects little of the widespread dissatisfaction with modernism after 1960. Index.

Curtis, William. *Modern Architecture Since 1900.* Englewood Cliffs, N.J.: Prentice-Hall, 1983. A general textbook that devotes much attention to Le Corbusier and defends his achievements against contemporary and later critiques. Synthesizes the insights of Benton, Blake, and Colin Rowe (see below), while stressing the classical features of the Villa Savoye and other work of the 1920's. Endnotes, index.

Le Corbusier. *Precisions: On the Present State of Architecture of City Planning.* Translated by Edith Schreiber Aujame. Cambridge, Mass.: MIT Press, 1991. The 1929 Buenos Aires lectures in which Le Corbusier explained the Villa Savoye as the synthesis of his principles. Illustrated by the architect's own sketches. No index or later editorial matter.

Jencks, Charles. *Le Corbusier and the Tragic View of Architecture.* Cambridge, Mass.: Harvard University Press, 1973. An often complex analysis that convincingly links the biographical, artistic, and theoretical in the architect's work. More inclusive than Benton's account, but more speculative. Index.

Rowe, Colin. *The Mathematics of the Ideal Villa and Other Essays.* Cambridge, Mass.: MIT Press, 1976. The title essay introduced the idea that Le Corbusier's architecture had classical as well as functionalist sources. This and the other essays illuminate how architects can be inspired by the past in indirect ways, but Rowe often relies more on hunches than on scholarship. Endnotes, no index.

M. David Samson

Cross-References

The Deutscher Werkbund Combats Conservative Architecture (1907), p. 181; Behrens Designs the AEG Turbine Factory (1909), p. 219; German Artists Found the Bauhaus (1919), p. 463; Wright Founds the Taliesin Fellowship (1932), p. 902; Aalto Designs Villa Mairea (1937), p. 1067; Le Corbusier Designs and Builds Chandigarh (1951), p. 1503.

THE GROUP THEATRE FLOURISHES

Category of event: Theater
Time: 1931-1941
Locale: New York, New York

The Group Theatre, founded in 1931 as a permanent theater company, flourished during the Great Depression before folding in 1941 after the United States' entry into World War II

Principal personages:
STELLA ADLER (1902-   ), an actress who figured prominently in Group Theatre productions
MORRIS CARNOVSKY (1897-   ), a character actor whose continuing involvement with the Group Theatre influenced it greatly
HAROLD CLURMAN (1901-1980), one of the founders and directors of the Group Theatre
CHERYL CRAWFORD (1902-1986), a founder and director of and a major force in the Group Theatre
PAUL GREEN (1894-1981), a North Carolina playwright, an early associate of the Group Theatre
ELIA KAZAN (ELIA KAZANJOGLOU, 1909-   ), an actor and director who learned his craft in the Group Theatre
CLIFFORD ODETS (1906-1963), an actor in the Group Theatre who became its most prominent playwright
LEE STRASBERG (ISRAEL STRASSBERG, 1901-1982), a founder and director of and a major force in the Group Theatre

Summary of Event

Harold Clurman, Cheryl Crawford, and Lee Strasberg founded the Group Theatre as a permanent acting company in 1931, when the United States was in the depths of the Great Depression. Clurman had been a play reader for the Theatre Guild, where Crawford was a casting director. Lee Strasberg was an actor who had learned the Stanislavsky method at the American Laboratory Theater.

American theater grew rapidly during the 1920's. Eugene O'Neill had emerged after World War I as a towering theatrical figure in a country that had little high-quality indigenous drama to stage until O'Neill's plays. A new freedom of language and outlook affected the emerging drama.

Most theater of the early century consisted of dramas by European playwrights or by such canonical playwrights as William Shakespeare. Broad Jewish comedies in Yiddish or "Yinglish," as the dialect that combined Yiddish and English came to be called, were also popular.

Earlier American playwrights such as George Henry Boker, Robert Montgomery

Bird, Dion Boucicault, and Clyde Fitch made little artistic impact on American theater. Their plays were mere vehicles for the stars, who dominated the theater. The star system was sufficiently entrenched that Eugene O'Neill's father, James, could spend most of his acting life playing one character: the count in the stage version of Alexandre Dumas' novel *Le Comte de Monte-Cristo* (1844-1845; *The Count of Monte-Cristo*, 1846).

Most plays revolved around stars of legendary proportions. Stages were filled with a supporting cast—sometimes a large supporting cast—but all attention was focused essentially on one or two actors (occasionally actresses) who dominated. The Theatre Guild, founded in 1918 to support living theater, bowed to the star system.

One of the Theatre Guild's experiments during 1929 involved its Studio Program, special Sunday performances of serious dramas. Cheryl Crawford, Lee Strasberg, and Harold Clurman were all involved in putting on the first—and only—performance of the Studio Program. The play was a Russian drama, and it brought all sorts of Communist sympathizers to the theater.

After the Studio Program collapsed, Clurman dreamed of organizing an acting company unlike any in the United States. He wanted to develop a permanent—but not a repertory—company that would have its own cadre of actors, playwrights, and directors. Clurman knew that Strasberg could help in the implementation of this dream, but he knew as well that Strasberg was not a good organizer and that, despite his intelligence and talent, Strasberg could be devastatingly tactless.

Clurman needed Strasberg, but he also needed a practical, down-to-earth organizer to carry on the day-to-day operation of the theater he envisioned. Cheryl Crawford's handling of the production for the Studio Program convinced Clurman that she could offer his project precisely the skills he required.

During the next months, the three worked toward establishing a theater company the express aim of which was to scrap the star system. Its plays, written by various playwrights associated with the company, would have fewer than ten parts, each as equal in prominence as the playwright could manage. Actors would play lead roles one week, smaller roles or no roles the next. The favored acting technique was the Stanislavsky method of affective acting.

Everyone associated with the group would share equally in any profits, again a blow to any vestigial thoughts the members might have about a star system. Nor were the playwrights to be stars. Rather, the plays were viewed as instruments for the expression of ideas and the formulation of philosophies. Playwrights received an equal share of the meager profits the Group Theatre's plays usually generated.

By late 1930, Clurman's dream was in the first stages of becoming a reality. He and his two fellow founders enticed many theater people to meet with them in strategy sessions. People including Franchot Tone, Morris Carnovsky, J. Edward Bromberg, Phoebe Brand, Dorothy Patten, and Stella Adler and her brother Luther became interested in the concept of the Group Theatre. Clurman held meetings every Friday night to draw Broadway people into his scheme.

When these meetings grew too large to fit into Clurman's room at the Hotel Meurice, they were moved to Cheryl Crawford's apartment. When the enthusiastic crowd overflowed the apartment, the Friday night sessions moved to Steinway Hall.

By June, 1931, the Group Theatre—twenty-eight actors, various spouses, children, and others—left New York for the compound Cheryl Crawford had found for them at Brookfield Center, near Danbury, Connecticut, and prepared for the theater's initial summer of operation. The first play scheduled for production was *The House of Connelly* (1931) by Paul Green of North Carolina.

Clifford Odets was among the actors at Brookfield Center for the Group Theatre's first summer together. He remained with the Group Theatre for most of its existence, leaving only to accept a tempting offer to write for Hollywood. Such an act meant that Odets was prostituting himself in his own eyes, but he did so to make money he could send back to Clurman to keep the financially strapped Group Theatre afloat.

The summer over, the Group Theatre returned to New York. Its members rented a ten-room apartment on West Fifty-seventh Street for fifty dollars a month, and the Group Theatre continued to operate during the winter. During its first few years, the organization presented important new plays by Group Theatre playwrights and also provided excellent experience for actors.

In 1935, Odets burst upon the dramatic scene with the January production of his *Waiting for Lefty* (1935), a tour de force that was precisely right for its time. By summer, Odets had two more plays on Broadway, *Till the Day I Die* (1935) and *Awake and Sing* (1935). In the autumn, his *Paradise Lost* (1936) was brought to Broadway, transforming an unknown actor who claimed to live on ten cents a week into the toast of New York.

The Group Theatre produced all Odets' subsequent plays through *Night Music* (1940). Its financial problems intensified when the United States entered World War II, a development that reduced the size of audiences. The Group Theatre was finally disbanded in 1941. With its disappearance, a significant chapter in the history of American drama ended.

Impact of Event

The Group Theatre affected American drama in many ways. Even with the emergence of Eugene O'Neill as a full-fledged, high-quality American playwright, American theater was somewhat without a compass until the Group Theatre redefined the place of drama in society. Much of the drama of the 1920's—excluding that by O'Neill—was a drama of manners. It did not seek to engage its audiences in penetrating thought along socioeconomic lines; nor, in the roaring 1920's, could it have.

The Group Theatre productions staged in the grim years of the Great Depression, however, raised thorny social questions relating to economics, the place of the individual in society, the role of government, pacifism and conscientious objection to war, and ethnically generated social injustice. One did not come to Group Theatre productions with the expectation of laughing, of being lulled into complacency, or of being amused. Nevertheless, people came, perhaps to have their consciences tweaked, their awareness of daunting economic problems raised.

The social backdrop against which Group Theatre productions played was one of poverty, joblessness, insecurity, and social alienation. The plays the Group Theatre presented dealt with all of these problems, although they played to audiences who certainly had the financial means to rise above the immediate problems that surrounded them. Theatrical audiences obviously have enough disposable income to enable them to attend plays; the theatrical audiences of the early 1930's seemed as well to have enough social conscience to encourage and patronize the kind of drama the Group Theatre favored.

That the Group Theatre changed permanently the structure of American drama cannot be denied. By moving away from the star system and encouraging playwrights whose plays had a balance of significant roles, the philosophy of the Group Theatre opened new possibilities to playwrights, particularly to such later practitioners of the art as Arthur Miller, Tennessee Williams, William Inge, and Edward Albee. It is interesting to note that in a work such as Albee's *Who's Afraid of Virginia Woolf?* (1962), for example, the play's four characters (Martha, George, Honey, and her husband) have virtually equal dramatic stature, even if Martha's mouth gives her a slight advantage.

The same can be said of plays such as Miller's *Death of a Salesman* (1949), Inge's *Come Back, Little Sheba* (1950), and Williams' *The Glass Menagerie* (1945). In *Death of a Salesman*, the characters Willie and Linda Loman and their two sons, Happy and Biff, are virtually dramatic equals; Lola, Doc, Marie, and Turk are almost equivalent characters in the Inge play; Amanda, Tom, Laura, and Jim are essentially equals in *The Glass Menagerie.*

The Group Theatre was also largely responsible for emphasizing method acting in the United States. The technique had been taught previously by such organizations as the American Laboratory Theater, but the Group Theatre made it clear that this was the most effective way to act, and its mandate to advance the Method in its training sessions stuck.

The actors and actresses produced by the Group Theatre included Franchot Tone, Stella Adler, Luther Adler, Jacob Adler, Morris Carnovsky, J. Edward Bromberg, Lee Cobb, Katharine Cornell, John Garfield, Frances Farmer, Luise Rainer, Brock Pemberton, and countless others. The greater legacy, however, is that which accrued to the next generation, to actors such as Marlon Brando, James Dean, Marilyn Monroe, and others whose training, often by people who had been trained in the Group Theatre, emphasized method acting.

Among those who act and write plays, the Group Theatre remains well known, and its impact is readily acknowledged. Although the Group Theatre existed for only a decade, it forged professional relationships and encouraged approaches to drama that were, until its existence, all but unimaginable.

Bibliography

Brenman-Gibson, Margaret. *Clifford Odets, American Playwright: The Years from 1906 to 1940.* New York: Atheneum, 1981. This first volume of the comprehensive biography of Clifford Odets has almost a column and a half of references to the Group Theatre in its index. This is an unusually well-documented biography that goes far beyond the narrow limits of a book about one person. It embraces an entire period of great change in American drama. Not for the casual reader, but a treasure trove for the scholar.

Clurman, Harold. *The Fervent Years: The Story of the Group Theatre and the Thirties.* New York: Hill & Wang, 1945. The authoritative history of the Group Theatre by one of its founders and directors. A warm narrative that deals with the Group Theatre and the people who made it possible. Certainly the most important book on the topic. Eminently readable.

Cohn, Ruby. *Dialogue in American Drama.* Bloomington: Indiana University Press, 1971. Cohn has an intense interest in the proletarian drama of the 1930's, much of which was dialect drama. She appreciates the lyricism of such playwrights as Clifford Odets and Thornton Wilder, relating their use of language to that of later playwrights such as Arthur Miller, Tennessee Williams, and Edward Albee. A specialized book written to be accessible to nonspecialists with a general interest in drama.

French, Warren G., ed. *The Thirties: Fiction, Poetry, Drama.* Deland, Fla.: Everett/ Edwards, 1967. The best chapters in this book for one interested in Group Theatre are Gerald Rabkin's on the Federal Theatre Project, Robert J. Griffin's on Clifford Odets, and Jordan Y. Miller's on Maxwell Anderson. Well balanced; quite accessible to the general reader.

Gassner, John. *Dramatic Soundings: Evaluations and Retractions Culled from Thirty Years of Dramatic Criticism.* New York: Crown, 1968. This collection contains John Gassner's essays and theatrical reviews from 1935 until 1965. He was much interested in the Group Theatre and its playwrights, particularly Clifford Odets, Paul Green, Philip Barry, and Maxwell Anderson, and wrote perceptively about them. Gassner focuses specifically on the Group Theatre, on the Actors' Studio, and on the Theatre Guild.

Krutch, Joseph Wood. *The American Drama Since 1918.* Rev. ed. New York: George Braziller, 1957. Krutch's is one of the most engaging overviews of American drama between the two wars. Krutch's discussion of playwrights associated with the Group Theatre and of the Group Theatre itself is important and is written at a level that most lay people can understand. One of the essential books for anyone who wishes to understand the drama of the period in which the Group Theatre flourished.

Odets, Clifford. *The Time Is Ripe: The 1940 Journal of Clifford Odets.* New York: Grove Press, 1988. The Group Theatre figures centrally in this journal, kept at a time when Odets' life was changing drastically. His marriage to Luise Rainer was deteriorating, his artistic integrity was on the line, and the Group Theatre, which was as close to having a real family as Odets ever came, was dissolving. The pages are interspersed with cogent references to the Group Theatre and what it meant to him.

Taylor, William E., ed. *Modern Drama: Essays in Criticism.* Deland, Fla.: Everett/

Edwards, 1968. Although this source has only three direct references to Group Theatre, it provides a valuable context for the period in which the Group Theatre flourished. The eleven contributors to the volume are well chosen.

Williams, Jay. *Stage Left.* New York: Charles Scribner's Sons, 1974. In its way, this book is an informal history of the Group Theatre. Focuses on several of the Group Theatre's playwrights—Clifford Odets, Sidney Kingsley, Paul Green—and addresses in important ways the shift in society that made proletarian drama, the mainstay of the Group Theatre, possible. An engaging book.

R. Baird Shuman

Cross-References

Stanislavsky Helps to Establish the Moscow Art Theater (1897), p. 1; The Federal Theatre Project Promotes Live Theater (1935), p. 989; Odets' *Awake and Sing* Becomes a Model for Protest Drama (1935), p. 1006; Kazan Brings Naturalism to the Stage and Screen (1940's), p. 1164; *A Streetcar Named Desire* Brings Method Acting to the Screen (1951), p. 1487.

THE EMPIRE STATE BUILDING OPENS AS THE WORLD'S TALLEST BUILDING

Category of event: Architecture
Time: May 1, 1931
Locale: 350 Fifth Avenue, New York, New York

The 1931 opening of the Empire State Building expressed the culmination of sky-scraper technology and introduced to the world an enduring symbol of American ingenuity and progressiveness

Principal personages:
JOHN JACOB RASKOB (1879–1950), the New York City financier who established the Empire State Corporation and spearheaded a plan to build the world's tallest skyscraper
WILLIAM F. LAMB (1883–1952), the New York City architect who used a functional approach in his design of the Empire State Building
ALFRED EMANUEL SMITH (1873–1944), the popular and charismatic ex-governor of New York City who fulfilled an important public relations role as president of the Empire State Corporation

Summary of Event

To many, the image of a sleek modern skyscraper was the quintessential symbol of America. When it opened during the Great Depression, the Empire State Building presented an image of strength and spirit of which New Yorkers and, by extension, all Americans could be proud.

On August 29, 1929, *The New York Times* headlined an announcement that the Empire State Corporation would begin construction on an important commercial venture at Thirty-fourth Street and Fifth Avenue, site of the famous Waldorf-Astoria Hotel. The five New York financiers involved intended to erect the world's tallest building on the two-acre site. Their plan was to offer prestigious rental office space in a skyscraper that would embody the richness and achievement of New York, the Empire State.

This building was the inspiration of John Jacob Raskob, an influential New Yorker who was head of the Empire State Corporation and a vice-president and shareholder in the General Motors Corporation. Politically active, he served as the Democratic National Chairman and acted as campaign manager for presidential candidate Alfred E. Smith, New York's popular four-time governor. Smith lost to Herbert Hoover in the 1928 election, providing Raskob with the opportunity to offer him the position of president of the Empire State Corporation and manager of the proposed Empire State Building. Raskob's shrewd decision to hire the charismatic Smith proved to be crucial to the success of the project. In late October of 1929, the stock market crashed, plunging an unprepared America into the midst of the Great Depression. Many construction and skyscraper projects were criticized as being too frivolous, given the severe economic slump. The Empire State Building project survived, however, largely as a result of Smith's association with the project. The man's powerful identity with New York, his obvious pride in the city, and his immense personal appeal and reputation for integrity helped to secure a $27.5 million loan from the Metropolitan Life Insurance Company.

The architectural firm of Shreve, Lamb, and Harmon was hired to design the Empire State Building. It was a young partnership with excellent credentials and a reputation for taking a practical, functional approach to commercial building. Together with chief architect William F. Lamb, Raskob calculated that 36 million cubic feet of rentable space would be needed to make the venture a profitable one. It soon became clear to Lamb that the skyscraper mass would be shaped primarily by practical matters: the size of the site (200 feet by 425 feet), a fixed budget of $60 million, a May 1, 1931, deadline, and city zoning laws. Adherence to the deadline date was of particular concern to Raskob, who wanted to avoid financial loss by ensuring immediate availability of rental space on the day for signing commercial leases.

Of all the practical elements involved in the design of the Empire State Building, New York's 1916 Zoning Law restrictions most significantly contributed to the building's final shape. Aimed at protecting the city from overbuilding and ensuring sufficient light and air for all streets and offices, these regulations required street setbacks above the thirtieth floor for any building mass and required that no floor be more than one quarter the area of the site. The pyramidal style common to many New York City skyscrapers clearly was a reaction by local architects to these restrictions.

Lamb designed from the top down. His sixteenth attempt (Plan K) at shaping the skyscraper resulted in the final design for the Empire State Building. Following the form of the classical column, the mass was divided into three parts: a five-story base topped by a sixty-foot terrace (meeting the required setback restriction), a limestone office tower that soared to the eighty-sixth-floor observation deck, and a cap composed of a rounded fourteen-story glass and metal mooring mast for dirigibles. It was Raskob's intent that with the continuation of transatlantic dirigible travel, the top floor of New York City's tallest building would make the ideal international arrival lounge. The style of the building was restrained Art Deco and blended traditional motifs with the streamlined look of the Machine Age. Fully conceived, the image of the Empire State Building was sleek, glamorous, and uplifting.

The construction firm of Starrett Brothers and Eken was engaged, and an elaborate strategy was mapped out in minute detail, complete with a set of overlapping monthly schedules. By October 1, 1929, the demoliton of the Waldorf-Astoria was begun. The hotel would relocate to a chic uptown location. On March 30, 1930, excavation for the Empire State Building was under way. The speed with which the structure rose was surprising even to those who worked on the project.

Lamb planned to meet the May 1 deadline by doing away with handwork wherever possible, instead using glass, stone, and steel elements capable of being accurately mass produced and speedily assembled. A new method of fenestration was used that cut time and costs as well as saving office space: Glass for the sixty-five hundred windows was applied to the outside wall, or skin, of the skyscraper with metal brackets, rather than setting each pane into an individual stone frame. This also created the building's characteristic smooth and shimmery exterior. Another time-saving innovation involved a temporary miniature railway that made tightly scheduled runs to each floor, carrying needed tools and materials.

On April 11, 1931—having broken several construction records—the completed Empire State Building towered 1,250 feet and 102 stories above New York City's busy avenues. Built in one year and forty-five days at a cost of approximately $41 million, the world's tallest skyscraper had, incredibly, been finished ahead of schedule and under budget.

The building officially opened at 11:15 A.M. on May 1, 1931. Standing before a festive crowd of onlookers, Alfred E. Smith assisted his two young grandchildren in a traditional ribbon-cutting ceremony at the magnificent Fifth Avenue entrance. At 11:30 A.M., President Herbert Hoover pushed a button in Washington, D.C., bathing the main corridors of the Empire State Building in light. Later, at a luncheon celebration on the eighty-sixth-floor observation deck, Governor Franklin D. Roosevelt noted that, as a creation of vision and faith, the Empire State Building ". . . is needed in the city of New York. It is located at a strategic center. . . . It is needed by the whole nation." The Empire State Building officially entered its four-decade reign as the tallest skyscraper in the world.

Impact of Event

The Empire State Building is as much an icon as it is an outstanding example of architectural achievement. Since its opening in 1931, it has become an important and dramatic source of identity for the people of New York and an internationally recog-nized symbol of the wealth and strength of the American nation. As such, the Em-pire State Building remains one of New York City's biggest tourist attractions. More than 65 million visitors flock to the eighty-sixth-floor observation deck annually. They go to experience the dizzying sensation of height, to see the magnificent views (more than fifty miles on a clear day), and to buy millions of souvenirs. Pencils, pens, postcards, glasses and mugs, key chains, spoons, snowy paperweights, and at least nine different variations of the Empire State Building in miniature serve to carry its famous image to even the most remote areas of the world.

Architecturally, the Empire State Building represents the culmination of the Amer-ican skyscraper race of the 1920's and 1930's, when monumentality was expressed by hugeness of mass and soaring height. This notion of height, which became an over-riding concern among New York architects in particular, gave New York City a distinctive skyline and a progressive image that applied not only to it but to all American cities of maturity. The building signified the nation's vitality. It became a symbol of skyscrapers everywhere and of a force that would forever change Amer-ica's urban environment. Its sheer size served to heighten controversy about the potential dangers of populating modern cities with densely packed high-rise build-ings. Some perceived the great American skyscrapers as symbols of greed and profit.

As the nation trudged along through the difficult Depression years, interest in the skyscraper movement waned.

From an artistic standpoint, the Empire State Building's restrained Art Deco style sent a message to the world about the successful marriage of art and technology in the Machine Age. It was a theme common to many major skyscrapers of that era. By blending progressive, eclectic, and traditional European stylistic elements, Art Deco skyscrapers such as the Empire State Building expressed the forces of motion, energy, and life, integrating these with the streamlined nature of the machine. The move away from the manual way of doing things was projected, and the future of technology was glorified. American skyscrapers became linked symbolically to national dreams and expectations.

During the Depression, construction of the Empire State Building provided positive images to the suffering populace. In May of 1930, American photographer Lewis W. Hine was commissioned to chronicle the rise of the building. He took more than a thousand photographs, concentrating on the energy and fearlessness of the thousands of workers involved. In Hine's *Men at Work: Photographic Studies of Modern Men and Machines* (1932), workers were portrayed as heroes. The collection revealed heartening images of courage, tenacity, and teamwork at a time when Depression hardships seemed almost insurmountable.

The Empire State Building remains a focal point for New Yorkers. In the 1930's, a television antenna was mounted to the top of the building and transmitted pioneering images of Mickey Mouse and Felix the Cat to homes within a fifty-two-mile range. Later, topped by a sixty-foot metal pole, the building was transformed into an immense lightning rod so that studies of the phenomenon could be made. Tragically, the famed building received national attention in 1945, when a B-25 bomber became lost in Manhattan's foggy maze of skyscrapers and crashed into the seventy-ninth floor. Lives were lost, yet only one steel beam in the entire structure was damaged. The accident briefly renewed negative comments about the continued construction of skyscrapers.

The Empire State Building is an easily identifiable image and a part of American lore. Over the years, it has played a part in more than 150 films, including *King Kong* (1933) and *An Affair to Remember* (1957). Artists such as Georgia O'Keeffe and photographers such as Alfred Stieglitz have incorporated it into their works. Suicides and celebrities alike have been drawn by the mystique and majesty of the towering structure. Visitors have included Albert Einstein, Winston Churchill, Queen Elizabeth II, and Helen Keller.

The Empire State Building is about many things—glamour, identity, commerce, entertainment, technology, opportunity, and, most important, achievement. Although it was surpassed in height when New York's World Trade Center opened in 1972, its image and symbolism endure.

Bibliography

Goldberger, Paul. *The Skyscraper.* New York: Alfred A. Knopf, 1981. Excellent discussion of the Chicago versus New York skyscraper movements. Chapter 5 focuses on the skyscraper races of the 1930's that produced the Chrysler, Chanin, and Empire State buildings. Photos, reference notes, and index included.

Goldman, Jonathan. *The Empire State Building Book.* New York: St. Martin's Press, 1980. An entertaining history of the Empire State Building. Ninety-six pages of facts, information, and anecdotes. Excellent photos and an interesting collection of postcard pictures, artists' renditions, and other memorabilia. No index, but two appendices.

James, Theodore, Jr. *The Empire State Building.* New York: Harper & Row, 1975. An exuberant, almost emotional, history and discussion, including many unusual facts and anecdotes. Photos (many taken by Louis W. Hine), an appendix of interesting facts, bibliography, and index are included.

Macauley, David. *Unbuilding.* Boston: Houghton Mifflin, 1980. This author/illustrator combines meticulous and playful pen-and-ink drawings with a unique fictional tale about the dismantling of the Empire State Building in the year 1989. The story is merely a vehicle to reveal architectural elements of the building. Eighty pages in length. This book will appeal to both juvenile and adult readers. Glossary.

Messler, Norbert. *The Art Deco Skyscraper in New York.* New York: Peter Lang, 1986. A sophisticated treatment of the cultural and historical significance of New York City's Art Deco skyscrapers of the 1920's and 1930's. Highlights and interprets the architectural elements unique to this style and discusses America's focus on technology and the Machine Age. Some photos, extensive reference notes, and an index are included.

Reynolds, Donald Martin. *The Architecture of New York City.* New York: Macmillan, 1984. Interesting and highly informative survey of New York City architecture from the seventeenth to the twentieth centuries. Author/art historian Reynolds uses a chronological approach to give the reader details about a wide range of significant buildings and structures. The Empire State Building is covered in Chapter 12, which is devoted to a study of the Art Deco skyscrapers. Glossary, extensive bibliography, and an index.

Schleier, Merrill. *The Skyscraper in American Art, 1890-1931.* Ann Arbor, Mich.: UMI Research Press, 1986. Discusses the significance and meaning of skyscraper imagery in the arts as a direct reflection of the effects of skyscraper technology on American culture. Highlights artists such as photographers Alfred Stieglitz and Margaret Bourke-White and painter Georgia O'Keeffe. Reference notes, extensive bibliography, and index.

Cynthia L. Breslin

Cross-References

A Paris Exhibition Defines Art Deco (1925), p. 654; NBC Launches American Television at the World's Fair (1939), p. 1143; Rockefeller Center Is Completed (1939), p. 1149; Saarinen Designs Kennedy Airport's TWA Terminal (1956), p. 1716; The AT&T Building Exemplifies Postmodernism (1978), p. 2407.

THE WHITNEY MUSEUM IS INAUGURATED IN NEW YORK

Category of event: Art
Time: November 17, 1931
Locale: New York, New York

The Whitney Museum helped to give American artists public importance and gained international recognition for American art as a distinct and viable movement

Principal personages:

GERTRUDE VANDERBILT WHITNEY (1875-1942), an heiress and recognized artist whose unflagging support and patronage made possible the Whitney Museum

JULIANA RIESER FORCE (1876-1948), a dedicated organizer who promoted the idea of the Whitney Museum and became its first director

ROBERT HENRI (1865-1929), an outstanding artist whose firm belief that American art should be indigenous and free of foreign influence greatly influenced Whitney

JOHN FRENCH SLOAN (1871-1951), a noted American artist who helped to focus the artistic objectives of the Whitney Museum

FORBES WATSON (1880-1960), a knowledgeable art critic and public-relations expert who helped to shape the public image of the Whitney Museum

ALFRED STIEGLITZ (1864-1946), a pioneer photographer, promoter of American art, and gallery owner who demonstrated that dealing in art could be profitable

Summary of Event

In a short statement at the ceremony inaugurating the museum named in her honor, Gertrude Vanderbilt Whitney noted that she had been collecting American art for twenty-five years not only because she thought it worthwhile but also because she believed in American creative talent. The struggle to achieve recognition not only for American art but also for modernism had been difficult and was far from over.

When Whitney, at the turn of the century, had sought to escape the stifling social atmosphere into which she was born and to seek an identity for herself, she had no thought of establishing a museum. Turning to sculpture, for which she had some talent, she hired instructors and took classes. For the first time, she became aware of the struggles and often bleak world of the average American artist. American art, particularly modern American art, had no official recognition. The artistic establishment was firmly under the control of conservatives who saw merit in contemporary art only to the extent that it imitated the past.

In 1906, Whitney by chance met Robert Henri, a member of a group of avant-garde artists seeking to escape the regimentation of existing artistic standards, especially as to subject matter. Even though the United States was undergoing tremendous social change in the face of increasing industrialization and urbanization, "social realism" in art was not officially tolerated.

Henri was so persuasive that when Whitney organized a 1907 art exhibition in honor of the opening of the Colony Club, a fashionable club for women, she included works from his group. Seeking further to identify herself with the avant-garde, Whitney at the time of the exhibit also acquired a studio in New York's Greenwich Village. She also acquired the services of Juliana Rieser—an action that would change the lives of both. Exuberant, gregarious, efficient, and dedicated, Rieser gave focus and direction to her employer's artistic development and objectives.

The Colony Club exhibit set the stage for the mounting of an exhibit the following year that many consider to be the real beginning of the Whitney Museum of American Art. As one of the judges for the annual spring exhibit of the National Academy of Design, Robert Henri wanted to enter works by six of his colleagues. To his chagrin, all but one were refused by the academy's jury because of the "inappropriateness" of the works' subject matter.

The fallout resulted in the controversial "Exhibit of Eight" mounted in the Macbeth Gallery in 1908. The artists involved were Henri, George Luks, William Glackens, John Sloan, Everett Shinn, Ernest Lawson, Maurice Prendergast, and Arthur B. Davies. Because of the novelty of the new work, viewers flocked to the exhibit largely to express their disapproval. The artists were dubbed the "Apostles of Ugliness" and the "Black Gang." The name that stuck was the "Ashcan School."

Another, more comprehensive exhibit was immediately planned. Under the guidance of the cosmopolitan Davies, it was decided to dedicate the exhibit to modernism in general and to include the works of leading European artists. The result was the Armory Show of 1913, which included more than a thousand works by nearly four hundred artists. Americans were exposed to movements such as Fauvism, with its emphasis on pure color, and cubism. For the first time, the American public saw works by Paul Cézanne, Pablo Picasso, Paul Gaugin, and Vincent van Gogh. What was also painfully obvious to many American artists was how immature their works seemed in comparison to that of their European counterparts.

Gertrude Whitney was the largest purchaser of works from the Exhibit of Eight; she subsidized the group organizing the Armory Exhibit. With her capable new assistant (who had in the meantime married and changed her name to Juliana Force), Whitney was determined to play a more direct role in American art largely through her sizable financial resources. In 1913, she acquired a townhouse that abutted her studio and established the Whitney Studio to show the works of artists who could not exhibit elsewhere. Seeking further to assist artists, Whitney acquired another property and established the Whitney Studio Club, which enabled artists not only to display but also to actually work on the premises.

With no formal entrance requirements, the club grew to an unmanageable size, and both the studio and club faced the possibility of becoming little more than a form of artistic charity. Under the direction of Juliana Force and with the advice and guidance of John Sloan and Forbes Watson, greater focus and selectivity were given both to exhibitions and to purchases. Watson, as editor of an art magazine and with newspaper connections, not only was a capable adviser and discerning critic but also was able to manage the increasingly necessary publicity. A model for the Whitney group's objectives was the famous "291" New York gallery of the pioneer photographer Alfred Stieglitz. Limiting himself to a relatively small number of artists of promise, Stieglitz had promoted both American art and his artists, resulting in increasing sales and commissions.

During the 1920's, the Whitney group staged a number of exhibitions of works by artists who later became famous, including George Bellows, Jo Davidson, Edward Hopper, Rockwell Kent, Charles Demuth, Gaston Lachaise, and Elie Nadelman. To accommodate the increased activity, two buildings adjoining the studio building were acquired. The financial drain, however, began to be a burden even for Whitney, who began to think of the eventual disposition of her by-then-considerable collection of American art. A solution seemed to be to place the collection in an endowed separate wing of the Metropolitan Museum of Art. Whitney's offer, however, was summarily rejected by the museum, so strong still was the prejudice against modern or experimental American art.

Whitney was more disturbed by the rejection than was Juliana Force, who had been charged with making the offer. Force had always hoped that the Whitney collection would keep its separate identity; she believed that even if the Metropolitan were to accept the offer, modern American art would not receive the respect and attention it deserved. The decision was made to create a separate museum. A building on West Eighth Street in New York was acquired for the project; the new building's facade was decorated with a picture of an American eagle with outspread wings.

This was the first of the three homes of the Whitney Museum of American Art, which made subsequent moves necessitated by the growth and importance of the collection. Housed since 1966 in a striking building on Madison Avenue designed by Marcel Breuer, it has become one of the world's great museums and Gertrude Vanderbilt Whitney's most lasting monument.

Impact of Event

The primary impact of the establishment of the Whitney Museum of American Art was in legitimizing American art and recognizing it as as one of the world's great art movements, on par with and soon to surpass that of Europe. The objective had been planned. In her speech at the opening, Juliana Force, the first director, noted that the museum would be devoted to the difficult but important task of gaining for the art of America the prestige that theretofore had been reserved for the art of foreign countries and the art of the past.

An important step in validating the kind of art the Whitney promoted was the recognition of the free creative spirit of the nonacademic artist. Much of the battle waged by the founders of the Whitney had been against the narrow restrictions imposed by academic institutions such as the National Academy of Design. One of the consequences of increasing artistic freedom was the evolution of abstraction, which was central to the development of perhaps the first important American school of art, the New York School that developed in the decades after 1945. Central to the movement were the abstract expressionists such as Arshile Gorky and Jackson Pollock. Juliana Force was attracted to abstraction, and the Whitney purchased a Gorky work in 1937. The museum would later become a major repository for American abstraction.

The opening of the Whitney Museum also gave a major impetus to twentieth century art and to modern art in general. In the 1910's and 1920's, the Whitney Studio and the Whitney Studio Club were among the few places where so-called modern art could be seen. In the years between 1929 and 1931, an artistic explosion of a sort took place with the opening of the Museum of Modern Art and the Albert E. Gallatin Gallery of Living Art, and the beginnings of the Solomon R. Guggenheim Museum of Non-Objective Art and the Peggy Guggenheim Gallery.

The opening of the Whitney also did much to raise the prestige of American artists. Gone were the days when the artist John Sloan could pessimistically observe that the pioneer American artist was like a roach, not wanted, not encouraged, yet present. One of Gertrude Whitney's major objectives, from which she never deviated, was to assist artists. Therefore, her emphasis was on encouraging living artists, and the exhibits at both the Whitney Studio and the Whitney Studio Club were primarily staged to enable artists to promote and to sell their works.

An adjunct to the prestige gained by the artist and the growing value of artworks was the growth of the art industry, which would become a vital part of the economies of such cities as New York, Chicago, and San Francisco. When the Whitney Studio first opened, only a handful of American galleries existed, and almost none was willing to exhibit nonacademic works. By the time the Whitney Museum opened, there were dozens of galleries, and the number kept growing. Art indeed had become big business.

Perhaps the most pervasive impact of the opening of the Whitney Museum has been in making the public more aware and more appreciative of art. Appropriate publicity has always been part of the museum's operation, and the Whitney was among the first to arrange traveling exhibits both in the United States and abroad— realizing an objective stated by Gertrude Vanderbilt Whitney in her opening address: that the museum would grow and increase in importance as its public also grew.

Bibliography

Ashton, Dora. *The New York School: A Cultural Reckoning.* Berkeley: University of California Press, 1972. Stresses the beginnings of the modern American art movement; Ashton writes of its maturation in the form of the New York School associated with Surrealism and Abstract expressionism. Scant mention is made of the Whitney Museum, however, even when the artistic life of Greenwich Village is being discussed.

Berman, Avis. *Rebels on Eighth Street: Juliana Force and the Whitney Museum of American Art.* New York: Atheneum, 1990. Probably the best work available on the founding of the Whitney Museum. Stresses the role of Juliana Force, possibly because the author is persuaded that Force has not been given the credit she deserves. Excellent bibliography and index. Illustrations, all in black and white, are meager for a work on an art museum.

Friedman, B. H. *Gertrude Vanderbilt Whitney.* Garden City, N.Y.: Doubleday, 1978. Can be viewed as the history of the museum from the standpoint of Whitney. Most valuable is part 3, "Alone Again," in which the author largely credits the death of Gertrude's husband in 1930 for the energy with which she pursued the establishment of the museum. Friedman admits it was largely due to the influence of Juliana Force that the Whitney kept its identity.

Goodrich, Lloyd. *Pioneers in Modern Art in America: The Decade of the Armory Show, 1910-1920.* New York: Praeger, 1963. The "Exhibit of Eight" in 1908 and the Armory Show of 1913 were instrumental in establishing the environment for the founding of the Whitney Museum and the Museum of Modern Art. Goodrich, who was the third director of the Whitney, is knowledgeable about his subject, and he shows how an indigenous American art movement began to coalesce after the cultural vacuum of the early part of the century.

Sims, Patterson. *Whitney Museum of American Art.* New York: W. W. Norton, 1985. No understanding of a museum can come about without a knowledge of its collection. This contains reproductions of many of the Whitney's outstanding works, all in color. Two of the more interesting paintings are a portrait of Gertrude Vanderbilt Whitney by Robert Henri and George Bellow's *Dempsy and Firpo*, which greeted visitors when the Whitney opened its doors in 1931. Included is an excellent overview of the history of the museum and short biographies of its major artists.

Nis Petersen

Cross-References

Stieglitz Organizes the Photo-Secession (1902), p. 63; Avant-Garde Art in the Armory Show Shocks American Viewers (1913), p. 361; New York's Museum of Modern Art Is Founded (1929), p. 782; *Abstract Painting in America* Opens in New York (1935), p. 1001; Peggy Guggenheim's Gallery Promotes New American Art (1942), p. 1239; The Guggenheim Museum Opens in a Building Designed by Wright (1959), p. 1806; Breuer Designs a Building for the Whitney Museum (1966), p. 2064.

CÉLINE'S *JOURNEY TO THE END OF THE NIGHT* IS PUBLISHED

Category of event: Literature
Time: 1932
Locale: Paris, France

Louis-Ferdinand Céline's argot-filled novel radiated an earthy vigor and alternately shocked and inspired readers with its exuberant expressions of disgust for civilization

Principal personages:

LOUIS-FERDINAND CÉLINE (LOUIS-FERDINAND DESTOUCHES, 1894-1961), a French novelist whose checkered past as anti-Semitic pamphleteer and Nazi collaborator have somewhat compromised his stature as one of the century's most celebrated iconoclastic novelists

ANDRÉ GIDE (1869-1951), a renowned novelist who gave positive evaluations to Céline's first two novels

ÉMILE ZOLA (1840-1902), the progenitor of the naturalistic novel who received Céline's homage, largely on account of both men's common fascination with the seamy side of life

FYODOR DOSTOEVSKI (1821-1881), the distinguished Russian novelist who introduced a new type of aggressively bitter and alienated narrator that Céline would develop to new depths of despair and pugnacity

FRIEDRICH WILHELM NIETZSCHE (1844-1900), the German philosopher whose iconoclastic pronouncements on Western civilization resonate with the adamantly grim views Céline held about human civilization in general

MIGUEL DE CERVANTES (1547-1616), a Spanish writer who was one of the few significant Renaissance influences upon Céline

Summary of Event

The son of hard-pressed lower-middle-class Parisian shopkeepers, Louis-Ferdinand Destouches borrowed his pen name of Céline from his grandmother before making the transition from doctor to novelist in the 1930's. His maiden novel, *Voyage au bout de la nuit* (1932; *Journey to the End of the Night*, 1934), vaulted him into the front ranks of the French literary scene, typically eliciting polarized reactions of either enthusiastic praise or vehement criticism from reviewers. Supporters contended that Céline had squarely faced the hypocrisy and degradation of modern social life with unprecedented candor and sensitivity, while one of the many detractors who rejected the novel as lowbrow and morally corrupt wisecracked that a tax levied upon each of the myriad obscenities in the book would make a major dent in France's ballooning budget deficit. Subsequent novels by Céline would differ from

Journey to the End of the Night in various ways, but his maiden work established his lifelong pattern of writing darkly humorous picaresque novels featuring argot-peppered prose and a spirit of outspoken and often truculent pessimism.

Like other picaresque novels, *Journey to the End of the Night* follows the footloose peregrinations of a dominant protagonist. Ferdinand Bardamu doubles as narrator and protagonist, and the many resonances of his life story with Céline's make him at least a semiautobiographical figure. Bardamu's life mirrors Céline's as follows: He suffers a serious injury while fighting against Germany as a volunteer in World War I and soon comes to dismiss war as a totally absurd and vain ritual; he goes to Africa, where he experiences revulsion at both European colonialism and native folkways; he voyages to America, where he works for a period in the intimidating atmosphere of mammoth auto plants and indulges in flings with American women of low repute; and he returns across the Atlantic to France, where he settles down as a doctor in a seedy working-class neighborhood of Paris. Although the careful reader cannot go so far as to assume a relationship of absolute identity between Céline and Bardamu, the close overlap between the life stories of author and protagonist has persuaded most reviewers and interpreters to identify the major attitudes and values of Bardamu with those of Céline, even if many of the minor details in Bardamu's life bear the mark of poetic license. Indeed, Céline's subsequent novels would continue to adopt the first book's strange mixture of plodding confessional autobiography and mercurial, hallucinatory disjunctiveness.

The hallucinatory quality of *Journey to the End of the Night* emerges early in the novel. After Bardamu startles a somewhat conservative interlocutor at a Paris café with an outspoken exposition of his cynical and pessimistic view of the ordinary citizen as but a galley slave for the rich at the top of the social pyramid, a parade of men enlisting for military service in World War I rounds a street corner in the two young men's direction. Supposedly overcome by the spectacle of a largely female crowd lining both sides of the street and cheering the marching men, Bardamu impulsively leaps up from his chair and hurries to join the procession of enlistees. While the reader gradually becomes accustomed to the mercurial impulsiveness of Céline's picaro, Bardamu's cocksure rejection of his civilization as disgustingly corrupt and exploitative sits very uneasily beside the ebullient optimism with which he decides to defend his country. To say that this abrupt turn in attitude lacks verisimilitude would be understating the case, for Bardamu's apparent amnesia regarding what he has just been saying about a world of galley slaves reminds one more of a dream or hallucination than of a plausible state of waking consciousness.

After a war wound allows Bardamu to cheat the heavy odds against him at the battlefront and to return alive to convalesce in Paris, he has an affair with a young American woman, whom he eventually comes to despise. A subsequent trip to a French colony in sub-Saharan Africa seems to reinforce his jaundiced view of civilization as a whole, though he singles out a certain French petty official for adulatory praise, likening the man to an angel because of his selfless devotion to a young woman. Later on in the novel during Bardamu's wanderings in America, he briefly shows obeisance to another model of selflessness, on this occasion the familiar popular archetype of the prostitute with a heart of gold, specifically the elusive and hastily sketched figure of Molly. Céline's view of the human condition thus shows itself as highly polarized; the narrator views himself and the great majority of fellow humans as despicably selfish exploiters, while a tiny minority of saintlike and selfless characters such as Molly and the French official stand in stark contrast to the malevolent multitude. Yet in light of the relish with which Céline describes the failings of the majority and the brevity and sketchiness with which he portrays the tiny angelic minority, one can only conclude that the novelist attributes far more vitality and genuine significance to the wretched and ignoble majority.

Though Bardamu takes Molly as his lover and seems satisfied with her as a partner, his wanderlust knows no bounds, and both he and his American paramour soon agree that the two of them must part for no other reason than his yearning for the road. Soon back in France, Bardamu takes up the practice of medicine in the same seedy neighborhood that houses Léon Robinson, his old war buddy and fellow pessimistic cynic.

Robinson comes across as something of an alter ego or double for Bardamu. Robinson abruptly veers in and out of the narrative from beginning to end as Bardamu's companion in avoiding the front lines in war, sampling American factory life in Detroit, and hustling jobs and approachable women in a grim working-class Parisian neighborhood. Both men harbor too much bitterness toward their society to take the step of partially integrating themselves with it by settling down and raising families. As the two escort their paramours on a double date to a cheap amusement park, the reader encounters yet another example of a coarse and callow sensibility bent on perpetually extending the joyful irresponsibility of adolescent drifting while indulging in paranoid fantasies about a cruel society forever victimizing the innocent. When Robinson's lover suspects that she means little more to him than one of the passing entertainments at the amusement park, she begins to insist that he show some commitment to their relationship of several months and talk about how it might be made permanent. Robinson merely scoffs at this idea with a cackle. When he notices how furious his lover has become, he tries to gloss over things by insisting that he has nothing personal against her but simply has an aversion to sullying himself with what he views as the hypocritical conventions of love and marriage. When he sinks into a sullen silence in response to her increasingly overwrought demands that he follow through with the implied commitment he has made to her over the past several months, she finally goes berserk and shoots him in the abdomen, at which point she flees the scene. Like many of Céline's characters, she abruptly slips out of the narrative, never to be heard of again.

Instead of rushing Robinson to a hospital, where inconvenient questions from the despised police might be asked, Bardamu and his paramour carry the bleeding and half-conscious man to a bed in the narrator's sanatorium ward. Simply assuming that Robinson has no chance of surviving, Bardamu holds his dying sidekick's hand while waiting for internal hemorrhaging to finish him off. The thoughts that run through Bardamu's mind at this point well represent the caustically antihumanistic tenor of Céline's pessimism, for Bardamu confesses that he feels less pity for the dying Robinson, his best friend, than he would have felt for a dying dog. After all, Bardamu muses, a dog is not sly, whereas Robinson was sly, as are humans in general. Were the word "sly" replaced with the word "sinful," Céline would appear much like one of the religious zealots who pontificate about the utter depravity of man and the impossible state of the world as a vale of tears. Since Céline rules out the possibility of efficacious intervention on the part of either human or supernatural forces, however, his views wind up even more acridly bitter and negative. It is hardly surprising that he can find no more appropriate line with which to end *Journey to the End of the Night* than "Let us hear no more of all this."

Impact of Event

Heavily pessimistic fiction can hardly be considered rare, as any reader of Thomas Hardy's Wessex novels or Émile Zola's Rougon-Macquart series could attest. Yet novels such as Hardy's and Zola's not only offer the reader at least the possibility of a satisfactory resolution but also present the onset of disillusionment as a gradual development governed by intelligible relations of cause and effect. In contrast, *Journey to the End of the Night* does not even attempt to present an incremental rise in disillusionment of the protagonist; instead, the book offers the reader an antiheroic picaro who seems astonishingly free of "illusions" about wretched mankind from the very outset. Just a few pages into the novel, Bardamu self-assuredly likens the lot of both himself and the vast majority of humans to the miserable fate of galley slaves, who must row like the devil in a stinking ship's hold while the captain lounges on the breezy deck with a perfumed and nubile young woman on his lap. Rather than witnessing Bardamu's increasing understanding of human suffering over time, the reader of *Journey to the End of the Night* observes merely a repetitious piling-up of anecdotes, vignettes, and pronouncements on the theme of human degradation and vileness.

The degree to which the disjointedly connected episodes in *Journey to the End of the Night* can be appreciated independently of what occurs before or after in the novel seems extreme even by the loose standards of the picaresque novel; the overall effect is somewhat like that of a series of vaudeville acts united only by the sameness of the lead performer. Céline draws on his mastery of the spoken idiom and theatrical exuberance to forestall the monotony that tends to result from repetitiousness of attitude and disjointedness of incident, but his racy argot and theatricality can rarely make up for the absence of a larger order in the scheme of his novel. In lieu of setting up a structural framework for his novels, Céline draws on the concept of "lacework" to explain his proclivity for articulating an intricate but predictable pattern or motif time and time again, as if he were weaving a piece of lace.

Céline's antisocial and partly hooliganish picaro stands as an important intermediary between Fyodor Dostoevski's underground man of *Zapiski iz podpolya* (1864; *Notes from the Underground*, 1918) and the rebellious countercultural protagonists common in the works of Henry Miller and such Beat generation novelists as Jack Kerouac, Ken Kesey, and William Burroughs. Like Dostoevski's underground man, Bardamu angrily resents the civilization from which he hails, and he repeatedly lashes both it and himself with partially relevant but greatly overblown accusations of sickness and inequity. Céline goes a step further, however, in jettisoning the decorum of a somewhat restrained and literate narrative persona. It was one thing to allow one's characters to brawl and spout obscenities, as many a character in Zola's novels did, but quite another to create a narrator who similarly exulted in mouthing expletive-laden argot and slapping defenseless women around. Although the rough-and-tumble language and brutish antics of Céline's narrators scandalized many readers at first, more and more writers followed suit with narrative personae similarly contemptuous of decorum and delicate aesthetic sensibilities. As a result, the kind of narrator who had shocked Céline's readers in the 1930's became a more and more familiar figure in European and American fiction by the 1960's. In more recent years, Céline's writings have become so accepted within the canon of major modern French writers that passages from his novels have made their way into the very pillar of cultural traditionalism, the national *baccalauréat* examination.

Céline often referred to his picaros as traveling the "night subway" through the seamy side of modern social life that more genteel writers ignored, falsified or prettified. While even many of his admirers have noted the dangers posed by his amoral stance and irrational and intolerant turns of thought, his important stature and wide influence in the realm of twentieth century fiction can no longer be contested.

Bibliography

Booth, Wayne C. *The Rhetoric of Fiction.* Chicago: University of Chicago Press, 1961. In this book's concluding chapter, "The Morality of Impersonal Narration," Booth acknowledges Céline's literary talent. Yet he also emphasizes how the French author's hard-bitten distrust of virtually all human motivations contradicts his self-assured pronouncements on virtues and vices.

Buckley, William K., ed. *Critical Essays on Louis-Ferdinand Céline.* Boston: G. K. Hall, 1989. Apart from its lack of a bibliography, this is the most comprehensive volume of Céline criticism in English, containing a representative selection of positive, negative, and neutral evaluations of the novelist.

Céline, Louis-Ferdinand. *Journey to the End of the Night.* Translated by John H. P. Marks. New York: New Directions, 1960. The standard English translation of Céline's first and most famous novel.

Hewitt, Nicholas. *The Golden Age of Louis-Ferdinand Céline.* Leamington Spa, England: Berg, 1987. This survey of Céline's work includes a chapter on the novelist's 1920's nonfiction writings about medical hygiene as significant influences on his fiction.

Luce, Stanford L., and William K. Buckley. *A Half-Century of Céline: An Annotated Bibliography, 1932-1982.* New York: Garland, 1983. The most comprehensive bibliography in English of Céline criticism.

McCarthy, Patrick. *Céline.* London: Allen Lane, 1975. Perhaps the finest life-and-works study of Céline in English, McCarthy's book illuminates many connections between Céline's major novels and French politics of the 1930's.

Philip F. Williams

Cross-References

Freud Inaugurates a Fascination with the Unconscious (1899), p. 19; Surrealism Is Born (1924), p. 604; Sartre's *Being and Nothingness* Expresses Existential Philosophy (1943), p. 1262; The Beat Movement Rejects Mainstream Values (1950's), p. 1460; Foucault's *Madness and Civilization* Is Published (1961), p. 1877.

HUXLEY'S *BRAVE NEW WORLD* REFLECTS FEARS ABOUT THE FUTURE

Category of event: Literature
Time: 1932
Locale: England

Brave New World *titillated readers with a portrait of an anti-Utopian world in which science and technology have satisfied every need at the expense of human freedom*

Principal personages:
ALDOUS HUXLEY (1894-1963), a novelist whose work explores the plight of modern man in a world of conflicting values
D. H. LAWRENCE (1885-1930), a controversial literary giant whose naturalistic philosophy and views against science, technology, and orthodox religion influenced Huxley's thinking
JOHN B. WATSON (1878-1958), an American psychologist and pioneer of behaviorist theory, which Huxley adapted in recounting conditioning of Fordian children

Summary of Event

By *Brave New World*'s publication early in 1932, Aldous Huxley was reaching the zenith of his fame as a novelist. Although he would publish much more over the next thirty years, he would turn increasingly to nonfiction.

Huxley grew up in the stimulating intellectual atmosphere of a family of prominent scientists and literary figures. His exposure to writing and matters of style came about as a natural consequence of his father's editorship of the influential *Cornhill Magazine*. Huxley's early writings included his contributions to the University of Oxford's respected *The Athæneum*. During World War I, while still a student at Oxford, Huxley published two books of poetry. Another volume of poetry and a book of short fiction immediately preceded the 1921 publication of his first novel, *Crome Yellow*, which was a critical and popular success and established Huxley as a novelist of ideas and as a satirist.

Huxley's world, from the beginning of his literary career up until (and certainly after) the publication of *Brave New World*, was one in which satire seemed to be the writer's appropriate mode. The post-World War I era was crassly materialistic, skeptical, and cynical; at the same time, it was buoyantly optimistic owing to the explosion of research and knowledge in many areas of life. Huxley and his literary contemporaries also detected a moral and spiritual emptiness that focused their themes. Huxley's 1920's novels witheringly portrayed the same frivolous generation being explored and satirized in the works of Evelyn Waugh, W. Somerset Maugham, F. Scott Fitzgerald, and Sinclair Lewis. Disillusionment, loss of faith, and spiritual shallowness received equal though less satirical treatment by Ernest Hemingway, D. H. Lawrence, Virginia Woolf, Ezra Pound, and T. S. Eliot. Over them all loomed the genius of James Joyce, who liberated style and form in the novel and strengthened Huxley's conviction that satirical fiction was the proper vehicle for the exploration of the modern human condition.

The beneficial effects of the literary atmosphere in which Huxley evolved as a writer were offset by some of the unpleasant social realities of the 1920's and early 1930's. England's postwar economic woes belied the feverish consumerism of the privileged classes. The "Roaring Twenties" were punctuated by the 1926 General Strike and the global 1929 stock market crash and ensuing Great Depression. In the new Soviet Union, power struggles unfolded that resulted in the ascent of Joseph Stalin. His aggressive totalitarianism was repeated in the equally ominous comings to power of Adolf Hitler, Benito Mussolini, and Francisco Franco. The economic disarray of their nations provided fertile ground for these dictators' relentless repression of individual and cultural freedom; the progressive breakdown of European nations signaled the inevitability of another global war.

At the same time, exciting developments in the sciences, both physical and social, were occurring. These stimulated both Huxley's intellect and his imagination. For example, mass production was revolutionizing industry (including arms production) through use of the assembly line, making inexpensive, mass-produced consumer goods widely available. Air travel technology, glamorized by the exploits of Charles Lindbergh and Amelia Earhart, was rapidly developing, and the pace of achievement in communications technology was stunning. Explorations in genetics and genetic mutation were stirring public debate. Behaviorist and conditioning theories, pioneered by American psychologist John B. Watson, were stimulating controversy and influencing theories of child care and education. In 1928, Margaret Mead published *Coming of Age in Samoa: A Psychological Study of Primitive Youth for Western Civilisation*, forcing cultural anthropologists to redefine many ideas about human social behavior. Huxley's considerable scientific knowledge enabled him to consider these advances, carried to their satirical extreme, in *Brave New World*.

Because of Huxley's well-established literary fame, *Brave New World* provoked an immediate popular response when it appeared in the winter of 1932. In its first year, it sold a total of twenty-eight thousand copies in England and the United States. Eventually, it was translated into nineteen languages, and it continued to enjoy respectable sales throughout the remainder of the century. It evidently struck a chord in a population both fascinated by and fearful of the huge scientific and technological advances of an era beset by economic instability, the possibility of renewed global warfare, and a decline in traditional values.

As a novelist of provocative ideas and sophisticated style, Huxley viewed fiction as the vehicle through which the human experience, especially in his eventful times, could best be explored. Judging by *Brave New World*'s continuing popularity, it was the novel with which Huxley came closest to achieving his goal of examining the dilemma posed by humankind's equal impulses for good and evil, for creativity and self-destructiveness.

Impact of Event

Although all of Huxley's first four novels satirize contemporary life, *Brave New World* extrapolates the values and the scientific and technological achievements of that life into a world exactly six hundred years in the future. A global holocaust, the Nine Years War, has reshaped the world. Its spokesman in 632 A.F. (After Ford) is the world controller, Mustapha Mond. Early in the novel, he expounds the principles on which the society, portrayed largely in a transformed London, is founded. Stability is its cornerstone; relentless elimination of human individuality by biological engineering and superficially benign totalitarianism is its most chilling achievement.

Life is orderly and tranquil, owing largely to the technological wizardry applied to its daily functions. The showpiece is the assembly-line production of the five types of humans, ranging from the intellectually superior Alphas to the semimoronic Epsilons. The novel opens with a tour of the Central London Hatchery and Conditioning Center. Huxley's wit and evocative descriptive style are at their best here, as the hatchery's director proudly describes the fetuses' inexorable nine-month journey by bottle through a twilight world, controlled and manipulated at every phase, to "decanting" into a life already programmed and predestined. Although free of illness and old age, it is a sterile life without free will or emotional depth. All human endeavor is directed toward satisfying the population's carefully conditioned impulses for material consumption and immediate sexual gratification. As the novel progresses, every aspect of life is scrutinized and ultimately trivialized by the jingles and slogans that have replaced thought and idealism.

Little in the way of a satisfying alternative to this frighteningly shallow (some critics said misogynist) society is offered. In keeping with the traditions of satire, characters' names suggest to an alert reader the existing political and philosophical ideals that Huxley either rejects or admires. The central protagonists, everyday people through whose eyes the future society is mostly presented and who provide the measure of Huxley's satirical intent, are themselves flawed and hopelessly alienated. Short, dark Alpha-Plus Bernard Marx, a psychological counselor, is set apart by physical deviation from the handsome, strapping Alpha and Beta norm, represented, for example, by the "pneumatic," intelligent, but determinedly conformist Lenina Crowne.

Bernard abhors the casual, sterile sexual license that keeps the population docile. He also resists soma, the soporific drug carried by all citizens to provide them with an immediate "holiday" from any unpleasantness or stress, any pesky remnant of dissatisfaction or longing for a fuller life not quite bred out of the human psyche. Bernard consciously rejects the ideal of undisturbed, painless existence. Unfortunately, the courage he displays in doing this is offset by his tendencies toward egotism and whining. His eventual fate is exile to Iceland, suitably remote and cold for hopeless social deviants. John the Savage, nurtured (accidentally) on the poetry and humanism of William Shakespeare, also has been shaped by the degraded society of his birth, a New Mexican reservation where poverty, disease, brutality, and corrupted tribal tradition prevail. In England, to which Bernard brings John and his ruined Beta-Minus mother Linda, John is first an object of scientific interest and public fascination but finally a figure of fun. In both dystopian societies, he is an outcast from birth—indeed, by the very process of birth, natural reproduction being considered the most revolting of the old human habits known. Denied the nobility inherent in his Rousseau-esque life and name, his dignity, and his Shakespearean outlook, John's only possible response is suicide. The one protagonist clearly intended as sympathetic is Bernard's friend and confidant Helmholtz Watson, a peripheral character marked for exile from the outset.

Critical response to *Brave New World* was contradictory. Huxley's literary reputation caused the novel to command the immediate attention of a large group of intellectual heavyweights in whose circles Huxley had moved all of his life, and with whom he debated the heady ideas—literary, historical, philosophical, scientific, and religious—of the time. Much of the reaction was negative and focused on the novel's satirizing of current scientific thought and research. Influential novelist and historian H. G. Wells, for example, reportedly was deeply offended by what he regarded as Huxley's betrayal of science and the future. Critic Joseph Needham, a distinguished biologist, thought the novel would appeal only to special-interest readers such as biologists and philosophers. Other reviewers, unreceptive to the novel's satirical intent and tone, dismissed it as frivolous. Some reviewers thought that Huxley was promoting the ideals of his anti-Utopia and were disgusted. Perhaps the most telling observations came from such influential contemporary thinkers as Bertrand Russell, Rebecca West, and Hermann Hesse, who all recognized in *Brave New World* its application to the present world, the anxiety it expressed about the human condition, and the serious intent beneath the surface cleverness and playful wit. This latter view prevailed in successive generations of readers, especially as some of Huxley's projections about modern life seemed to come horribly true.

Brave New World was a watershed in Huxley's development as a writer and thinker. After his 1932 introduction to mystic Gerald Heard, his interest in the spiritual parameters of life led to his controlled experimentation with drugs, coloring his subsequent writing and thinking. He continued to ponder his achievement in *Brave New World*, in a foreword to a 1946 edition and finally in the full-length *Brave New World Revisited* (1958). Paramount among the novel's weaknesses, he thought, was his own failure to recognize the ominous potential of nuclear fission, "for the possibilities of atomic energy had been a popular topic of conversation for years before the book was written." Huxley came to believe, especially after the dropping of the atomic bomb, that individual freedom was much closer to extinction than he had suggested when he placed *Brave New World* six hundred years in the future. His fundamental optimism about humanity is also evident. He observed, "The theme of *Brave New World* is not the advancement of science as such; it is the advancement of science as it affects human individuals." One artistic failure, he thought, was the character John the Savage, because he was not offered sanity as a possible alternative to the shortcomings of future life. Huxley hoped throughout his life that sanity would prevail to pull humankind back from the brink of annihilation.

Ironically, *Brave New World* is best described today by the adjective "Orwellian," coined after George Orwell's *Nineteen Eighty-Four* (1948) described the nightmare world of Oceania and its successful assault on individual freedom. In a 1959 review of both novels, influential novelist, playwright, and essayist C. P. Snow dismissed both works on artistic grounds and especially for their pessimism about scientific progress and social purpose. Yet Huxley, like Orwell, simply tried to express the pervasive anxiety of the turbulent twentieth century, and above all acknowledged the contradictory creative and destructive forces of man's most potent capability, that of free will.

Bibliography

Brander, Laurence. *Aldous Huxley: A Critical Study.* Lewisburg, Pa.: Bucknell University Press, 1970. An exhaustive, readable study covering all of Huxley's writing except poetry. A short selected bibliography precedes an index listing topics related to Huxley's works and thought.

Firchow, Peter Edgerly. *The End of Utopia: A Study of Aldous Huxley's "Brave New World."* Lewisburg, Pa.: Bucknell University Press, 1984. In five chapters, Firchow examines the novel as literature, as prophecy of future science and technology, as consideration of future man, as political anti-Utopia, and in comparison to Orwell's *Nineteen Eighty-Four.*

Henderson, Alexander. *Aldous Huxley.* New York: Russell & Russell, 1936. Describes Huxley's life and assesses all of his writing to the mid-1930's. An interesting if a bit pedantic study of contemporary thought on Huxley's works to that time.

Kuehn, Robert E., ed. *Aldous Huxley: A Collection of Critical Essays.* Englewood Cliffs, N.J.: Prentice-Hall, 1974. A variety of critical response reflected in ten essays and a critical symposium written for *The London Magazine* (1955). A chronology and a selected bibliography are included.

Nance, Guinevera A. *Aldous Huxley.* New York: Continuum, 1988. The third of five chapters, "Heaven and Hell: The Utopian Theme in Three Novels," explores this aspect of *Brave New World.* Analyzes the progress of Huxley's vision from dystopian to positive. Interesting and readable. Hindsight gives a clear perspective on Huxley's achievement.

Watt, Donald, ed. *Aldous Huxley: The Critical Heritage.* London: Routledge and Kegan Paul, 1975. An indispensable collection of critical reviews of Huxley's writings from beginning to end, listed chronologically by title and date of work. Also includes an intelligent biographical introduction, interesting appendices, bibliography, and index.

Jill Rollins

Cross-References

Lang Expands the Limits of Filmmaking with *Metropolis* (1927), p. 707; *The Bedbug* and *The Bathhouse* Exemplify Revolutionary Theater (1929), p. 787; Socialist

WRIGHT FOUNDS THE TALIESIN FELLOWSHIP

Category of event: Architecture
Time: 1932
Locale: Spring Green, Wisconsin, and Scottsdale, Arizona

The great architect invited apprentices to work with him during the third and most productive period of his career

Principal personages:

FRANK LLOYD WRIGHT (1867-1959), a visionary architect

OLGIVANNA LLOYD WRIGHT (1900-1985), his third wife, who organized domestic life, entertainment, and educational projects at Taliesin

WILLIAM WESLEY PETERS (1912-1991), one of the original Taliesin Fellows, who became Wright's son-in-law and chief architect of Taliesin Associated Architects

EDGAR KAUFMANN, JR. (1910-1989), an early Taliesin Fellow who convinced his father to commission Fallingwater, Wright's masterpiece

EDGAR TAFEL (1912-   ), one of the original Taliesin Fellows, who helped to engineer and supervise many buildings

Summary of Event

At the age of sixty-five in 1932, Frank Lloyd Wright had fallen on hard times. Taliesin, his home, had been struck by lightning and burned. Having fallen in love with another woman during a messy divorce, he was hounded by police and forced to spend a night in jail before they could be married. The Great Depression was making money for big buildings scarce. In nearly five years, he had built buildings for only two paying clients, one a cousin. With his new bride, he returned to rebuild Taliesin and write his autobiography.

Genius struck again. Wright decided to found the Taliesin Fellowship. Apprentices around the world were invited to live and work with him at Taliesin, where they could learn architecture from the ground up. It was a self-sufficient community; the fellows generated electricity, grew their own food, lumbered forests, quarried stone, and built buildings to live and study in. Having learned design and construction, the fellows helped to engineer and superintend construction of Wright's greatest buildings.

Twenty-three fellows gathered at Taliesin in October, 1932. A few soon left, daunted by the work; some stayed a decade or more. The fellowship flourished. The members' numbers doubled and tripled.

To escape the brutal winter of 1937, Wright led them by caravan to Arizona, where they built winter quarters near Phoenix. A frontier camp at first, its great drafting room was lit by sunlight through a canvas roof. Based on Wright's principles of organic architecture, the headquarters was designed to blend with the desert landscape and was made mostly of materials at hand.

Wright remained young at heart, especially in old age. With his young apprentices, he formed a natural bond. He believed buildings should not be decided by politicians with grudges or old people with prejudices to preserve, but by fresh young minds. His own creative vigor was spurred by theirs. The Taliesin Fellowship thrust Wright's career into a second golden age.

Among the first to join him at Taliesin was Edgar Kaufmann, Jr., who persuaded his father to commission a vacation home in the wild woods of western Pennsylvania. Wright visited the spot, and the result was Fallingwater, perhaps the most famous private home ever built for a person not of royal blood. Senior Taliesin Fellows superintended the construction.

A boulder by a stream, which had been the family's favorite picnic spot, shoulders through the floor beside the hearth. Anchored to that rock, the house sweeps out horizontally over the waterfall on cantilevered, reinforced concrete balconies. Light and sound from the rippling waters reverberate on slabs of stone, glass, and concrete. Indoors and outdoors blend. United with nature organically, interior space seems unenclosed, reaching out from within.

In the same year, Herbert Johnson asked Wright and his fellows to make a new headquarters for his wax company. They presented him with the most astonishingly original, aesthetically pleasing commercial building ever erected. One newspaper reviewer said it was "like a beautiful naked woman bathing in a forest pool," a rare compliment for an office building.

Fashioned on low horizontal curves without corners, the building is entered from behind and beneath, through a carport. Its windowless walls afford no view of drab downtown Racine, Wisconsin, yet there is no feeling of containment, for bands of glass tubing encircle the building, shedding natural daylight on a great communal workspace without cubicles or partitions. As the tubes of glass disperse consciousness of walls, so the ceiling is effaced by giant columns shaped like lily pads; the columns are twenty-four feet in diameter at the top, slimming down to nine inches wide at the floor.

Building code inspectors balked. Each column had to support seven tons. Wright staged a public demonstration. With sixty tons loaded up on one column, the permit was issued. The spectacle drew nationwide attention. Johnson declared the building was worth more than five times its cost in publicity alone; he gave the fellowship a twenty-thousand dollar tip and renewed it every year.

One of the fellowship's first projects had been a scale model of Broadacre City, Wright's visionary plan for a community with a tillable acre of land for each family. The model had featured low-cost "Usonian" (American) homes incorporating Wright's functional concepts. Madison newspaperman Herbert Jacobs commissioned the first truly Usonian home actually built. Without plaster, radiators, attic, or cellar, the famous five-thousand-dollar house was built of concrete blocks and glass on a concrete slab heated by hot-water pipes. Jacobs also commissioned another home that made history, a rounded structure with a berm in back and glass in front for exposure to the sun. Called the solar hemicycle, it was the prototype for passive solar design.

One of the last great projects undertaken by Wright and his fellows proved their most controversial: the Guggenheim Museum in New York City, an art gallery for nonfigurative art. Wright designed a circular structure that looked more like a concrete eggshell than a regular building. Inside, he coiled a three-fourths-of-a-mile-long walkway down from a glass skylight dome on a three-percent grade. Visitors elevator up to the top and then stroll past paintings hung on luminous walls. A turn toward the center presents a prospect of the whole collection. One floor flows into another imperceptibly. Nowhere does the eye meet with any abrupt change of form; all lines flow together in unified harmony. The whole effect is quite serene. Wright, though, died months before the museum was opened.

Impact of Event

The impact of the Taliesin Fellowship was felt upon Wright's own career, by the fellows themselves, and by modern architecture in America and abroad.

Taliesin is a Welsh word that means "the shining brow." Wright took it as a name for his sparkling house of rock and glass built on the brow of a hill in rural Wisconsin. Taliesin was also the name of a mythical Welsh bard who entertained King Arthur and his knights of the Round Table. For Wright, the name thus suggested artistic inspiration, and he used it to christen the fellowship that lifted him late in life with abundant inspiration. With his fellows around the drafting board, he could play King Arthur with his court. They built a new Camelot for themselves and enlivened architecture around the world.

The commission that relaunched the great architect's career came from the father of a Taliesin Fellow. The worldwide acclaim paid to Fallingwater was unprecedented and led to dozens of other residential commissions, the bread and butter of an architect whose scandalous private life had turned away many corporate and governmental customers.

The fellowship itself drew much publicity. Its work-camp ethic appealed to American values during Depression years. Much was made of receiving visitors at Taliesin. For fifty cents, fellows would conduct a tour of the house and grounds, the Taliesin orchestra or chorus would perform, and Wright would greet his guests in person. The fellowship gained many clients and allies in this way, among them Herbert Johnson, Carl Sandburg, Adlai Stevenson, Henry and Claire Boothe Luce, and other influential shapers of public opinion.

The most immediate and long-range effect the Taliesin Fellowship had on architecture was to spread the fame and influence of Frank Lloyd Wright around the world. Their success with Fallingwater and the Johnson Wax headquarters early in the life of the fellowship reestablished Wright's professional reputation. In 1938, a special edition of the influential journal *Architectural Forum* was devoted to Wright's recent work, and his portrait appeared on the cover of *Time*. In 1939, Wright was asked to lecture at the Royal Institute of British Architects. Taliesin Fellows put together a major retrospective exhibition shown at the Museum of Modern Art in 1940. In the 1950's, Philadelphia architect Oscar Stonorov organized an exhibition called "Sixty Years of Living Architecture" and presented it in several cities in the United States, Europe, and Mexico.

Wright was the first American architect to gain worldwide fame and influence. The fascination with his work revived after the founding of the Taliesin Fellowship has hardly abated. A comprehensive bibliography of publications by and about Wright published in 1978 listed more than two thousand items.

Individually and as an organization, many of the fellows carried on after Wright's death. The fellowship was transformed into Taliesin Associated Architects, a firm that extended Wright's organic principles of design across America. The Frank Lloyd Wright Foundation and School of Architecture were established to promulgate his philosophy and provide professional education in architecture.

Taliesin Associates completed several important projects unfinished at the time of Wright's death: the buildings at Florida Southern College, the Marin County Civic Center complex, and the Grady Grammage Memorial Auditorium at Arizona State University. Some of Wright's designs were executed as late as the 1970's, such as the Pfeiffer House at Taliesin West, the Feldman House in Berkeley, California, and the Loveness Guest House in Stillwater, Minnesota.

Many fellows went on to achieve prominence in their own right in architecture and related fields, among them Edmund Thomas Casey, Bruce Gobb, Aaron Green, John deKoren Hill, John H. Howe, Edgar Kaufmann, Jr., Eugene Masselink, Charles Mantooth, Robert Mosher, Wesley Peters, Ling Po, John Rattenbury, Paolo Soleri, and Edgar Tafel. Moreover, Taliesin Associated Architects was responsible for several significant structures erected in the decade after Wright's death, such as the Ascension Lutheran Church in Scottsdale, designed by Wesley Peters, the Prairie School in Racine, designed by Charles Mantooth, the Rocky Mountain National Park Center, the Lincoln Income Life Insurance Company in Louisville, Kentucky, the Spring Green resort development near Taliesin, and the Lescohier House in Madison, designed by Peters.

Wright regretted that his effects on architecture had been more imitative than emulative, but they were both. The course of modern architecture was charted by the possibilities of concrete, steel, and glass that he and his Taliesin Fellows pioneered. Indeed, his concepts of the prairie house, the Usonian house, and passive solar design revolutionized residential architecture, especially in American suburbs. City planners, of course, never realized the concepts Wright envisioned for Broadacre City in full, but they did try to bring more of the country into the city. In the 1970's and 1980's, many downtowns were redesigned as pedestrian malls and gardens to minimize or eliminate the presence of private automobiles. Suburban shopping malls, with their wide-open spacing and horizontal sweep, reflect the massive indirect influence of Wright's Taliesin period.

If Wright had retired at sixty-five instead of founding the Taliesin Fellowship, he would be remembered as a daring experimentalist in residential architecture and interior design. The impact of his creative innovations and organic philosophy on subsequent architecture, though, would have been marginal, as it was before 1932, and his impact on modern building would have been a fraction of what it was and is.

Bibliography

Costantino, Maria. *Frank Lloyd Wright.* New York: Crescent Books, 1991. An oversized, lavishly illustrated picture book of Wright's architecture, with brief commentary, covering all periods of his work in chronological order. Eighty-nine full-color photographs and nineteen black-and-white illustrations feast the eye with glimpses of the monumental buildings and spacious interiors Wright designed. Includes a biographical introduction, 111 pages of photographs, and an index.

Smith, Norris Kelly. *Frank Lloyd Wright: A Study in Architectural Content.* Englewood Cliffs, N.J.: Prentice-Hall, 1966. An intriguing portrait of the architect; not a biography, but an analysis of his political, religious, social, aesthetic, and philosophical beliefs. Smith finds Wright a romantic spirit committed to the universal salvation of mankind, a fundamentally conservative and religious cause. Includes illustrations and footnotes.

Storrer, William Allin. *The Architecture of Frank Lloyd Wright: A Complete Catalog.* Cambridge, Mass.: MIT Press, 1974. Provides a photograph or sketch of every building known to have been designed by Wright, with brief, cogent commentary, 433 entries in all. Arranged in chronological order. Much scholarship and detective work went into locating, dating, and photographing each structure. Includes an introduction, several floorplans, maps, and geographical and alphabetical indexes.

Tafel, Edgar. *Apprentice to Genius: Years with Frank Lloyd Wright.* New York: McGraw-Hill, 1979. The fullest and most reliable account of the Taliesin Fellowship, by one of Wright's greatest protégés. Lavishly illustrated with dozens of photographs, maps, and designs, many in color, including photographs of apprentices at work and buildings under construction. An index and a list of buildings open to the public are included.

Twombly, Robert C. *Frank Lloyd Wright: An Interpretive Biography.* New York: Harper & Row, 1973. The best popular interpretation of Wright's life, work, and thought. Twombly offers cogent commentary on the major designs and an appreciative yet balanced assessment of Wright's political and social ideas and their impact on his work. Marred, though, by vituperative attacks on Wright's followers. Illustrated, with notes, index, and an annotated bibliography.

Wright, Frank Lloyd. *An Autobiography.* Rev. ed. New York: Horizon Press, 1977. The basis for most books about Wright, his own revelations of amazing experiences and overwhelming adversity remain lively, fresh, and intriguing. The first edition was revised and enlarged in 1943. The 1977 edition incorporates corrections and eighty-two photographs of people and works built as late as 1976. A separate index by Linn Ann Cowles was published in 1976.

Wright, Olgivanna Lloyd. *Frank Lloyd Wright: His Life, His Work, His Words.* New

York: Horizon Press, 1966. A laudatory first-person account of the architect by his beloved wife. Interesting as an insider's view of life at Taliesin and as a sampler of Wright's lectures to his Taliesin Fellows. Includes many black-and-white photographs of people and buildings, a chronological list of Wright's architectural innovations, a catalog of his buildings and unfinished projects, and several sketches of later designs by Taliesin Fellows.

John L. McLean

Cross-References

German Artists Found the Bauhaus (1919), p. 463; Le Corbusier's Villa Savoye Redefines Architecture (1931), p. 869; Prouvé Pioneers the Prefabrication of Buildings (Late 1930's), p. 1021; Fuller's First Industrial Geodesic Dome Is Erected (1953), p. 1579; The Guggenheim Museum Opens in a Building Designed by Wright (1959), p. 1806.

SOCIALIST REALISM IS MANDATED
IN SOVIET LITERATURE

Category of event: Literature
Time: April, 1932-August, 1934
Locale: Union of Soviet Socialist Republics

The Communist state regimented the Soviet literary world, reversing the tolerance for artistic innovation shown in the years immediately following the 1917 revolution

Principal personages:

JOSEPH STALIN (JOSEPH VISSARIONOVICH DZHUGASHVILI, 1879-1953), the dictator of the Soviet Union from 1924 to 1953, under whose rule Socialist Realism was imposed on Russian writers

LEOPOLD AVERBAKH (1903-1939), a Communist literary critic, and leader of the Russian Association of Proletarian Writers (RAPP)

NIKOLAI IVANOVICH BUKHARIN (1888-1938), a political rival of Stalin who advocated freedom for writers

ANDREI ALEKSANDROVICH ZHDANOV (1896-1948), an enforcer of cultural conformity who spoke at the 1934 Writers' Congress

MAXIM GORKY (ALEKSEY MAKSIMOVICH PESHKOV, 1868-1936), a writer of the late czarist and early Soviet eras who was the first president of the Soviet Writers' Union

Summary of Event

The year 1932 was not really a turning point in Russian literary history, although it was a milestone. Persecution of literary figures began even before 1932, and even more rigorous regimentation of the arts came later.

Under Communism, the age of broadest freedom for Soviet writers before the late 1980's was the New Economic Policy Era (1921-1928). Led by Vladimir Ilich Lenin, the Bolsheviks, victors in the Russian Revolution of 1917 and the subsequent civil war, did not at first try to enforce a literary conformity. A spirit of experimentation flourished in poetry, fiction, the theater, music, and the cinema. Vladimir Mayakovsky, a fiery young poet and playwright who would commit suicide in 1930, ardently defended both the new regime and avant-garde literature. Exile was not yet permanent; the literary portrayer of late czarist Russia's urban poor, the novelist and playwright Maxim Gorky, left Russia in 1921 but was later allowed to return home. Writers could maintain contacts with Western European publishing houses. In contrast to later periods, varied literary schools of thought were permitted.

Two principal types of Soviet writers coexisted in the 1920's: the proletarians, who glorified the new regime in works of fiction about the Russian Civil War and the tasks of reconstruction, and the fellow travelers, who, although they did not make propaganda for the new regime, were non-Communist rather than anti-Communist. Proletarian novelists included Fyodor Gladkov, Alexander Fadeyev, and Mikhail Sholokhov; the satirist Evgeni Zamyatin, the short-story writers Boris Pilnyak and Isaac Babel, and the novelists Konstantin Fedin, Alexei Tolstoy, Yuri Olesha, and Leonid Leonov were fellow travelers. Mediating between the two was Alexander Voronsky, a literary critic and editor of the journal *Red Virgin Soil*, who urged both government aid to and broad freedom for writers. In June, 1925, the Communist Party Central Committee, while explicitly encouraging proletarian literature, ordained continued freedom for other approaches as well.

Politics destroyed this climate of tolerance. After Lenin died in 1924, Nikolai Bukharin, Leon Trotsky, and Joseph Stalin vied for power; by the end of 1929, Stalin had won the upper hand. Stalin believed in agricultural collectivization and rapid industrialization, but not in freedom for the arts. In 1927, Voronsky had to resign the editorship of *Red Virgin Soil*. Mayakovsky's satirical plays *Klop* (pr., pb. 1929; *The Bedbug*, 1931) and *Banya* (pr., pb. 1930; *The Bathhouse*, 1963) were withdrawn from the stage after sharp official criticism. In August, 1929, the leader of the Russian Association of Proletarian Writers (RAPP), Leopold Averbakh, attacked Pilnyak and Zamyatin as traitors. Pilnyak's career was ruined; Zamyatin left Russia in 1931. RAPP seemed about to take over the literary world.

On April 23, 1932, the Communist Party suddenly called a halt to the strife by ordering that all competing literary associations be dissolved, to be replaced by a single Soviet Writers' Union. The term "Socialist Realism," first used by *Izvestia* editor Ivan Gronsky in a speech of May 20, 1932, was defined publicly by Stalin's spokesman Andrei Zhdanov at the First Congress of the Soviet Writers' Union held in August, 1934. Although this Congress had a pro-Stalin majority, it was attended by writers of all viewpoints, including such mavericks as Babel, Olesha, and the poet Boris Pasternak, as well as by the out-of-favor Communist Bukharin, who praised Pasternak's poetry. Gorky, back from Italian exile, was named president of the new union; his novel *Mat* (1906; *The Mother*, 1906), about a woman converted to the revolutionary cause by her son, was now praised as a model of Socialist Realism. The adoption by the Congress of socialist realism as an official creed was a bad omen, yet some writers, tired of the zealotry of RAPP, mistakenly thought that a new era of tolerance was at hand.

After Leningrad Party boss Sergei Kirov was assassinated in December, 1934, Stalin's purges began. In 1938, Bukharin was tried and executed. Vladimir Stavsky, who headed the Writers' Union after Gorky's death in 1936, ferreted out suspected anti-Stalinists among the literati. Artist victims of the purges included Ivan Katayev, who had once written a short story expressing doubts about agricultural collectivization; Pilnyak; Babel; the poet Osip Mandelstam; and the innovative theatrical director Vsevolod Meyerhold. Ironically, Averbakh himself was purged as an alleged Trotskyite; fellow RAPP member Fadeyev survived to become a key Writers' Union bureaucrat. The purge was the final stage in the regimentation of literature.

Socialist Realism mixed methodological conservatism with ideological radicalism; initially applied to fiction, it was later imposed on the theater, motion pictures, the visual arts, and music. The novel was seen as the highest expression of literature;

its protagonist, according to the doctrine, should be a positive hero who fights for the goals of socialism and attains these goals despite stiff social or natural obstacles. A novel should pay heed to the Communist Party's role in guiding people toward a new society; its ending must be happy for the community as a whole, if not for individuals. Writers were urged to use a simple style, avoiding any experimentation that might make their works difficult for ordinary people to comprehend, yet they were also commanded to go beyond mere realism and to educate people toward socialism. Ironically, such "Realist" literature often ended up sugar-coating some of the harsher realities of life in the Soviet state.

Impact of Event

Any discussion of the impact of the imposition of Socialist Realism must treat both the effect on individual writers and the effect on writers as a group. Even in the Stalinist era, not all writers who strayed from Socialist Realism were purged. Some, unwilling to produce literature of the approved type, simply stopped writing original work altogether. Olesha, who published nothing from 1934 until the 1950's, was one of these; so was Pasternak, who turned from poetry writing to translation. If permitted to remain writers, those literati who were judged to have deviated from the creed either revised their own works or saw them revised by others.

Loyalty to the creed of Socialist Realism was enforced by carrots as well as sticks. After 1934, writers who became members of the Writers' Union and steered clear of Stalin's wrath were guaranteed a market for their writings; various material perquisites were also attached to membership in the Writers' Union. Those recognized as writers by the state came to enjoy both high social status and a privileged life-style, an important consideration in light of the narrow range of white-collar occupations permitted in a socialist economy. Just how seductive the allure of privilege could be is shown by the fact that some of the writers who did well under Stalin (such as Alexei Tolstoy) had been fellow travelers rather than proletarian writers in the 1920's.

The enforcement of Socialist Realism was somewhat capricious. Once the creed was imposed, works published by first-time writers under official auspices adhered to Socialist Realism slavishly. Hence a book such as the autobiographical novel *Kak zakalyalas stal* (1932-1934; *How the Steel Was Tempered*, 1934), by Nikolai Ostrovsky, about a boy from a poverty-stricken background who fights bravely for Bolshevism despite severe physical handicaps, is regarded as an example of Socialist Realism by both Russian and Western critics. Yet some works published before 1932 that are cited by Russian literary critics as models of Socialist Realism are found by Western critics to deviate from that literary creed in some way.

Thus, Sholokhov's *Tikhy Don* (1928-1940; translated in two parts as *And Quiet Flows the Don*, 1934, and *The Don Flows Home to the Sea*, 1940), the first two volumes of which were published in 1928-1929, is not only beautifully written but also remarkably impartial. In this novel of the civil war in the Don Cossack country, the Bolsheviks are not portrayed as plaster saints, nor their enemies as cartoon villains; the protagonist, no positive hero, switches back and forth between the Bolshevik and anti-Bolshevik sides, and the ending is not a happy one. Yet because of the enormous popularity of the novel both in the Soviet Union and abroad, Communist critics praised it as a Socialist Realist classic; Sholokhov's fame may even have saved him from being purged in the 1930's. In his hurriedly produced novel about agricultural collectivization, *Podnyataya tselina* (1932; *Virgin Soil Upturned*, 1935), Sholokhov tried harder to glorify the role of the Communist Party without glossing over entirely the disruptions collectivization had imposed on the peasantry.

On the other hand, Leonov's *Doroga na okean* (1935; *Road to the Ocean*, 1944), was severely criticized for its pessimism, individualism, and emphasis on personal tragedy and death and was practically suppressed. Leonov, turning to the writing of plays, did not publish another novel until 1953. Fedin was not punished in the 1930's for his somewhat unorthodox (by 1934 standards) work of the 1920's; he did, however, try to ingratiate himself with Stalin's new order in art by writing a cliché-filled novel, *Pohkishchenie Evropy* (1933-1935; the rape of Europe). In the cases of Sholokhov, Fedin, and Leonov, one could argue that the contortions necessary to make their literary works politically acceptable stultified to some extent the creativity that all three had shown in the 1920's.

During World War II, controls were relaxed; the strictest enforcement of Socialist Realism came after the War, in the period from 1945 to 1953. In 1946, the satirist Mikhail Zoshchenko, tolerated up to that time, was driven from his profession by Zhdanov, Stalin's cultural watchdog, for a story that seemed to compare Soviet man to an ape. Even Fadeyev, a Party literary stalwart, was compelled to rewrite his World War II novel, *Molodaya gvardia* (1946; the young guard), because it did not sufficiently emphasize the role played in the war effort by the Communist Party. Writers were now expected to refrain from portraying either the less pleasant sides of Soviet society or the conflicts within it. During the period from 1945 to 1953, Socialist Realism was also imposed on the literary world in those Eastern European states upon which Stalin had imposed Communist regimes.

The extent to which Russian literature, after Stalin's death in 1953, was forced to follow the rules of Socialist Realism is disputed by scholars. Relatively tolerant periods, such as 1953-1956 and 1960-1963, were followed by relatively repressive ones. As late as 1958, Pasternak was forbidden to receive the Nobel Prize because his novel *Doktor Zhivago* (1957; *Doctor Zhivago*, 1958) expressed too much skepticism about the blessings bestowed on humanity by the Bolshevik Revolution of 1917; the hero of the novel is a totally apolitical man in an era of fighting political faiths. Between 1964 and 1985, there was a lively underground dissident literature (*samizdat*) in opposition to the official Writers' Union. Yet only with the introduction of the policy of *glasnost* (openness) after 1985 and the collapse of Communism in 1991 can the effort to impose on Russian writers an official literary creed be truly said to have ended.

Bibliography

Brown, Edward J. *The Proletarian Episode in Russian Literature, 1928-1932.* New

York: Columbia University Press, 1953. This study of the rise and fall of Leopold Averbakh and RAPP emphasizes the diversity of viewpoints within the proletarian literary movement. Views proletarian writers not as mere fanatics but as defenders of artistic autonomy and victims of Stalin's regimentation of literature. Endnotes, selected bibliography, index.

Clark, Katerina. *The Soviet Novel: History as Ritual.* Chicago: University of Chicago Press, 1981. Using the tools of anthropology and literary criticism, Clark, examining novels by various authors, outlines a prototypical Socialist Realist plot. Denies that Socialist Realism was simply imposed by bureaucrats; sees its roots in pre-revolutionary literature and its influence in the writings of post-1953 dissidents. Endnotes, bibliography, index.

Ermolaev, Herman. *Soviet Literary Theories, 1917-1934: The Genesis of Socialist Realism.* Vol. 69 in *University of California Publications in Modern Philology.* Berkeley: University of California Press, 1963. A pathbreaking study, repeatedly cited by scholars of Communist-era Russian literature. Analyzes critical articles, speeches, resolutions, and debates. The treatment of the period from 1932 to 1934, when an official definition of Socialist Realism was hammered out, is especially good. Sees Socialist Realism as imposed by Stalin. Endnotes, bibliography, index.

Garrard, John, and Carol Garrard. *Inside the Soviet Writers' Union.* New York: Free Press, 1990. Contains two historical chapters that treat the Stalin era. The account of the 1934 Writers' Congress relies partly on survivors' testimony published in the 1980's. Tries to estimate exactly how many writers were purged by Stalin. No analysis of literary works. Endnotes, index.

Maguire, Robert A. *Red Virgin Soil: Soviet Literature in the 1920's.* Princeton, N.J.: Princeton University Press, 1968. A history not just of Voronsky's journal but of literary politics in the 1920's. Suggests that writers' poverty spurred them to form associations to secure government help and argues that Socialist Realism combined Voronsky's reverence for past literary models with the activism of the proletarian writers. Footnotes, index, bibliography.

Simmons, Ernest J. *Russian Fiction and Soviet Ideology: Introduction to Fedin, Leonov, and Sholokhov.* New York: Columbia University Press, 1958. Shows how three writers who had made their reputations in the relatively liberal 1920's adapted to the literary dogmatism prevalent in the 1930's; the damage done to artistic integrity varied with each writer, being probably greatest with Leonov. List of works discussed, index, photographs of each writer.

Struve, Gleb. *Russian Literature Under Lenin and Stalin, 1917-1953.* Norman: University of Oklahoma Press, 1971. A useful survey. Nine chapters out of thirty treat the 1930's; the 1934 Writers' Congress gets an entire chapter. Sees proletarian writers as accomplices in, as well as victims of, Stalin's regimentation of literature. Discusses influence of Socialist Realism on fiction, poetry, and drama. Bibliography, footnotes, index.

Paul D. Mageli

Cross-References

The Soviet Union Bans Abstract Art (1922), p. 544; Eisenstein's *Potemkin* Introduces New Film Editing Techniques (1925), p. 615; Kuleshov and Pudovkin Introduce Montage to Filmmaking (1927), p. 701; *The Bedbug* and *The Bathhouse* Exemplify Revolutionary Theater (1929), p. 787; Stalin Restricts Soviet Composers (1932), p. 914; Shostakovich's *Lady Macbeth of Mtsensk* Is Condemned (1936), p. 1042; Hitler Organizes an Exhibition Denouncing Modern Art (1937), p. 1083; Zhdanov Denounces "Formalism" in Music (1948), p. 1388; Pasternak's *Doctor Zhivago* Is Published (1957), p. 1747; *The Gulag Archipelago* Exposes Soviet Atrocities (1973), p. 2277.

STALIN RESTRICTS SOVIET COMPOSERS

Category of event: Music
Time: April 23, 1932
Locale: Moscow, Union of Soviet Socialist Republics

Joseph Stalin's concept of Socialist Realism was an attempt to transform all Soviet arts from a portrayal of what was to a portrayal, in Communist ideology, of what ought to be

Principal personages:

JOSEPH STALIN (JOSEPH VISSARIONOVICH DZHUGASHVILI, 1879-1953), the brutal dictator who ruled the Soviet Union for almost thirty years

KARL RADEK (1885-1939?), a Soviet official who was instrumental in defining the concept of Socialist Realism from 1932 to 1936

ANDREI ZHDANOV (1896-1948), a key Stalinist who led major purges of musicians, writers, and other artists who did not adequately conform to the doctrine of Socialist Realism

SERGEI PROKOFIEV (1891-1953), a major Russian composer who sought to conform, at least outwardly, to Socialist Realism

DMITRI SHOSTAKOVICH (1906-1975), the best-known of younger Soviet composers, who more easily conformed to Socialist Realism than their elders did

Summary of Event

Socialist Realism was an outgrowth of basic Marxist-Leninist philosophy. "Realism," in the context of socialism, could better be defined as "idealism," since the goal of socialism is the elusive concept of a perfect, harmonious life for all.

The Bolshevik Revolution of 1917 established Marxist-Leninist socialism in what then became the Union of Soviet Socialist Republics. The result was the creation of a totalitarian society that provided a fertile ground for the forced application of socialist goals to all areas of life, including arts and culture.

In 1925, Soviet leadership was seized by Joseph Stalin, who wanted every aspect of Soviet life under his direct control; his massive ego led to the creation of the "Stalin cult" by 1929. This, in turn, allowed Stalin to begin enforcing his brand of socialism throughout the Soviet Union. His first Five-Year Plan (1928-1933) called for all Soviet artists, writers, and musicians, in their creative works, to support his socialist goals by glorifying the real and imaginary accomplishments of the workers and peasants.

From 1929 to 1932, the idea of Socialist Realism emerged. The term is attributed to Stalin himself. In an early definition of the idea, Karl Radek emphasized that reality, in socialist terminology, is not only what it is but also what will be. All Soviet citizens involved in the creative arts were thus expected not only to portray the future but also to help to create it. They were to become, again in Stalin's words, "engineers of the human mind." The result of that engineering was that the Soviet Union entered a cultural wilderness from which the country did not emerge until after Stalin's death in 1953.

Since Stalin was an avid reader, it was natural that the first application of the doctrine of Socialist Realism should have been in the field of literature. Andrei Zhdanov, a top Stalinist official, led the efforts to silence Soviet writers who would not confess their past "errors" of espousing Western views and who would not conform to Socialist Realism. Zhdanov's efforts were soon felt in other cultural areas, including music. Soviet writers, musicians, and others were soon being compelled to produce works envisioning a glorious socialist future.

In the field of music, the major enemy of Socialist Realism was Western formalism. "Formalism" soon came to mean anything that Stalin and his top officials did not like or did not understand—and since Stalin rarely attended concerts and apparently knew little about music, the latter category was broad. Certain musical concepts, either correctly or incorrectly identified as Western, were soon officially banned. One of these concepts was atonality, the perceived absence of a tonal center in musical compositions.

The rich heritage of Russian music soon began to suffer. Earlier Russian composers such as Mikhail Glinka, Nikolay Rimsky-Korsakov, Modest Mussorgsky, and Peter Ilich Tchaikovsky had used the age-old themes of Russian nationalist folk music. Soviet composers laboring under Socialist Realism were expected not to renounce the folk traditions but to project them into the socialistic future. Of the earlier musicians, Mussorgsky was the most useful to the architects of Socialist Realism because of his belief that music had to be "true" as well as beautiful. Tchaikovsky was also useful as a model, since his music was international in its scope, thus conforming more readily to the vision of a socialistic world order.

Since music is more abstract than the other arts, it was less easily brought under government control. As long as Soviet composers paid lip service to the dogmas established by the Central Committee of the Communist Party, they were able to maintain more individuality than other artists.

Music with a vocal text, such as opera and ballet, was best suited for Socialist Realism. Stalin enjoyed these forms because they could combine the rich folk heritage with a plot expressing socialistic goals. Even nonvocal music, however, was expected to project those same goals.

Long before the official proclamation of Socialist Realism, organs were in operation to support its goals. On January 1, 1929, a magazine called *Proletarian Musician* began publication in Moscow. In the preface of the first issue, the editors declared that they would be opposing the decadent influence of Western bourgeois music, supporting the ideologically acceptable contributions of the past, and promoting new styles of proletarian music. The editors, however, had not yet been told what those new styles were.

In March, 1931, the Russian Association of Proletarian Musicians held its first convention in Moscow. This group, and similar groups in other cultural arts, was controlled by its own leaders, who were then to obey the dictates of the Central Committee. This arrangement, however, did not give the Central Committee the immediate control that they desired.

On April 23, 1932, the Central Committee dissolved by decree the Russian Association of Proletarian Musicians and the other cultural organizations, an event that marked the official beginning of Socialist Realism. From that date until Stalin's death, cultural leadership was in the largely uncultured hands of the members of the Central Committee.

In September, 1934, the Soviet government decreed the amount of money that composers would get for their work; it thus became financially advantageous for composers to create works that supported Socialist Realism. The obvious result was that some musicians, especially the younger ones who were trained after the Bolshevik Revolution in 1917, began to compromise their creativity in order to gain favor with Stalin and other government leaders. Sergei Prokofiev, an older composer, dared to remark that Socialist Realism in music really meant the writing of tunes that Stalin could whistle. Later, though, even Prokofiev helped to create those tunes.

Impact of Event

The first impact of Socialist Realism on music was its application to composers of worldwide fame. Since Stalin enjoyed the music of Ludwig van Beethoven, Beethoven was declared in conformity to Socialist Realism. In fact, some Soviet leaders classified Beethoven as the first Socialist Realist composer. The work of Johann Sebastian Bach, on the other hand, was respectfully rejected by Stalin; Stalin could not perceive the meaning of Bach's compositions. It is obvious that Igor Stravinsky, a Russian composer in exile, was a major factor in the rejection of Bach. Stravinsky sought to return to many of Bach's principles; Stalin interpreted this as an expression of preference for the past rather than for the bright future of socialism.

In 1934, when Stalin's bloody purges of the Soviet Union began, the avalanche of Socialist Realism buried the once-rich Russian culture. Replacing it was the ideologically uniform culture of the Communist Party. This new culture was molded around the personality of Joseph Stalin. The terror of the purges had a savage, sadistic twist when it was applied to cultural leaders. Writers and musicians were often forced to be the instruments in declaring their own condemnations. One by one, Soviet composers and other cultural greats either capitulated to the dictates of Socialist Realism or disappeared into the oblivion shared by many others who were a perceived threat to Stalin's tyranny.

Sergei Prokofiev provides a classic example of the impact of the constant and ever-increasing pressure of Socialist Realism. After living and working in Paris during the 1920's, Prokofiev returned to the Soviet Union in 1934. He first tried to ignore the concept of Socialist Realism, but this soon proved to be impossible. Prokofiev's music then became more practical and even propagandistic. For the remainder of his life, Prokofiev fell in and out of favor with the leaders of Socialist Realism. The reasons for the periodic attacks on Prokofiev remained obscure to Western observers, since most of his music appeared to conform to the dictates of Socialist Realism.

Dmitri Shostakovich is the best example of the official cultural policy toward the younger Soviet composers who were trained after 1917. The starting point for the music of Shostakovich is Beethoven, which put Shostakovich in good favor with the government of Stalin. Shostakovich, however, soon exhibited a spirit of individuality that evoked official criticism. His famous opera *Lady Macbeth of Mtsensk* (1932) is an intense satire that fell far short of Socialist Realism. Trouble for Shostakovich began when Stalin attended a performance of this opera. After being sharply attacked, Shostakovich tried, without immediate success, to redeem himself. Finally, his Fifth Symphony in 1937 sufficiently conformed to accepted standards, and Shostakovich settled down to produce a series of patriotic works with heroic themes. His later *Leningrad Symphony* (1941) expressed both the fury of the German invasion of the Soviet Union and the successful Soviet defense of their city and country.

Two other composers of the post-1917 generation, Aram Khachaturian and Dmitry Kabalevsky, were sufficiently able to uphold the ideals of Socialist Realism so as to avoid serious criticism. To some Western critics, however, the music of these men had a superficial character that might have been absent in a free environment.

Fortunately for Soviet composers, the bloody purges of the late 1930's concentrated on perceived political and literary threats to Stalin. The purges were soon followed by World War II (called the "Great Patriotic War" in the Soviet Union), when all energies were directed toward survival.

The end of World War II in 1945, and the simultaneous advent of the Cold War with the West, initiated a revival of Socialist Realism in the Soviet Union. A pathetic scene was created in 1946 when Prokofiev, Shostakovich, and Khachaturian were forced to repent publicly for some of their earlier works that did not uphold the tenets of Socialist Realism. Soviet citizens were accustomed to seeing their political leaders publicly confess to imaginary crimes, but seeing their composers and other cultural leaders grovel at the feet of Stalin was indeed a shock.

For most of the remainder of his life, Prokofiev conformed, at least outwardly, to Socialist Realism, although not without criticism. Vocal texts were often added to his compositions to help achieve the desired goals. One of his last works, *On Guard for Peace* (1950), was widely hailed by Soviet leaders.

From 1946 to 1948, this revival of Socialist Realism was led by its earlier spokesman, Andrei Zhdanov. By then a secretary of the Central Committee of the Communist Party, Zhdanov demanded the total abolishment of Western cultural influences. Since independence was the greatest threat to Socialist Realism, the most independently minded composer, Shostakovich, was specifically attacked. Shostakovich then performed the usual repentance and produced several works in honor of Stalin.

Zhdanov's death in 1948 did not mean the end of his campaign. Although his replacement, Mikhail Suslov, preferred to work behind the scenes, the pressure of

Socialist Realism did not weaken. Once again, Prokofiev was attacked and forced to recant in a letter to the Central Committee.

The total impact of Socialist Realism on Russian culture becomes clear when it is realized that professional composers were compelled to produce their work according to the dictates of professional politicians who knew little or nothing about music. The very livelihood of the composers, who were under contract to the State Committee on Arts, depended on their conformity to those dictates.

This did not mean that the composers were mere stooges of the Communist Party. The subtle nature of music, combined with the musical ignorance of most party leaders, meant that the good composers could still manifest their independence. Yet one cannot but wonder what the work of Prokofiev, Shostakovich, and others would have been like if they had not been compelled to labor under the weight of Socialist Realism.

The death of Stalin in March, 1953, brought sighs of relief in many areas of Soviet life. One of these areas was culture. The full weight of Socialist Realism died with Stalin; Stalin's successors found milder means of cultural control. As the reality of this began to spread, musicians and others began to produce new and more independent works. Not until the demise of the Soviet Union in 1991, however, were the country's musicians completely free from government control.

Bibliography

Fitzsimmons, Thomas, Peter Malof, and John C. Fiske. *U.S.S.R.: Its People, Its Society, Its Culture.* New Haven, Conn.: HRAF Press, 1960. The author provides an excellent overview of Soviet life and culture. Published just seven years after Stalin's death, this book is valuable to readers who are not familiar with Stalin and the oppression of his regime.

Heller, Mikhail, and Aleksandr Nekrich. *Utopia in Power.* New York: Summit Books, 1985. Written originally in Russian by authors who were raised and educated in the Soviet Union, this book reveals the tragic effects of Marxist-Leninist socialism on Russia. Particularly valuable in showing the reader the progress of Socialist Realism after World War II.

Kulski, W. W. "The Party and the West." In *The Soviet Regime: Communism in Practice.* Syracuse, N.Y.: Syracuse University Press, 1954. This chapter by Kulski presents a detailed picture of Stalin's attempt to rid the Soviet Union of all Western influences, including music styles. The author defines what the Central Committee of the Communist Party meant in classifying Western music as "pathological." Readers familiar with composers such as Prokofiev and Shostakovich will better understand the pressure under which they labored.

Randall, Francis B. "The Culture." In *Stalin's Russia.* New York: Free Press, 1965. Randall tries to analyze Stalin's personality in order better to understand Socialist Realism. He emphasizes the use of censorship and terror to discourage dissent by cultural leaders. Compares what Stalin called the "bourgeois realism" of the nineteenth century with the Socialist Realism of the twentieth century.

Salzman, Eric. "National Styles." In *Twentieth Century Music: An Introduction.* Englewood Cliffs, N.J.: Prentice-Hall, 1974. Salzman presents an excellent survey of twentieth century music styles. Himself a composer, the author in this chapter discusses the influence of Socialist Realism on Soviet composers and also describes the changes it produced in the Soviet Union's nationalist music styles.

Treadgold, Donald W. "Stalin's Cultural Policy: 1927-1945." In *Twentieth Century Russia.* 7th ed. Boulder, Colo.: Westview Press, 1990. In this chapter, the author, a respected scholar of Soviet studies, evaluates Socialist Realism in light of Stalin's full totalitarian rule. Reveals the influence of the Communist Party and officials such as Zhdanov in determining what was or was not acceptable in music and other cultural areas.

Glenn L. Swygart

Cross-References

The Soviet Union Bans Abstract Art (1922), p. 544; Eisenstein's *Potemkin* Introduces New Film Editing Techniques (1925), p. 615; Kuleshov and Pudovkin Introduce Montage to Filmmaking (1927), p. 701; *The Bedbug* and *The Bathhouse* Exemplify Revolutionary Theater (1929), p. 787; Socialist Realism Is Mandated in Soviet Literature (1932), p. 908; Shostakovich's *Lady Macbeth of Mtsensk* Is Condemned (1936), p. 1042; Hitler Organizes an Exhibition Denouncing Modern Art (1937), p. 1083; Zhdanov Denounces "Formalism" in Music (1948), p. 1388; Pasternak's *Doctor Zhivago* Is Published (1957), p. 1747; *The Gulag Archipelago* Exposes Soviet Atrocities (1973), p. 2277.

JOOSS'S ANTIWAR DANCE *THE GREEN TABLE* PREMIERES

Category of event: Dance
Time: July 3, 1932
Locale: Théâtre des Champs-Élyseés, Paris, France

Kurt Jooss's The Green Table, *a powerful commentary on the futility of war, extended the subject matter and technical range of modern dance*

Principal personages:
> KURT JOOSS (1901-1979), the choreographer and creator of *The Green Table* who also danced the principal role
> FRITZ A. COHEN (1904-1967), the composer who scored the music for *The Green Table*
> HEIN HECKROTH (1901-1970), the designer of the set, costumes and masks for *The Green Table*

Summary of Event

The Green Table is a danse macabre in contemporary terms. Consisting of six scenes, a prologue, and an epilogue, the work presents the consequences of war and their related social results realistically in a stylized, unromanticized manner. Before the dance begins, discordant piano sounds foretell the ominous atmosphere of the ballet that will unfold. The music changes into a lighthearted cabaret tango. The curtain opens to reveal a rectangular conference table covered in green; the table is lined on two sides by diplomats dressed in black morning coats and spats and wearing grotesque masks. The two factions engage in rituals of diplomacy, each side making points and counter points, bickering amongst themselves and almost coming to blows with the opposing group. A feigned mood of courtesy prevails as the arbiters gesticulate in puppet-like fashion. The scene concludes in response to the rising unsurmountable tensions among the diplomats. Finding no solution to the discussion, they remove pistols from their vests, bow politely to one another, lift their arms upward, and shoot the pistols into the air, symbolically releasing a pattern of violence that will bring death, injury, and tragedy. The stage goes dark.

The grisly image of Death is gradually revealed out of the blackness. Death, who dominates the work, is humanized as a skeleton and is garbed in the breastplate and helmet of Mars, the god of war. His menacing, repetitive, march-like steps evoke a sense of doom.

The Standard Bearer enters holding a banner and rallying troops. Forces for battle are assembled, trained, and called to action. The combatants take leave of their sweethearts and mothers, and the story of war continues. The cunning Profiteer, a sleazy character whose pleasure derives from the misfortunes of others, is portrayed. The hovering, ever-present Death claims his victims one by one and triumphantly leads them in a procession of the dead. The figure of Death fades into blackness. Pistol shots ring out, and the scene returns to the conference table. Friendly relations are resumed, and the politicians once more enact their charade, which freezes in a stalemate.

The conceptualization of the libretto for *The Green Table* gradually grew over a ten-year period. Jooss had seen a sequence of medieval drawings of individuals from various walks of life dancing with Death, personified as a skeleton. Jooss found the dance of death a fascinating subject and thought the idea could be a proposal for an actual dance work. Memories of World War I and the Depression also were interpolated into the piece. Jooss was an avid reader of *Die Weltbühne*, a German periodical edited by Carl von Ossie. The magazine published political writings by Kurt Tucholsky that concerned moral integrity and the struggle for human decency; Tucholsky's work directly affected the political overtones of *The Green Table*.

Movement for the ballet stemmed, in part, from Jooss's study with Rudolf Laban, an innovative teacher and theorist of the style of "plastic rhythm," or motion for its own sake. This extremely different form of dance expression rejected the artificiality and structure of classical ballet existing in German dance prior to World War I. Laban elaborated on the principles of anatomical expression and gesture set forth by François Delsarte in the mid-nineteenth century. In 1921, Jooss began to study with Laban at the National Theater in Mannheim, Germany, later becoming his assistant and principal dancer. Subsequently, Jooss founded Neue Tanzbühne (New Dance Stage), a separate entity of the state theater in Münster. The group included the dancers Sigurd Leeder and Aino Sümola, the composer and conductor Fritz Cohen, and the designer Hein Heckroth. The company toured throughout Germany for a two-year period presenting a repertoire of Jooss's works.

Jooss's search for expression in a personal manner led him to merge and reorganize new ideas in theater dance continually. He traveled to Paris and Vienna in the winter of 1926 with Sigurd Leeder to study, both in mind and body, the system of classical ballet. While gaining physical mastery of classical dance, Jooss examined its technique and pedagogy. He adapted some of these ideas into his choreographic endeavors as he sought to give clarity to performance. Jooss earned the hostility of his classical as well as his modern colleagues in 1928, when he candidly stated that the rivalry between the two dance forms was absurd.

The Green Table synthesizes these two forms of dance, combining the dramatic expression of modern dance with ballet technique. The choreography utilizes the range of everyday movement while adding strong distinctive patterns for the soldiers, diplomats, and other dancers. Identifying movements used only by the Profiteer and Death were created.

The music moves along with the dancing and does not influence the shape of the choreography or its movement. At times, the score conveys the atmosphere, which ranges from foreboding to lyrical to plaintive.

The masks used for *The Green Table* evolved in response to practical considerations. With only sixteen dancers in the piece, which required a quick change of the opening scene and a change of costumes, the possibility of applying makeup was negligible. As the dancers had to look grotesque for the prologue and epilogue, masks were designed to transform their appearance in a rapid fashion.

Impact of Event

The Green Table won first prize in a choreographic competition organized by the Archives Internationales de la Danse in Paris, and the success led to an offer to participate in a season of innovative dance at the Casino de Paris in the fall of 1932. The event called for the inclusion of *The Green Table* and the competition's other prizewinners in a production during the dormant period between the casino's regular shows. The Jooss dancers, though, arrived in Paris to learn that the other groups were unavailable and that the casino was continuing to present its revues. The fall season's offering began with the casino's attractions of nudity, risqué songs, and other suggestive happenings. Following the intermission, *The Green Table*, with its sober commentary, was presented. The ballet, in sharp contrast to the previous happenings, was met with such commotion that the music could not be heard. In a short time, however, as the Parisian public learned of the performance, a different type of audience began to attend and gave their approval to the work.

A proper theater season in Paris and Europe was arranged for the following spring, which firmly established Ballets Jooss, as the company had become known. *The Green Table* was presented along with other works by Jooss.

Created a year before Adolf Hitler seized power, the ballet expressed a message that was comparable to those expressed in many antiwar novels of the time. Sentiments portrayed in *The Green Table* were not, however, in keeping with the views of Hitler and the Nazi Party. As a result of this and of Jooss's support of Jewish and partly Jewish colleagues, of necessity, Jooss and his company fled Germany.

During World War II, while Ballets Jooss was performing in England, the decision was made by Jooss to withdraw *The Green Table* from the repertoire. Jooss believed that the effects of war were too near at hand and that, in wartime, people attended the theater for relaxation. Audiences, however, requested the ballet, and *The Green Table* was restored to the programs. With the final days of World War II approaching, Jooss again believed the end of *The Green Table*'s performance life was near. He was proved wrong once more. Audiences continued to request the ballet, and so Ballets Jooss continued performing the work.

In 1948, Jooss was invited to Santiago, Chile, by former soloists of Ballets Jooss who had performed in the original production of *The Green Table*. There, Jooss staged *The Green Table* for the Chilean National Ballet, which his dancers had founded. During this production, Jooss made his final appearance as a dancer in the role of Death.

The enduring quality of *The Green Table* led to its incorporation into the repertoires of ballet companies worldwide. Productions have been staged by the Bayerische Staatsoper, Munich (May, 1964), the City Center Joffrey Ballet, New York (March, 1967), the Tanz-Forum, Cologne (December, 1971), the Royal Winnipeg

Ballet, Toronto (November, 1974), the Batsheva Dance Company, Tel Aviv (November, 1975), the José Limon Dance Company, New York (April, 1977), the Opernhaus, Zürich (May, 1978), the Cleveland Ballet, Cleveland (April, 1979), the Hartford Ballet, Hartford (August, 1981), the Suomen Kansallisbaletti, Helsinki (November, 1982), the Companhia Nacional de Bailado, Lisbon (May, 1984), and the Bühnen der Stadt, Essen (March, 1985), among others.

The Green Table has been documented in two styles of dance notation. Three different sources have "Labanotated" the work, and in 1974, Juliet Kando recorded the work in Benesh dance notation.

Continued interest in *The Green Table* has led to several televised productions of the ballet. A German production of the piece was televised in 1963, and in 1966 the British Broadcasting Corporation (BBC) televised a performance directed by Peter Wright. A Swedish version was broadcast in 1977 and a Japanese version in 1979. In 1982, the Joffrey Ballet undertook a production for public television's "Dance in America" series.

The Green Table's significance extends beyond the ballet's message and reflects Jooss's innovative use of choreography, stagecraft, and lighting. A period of development for Jooss in which he formulated his beliefs and experimented in dance movement and in stagecraft preceded *The Green Table*. His dance technique negated many premises that were accepted by ballet choreographers of the time. To Jooss, a painted set, a corps de ballet, and the sound of an orchestra were nonessential; instead, the dramatic effect of dance was underlined by stagecraft. Emphasis was placed on costume rather than decor; costumes were used to accentuate symbolism rather than merely to serve decorative purposes. Jooss also used costumes to make his dancers appear more vividly three-dimensional to the audience.

The use of lighting in an unusually fluid manner contributed to the three-dimensional concept. The stage space was altered by filling or emptying different areas, surfaces, and levels with light. Lighting was used to mask, reveal, or emphasize a solo figure or group; the color, volume, and direction of Jooss's lighting was constantly changing to reveal the space necessary for action at any moment.

All aspects of Jooss's style of theatrical dance were first completely realized in *The Green Table*. Jooss blazed a trail in dance with *The Green Table*; until the piece's premiere, dance, with few exceptions, was escapist in its audience appeal.

The Green Table is acknowledged as Jooss's greatest, most successful, and most enduring work. The ballet remains a powerful indictment of war.

Bibliography

Chujoy, Anatole, and P. W. Manchester, eds. *The Dance Encyclopedia.* Rev. ed. New York: Simon & Schuster, 1967. Gives brief accounts of *The Green Table*, Kurt Jooss, and the Ballets Jooss. A photograph of Jooss as Death holding the Old Woman is included.

Clarke, Mary, and Clement Crisp. *The Ballet Goer's Guide.* New York: Alfred A. Knopf, 1981. Presents a capsule view of Jooss's career. A brief synopsis of the ballet is presented. Photographs include the tableau that opens and closes the work and Jooss as Death holding the Old Woman.

Coton, A. V. *The New Ballet: Kurt Jooss and His Work.* London: Dennis Dobson, 1946. Deals extensively with Jooss's work. Discussion of the background of twentieth century ballet places the development of Ballets Jooss in proper context. Excellent information on *The Green Table* and selected works of Jooss, including notes for references in text and descriptions of ballets. A valuable source on Jooss, replete with photographs and line drawings.

Gruen, John. *The World's Greatest Ballets.* New York: Harry N. Abrams, 1981. An excellent descriptive synopsis of *The Green Table.* The vivid narrative accurately follows the action of the ballet, and an account of Jooss's career is presented.

Markard, Anna, and Hermann Markard. *Jooss.* Cologne: Ballett-Buhnen-Verlag, 1985. Based on part of an exhibition, "Kurt Jooss and His Work," for a 1981 Venice dance festival. Includes a biography of Jooss, a record of the tours of Ballets Jooss, and a list of Jooss's choreographies. Photographs of ballets and of soloists include some taken at productions of *The Green Table.* Excellent source on Jooss.

Mondadori, Arnoldo, ed. *The Simon & Schuster Book of the Ballet.* New York: Simon & Schuster, 1980. Provides a brief description of the ballet. Also included are remarks regarding the atmosphere of the times, with brief comments on the choreography.

Williamson, Audrey. *Contemporary Ballet.* London: Rockliff, 1946. Provides a chapter of commentary on Ballets Jooss, which made its home in England during World War II. The major ballets of Jooss are critiqued, and an insightful commentary on *The Green Table* is included.

Mary Pat Balkus

Cross-References

The New Objectivity Movement Is Introduced (1925), p. 631; Berg's *Wozzeck* Premieres in Berlin (1925), p. 680; *All Quiet on the Western Front* Stresses the Futility of War, (1929), p. 767; Tudor's *Jardin aux lilas* Premieres in London (1936), p. 1036; Hitler Organizes an Exhibition Denouncing Modern Art (1937), p. 1083; The Nazis Ban Nolde's Paintings (1941), p. 1217.

BERKELEY'S *42ND STREET* REVOLUTIONIZES FILM MUSICALS

Category of event: Motion pictures
Time: 1933
Locale: Hollywood, California

With film studios near bankruptcy at the height of the Depression, Busby Berkeley revitalized film musicals with new camera and staging techniques

Principal personages:
> BUSBY BERKELEY (WILLIAM BERKELEY ENOS, 1895-1976), a Broadway dance director who created a musical form unique to film
> RUBY KEELER (1909-1993), a former Broadway performer who became a film star in *42nd Street*
> DICK POWELL (1904-1963), an actor who played Keeler's love interest in the film
> WARNER BAXTER (1891-1951), a distinguished character actor who played a Broadway producer
> LLOYD BACON (1890-1955), a former silent-screen actor who directed the nondancing part of film

Summary of Event

In the late 1920's, when sound films began to replace silent films, Hollywood studios produced a flood of musicals. Early sound cameras were almost immobilized, since any motion created noise that was magnified on the sound track; most early musicals were therefore photographed as if the camera were a member of the audience. Studio directors also apparently did not realize that sloppy dancing, tawdry sets, and poor costumes, sometimes effective on the stage, would appear ridiculous when magnified many times over on the screen. As a result, musicals failed at the box office. In 1928, sixty were released; by 1932, only fifteen were released, and only two of those made a profit. By then, the Depression had forced many studios near bankruptcy; in 1933, some twenty-five hundred theaters had been forced to close.

Darryl Zanuck, then employed by Warner Bros., believed the musical still had a future. Supposedly, though, he did not tell his bosses that he had a musical in mind when he brought Busby Berkeley to the studio. Berkeley had been dance director for twenty-one Broadway musicals, and as a soldier during World War I, had devised trick drill patterns for the movement of masses of men in close formation. Both experiences would influence his Hollywood career. He had never had a dancing lesson, and he knew little of cameras or photography when he was brought to Hollywood in 1930 to direct dance numbers for Eddie Cantor and Mary Pickford. He had then run out of work.

Assigned to *42nd Street*, he directed production numbers at one site, while Lloyd Bacon worked with the rest of the script at another. Veteran cameraman Sol Polito was in charge of filming at both. The directors emphasized the Cinderella theme of this backstage musical, replacing the tearful sentimentality of many earlier musicals such as Al Jolson's *The Singing Fool* (1928), which had involved, among other things, a dying child. Both directors understood that the Depression audience needed hope, not more depression.

Both the film's script and its first production numbers are grounded fully in the realities of the Depression. The threat of unemployment hangs over the characters who appear early in the film, from Julian Marsh (Warner Baxter), a Broadway producer who has lost his money and health, to girlish Peggy Sawyer (Ruby Keeler). Given a place in the chorus, Sawyer faints in rehearsal from hunger and fatigue. Chorus girls, desperate for work, stoically endure brutally crude sexual remarks and groping hands. Even the fictitious show's star endures the witless sexual aggression of the show's lecherous financial backer until, driven beyond her capacity, she rejects him. Shortly afterward, she is injured and must be replaced.

As Cinderella, Peggy Sawyer steps in. In one grueling rehearsal scene, she is forced to prove her talent, courage, and capacity for hard work. At that point, Berkeley inserted production numbers that proved to the Depression audience that those character traits could take Cinderella to a fantasy land such as an audience had never before seen.

When Sawyer becomes a star, music and staging change. She does not appear in the first major production number, "Young and Healthy," sung by Dick Powell, which introduced the moving platforms and geometric designs for which Berkeley was to become famous. The second major number, "Shuffle Off to Buffalo," depicts Sawyer as a young bride, but the Pullman sleeping car in which she is traveling surrealistically splits in half, and she finds herself surrounded by chorus girls wearing night cream and mouthing cynical asides about love and marriage. Then these numbers are dwarfed by "42nd Street," which closes the film and which made Berkeley's reputation.

As that number begins, Sawyer is dancing, as if on a stage. The camera pulls back, and she is seen to be on top of a taxi. She climbs down and is surrounded by New Yorkers—police officers, nursemaids, ordinary pedestrians—going about their everyday dramas. A woman appears in an upstairs window. She is terrified, and she flees from a man who pursues her into the street and stabs her. Her death attracts no more than a moment's attention, as Powell sings "42nd Street" from an upstairs window. An instant later, both are forgotten as a chorus of precisely choreographed and beautifully costumed dancers tap out the title song. They mount a staircase and, turning, reveal cardboard cutouts that form the Manhattan skyline. The skyline dances, stabilizes, and opens to reveal a skyscraper, at the top of which are Powell and Keeler embracing. Berkeley had created a fairy-tale ending to a dazzling fantasy, and in doing so, he had created a world that could exist nowhere except on film and could be staged nowhere except on huge Hollywood sound stages.

The techniques he used changed Hollywood musicals. He worked with a single camera rather than with the customary four, planning out each number so that it unrolled smoothly; the camera's eye was the audience's eye, but he photographed from every possible angle. He respected the integrity of the production number and showed it without interruption. He demanded both beauty and intelligence of his dancers, and while critics complained about his tendency to focus on their bodies, he was careful to let his camera also caress their faces and the intelligence in their eyes. He allowed greater variation of face and body types than would later be permissible, but he demanded precise movement, proud posture, and precision of tapdancing. He juxtaposed violence and musical exuberance; the audience was reminded of the world they were escaping even as they escaped it. All of this was to affect the Hollywood musical until the mid-1950's, when the decline of the Hollywood studio system virtually ended the production of these expensive films.

Impact of Event

The immediate effect of *42nd Street* was to give Berkeley a free hand and almost unlimited financial support at Warner Bros., allowing him to develop his vision. The film's success was to motivate other Hollywood studios to rival him.

Among the first of a series of imitations was the Metro-Goldwyn-Mayer (MGM) production *Dancing Lady* (1933), which attempted to exploit the popularity of Clark Gable and Joan Crawford, neither of whom was suited for musical films. Crawford's dancing was strained and ungainly. Fred Astaire, then new to Hollywood, played a bit part. MGM's 1936 *The Great Ziegfeld*, with its giant wedding cake and beautifully costumed tiers of girls, owes more to Berkeley than to anything the real Florenz Ziegfeld could have produced on the narrow confines of a Broadway stage. RKO then gave Astaire a role—along with Ginger Rogers, who had attracted attention in a bit part in *42nd Street*—in its new film, *Flying Down to Rio* (1933), and the pair's famous partnership was formed. Berkeley's influence can be seen in the spectacular aerial ballet that ends the RKO film and in the precision dancing of the "Carioca" production number that is the Rogers-Astaire showpiece of the film. Twentieth Century (later Twentieth Century-Fox) imitated Berkeley with *Stand Up and Cheer* and *George White's Scandals*, both in 1934, but was not to find a successful formula until, later in the 1930's, it featured singer Alice Faye, child star Shirley Temple, and ice-skating champion Sonja Henie.

While being imitated, Berkeley polished forms introduced in *42nd Street* and developed new ones. His *Gold Diggers of 1933* featured, among others, the spectacular "We're in the Money" number, in which Ginger Rogers led the Berkeley dancers, dressed in oversized gold coins, against a backdrop of gigantic coins. His "Shadow Waltz" in that film showed his chorus playing illumined violins and finally shaping themselves into the pattern of a lighted violin. In "Remember My Forgotten Man," a parade of World War I soldiers, filmed in silhouette, becomes a ragged procession of the unemployed, and an out-of-work drunk, wearing a combat medal, is arrested. In *Footlight Parade* (1933), Berkeley shot a water ballet from over, under, and around a specially designed pool, and he incorporated "Shanghai Lil," a number sung and danced by Keeler and James Cagney, which begins in barroom violence and ends, some time later, in one of the military formations that Berkeley frequently used. In *Roman Scandals* (1933), he filmed dancers naked except for their hair.

In *Gold Diggers of 1935*, he filmed what is generally considered his best work, "Lullaby of Broadway." In this production number, the audience sees the life and death of a Broadway party girl; an army of precision tap dancers paces out the cadence of her life. Singer Wini Shaw's face is first seen as a small white dot on a black screen. She sings "Lullaby of Broadway" as the camera moves gradually into close-up, and her face dissolves into a view of Manhattan. The audience sees her story. She arrives home after a night of fun, feeds her cat, sleeps all day, and sets out with Dick Powell for another night of entertainment. They go to an enormous nightclub, where two dancers begin the "Lullaby." Suddenly, the dancers become an army of men and women who engage in a dazzling display of precision dancing without, for many beats, musical accompaniment. They become threatening and overpowering. As they almost engulf Shaw and Powell, Shaw flees to a balcony and then falls screaming to her death. The camera moves back to the New York scene. The cat waits to be fed. Shaw's face fades back to the tiny white dot first seen and then disappears.

In the late 1930's, Berkeley moved to MGM, where his dance direction included *Ziegfeld Girl* (1941). His MGM credits also included *Lady Be Good* (1941), with dancer Eleanor Powell, and three of the most popular Mickey Rooney-Judy Garland musicals, *Babes in Arms* (1939), *Strike up the Band* (1940), and *Babes on Broadway* (1941), all backstage musicals with variations on the Cinderella theme. He directed the eccentric dance by Scarecrow Ray Bolger, "If I Only Had a Brain," for the *Wizard of Oz* (1939) and designed spectacular swimming ballets for Esther Williams in *Million Dollar Mermaid* (1952) and *Easy to Love* (1953).

While he was frequently imitated, certain of his techniques remained distinctly his. Far more than most dance directors, he stressed the precision movement of masses of people more than dance steps. No other director chose so often to turn dancers into geometric patterns, flattening conventional perspective. At the same time, more than most other directors, he featured the dancers' faces; his stars had to work harder to prove themselves than did the stars of more conventional musicals, which often showed the star figure alone against a vaguely photographed background of anonymous bodies. His juxtaposition of violence and exuberance was to be imitated many times, but never so forcefully, since Berkeley would not permit mood music to signal the coming of tragedy. Berkeley's gift was to give his audience a reality that they understood, one in which violence and agony come without warning, while at the same time giving his Cinderella figures an escape even more fantastic than the most imaginative of his audiences could dream. He was best known for his camera angles, but these were more easily imitated than the other qualities that made him unique.

Bibliography

Altman, Rick. *The American Film Musical*. Bloomington: Indiana University Press, 1989. Made unnecessarily difficult by scholarly jargon, this book contains two sets of chapters, difficult ones on theory and more readable chapters of practical application. The latter can be read separately and provide an excellent categorization of folk musicals, fairy-tale musicals, and backstage musicals. The backstage musical material necessarily includes much about Berkeley.

Delameter, Jerome. *Dance in the Hollywood Musical.* Ann Arbor, Mich.: UMI Research Press, 1981. This scholarly but relatively readable work includes two chapters, "Dance in Film Before 1930" and "Busby Berkeley at Warner Brothers," which are useful for an understanding of Berkeley's importance. Delameter, primarily interested in technical dance, thinks little of Berkeley but rightfully associates him with the French surrealistic movement in art.

Mordden, Ethan. *The Hollywood Musical.* New York: St. Martin's Press, 1981. Mordden's witty, opinionated, and readable work remains a standard starting place for students of the film musical; he offers a general overview of Berkeley's role in reviving musicals and influence on the genre.

Pike, Bob, and Dave Martin. *The Genius of Busby Berkeley.* Reseda, Calif.: Creative Film Society, 1973. This poorly produced book contains a lengthy interview with Berkeley, most of which is accessible in Tony Thomas' book (see below). Also includes a filmography, some review material, and a biography that largely repeats the interview.

Schatz, Thomas. *The Genius of the System: Hollywood Filmmaking in the Studio Era.* New York: Pantheon, 1988. Easily the best readily accessible source for information about the business side of filmmaking, including the making of *42nd Street.* Provides an excellent list of archival sources and a reliable bibliography.

Sennett, Ted. *Warner Brothers Presents: The Most Exciting Years—From the "Jazz Singer" to "White Heat."* New Rochelle, N.Y.: Arlington House, 1971. Discusses Berkeley as a film director, a role in which he was relatively unsuccessful, as well as a dance director. Sennett gives an overview of Berkeley's creative use of cameras, his inventiveness, and his contribution to the revival of the studio.

Thomas, Tony, and Jim Terry, with Busby Berkeley. *The Busby Berkeley Book.* Greenwich, Conn.: New York Graphic Society, 1973. This is the single essential work for a study of Berkeley. Lavishly illustrated, it contains a foreword by Ruby Keeler, a biography, and a filmography.

Betty Richardson

Cross-References

The Jazz Singer Premieres in New York (1927), p. 734; Sound Technology Revolutionizes the Motion-Picture Industry (1928), p. 761; *Hallelujah* Is the First Important Black Musical (1929), p. 772; Hollywood Enters Its Golden Age (1930's), p. 822; Lubitsch's *The Merry Widow* Opens New Vistas for Film Musicals (1934), p. 941; *Top Hat* Establishes the Astaire-Rogers Dance Team (1935), p. 984; The Classic *The Wizard of Oz* Opens (1939), p. 1109.

BILLIE HOLIDAY BEGINS HER RECORDING CAREER

Category of event: Music
Time: 1933
Locale: New York, New York

Producer John Hammond's recording of Billie Holiday singing with Benny Good-
man's band in 1933 brought her to the attention of jazz aficionados

Principal personages:
BILLIE HOLIDAY (ELEANORA FAGAN, 1915-1959), a jazz and blues singer
whose recordings and innovative techniques would prove widely in-
fluential
LESTER YOUNG (1909-1959), a celebrated saxophonist who teamed with
Holiday on many of her best recordings
TEDDY WILSON (THEODORE SHAW, 1912-1986), a pianist who recorded
with Holiday and helped to launch her career
JOHN HAMMOND (1910-1987), a Columbia Records producer who signed
Holiday to her first recording contract
BENNY GOODMAN (1909-1986), a renowned bandleader with whom Holi-
day made her first recordings

Summary of Event

Billie Holiday was born Eleanora Fagan in Baltimore, Maryland, on April 7, 1915,
to Sadie Fagan and guitarist Clarence Holiday, a guitarist in the renowned band led
by Fletcher Henderson. Her parents were later married briefly. After they separated,
she was left with relatives while her mother went to New York to find work. There
are several stories about the origin of the name "Billie." She was a tomboy, and her
father called her "Bill"; moreover, actress Billie Dove was her idol.

When Holiday was ten years old, she was raped by a forty-year-old man. He went
free; she was sent to a Catholic "correctional" home. At thirteen, she went to live
with her mother in Harlem. She smoked marijuana and was jailed as a prostitute.
She said she ran errands for a "madam" so that she could hear the Bessie Smith and
Louis Armstrong records played in the parlor of the brothel.

At seventeen, she began to sing professionally in Harlem at Monette Moore's
speakeasy on 133rd Street for ten dollars a week. She soon began working at other
Harlem clubs; eventually, Columbia Records producer John Hammond heard her and
arranged for her to record with Benny Goodman's band on Columbia in 1933. The
two sides were "Riffin' the Scotch" and "Your Mother's Son-in-Law." In that same
year, Teddy Wilson came to New York and signed with Brunswick Records. Wilson
played piano with Goodman's small group, with Lionel Hampton on vibes. Wilson
recorded pop tunes for Brunswick in 1935. He had earlier been allowed to record

with Goodman for Victor Records; in return, Goodman had agreed to record as a sideman with him for Brunswick. There were no arrangements. The vocalist was Billie Holiday. These recordings created a following among jazz musicians and jazz buffs, and Holiday was soon in demand.

In 1936, Holiday became known as "Lady Day" or "The Lady." The Count Basie band came to New York City. "The Count" had a Decca Records contract and could not play on the Wilson-Holiday recordings, but his sidemen could—Buck Clayton, Freddie Greene, Walter Page, and "Prez," Lester Young. It supposedly was Lester Young who nicknamed Holiday "Lady." In the jazz world, there was a Duke (Ellington), there was a Count, there was a "Prez"—short for "President"—and now a Lady.

On the 1936 recordings as Teddy Wilson's vocalist Holiday was surrounded by other fine musicians such as Jonah Jones, Johnny Hodges, Harry Carney, John Kirby, Cozy Cole, Vido Musso, Ben Webster, and of course, Teddy Wilson, whose playing with the left hand was far ahead of that of most pianists of the day. For eight months, Holiday was Count Basie's vocalist, and three "airchecks," recordings of the Basie band live at the Savoy Ballroom in Harlem in 1937, were later released commercially. She was also bandleader Artie Shaw's vocalist for a short time, including on a miserable trip on the band bus through the segregated South. After that, she worked on her own.

In 1936, too, she recorded with her own group for Vocalion Records. Shaw was a sideman on one session along with Bunny Berigan and Joe Bushkin. She again recorded for Vocalion in 1938 and 1939 and for Columbia as Wilson's vocalist; she also recorded for Columbia as the leader of "Billie Holiday and Her Orchestra."

From 1939 through 1941, she recorded with her own band for OKeh Records and as vocalist with Teddy Wilson and his orchestra. On a number of the OKeh recordings, Lester Young, Walter Page, Freddie Greene, and Jo Jones again recorded with her. Roy "Little Jazz" Eldridge played trumpet on several of the recordings; Charlie Shavers played on one. Young, Eddie Heywood on piano, and Kenny Clarke on drums were among the personnel who recorded "Georgia on My Mind" in 1941.

In the late 1940's, some of the Teddy Wilson recordings were reissued by Commodore Records, among them "Gloomy Sunday," which was neither jazz nor popular song but took on the dimensions of folklore and was forever after identified with Holiday. The recording was purportedly a version of a Hungarian "suicide song" that had, it was said, been banned from radio because some listeners who heard the song had killed themselves—although a disclaimer toward the end of the song noted that the singer was "only dreaming."

Another song that was neither jazz nor pop belongs to Holiday alone. "Strange Fruit," a poem set to music, describes the contrast between the ugly violence of lynchings and the physical beauty of the South. She recorded it in 1939, a brave act at the time; issuing such a racially charged song could have wrecked her career or led to physical harm. Southern writer Lillian Smith used the song's title as the title of a novel about racial violence in the South.

Impact of Event

Billie Holiday created some songs that will always be identified with her, including "God Bless the Child," which has the structure of a pop tune but the feel of a blues lament and is still recorded by both black and white vocalists. Several original blues performed by her have stayed in the jazz vocalist repertoire, including "Fine and Mellow" (the title of which is a good description of her vocal), "Billie's Bounce," "Long Gone Blues," and "Billie's Blues."

She made more than one later recording of the tunes first recorded in the 1930's and early 1940's, but the early recordings give the listener a strong, young Holiday at home within the structure of the song and the performance of the other musicians, comfortable enough to "lay back on the beat" in the manner of a young Louis Armstrong. Among these repeatedly recorded early performances are "Them There Eyes," "Love Me or Leave Me," "I Cover the Waterfront," "I Can't Get Started," "These Foolish Things," "No Regrets," and "Some Other Spring." Later songs also identified with Holiday include "Trav'lin' Light," "Don't Explain," "Good Morning, Heartache," and "Easy Livin'." Even some songs originally identified with blues giant Bessie Smith came to be known as Holiday's, including "Gimme a Pigfoot" and "Ain't Nobody's Business."

In 1938, she had moved from Harlem downtown into Manhattan, as Lena Horne would do a few years later. She began performing at the well-known Café Society, and until the late 1940's she worked at various Manhattan jazz clubs. In 1947, she appeared, dressed as a maid, in the film *New Orleans*. In that same year, however, she was arrested for possession of heroin and sentenced to a year and a day in a federal prison in Alderson, West Virginia. Ten days after her release, she performed to a capacity crowd at Carnegie Hall. She could not, however, work in any jazz club in New York City; an archaic law required performers in establishments that sold liquor to obtain a "cabaret card" permitting them to work there. Cabaret cards were unavailable to musicians with drug convictions. Holiday thus could not work in her town, the center of live jazz performance in America at that time.

In the early 1950's, Steve Allen, the host of an early New York television variety show that would later become *The Tonight Show*, featured a number of notable jazz performers, including Holiday, on his program. In 1957, a television special with Lester Young and others let fans see and hear her one more time; the soundtrack to the special was released as the album *The Sound of Jazz*.

In 1956, with coauthor William F. Dufty, she wrote her autobiography, *Lady Sings the Blues*. A hit 1972 film based on the book starred Diana Ross as Holiday. Although Ross was musically miles away from Holiday, the film's sound track introduced a generation to Holiday's songs.

Holiday toured Europe in the last few years of her life and was received enthusiastically. Her last performance in New York City was a 1959 benefit performance at the Phoenix Theater. On May 31, 1959, she collapsed at her Manhattan apartment. In a coma, she was taken by a police ambulance to a private hospital, where she lay unattended for an hour. She was then taken to Metropolitan Hospital in Harlem. She lingered, under an oxygen tent, for more than two weeks, with a policeman outside her door. Authorities denied that he was waiting to arrest her, but her public certainly thought so. The officer was removed by court order the day before Holiday died.

When she collapsed, she had seventy cents in her bank account and $750 in cash taped to her leg. Three thousand people attended her funeral at St. Paul the Apostle Catholic Church in Harlem. She was buried in Raymond's Cemetery in the Bronx. For some time, her grave was not marked by a headstone, a fact that resulted in an angry article in *Downbeat* magazine. (Ironically, she never won the top spot in any of *Downbeat*'s celebrated polls.)

What was it about Billie Holiday that brought three thousand people to her funeral, that made young white Southerners who had not heard of Lester Young and Roy Eldridge buy her records and learn the words to "Easy Livin'" and "God Bless the Child"? Her many fans did not see her perform in films, as they did, for brief moments, Lena Horne. Moreover, unlike other popular black stars of the day such as Ella Fitzgerald, Fats Waller, the Ink Spots, and the Mills Brothers, she did not often have her music featured on juke boxes in white establishments.

She simply recorded the popular songs of the day, some of which became standards; some, like "Miss Brown to You" and "I Wished on the Moon," did not but live anyway because Billie Holiday sang them.

What made Holiday's music so compelling was her much-discussed "style." Many people have written about the way she altered the melodic line of a song. In fact, though, she did not play around with melody very much—no more, for example, than the young Miles Davis, who played "Blue Room" almost note for note.

To say that she sang "like a horn player" is not quite right, either. A listener to early Armstrong vocals is struck by the swinging way he played with the time. The effect is much more noticeable to a nonmusician on early Armstrong records, when the rhythm sections still played tight four-beat patterns. The listener hears Billie Holiday do the same thing on the "up" tunes on her 1930's recordings; moreover, on such songs the last bars of her chorus leading into a musician's solo often anticipate the solo, "inviting" the instrumentalist into the tune.

Her talent is not merely evident in the "room" she could make, however, inside those four-beat rhythms. Sometimes it shows in what Louis Armstrong talked about as leaving spaces between the notes. Sometimes her ability is apparent in the notes, words, or syllables she accents. "Percussive" is too strong a term to describe the technique—it is rather almost percussive, almost syncopated. Whatever the secret of her style is, it is as unmistakable as a fingerprint. It is her signature. To this unique element she added "bent," gliding notes, all with a voice that could seem both sweet and sassy.

Toward the end, her health and breath gone, she sometimes sounded like an imitation of herself, though there were still moments in which her talent shone. Many people liked her toward the end of her career, though, simply because she seemed to symbolize everybody's suffering.

After her death, her power remained in her recordings, together with some all-too-brief moments on film and videotape. Her influence is still apparent, too, in the work of legions of jazz singers. The listener hears it in the work of the young Peggy Lee, for example, sometimes subtly, sometimes in open tribute, as on Lee's recording of "Them There Eyes." (Lee's guitarist husband, Dave Barbour, recorded a few sides with Holiday.)

Carmen McRae has perhaps done more than anyone else to keep Holiday's memory alive. A fine instrumentalist on the piano, McRae also uses her voice like an instrument. There are moments in her performances—an emphasis on a syllable, a bend in a note—when she expects her listeners to hear Holiday.

McRae nearly always includes a Holiday song in her concerts, and she once recorded a whole album of songs with which Holiday is identified. A more recent live recording by McRae of Thomas "Fats" Waller's "Black and Blue" evokes an emotion that can only make a Holiday admirer remember "Strange Fruit" and the sound of Holiday's voice in the last line.

Holiday never had much room on her recorded sides, most of which were short 78 rpm records. Moreover, most of her recordings were monaural and only later "enhanced" for stereo. A new listener thus will not get the full impact of Holiday's unique talent in two minutes. After an hour or an evening of listening to Billie Holiday at her best, however, the listener will always hear those tunes differently.

Billie Holiday ultimately will be remembered not for the tragedy of her life but for the triumph of her music. Perhaps the essence of her spirit can be found in the title of her joyous, swinging 1936 recording "No Regrets."

Bibliography

Friedwald, Will. *Jazz Singing: America's Great Voices from Bessie Smith to Bebop and Beyond.* New York: Charles Scribner's Sons, 1990. An excellent illustrated overview of the contributions of great jazz vocalists, from Louis Armstrong and Bing Crosby through Betty Carter. The author contrasts Holiday's singing with that of Ella Fitzgerald, noting that the two singers "travel completely different ways to the same destination." Lucid, scholarly, and comprehensive.

Holiday, Billie, with William Dufty. *Lady Sings the Blues.* Garden City, N.Y.: Doubleday, 1956. Holiday's autobiography. Frank in its presentation of details about her painful childhood and drug addiction, although some people who knew Holiday later in life have criticized the book as unreliable.

James, Burnett. *Billie Holiday.* New York: Hippocrene Books, 1984. A useful short biography of the singer produced as part of the "Jazz Masters" series. Illustrated; helpful selective discography.

Kliment, Bud. *Billie Holiday.* New York: Chelsea House, 1990. A profusely illustrated biography directed toward younger readers. Contains an introductory essay, "On Achievement," by Coretta Scott King.

Pleasants, Henry. *The Great American Popular Singers.* New York: Simon & Schuster, 1974. An interesting though somewhat dated overview of the topic. Useful, and somewhat unusual, in its discussion of Holiday and other jazz and blues artists alongside singers such as Elvis Presley and Hank Williams, who earned their fame in other genres. Illustrated, with a glossary of singing terms.

Katherine Lederer

Cross-References

Harlem Renaissance Celebrates African-American Culture (1920's), p. 480; Bessie Smith Records "Downhearted Blues" (1923), p. 572; Armstrong First Records with His Hot Five Group (1925), p. 670; *The Jazz Singer* Premieres in New York (1927), p. 734; Ellington Begins an Influential Engagement at the Cotton Club (1927), p. 739; Goodman Begins His *Let's Dance* Broadcasts (1934), p. 968; Marian Anderson Is Barred from Constitution Hall (1939), p. 1126; *Stormy Weather* Offers New Film Roles to African Americans (1940's), p. 1149; Sinatra Establishes Himself as a Solo Performer (1943), p. 1250; Parker's Playing Epitomizes Bebop (1946), p. 1318.

COWARD'S *DESIGN FOR LIVING* EPITOMIZES THE 1930'S

Category of event: Theater
Time: January 2, 1933
Locale: Hanna Theatre, Cleveland, Ohio

Noël Coward kept a promise to Alfred Lunt and Lynn Fontanne and wrote a comedy that epitomized the laughter and despair of the 1930's

Principal personages:

NOËL COWARD (1899-1973), an actor and leading English playwright of the 1920's, who promised to write a play for his friends when all became stars

LYNN FONTANNE (1887-1983), an English-born actress who became half of the foremost acting team of her generation

ALFRED LUNT (1892-1977), a Wisconsin-born actor, often considered the greatest of his generation, who rarely appeared without Fontanne after their 1922 marriage

MAX GORDON (MECHEL SALPETER, 1892-1978), a son of impoverished immigrants who became Broadway's most successful producer of the 1930's

Summary of Event

Design for Living resulted from an eleven-year-old promise. In 1921, Noël Coward, Alfred Lunt, and Lynn Fontanne were relatively unknown. They dreamed of stardom, and they agreed that, when fame arrived, Coward would write a play to star all three.

Coward had begun to perform in 1910; he had worked in Charles Hawtrey's company in 1911 and, among other appearances, had briefly acted in D. W. Griffith's film *Heart of the World* (1918). His first major hit was the 1923 revue *London Calling*, based largely on his lyrics. He performed in it with Gertrude Lawrence. Fontanne made her English debut in *Cinderella* (1905) before coming to America in 1910. She met Lunt in *A Young Man's Fancy* (1916), and, in 1921, made her reputation in George S. Kaufman and Marc Connelly's *Dulcy*. Lunt's first major recognition was for his Broadway performance as the title character in Booth Tarkington's *Clarence* (1919). Lunt and Fontanne achieved the kind of fame they desired with their appearance as a team in a Theatre Guild production of Ferenc Molnar's *The Guardsman* (1924).

Coward's major breakthrough came with his serious drama *The Vortex* (1924). Coward played the role of Nicky. *The Vortex* provided a considerable and scandalous sensation; it presented a theme that was to remain a constant in Coward's work: the struggles of post-World War I characters to work out their own values, since the values of the past had become outmoded or bankrupt. The principal characters in

The Vortex are Nicky, addicted to drugs, and his mother, addicted to eternal youthfulness. She refuses to admit her maturity, takes lovers her son's age, and cannot relinquish her own pleasures to play mother to her son. At the end, mother and son vow to reform, but they leave the audience with no particular reason to believe that they will.

This contrast between the meaningless lives of moderns and the values of the past that are lost underlies many of the Coward hits that followed. In *Cavalcade* (1931), a panorama of England from the Boer War to 1929, Coward ends by juxtaposing the weary song "Twentieth Century Blues" with the figures of six basket-weaving wounded World War I veterans as well as with a cacophony of noise from planes, jazz, and loudspeakers; these suddenly give way to a singing of the traditional "God Save the King." At the end of Coward's musical *Bitter Sweet* (1929), heroine Sari Linden sings of the enduring loves and loyalties of the past only to find herself abandoned by her uncomprehending audience of Jazz-Age young people. Most bitterly in *Post Mortem* (1931), Coward shows his affinity with the great wave of revulsion that swept Europe, England, and, to some extent, America in reaction to the traditional values that had produced the devastation of World War I, with its aerial bombardment, gas and trench warfare, and millions of casualties. In *Post Mortem*, young John Cavan, killed in action, returns from the dead to learn that his death, apparently, meant little. Attitudes have not changed; platitudes and hypocrisy that made the war possible still conceal its brutal reality. Young people, survivors of the war, cannot accept these values but have nothing with which to replace them.

Design for Living moved to the Ethel Barrymore Theatre in New York on January 24 after its Cleveland opening. Although the play is high comedy, indirectly it reflects the grim world of the 1930's, a world in which frivolous laughter barely conceals despair. The play reflects the decade's insecurity, recorded in Coward's autobiography and letters, about the Depression and the European situation that was to lead to World War II. Coward wrote the play very quickly on his way back from Chile, where he had received a cable from the Lunts informing him that their Theatre Guild commitment was over and asking him about their play. He returned to California, the lone passenger on a Norwegian freighter, and completed the play two days before the ship docked at Los Angeles. Clearly, the play emerged from preoccupations, especially the idea, suggestive of George Bernard Shaw's beliefs, that moderns must overthrow traditional moral and social sanctions to create their own lives and values. Coward's play is light, seemingly frivolous, but its action points irrevocably to this single conclusion.

Gilda, Leo, and Otto are the play's principal characters. Leo (played by Coward) is a playwright, Otto (Lunt) a painter, and Gilda (Fontanne) loves both. In the first act, Gilda lives with Otto in Paris. She and picture dealer Ernest Friedman (played by Campbell Gullen) are talking as Otto returns from a trip. Leo emerges from the bedroom. Conventionally furious, Otto stalks off, feeling betrayed. In the second act, Gilda is living with Leo in London. Leo leaves for a country weekend but returns early to find Otto with Gilda. Disgusted with both men's reactions, Gilda stalks out. She marries Ernest, a merchant, not a creator, and tries to live a conventionally money-hungry life in New York. The third act takes place in their New York apartment, where their pictures and even their furniture are for sale. Otto and Leo enter and scandalize some guests. Gilda walks out again. Ernest returns the next morning to find both Otto and Leo emerging from the bedroom, wearing his pajamas. They claim they want Gilda. Conventional Ernest is horrified and flies into a fury, mouthing the platitudes of an outraged moralist, when Gilda returns to say she is leaving with Otto and Leo. She cannot live without them both. It is Ernest's turn to stalk out, but he trips and falls flat, and the play ends with the laughter of Otto, Leo, and Gilda.

Impact of Event

Like many other Coward plays, *Design for Living* was a success, but critical reviews were mixed. Having exhausted himself during the run of *The Vortex*, Coward had promised himself to appear in no more than a three-month run, but *Design for Living* was so successful that he extended this to five months. Biographer Cole Lesley records that, during the final week, police had to be called out to control the crowds. For the only time in his life, Coward had to hire a bodyguard. He had rented a secluded cottage and was receiving threatening letters.

These letters may have been related to the play. Critics, while praising the performance, often cited it as decadent or amoral. The most famous still photograph from the play emphasizes a possible homosexual relationship between Leo and Otto; one man reclines in the arms of the other while reaching out to Gilda, who sits separately. Then, too, the play supports an aristocracy of the elite, whose duty is to live by its own precepts regardless of the conventional morality for which Ernest, as his name suggests, is the humorless spokesman. Finally, Gilda walks out on her marriage to Ernest, not for high principles, as was true of Henrik Ibsen's Nora in *Et dukkehjem* (1879; *A Doll's House*, 1880), but simply because she wants to do so. In fact, problems with British censorship probably explain why the play was not performed in England until 1939. Paramount filmed the play in 1933, with Ernst Lubitsch as director, but filmwriter Ben Hecht threw out most of Coward's script. (The film starred Fredric March, Gary Cooper, Miriam Hopkins, and Edward Everett Horton.)

The popularity of Lunt, Fontanne, and Coward himself, however, was such that would-be censors had no power over the production, thus opening up hitherto questionable material for future playwrights, such as Coward's admirer Edward Albee. Of those involved, only Max Gordon's career was profoundly affected, and that positively. Coward had been impressed by Gordon's frank critique of his performance in *Private Lives*. When Coward offered Gordon *Design for Living*, he apparently did not know Gordon's financial problems were so severe that they had brought him near bankruptcy; he was suicidal and had been hospitalized. Gordon saw *Design for Living* as the lifeline that had saved him; he became solvent again and went on to produce such hits as *Roberta* (1933), *The Great Waltz* (1934), *The Women* (1936), *My Sister Eileen* (1940), and *Born Yesterday* (1945). The Lunts, too, went on from this success to others such as *Reunion in Vienna* (1931), *Idiot's Delight* (1936), *Amphitryon 38* (1937), *There Shall Be No Night* (1940), and *The Pirate* (1942).

Coward's career was at its height with *Design for Living*. He followed it with *Conversation Piece* (1934), written for French singer Yvonne Printemps, and, in that year, the first volume of his collected plays appeared. Of the many plays that followed, the two most important are *Tonight at Eight-Thirty* (1935) and *Blithe Spirit* (1941). In 1942, he gained wartime celebrity for writing and acting in the patriotic film *In Which We Serve*, which also starred John Mills and Michael Wilding. This was a starkly realistic account of the German destruction of a British ship and its effects on the people involved.

In the post-World War II world, Coward lost critical favor but retained his popular audience. John Osborne's 1956 *Look Back in Anger* introduced a new kind of realism, as shocking in its way as Coward's had been two decades earlier. Coward continued to write plays, but he rarely repeated his earlier successes. Yet he continued not only writing but also entertaining. In 1953, for example, he appeared as King Magnus in a London production of Shaw's *The Apple Cart*; Shaw's advice had early influenced him, and a continuing influence is to be found in the structure and dialogue of Coward's plays.

By that time, the critical tide again turned, and he became celebrated as the grand old man of British theater. He appeared several times in the 1950's at London's Café de Paris, and in 1954 he gave a royal command performance at London's Palladium. In the following year, he wrote and directed *Together with Music*, a U.S. television review, for himself and Mary Martin. He made other television appearances, including, in 1967, a role in a U.S. performance of Shaw's *Androcles and the Lion*. A number of his own plays were adapted for television. In 1955, to his astonishment, he was offered $40,000 a week to appear at the Desert Inn in Las Vegas; it was a personal triumph. In that year, he appeared in the film version of *Around the World in 80 Days*. He followed this with a noteworthy performance in the 1959 film of Graham Greene's *Our Man in Havana*. A London revival of *Private Lives* led to major revivals of many others. He received an honorary Tony Award for his career, an honorary doctorate from the University of Sussex, and, in 1970, a knighthood. In 1971, *Cowardly Custard* played in London and *Oh! Coward* in New York; these were revues, essentially anthologies of his lyrics.

Bibliography

Castle, Charles. *Noël*. Garden City, N.Y.: Doubleday, 1973. An informal compilation of biographical notes, photographs, texts of songs, extracts from plays, and recollections of friends that provides an interesting supplement to more formal biographies.

Coward, Noël. *Noël Coward: Autobiography*. London: Methuen, 1986. Contains his three autobiographies, *Present Indicative* (1937), *Future Indefinite* (1954), and *Past Conditional* (an unfinished work, first published here); the most valuable volume is the first.

_____. *Play Parade.* Garden City, N.Y.: Doubleday, Doran, 1933. This volume was published alone in the U.S.; it includes *Design for Living, Cavalcade, Private Lives, Bitter Sweet, Post Mortem, The Vortex,* and *Hay Fever* (1925). In England, this was the first of a six-volume edition.

Gordon, Max, with Lewis Funke. *Max Gordon Presents.* New York: Bernard Beis, 1963. A readable, generally anecdotal account of Gordon's rise from New York slums to prominence, with some coverage of his work with Coward.

Lahr, John. *Coward the Playwright.* London: Methuen, 1982. One of the earliest studies to take full account of Coward's homosexuality. Lahr stresses that topic and Coward's desire for fame, sometimes at the expense of the plays' substance.

Lesley, Cole. *Remembered Laughter: The Life of Noël Coward.* New York: Alfred A. Knopf, 1977. First employed by Coward in 1936, Lesley remained companion and assistant until Coward's death; this well-written memoir is tipped slightly toward a personal, rather than professional, biography. It was published in London by Jonathan Cape in 1976 as *The Life of Noël Coward.*

Levin, Milton. *Noël Coward.* Rev. ed. Boston: Twayne, 1989. A colorless, workmanlike study with chronology, bibliography of Coward's works, and limited bibliography of works about him.

Mander, Raymond, and Joe Mitchenson. *Theatrical Companion to Coward.* New York: Macmillan, 1957. Extremely useful for early plays and other works. Contains cast lists, production dates, synopses, discography, list of plays unproduced and unpublished at time of publication, list of individual songs, a tribute by playwright Terence Rattigan, and much else.

Morley, Sheridan. *A Talent to Amuse: A Biography of Noël Coward.* Rev. ed. Boston: Little, Brown, 1985. First published in 1969, reissued with new prologue and epilogue in 1985, this volume is slightly more oriented to Coward's professional than personal life and contains a valuable chronology, listing his work as playwright, performer, composer, author, and director as well as listing major revivals of his work.

Zolotow, Maurice. *Stagestruck: The Romance of Alfred Lunt and Lynn Fontanne.* New York: Harcourt, Brace & World, 1965. One of several studies of the Lunts, this contains considerable material about their relationship with Coward.

Betty Richardson

Cross-References

Shaw Articulates His Philosophy in *Man and Superman* (1903), p. 85; Lubitsch's *The Merry Widow* Opens New Vistas for Film Musicals (1934), p. 941; The Classic Screwball Comedy Reaches Its Height in Popularity (1934), p. 951; Ealing Comedies Mark a High Point in British Film (1949), p. 1427; Allen's *Annie Hall* Captures Complexities of 1970's Life (1977), p. 2381.

LUBITSCH'S *THE MERRY WIDOW* OPENS NEW VISTAS FOR FILM MUSICALS

Category of event: Motion pictures
Time: 1934
Locale: Metro-Goldwyn-Mayer studios, Culver City, California

Ernst Lubitsch brought visual and verbal wit, European sophistication, dance, and song together into a fully integrated musical myth that popularized cinematic operetta

Principal personages:
ERNST LUBITSCH (1892-1947), a German actor and director who introduced a wit and sophistication known as the "Lubitsch touch" to Hollywood
JEANETTE MACDONALD (1901-1965), a onetime Broadway chorus girl who played Sonia, the title character in *The Merry Widow*
MAURICE CHEVALIER (1888-1972), a former French cabaret singer turned international film star who played Captain Danilo in *The Merry Widow*
EDWARD EVERETT HORTON (1886-1970), a comedian who played fussy, blundering Ambassador Popoff

Summary of Event

Early film musical directors were troubled by the role of song and dance, wondering what justification there was for a performer to stop the action, turn to the audience, and begin to sing. Efforts to justify production numbers explain why many early musicals were set in theaters or nightclubs, where music was the logical outgrowth of the setting. On stage, operetta came closer than any other form to fully integrating music, dance, plot, and character development into a coherent whole. That integration was most successful in Jerome Kern's *Show Boat*, which opened on Broadway in 1927.

In Germany, Ernst Lubitsch, once a comic and a student of famed director Max Reinhardt, had himself turned director. His first success as director was *Schuhpalast Pinkus* (*Shoe Salon Pinkus*), a silent musical released in 1916. (Silent films were not, to their audiences, silent; they were always accompanied by music, and in urban centers, the films might be accompanied by full orchestras.) After Lubitsch's arrival in the United States, he made *Rosita* (1923), which featured Mary Pickford as a street singer; *So This Is Paris* (1926), with an extravagant production number; *The Student Prince* (1927), one of its sources the Sigmund Romberg operetta; and *Love Parade* (1929), with Jeanette MacDonald and Maurice Chevalier.

The Merry Widow had been filmed before. In fact, Lubitsch's film was overshadowed, at the time, by the 1925 silent version, which starred screen idol John Gilbert and popular actress Mae Murray; the director of the earlier version was Erich von

Stroheim. Lubitsch, however, brought a new perspective to the film, as well as new and witty songs by Richard Rodgers and Lorenz Hart and by Gus Kahn. The major characters, Sonia and Danilo, are treated both tenderly and poignantly. Comedy derives partly from his vanity and her pride but primarily from the struggles of the two to resist the social order and the necessary cycles of marriage—and, by implication, reproduction—to which both must ultimately yield.

The plot of Franz Lehár's operetta, first staged in Vienna in 1905, is simple. Sonia, wealthy and widowed, is lonely and bored. Captain Danilo, a happy womanizer, is eager to meet the heavily veiled widow, but he has been spoiled by the bored women of Maxim's bordello in Paris, the equally bored peasant women of Marshovia, and the even more bored Queen Dolores (played by Una Merkel) of that country. When he meets Sonia, his remarks are directly sexual. She is attracted, but her pride causes her to rebuff him. She flees to Paris. Danilo's government sends him after her to marry her and keep her wealth in the country. He wins her at an embassy party, but she learns he is courting her under orders. Now truly in love, Danilo refuses to defend himself. He is arrested and returned to Marshovia to be tried for treason. She appears at his trial and visits him in jail. There, the king and ambassador lock them in until they agree to be married by a priest the king has conveniently provided.

What Lubitsch adds is a story told in contrasts. Chevalier's untrained French cabaret voice represents the forces of passion and freedom; MacDonald's trained operatic soprano is the voice of love and marriage. At Maxim's, where Sonia follows Danilo, the audience first sees a cancan, an exhibitionist dance in which women display themselves to male viewers. That dance gives way to an awkward hopping dance that Chevalier performs with a crowd of women, not with a single partner. The scene switches to the embassy, where a disciplined folk dance balances the cancan of the earlier scene. Then the waltz begins. In contrast to Danilo's hopping dance at the club, the circles of the waltz are disciplined. They represent the eternal cycles of mating, childbirth, and death, a notion given particular poignancy by a single shot of viewers in a balcony, older people, whose time of youth and joy is ended. They are observers, as Sonia and Danilo must someday be. Below, the lovers dance alone, merge into the crowd, dance alone, and are surrounded by dancers again, symbolic of the difficulty they are having accepting their destiny. When Sonia rejects Danilo, however, and he is arrested, she begins a hysterical parody of the waltz; in its disorder, it is comparable to Danilo's earlier hopping dance.

Both visual and verbal wit suggest that social order is necessary but not flawless. Much of the film's considerable comedy is at the expense of government. In the opening credits, a magnifying glass appears over a map of central Europe so that the audience can find tiny Marshovia. Marshovian government, though, takes itself very seriously. King Achmed communicates clichés and trivia to Popoff in an elaborate secret code. He tolerates his queen's adultery because he possesses a politician's desire to avoid scandal. Yet livestock must be removed from a Marshovian courtroom before Danilo can be tried for treason; significantly, a goat is led out as Danilo is led in.

Set design and costume also develop the mythic dimension. Exteriors of Sonia's castle are nonrealistically presented in ways suggestive of the German expressionist theater. Hers is a fairy-tale castle in which a widow is imprisoned by convention. Surprisingly in a black-and-white film, the stark contrast between black and white effectively stresses the contrast between the white of freedom and the black of convention. Alone in her castle, Sonia wears a widow's deep mourning. The audience sees a closet of mourning gowns, of mourning veils, of mourning corsets; even her dog is black. When she resolves to leave for Paris, all, even the dog, turns white. In the cancan at Maxim's, the girls' costumes are white edged in black; at the embassy, waltzers wear, at first, black and white in balance.

Impact of Event

Lubitsch popularized operetta on film, but for Lubitsch himself, *The Merry Widow* was an ending, not a beginning. He made more than forty films in Hollywood, but no other musicals. His later credits include *Ninotchka* (1939), with Greta Garbo; *The Shop Around the Corner* (1940), with Margaret Sullavan and James Stewart; *To Be or Not to Be* (1942), with Carole Lombard and Jack Benny; *Heaven Can Wait* (1943), with Gene Tierney; and *Cluny Brown* (1946), with Charles Boyer and Jennifer Jones. The film also was an ending for Chevalier. After appearing in *Folies Bergère* (1935), he returned to Europe and made no more Hollywood films until *Gigi* (1958).

The Lubitsch touch was affected by increasing censorship. Following a decade of Hollywood scandals, the institution of the Catholic Church's League of Decency in 1933 caused Hollywood to enforce the Hays Production Code which prohibited the type of wit that had informed *The Merry Widow*. Danilo's casual promiscuity would become unacceptable; clearly, in the film, when he marries Sonia, he gives up a life that has given him great pleasure. This is sacrifice, not repentance. The obvious sexual reference of the trial scene—when the entrance of Danilo, now romantically in love, is associated with the exit of the goat, a traditional symbol of lechery— would also be unacceptable, as would the blatant sexuality of the queen and the obvious prostitutes at Maxim's. Specific kinds of stage business would not be seen again for two decades. For example, there is considerable symbolic byplay involving a comparison of swords and swordbelts in the scene in which the king learns of his wife's adultery with Danilo. When Danilo thinks the king is gone, he suggestively sheaths his sword before entering the queen's bedroom. The king, however, returns. He has forgotten his sword and belt. Accidentally, he picks up the now-abandoned sword and belt of Danilo, which obviously belong to a younger, trimmer, and by implication more virile man. This broadly sexual visual humor would go underground until such films as the Beatles' *A Hard Day's Night* (1964) and *Help!* (1965), after censorship had ended.

It is possible, too, that with Adolf Hitler and Benito Mussolini on the march in Europe, neither public nor studio heads, many of them Jewish, would be so much amused as before by the self-important caperings of heads of small European nations. Certainly, Lubitsch was harshly criticized for bringing humor to bear on the

European situation in his later *To Be or Not to Be*. *The Merry Widow* depends heavily on such topical humor. For example, when Sonia leaves Marshovia, the threat to the economy is so great that the king hears of impending revolution. The shepherds, he is told, are threatening to organize into a Black Sheep movement. The king, however, is relieved to hear that the leaders are merely "left bank intellectual" shepherds and, consequently, not a force to be feared. Such humor savors more of the Weimar Republic than of the America of the 1930's and 1940's.

Yet Lubitsch's use of operetta was influential. It simply underwent changes, the tracing of which offers a revealing insight into the popular culture of the 1930's. With the heightening impact of the Depression and the increasing threat of war in Europe, the public demanded simpler emotions and more stereotyped characters than were to be found in Lubitsch musicals; it clearly rejected his characters' sophisticated ambivalence about their proper roles.

Chevalier's European sophistication was thus replaced by Nelson Eddy's boyish earnestness. Eddy and MacDonald, "America's Sweethearts," were rivaled only by Ginger Rogers and Fred Astaire as the most popular couple in film history. Eddy had a trained operatic voice; he had sung with the Philadelphia Civic Opera. Without acting ability, he simply portrayed manly courage, protectiveness of women, and American virtue. Even in films such as the disastrous *I Married an Angel* (1942), which concluded the Eddy-MacDonald series and in which Eddy is described as a womanizer, he obviously views women with great alarm. Unlike Chevalier's Danilo, he greets his rescue by a virtuous woman with absolute relief. MacDonald played innocent girls, not experienced women, until, in *I Married an Angel*, the camera shows her forty-one years in her chinline and eyes—even as she simpers like a teenager in a film caught between pure sentimentalism and self-parody. The MacDonald-Eddy partnership began in 1935 with *Naughty Marietta* and continued through *Rose Marie* (1940), *Bitter Sweet* (1940), and *The Chocolate Soldier* (1942), among others. Worldliness and social satire were replaced with sentimentality.

Lubitsch's synthesis of fairy-tale musical and myth was to wait much longer to reappear. A number of films in the folk musical tradition subordinated romance and melodrama to mythic structure; these began with King Vidor's 1929 *Hallelujah* and continued through the various filmings of *Show Boat* (1936 and 1951), *The Wizard of Oz* (1939), and such later musicals as *Carousel* (1956) and *Oklahoma!* (1955). Audience acceptance of the more sophisticated Lubitsch myth, though, would not reappear until after World War II. Lubitsch's aware and experienced couple, afraid of commitment but pulled, by forces greater than they, into cycles of life, were to appear again in *South Pacific* (1958); a similar story is told in *Gigi*, in which Chevalier also reappears. Lubitsch's mythic kingdom is alive, but sentimentalized, in the 1967 *Camelot*. These films shared something of Lubitsch's archetypes, but no audience was again to see his ideas portrayed with such dazzling effect and such wit.

Bibliography

Altman, Rick. *The American Musical*. Bloomington: Indiana University Press, 1989.

The reader put off by academic jargon should avoid the theoretical chapters here, but the chapter "The Fairy Tale Musical" contains an excellent analysis of Lubitsch, and "The Folk Musical" introduces the use of mythic elements.

Eisner, Lotte H. "Lubitsch and the Costume Film." In *The Haunted Screen: Expressionism in the German Cinema and the Influence of Max Reinhardt.* London: Thames and Hudson, 1969. Eisner is annoyingly condescending to Lubitsch as a lower-middle-class Jew, but Eisner's work, first published in France in 1952, recognizes expressionistic and mythic elements overlooked by most critics.

Manvell, Roger, and Heinrich Fraenkel. *The German Cinema.* New York: Praeger, 1972. The first two chapters provide a solid overview of the German film from 1895 to the 1920's, when Lubitsch was learning acting and directing. The authors emphasize spectacular films, such as Lubitsch's *Madame Dubarry* (1929), and the influence on Lubitsch's later, more intimate work of such directors as Mauritz Stiller.

Poague, Leland. *The Cinema of Ernst Lubitsch.* South Brunswick, N.J.: A. S. Barnes, 1978. Deals somewhat superficially with Lubitsch's American work, but provides good synopses of these films, although Poague's conclusions about Lubitsch's dawning self-awareness are dubious. Contains a valuable filmography of Lubitsch's American films and a useful, if brief, bibliographical note.

Pratt, George C. "Foreign Invasion (II) Ernst Lubitsch." In *Spellbound in Darkness: A History of the Silent Film.* Rev. ed. Greenwich, Conn.: New York Graphic Society, 1973. Less a history than a filmography, but contains valuable extracts from hard-to-find feature articles and reviews, the latter only concerning Lubitsch's American silents. Only one illustration.

Sennett, Ted. "The First Sounds of Music." In *Hollywood Musicals.* New York: Harry N. Abrams, 1985. This lavishly illustrated coffee-table volume contains an intelligent, if superficial, overview of Lubitsch's work and a brief bibliography.

Weinberg, Herman G. *The Lubitsch Touch: A Critical Study.* 3d ed. New York: Dover, 1977. This is the best book on Lubitsch's total career, but it is crippled by the author's coy prose style, by some thirty-five pages of tributes from contemporaries given without the documentation that would allow readers to consult the sources, and by a bibliography arranged, inexplicably, in chronological rather than alphabetical order.

Betty Richardson

Cross-References

Reinhardt Becomes Director of the Deutsches Theater (1905), p. 145; *The Cabinet of Dr. Caligari* Opens in Berlin (1920), p. 486; *The Jazz Singer* Premieres in New York (1927), p. 734; *Show Boat* Introduces American Musical Theater (1927), p. 745; Sound Technology Revolutionizes the Motion-Picture Industry (1928), p. 761; Hollywood Enters Its Golden Age (1930's), p. 822; Berkeley's *42nd Street* Revolutionizes Film Musicals (1933), p. 925.

HITCHCOCK BECOMES ENGLAND'S FOREMOST DIRECTOR

Category of event: Motion pictures
Time: 1934-1935
Locale: Great Britain

With The Man Who Knew Too Much *and* The Thirty-nine Steps, *Hitchcock revitalized a sagging career, creating a mixture of themes and cinematic techniques that would make his name synonymous with suspense*

Principal personages:
ALFRED HITCHCOCK (1899-1980), the British director who would establish his reputation with thrillers
MICHAEL BALCON (1896-1977), a British film producer who would help Hitchcock to reemerge as an important filmmaker
ROBERT DONAT (1905-1958), the lead actor in *The Thirty-nine Steps* and the first truly Hitchcockian hero
MADELEINE CARROLL (1906-1987), the actress whose portrayal of Pamela in *The Thirty-nine Steps* created the prototype of the Hitchcock blonde
PETER LORRE (1904-1964), the actor who was able to make evil somewhat sympathetic in *The Man Who Knew Too Much*

Summary of Event

By 1933, Alfred Hitchcock was stymied; his career appeared to be going nowhere. In 1926, he had made *The Lodger*, a melodramatic thriller involving a Jack-the-Ripper motif that had won stunning praise and instantly placed him among Great Britain's top directors. *The Lodger* had been his third film, but since then he had directed thirteen more, none matching *The Lodger*'s popularity. Although some of his pictures had been well received, most met with indifference, and his last few films had been outright flops. He had tried other thrillers, romance, comedy, filmed plays, and even musicals, but nothing seemed to work. At this point, as he seriously questioned whether he had any future in the film industry, Hitchcock was approached by an old colleague, Michael Balcon. Balcon, who had produced some of Hitchcock's early pictures, including *The Lodger*, was now in charge of production for the Gaumont-British Studio, and he wanted Hitchcock for his film company. Some of Hitchcock's problems in the past had stemmed from his working for studios that gave him little control over which films he was to direct. Balcon offered Hitchcock freedom of choice and personal moral support. Agreeing to join with Balcon, Hitchcock decided to return to the genre that he personally preferred and that had given him his first success—the thriller. He would first make *The Man Who Knew Too Much* and *The Thirty-nine Steps*, and his career would be transfigured.

The Man Who Knew Too Much, released in 1934, was a tale of murder, kidnapping, and attempted assassination centering on an English family caught in a web of international intrigue. While vacationing in Switzerland, Bob and Jill Lawrence (Leslie Banks and Edna Best) inadvertently stumble on a plot to slay a leading European statesman in London. Their young daughter Betty (Nova Pilbeam) is then abducted by the conspirators. Bob and Jill return to England and, through a series of adventures, foil the assassination and rescue Betty.

The Man Who Knew Too Much reawakened interest in Hitchcock, capturing public and critical acclaim. *The Thirty-nine Steps* in 1935 would be an even greater triumph. *The Thirty-nine Steps* also deals with espionage; Richard Hannay (Robert Donat), a Canadian visiting London, meets a mysterious woman who tells him that she is trying to stop a group of spies from smuggling an important military secret out of the country. She is murdered in Hannay's apartment; Hannay is suspected and flees from the police. Soon, he discovers that the foreign agents are also trying to kill him before he can reveal anything about their plot. From London to the Scottish Highlands, across fog-swept moors and back to London, Hannay is pursued. In the process, he becomes romantically involved with Pamela (Madeleine Carroll), a young woman who at first believes he is a killer and who then becomes convinced of his innocence. Together, Hannay and Pamela save the secret, help break up the spy ring, clear Hannay's name, and go off to live happily ever after.

Impact of Event

The Man Who Knew Too Much and *The Thirty-nine Steps* reestablished Alfred Hitchcock as Great Britain's premier director, setting him on a path that would lead to Hollywood and greater fame. In the two films can be seen the mature realization of several of Hitchcock's trademark techniques and approaches. He had always favored spectacular scenes, an expressionist mood, and editing that kept viewers off balance and the pace moving. Both films mix these elements skillfully. *The Man Who Knew Too Much* features several exciting moments, including three scenes that have become part of Hitchcockian lore: the assassination attempt during a symphony in the vast Albert Hall; a shootout with besieged conspirators that seemingly engages half of London's police force; and a desperate moment at the picture's conclusion, when one of the assassins stalks Betty across a high roof, seeking to kill her before she can be saved. While *The Thirty-nine Steps* does not offer as many memorable scenes, it does have a striking conclusion in London's Palladium; it is also a faster film, with almost nonstop action. Both films are darkly expressionistic, and both are filled with sudden, jarring changes of mood.

Although sound was still a primitive art in the industry, Hitchcock had been among the first to experiment with the different ways sound could be used to enhance films. In these two pictures, he moved some distance. The films' use of dialogue is more extensive and more assured than in Hitchcock's previous talkies. In *The Man Who Knew Too Much*, he employs sound to accompany the assassination; the attempt is made in the midst of a symphonic performance, at the precise instant when the drums beat and the cymbals clash. The music becomes an integral part of the plot, heightening the anxiety for the viewer. In *The Thirty-nine Steps*, when a maid finds the murdered woman in Hannay's apartment, she opens her mouth to scream; what the audience hears is the whistle of the train on which Hannay is fleeing London. Sudden, unsettling, the segue became one of the historic cinematic moments. With it, Hitchcock broke with the convention of early sound films that required the camera and the soundtrack to stay in sync; he thus enlarged the possibilities for the use of sound in films.

Hitchcock liked to utilize humor to relieve tension; he also liked to follow comic incidents with the return of menace, allowing the humor to make the shift to danger all the more potent. *The Man Who Knew Too Much* was, to that point, his most extensive melding of the comical into the thriller, but the film's humor is largely limited to witty dialogue. Humor, though, permeates *The Thirty-nine Steps*. The banter is even sharper than that of *The Man Who Knew Too Much*, and the film is replete with laughable situations that temporarily mask Hannay's peril. Hannay is sitting in a railway car, expecting soon to be caught, and he finds himself having to listen to a lingerie salesman display his wares and make risqué jokes. Running from the police, Hannay stumbles into a political meeting, is mistaken for a speaker, and gives an absurd oration. Pamela and Hannay are handcuffed together and awkwardly try to eat and sleep together. These are diverting, antic scenes; however, they soon give way to renewed suspense. One cannot relax too long in *The Thirty-nine Steps*.

These two films also introduced new elements that would be crucial in the evolution of the Hitchcock film. *The Man Who Knew Too Much* was his first foray into espionage. By 1934, Fascism was entrenched in Italy, Adolf Hitler had taken power in Germany, and the English were beginning to feel the onset of war jitters. Fear was in the air, and Hitchcock's ability to tap this apprehension helped to ensure the success of *The Man Who Knew Too Much* and *The Thirty-nine Steps*. After 1934, a significant proportion of Hitchcock's work would revolve around international intrigue. The world would be plagued by tension and conflict for the rest of his life; the espionage film would become a special type of thriller and Alfred Hitchcock one of its most skilled practitioners. Part of the reason was financial—spies could be big box office, as he discovered with *The Man Who Knew Too Much*—yet he also found he enjoyed fashioning cinematic stories around the shadowy life of the secret agent.

The archetypal Hitchcock hero, heroine, and villain were first seen in these films. *The Man Who Knew Too Much* provides the villain in the leader of the conspirators, played by Peter Lorre. Dangerous, yet perversely appealing, a terrorist at once droll, sophisticated, and menacing, Lorre is the most dynamic character in the film; his character was the first of a number of similarly fascinating evil figures who would energize many of Hitchcock's future films. After *The Thirty-nine Steps*, moreover, Hitchcock's male and female protagonists would be made to resemble Hannay and Pamela. His previous heroes and heroines, including the Lawrences in *The Man Who Knew Too Much*, tended to be one-dimensional; their characters were secondary to plot and to Hitchcock's special cinematic techniques. In *The Thirty-nine Steps*, both primary roles are multifaceted, central to the story's development, and played by actors of major talent and star presence. Hannay, as envisioned by Hitchcock and realized by Robert Donat, is witty and courageous, a man of action and charm. Similar characters would reappear in Hitchcock films over the years played by Michael Redgrave, Jimmy Stewart, Paul Newman, and Cary Grant. Madeleine Carroll is the original "Hitchcock blonde"; strong blondes, seemingly icy but actually passionate, would become a Hitchcock hallmark. While he had featured blonde actresses in films before *The Thirty-nine Steps*, Madeleine Carroll as Pamela first personified his ideal heroine. Later Hitchcock stars such as Grace Kelly, Eva Marie Saint, and Tippi Hedren were cast in her lineage.

The Thirty-nine Steps presents one of Hitchcock's favorite thriller structures: an honest man, made to look guilty by circumstances, is chased over long and picturesque distances while trying to establish his innocence. It also contributes the legendary Hitchcock device, the "MacGuffin." The MacGuffin is a secret that inaugurates the action, a secret apparently so crucial that everyone wants to control it, although it ultimately turns out to be rather inconsequential. In *The Thirty-nine Steps*, the MacGuffin is a military secret, a type of aircraft engine design. The viewer never really learns much about it, and indeed, the secret is soon lost sight of in the plot. The film is not about the engine design; it is about Hannay's attempt to prove his innocence and his growing relationship with Pamela. The MacGuffin could have been anything; its only real importance is to get events started. After *The Thirty-nine Steps*, Hitchcock incorporated the MacGuffin into his repertoire, and a favorite game for Hitchcock buffs would be to look for the MacGuffins in his pictures.

Of the two films that restored Hitchcock's reputation, *The Thirty-nine Steps* is the more significant. Audiences at the time felt this was so, as did critics. Hitchcock himself believed it a richer, more professional accomplishment, and cinema scholars have agreed. They see it as a compendium of his best early work and the first clear indication of the Hitchcock that was to come. Nevertheless, *The Man Who Knew Too Much* is not without its importance. The film did begin Hitchcock's relationship with the spy thriller and was quite popular, and its success was the turning point of Hitchcock's career. After that film, there was no doubt of Hitchcock's ability as a director.

Hitchcock crafted two more espionage thrillers for Michael Balcon, *Secret Agent* (1936) and *Sabotage* (1936). While neither was as admired as *The Man Who Knew Too Much* or *The Thirty-nine Steps*, both added to his indisputable standing as Great Britain's finest director. The fruitful collaboration with Balcon, however, did not last. Gaumont-British, destroyed by executive wrangling, gave up film production. Hitchcock made two films for Gainsborough Studios, *Young and Innocent* (1937), a lighthearted thriller, and *The Lady Vanishes* (1938), a spy film that many consider one of his best. Then Hitchcock decided to quit Great Britain for the United States. Ever since making *The Man Who Knew Too Much* and *The Thirty-nine Steps*, he had received approaches from Hollywood. After much hesitation, he finally chose to accept an offer from David O. Selznick. The working relationship with Michael Balcon was gone, and there would be more money, better production facilities, and perhaps more artistic challenges in the United States. Before he left, he directed one last film, *Jamaica Inn* (1939), a pirate melodrama, for actor and producer Charles Laughton. Although the film earned money, it was a critical failure and confirming evidence that his strength lay in thrillers.

Hitchcock went to the United States in 1939; he would die there in 1980. The forty-one years in Hollywood would make him perhaps the best-known filmmaker in the world. Building upon his British experience, he would create a remarkable number of varied landmark thrillers, including *Rear Window* (1954), *Vertigo* (1958), *North by Northwest* (1959), *Psycho* (1960), and *The Birds* (1963). He would influence generations of filmmakers, especially in the suspense genre. His films continue to be watched, and universities and film schools produce studies in ever-increasing numbers interpreting his pictures in minute detail. If Hitchcock had not made *The Man Who Knew Too Much* and *The Thirty-nine Steps*, none of this might have happened.

Bibliography

Durgnat, Raymond. *The Strange Case of Alfred Hitchcock*. Cambridge, Mass.: MIT Press, 1974. Durgnat is especially helpful in illuminating Hitchcock's 1920's and 1930's work. Quite intellectual in its approach, but written clearly enough for the general reader. Bibliography, filmography, and index.

Harris, Robert A., and Michael S. Lasky. *The Films of Alfred Hitchcock*. Secaucus, N.J.: Citadel Press, 1976. A fully illustrated analysis of all Hitchcock's work, picture by picture. Despite its slick appearance, this is a serious, well-written overview of the films.

Spoto, Donald. *The Art of Alfred Hitchcock*. Rev. ed. New York: Doubleday, 1992. An updated revision of Spoto's 1976 work, this massive book also looks at each film separately. Spoto's style is accessible, his insights rewarding. A necessary source. Index and filmography.

Truffaut, François. *Hitchcock*. Rev. ed. New York: Simon & Schuster, 1984. A revised edition of the 1967 series of interviews of Hitchcock by Truffaut, the noted French director. Hitchcock tells his own story in these interviews. Illustrated, extended filmography, short bibliography, index.

Taylor, John Russell. *Hitch: The Life and Times of Alfred Hitchcock*. New York: Pantheon Books, 1978. Perhaps the best biography of Hitchcock; easy to read and comprehensive. Index.

Clarke Wilhelm

Cross-References

Sound Technology Revolutionizes the Motion-Picture Industry (1928), p. 761; *Little Caesar*, *Public Enemy*, and *Scarface* Launch the Gangster-Film Genre (1930), p. 839; Welles Broadcasts *The War of the Worlds* (1938), p. 1103; The Sherlock Holmes Film Series Begins (1939), p. 1131; The French New Wave Ushers in a New Era of Cinema (1956), p. 1710; *Psycho* Becomes Hitchcock's Most Famous Film (1960), p. 1855.

THE CLASSIC SCREWBALL COMEDY REACHES ITS HEIGHT IN POPULARITY

Category of event: Motion pictures
Time: 1934-1938
Locale: The United States

Romantic Hollywood comedies featuring bickering lovers flourished with the release of such films as It Happened One Night *and* Bringing Up Baby

Principal personages:

FRANK CAPRA (1897-1991), the director of *It Happened One Night*

CLAUDETTE COLBERT (CLAUDETTE LILY CHAUCHOIN, 1905-   ), the leading actress in *It Happened One Night*

CLARK GABLE (1901-1960), the leading actor in *It Happened One Night*

HOWARD HAWKS (1896-1977), the director of *Bringing Up Baby*

CARY GRANT (ARCHIBALD LEACH, 1904-1986), the leading actor in *Topper, The Awful Truth,* and *Bringing Up Baby*

KATHARINE HEPBURN (1907-   ), the leading actress in *Bringing Up Baby*

CAROLE LOMBARD (JANE ALICE PETERS, 1908-1942), the leading actress in *Twentieth Century, My Man Godfrey, Nothing Sacred,* and *True Confession*

WALTER CONNOLLY (1887-1940), a character actor who appeared in *It Happened One Night, Twentieth Century, Libeled Lady,* and *Nothing Sacred*

Summary of Event

When films learned to talk, they also learned to be naughty. Many American films of the early 1930's, especially those starring Mae West and Jean Harlow and the sophisticated comedies directed by Ernst Lubitsch, featured strong sexual innuendoes. Fear of government censorship led in 1934 to the implementation of a production code that severely restricted the amount of sex and violence in American films. One of the sillier results of the code, ferociously enforced by Joseph L. Breen of the Motion Picture Producers and Distributors of America, was that two people of the opposite sex could not appear on a bed together unless one had at least one foot on the floor. The production code remained in effect, with only slight modifications, until 1966.

The screwball comedy evolved in part as a response to the limitations of the code. The inability of filmmakers to spell out the sexual attraction of their films' protagonists resulted in the production of films in which the romantic leads battled both verbally and physically for much of the running time. Quarreling lovers on the stage go back at least as far as William Shakespeare's *The Taming of the Shrew* (1593-1594). By the 1930's, they had become prominent in such Noël Coward plays as

Private Lives (1930). One of the main precursors of the screwball comedy is Lubitsch's Americanized 1933 version of Coward's *Design for Living*, in which two young Americans in Paris, Tommy Chambers (Fredric March) and George Curtis (Gary Cooper), fall in love with the same woman, Gilda Farrell (Miriam Hopkins). Despite discreet fadeouts, Lubitsch clearly implies that Gilda has sex with both George and Tommy. After the implementation of the production code, sexual innuendo became more subtle and was often hidden behind a veil of slapstick.

Most experts consider *It Happened One Night* (1934) to be the first screwball comedy. Directed by Frank Capra and written by Robert Riskin (based on two short stories by Samuel Hopkins Adams), *It Happened One Night* presents the efforts of spoiled heiress Ellie Andrews (Claudette Colbert) to escape her father, Alexander Andrews (Walter Connolly), and marry playboy King Westley (Jameson Thomas). On a bus from Florida to New York, Ellie meets newspaper reporter Peter Warne (Clark Gable), who eventually offers to help her in exchange for her story. After numerous adventures, she finds herself in the middle of an elaborate wedding ceremony only to forsake Westley for Peter.

Although the film's studio, Columbia, had no such expectations, *It Happened One Night* was an enormous success and had a tremendous influence on Hollywood. According to legend, the film popularized bus travel, saving the Greyhound Bus Company from bankruptcy; a scene in which Gable undressed to reveal he wore no undershirt drastically affected the sales of men's underwear. The film won Academy Awards for best picture, best actor, best actress, best director, and best adapted screenplay.

It Happened One Night introduced several elements soon to become familiar as the screwball genre flourished through the early 1940's. The most significant element is the constant bickering between the film's protagonists. When Ellie and Peter meet, they argue over the last remaining bus seat, and Peter forces Ellie, who is used to sharing nothing, to give him enough room to sit. Throughout the trip, they argue over money, food, and sleeping arrangements. When they are compelled to share a motor-camp cabin after roads are flooded, Peter erects a blanket between their beds to ensure, he says, his privacy. Peter calls the blanket, suspended on a rope, "the walls of Jericho." These walls represent the sexual tension between Peter and Ellie. Ellie is drawn to a man who stands up to her peevishness, Peter to her spunk. The film ends with Capra's camera outside another motel cabin; a trumpet is heard inside, as the walls of Jericho come down at last.

In most screwball comedies, the protagonists battle on almost equal terms. Ellie's audacity allows her to escape her father's yacht by jumping into water fully clothed. When detectives confront them at the first motor camp, Peter begins a mock argument to divert suspicion, and Ellie is quick-witted enough to assume immediately the persona of a crying Southern belle. In the film's most famous sequence, Peter attempts to show Ellie his foolproof hitchhiking techniques and fails miserably; Ellie then raises her skirt to stop the next passing car, proving to Peter that she has resources of which he is incapable.

It Happened One Night also conveyed a notably sympathetic attitude toward the rich that was evident in many screwball comedies. Ellie is condemned more for being spoiled than for being privileged, and her father, far from being a capitalist ogre, immediately perceives that the earthy Peter will make a much better son-in-law than the oily Westley.

Impact of Event

This attitude is taken to further extremes in Gregory La Cava's *My Man Godfrey* (1936) and Mitchell Leisen's *Easy Living* (1937). In the former, a homeless man turned butler (William Powell) is really a Boston Brahmin who has chosen poverty after an unhappy love affair. When the family employing him faces financial disaster, Godfrey uses his understanding of the stock market to rescue them, essentially rewarding them for their selfishness, eccentricity, and incompetence. *Easy Living*, written by Preston Sturges, pokes fun at the pompous banker J. B. Ball (Edward Arnold) by having his servants and secretary make sneering remarks, but the film ends with another narrow escape from ruin, thereby justifying Ball's way of life.

It Happened One Night initiated the tradition of spoiled heiresses and cynical reporters at the center of screwball comedies, including Carole Lombard's exceedingly empty-headed rich girl in *My Man Godfrey* and Fredric March's tough newspaperman in William Wellman's *Nothing Sacred* (1937). March's character falls in love with a young woman (Lombard again) who is supposedly dying of radium poisoning. Hostilities between heiresses and reporters that dissolve into romance appear in several screwball comedies, most notably with Myrna Loy and William Powell in Jack Conway's *Libeled Lady* (1936) and Barbara Stanwyck and Henry Fonda in Leigh Jason's *The Mad Miss Manton* (1938).

The most important influence of *It Happened One Night* is the bickering tradition. Among the many variations on the Ellie-Peter model are the married couple (Irene Dunne and Cary Grant) who cannot stop their altercations even after divorcing in Leo McCarey's *The Awful Truth* (1937) and the multiple battling couples of *Libeled Lady*: Jean Harlow and Spencer Tracy, Loy and Powell, and Harlow and Powell.

Before the genre reached its apex with *Bringing Up Baby* (1938), several more essential screwball elements had to be introduced, the most significant being slapstick. Since the production code prohibited suggestive physical contact between the battling lovers, pratfalls were substituted as a means of releasing pent-up sexual energy. In William A. Seiter's *The Moon's Our Home* (1936), an heiress (Margaret Sullavan) and an explorer (Henry Fonda) take spills off a sled, a sleigh, and skis. They are thrown from their sleigh when their horse, a mare, takes off in romantic pursuit of another horse. In *Nothing Sacred*, Lombard and March knock each other out, and in Alfred Santell's *Breakfast for Two* (1937), an heiress (Barbara Stanwyck) conceals a doorknob in a boxing glove to give a black eye to a playboy (Herbert Marshall).

Many screwball comedies offered satirical elements: *My Man Godfrey* made fun of the trivialities of the Park Avenue rich, *Nothing Sacred* punctured the excesses of the sensationalist press, and *The Moon's Our Home* attacked the inflated egos of celebrities. The most penetrating satire came in Richard Boleslawski's *Theodora Goes Wild* (1936), based on a story by Mary McCarthy. In the film, a young woman (Dunne) writes a best-seller the sexual suggestiveness of which is condemned by her puritanical hometown. The smug hypocrisy of small-town America is constantly ridiculed, especially when Theodora delights in making the community think she has given birth to an illegitimate child.

Bringing Up Baby, though it lacks a satiric edge, is the culmination of these screwball elements. Directed by Howard Hawks and written by Dudley Nichols and Hagar Wilde, it presents the dizziest of dizzy heiresses, Susan Vance (Katharine Hepburn), who hopes for a million-dollar bequest from her Aunt Elizabeth (May Robson). Paleontologist David Huxley (Cary Grant) wants the same million for his museum. Susan soon falls in love with David and wants him to get the money, but all of her assistance leads to disaster.

Her brother has sent a domesticated leopard from South America as a present for Aunt Elizabeth. Susan tricks David into helping her take the leopard, called Baby, to her aunt's Connecticut farm so that he will miss his wedding to the stuffy Alice Swallow (Virginia Walker). Aunt Elizabeth's fox terrier steals and buries the bone David has just received to complete the dinosaur skeleton he has been working on for years; Baby escapes; Susan releases a dangerous leopard she thinks is Baby from a circus van; and all the protagonists end up in jail suspected of a variety of offenses.

Aunt Elizabeth becomes convinced of David's instability and gives her money to Susan. Alice is also shocked by his behavior and decides not to marry him. *Bringing Up Baby* ends with Susan giving the million to David, who has spent the entire film resisting her aggressive advances. As Susan climbs upon his dinosaur skeleton to express her love, causing the skeleton to collapse, David finally accepts the inevitable.

The collapsing dinosaur is a fitting conclusion to a film filled with slapstick. David and Susan are constantly falling down. Aunt Elizabeth's explorer friend, Major Horace Applegate (Charles Ruggles), and her drunken servant Gogarty (Barry Fitzgerald) chase and are chased by the leopards. Viewers and reviewers of 1938 apparently felt that the physical humor was excessive, since the film was a commercial and critical flop. Audiences and film historians in the years since have embraced the silliness, which includes Grant's dressing up in a woman's fluffy dressing gown, as essential to the genre.

The romance at the center of the film is notable for the extroverted antics of Susan, who is willing to try anything that might lead to fun. Stiff and humorless at the beginning of the film, David is taught to accept the unpredictability of life by Susan and becomes more human.

Physicality was important in screwball comedies, and the preeminent performers of the genre were Grant, who displayed his debonair athleticism in *The Awful Truth*, Norman Z. McLeod's *Topper* (1937), and *Bringing Up Baby*, and Lombard, who showcased her combination of beauty, vulnerability, physical vitality, and buffoonery in Howard Hawks's *Twentieth Century* (1934), *My Man Godfrey*, Wesley Ruggles' *True Confession* (1937), and *Nothing Sacred*.

As important as the stars of screwball comedies were the contributions of the supporting performers. More notable character actors appeared in Hollywood films during the 1930's and early 1940's than at any other time, and many received their best parts in screwball comedies. In addition to Robson, Ruggles, and Fitzgerald, *Bringing Up Baby* offered Walter Catlett as a hot-tempered, easily confused sheriff and Fritz Feld as a stodgy psychiatrist. The most significant supporting performer in these films may be Walter Connolly, who played the father in *It Happened One Night*, the assistant constantly being fired by theatrical producer John Barrymore in *Twentieth Century*, Myrna Loy's fishing-obsessed father in *Libeled Lady*, and the easily angered editor in *Nothing Sacred.*

Other notable supporting performers in screwball comedies included Luis Alberni and Franklin Pangborn (*Easy Living*); Mischa Auer, Alice Brady, Eugene Pallette, and Gail Patrick (*My Man Godfrey*); Eric Blore and Donald Meek (*Breakfast for Two*); Charles Butterworth and Margaret Hamilton (*The Moon's Our Home*); Spring Byington (*Theodora Goes Wild*); Roscoe Karns (*It Happened One Night* and *Twentieth Century*); Edgar Kennedy and Una Merkel (*True Confession*); and Maxie Rosenbloom and Charles Winninger (*Nothing Sacred*).

Bringing Up Baby is especially praiseworthy for the speed and surety of its comic timing. Screwball comedies are generally fast-paced, but those directed by Hawks are the fastest of all. The director made films in this genre longer than anyone, continuing into the 1940's with *His Girl Friday* (1940), with Grant and Rosalind Russell, *Ball of Fire* (1942), with Stanwyck and Cooper, *I Was a Male War Bride* (1949), with Grant and Ann Sheridan, and *Monkey Business* (1952), with Grant and Ginger Rogers.

Other important screwball comedies made after *Bringing Up Baby* included Leisen's *Midnight* (1939), with Colbert and Don Ameche; Garson Kanin's *My Favorite Wife* (1940), with Dunne and Grant; Alfred Hitchcock's only comedy, *Mr. and Mrs. Smith* (1941), with Lombard and Robert Montgomery; Preston Sturges' *The Lady Eve* (1941), with Stanwyck and Fonda, and *The Palm Beach Story* (1942), with Colbert and Joel McCrea; Billy Wilder's *The Major and the Minor* (1942), with Rogers and Ray Milland; and George Stevens' *The More the Merrier* (1943), with McCrea and Jean Arthur. The latter is perhaps the most romantic screwball comedy, since the sexual longing of the protagonists is made as explicit as the code allowed.

Screwball elements continued to appear in varying degrees after the genre's heyday, resurfacing, for example, in Wilder's *Some Like It Hot* (1959). In 1972, Peter Bogdanovich attempted a contemporary version of *Bringing Up Baby*, *What's Up, Doc?*, with Barbra Streisand and Ryan O'Neal. Although the film was a popular success, most reviewers condemned it as heavy-handed, cartoonish, and mean-spirited. Many critics have claimed that the classic screwball comedy is extinct, since attaining the appropriate combination of versatile performers, sophisticated writing, and perfect timing is so difficult. Of recent works, perhaps Sydney Pollack's *Tootsie* (1982), with Dustin Hoffman and Jessica Lange, comes closest to the classic formula.

Bibliography

Cavell, Stanley. *Pursuits of Happiness: The Hollywood Comedy of Remarriage.* Cambridge, Mass.: Harvard University Press, 1981. Examines seven comedies of the 1930's and 1940's, including *It Happened One Night, Bringing Up Baby,* and *The Awful Truth,* to show how they create a comic genre of remarriage. Shows how the genre grows out of Shakespearean comedy. Photographs and index.

Everson, William K. "Screwball Comedy: A Reappraisal." *Films in Review* 34 (December, 1983): 578-584. Thought-provoking but unconvincing argument that screwball comedies are period pieces of little interest to modern audiences.

Harvey, James. *Romantic Comedy in Hollywood from Lubitsch to Sturges.* New York: Alfred A. Knopf, 1987. Analyzes comic style of the 1930's and 1940's, with particular attention to the films of Lubitsch and Sturges. Also discusses such directors as Capra and Hawks and such performers as Colbert, Grant, and Lombard. Includes photographs, index, and interview with Dunne.

Kendall, Elizabeth. *The Runaway Bride: Hollywood Romantic Comedy of the 1930's.* New York: Alfred A. Knopf, 1990. Traces the device of the runaway bride and its variations through several films of the 1930's and early 1940's, including *It Happened One Night, My Man Godfrey,* and *The Awful Truth.* Provides considerable background about the stars and directors. Excellent study includes photographs, bibliography, and index.

Sarris, Andrew. "The Sex Comedy Without Sex." *American Film* 3 (March, 1978): 8-15. Discusses the difficulty of defining the genre and of determining what films are truly "screwball." Argues that comediennes are the most crucial ingredient. Excellent brief introduction to the genre.

Sikov, Ed. *Screwball: Hollywood's Madcap Romantic Comedies.* New York: Crown, 1989. The most thorough examination of the genre. Analyzes the major examples and divides screwball comedies into clearly defined categories. Extensively and beautifully illustrated. With excellent filmography and bibliography. Index.

Weales, Gerald. *Canned Goods as Caviar: American Film Comedy of the 1930s.* Chicago: University of Chicago Press, 1985. Attempts to place twelve 1930's comedies in the context of the social and political life of the decade. Analyzes *Bringing Up Baby, My Man Godfrey, Libeled Lady,* and *Nothing Sacred.* Photographs and index.

Michael Adams

Cross-References

Sennett Defines the Slapstick Comedy Genre (1909), p. 230; Chaplin Produces His Masterpiece *The Gold Rush* (1925), p. 659; Keaton's *The General* Is Released (1926), p. 691; Hollywood Enters Its Golden Age (1930's), p. 822; Ealing Comedies Mark a High Point in British Film (1949), p. 1427; Allen's *Annie Hall* Captures Complexities of 1970's Life (1977), p. 2381.

RIVERA'S ROCKEFELLER CENTER MURAL
IS DESTROYED

Category of event: Art
Time: February, 1934
Locale: New York, New York

When Diego Rivera included an image of Soviet leader Vladimir Ilich Lenin in a mural for the newly constructed RCA Building, controversy arose and the painting ultimately was destroyed

Principal personages:
DIEGO RIVERA (1886-1957), a painter and muralist who vibrantly depicted Mexican folk and American working classes
NELSON A. ROCKEFELLER (1908-1979), a millionaire philanthropist and art collector who commissioned and later dismissed Rivera
JOSÉ CLEMENTE OROZCO (1883-1949), a renowned muralist
DAVID ALFARO SIQUEIROS (1898-1974), a renowned muralist
FRIDA KAHLO (1919-1954), Rivera's second wife, a respected painter in her own right

Summary of Event

Painter and muralist Diego Rivera managed to earn commissions from mainstream government and corporate leaders while simultaneously portraying the struggles and epics of the laboring classes. His Mexican murals, frequently embellishing the walls of public buildings, drew attention to native farmers, peasants, and urban dwellers. In the United States, he often focused on those who worked on assembly lines and thereby fueled industrial processes.

Rivera's subject matter evolved from his political beliefs. An activist who was kicked out of but later reinstated into the Mexican Communist Party, his artistic interpretations of doctrine were direct and uncomplicated. Rivera's murals also displayed an understanding of higher mechanics, the ways in which various physical and human elements interacted. From a political perspective, then, his work could move the masses; from a technical perspective, it appealed to the cognoscenti.

The collision between subject matter and patronage had surfaced before Rivera was commissioned to do the Rockefeller Center (RCA Building) mural, but to a different degree. In the United States, the conflict proved to be more acute than in Mexico, where the revolution of 1910 had empowered the country's vast citizenry and diminished the European, particularly Spanish, influences of the reigning elite.

Rivera's American debut took place in San Francisco during 1930. His murals soon graced the walls of the local stock exchange and the California School of Fine Arts. Although some condemned the painter for being a Communist, his San Francisco tenure proved personally enjoyable and ended without incident.

Rivera's next major assignment foreshadowed what would transpire in New York City. The Detroit Art Commission, under the chairmanship of automaker Edsel Ford, gave the artist complete freedom to decorate the courtyard of the Detroit Institute of Arts. The resulting epic consisted of twenty-seven panels, the artist's self-described vision depicting "in color and form the story of each industry and its division of labor." Given the sheer number of political statements that could be interpreted in such a massive work, controversy was hardly surprising. Father Charles Coughlin, the conservative, virulently jingoistic, Detroit-based priest then at the height of his national influence, proved to be one of the most threatening critics. Rivera's creation provoked extreme reactions on all fronts, drawing support as well as criticism. A disparate group of workers coalesced solely for the purpose of protecting the murals, with force, if necessary.

Nelson Rockefeller was a Rivera supporter, and his wife, Mary Todhunter Clark Rockefeller, boasted several of the artist's works in her collection. Having expressed a desire to see the Detroit murals, the millionaire philanthropist soon followed up with a letter describing another project: decoration of the new RCA Building in Manhattan.

The New York project's parameters appeared to be circumscribed from the start. Rockefeller's contractors sent proposals to three chosen artists—Pablo Picasso, Henri Matisse, and Rivera—inviting them to participate in a "contest." Instructions were clear, down to the size of the figures, color scheme (black and white), and varnishing requirements. All three painters, well respected enough by this time to demand artistic freedom, rejected the offer. Rockefeller personally set out to persuade Rivera. After some of the rules were softened, including allowing the use of color, the muralist acceded.

Rivera submitted a sketch addressing the predesignated theme, "Man at the Crossroads Looking with Hope and High Vision to the Choosing of a New and Better Future." The design concept, extolling workers and shunning some of the more egregious facets of industrial society, won Nelson Rockefeller's approval. Work commenced in March, 1933.

The technical aspects of mural painting, as perfected by Rivera, were labor intensive. A cadre of assistants applied three surface coatings to ensure stability and enhance color, ground the paints, and transferred the lines of the artist's sketches to the wall. Rivera then proceeded with his brushwork.

As the painting neared completion in late April, a New York *World-Telegram* reporter, Joseph Lilly, visited the RCA Building for a preview. The resulting article, titled "Rivera Paints Scenes of Communist Activity and John D. [Rockefeller] Jr. Foots Bill," highlighted many themes that were not new to those familiar with the artist's work. Representations of toxic materials and poisonous gases, for example, had appeared in the Detroit murals. One element was to make its debut: the figure of Russian revolutionary leader Vladimir Ilich Lenin.

Nelson Rockefeller subsequently viewed the mural. Claiming to find it "thrilling," he nevertheless wrote Rivera a letter requesting that another figure be substituted for that of Lenin. Rivera sought the counsel of his friends and assistants. He then responded to Rockefeller. Lenin would remain, but perhaps some additional elements, such as the figure of a great American, could be used for balance.

Several days later, Rockefeller's contractors and a band of security guards escorted Rivera off the scaffold, paid his full $21,000 commission, and placed canvas over the mural. Workers protested by picketing outside. Intellectuals, artists, and businesspeople mounted strong pro- and anti-Rivera campaigns.

After he paid his expenses and reimbursed his assistants, Rivera retained almost $7,000 from the RCA job. He used his "Rockefeller money" to paint murals in two American Communist institutions, the New Workers' School and Trotskyite headquarters. Harmony between content and venue now came to the man who once unhesitatingly decorated the walls of the San Francisco Stock Exchange. The New York frescoes were to be Rivera's last permanent works in the United States, as commissions were cancelled or failed to be offered. Rivera did, however, continue to exhibit and paint on movable panels.

In February, 1934, after returning to Mexico, Rivera learned that his previously covered RCA mural had been extricated forcibly from the wall. He gained a commission from the Mexican government and reconstructed the work, with several changes. As Rivera himself described it, a scene of nightclub carousing now included John D. Rockefeller, Jr., "his head but a short distance away from . . . venereal disease germs."

Impact of Event

Although Rivera received no more large American commissions after the Rockefeller incident, offers came from around the world. Nevertheless, the artist soon turned to easel painting and to the interests of private collectors who would use his work to decorate their private homes, galleries, and offices. Mural painting, however, had not yet reached its pinnacle in either the United States or Mexico. Rivera surely contributed to the explosion that followed, but he left the genre before it could be considered common.

Sometimes an extraordinary event can push politics or culture in a certain direction. The RCA mural may have had such an effect. Left-wing politics, wrought out of the Great Depression and Soviet influence, brought about two related art forms, social realism and Socialist Realism. Both elevated the ordinary person, celebrating daily existence and calling attention to widespread social and economic inequities. Socialist Realism suggested a political, clearly Marxist answer to working-class dilemmas; it was the more blatantly propagandistic of the two schools. In the Soviet Union, Joseph Stalin mandated Socialist Realism as the cultural medium. Artists who did not pursue it were denied commissions, were banished, or worse.

Some historians have pointed out that the RCA murals represented a leap for Rivera from social realism to Socialist Realism. In the United States, too, critics simultaneously wondered whether President Franklin D. Roosevelt was leading the country toward socialism. If that were the case, however, the course was temporary and motivated by economics. Roosevelt's first term, beginning in 1933, saw a flurry of progressive legislation aimed at reducing widespread unemployment. One of these programs was the Works Progress Administration (WPA), initiated in 1935. Part of that program engaged artists and writers in the celebration and documentation of American cultural heritage. WPA commissions soon enlivened post office walls, government buildings, and many other public venues. Rivera's influence radiates from these brightly colored murals, often rendered in social realist style, filled with historical references, and illustrating themes inspired by the working class. Indeed, the rich collection of WPA wall paintings remains a legacy, outliving Rivera by decades.

It is impossible to talk about Diego Rivera without mentioning two of his contemporaries, José Clemente Orozco and David Alfaro Siqueiros. In 1923, Siqueiros helped to organize the Syndicate of Revolutionary Painters, Sculptors, and Engravers, a sort of postrevolutionary union ultimately responsible for instituting mural painting as a Mexican national art form.

The *tres grandes*, or big three—Rivera, Siqueiros, and Orozco—differed in technique and in their personal and artistic responses to political events, yet they collectively elevated their chosen genre. According to one expert, Mexican mural commissions reached their peak in the late 1950's. A whole new generation of Mexican artists, who came of professional age during the following decade and were concerned with the social values of the era, drew their inspiration from the great muralists. It also is interesting to note that the *tres grandes* experienced the United States in similar ways. All worked there during the Depression, and after the Rockefeller Center incident, they were never again to receive large, permanent commissions.

Rivera possibly held more of a universal appeal than did either Siqueiros or Orozco. Unlike his respected colleagues, he benefited from a solid general education and European art training. Rivera first studied in Spain, then moved to Paris, where he was mentored by Picasso and was captured on Amedeo Modigliani's canvas. His use of color is said to have been derived from classical Italian frescoes, and for a while, he dabbled in cubism. Europe during Rivera's stay (1907-1921) also blazed with differing political philosophies, nationalism and Marxism not least among them. The artist therefore gained a sense of history, learning how to incorporate his ideas into unique and timely contexts. He conducted various interviews when working on his Detroit commission and sent his assistants to research American historical figures for the RCA mural. In the midst of the controversy concerning his Communist credentials, during 1936, Rivera was invited by fascist leader Benito Mussolini to paint in Italy.

The muralist exuded a personal charm that drew fledgling artists to him. His wife, the painter Frida Kahlo, respected for her sensitive portrayal of women's emotional needs and feelings, declared at the age of thirteen that she wanted to have a child by Rivera. In a different way, his assistants formed a cadre of steadfast supporters. There is evidence, for example, that Rivera might have acceded to Rockefeller's demands if these young men and women had not threatened to strike over such terms. In addition to his own enduring artistic legacy, the Rivera influence survived through the work of assistants Lucienne Bloch, John Hastings, and, most notably, social realist painter Ben Shahn.

Decades after his death, Rivera's influence endures. During the early 1990's, the Mexican government promoted a cultural exchange with the United States. The traveling art exhibit was so large that, with some extra borrowing or digging into their permanent collections, museums could focus on any number of styles, historic eras, or themes. The ever-buoyant Diego Rivera thus was introduced to a new generation. Frida Kahlo, too, enjoyed a revival during the early 1990's. Initially brought to public attention by the pop singer Madonna, Kahlo now attracted young women who could relate to her style and empathize with her spirit. This time, Rivera may have ridden on his wife's coattails as the subject of paintings such as *Diego and Me*.

Immersed in many artistic movements and historic moments, Diego Rivera was a creative bridge between the early and late twentieth century. His style was a unique contemporary amalgamation, but his genre, subject matter, and accessible political expression have proven to be perennially inspirational.

Bibliography

Chavez, Augustin Velazquez. *Contemporary Mexican Artists*. New York: Covici-Friede, 1937. Thumbnail sketches, typically two pages in length, and four black-and-white plates are used to present each of the twenty-five artists included here. A short introductory section lends unity to the book.

Goldman, Shifra M. *Contemporary Mexican Painting in a Time of Change*. Austin: University of Texas Press, 1977. Although focusing on a later generation, this work portrays Rivera and other muralists as wellsprings of modern Mexican art. Goldman demonstrates the interrelationships between various painters, how they inspired each other and split to create new schools or perspectives. The historic and political nature of art is an important theme.

Helm, MacKinley. *Modern Mexican Painters*. New York: Dover, 1974. A chapter on Rivera lends insight into the artist's technique and evolution over the years. It is evident that Helm, a collector with informed opinions, came to know the muralist through both personal interviews and exhibitions. Their conversations periodically surface on these pages. A good discussion of the differences between Rivera the person and Rivera the artist.

McMeekin, Dorothy. *Diego Rivera: Science and Creativity in the Detroit Murals*. Lansing: Michigan State University Press, 1985. A massive mural project—twenty-seven frescoes in the courtyard of the Detroit Institute of Arts—is used to illustrate Rivera's comprehension of biology, geology, and technology. The broader political feelings are apparent, too, thus providing a good basis of comparison with the Rockefeller Center work.

Museum of Modern Art (New York). *Diego Rivera*. New York: Arno Press, 1931. Published to celebrate Rivera's one-person show at the museum, this catalog contains more than one hundred black-and-white plates. A short bibliography and time line offer an excellent perspective on early, enduring influences including the artist's nurturing and liberal family; impressive general education; and encouragement, from the age of three, to pursue creative avenues.

Rivera, Diego, with Gladys March. *My Art, My Life: An Autobiography.* New York: Citadel Press, 1960. Rivera writes in an informal voice, divulging details and presenting his side of an often controversial life story. The appendix features "statements" from each of the four women whom he lived with or married.

Wolfe, Bertram D. *The Fabulous Life of Diego Rivera.* New York: Stein & Day, 1963. Perhaps the most comprehensive basic biography of Rivera, this book includes a chapter on "The Battle of Rockefeller Center." The author was an adviser to the artist during the episode, and he uses correspondence, business documents, and contemporary accounts to describe it.

Lynn Kronzek

Cross-References

The Roosevelt Administration Creates the WPA/FAP (1935), p. 995; Picasso Paints *Guernica* (1937), p. 1062; Hitler Organizes an Exhibition Denouncing Modern Art (1937), p. 1083; Rockefeller Center Is Completed (1939), p. 1149; Blacklisting Seriously Depletes Hollywood's Talent Pool (1947), p. 1340.

MILLER'S NOTORIOUS NOVEL *TROPIC OF CANCER* IS PUBLISHED

Category of event: Literature
Time: September 1, 1934
Locale: Paris, France

Henry Miller's autobiographical novel Tropic of Cancer, *which was based on his first two years as an expatriate in Paris, created a sensation and began a new phase in American literature*

Principal personages:

HENRY MILLER (1891-1980), an American writer who used his life as the basis for his art

ANAÏS NIN (1903-1977), a Paris-born writer who befriended Miller during his exile in Paris and who was instrumental in getting *Tropic of Cancer* published

JACK KAHANE (1887-1939), an English expatriate who owned the Obelisk Press in Paris and who first published *Tropic of Cancer*

MICHAEL FRAENKEL (1896-1957), a writer who let Miller share his Paris apartment in 1931 and who encouraged Miller in the writing of *Tropic of Cancer*

JUNE EDITH SMITH (1902-   ), a dancer and would-be actress whom Miller married in 1924

Summary of Event

It is now the fall of my second year in Paris. I was sent here for a reason I have not yet been able to fathom.

I have no money, no resources, no hopes. I am the happiest man alive.

Thus begins Henry Miller's opus of self-liberation and rebirth, *Tropic of Cancer.* *Tropic of Cancer* records Miller's unflinching look at himself as he struggled to survive amid the bohemian milieu of Paris in the early 1930's. It is the record of an odyssey of the spirit in which Miller experiences the hard, essential truth of what it means to be truly alive and open to the moment as it unfolds. By transforming the chaos of his struggle into art, he fashioned a document that captures the turbulent spontaneity of existence.

Henry Miller was born the son of lower-middle-class parents in the Yorkville section of New York City on December 26, 1891. In 1892, Miller's family moved to Brooklyn, where he was reared. As a child, he learned to play the piano and developed a love for the romantic adventure stories of Knut Hamsun and the poetry of Walt Whitman. In 1909, Miller attended the City College of New York, but he left after two months.

He spent the next several years traveling through the Southwest, working at odd jobs. When he returned to New York City, he assisted his father in the family tailor shop. In 1917, he married Beatrice Wickens, a piano teacher, and had a daughter, Barbara. In 1920, after a succession of dreary jobs, he was hired as employment manager for the Western Union Telegraph Company in Manhattan. In 1924, Miller divorced his wife and married a Broadway taxi dancer, June Smith, whom he had met during his late-night wanderings in the city. Their relationship was tumultuous, and June's promiscuity was destructive for Miller. June, however, encouraged his aspirations to become a writer, and with her support, Miller quit his job to write full time.

His early efforts met with little success, and in 1928, Henry and June left for Europe for a brief stay. Running low on funds, they returned to America after eight months. In 1930, with June's urging and promises of financial support, he returned alone and settled in Paris. Finally separated, their marriage fell apart under the weight of June's emotional instability. Four years later, June obtained a Mexican divorce. In Paris, Miller was at last free to be a writer, without the demands of the society he had left behind, but there were new problems to be faced. Miller was an exile in a strange country where he had no friends, little money, and no prospects. He did not even speak the language. What he did have, though, was the strength and determination to beat out his exile, no matter what unpleasant realities he would have to face. He was to achieve his goal of becoming a writer both because of and in spite of his sufferings.

After arriving in Paris in 1930, Miller moved to a cheap hotel on the rue Bonaparte. From there, he began wandering the streets of Paris, taking notes and keeping a daily record of his life, the things he saw and the people he met. He would relate these adventures in long letters to his friends in America; many of these letters were later included in *Tropic of Cancer*. His adventures with prostitutes and the characters he met on the street and in cafés became the fabric of his Paris book.

When Miller's money ran out, he was forced to panhandle and find lodging wherever he could. He had, in reality, become homeless, dependent upon fate and the charity of others. Miller, though, did not become dejected. Rather, by using these deprivations and desperate situations as the raw material for his letters, he turned his destitution into a testament to the human spirit.

Miller met a number of writers, artists, and intellectuals in Paris who befriended him. After months of living hand-to-mouth, he landed a job as a proofreader for the Paris edition of the *Chicago Tribune*. While there, he met Michael Fraenkel, a writer and occasional publisher who let Miller move in with him. While living with Fraenkel, Miller began to work on *Tropic of Cancer*. Fraenkel, a man given to abstract debates about death, is portrayed in the novel as Boris, a character frozen by philosophical introspection. Miller, on the other hand, is the hero who opens himself to the richness and sensuality of life in Paris.

Although he was still very much in love with June, who was back in New York, Miller met and began an intimate relationship with the French writer Anaïs Nin.

When they met, they were immediately drawn to one another, and though Nin lived outside Paris with her husband, Miller visited her frequently. During 1931 and 1932, they exchanged a voluminous correspondence. At one point, when Miller was depressed over his estrangement from June, Nin arranged for him to teach English at a preparatory school in Dijon. The position paid little, and Dijon was a depressingly provincial town that added to Miller's sense of isolation. He left after two months. Back in Paris in the summer of 1932, he completed work on the manuscript of *Tropic of Cancer.*

An American literary agent in Paris read *Tropic of Cancer*, liked it, and gave it to English expatriate Jack Kahane, who owned the Obelisk Press. Kahane read the novel and was so impressed that he offered Miller a contract. Written in Miller's raw, uninhibited style, *Tropic of Cancer* contained obscene language and graphic accounts of sex. Though the Obelisk Press had a reputation for publishing risqué novels, Kahane stalled publication because of fears of French censorship laws. Kahane persuaded Miller to write another more "serious" book, one that would give his work an air of respectability. Though Miller attempted a scholarly study of D. H. Lawrence, he failed to produce a publishable book. Finally, after nearly two years of delays, Anaïs Nin came to the rescue with six hundred dollars to underwrite the publication of *Tropic of Cancer* with the Obelisk Press. Miller's turbulent and euphoric autobiographical novel went to press on September 1, 1934.

Impact of Event

Miller began receiving praise for *Tropic of Cancer* soon after its publication. Among the writers and artists who applauded *Tropic of Cancer* were Ezra Pound, T. S. Eliot, Marcel Duchamp, and Blaise Cendrars.

As his reputation grew during the next several years, Miller became the subject of much interest by writers and publishers. Other publishers such as Alfred A. Knopf in New York and Faber & Faber in London expressed interest in Miller's work but did not make definite offers to publish him.

After completing *Tropic of Cancer*, Miller had begun his second autobiographical novel, *Tropic of Capricorn*. Whereas the first book had been set in Paris, *Tropic of Capricorn* was about his life in New York City and his exploration of sexuality during a period of personal frustration and upheaval. In 1939, it too was published by the Obelisk Press.

Another work that Miller had begun writing in 1933 was a surrealistic self-portrait filled with fragments of letters, dreams, and reminiscences. Finally given the title *Black Spring*, it was published in Paris in 1936. Meanwhile, Miller's life had begun to settle somewhat. While there, he wrote steadily and worked on various publishing projects.

With the outbreak of war in Europe and the threat of invasion by the Germans, Miller decided to leave his Paris home for good. After nearly ten years, his exile was drawing to an end. In 1939, he sailed for Greece at the urging of his friend Lawrence Durrell. Arriving in Corfu, he stayed with the Durrells and then traveled around

Greece. His adventures were later published as *The Colossus of Maroussi* (1941), a kind of spiritual travelogue praised as one of his best books.

In 1940, Miller left Greece for New York. Although his books had continued to sell briskly in Paris, he was unable to obtain royalties owed him. Thus, when he arrived back in America, he was almost as broke as when he had left ten years ealier. Miller eventually moved to California and settled in Big Sur, where he became the focus of a growing artists' colony. There he worked on the three volumes of *The Rosy Crucifixion: Sexus* (1949), *Plexus* (1953), and *Nexus* (1960), the story of his ill-fated relationship with June Smith.

All through the 1930's, *Tropic of Cancer* continued to sell in Paris, though it was not until the German occupation of the 1940's that sales increased dramatically. By the war's end, Miller's accumulated royalties from French sales of *Tropic of Cancer* totaled some forty thousand dollars. By 1947, he was owed ten times that amount. Because of postwar restrictions and a rapid devaluation of the franc, however, he was unable to collect his earnings.

Miller's Paris publisher faced other problems. In 1946, French authorities brought charges against the owners of the Obelisk Press and managed to convict them of distributing pornographic materials. Fortunately, several famous and influential French writers, including Albert Camus, Paul Éluard, and Jean-Paul Sartre, came to the book's defense, and the verdict was overturned. Meanwhile, *Tropic of Cancer* had still not been published in America.

For years, *Tropic of Cancer* and *The Rosy Crucifixion* were deemed to be obscene and were banned from publication in the United States. In 1961, however, Grove Press brought out an American edition of *Tropic of Cancer*. Sales of the book were phenomenal, and Miller became an overnight celebrity. The publication was met with controversy, however, and numerous attempts were made to have the book banned. Finally, in 1963, a United States Supreme Court decision ended censorship of Miller's books.

In spite of—or perhaps because of—such controversy, *Tropic of Cancer*'s effect on American literature was significant. Miller's form of autobiographical novel, with its unrestrained language and lack of literary pretenses, influenced such writers as William Burroughs, Jack Kerouac, and Norman Mailer. Miller's work explored the meaning of what it was to be alive in a civilization that was being torn apart by forces it had unleashed upon itself. Dehumanizing technology, the forced conformity of the masses, poverty, and war all threatened to destroy the individual's spirit and imagination. *Tropic of Cancer* is a record of Miller's fight to save his own soul. In doing so, he delivered a work that reverberates with a desperate energy and a liberating vision.

Bibliography

Dearborn, Mary V. *The Happiest Man Alive: A Biography of Henry Miller.* New York: Simon & Schuster, 1991. A valuable biography that raises questions about the lack of serious academic criticism of Miller's work. Successfully depicts the man and all of his contradictions. Includes numerous photographs and detailed notes.

Durrell, Lawrence. *Durrell-Miller Letters, 1935-80.* Edited by Ian S. MacNiven. London: Faber & Faber, 1988. A collection of letters that nearly doubles the published correspondence between the two writers. The letters illustrate and confirm the affection between them and the vitality of their relationship.

Gordon, William A. *The Mind and Art of Henry Miller.* Baton Rouge: Louisiana State University Press, 1967. The first serious, full-length study of Henry Miller as an artist. Insightful and objective. Examines Miller's principal themes and studies his growth toward self-liberation through his writing.

Lewis, Leon. *Henry Miller: The Major Writings.* New York: Schocken Books, 1986. An examination of Miller scholarship and a perceptive discussion of Miller's life and major works. Offers insight into reasons for Miller's enduring popularity.

Miller, Henry. *Letters to Emil.* Edited by George Wickes. New York: New Directions, 1989. A collection of several dozen letters from Henry Miller to Emil Schnellock, written when Miller was in Paris. The letters offer a unique record of Miller's literary apprenticeship.

Winslow, Kathryn. *Henry Miller: Full of Life.* Los Angeles: J. P. Tarcher, 1986. A memoir by a longtime friend of Miller who met the novelist in 1944, after he had moved to Big Sur.

Francis Poole

Cross-References

Stein Holds Her First Paris Salons (1905), p. 129; Surrealism Is Born (1924), p. 604; Hemingway's *The Sun Also Rises* Speaks for the Lost Generation (1926), p. 696; Mailer Publishes *The Naked and the Dead* (1948), p. 1373; The Beat Movement Rejects Mainstream Values (1950's), p. 1460.

GOODMAN BEGINS HIS *LET'S DANCE* BROADCASTS

Category of event: Music
Time: December 1, 1934
Locale: New York, New York

Benny Goodman's Let's Dance *broadcasts on network radio led to the launching of the Swing Era, in which big-band music achieved huge popularity*

Principal personages:

BENNY GOODMAN (1909-1986), a virtuoso clarinetist and bandleader whose jazz-influenced dance band led in establishing "swing music" as the dominant popular style of the 1935-1945 period

FLETCHER HENDERSON (1897-1952), a pioneering black orchestrator and bandleader whose arrangements were sold to Goodman

JOHN HAMMOND (1910-1987), the scion of a wealthy family who supported social and racial equality and discovered, promoted, and recorded some of America's most important musicians

GENE KRUPA (1909-1973), the drummer whose drive and showmanship contributed to the popularity of the Goodman band

TEDDY WILSON (1912-1986), the black pianist who joined Goodman's trio and became part of the first famous integrated group in American music

LIONEL HAMPTON (1913-   ), the vibraphonist and drummer who helped turn Goodman's trio into an influential jazz quartet

Summary of Event

Benny Goodman's prodigious talent as a clarinetist freed him from an early life of poverty in a Chicago Jewish ghetto; by the age of thirteen he was a member of the American Musicians Union and within a year following that was a full-time professional. He quickly combined his traditional European classical training with an interest in the New Orleans-style jazz that was flourishing in Chicago and paid special attention to important players such as Jimmy Noone, Albert Nicholas, Johnny Dodds, and Barney Bigard. Goodman played with various dance bands and at the age of sixteen joined drummer Ben Pollack's Chicago-based band, which was then working in California. Goodman made his first recordings with Pollack in 1926 and had recorded under his own name by 1928. He played with most of the promising white jazz players in Chicago, including Dave Tough, Bud Freeman, Gene Krupa, and the visiting Bix Beiderbecke before moving with Pollack to New York, where he continued to record and broaden his experience. As the economic times became increasingly difficult, the talented Goodman found work in a variety of dance bands and as a free-lance musician playing in theater pit bands, film soundtrack studios, and radio studio orchestras. His first love was jazz, and in 1934 he decided to form a big band that would satisfy both his musical taste and his need for stable employment.

Goodman assembled a band on a shoestring budget and, with the encouragement of his future brother-in-law John Hammond, landed an engagement at the new Billy Rose Music Hall. After four months, the management changed and the band was fired. During this period, Goodman was struggling to give his undistinguished band a musical identity. Plans to take an all-star racially mixed band to England fell through, and Goodman hung all his hopes on being hired for an exciting new radio program sponsored by the National Biscuit Company (later Nabisco) to advertise its new product, Ritz Crackers.

Let's Dance was to feature a "sweet" band, a Latin band, and a "hot" or jazz band in a three-hour program broadcast on Saturday nights to fifty-three stations nationwide on the National Broadcasting Company (NBC) network. Goodman narrowly won the audition in the hot band category, playing a brassy and rhythmic jazz-oriented dance music that was becoming known as swing.

On December 1, 1934, the Benny Goodman Band made its first broadcast in the *Let's Dance* series, before a large studio audience. Goodman's contract provided for generous salaries and the purchase of the musical arrangements necessary to supply a band of fourteen musicians with fresh material for each program. These written arrangements were essential elements in establishing a band's identifying and distinctive sound, and Goodman, not an arranger himself, set about commissioning writers who could work to his specifications. Goodman's ideal was to have a band that featured ample room for improvised solos, a disciplined yet swinging ensemble, and an inspiring rhythm section. As he would throughout his career, Goodman, by most accounts a difficult man to work for, made frequent personnel changes in an attempt to find better musicians. The most significant of the early additions were the flamboyant drummer Gene Krupa and the gifted trumpet player Bunny Berigan, both soon to become famous.

Goodman had long been an admirer of the Fletcher Henderson orchestra, a black aggregation that had been well known among musicians since the mid-1920's. Henderson and his collaborators are usually credited with perfecting the basic formulas used by most large jazz-oriented bands in their written orchestrations. Unfortunately, Henderson's abilities as a leader did not match his musical talent; by 1934 his influential band was disintegrating and the Depression was exacerbating his financial problems. John Hammond, a member of the Vanderbilt family and one of the most important nonmusicians in American musical history, was a lifelong supporter and promoter of black artists. Hammond encouraged Goodman to buy some of Henderson's arrangements for his own band. In effect, this meant adopting the Henderson sound. The influence was strengthened when Henderson also agreed to write orchestrations especially for Goodman, whose well-trained band executed them flawlessly and with a rhythmic drive seldom heard in the white bands of the day. Although Goodman continued to use a number of talented arrangers, the bulk of his band's repertoire (including important pieces such as "King Porter Stomp" and

"Down South Camp Meetin'") and much of its fundamental style originated with Fletcher Henderson. Goodman put his own stamp on the band through his insistence on excellence and his meticulous attention to nuance and musical detail. His virtuoso clarinet playing became a trademark that appealed to a wide audience while remaining true to its jazz roots. The national exposure afforded by the *Let's Dance* broadcasts started Goodman on the road to stardom if not immediate popular success.

When the *Let's Dance* series was canceled after twenty-six broadcasts as a result of the sponsor's labor troubles, Goodman found himself out of work. Hired to replace Guy Lombardo and his orchestra at New York's prestigious Hotel Roosevelt, Goodman's band was abruptly fired as too loud and jazzy. In a desperate attempt to save the band, Goodman embarked on a long cross-country tour. Audiences ranged from mildly enthusiastic to indifferent, and the dispirited Goodman expected that he would be forced to disband in California. When the band appeared at the Palomar Ballroom in Los Angeles, however, it was greeted by excited crowds of mainly young people who came not only to dance but also to listen. The way had been prepared by the *Let's Dance* live broadcasts, the local disc jockeys who often featured Goodman's recorded music, and the increased availability and sales of the records Goodman had made during and after the period of his network broadcasts. Crowds grew in size and enthusiasm, and the Palomar engagement was extended from one month to two. Public taste was shifting and Goodman, soon to be dubbed "The King of Swing" by a press agent, had caught the crest of the wave.

Impact of Event

After his triumph at the Palomar, Goodman's next major appearance was at Chicago's Congress Hotel, where an engagement of one month was extended to six. During this period, the popular press joined jazz journalists in paying increasing attention to Goodman's music, which was now labeled as "swing." Goodman's success allowed him, with the encouragement of some Chicago socialites, to confront the de facto racial segregation that existed in American entertainment. At a specially arranged benefit performance, both Goodman and Krupa played on stage with a group of black musicians in what Goodman believed was the first integrated performance before a paying audience in the United States.

Jazz is essentially the product of African-American culture, and most white jazz musicians had taken outstanding black musicians as their models. Interracial performances were common at informal jam sessions and had occurred from time to time in public, but seldom at important venues. Goodman himself was one of many who had played with racially mixed groups on recordings, where color could be ignored, but those who controlled the music industry were convinced that the public would not accept black and white musicians openly performing together on an equal basis. Despite his own concern about the financial and other consequences, Goodman decided to use his growing popularity to challenge publicly the prevailing racist practices.

Goodman already had made several popular trio recordings with Gene Krupa and the impressive young black pianist Teddy Wilson. With the urging of John Hammond and others, he introduced his trio as part of a special concert. When the feared adverse reaction did not materialize, Goodman made trio appearances a part of his regular band performances, but he did not yet dare to actually integrate his band. Instead, he presented the trio as a unit by itself. Despite the tentative nature of Goodman's initial actions, he showed considerable courage in breaking the color barrier, and his success was well publicized. When Goodman expanded his trio to a quartet in 1936, he hired another black musician, vibraphonist Lionel Hampton. Wilson and Hampton's association with Goodman made both famous, and Hampton credited Goodman's example with opening up opportunities for African Americans not only in music but also eventually in baseball and other fields. Although notoriously parsimonious, Goodman accepted the financial and social problems that threatened integrated groups. He wanted the best musicians he could find and continued to employ African Americans throughout the rest of his career. His actions in the mid-1930's stand as important milestones in the evolution of American society.

Goodman's small groups also had a musical influence on American culture. He often set up his trio or quartet on the dance floor so that audiences were enticed to pay close attention to these exciting ensembles. This chamber-music approach introduced a broad audience to the conventions and delights of superior small-group jazz performance and presented jazz not only as an accompaniment to dancing and socializing but also as music worthy of serious listening. Goodman's example was copied frequently by other big-band leaders such as his rival for clarinet supremacy Artie Shaw, who formed a small group called the Gramercy Five. Some critics who find Goodman's big-band performances artistically uneven point to his trio, quartet, and sextet recordings as examples of his highest musical achievements.

As Goodman's fame and success increased, the jazz that his band and others like it played became the popular music of the day. For about a decade, commercial success accompanied a significant elevation in the public's musical taste. Not only leaders but also sidemen such as Goodman's outstanding trumpet soloist Harry James became celebrities on a par with the most famous film stars. Goodman's band itself appeared in a number of Hollywood films, as did other swing bands such as those of Duke Ellington, Tommy Dorsey, and Glenn Miller.

Goodman's success in presenting jazz as a respectable music purely for listening was demonstrated triumphantly in 1938 by his historic concert at Carnegie Hall, a hallowed venue previously reserved for "serious" music. The absent-minded Goodman discovered twelve years later that he had recordings of the concert. The records have sold more than one million copies and have been available continuously, making them among the most popular jazz recordings of all time. As Goodman sought to make jazz more respected, his performances of classical music enhanced his own credibility and that of other jazz musicians. Many who had disparaged jazz and its players came to see that their artistic boundaries were artificial, as Goodman commissioned and performed music by such composers as Béla Bartók, Aaron Copland, and Paul Hindemith.

During the height of swing music's popularity in the late 1930's and early 1940's, there were at least fifty dance bands with national reputations and significant followings and hundreds of lesser-known and local professional orchestras. Dance styles such as the jitterbug were based on swing music, fan clubs boosted individual bands, and thousands of high-school and college students, especially young women, flocked to performances, often mobbing the bandstands and drowning out the music in their enthusiasm, as occurred in 1937 at Goodman's legendary Paramount Theater appearances in New York City. Radio broadcasts, record sales, public dances and performances, and extensive media coverage all confirmed that swing was the period's dominant form of American musical entertainment. Goodman had played a central role in making it so.

Bibliography

Baron, Stanley. "Introduction." In *Benny, King of Swing: A Pictorial Biography Based on Benny Goodman's Personal Archives* by Benny Goodman. New York: William Morrow, 1979. The handsome coffee-table book has more than two hundred photographs and Baron's long introduction, replete with interesting anecdotes and biographical details but little musical commentary. No index.

Collier, James Lincoln. *Benny Goodman and the Swing Era*. New York: Oxford University Press, 1989. A comprehensive and detailed study of Goodman, his many sidemen, and their music within the musical, social, and historical context of the swing period. Its scholarly method and personal opinion make this a lively if at times quirky approach to the subject. An attempt is made to debunk many popular myths. Photographs, a selected discography, and index.

Connor, D. Russell, and Warren W. Hicks. *BG on the Record: A Bio-Discography of Benny Goodman*. New Rochelle, N.Y.: Arlington House, 1969. A standard and highly detailed reference for the study of most of Goodman's recordings, including dates, locations, and personnel. Biographical details and anecdotes place the recordings in context. Photographs and a variety of indexes including song titles, artists, and arrangers.

Goodman, Benny, and Irving Kolodin. *The Kingdom of Swing*. New York: Frederick Ungar, 1939. Goodman's autobiography, written near the height of his success. Highly readable. A few photographs, no index.

Hammond, John, with Irving Townsend. *John Hammond on Record: An Autobiography*. New York: Penguin Books, 1981. By the man who discovered and first recorded performers ranging from Billie Holiday and Count Basie to Bob Dylan and Bruce Springsteen. Hammond, associated with Goodman through common interests and family ties (Goodman married his sister several years after the men had first met), provides an insider's view of Goodman's career. Photographs, a selective discography, and index.

Schuller, Gunther. "The 'King' of Swing: Benny Goodman." In *The Swing Era: The Development of Jazz, 1930-1945*. New York: Oxford University Press, 1989. A valuable and at times technical evaluation of Goodman's musical achievements by one of the foremost experts in the field. Transcribed musical illustrations, a selected discography, glossaries, and indexes.

Douglas Rollins

Cross-References

Armstrong First Records with His Hot Five Group (1925), p. 670; Ellington Begins an Influential Engagement at the Cotton Club (1927), p. 739; Billie Holiday Begins Her Recording Career (1933), p. 930; Sinatra Establishes Himself as a Solo Performer (1943), p. 1250; Parker's Playing Epitomizes Bebop (1946), p. 1318; Davis' *Birth of the Cool* Recordings Spawn 1950's Cool Jazz (1949), p. 1438; The First Newport Jazz Festival Is Held (1954), p. 1617; Davis' *Bitches Brew* Vitalizes Jazz-Rock Fusion (1969), p. 2153.

BALANCHINE'S *SERENADE* INAUGURATES AMERICAN BALLET

Category of event: Dance
Time: December 6, 1934
Locale: Avery Memorial Theater, Hartford, Connecticut

George Balanchine's Serenade *presaged a new era for ballet in the United States*

Principal personages:
GEORGE BALANCHINE (GEORGI MELITONOVITCH BALANCHIVADZE, 1904-1983), one of the most influential choreographers of the twentieth century, who did much to establish the style and content of contemporary ballet in America
LINCOLN KIRSTEIN (1907-   ), a ballet cognoscente who persuaded Balanchine to form an American ballet company
EDWARD WARBURG (1908-   ), a patron of the arts who supported the fledgling enterprise from its inception

Summary of Event

Born Georgi Melitonovich Balanchivadze in St. Petersburg, Russia, George Balanchine was enrolled in the Imperial Ballet School in that city at age ten and danced in productions at the Maryinsky Theatre. After becoming known for his experimental choreography, he formed a small troupe of dancers to tour Germany in 1924 with the full intention never to return to the revolutionary turmoil in Soviet Russia. He joined Sergei Diaghilev's Ballets Russes the next year and remained its chief choreographer until the company split asunder after Diaghilev's death four years later. For the next three years, Balanchine worked in London, Paris, Monte Carlo, and Copenhagen for various theaters, but the insecurity of this peripatetic life did not appeal to him. When Lincoln Kirstein appeared on the scene in 1933 and offered him the directorship of a company that was yet to come into existence, Balanchine took a gamble and moved to the United States, a country that had fascinated him for much of his life. This decision was to change the shape of ballet in America.

Balanchine was not the first Russian dancer to seek his fortune in the United States. Anna Pavlova had toured the country from coast to coast beginning in 1910, and several of her partners had settled in the United States to teach. Vaslav Nijinsky led Diaghilev's Ballets Russes for a series of American appearances in 1916. Other of Diaghilev's chief choreographers and dancers, most notably Michel Fokine and Adolf Bolm, had come to America to teach and perform. By the time that Balanchine arrived on October 17, 1933, there were well-established pockets across America where young dancers could receive adequate training in ballet.

Yet Balanchine recognized the need for an academy with unified standards where talented dancers could be molded to suit his stylistic needs. Auditions for the School of American Ballet were held on January 1, 1934, and a first performance was scheduled for that June.

Balanchine chose as music for the ballet a piece that he had loved ever since he was a child, Peter Ilich Tchaikovsky's *Serenade in C for String Orchestra* (1880). The composer was one with whom Balanchine felt a close spiritual affiliation all of his life. More practical considerations were involved as well; the piece required only a small orchestra, which was all the company could afford. For the premiere, Balanchine utilized the first three movements of Tchaikovsky's work; in 1940, he added the final section (which he interposed before the third movement).

Working in a style that anticipated modern dancer Merce Cunningham's "chance" choreography, in which a flip of a coin may determine dance sequences, Balanchine choreographed *Serenade* with whichever dancers happened to show up that day for rehearsal. For example, the beginning section of *Serenade* has a corps de ballet of seventeen female dancers—because that was how many were enrolled in the class. Not until Charles Laskey joined the rehearsals was a male dancer introduced into the second section. A dancer entered late one day and walked through the lines to search out her place; Balanchine mischievously retained the sequence, a pointed lesson to remind others to come on time. Another dancer slipped, fell, and began to cry, and Balanchine told her to repeat the incident thereafter at the exact same spot in the piece. The ballet, then, became a living witness of the company's transition from amateur into professional, a veritable history of individual growth.

Serenade begins with daring simplicity: seventeen girls pose with right arms lifted in salute. They perform standard *ports de bras* exercises with arms moving slowly along circular paths, movements drawn from the five classic positions of ballet. Then, with deliberate abruptness, the dancers face forward toward the audience. Suddenly, their legs rotate outward so that they stand resolutely with heels touching. The underlying message is obvious: They acknowledge the three-hundred-year-old tradition of classic ballet and yet announce that they are fully prepared to face whatever the future may bring. They are ready to dance. Extravagantly full-blown movements follow, with great arm sweeps, full backbends, and the fleet footwork that was to become a Balanchine signature.

The ballet's most gripping sequence is its conclusion, a dreamlike scene in which a man walks slowly across the stage followed by a darkly dressed woman, who covers his eyes with one hand and holds her other hand over his heart. The man's eyes open, and he beholds a woman at his feet. The three begin to dance, but they are interrupted by streams of dancers who throw themselves into the man's arms. He attempts to express his love for the woman, but when he places his hand over his heart to pledge his devotion, the dark shadow behind him again covers his eyes and places her chill hand over his heart. He walks away, and the distraught woman is borne offstage by a solemn procession of dancers.

The final scene is noteworthy for its psychological ambiguity: Strong emotions appear to underlie the dancers' relationships, yet the ballet's creator denied any attempt to portray a story. Balanchine prided himself on his innovative "plotless" ballets, which discarded the dramatic storyline and lush scenery characteristic of many Diaghilev ballets. When a puzzled dowager once demanded to know what one particular ballet was about, he is alleged to have replied pertly, "About twenty minutes." Yet *Serenade* evidently held a special meaning for him; one night he confessed to a friend that the final scene was "like fate . . . Each man going through the world with his destiny on his back. He meets a woman—he cares for her—but his destiny has other plans."

The Hartford premiere was adjudged a glamorous event by its fashionable audience, which included George Gershwin and Salvador Dalí. The American Ballet made its New York City debut with *Serenade* on March 1, 1935, and Balanchine was to retain his ties with the city, except for a brief period, from then on; however, neither the puzzled critic of *The New York Post* nor John Martin of *The New York Times* were particularly impressed with *Serenade*. Martin even had the effrontery to suggest that Balanchine ought to be sent back to Paris, where his avant-garde "Riviera esthetics" really belonged, so that he could be replaced by an American-born director.

Kirstein, however, praised *Serenade*'s "cool frankness, a candor that seemed at once lyric and natively athletic; a straightforward yet passionate clarity and freshness suitable to the foundation of a non-European academy." He was echoed by the critic of *The Dancing Times* in London, who commented that "*Serenade*, which opened the bill, contains some of Balanchine's most unusual groupings, breathtaking in the sheer beauty of their arrangement. The 'Elegy,' which forms the closing movement of this ballet, is a little masterpiece of choreographic design."

Impact of Event

The original twenty-eight dancers who performed in Hartford that December grew in number to forty-five within the next nine months. The season, boasted Edward Warburg, proved that a first-rate company of American-born dancers could be put together, and that these dancers could even be comparable on a technical level with European imports. John Martin of *The New York Times* had "nothing but praise" for these "hard-working youngsters," who conveyed "the dignity and purity of the classic style at its best." The writer in *The Dancing Times* agreed that inexperienced dancers had been magically transformed into skilled dancers, but pointed out that their artistic maturity still lagged behind.

The company not only proved that Americans could dance well but also raised hopes of establishing an American tradition of ballet that would equal the Russian tradition. Martin had originally welcomed the company in "An Open Letter of Greeting," in which he complimented the organizers for their "sincere and almost passionate purpose to create an American ballet." He expressed reservations about the choice of a Russian choreographer—one who would take many years to acquire "a feeling of America, its life and background" and who would "inevitably put the stamp of Europe upon his pupils and dancers in these sensitive and formative years." The directors of the American Ballet, however, remained adamant in their conviction that their work would one day come to be seen as the building of an American tradition in classical dance. In their brave aspirations and high expectations, they could cite the successes of the early modern dancers of the time such as Martha Graham, Doris Humphrey, Charles Weidman, and Helen Tamiris, who were founders of an American dance form of great originality. After the company moved to New York, the American Ballet joined with the Metropolitan Opera ballet for the 1935 to 1938 seasons; in 1946, Balanchine and Kirstein founded the Ballet Society, and in 1948 they were invited to join the New York City Center with the company that became known as the New York City Ballet. *Serenade* became the company's signature piece.

The New York City Ballet style associated with Balanchine became an international standard by the end of the twentieth century, and plotless ballets, once dismissed as mere avant-garde experiments, became the norm. The cool neoclassicism of the so-called Balanchine ballerina was soon imitated everywhere. The choreographer acknowledged that women had primacy in his ballets—"Ballet is Woman," he was fond of saying. His women all looked alike, even down to the diamond studs flashing in their ears; he declared that ballerinas must have "skin the color of a peeled apple," and he chose dancers with coltishly long legs, long necks, small heads, long hair, and prepubescent, even anorexic, physiques. Balanchine's vision came to dominate the ballet world, with the unfortunate consequence that, even years after his death, many talented dancers, including African-American women and ballerinas with bustlines, could find only limited performance opportunities in ballet.

In the end, Kirstein and Warburg's faith in Balanchine was confirmed, and John Martin was to confess error. At the moment of *Serenade*'s premiere, Kirstein was beside himself with impatience to get the company moving, for he had set a deadline to deliver "an American ballet," freed of alien influences and danced by American youths, within a few years after Balanchine's arrival. It was going to take longer than that, but their vision eventually made debtors of everyone in the ballet world.

Bibliography

Balanchine, George, and Francis Mason. "Serenade." In *Balanchine's Complete Stories of the Great Ballets.* Rev. ed. Garden City, N.Y.: Doubleday, 1977. A description of the ballet action, with a rare commentary by Balanchine on his own work in which he rejects the notion of "storytelling." Index and descriptions of other Balanchine works. A useful reference source.

Barnes, Clive. "*Serenade.*" In *Dance and Dancers.* London: Hansom Books, 1976. A description of *Serenade* for British readers, in honor of the ballet's performance by the Royal Ballet in 1964. Most writers focus on the ballet's historical importance as the first Balanchine ballet in America, so Barnes's reactions to the Royal Ballet version, although more journalistic than scholarly, are refreshing. Photographs of the British dancers are lavish and lovely.

Buckle, Richard, with John Taras. *George Balanchine: Ballet Master.* New York:

Random House, 1988. Perhaps the most comprehensive biography of Balanchine, with much new information gleaned about his early life in Russia. The author unfortunately tends to be effusive in his praise, which only does a disservice to a subject known for excessive modesty. Index, limited bibliography, source notes (omitted in most other Balanchine biographies), and some previously unpublished photographs.

Kirstein, Lincoln. *The New York City Ballet.* New York: Alfred A. Knopf, 1973. The text is somewhat confusing, as it is divided between Kirstein's intensely personal diary jottings, which were contemporaneous with the event, and emotions re-collected later. Since Kirstein was intimately involved with the origins of the ballet and the founding of the American Ballet, his insights, even if highly partisan, are invaluable. The appendix contains a list of premiere performances produced by all the Balanchine companies. Useful index; profusely illustrated with exquisite photographs.

Volkov, Solomon. *Balanchine's Tchaikovsky: Interviews with George Balanchine.* Translated by Antonia W. Bovis. New York: Simon & Schuster, 1985. Balanchine was notoriously shy in talking about his sources of creative inspiration or working methods, but he opened up to a fellow Russian émigré. The author, a trained musicologist, edited the comments, rearranged the sequences, and succeeded in making this provocative book much more than a series of formulaic questions and answers. While Balanchine says very little about *Serenade* per se in this volume, he reveals a mystical affinity to Tchaikovsky and thus sheds indirect light on his own emotional life during the creative process. Index and parallel chronologies of events in Tchaikovsky's and Balanchine's lives.

Maureen Needham Costonis

Cross-References

Diaghilev's Ballets Russes Astounds Paris (1909), p. 241; Fokine's *Les Sylphides* Introduces Abstract Ballet (1909), p. 247; Graham Debuts *Appalachian Spring* with Copland Score (1944), p. 1284; Balanchine and Kirstein Make New York a World Center for Ballet (1946), p. 1301; Cunningham Stages His First Dance "Event" (1964), p. 2011.

SCHIAPARELLI'S BOUTIQUE MINGLES
ART AND FASHION

Category of event: Fashion and design
Time: 1935
Locale: 21 place Vendôme, Paris, France

Elsa Schiaparelli collaborated with Surrealist artists to create a reputation for outrageous fashion designs while developing new and successful means of marketing her creations

Principal personages:

ELSA SCHIAPARELLI (1890-1973), a fashion designer who linked high society, the fine arts, and haute couture

SALVADOR DALÍ (1904-1989), a Surrealist painter who collaborated with Schiaparelli on designs for clothing and furniture

JEAN COCTEAU (1889-1963), a poet, essayist, and film writer whose drawings were adapted by Schiaparelli for clothing

JEAN-MICHEL FRANCK (1897-1941), the interior designer responsible for the Schiaparelli boutique and home

LEONOR FINI (1908-   ), a Surrealist painter, sculptor, and designer who worked closely with Schiaparelli

Summary of Event

In January, 1935, Elsa Schiaparelli moved her couture house into new quarters at 21 place Vendôme in Paris. Though she had been showing her designs since 1926, she had presented major collections for only six years. Beginning with sportswear and her signature knits—it was her *trompe l'œil* sweaters that first made fashion news—she expanded to designing daywear and, in 1930, to evening wear. She defined the feminine silhouette of the 1930's, with its broad and squared shoulders, and she repeatedly shocked the establishment with new fabrics, refined shapes, and unusual buttons and accessories. In six years, she gained significant recognition. Recognition translated into financial success, and the new house, at the center of one of Paris' most exclusive districts, symbolized that success.

The move, however, meant more than a larger space. In addition to her studio, workrooms, and sales salons, Schiaparelli dedicated three rooms with windows fronting on the square to the display and sale of separates, perfumes, and accessories—the daring hats, scarves, gloves, and jewelry on which her reputation was in part based and which had become known as "Schiaparelli-isms." Unlike the designs offered in the salons upstairs that were custom made for individual clients, these items could be purchased "ready-to-wear." Schiaparelli's boutique combined high-fashion appeal with remarkable business acumen and the outrageousness of the avant-garde. It took a person of Schiaparelli's background to hit upon the idea.

Unlike the Parisian designers with whom she competed, Schiaparelli was born to the class that made up her clientele. Her family combined Italian aristocracy and intelligentsia; a brief marriage had given her the title of countess. She had lived in Rome, London, New York, and Paris, and she spoke four languages, three of them fluently. Her society connections, especially those with Americans in Paris, were useful and helped to provide her with financing, expertise, and notoriety, as well as with clients. Her connections with the cultural elite were essential for her sense of design, and her collaboration with the Surrealist avant-garde resulted in the creations for which she became best known.

The boutique itself was an act of collaboration: The idea was pure Schiaparelli, but the interior was designed by Jean-Michel Franck to resemble a great gilded cage. Schiaparelli's longtime American associate Bettina Jones broke new ground in creating the striking window displays. Spanish expatriate Salvador Dalí designed a couch in the form of enormous Surrealist lips, which Schiaparelli had made in shocking pink, her signature color, which she developed and introduced in 1936. Her perfume bottles were designed by Leonor Fini, an artist known for Surrealist erotica.

Throughout the mid-1930's, the cross-fertilization between Schiaparelli and artists stamped her more characteristic designs. To her, fashion design was an art. As such, it had to be daring, shocking; and the images and techniques of Surrealism gave her the means. Surrealism sought to de-structure the world of experience by means of metamorphosis, fragmentation, and dislocation; the designs of Schiaparelli and her Surrealist friends between 1935 and 1939 achieved those ends. A Jean Cocteau drawing of a vase of flowers that is transformed, by the addition of eyes, into a picture of two lovers kissing was applied by Schiaparelli to an evening coat in 1937. In the same year, Schiaparelli produced a jacket animated by Cocteau's drawing of a female figure whose hair cascades down the jacket's sleeves and whose hands clasp the wearer's waist.

Schiaparelli worked with many artists but with Dalí most frequently and with the most notorious results. To celebrate the boutique, Dalí presented her with a life-sized model of a bear into whose body he had constructed drawers reminiscent of his *Venus de Milo with Drawers*. Under this influence, Schiaparelli in 1936 created her "desk suit," on which real and false pockets are treated as drawers, with drawer pulls substituting for buttons. In the following year, she showed several Dalí-inspired designs: a dress made of fabric painted by Dalí with a depiction of a large cooked lobster across the center of the skirt (a garment chosen by Wallis Simpson as part of her trousseau when she married the Duke of Windsor). The evening gown known as the tear dress had both painted tears and actual rends in the fabric, calling into question the function of clothing and the gap between the wealth of couture and the poverty of rags. It was in the creation of hats, the perfect Freudian vehicle for social and sexual displacement, that Dalí and Schiaparelli were at their most outrageous. Under his influence, she designed a hat that was a shoe; in one version, the fetishized high heel was shocking pink. Another hat, which, like the lobster dress, alluded to the woman wearer as comestible object, was in the shape of the lamb chop, complete with white patent-leather frill to mimic paper "panties" at the bone end.

Only Schiaparelli was audacious enough to wear this version.

Beyond such examples of specific influence, many of Schiaparelli's creations bore the imprint of Surrealism. The early *trompe l'œil* sweaters presented one thing as something else. Her buttons were often adapted from unusual objects—fruit forms, kitchen utensils, insects, and more. She designed a line of gloves that mimicked the hands within. She was the first designer to engage artists to paint designs,—including musical notes, circus performers, and poodles—which she then had translated to fabrics.

In these examples of collaboration and the many other designs of Surrealist appeal, Schiaparelli bridged the worlds of fashion, high society, and art.

Impact of Event

Schiaparelli's appropriations of Surrealism and her marketing of them through her boutique as well as through her custom designs were in keeping with the times; her work has continued to affect the shape of fashion. Paris in the 1930's placed great emphasis on youth, style, and bravura: Gaiety in the face of an absurd and darkening world was the order of the day. Furthermore, the economics of fashion were changing. Style was no longer only for the upper classes. More women worked and had wages to spend; fashion publications were growing in circulation and influence; skilled copyists were imitating couture designs before models had left the runway; and American designers were pioneering moderately priced ready-to-wear clothing. Schiaparelli-isms and the boutique that offered them for sale captured these trends.

Schiaparelli altered the relationship between social class and fashion in two ways. First, there was Schiaparelli herself. She was the first of the socialite designers, women of high station who turned to fashion design and merchandizing as genteel employment and diversion. Schiaparelli capitalized on the panache of her own breeding, and she capitalized on that of others as well, employing a number of wealthy or titled women as models and associates. She and her aristocratic models could not only display designs within the salon but also wear such designs at the social events for which they were created. Second, the boutique offered items of high fashion to buyers who had neither the courage nor the money for couturier designs. The boutique became a tourist attraction, and Schiaparelli-isms were carried home by many upper-middle-class travelers as souvenirs of Paris.

Schiaparelli's designs had a continuing impact in fashion as well. Her early collections emphasized coordinated separates, the economy and logic of which have been the basis for the feminine wardrobe ever since. She also pioneered the use of many synthetic fabrics and of the zipper for closures. Her suited silhouette of the 1930's, as popularized by film stars such as Joan Crawford, became the uniform for career women of the prewar period, what one historian has called the "armor" of the New Woman. Schiaparelli also had followers in her exploitation of fantasy and the absurd, most notably the Parisian designers Yves Saint-Laurent and Jean-Paul Gauthier and the "punk" designers of 1970's Great Britain.

One of the characteristics of Schiaparelli as a business woman was the ability to identify talent in young people and the willingness to turn such talent loose to create. It is no surprise, therefore, that several of her associates went on to spectacular careers of their own. For example, both Hubert de Givenchy and Pierre Cardin served apprenticeships in her establishment in the postwar period. She also early recognized the talents of a young jewelry designer, Jean Schlumberger, who worked in association with her from 1937 to 1939.

While few designers have continued such close collaboration with artists of the avant-garde, the links between fashion and art Schiaparelli forged would continue to hold. Through her work, Surrealism came to be recognized by a broader public, and fashion publishers came to realize the potential it offered for representation. Surrealism's stress on the eroticism of the female form, the potential of the fragmented, fetishized image, the linking of fashion with the subconscious and the absurd—all aspects explored in the illustration of Schiaparelli's designs by such artists as Leonor Fini, Man Ray, Cecil Beaton, and others—have been utilized in fashion layouts ever since. Also, artists accustomed to working in the more commercialized world of fashion often continued that association long after Schiaparelli ceased major design activities. Dalí, for example, continued to design for fashion publications long after World War II.

It is probably in the field of fashion merchandising, however, that Schiaparelli and her boutique had the greatest influence on the world of fashion. Her boutique was the first of its kind. Other designers before her had brought out perfumes linked to their design houses; Schiaparelli, though, added designer cosmetics and beauty supplies. She made her scarves such fashion accents that they were in much greater demand than the clothes they accessorized. Moreover, no one before her had combined these cosmetics and accessories with a true ready-to-wear line for direct sale to customers. While it was through her one-of-a-kind couture creations that she made her reputation, it was the boutique, and especially the perfume business, that made her fortune.

Since Schiaparelli began the practice, most designers have exploited the financial potential of licensing, and most have operated boutiques. In fact, while designers now base their reputations on couture designs shown in fall and spring exhibitions, such designs are so labor-intensive and costly to produce that designers depend upon the proceeds from the sale of everything from perfumes to bed sheets to finance and make truly profitable their operations.

Bibliography

De Marly, Diana. *The History of Haute Couture, 1850-1950.* London: B. T. Batsford, 1980. A history of the beginnings of haute couture, with emphasis on the late nineteenth and early twentieth centuries. Interesting chapters on the organization and financial aspects of the couture industry and on clients and their wardrobe requirements. Schiaparelli is dealt with primarily in chapter 9. Black-and-white illustrations; brief bibliography.

Hall, Carolyn. *The Thirties in "Vogue."* New York: Harmony Books, 1985. A montage of images and ideas covered in *Vogue* magazine during the decade. Divided into broad groupings—the social scene, arts and entertainment, and travel and leisure. Important for the flavor of the times and for photographs of celebrities in couture creations, including those by Schiaparelli. A brief section on the magazine's coverage of and links with Surrealism.

Martin, Richard. *Fashion and Surrealism.* New York: Rizzoli, 1987. A richly illustrated overview of the interactions between clothing design and Surrealist art. Discussion of Schiaparelli is scattered throughout; a chapter is dedicated to her collaborations with Dalí. Of particular interest are many illustrations of otherwise seldom shown Surrealist pieces. Gives attention to contemporary Surrealist designs.

Mulvagh, Jane. *"Vogue" History of Twentieth Century Fashion.* London: Viking, 1988. A chronological discussion of fashions featured in *Vogue*. The period is divided into segments of six to nine years; the sections dealing with each segment are introduced with brief essays. Useful because so many other works are cavalier about the specific dates of fashion events. Copiously illustrated, but in small black-and-white reprints from the magazine.

Schiaparelli, Elsa. *Shocking Life.* New York: E. P. Dutton, 1954. The autobiography of Schiaparelli. A good source for information about her cultural background, the network within which she operated in the 1930's, her career, and her travels. Considerably less revealing of the inner life and personal life of the subject.

Steele, Valerie. *Women of Fashion: Twentieth Century Designers.* New York: Rizzoli, 1991. A history of women in fashion, written from a contemporary feminist perspective and highlighting the major role played by female designers in the period between the two world wars. Attention is also given to an international range of contemporary women designers. Moving postscript about acquired immune deficiency syndrome (AIDS). Extensive notes and bibliography. Many illustrations, some in color.

White, Palmer. *Elsa Schiaparelli, Empress of Paris Fashion.* New York: Rizzoli, 1986. Best biography of the designer, based largely though not entirely on Schiaparelli's autobiography. In many ways more complete than the autobiography and more informative about her personality. Lavishly illustrated, with fine color depictions of Schiaparelli designs.

Jean Owens Schaefer

Cross-References

Chanel Defines Modern Women's Fashion (1920's), p. 474; Man Ray Creates the Rayograph (1921), p. 513; Surrealism Is Born (1924), p. 604; A Paris Exhibition Defines Art Deco (1925), p. 654; Buñuel and Dalí Champion Surrealism in *Un Chien andalou* (1928), p. 750; Punk's Antifashion Style First Appears (1974), p. 2299; A Dalí Museum Opens in Figueras, Spain (1974), p. 2310.

TOP HAT ESTABLISHES THE
ASTAIRE-ROGERS DANCE TEAM

Categories of event: Dance and motion pictures
Time: 1935
Locale: Los Angeles, California

Fred Astaire and Ginger Rogers sang and danced to Irving Berlin's music in Top Hat, *one of a series of Astaire-Rogers films that helped to popularize and define the screen musical*

Principal personages:

FRED ASTAIRE (FREDERICK AUSTERLITZ, 1899-1987), the performer who appeared with Ginger Rogers in *Top Hat* and eight other RKO musicals

GINGER ROGERS (VIRGINIA KATHERINE MCMATH, 1911-   ), Astaire's dancing and acting partner

IRVING BERLIN (1888-1989), a well-known American songwriter who composed five songs for the film

PANDRO S. BERMAN (1905-   ), the studio head at RKO who oversaw the development of the Astaire-Rogers series

MARK SANDRICH (1900-1945), the director of *Top Hat* and four other Astaire-Rogers musicals

HERMES PAN (HERMES PANAGIOTOPOLOUS, 1910-1990), the dance director for the Astaire-Rogers musicals

DWIGHT TAYLOR (1902-1986) and ALLAN SCOTT (1909-   ), the writers of the screenplay for the film

VAN NEST POLGLASE (1898-1968) and CARROLL CLARK (1894-1968), the set designers for the Astaire-Rogers series

EDWARD EVERETT HORTON (1886-1970), a character actor who appeared in *Top Hat* and in two other Astaire-Rogers films

ERIC BLORE (1887-1959), a British comic actor who appeared in *Top Hat* and in four other Astaire-Rogers films

Summary of Event

Fred Astaire and Ginger Rogers both made their screen debuts in the early 1930's, Astaire in a small role supporting Clark Gable and Joan Crawford in *Dancing Lady* (1933) and Rogers as a wisecracking supporting player in *Young Men of Manhattan* (1930). They began to define their more familiar screen characters when paired by producer (soon to be studio head) Pandro Berman at RKO. Astaire and Rogers first appeared together in *Flying Down to Rio* (1933), though Dolores del Rio and Gene Raymond played the leads. The first true Astaire-Rogers musical was their next vehicle, *The Gay Divorcee* (1934), adapted from a Cole Porter show in which Astaire had recently starred on Broadway. Although only one Porter song ("Night and Day") was kept in the film, the concluding set piece "The Continental" (by Con Conrad and Herb Magidson) won the first Oscar ever awarded for best song and, along with the chemistry of Astaire and Rogers, helped to make the film profitable.

Profits were something that RKO, the smallest of the major studios, needed badly. The studio's initials stood for Radio-Keith-Orpheum, the names of the theater circuits (some of them former vaudeville houses) through which the studio's films were distributed to exhibitors. In 1933, RKO was bankrupt and under the receivership of a New York bank; the young studio head Berman eagerly pursued any film property that looked financially promising. Berman also overrode Astaire's objections to being part of a film couple. Astaire had previously been teamed on Broadway with his sister Adele, who had received the greater acclaim. Now he wanted to be a solo performer, but the financial straits of the studio allowed Berman to offer Astaire the unheard-of incentive of profit points. Astaire relented, and the success of his early films with Rogers—*Roberta* (1934) followed *The Gay Divorcee*—pulled RKO out of debt. With their fourth teaming, *Top Hat* (1935), in preparation, Astaire's contract called for him to receive ten percent of the profits above his regular salary.

Berman assigned Mark Sandrich to direct *Top Hat*; Sandrich would also direct four other Astaire-Rogers films. Sandrich had an engineering background, and he took a systematic approach to filming dance musicals. He reduced a film's sequences (dialogue, action, music, dance) to a color-coded diagram that showed the order and duration of each activity in the shooting script. Sandrich understood the structural purpose of every scene, and he wanted songs that advanced the plot. For the music, Berman hired Irving Berlin. Somewhat disappointed by his previous experiences with film productions (*Puttin' on the Ritz* and *The Cocoanuts* in 1929), Berlin, a perfectionist, this time found a kindred spirit in the meticulous Astaire. Berlin's respect for Astaire would last his entire life; Berlin would later join the film *Holiday Inn* (1942) only because Astaire was part of the project. Berlin even claimed that he would rather have Astaire introduce his songs than any other performer (quite a statement, considering that Bing Crosby had performed Berlin's enormously popular "White Christmas"). The composer stayed for six weeks at a Los Angeles hotel, working sometimes for twelve hours at a stretch. "Cheek to Cheek," Berlin's longest-ever popular tune (at sixty-four bars), was written in one day; on the other hand, "The Piccolino," the big production number to conclude the film, was a throwback to the type of music Berlin had composed for Broadway revues in the 1920's and required as much work as the rest of the score.

The remainder of the creative team also worked on many of the Astaire-Rogers films. Dwight Taylor wrote the script for *Top Hat*, which emphasized romantic comedy and mistaken identity and was a virtual rewrite of *The Gay Divorcee*. Allan Scott reworked the screenplay and went on to contribute to the scripts for the next four Astaire-Rogers films: *Follow the Fleet* (1936), *Swing Time* (1936), *Shall We Dance* (1937), and *Carefree* (1938). Hermes Pan is listed in the screen credits of *Top Hat* for staging the ensembles, but he was really assigned by RKO to Fred Astaire as his assistant. Pan had heard of Astaire's broken-rhythm dancing, and, like Astaire, had relocated from Broadway to Hollywood. Physically, he closely resembled Astaire, and he would rehearse routines with him, help him to solve tricky problems of choreography, and teach the completed steps to Rogers. Astaire and Pan would collaborate throughout their long careers. As the head of the art department, Van Nest Polglase is listed in the credits for nearly all RKO motion pictures of the time, but his assistant Carroll Clark may have been more responsible for giving the musicals their sleek visual shine. Viewers of the films remember their distinctive Art Deco style nearly as much as the dance numbers.

The stars were assisted by an able group of supporting players who formed what could be called the Astaire-Rogers repertory company. The British comic actor Eric Blore, for example, plays the butler Bates in *Top Hat*; Blore embodied the prototypical gentleman's gentleman. Edward Everett Horton took the role of the fussy but likable theatrical producer, and Helen Broderick appears as his sarcastic wife. Erik Rhodes drew on his supply of accents to play Beddini (Rhodes had played a Frenchman in *The Gay Divorcee*). The studio contract system also resulted in the casting of some performers who would become famous years later: For a few seconds, a platinum-blonde Lucille Ball can be glimpsed as a clerk in a flower shop.

What made the team work? Astaire would later appear with more technically proficient dancers than Rogers, but none of them generated the same magnetism with him that she did. Though Rogers would later win an Academy Award for her dramatic performance in RKO's *Kitty Foyle* (1940), she will always be remembered first for her work with Astaire. Did audiences simply find the two of them indigenous to the deliberately artificial film world they inhabited? Perhaps each complemented the other in ways that would remain incomplete in their other films. Katherine Hepburn explained it more succinctly in her often-quoted remark that Ginger gave Fred sex appeal and he gave her class.

Top Hat opened at the new Radio City Music Hall (partly owned by RKO) on September 6, 1935, and became an instant hit. The *New York Daily News* called it the best movie musical ever. Produced at a cost of $600,000, the film brought in more than $3 million. Only *Mutiny on the Bounty* (1935) earned more money that year.

Impact of Event

The Astaire-Rogers series was begun at a time when the techniques for filming screen musicals were changing. Director Mark Sandrich has been credited with formulating the playback method of prerecording the performers' songs with the orchestra and then having the actors lip-sync the lyrics during shooting. The advantages of this approach can be seen by comparing any of the Astaire-Rogers films with a musical such as *The Cocoanuts*, an early talkie starring the Marx Brothers. In that film, the usually fast-moving comedians are noticeably more stationary because of their need to hear the off-camera accompaniment and because of the immobile camera and sound apparatus of the time. Sandrich's playback method and the comparatively lighter equipment by then in use enlivened musical numbers and made possible more ambitious dance sequences.

These dance numbers are enormously effective and, more than any other element, give the Astaire-Rogers films their stamp of individuality. Other musicals may linger in the mind because of their setting, their songs, or their sentiment, but the Astaire-Rogers films are rightly remembered for their dancing. Dancing became Astaire's way of reshaping the film medium. In the same way that Alfred Hitchcock would shoot his suspense scenes by trying to avoid clichéd situations and by emphasizing the visual and Ernst Lubitsch would find fresh ways to film romantic scenes, Astaire brought innovations that forever changed dance musicals.

This change had both a technical and a dramatic facet. Astaire insisted that dance numbers be shot and shown as much as possible in one continuous camera take. By minimizing editing, he hoped that the audience would notice that a dance number was not a spliced-together sequence representing the best of numerous takes on the sound stage but rather a single perfect performance captured on film. He opposed cutaways and reaction shots, since they interrupted a scene's fluidity and hinted that camera tricks might be involved (and, indeed, the few reaction shots that remain in the dance numbers are always intrusive). Filming in one unbroken take placed greater demands on Astaire and Rogers, since one wrong step would mean reshooting the entire dance from the beginning. Hermes Pan and Astaire also gave attention to camera placement. To move a dancer toward the camera, for example, tended to lessen the audience's overall impression of movement; moving the camera at times with the performer, however, created more kinetic excitement.

Dramatically, the dances develop character and advance the plot. The first number in *Top Hat*, "No Strings," is an anthem of independence for Astaire's character Jerry Travers. After he sings about his freedom from emotional ties, he dances with syncopated squirts from a seltzer bottle and slaps on the furniture to express rhythmically and pictorially his happy bachelorhood. Berlin's second song "Isn't This a Lovely Day (To Be Caught in the Rain)?" becomes a courtship dance for Astaire and Rogers. Trapped on a deserted bandstand when a cloudburst hits, they stroll about and cautiously ease into concurrent steps, two people musically releasing their inhibitions. The visual contrast between the downpour outside and the couple moving in graceful rhythm under the roofed bandstand works well. At the start of the song, she is antagonistic toward him; at the end, they are in love. It is a cinematic courtship accomplished wordlessly in the language of dance.

The Astaire-Rogers films may have established and popularized the film musical, but they did not spawn a series of close imitations at other studios. Does this mean that the films are inimitable? They certainly exist in their own world of 1930's fantasy romance, an invention of the RKO creative team. Audiences have continually cherished the films not because they are time capsules of an age gone by, since such total stylization—people who always wear dinner jackets and formal dresses, drawing rooms as big as gymnasiums—never existed. Woody Allen gently satirized such films in *The Purple Rose of Cairo* (1985) and even included a clip from *Top Hat*. The Astaire-Rogers films show a 1930's that never was or, as Arlene Croce has suggested, provide a memory of how the Jazz Age and prosperity were reshaped in the

Depression. The films' cultivated artificiality is the point; they facilitated the wish-fulfillment and escapism that audiences wanted. Like Restoration comedy and the novels of P. G. Wodehouse, the films can be enjoyed and appreciated but not imitated.

Bibliography

Bergreen, Laurence. *As Thousands Cheer: The Life of Irving Berlin.* New York: Viking Press, 1990. The most thorough and authoritative biography of the famous composer and the first published after his death. Chapter 14 discusses the making of *Top Hat.*

Carrick, Peter. *A Tribute to Fred Astaire.* Salem, N.H.: Salem House, 1984. Carrick's biography describes *Top Hat* more fully than any other Astaire-Rogers film, seeing it as representative of the very best of the series.

Croce, Arlene. *The Fred Astaire/Ginger Rogers Book.* New York: Vintage Books, 1972. Not merely good on the Astaire-Rogers series, Croce's excellent study is one of the best books ever about film. Thoughtfully written and a pleasure to read, the work also cleverly features two series of still frames printed in page corners, so that by flipping pages, one can see Fred and Ginger dance.

Jewell, Richard B. *The RKO Story.* New York: Crown, 1982. Though oversized and filled with photographs, Jewell's study is good for reading as well as for browsing. He covers every film RKO produced year by year and includes useful facts about the costs of productions and the box-office receipts of notable successes and failures.

Mueller, John E. *Astaire Dancing: The Musical Films.* New York: Alfred A. Knopf, 1985. Rich analysis of each of Astaire's dances from every film. Mueller's book is rightfully viewed as one of the best on Astaire and dance musicals.

Rogers, Ginger. *Ginger: My Story.* New York: HarperCollins, 1991. Somewhat slight and anecdotal, and obviously geared toward a popular audience. Nevertheless, valuable for its first-person view, albeit a highly selective one.

Thomas, Bob. *Astaire, the Man, the Dancer: The Life of Fred Astaire.* New York: St. Martin's Press, 1984. A popular biography that includes comments by Astaire. Readers interested in more of Astaire's point of view should consult his autobiography, *Steps in Time* (1959).

Glenn Hopp

Cross-References

The Jazz Singer Premieres in New York (1927), p. 734; *Show Boat* Introduces American Musical Theater (1927), p. 745; Hollywood Enters Its Golden Age (1930's), p. 822; Berkeley's *42st Street* Revolutionizes Film Musicals (1933), p. 925; Lubitsch's *The Merry Widow* Opens New Vistas for Film Musicals (1934), p. 941; The Classic Screwball Comedy Reaches Its Height in Popularity (1934), p. 951; Kelly Forges New Directions in Cinematic Dance (1949), p. 1432.

THE FEDERAL THEATRE PROJECT PROMOTES LIVE THEATER

Category of event: Theater
Time: 1935-1939
Locale: The United States

From 1935 to 1939, the Federal Theatre Project brought live theater to the general public by funding small and regional theaters all over the United States

Principal personages:
> HALLIE FLANAGAN (1890-1969), a Vassar college theater director who was appointed to organize and direct the Federal Theatre Project
> ORSON WELLES (1915-1985), an actor with the Federal Theatre Project who went on to found the Mercury Theatre and become famous as an actor
> JOHN HOUSEMAN (1902-   ), an actor with the Federal Theatre Project, Welles's partner in the Mercury Theatre and later a famous actor

Summary of Event

In May, 1935, Vassar College theater professor and director Hallie Flanagan received a call from Harry Hopkins, head of the Works Progress Administration, asking her to come to Washington to discuss what to do about unemployed theater people. Out of that phone call came the Federal Theatre Project, which was designed to provide subsistence income for unemployed theater workers.

In 1935, there were fifteen million unemployed people in the United States. Six million were on relief rolls. An estimated forty thousand theater people across the country were out of work. The project was to employ as many theater people then on relief rolls as possible. Approximately ten thousand people found work with the Federal Theatre Project. By the time of its demise, nearly three thousand of those workers had found employment within the private sector.

In President Franklin D. Roosevelt's famous first hundred days in office in 1933, he set up a number of agencies to alleviate the conditions under which ordinary Americans had suffered since 1929. Businesses had gone bankrupt. Banks and savings and loans had failed, impoverishing the people whose uninsured savings were wiped out. Unemployed men sold donated apples on street corners. They asked for food at the back doors of those lucky enough still to have homes.

Roosevelt's Civilian Conservation Corps gave unemployed urban men work in rural areas, where they built roads, replanted deforested areas, and built picnic areas along highways. His Public Works Administration and Works Progress Administration (WPA) built post offices, schools, community swimming pools, and recreation buildings in city parks. The WPA also found work for writers, who were assigned to write books about each state. Other writers and photographers documented the plight of farmers in the Southern states. Under WPA auspices, people interviewed ex-slaves and sent interview transcripts to Washington, D.C. Artists painted murals for local post offices and other public buildings. The Federal Theatre Project, begun under the Emergency Relief Act of April, 1935, as a relief measure to provide minimal wages for ten thousand unemployed theater people, was part of the same effort to combat unemployment, as well as bringing performance art to wider audiences.

The Federal Theatre Project kept thousands of future professionals in the theater. Many became famous in later years. They covered the spectrum of the arts, including among their numbers composers, set and costume designers, directors, playwrights, and actors. Among project employees were Will Geer, Canada Lee, Joseph Cotten, Virgil Thomson, Paul Bowles, Arthur Miller, Sidney Lumet, Orson Welles, John Houseman, Dan Dailey, Gene Kelly, and Burt Lancaster (as an acrobat with a Federal Theatre circus).

The Caravan Theatre, with its portable stage, presented productions in New York City parks. Multilingual productions brought theater to Spanish Harlem and presented plays in Yiddish. Admission prices ranged from nothing to a nickel to, on Broadway, one dollar. There was also children's theater, including puppeteers and magicians, as well as regional and community dramas.

The project's national headquarters, directed by Hallie Flanagan, was located in New York City. There were five regional organizations, each with a regional director: East, Midwest, South, West, and New York City. In each region, there were various subgroups of theatrical performance. The regional organizations were either attached to already existing nonprofit theaters or, where those were lacking, set up as independent companies.

Flanagan had a plan for regional theater, to establish theaters that had the possibility of growing into social institutions in communities in which they were located. In addition to plays with nonregional content produced by these regional centers, some work based on local history and folklore was produced, such as *The Sun Rises in the West*, produced in Los Angeles, and *The Lost Colony*, produced in North Carolina.

The immediate impact of the project, in addition to removing thousands from public assistance programs, was to draw hundreds of thousands of people to performances all over the country. It is estimated that project performances drew audiences of half a million weekly and that by the project's end in 1939, thirty million people had seen its productions. Approximately 65 percent of those people, it was estimated, had never before seen live theater.

There was trouble with Congress, the source of funding for the project, almost from the beginning; project employees were accused of "boondoggling" and of serving as fronts for New Deal and Communist propaganda. Attacked by the House Committee on Un-American Activities in 1938, the Federal Theatre Project came to an end on June 30, 1939, after the congressional committees in charge of appropriations decided not to continue funding.

In its brief life, the Federal Theatre Project brought free or nearly free live theater to new mass audiences and created work for thousands. Some few of them later became famous in the arts. Some production devices of its "Living Newspaper" productions were later used in professional theater. Its research division created histories of local and regional theaters. Its neighborhood ethnic productions, often performed on specially designed trucks, were the prototype for productions in the late twentieth century in New York City.

Perhaps most important, the project left a dream of the possibilities of a government-funded national theater. In television and radio in the last decades of the twentieth century, its closest counterparts may be the Public Broadcasting System and National Public Radio.

Impact of Event

Difficulties with Congress began before the first production opened. The directors of the Living Newspaper, a subunit of the project, chose to do a piece about the Italian invasion of Ethiopia. Playwright Elmer Rice, selected by Flanagan to head New York projects, agreed with her that the productions should be fluid and timely, like a newspaper. Rice selected Morris Watson, vice-president of the American Newspaper Guild, to run the Living Newspaper group, and a staff of real reporters researched the material on which the plays were based. Employing devices of agitprop (agitation-propaganda) plays Flanagan had seen recently in Europe, the Living Newspaper productions were total theater, using light, music, dance, mime, posters, graphs, charts, and direct speeches to the audience. Many of the techniques became staple devices of later Broadway theater. The first production, *Ethiopia*, nevertheless was killed by congressional fiat before it could open. Elmer Rice quit in protest.

Because the subject matter of Living Newspaper plays was contemporary social and political problems, these plays always found criticism from politicians and columnists. *Triple-A Plowed Under* dealt with the plight of the farmer; *Power* with Tennessee Valley Authority attempts to control floods and harness water power for electricity; *One-Third of a Nation*, taking its title from Franklin D. Roosevelt's "one-third of a nation ill-housed, ill-clad, ill-nourished," championed public housing for the urban poor.

Until the creation of the Federal Theatre Project, African-American actors and playwrights who did not want to conform to white stereotyping of their lives had little access to theater. In New York, there were the Harlem Suitcase Theater and the Rose McClendon Players' Theater Workshop, and in Cleveland the Karamu Theater. In addition to creating its New York group, the project set up black production groups in Chicago, Birmingham, Los Angeles, Philadelphia, Seattle, and other cities and developed a repertory of fifty-five plays, nearly all original scripts.

The New York company, in particular, was highly successful. Orson Welles and John Houseman directed an all-black cast in a production of *Macbeth* set in Haiti in which the play's witches were voodoo practitioners. Productions of works by W. S. Gilbert and Sir Arthur Sullivan by white project performers were popular, but the black group had a smash hit with an all-black cast and updated music in *The Swing Mikado*. It also produced W. E. B. Du Bois's *Haiti*, depicting the rebellion led by

Toussaint l'Overture. *Walk Together Chillun* dealt with the need for unity among African-American factory workers.

Critics of "that man in the White House," as hard-core Republicans referred to Roosevelt, argued that the Works Progress Administration was created to buy votes by paying "boondogglers," a word coined to describe workers who allegedly did nothing. Roads, buildings, and dams provided visible evidence that somebody must be doing something; it was easier to attack the arts, which had few such tangible products. Even the Federal Theatre Project's Children's Theatre did not escape the criticism that the project was full of Communists and that its productions were Communist propaganda. The Children's Theatre performed free of charge in playgrounds, parks, and public schools and had some long-running hits, notably *The Emperor's New Clothes*. A play called *The Revolt of the Beavers*, however, in which the subjects of an evil king throw him out so that they can remain nine years old and eat ice cream, was described by project haters as Communist allegory.

Among the project's more striking socially conscious plays were *The Cradle Will Rock* and *It Can't Happen Here*. Technically, *The Cradle Will Rock* is not a Federal Theatre Project play, since Congress canceled funding for it. Unpaid theater owners padlocked their doors on opening night, and Equity actors could not appear in roles in costume. Directors Orson Welles and John Houseman led the cast and the audience that had showed up to see the show down the street to a hastily rented vacant theater, where composer Marc Blitzstein played the score on a piano and actors in street clothes stood up in the audience and sang when their cues came. The performance received great publicity and gave impetus to the Welles-Houseman Mercury Theatre, which the directors left the project to form. *It Can't Happen Here* is remembered for the conditions of its staging. Novelist Sinclair Lewis, his political consciousness raised by his wife, columnist Dorothy Thompson, wrote a novel about the way in which a Fascist pretending to be an anti-Fascist could be elected president and become a dictator. He adapted it for the stage, and on October 27, 1936, the Federal Theatre Project produced it simultaneously in seventeen theaters across the country. Hallie Flanagan canceled productions in St. Louis and New Orleans; Louisiana politicians protested that the play was really about Governor Huey Long, and Missourians wanted script changes. Most reviews, though, were favorable. The simultaneous productions reached the largest audience ever to see a play at the same time until the advent of television.

The project did not neglect the classics, performing works by William Shakespeare and the Greek playwrights, including the first performance in America of Euripides' *Lysistrata* as well as medieval miracle and morality plays. George Bernard Shaw let the project produce his plays for only token royalties, and T. S. Eliot's *Murder in the Cathedral* was given its premiere performance on Broadway by project actors.

Under attack from its inception by critics of Roosevelt's New Deal relief acts and by those who labeled it a hotbed of Communist propaganda, the Federal Theatre Project was weakened slowly by financial cuts and attempts at censorship. In 1938,

Martin Dies's House Committee on Un-American Activities attacked the project and refused to allow Hallie Flanagan and other project officials to testify at the Committee's hearings. Republican Representative J. Parnell Thomas accused the project's plays of being propaganda for Communism or the New Deal. Flanagan finally was allowed to testify before the committee in December, 1938. When she managed to refute the so-called "evidence," the hearings were ended, and Flanagan was not allowed to finish her testimony.

The end of the project came in 1939, after the committees in the House and Senate that controlled appropriations for the project debated ending funding. Republican Representative Clifton Woodrum said that "every theatre critic of note has expressed his disapproval of projects of this type." The day following his statement, he received a telegram denying its truth, signed by every major critic in New York City.

The House committee voted to end appropriations but the Senate committee approved funding. A joint committee passed a compromise bill that omitted funding. On June 30, 1939, the Federal Theatre Project was killed.

Two project productions, *Pinocchio* and *Sing for Your Supper*, were still running on Broadway. As funding expired, *Pinocchio* was given a different ending. Instead of becoming a real boy at the end, Pinocchio died and was placed in a pine coffin bearing a death date of June 30, 1939. Leaving the curtain up, the stagehands struck the set; the audience then followed the cast and crew outside and down the street in a "funeral march."

Representative Woodrum, attacking *Sing for Your Supper*, said that he would eat the manuscript if there was a line in it that "contributed to the cultural or educational life of America." The next year, the closing song from the show, "Ballad for Americans," was the theme song of the Republican National Convention.

Many people involved in the Federal Theatre Project went on to professional fame. Of the rest of the ten thousand, Hallie Flanagan wrote, "The 10,000 anonymous men and women—the et ceteras and the and-so-forths who did the work, the nobodies who were everybody, the somebodies who believed it—their dreams and deeds were not to end. They were the beginning of a people's theatre in a country whose greatest plays are still to come."

Bibliography

Bentley, Eric, ed. *Thirty Years of Treason.* New York: Viking Press, 1971. Contains transcripts of the testimony of artists, writers, and other theater people before various congressional committees. Includes Flanagan's testimony before the House Committee on Un-American Activities.

Buttita, Tony, and Barry Witham. *Uncle Sam Presents: A Memoir of the Federal Theatre, 1935-1939.* Philadelphia: University of Pennsylvania Press, 1982. Buttita worked on *The Federal Theatre Magazine* and was press agent for some of the New York productions. Gives an eyewitness account of the project, particularly of the New York City center.

Flanagan, Hallie. *Arena.* New York: Duell, Sloan and Pearce, 1940. A personal his-

tory of the Federal Theatre Project by its founder and director, written immediately after it ended. Still interesting and useful, particularly for its eyewitness
accounts.
Himelstein, Morgan Yale. *Drama Was a Weapon: The Left-Wing Theatre in New
York, 1929-1941.* New Brunswick, N.J.: Rutgers University Press, 1963. Chapter 5
concerns the Federal Theatre Project. Other chapters describe various efforts in
the theater conducted by the Communist Party. Notes, bibliography, and index.
Kazacoff, George. *Dangerous Theatre.* New York: P. Lang, 1989. A scholarly and
useful doctoral dissertation focusing primarily on new plays produced by the Federal Theatre Project, including those criticized as political. Contains a useful bibliography, particularly for material in the Federal Theatre Project Collection at
George Mason University in Fairfax, Virginia.
Williams, Jay. *Stage Left.* New York: Charles Scribner's Sons, 1974. Chronicles the
early years of left-wing theater in the United States, ending with a discussion of
the Federal Theatre Project. Discusses many of the theater groups involved in
socially conscious drama. Index and photos.

Katherine Lederer

Cross-References

The Group Theatre Flourishes (1931), p. 874; The Roosevelt Administration Creates
the WPA/FAP (1935), p. 995; Odets' *Awake and Sing* Becomes a Model for Protest
Drama (1935), p. 1006; Kazan Brings Naturalism to the Stage and Screen (1940's),
p. 1164; Welles's *Citizen Kane* Breaks with Traditional Filmmaking (1941), p. 1200.

THE ROOSEVELT ADMINISTRATION CREATES WPA/FAP

Category of event: Art
Time: 1935-1943
Locale: Washington, D.C.

The Roosevelt Administration's New Deal programs provided a role and a place in society for the artist to an extent that was unprecedented in American history

Principal personages:
EDWARD BRUCE (1879-1943), a lawyer, businessman, and professional painter who guided the specific direction of the federal art programs
HOLGER CAHILL (1893-1960), a writer, museum curator, and art expert who was director of the WPA/FAP
HARRY L. HOPKINS (1890-1946), a key administrator in Franklin D. Roosevelt's New Deal who established the WPA/FAP in August, 1935
GEORGE BIDDLE (1885-1973), a well-known artist and longtime friend of Roosevelt who first presented to the president the idea of a new nationalism in art to represent the spirit of the New Deal

Summary of Event

The story of the Works Progress Administration's Federal Art Project (WPA/FAP) begins with the crash of the New York stock market on October 29, 1929, that ushered in the Great Depression of the 1930's. All across the country, banks failed, farm prices fell to unprecedented lows, and jobs vanished. Americans saw their security and their life savings disappear. As cities struggled to cope with the large numbers of people who were now on relief, it seemed that the American Dream of a better life for anyone willing to work had ended.

During the last months of President Herbert Hoover's administration, as hunger marchers descended upon Washington, D.C., and as Americans from all walks of life tried to understand and adjust to the changed world in which they now found themselves, talk of social revolution became common—and many predicted that such a revolution would occur. Instead, American voters rejected Hoover's New Order in favor of Franklin Delano Roosevelt's New Deal.

In 1930, at the start of the Depression, four million people were out of work. By 1933, when Roosevelt's administration began, that figure had jumped to 15 million unemployed—more than one-fourth of the American labor force. Thus, one of the first priorities of the New Deal was providing relief for the unemployed, although the Roosevelt Administration believed that this relief would be temporary and would be phased out as the private sector recovered. These emergency relief measures took two basic forms: direct payments to the needy and work relief, which provided various jobs for the unemployed.

The economic crisis hit American artists as hard as or harder than any other sector of society; their unemployment rate was eventually greater than that in the general population. Following the art boom of the 1920's, however, many artists and gallery owners were slow to realize the seriousness of the situation. As late as October, 1932, for example, *Art News* proclaimed that a definite improvement being felt in the business world would soon be followed by a parallel upward movement in the art market.

As more and more artists found themselves unemployed and more galleries were forced to close, the earlier optimism evaporated, and some efforts were made in the private sector to help artists. In April, 1932, five hundred artists in New York's Greenwich Village received permission to sell their works in Washington Square, and the Syracuse Museum held a barter show in which artists exchanged works for food and medical care. The College Art Association (CAA) in New York also tried to help by providing exhibit space and a rent-a-painting scheme that was adopted in several locales across the country. The Emergency Work and Relief Bureau of the privately financed Gibson Committee in New York collaborated with the CAA to establish a program for unemployed artists to paint murals in churches and community centers and to teach art in settlement houses. When the Gibson Committee ran out of funds, its art program was taken over by the New York Emergency Relief Administration (ERA). None of these efforts, however, could keep pace with the rising rate of unemployment among artists.

In November of 1933, responding to demands for action, the federal government established the Civil Works Administration (CWA) under the direction of Harry L. Hopkins, a Grinnell College graduate with extensive social work experience. The CWA employed four million people on federal projects such as repairing roads, improving schools, and maintaining parks—but nothing, thus far, was being done to help artists in particular.

Meeting in New York, members of several professional organizations—the Society of Independent Artists, the National Academy of Design, the Whitney Museum of American Art, and the CAA—wrote to Hopkins expressing concern for the plight of artists and calling for a federal program to support the arts. This was followed by a letter to the president from George Biddle, a prominent artist and a boyhood friend of Roosevelt. Biddle's letter declared that American artists, with government support, could produce a timely and exciting mural art depicting the ideals of the New Deal on the walls of public buildings in the same way that Mexican muralists had celebrated the social ideals of the Mexican Revolution in the 1920's. Roosevelt liked this idea of a new nationalism in art and discussed the proposal with Assistant Secretary of the Treasury Lawrence L. Robert, Hopkins, and several others in his administration, all of whom expressed their interest. Biddle's concept did not fulfill the national aims of the New Deal, however, since it called for a limited number of artists and did little to help the thousands of unemployed artists across the country. It did, however, show the Roosevelt Administration what the possible function of the artist could be in a government-sponsored program.

Robert then contacted Edward Bruce, a lawyer, a Treasury Department administrator, and an internationally recognized artist himself, for his advice in developing a fine arts program. Gathering support from other Treasury Department officials, from the Treasury Secretary's wife, Mrs. Henry Morgenthau, Jr., and from Eleanor Roosevelt, in December of 1933 Bruce implemented the first federal program for artists—the Public Works of Art Project (PWAP)—and became the first director. The program employed approximately thirty-seven hundred artists at a cost of about $1,312,000.

The second program, the Section of Painting and Sculpture—later called the Section of Fine Arts—was also administered by the Treasury Department. Its purpose was to obtain, through anonymous competitions, paintings and sculptures to decorate new federal buildings, especially post offices and courthouses. Beginning in 1934 and ending in 1943, this program awarded some fourteen hundred contracts and cost about $2,571,000.

The Treasury Relief Art Project (TRAP), the third program, was financed in 1935 by an allocation of funds from the WPA to the Treasury for the decoration of federal buildings. It was administered according to the same relief rules specified by the WPA, meaning that between ten and twenty-five percent of the program's participants had to be certified for relief. Actually, TRAP employed 446 artists, about seventy-five percent of whom were on relief. Before it was discontinued in 1939, the program cost approximately $833,784.

The Works Progress Administration's Federal Art Project, the largest relief program for the visual arts, was part of a broader program that included drama, literature, and music. Begun in August of 1935 under the direction of Holger Cahill, the WPA/FAP was also administered according to the relief rules of the WPA. Before the program ended in June of 1943, it cost about $35,000,000 and employed more than five thousand artists, who created more than twenty-five hundred murals, seventeen thousand sculptures, 108,000 easel paintings, and eleven thousand designs. The WPA/FAP also operated more than one hundred Community Art Centers and compiled a twenty-thousand-piece Index of American Design.

Impact of Event

Since the end of the Roosevelt era, scholars have analyzed the motives behind the creation of the New Deal's art programs. Claiming that human economic relief was the sole reason for the programs' existence and the reason for their ready acceptance by both public and politicians, some writers have insisted that without the Depression the government would not have increased its support of the visual arts beyond the minimal levels of earlier periods. Others have maintained that the New Deal's art programs resulted from the combination of Roosevelt's own background and education, which included a respect and appreciation for the traditional arts, with a certain strong sense of noblesse oblige that prompted him to speak frequently of his desire for Americans to have "a more abundant life"—meaning cultural as well as material abundance. Other explanations of the impetus behind the New Deal art programs include the phenomenon of nationalism and patriotic self-awareness that arose during the Depression and that was evidenced by a renewed interest in all things uniquely American. Additionally, a strong political radicalism in the 1930's stressed the idea that cultural awareness was the right of the masses and promoted the creation of art forms that reflected a radical ideology. The new nationalists and the radicals both supported the creation of New Deal art programs, although neither group was really satisfied with the results.

New Deal art was derived from three basic cultural sources: the social, economic, and political conditions of the Depression itself, the rejection of European styles in favor of American ones, and the Mexican mural movement of the 1920's.

The adverse conditions of the Depression influenced American artists' approach to landscape painting. Nineteenth century American painters had interpreted nature as the sublime creation of God, unspoiled by human contact, but the painters of the 1930's saw nature as the background for human suffering, and their works are filled with images of migrant workers, dust-bowl farmers, and homeless families wandering the countryside. Yet the idealism of the New Deal gave the artist a contrasting view—the hope that the American promise of a good life for all could somehow be revived.

The New Deal artists' extensive use of American themes emphasized the rejection of European styles and conventions that had dominated American art throughout the 1920's. The movement known as American Regionalism was on the rise, and examples from the period include the murals of Thomas Hart Benton at the New School for Social Research in New York City, John Steuart Curry's dramatic paintings, and Grant Wood's immortal apotheosis of the American farmer, *American Gothic* (1930). There was an almost total rejection of the European idea of art for art's sake by many American artists, museum directors, and art critics. The writer and critic Thomas Craven supported the American theme over what he called "the curse of French trivialities" and declared that any indigenous expression in American art would have to come from strong native impulses, simple ideas, and the popular taste. Holger Cahill, the director of the WPA/FAP, was in sympathy with Craven's viewpoint, declaring that, in a time of critical reevaluation, art for art's sake was a worn-out symbol. Although some artists continued to debate the issue, American nationalism definitely had the upper hand in the art world of the 1930's.

From the Mexican muralists of the 1920's came the concept of a "people's art" that could be seen on public walls. The Mexican mural movement itself had grown out of the desire of artists to celebrate the social ideals exemplified by the Mexican Revolution of 1910. When two prominent Mexican muralists, José Clemente Orozco and Diego Rivera, came to the United States in the late 1920's, the socially conscious murals they painted prompted New Deal artists to create their own mural art depicting the people's determination to revive the American Dream.

Government patronage of public art was surprisingly well supported, in spite of objections from those who felt that art, by its very nature, should be elitist and despite protests from those who opposed any government support of the arts on principle. Because of limitations of both time and money, the New Deal art programs were not able to accomplish all that the participating artists and administrators might have wished; nevertheless, those who worked within the programs have been almost unanimous in their enthusiasm for what was accomplished. Moreover, many of the achievements of the New Deal art programs were intangible and experiential. Government support gave thousands of artists freedom to experiment and to continue their work relatively free of economic worries. Furthermore, working in the programs gave the artists a strong sense of camaraderie, bringing them together for discussion and interchange of ideas and encouraging them to learn from one another. Program artists also had an almost unprecedented opportunity to reach a large segment of the public with their art. The program's community art centers and art classes, along with the allocation nationally of original works of art, resulted in a new acceptance of art and in the creation of art departments in many colleges and universities. Many of these departments were staffed by artists who had received their first teaching experience in the federal programs.

In the final analysis, however, the most important and enduring legacy of the New Deal art programs is simply the fact that a precedent was set for the idea of art as an integral part of American society and an essential feature in the public environment.

Bibliography

Contreras, Belisario. *Tradition and Innovation in New Deal Art.* London: Associated University Presses, 1983. Discusses both the politics and aesthetics of New Deal art. Points out what was traditional and what was innovative in the art of the PWAP and the WPA/FAP. Thoroughly documented and well illustrated (black-and-white plates only).

DeNoon, Christopher. *Posters of the WPA.* Los Angeles: Wheatley Press, 1987. Identifying the period from 1935 to 1943 as one of the most innovative in the history of American graphic design, the author discusses the developments that took place as the WPA printed two million posters from thirty-five thousand designs. Illustrated with accurate color reproductions of the original posters.

McKinzie, Richard. *The New Deal for Artists.* Princeton, N.J.: Princeton University Press, 1973. Emphasizes the social and political forces behind the establishment of the WPA/FAP; does not focus on the evaluation or explication of the art produced under the program's auspices. A carefully documented study of the relationship between a government bureaucracy and the arts.

O'Connor, Francis, ed. *Art for the Millions.* Greenwich, Conn.: New York Graphic Society, 1973. A collection of essays written by many of the artists and administrators who were in the WPA/FAP. One of the best sources of information about the program. Also contains complete documentation: inventories of works and manuscripts, reports of expenditures, a list of community art centers, and bibliography.

Park, Marlene, and Gerald Markowitz. *Democratic Vistas: Post Offices and Public Art in the New Deal.* Philadelphia: Temple University Press, 1984. Focuses upon the Treasury Department's Section of Fine Arts, which commissioned murals and sculpture for federal buildings and for eleven hundred post offices. Authors concentrate on choice of themes as well as style, while also giving helpful data on individual artists. Profusely illustrated.

LouAnn Faris Culley

Cross-References

Guthrie's Populist Songs Reflect the Depression-Era United States (1930's), p. 810; Rivera's Rockefeller Center Mural Is Destroyed (1934), p. 957; The Federal Theatre Project Promotes Live Theater (1935), p. 989; The Ford Foundation Begins to Fund Nonprofit Theaters (1957), p. 1736; The National Endowment for the Arts Is Established (1965), p. 2048.

ABSTRACT PAINTING IN AMERICA OPENS IN NEW YORK

Category of event: Art
Time: February 12-March 22, 1935
Locale: Whitney Museum of American Art, New York, New York

The Whitney Museum mounted the first comprehensive exhibition of American abstract painting

Principal personages:

STUART DAVIS (1894-1964), a leading American abstract painter who exhibited in *Abstract Painting in America*, wrote the essay for the exhibition catalog, and drew the catalog's cover illustration

HERMON MORE (1887-1968), the chief curator at the Whitney Museum who mounted the 1935 exhibition

JULIANA FORCE (1876-1948), the director of the Whitney Museum of American Art from its inception in 1917 until her death

DAVID SMITH (1906-1965), a young sculptor who wrote to the museum on behalf of several artists demanding inclusion in the 1935 exhibition

BYRON BROWNE (1907-1961), an abstract painter who participated in the exhibition and helped to found the influential "American Abstract Artists" group

ARSHILE GORKY (VOSDANIG ADOIAN, 1905-1948), a leading abstractionist who exhibited in the 1935 show

ALFRED STIEGLITZ (1864-1946), a renowned photographer and art dealer who earnestly promoted modern art in America

EDITH HALPERT (1900-1970), the director of the influential Downtown Gallery, which handled Davis' work

ISRAEL BER (J. B. NEUMANN, 1887-1961), the director of the New Art Circle Gallery

Summary of Event

In February, 1935, the Whitney Museum of American Art mounted an exhibition entitled *Abstract Painting in America* that traced the development of an abstract style of painting in the United States during the early part of the twentieth century. The show also examined the extent of the commitment by American artists to abstraction. This attempt at a comprehensive examination of artists working in an abstract idiom was a serious attempt to address artistic modernism in the United States. Although the exhibit fell short of some expectations, nevertheless it did openly address the issue of abstraction. American abstract art during this period was closely tied to European models and employed a broad range of artistic expression. Whether avant-garde American artists employed a cubist breakup of space, the geometry of nonobjective form, or merely stylized form, "abstraction" was the rubric under which all of their work was grouped. Some of these artists were committed to an agenda of abstraction, while some only dabbled in an abstract stylization of form. Many of those represented in the Whitney's exhibit had already abandoned abstraction by the time of the show, and it was generally thought that the American abstract movement, as such, was over. Nevertheless, the exhibition was the first attempt by a major museum to deal with the issue of abstraction in American art; it stands as an important historical event, crucially tied to the art production of the time and to the political and social matrix in which such art was made.

The issue of abstraction in American art had been blurred during the 1930's. An ideological schism erupted between figurative and abstract painters, between social realist and "American Scene" artists on one side and their abstract counterparts on the other. American Scene painters such as Thomas Hart Benton and Grant Wood received support from galleries and museums, while the abstract artists were considered outsiders and often felt disfranchised. Yet American abstractionists continued their engagement with the abstract, and some formed a coalition with European abstract and nonobjective artists called the "Abstraction-Création" group.

This debate over figurative and abstract art was a major concern for artists, and the Whitney responded by holding a symposium on April 10, 1933, to discuss the issue. Led by Cooke Glassgold, the panel included Whitney curator Lloyd Goodrich, art critic and artist Walter Pach (who had been one of the organizers of the 1913 Armory Show), and artists Leo Katz and Morris Davidson; the panel discussed the topic "The Problem of Subject Matter and Abstract Esthetics in Painting." The Whitney curators were more comfortable with figuration, and Goodrich spoke on behalf of that style of imagery. The young Arshile Gorky spoke up and challenged their view, calling for recognition of abstract art as a valid means of expression, one that could be judged and evaluated by the same criteria employed for more traditional work. Gorky was represented by four paintings in the 1935 abstract show; in 1937, Goodrich would reconsider his position, and the Whitney would purchase a painting by Gorky for its permanent collection. The sale was the artist's first to a major public collection.

By 1935, with all the interest and discussion surrounding abstraction in America, the Whitney decided to mount an exhibition. The museum's curator, Hermon More, along with his assistant, Karl Free, and museum director Juliana Force, proceeded to make plans for a comprehensive show. More was well regarded for his installation techniques, and his judgment of American art was sound. He asked Stuart Davis, a leading American abstract painter and the editor of *Art Front* magazine, to write the introductory essay for the exhibit's catalog; a drawing of Davis' was used for the catalog's cover illustration. It is ironic that the cover drawing by Davis is an ordinary line drawing, a representational still life, rather than an abstraction. Davis' abstract work was well represented in the show, however, by five oil paintings and one gouache, including two paintings from his seminal *Eggbeater* series. Yet the cover illustration and the accompanying essay had further resonance for the exhibition. In his essay, Davis stated that the greatest period of abstract art had occurred between 1915 and 1927. The outlook of the museum's curators and its spokesman artist, therefore, was that abstraction for the most part was over, and that the Whitney's exhibition was an overview of a movement that was now part of the historical past.

While Davis seemed to think that the abstract movement had waned, he did state eloquently the objectives of the abstract artist. He wrote that "the generative idea of abstract art is alive. It changes, moves and grows like any other living organism." Davis continued his opinion on the nature of abstract art by explaining that "Art is not and never was a mirror reflection of nature. All efforts at imitation of nature are foredoomed to failure. Art is an understanding and interpretation of nature in various media." While key figures of abstraction were represented in the Whitney's show, many of the artists included were mere stylists; some, too, had by then abandoned abstraction altogether. The Whitney may have mounted a less than inspired show, but the mere fact of the exhibition was itself important. The Museum of Modern Art, New York's other leading venue for the exhibition of modern works, was entrenched in European modernism and was virtually closed to American artists. Countering the Museum of Modern Art's disregard for American modernism, the Whitney championed neglected American talent.

When American abstract artists heard of the upcoming exhibition, they were heartened that the museum was going to address the issue of abstraction; many hoped that the show would somehow validate their position and promote their ideas and their careers. This was an invitational exhibition, but many lesser-known artists openly solicited the museum for inclusion. One such artist was the young sculptor David Smith, who, together with a group of artist friends—including Willem de Kooning, Arshile Gorky, John Graham, Edgar Levy, and Mischa Resnikoff—drafted a letter to the museum stating that they had formed an alliance and would exhibit in the show only if they all were accepted. Only three, however, were invited to participate, and the group disbanded.

A number of galleries were asked to contribute work to the show, including that of Alfred Stieglitz, who secured the work of Arthur Dove, Marsden Hartley, John Marin, Georgia O'Keeffe, and Stanton Macdonald-Wright, members of his illustrious gallery. Edith Halpert's Downtown Gallery supplied the works of several of the Precisionist painters, including George Ault, Preston Dickinson, and, most notably, Stuart Davis. Work by Gorky was secured through the J. B. Neumann Gallery, which handled the work of many leading European painters. All the artists, collectors, and dealers concerned cooperated with the museum in the venture, and *Abstract Painting in America* opened on February 12, 1935.

Impact of Event

Abstract Painting in America baffled most New York critics; even abstract stylization was too much for many of them to comprehend and appreciate. The only critics who offered favorable reviews of the show were Forbes Watson and Henry McBride. The Whitney's next exhibition was *American Genre: The Social Scene in Paintings and Prints*, which, as art historian Avis Berman has noted, was certainly a retrenchment to safer ground.

The following year, however, the Museum of Modern Art mounted an abstract exhibit assembled by Alfred H. Barr, Jr. Barr's impressive *Cubism and Abstract Art* show traced the genesis of abstraction from its Postimpressionist roots through neoplasticism and beyond. The only American artist included was Alexander Calder; the show's Eurocentric emphasis gave a stamp of approval to artists across the Atlantic. Barr had said that he felt that abstraction was a European feature, not an American one, and that Americans were not, by nature, abstract. A decade later, he would change his mind, but in the mid-1930's the Modern's edicts were law. In December, 1935, Barr mounted another important show, *Fantastic Art, Dada, and Surrealism*, which dealt another blow to the Americans by exhibiting yet more examples of important art from abroad.

Although the Whitney's show had not done much to further the cause of American abstraction, at least it had addressed the issue. U.S. artists knew that galleries, museums, and critics remained hostile to abstraction, but a new idea emerged: American abstractionists would form an exhibition group to popularize abstract art, and they would hold group exhibitions promoting abstraction. At Ibram Lassaw's studio, a band of artists, including Burgoyne Diller, Balcombe and Gertrude Greene, Harry Holtzman, and Byron Browne, met to discuss exhibitions and the creation of a school for modern art. While the school idea was abandoned, the idea of an exhibition group took root. Browne took a major role in the group, which in 1936 formed the American Abstract Artists.

Browne was one of the younger artists included in the Whitney exhibition, and as a founding member of the American Abstract Artists, he helped to mount the group's first annual exhibition on April 3, 1937, at the Squibb Building Gallery on New York's Fifth Avenue. The exhibit was the largest abstract show held outside a museum venue. Large numbers of visitors filled the gallery, and New York's art critics did review the show—although not altogether favorably. The artists involved wanted to make a strong statement about abstract art, and Václav Vytlacil compiled a portfolio of lithographs by the exhibitors to be sold inexpensively to the public to help acquaint them with the new work. At the lively opening, Gorky carried around a large reproduction of a painting by the nineteenth century French classicist Jean-Auguste-Dominique Ingres and pointed out the painting's abstract qualities. This group established the viability of abstraction in America, providing a forum for young abstract artists to discuss their ideas and to display their work. Many of the group's members would later go on to establish the "New York School" of abstract expressionism.

The Whitney's initial attempt to acknowledge the early American abstract movement opened up a dialogue between curators, dealers, critics, the public, and the abstract artists themselves. Although it took some time for the discussion the show inspired to bear fruit, *Abstract Painting in America* helped to set the stage for a revitalization of painting in America and served as a harbinger of things to come.

Bibliography

Berman, Avis. *Rebels on Eighth Street: Juliana Force and the Whitney Museum of American Art.* New York: Atheneum, 1990. An excellent history of the founding of the Whitney and of the leading artists and art-world figures involved. An engrossing look at a pivotal period in American art.

Chipp, Herschel B. *Theories of Modern Art.* Berkeley: University of California Press, 1968. An anthology of writings by various critics, historians, and artists. Includes "The Artist Today," written by Stuart Davis in 1935, and "Is There an American Art," dated 1930, which first appeared in *Creative Art* magazine as a reply to critic Henry McBride.

Lane, John R., and Susan C. Larsen, eds. *Abstract Painting and Sculpture in America, 1927-1944.* New York: Harry N. Abrams, 1983. A thorough examination of abstract painting in America during an important period.

Rose, Barbara. *American Art Since 1900.* Rev. ed. New York: Praeger, 1975. A good survey of the development of modern art in twentieth century America.

Schapiro, Meyer. "Nature of Abstract Art." In *Modern Art, Nineteenth and Twentieth Centuries.* New York: George Braziller, 1982. A seminal essay showing the political matrix involved in abstract painting during this period of early modernism.

Nancy Malloy

Cross-References

Kandinsky Publishes His Views on Abstraction in Art (1912), p. 320; Duchamp's "Readymades" Challenge Concepts of Art (1913), p. 349; The Formation of the Blue Four Advances Abstract Painting (1924), p. 583; New York's Museum of Modern Art Is Founded (1929), p. 782; The Whitney Museum Is Inaugurated in New York (1931), p. 885; Peggy Guggenheim's Gallery Promotes New American Art (1942), p. 1239; Rosenberg Defines "Action Painting" (1952), p. 1557.

ODETS' *AWAKE AND SING* BECOMES A MODEL FOR PROTEST DRAMA

Category of event: Theater
Time: February 19, 1935
Locale: New York, New York

Awake and Sing *depicted the social and economic consequences of the Great Depression for three generations of a working-class Jewish-American family in the Bronx*

Principal personages:
 CLIFFORD ODETS (1906-1963), the Group Theatre's most successful play-
 wright
 LEE STRASBERG (ISRAEL STRASSBERG, 1901-1982), a founder of the Group
 Theatre and a prominent director
 STELLA ADLER (1902-   ), a Group Theatre actress for whom Odets
 designed the part of Bessie Berger

Summary of Event

Awake and Sing is largely a product of Clifford Odets' success after *Waiting for Lefty* (1935) catapulted him to instant prominence in 1935 by winning the New Masses/New Theatre Award and galvanizing audiences during its first performance at the Civic Repertory Theatre in lower Manhattan. *Waiting for Lefty*, about a strike of taxicab drivers, was written in three days and could not have been more appropriate to its times.

Odets, a member of the Group Theatre, had acted in a few of its plays and was an indifferent actor. He lived with members of the Group Theatre during summers in the countryside outside New York City and during winters in the sprawling tenement they had rented collectively on New York's West Fifty-seventh Street. In 1933, he wrote *I've Got the Blues*, which later that year was retitled *Awake and Sing*. The play was optioned to Frank Merlin, who shortly afterward went bankrupt. Odets read his script to members of the Group Theatre in hopes that they would produce it.

The play focuses on the social adjustments that a three-generation working-class Jewish-American family in the Bronx faces as the Great Depression gradually robs them of their livelihoods and security. Lee Strasberg, the most dyspeptic of the Group Theatre's three directors, disliked the play, and his disapproval scuttled its chances of being staged, even though its second act was given a reading by the group during the summer of 1933 in Warrensburg, New York. Strasberg had reservations about *Waiting for Lefty* as well.

Awake and Sing was resurrected in 1935 because *Waiting for Lefty* had left the public clamoring for more Odets. Under pressure to capitalize on the enthusiastic recognition *Waiting for Lefty* had brought him, Odets quickly polished the earlier play, which opened on February 19, 1935, at New York's Belasco Theatre to favorable reviews.

Like most plays written with the Group Theatre in mind, *Awake and Sing* has a cast of seven characters of relatively equal importance. An eighth character, Schlosser, is minor, but he advances some of the business of the narrative and carries part of its philosophical burden. Odets' manuscript of *I've Got the Blues* shows that he had Stella Adler in mind for the role of Bessie Berger when he originally conceived of the play; he often referred to Bessie as "Stella" in the typescript that is in the Library of Congress.

Bessie, the mother of the family, belongs to the middle generation. Her father, Jacob, lives with the family in their respectable Bronx apartment. Bessie's husband, Myron, once had potential; Bessie worked in a stocking factory for two years so that he could attend law school, which he did not complete. Myron has eked out an existence for his family, but his idealism is now badly tarnished and emerges only vestigially when, after Myron spends fifty cents for an Irish Sweepstakes ticket, he tells his skeptical brother-in-law, Morty, that the contest cannot be rigged because the government would not allow it.

The children in the family, Ralph and Hennie, are both grown, Ralph is in love with Blanche, whose name heavy-handedly suggests her purity. The two cannot realistically consider marriage, however, because Ralph does not earn a decent living; the future holds little hope for him. Ralph's sister Hennie, pregnant and unmarried, has no more hope for her future than her brother has for his.

The only people Odets brings onto the stage who have some sort of security are Moe Axelrod, the Berger's boarder, who makes no secret of his attraction to Hennie, and Uncle Morty, Bessie's cigar-chomping brother, who, although he has money, shares little of it with his aged father, Jacob. Moe Axelrod has been injured in the war and has the security of a government pension. Uncle Morty represents the dirty, self-centered capitalist indifferent to anyone's problems except his own.

Bessie lives daily in a hell of insecurity. She recounts to her family how a respectable old lady on the next block has been evicted because she lacks the money to keep her house; the woman is out on the street over on Dawson Avenue, surrounded by her belongings. The old woman's plight embodies Bessie's worst nightmare. Bessie's urgent need is to keep her family intact. She is the caregiver and the manager in a family whose father, the natural provider, has been worn down by a socioeconomic system that, in Odets' eyes, is destroying the working class. Myron, robbed of his maleness by society (and by a very domineering wife), has been neutered emotionally.

When Hennie turns up pregnant, Bessie has to find a husband for her. To do otherwise would be to jeopardize the family's respectability in its neighborhood, the limit of Bessie' encapsulated world. In order to protect this precious image, which could, in her eyes, easily be shattered, Bessie has no qualms about marrying Hennie off to Sam Feinschreiber, a hapless immigrant who is duped into thinking that Hennie's baby is his.

Both the representatives of the younger generation escape by the play's end, but the escape is not a happy one. Hennie runs off with Moe Axelrod, leaving her husband and child behind. Distant places have been calling. Odets uses the leitmotif of the evening mail plane that flies over the Berger house in the same way that earlier generations of writers used train whistles to suggest escape to some land of heart's desire.

Ralph is given his chance when Jacob, who has made Ralph the beneficiary of his small insurance policy, throws himself from the roof. Because Ralph and Hennie have been robbed of their hope, the escape Odets offers them does not involve their doing anything productive to overcome their problems. The point of the play clearly is that the accommodation each of them finds offers no realistic hope for the future, either theirs or society's.

Impact of Event

Awake and Sing presents a stinging critique of the capitalist society that, Odets suggests, robs people of their dignity, their hope, and their potential. One cannot really call the play "angry"; the hopeless characters are too demoralized to be angry in the way that Odets' taxicab drivers were. Instead, the play touched the inner beings, the social consciences, of large audiences—the affluent audiences that sat in the expensive seats as well as the audiences that squeezed into the dollar seats in the balcony on matinee days.

In writing the play, Odets benefited from the new freedom of language that the 1920's—especially the work of Eugene O'Neill—had brought to American drama. Odets wrote in the vernacular of common people, a vernacular he had learned growing up in a Jewish-American family in Philadelphia and New York. The language of *Awake and Sing* is both lyrical and authentic. It employs the accents, the clichés, and the wisecracks that working-class people use naturally in their daily speech.

Awake and Sing also pointed the way to a drama of the people. Odets' heroes are antiheroes. If their tragedy comes about because of a fall, they do not have far to fall. They are not Oedipuses or Lears or Macbeths. They are, rather, the people next door or around the corner. Their kinship is more to Everyman or to Geoffrey Chaucer's Wife of Bath than to the classical heroes of ancient Greek or Elizabethan tragedy.

Playwrights associated with the Group Theatre—Paul and Claire Sifton, Paul Green, Sidney Kingsley, Maxwell Anderson, John Howard Lawson—wrote generally about the proletariat, about common people rather than about the famous or highly placed. Odets and his compatriots during the 1930's opened new worlds for such later playwrights as Tennessee Williams, Arthur Miller, and William Inge, all of whom drew sustenance from the drama that immediately preceded their emergence as playwrights.

The trend of writing about common people continued in the work of such later playwrights as Lanford Wilson, August Wilson, Tom Stoppard, Edward Albee, and Samuel Beckett. Eugene O'Neill had made strides in this direction during the 1920's with such plays as *Anna Christie* (1921), *The Hairy Ape* (1923), and *Desire Under the*

Elms (1925). Writers such as Odets benefited greatly from O'Neill's daring ventures and built on them in ways that moved American theater forward into unexplored dramatic territory.

An earlier generation in Europe—Gerhart Hauptmann, Anton Chekhov, Maxim Gorky, Henrik Ibsen—had already used drama as a vehicle for advancing proletarian ideas. Those who wrote for the Group Theatre eagerly plugged into the currents these dramatic pioneers had sparked. They made their own advances, which in turn led to a burgeoning of plays about common people in the 1940's and after.

Awake and Sing is a prime example of a play that departs from a blind acceptance of the star system. The counterbalancing of seven significant characters in the play replicates the actual dynamics of the informal human relationships that characterize family existence and interaction. The star system makes protagonists of Shakespearean proportions obligatory; the Group Theatre approach, however, reduces those proportions to dimensions common people understand.

In many respects, *Awake and Sing* was a key element in the advance toward much of the drama in vogue in the late twentieth century. Although its impact is essentially socialistic, *Awake and Sing* is also a significantly democratic play in that it takes seriously the lives of people who, in cultures that are less egalitarian, probably would evoke little interest or attention.

Bibliography

Bentley, Eric, ed. *Thirty Years of Treason: Excerpts from the Hearings Before the House Committee on Un-American Activities.* New York: Viking Press, 1971. It is difficult to understand Odets fully without understanding his reaction to being summoned before the House Committee on Un-American Activities when his national loyalty and that of many others working in theater and film was questioned. Bentley details the facts accurately. For anyone interested in the political ramifications of Odets' work, this book is indispensable.

Brenman-Gibson, Margaret. *Clifford Odets, An American Biography: The Years from 1906 to 1940.* New York: Atheneum, 1981. Although another volume of this comprehensive biography of Odets is promised, this well-documented, thoroughly researched book is a monument in its field. It covers Odets' early life in greater detail than any previous biography has. Its psychoanalytical interpretation of *Awake and Sing* is brilliant and original. Masterful organization of a huge amount of disparate material into a compelling narrative.

Cantor, Harold. *Clifford Odets: Playwright-Poet.* Metuchen, N.J.: Scarecrow Press, 1978. This review of Odets' use of language, especially of dialects, is particularly relevant to *Awake and Sing*, the lyricism and authenticity of which have been widely acknowledged. Chapter 3 is central to the discussion of Odets' use of language. It broaches such areas as his use of the cliché, of wisecracks, and of epigrams.

Clurman, Harold. *The Fervent Years: The Story of the Group Theatre and the Thirties.* New York: Alfred A. Knopf, 1945. This is the quintessential history of the

Group Theatre, out of which much of Odets' work grew. Clurman goes into great detail about the genesis of *Awake and Sing*, which existed under a different title before it was rushed into production in 1935.

Cooperman, Robert. *Clifford Odets: An Annotated Bibliography, 1935-1989.* Metuchen, N.J.: Scarecrow Press, 1990. The bibliographical essay with which this book begins is thoughtfully conceived and well presented. Part 2 of the text provides the most comprehensive list in print of Odets' writing; part 3 contains an extensive bibliography of writing about Odets.

Griffin, Robert J. "On the Lovesongs of Clifford Odets." In *The Thirties: Fiction, Poetry, Drama*, edited by Warren G. French. Deland, Fla.: Everett/Edwards, 1967. Griffin focuses on Odets' two most notable family plays, *Awake and Sing* and *Paradise Lost* (1935). This brief essay is valuable for its comments on Odets' language and on his social outlook as reflected in these plays.

Miller, Gabriel, ed. *Critical Essays on Clifford Odets.* Boston: G. K. Hall, 1991. Presents essays on Odets by such critics as Joseph Wood Krutch, Brooks Atkinson, and John Mason Brown. Also includes interviews with Odets conducted by Michael Mendelsohn, Arthur Wagner, and Armand Aulicino. The book contains three entries specifically on *Awake and Sing*. Moderately easy reading level for the uninitiated.

Weales, Gerald. *Clifford Odets: The Playwright.* Reprint. New York: Methuen, 1985. The best brief critical biography of Odets. Gives valuable insights into each of his major plays, including *Awake and Sing*. Weales relates Odets well to the sociopolitical currents of the period in which he was most productive.

R. Baird Shuman

Cross-References

Stanislavsky Helps to Establish the Moscow Art Theater (1897), p. 1; The Group Theatre Flourishes (1931), p. 874; The Federal Theatre Project Promotes Live Theater (1935), p. 989; *Our Town* Opens on Broadway (1938), p. 1099; Kazan Brings Naturalism to the Stage and Screen (1940's), p. 1164; *A Streetcar Named Desire* Brings Method Acting to the Screen (1951), p. 1487; The Ford Foundation Begins to Fund Nonprofit Theaters (1957), p. 1736.

TEMPLE RECEIVES A SPECIAL ACADEMY AWARD

Category of event: Motion pictures
Time: February, 27, 1935
Locale: Los Angeles, California

Shirley Temple, America's cinema sweetheart and the top box-office draw from 1935 to 1938, received a special miniature Academy Award for her outstanding contribution to the film industry

Principal personages:
SHIRLEY TEMPLE (1928-   ), a child cinema star whose work provided escapist fare during the Depression era
DAMON RUNYON (1884-1946), an American author who wrote the story on which *Little Miss Marker* was based
ADOLPHE MENJOU (1890-1963), the male lead and dramatic foil for Shirley Temple in *Little Miss Marker*
DARRYL F. ZANUCK (1902-1979), a Hollywood producer who hired Shirley Temple for Twentieth Century-Fox Pictures

Summary of Event

Following the stock market crash of 1929, Shirley Temple, a cheery child screen star of the 1930's, quickly rose to fame by capturing the hearts of the moviegoing audience and freeing them momentarily from the worries of joblessness, homelessness, breadlines, bank failures, and other monetary disasters. For her popularity and skill in dance, voice, and acting, she was awarded a special child-size Oscar—the slender gold statuette coveted by film professionals since it was first awarded in 1929—at the 1935 Academy Awards presentation banquet. The event, as usual, was attended by the elite of Hollywood society and agency professionals, and announced by searchlights, press releases, film magazine interviews, and nationwide radio coverage.

Temple, the youngest star to receive an Oscar, earned the admiration of the American Academy of Motion Picture Arts and Sciences chiefly for *Little Miss Marker* (1934), a black-and-white film adapted from a Damon Runyon story, starring Adolphe Menjou, Dorothy Dell, Charles Bickford, Lynne Overman, Frank McGlynn, and Willie Best in addition to Temple. The plot, which reveals how a seedy racetrack gambler adopts a small girl who eventually rescues him from his adversaries, features the predictable Runyon components—cynical underworld figures and appealingly helpless ingenues who employ their charms to soften hardened hearts and bring about a quick rescue. The story concludes with a satisfying reward for good and an appropriate penalty for evil. *Variety* lauded the film for its blend of melodrama and compassion.

Shirley Temple's unprecedented success sprang from a pairing of genes and luck, with a little family push thrown in for good measure. Born in Santa Monica, California, the third child and first daughter of Francis George Temple, a bank officer, and

Gertrude Krieger Temple, Shirley, a sunny, smooth-limbed blonde, enhanced her natural appeal by studying tap dance beginning when she was three years old. Scouted in her kindergarten classroom by an agent from Educational Studios and accompanied on location by her famous stage mother, Shirley began her screen appearances in the "Baby Burlesk" series before advancing to major roles. At the age of five, she bested two hundred candidates for her first cinema part in *Stand Up and Cheer* (1934). Success brought a contract for $1,250 a week, a phenomenal salary for Depression times.

Temple's image—the stereotypical lighthearted, dimple-cheeked minx—evolved from good grooming in little-girl fashions, including patent leather Mary Janes and anklet socks, starchy sailor suit, immaculate gloves, and saucy, cylindrical curls highlighted with a matching bow. A disarmingly bright, poised, mischievous moppet, Temple delighted fans with her self-confident, insouciant air. Hordes of worshipers and Temple look-alikes followed her wherever she appeared, at airports, the circus, beaches, or visits to department store Santa Clauses. Notables such as Albert Einstein, J. Edgar Hoover, and President Franklin D. and Eleanor Roosevelt counted her among their personal favorites; fans the world over recognized her at once by her characteristically bumptuous posturing and mugging and Kewpie-doll smile.

The epitome of little-girl sweetness, Temple parlayed her charms into success by maximizing talent, concentration, and hard work. She could mimic her contemporaries, including Fred Astaire and Ginger Rogers, and match the complicated dance routines of veteran hoofer Bill "Bojangles" Robinson. She balanced a variety of male costars, from Randolph Scott, Joseph Cotten, Cary Grant, and Buddy Ebsen to Ronald Reagan. Even though the plots of her films provided meager challenges to a thinking audience, much to the moviemakers' benefit, the rush to see Temple singing, dancing, and mugging in her costume-rich scenarios kept theater lines long.

Eager to make the most of their pint-sized box-office wonder during a period when money for film tickets was growing scarce, the studios moved swiftly to exploit every moment of her childhood. Two subsequent 1934 films, *Now and Forever*, a Paramount production starring Gary Cooper and Carole Lombard, and *Stand Up and Cheer*, with James Dunn, Nigel Bruce, and Stepin Fetchit, influenced her Academy Award nomination. The former, a likable mix of thrills and comedy, as was *Little Miss Marker*, depicts the power of a small child to transform her father, a jewel thief, and his hard-boiled mistress. *Now and Forever* received high marks from both the *New York Post* and *Variety*. In contrast, *Stand Up and Cheer*, a Fox production about a child performer who helps the fictional U.S. secretary of amusement to boost the country's Depression-racked spirits, received less favorable press because of its contrived plot. The film redeemed itself primarily through audience reaction to the engagingly talented, cherubic six-year-old star.

Impact of Event

The Shirley Temple phenomenon peaked in 1939, when the child lost her rounded cuteness and entered adolescence. Up until that point, she had been a major moneymaker for the studios. In her biography, she noted bitterly the commerciality of her success and how she was marketed like a grocery-store commodity. Signed by Darryl F. Zanuck to a Twentieth Century-Fox contract and insured by Lloyd's of London, Temple lived in a special on-site four-room cottage, complete with rabbit hutch, picket fence, and rope swing. To restrict the public's access to her, she was tutored privately. In the 1940's, returned to a semblance of normalcy, she attended the Westlake School for Girls, from which she was graduated at the age of seventeen. She contributed greatly in her childhood to film history, with forty film and fifty television productions, including hits such as *Baby Take a Bow* (1934), *Bright Eyes* (1934), *Curly Top* (1935), *The Little Colonel* (1935), *Poor Little Rich Girl* (1936), *Wee Willie Winkie* (1937), *Heidi* (1937), *Rebecca of Sunnybrook Farm* (1938), *The Little Princess* (1939), and *The Blue Bird* (1940).

In her teens, Temple, taller but unmistakably dimpled and winsome, continued to please faithful fans. Her teen and post-teen roles in *Since You Went Away* (1944), *Kiss and Tell* (1945), *The Bachelor and the Bobby-Soxer* (1947), *That Hagen Girl* (1947), *Fort Apache* (1948), and *A Kiss for Corliss* (1959) received less adulation, primarily because they could not play on the cuteness of childhood. About the time that Temple met John Agar, a soldier turned actor whom she married to relieve the loneliness and isolation engendered by too much fame, the studio, searching for a replacement child star, considered Sybil Jason, Gigi Perreau, and others. Among the most successful post-Temple child stars were Margaret O'Brien, who premiered at the age of four in *Babes in Arms* (1939) and won an honorary Oscar in 1944, and Natalie Wood, who debuted at the age of eight in *Tomorrow Is Forever* (1946). Never as appealing as Shirley Temple, Wood earned lasting fame in the Christmas classic *Miracle on Thirty-fourth Street* (1947), then grew more voluptuous and appealing to cinema audiences. Her later successes included *Splendor in the Grass* (1961), *West Side Story* (1961) and *Marjorie Morningstar* (1958).

Some male child stars met with equally long-lived popularity. Jackie Cooper scored with *The Champ* (1931) and *Skippy* (1931), for which he was nominated for an Academy Award for best actor. A stream of other cute-child scenarios brought him work in *Sooky* (1931), *Donovan's Kid* (1931), and *Divorce in the Family* (1932). Along with a coterie of children who composed the *Our Gang* cast, he made a notable effort that resulted in years of reruns. Temple certainly influenced, through her success, the trend toward child-oriented films.

An extended film career is not a part of the Shirley Temple legend. After her divorce from Agar, Temple, already the mother of a daughter, suffered intense depression. Following a relaxing vacation in Hawaii, she met businessman Charles Alden Black, son of a wealthy family, whose emotional maturity provided the stability she needed at the nadir of her young womanhood. After their marriage, she bore a son and a second daughter, settled south of San Francisco, and involved herself in volunteerism for the National Wildlife Federation and the National Multiple Sclerosis Society. At one point, she served as receptionist in a children's orthopedics hospital.

From local activism, she moved into politics. To maintain a dignified professional image, she was forced to transcend the public's image of a dimpled darling in frills and tap shoes. In 1967, she failed to unseat Pete McCloskey in a bid for a seat in the U.S. House of Representatives, but from 1974 to 1976 she held the ambassadorship to Ghana. Her return to the public eye brought new audiences of children to her old films, which had fallen into neglect. Hollywood, capitalizing on her late-in-life achievements, returned the spotlight to her. Honored at the fifty-seventh annual Academy Awards presentation ceremony, on March 25, 1985, Shirley Temple Black received a full-sized Oscar to replace the miniature version she accepted in 1935. To recapture the mystique of the toddler star, organizers of the ceremony ran clips of her greatest films. Three years later, the documentary *Going Hollywood: The War Years* received archival footage from her canon in a montage of films from the World War II era.

Recovered from breast cancer in 1989, Shirley Temple Black was named ambassador to Czechoslovakia. She studied in an immersion language course to expedite negotiations with President Gustav Husák, to whom she presented her credentials in his native tongue. She took particular pride in the nation's bloodless overthrow of an oppressive communist regime. As an outspoken supporter of the human rights that communism had violated, she remains difficult to typify as liberal or conservative, Democrat or Republican, but periodically she has been considered as a vice-presidential candidate or a cabinet post nominee.

Looking back on these honors, appointments, and opportunities, Shirley Temple Black has acknowledged that her film career, although it has little connection with her adult interests and capabilities, provided the requisite name recognition to people in power such as President George Bush, who nominated her for the ambassadorship to Czechoslovakia. Her prior fame opened possibilities to become involved with research programs on acquired immune deficiency syndrome (AIDS), assistance for homeless and disabled people, the campaign to ratify the Equal Rights Amendment, and the prochoice movement. In her 1988 autobiography, *Child Star,* she unleashed adult vengeance on Hollywood's corrupt star system, which exploited her in childhood, menaced her innocence, and enriched a cadre of opportunists, many of whom borrowed money for private use that they never repaid.

At her Woodside, California, residence, Shirley juxtaposed Ghanaian and Czech treasures alongside her Oscars. Still linked to fans by personal replies to some of their letters, she often dissuades parents and children who considered attempts to emulate her stardom. In her adult opinion, the vastly popular child prodigy of the 1930's enjoyed as normal a childhood as possible yet suffered a host of insecurities and lapses that led to divorce and prolonged despair. Her three children—Susan Black Falaschi, a prominent journalist and science-fiction writer; Charles, Jr., at one time a staff member of the Department of Commerce; and Lori, a photographer and New Wave musician—have avoided the glittering path of the film industry and chosen other fields in which to succeed.

Bibliography

Bell, Joseph N. "Shirley Temple: Her Movies, Her Life." *Good Housekeeping* 192

(February, 1981): 114-115, 185-190. A thorough biographical article, complete with seventeen photographs of her film career, featuring shots of costars Buddy Ebsen, Charles Farrell, James Dunn, and the most famous, Bill "Bojangles" Robinson, with whom she tap-danced and sang. The chronology covers its subject's bout with breast cancer, her role as first U.S. chief of protocol, and her service as ambassador to Ghana and Czechoslovakia.

Haskins, James. *Shirley Temple Black: Actress to Ambassador.* New York: Penguin, 1988. This illustrated overview carries Black's career from childhood to her appointment as U.S. ambassador to Ghana. Aimed at the elementary school market, this book summarizes information for readers from grades two through seven.

Michael, Paul. *The Academy Awards: A Pictorial History.* Rev. ed. New York: Crown, 1968. A chronological compendium of award details covering ceremonies from 1927 to 1967. The terse, cramped text, composed chiefly of isolated details, is accompanied by cinematic stills with cutlines. An "Index of Losers" and a meager index of titles and winners conclude the work.

Osborne, Robert. *Sixty Years of the Oscar.* New York: Abbeville Press, 1989. A thorough listing of Academy Award winners from the inception of the Oscar to 1987. Complete with full-color cinematic stills and cutlines plus color dust jackets from adapted novels and plays, this overview of the Oscar demands respect from historians, researchers, and serious cinema fans.

Temple, Shirley. *Child Star.* New York: McGraw-Hill, 1988. A definitive illustrated autobiography describing Temple's family, early training in dance and music, introduction into filmdom from kindergarten, starring film roles, and adolescent screen roles, along with critical opinions of her cinematic talents. Additional information details her eclipse in adolescence and failed marriage to John Agar. A worthy study for the cinema buff or student of Hollywood history.

Windeler, Robert. *The Films of Shirley Temple.* Secaucus, N.J.: Citadel Press, 1978. A critique of Temple's screen career, this overview, available in an illustrated paperback version from Citadel Press in 1983, focuses on information pertinent to cinema history and critical commentary on the child film genre. Well worth reading for detailed history.

Yorkshire, Heidi. "Shirley Temple Black Sets the Record Straight." *McCall's* 116 (March, 1989): 88-92. A commentary describing Temple's adult career and her decision to write *Child Star*, an autobiography describing the seamier side of cinema life from a child's point of view.

Mary Ellen Snodgrass

Cross-References

Pickford Becomes "America's Sweetheart" (1909), p. 224; The First Academy Awards Honor Film Achievement (1929), p. 799; Hollywood Enters Its Golden Age (1930's), p. 822; The Classic Screwball Comedy Reaches Its Height in Popularity (1934), p. 951; The Classic *The Wizard of Oz* Opens (1939), p. 1109.

GERSHWIN'S *PORGY AND BESS* OPENS IN NEW YORK

Categories of event: Theater and music
Time: October 10, 1935
Locale: New York, New York

George Gershwin permanently blurred the distinction between musical theater and opera with Porgy and Bess *and opened the door to other ambitious experiments in form*

Principal personages:
GEORGE GERSHWIN (1898-1937), a composer who worked in jazz, classical, and show music
IRA GERSHWIN (1896-1983), George's brother, a lyricist who showed a unique feeling for and a determined loyalty to his brother's work
DuBOSE HEYWARD (1885-1940), a poet and playwright who originated the story of *Porgy and Bess* and worked on its various incarnations
ROBERT BREEN (1909-1990), a former director of the American National Theatre and Academy, who brought *Porgy and Bess* to international acclaim

Summary of Event

On the night of October 10, 1935, after a brief overture, the curtain rose at the Alvin Theater in New York City. The audience heard a solo soprano voice sing a plaintive lullaby, "Summertime." From there, the joys, sorrows, laughter, and tears of *Porgy and Bess* cascaded upon the audience. This opening, which seems so elegant and has seemed so right since 1935, was not the first choice. Like much else in musical theater, the opening went through drastic changes. Prior to the world premiere on September 30 in Boston, it was planned that *Porgy and Bess* would open with a black piano player playing jazz in a smoky dance hall. The change—eliminating the piano player and opening with the lullaby—was based purely on economy. The dance hall would have required another set. Such choices are part of the collaboration common in musical theater, and the story of *Porgy and Bess* is a story of collaboration.

Often referred to as George Gershwin's *Porgy and Bess*, the story about the crippled Porgy and his woman, Bess, had a genesis that was quite removed from the sophisticated composer. In 1924, an insurance salesman named DuBose Heyward decided to become a full-time writer. He had written some poetry as a hobby and had become involved in a summer writers' colony. Heyward set out to write a novel, and, as a subject, he chose the people of the poor black section of his native Charleston, South Carolina. Specifically, Heyward used as inspiration a crippled man named Sammy Smalls who moved about the poorer sections of Charleston in a cart pulled by a particularly pungent goat. Heyward read a short article in the Charleston *News and Courier* detailing Smalls's arrest for aggravated assault and attempted escape on his cart. Another inspiration was an area of Charleston called "Cabbage Row." It was an area of decay, with a courtyard fronted by vegetable stands. It was a place of poverty, crowds, and numerous calls to the police. Heyward passed it every day as he went to work. In his mind, he transformed it into "Catfish Row."

Heyward took these ideas with him to the MacDowell Colony, where he met and married a playwright named Dorothy Kuhns. He worked on his novel while she worked on plays and mysteries. Heyward's main character was first called Porgo. Like Smalls, he made his way on a cart pulled by a goat. Dorothy immediately saw dramatic potential in the unfinished manuscript, but Heyward was hesitant. He wanted to concentrate on his work as a novel. In addition, the mid-1920's was not a time to put a serious treatment of African Americans on the Broadway stage.

The novel was completed in 1925, renamed *Porgy*, and published to a very positive response. In very little time, the former insurance salesman became a literary celebrity. Cecil B. DeMille expressed interest in filming the novel for a group called the Producers Distributing Corporation, with Paul Robeson considered for the lead. Finally, however, the business minds at the corporation ended the project because it would not sell in the South.

Others had higher hopes for Heyward's novel. Dorothy Heyward was still at work, secretly, on a dramatic treatment. In the late summer of 1926, Heyward received a letter from George Gershwin indicating interest in and excitement about the possibility of turning *Porgy* into an opera. DuBose Heyward may have been unfamiliar to George Gershwin, but Gershwin was very familiar to Heyward. By 1926, Gershwin's name was quite well known.

Because he was the son of immigrant Jews, George Gershwin's name had changed several times. George began as Jacob. His elder brother went from Israel to Isadore to Ira. Their last name was Gershovitz in Russia and then became Gershvin, Gershwine, and, finally, Gershwin. George began piano lessons at the age of twelve and was playing in bars at fifteen. Soon, while working for a music publishing house, George became familiar with popular music and show music. By 1916, he had written a song for a revue. In 1919, Broadway saw the first George Gershwin musical, *La La Lucille*. Previously in that year, Al Jolson had sung Gershwin's song "Swanee" in *Sinbad*.

For the 1922 edition of *George White's Scandals*, Gershwin and Buddy DeSylva wrote a twenty-minute "jazz opera" called *Blue Monday*. It dealt with infidelity among African Americans, although the parts were played by white actors in blackface. After opening night, the piece was cut from the show, but it clearly indicated Gershwin's future work with *Porgy*. In 1924, Gershwin made important strides in several directions. Paul Whiteman, the orchestra conductor for *Blue Monday*, had admired the work and approached Gershwin with the idea of composing and performing a serious work using jazz idioms. The result was "Rhapsody in Blue." Later that year, Gershwin opened *Lady, Be Good!* on Broadway. This was his first collaboration with his brother, Ira.

George had worked with other lyricists and he would work with others in the future. Ira also had worked with other composers and he would work with more as well, but there was something special about the brothers working together. Their other shows included *Girl Crazy* (1930), *Strike Up the Band* (1930), and the Pulitzer Prize-winning *Of Thee I Sing* (1931), the first musical to win that award.

This was the reputation George Gershwin had started to build when he wrote to DuBose Heyward about turning *Porgy* into an opera. As Heyward considered a partnership with the great Gershwin, Dorothy Heyward confessed that she had been writing a dramatic version of *Porgy*. Both Heywards were convinced that the issue was a choice between a play or an opera. It did not occur to either that they could have both. Heyward was drawn to his wife's work not only out of loyalty but also because it was good. He was intrigued by how well she was able to make the story work on stage. Heyward told Gershwin of his decision, assuming that it would put an end to the opera. Gershwin's greater theater experience led him to believe that the two options were not mutually exclusive. In fact, Gershwin realized that working from a play would provide a needed structure.

With this news, the Heywards set to work revising the first draft. DuBose was able to make the unique contribution of accurate dialect. Dorothy, however, made the key suggestion of changing the novel's ending to show that Porgy's spirit had not been crushed. The play was produced by the Theatre Guild in October, 1927, under the direction of Rouben Mamoulian. It was a hit and only served to increase Gershwin's determination to create an opera from the material.

Other proposals were made, including a musical by Jerome Kern and Oscar Hammerstein II, to feature Al Jolson in blackface. By 1933, Heyward and Gershwin were committed contractually to the project. George wrote the music, and both Heyward and Ira Gershwin created lyrics. They had very different styles of working. According to Ira, it took the poet that Heyward was to create "Summertime," but when it came to up-tempo, rhythmic songs such as "It Ain't Necessarily So," Ira Gershwin would step in. Although he could not read music, he would listen to the melody his brother created and work from there. In at least one instance, the three collaborated. It was agreed that Porgy needed a happy song. George played a happy melody for the two lyricists. Ira immediately suggested the line "I got plenty o' nuthin', and nuthin's plenty for me." Heyward took that line and the music and finished the song.

Rouben Mamoulian, by this time a noted film director in Hollywood, was brought back to direct the opera, once again produced by the Theatre Guild. By the time of the much anticipated Boston premiere on June 24, 1935, Gershwin had made several cuts in the score. At the suggestion of the producers and the director, he made several more as the show was prepared for its New York opening. Following the New York opening on October 10, 1935, the reviews and the public response were mixed. Many realized the genius of each of the collaborators, but others were unsure as to exactly what had been created. George Gershwin was certain that this was his stage masterpiece. As fate would have it, it was his last major work for the stage. He and his brother worked on several films following *Porgy and Bess* and then, in 1937, he died of a brain tumor.

Impact of Event

Besides the obvious contributions of Gershwin's melodies and the story of Porgy told by Heyward and Ira Gershwin, the production of *Porgy and Bess* made several other unique contributions to music and theater. First was the use of black actors on stage. Clearly this was not the first time African Americans had been on stage; it was not even the first time black actors had serious singing roles on stage. *Show Boat,* by Jerome Kern and Oscar Hammerstein II, had in 1927 featured a character named Joe who sang "Ol' Man River." The original stage version of *Porgy* featured serious black actors. For the most part, however, black actors in Broadway musicals were in revues such as *Shuffle Along* (1921) and *From Dixie to Broadway* (1924).

Lack of experienced black actors made casting a challenge, and it meant that the performers who eventually were hired were in many cases in need of coaching. The original Porgy, Todd Duncan, was a music teacher from Washington, D.C. Anne Brown (Bess) and Ruby Elzy (Serena) were both graduates of Juilliard. A vaudeville performer, John W. Bubbles, was hired to play Sportin' Life. The Eva Jessye Choir, a black touring choir, was added to the chorus. As is the case with most productions that open and then tour, *Porgy and Bess* went through many cast changes over the years. It afforded unique opportunities for many black performers.

In the early 1950's, Robert Breen, the former general director of the American National Theatre and Academy, began a crusade to revive *Porgy and Bess* and tour it worldwide. Over the next seven years, the show toured with various casts to London, Italy, Germany, and the Soviet Union. It was the first American theatrical production to play in the Soviet Union since the 1917 revolution. There was some hesitation about a production there, as it might communicate a false impression to audiences about how black people lived and acted in America. Another view was that *Porgy and Bess* showcased members of a minority who were gifted artists and should be given the opportunity to share their gifts. That view won out. Otto Preminger directed a 1959 film version starring Sidney Poitier and Dorothy Dandridge.

A contradiction existed concerning the show itself. Some critics thought it was an opera. Others were sure it was a Broadway musical. The arguments are clear. It appeared first on the Broadway stage, though it became part of the repertoire of several leading opera companies. It was composed by a "popular" composer, and there are "standard" songs in the score. At the same time, this "popular" composer did work in the classical arena, and the score is filled with recitatives and choruses. *Porgy and Bess* does not have the characters usually found in opera. This is basically the same argument used in the 1950's concerning *Death of a Salesman's* status as a tragedy.

The debate concerning classification of *Porgy and Bess* becomes a question of attitude. Although *Porgy and Bess* may not be populated with the usual characters of opera, it certainly has the characteristics. Technically, it has elements of a sung-through score, grand passions, and tragedy. For some, the fact that it is in English— American English, no less—precludes it from consideration as an opera. Others perceive its blending of forms between Broadway and the opera as leading to Frank

Loesser's *Most Happy Fella* (1956), Tim Rice and Andrew Lloyd Webber's *Jesus Christ Superstar* (1971) and *Evita* (1979), and *Les Misérables* (1987). Whether George Gershwin wrote an opera therefore is debatable; he certainly wrote a great work of art that has led to other great works.

Bibliography

Alpert, Hollis. *The Life and Times of Porgy and Bess.* New York: Alfred A. Knopf, 1990. An exceptional study of the show. Alpert uses research and interviews to re-create the experience, going from the newspaper article that gave Heyward his idea to the 1959 film. Alpert is as interested in the art as in the business. The pictures and the summary of the actual show make this useful for the layperson as well as the scholar.

Engel, Lehman. *Words with Music.* New York: Macmillan, 1972. A serious look at the needs and problems of the libretto in the musical theater. Engel's background as a conductor and theorist of the musical makes his opinions especially important. Engel also includes a helpful discussion of opera and the differences between the opera and the musical. An essential book for serious study of the musical.

Laufe, Abe. *Broadway's Greatest Musicals.* New York: Funk & Wagnalls, 1977. A standard history, one of the usual places to start. Laufe gives a good, if basic, chronological study of the growth of musical theater. The pictures are quite good, and he tells the story well. Not a great deal of attention is paid to *Porgy and Bess*, but a sense of the time and Gershwin's other work comes across.

Smith, Cecil, and Glenn Litton. *Musical Comedy in America.* New York: Theatre Arts Books, 1981. An excellent overall history. The pictures are adequate, and the text is thorough and literate. Smith and Litton go beyond the expected chronology and discuss technique. Smith, who wrote the earlier section, is not willing to take a stand on the opera/musical debate concerning *Porgy and Bess* but explains the issues well.

Wilk, Max. *They're Playing Our Song.* Kingsport, Tenn.: Kingsport Press, 1973. A book for popular use, though not much help in research. The cover indicates a chapter on George Gershwin that does not exist, but there is a chapter on Ira. The material is basic and conversational. This is more of a personality study, good for background.

William B. Kennedy

Cross-References

Gershwin's *Rhapsody in Blue* Premieres in New York (1924), p. 598; *Show Boat* Introduces American Musical Theater (1927), p. 745; *Hallelujah* Is the First Important Black Musical (1929), p. 772; *Jesus Christ Superstar* Establishes the Rock Opera (1971), p. 2254; *The Wiz* Brings African-American Talent to Broadway (1975), p. 2334.

PROUVÉ PIONEERS THE PREFABRICATION OF BUILDINGS

Category of event: Architecture
Time: The late 1930's
Locale: France

Jean Prouvé initiated and refined the total prefabrication of homes and a variety of other structures in an effort to bring building into the industrial age

> *Principal personages:*
> JEAN PROUVÉ (1901-1984), a metal craftsman who pioneered the total art of architectural prefabrication
> WALTER GROPIUS (1883-1969), one of the twentieth century's great architects, leader of the Bauhaus School, and an influence on Prouvé
> LE CORBUSIER (CHARLES-ÉDOUARD JEANNERET, 1887-1965), an architect with whom Prouvé collaborated
> TONY GARNIER (1869-1948), another architect who worked with Prouvé
> EUGÈNE ELIE BEAUDOUIN (1898-   ), one of many architects who employed Prouvé's architectural products
> MARCEL LODS (1891-1978), one of Prouvé's architect collaborators
> BERNARD ZEHRFUSS (1911-   ), a leading architect who worked with Prouvé

Summary of Event

In 1937, near Buc, a French village too small to appear in atlases, construction was completed on the Roland Garros Aeroclub. Almost the entire building, including floors, walls, ramp, and roof—indeed, all the structure's pressed-metal components—were prefabricated. Dismantled by the Germans a few years later during World War II, the Aeroclub nevertheless has subsequently been identified by architectural historians as one of the twentieth century's most interesting and important buildings. Although the Aeroclub was less influential than Antonio Gaudí's Casa Milá flats, Le Corbusier's Villa Savoye, or Alvar Aalto's Villa Mairea, it was in many respects more innovative than any of these architectural milestones. So, too, was another structure built in 1938 in the Paris suburb of Clichy, the Maison du Peuple, a large market and auditorium with floors, walls, and a roof that moved electrically—all within an envelope of stressed-skin panels separated by coil springs. The Maison du Peuple was another novel building that was industrially designed and industrially produced. Moreover, while design of the Aeroclub and the Maison du Peuple engaged the talents of the same two notable architects, Eugène Beaudoiun and Marcel Lods, the buildings' distinctive characters were as much the work of a remarkable metal craftsman, engineer, and self-taught French architect named Jean Prouvé.

By 1946, barely a decade after erection of the Aeroclub, Prouvé was pioneering not only the total prefabrication of industrial and public buildings but—of equal importance from his perspective—the prefabrication of entire houses and housing units. Prouvé believed that neither architects nor builders had adequately availed themselves of industrialized materials or techniques and had therefore failed to recognize the efficiencies and potential afforded by an industrial age. Prouvé's convictions made him one of the leaders of the modern movement in building technology.

The son of Victor Prouvé, a painter prominent in the decorative arts that flourished in Nancy (France) around 1900, Jean was born in Paris in 1901. Nancy—the home to which the Prouvés soon returned—was a manufacturing center lying at the heart of an iron-mining region with major ironware and steel industries. Consequently, after his preliminary education, the young Prouvé, under the aegis of master craftsmen in Paris, trained from 1916 to 1923 as a blacksmith and metal worker. Back in Nancy by 1924, he married and, as a qualified engineer, founded his own metal-fittings and furniture establishment. Like many of the century's famed and formally educated architects such as Walter Gropius, Le Corbusier, Alvar Aalto, Marcel Breuer, and Ludwig Mies van der Rohe, Prouvé came to an understanding of architecture early in his career through the design and manufacture of furnishings.

He rapidly became a master of modern building materials, and his designs and the works of his establishment were avidly sought by the greatest architects. In the early 1930's, for example, Prouvé collaborated with Tony Garnier, producing operating theaters and sliding windows for a Lyon hospital and doors, partitions, and furniture for the Boulogne-Billancourt town hall. In the mid-1930's, too, Prouvé began more than thirty years of intermittent collaboration with Le Corbusier. Prouvé entered this association modestly with the design of a portable toilet for the Paris World's Fair. In the ensuing years, he provided such design and building components as the suspended ceilings for Le Corbusier's Unité d'Habitation as well as the staircases, kitchens, and furnishings for the Cité Radieuse, both major projects of Le Corbusier in Marseille. Over the years, Prouvé did similar business with other notable French architects who had international repute, including Bernard Zehrfuss and Robert Mallet-Stevens. His work was also solicited by leading corporations, banks, hospitals, research institutions, schools, oil companies, hotels, subway systems, and cinema and television chains, as well as by the governments of France and many other European and African nations.

Prouvé's industrialized design and production of prefabricated housing was the result of several factors. First, his own mastery of modern building technology and materials, in addition to his familiarity with the manufacture and installation of nearly every modern structural component, brilliantly equipped him to carry his work into the production of entire dwelling and structural units. Second, France's preparations for and engagement in World War II created huge demands for swiftly constructed housing. Third, Prouvé, along with the great architects with whom he collaborated, believed that the industrialized production of housing more honestly reflected the efficiency, character, and potential of an industrial era than did traditional design.

Prouvé's first experiment with full prefabrication was the creation of eight hundred units in Lorraine for the Ministry of Reconstruction and Town Planning, a project closely followed by the construction of a house in Vesoul; both projects took place in 1944, while Prouvé still worked with the French Resistance. Pressures for housing increased at war's end, and his work began maturing with construction of Nancy's Cité Universitaire student quarters. The following year, he produced the fully prefabricated Portico House for his own workshop as well as boarding facilities for the Apprenticeship Glassworks Center and a more modest private home in Carnac. In 1948, he continued his prefabrication for the ministry, producing demonstration houses in four French towns. In 1949, serving as architect himself, he prefabricated so-called Metropole and Coque housing, again for the ministry, in Meudon. These were successful ventures, and he repeated construction of the Metropole houses in both Oran and Algiers for local utility companies. Until 1976, Prouvé averaged one commission on fully prefabricated structures per year. Always disdainful of the conservatism of professional architects and builders (not to mention the general public), Prouvé had difficulties with industrialized housing. As a consequence, he continued earning much of his living by supplying others with his superb prefabricated components and furnishings, which always spoke by their excellence of the aesthetic and economic possibilities of industrialized building.

Impact of Event

By the early twentieth century, prefabrication was an old idea and a frequently utilized construction technique. Many examples existed before Prouvé's work began. The prefabrication of Venetian galleys for Venice's great commercial fleet functioned effectively throughout the fifteenth century. Similarly, on the American and Canadian frontiers during the late nineteenth century, whole towns of individual homes and shops were preassembled, transported westward, and assembled again. More notably, London's spectacular Crystal Palace of 1850—one of the century's architectural landmarks—was premanufactured and, amazingly, assembled within a few days. Quite commonly by the 1880's, whole building façades of premanufactured cast-iron distinguished businesses on American Main Streets.

Until the twentieth century, however, prefabrication generally was definable as the manufacture and assembly of varied building components, not as the design and manufacture of industrialized structures that represented complete industrial products in themselves. For influential schools of architecture such as Germany's Bauhaus as well as for precedent-breaking architects—Gaudí, Garnier, or Le Corbusier, for example—the very objective of designs was to bring building, and life-styles, into the machine age. These innovators sought to explore and experiment with the qualities (and economies) of modern construction materials such as concrete, steel, aluminum, glass, and plastics and envisioned the "machining" of all sorts of structures. Gropius, for years the leader of the Bauhaus, was profoundly interested in this form of prefabrication; in the early 1930's, before Prouvé's industrialized structures had appeared, Gropius had contracted with the Hirsch Copper Company (a German firm) to manufacture scores of company houses. A few years later, he effected an identical arrangement with another German firm, though in each instance the materials to be employed were largely traditional ones such as wood. Undertakings like these united Gropius, Garnier, and Le Corbusier, among others, in mutual influences and collaborative enterprises.

In the United States, R. Buckminster Fuller had begun experiments with manufactured housing and other buildings in an attempt to provide light, sturdy structures that were easy to erect and that used not only modern materials such as steel, prestressed concrete, and aluminum but also paperboard, plywood, and bamboo. It was not until 1946, however, that Fuller succeeded in completing his famed Dymaxion House and geodesic domes. These and similar twentieth century experiments, though undeniably impressive, were nevertheless architectural "sports" developed beyond the pale of architecture's everyday business of building design and construction.

The steady impetus toward industrialized building came not only from the aesthetics and creative curiosities of a handful of architects but was also stimulated by the immense backlog of housing created by two world wars. In France and the rest of Europe, incentive stemmed more urgently from the requirements of national reconstruction and from the increasing intervention of governments in all areas of national life. Each of these circumstances directly informed Prouvé's expectations and experiments.

Prouvé's work and its analogues had profound consequences in the second half of the twentieth century. The testimonials to his influence stand as familiar parts of urbanized landscapes around the developed world. For industrialized building as a type of architecture, Prouvé set singular and exemplary standards. His sensitivity to the capacities and possibilities of materials and machines opened architects' eyes to new structural vistas for individual homes, housing complexes, towns, offices, and schools.

Nevertheless, it is more common to witness the drab, monotonous expanses of wartime prefabrications, of construction camps, and trailer towns, than it is—as Prouvé complained before his death—to know the whereabouts of factories that produce houses much as other types of factories mass-produce automobiles. Acknowledging by the 1980's that both the principles and practice of what he meant by "prefabrication" had taken root, Prouvé was still aware of the shortfall of his expectations. Architects, he advised, needed to be intimate parts of manufacturing, which as yet they were not. Too much industrialized building, he thought, unnecessarily continued employing new materials in traditional ways—a fault of both architects and builders. Having designed and manufactured his own products as if nothing had ever been built before, he deplored adaptations of buildings to existing machine processes, many of which he disdained. The general approbation for his industrialized pressed-metal structures—including his exhibition village, at Michel-sur-Orge, his Pierrelatte workshop for France's atomic energy workers, and his Fontainebleau holiday resort for Air France, all built in the 1960's—continue to goad architects and builders out of the past in which he believed them to be confined.

Bibliography

"Jean Prouvé." *Architecture* 2, nos. 11-12 (December, 1954). A solid appraisal of Prouvé's aims and contributions even before the peak of his public exposure and professional acclaim. Well-written professional assessments that are easy to read and invaluable. Photos and designs. Few notes, but plenty of references to those with whom Prouvé collaborated. Unfortunately, this journal can be hard to find.

Lavedan, Pierre. *French Architecture.* London: Scholar Press, 1971. A readable, scholarly survey that places Prouvé in a national setting and gives readers an understanding of just how innovative he and other modernists have been. A few notes, photos, bibliography, and index. Very useful.

Newton, Nigel. "Prouvé: Modern Movement Pioneer." *Building Design* 30 (March, 1984): 175-178. Essentially a tribute to Prouvé shortly after his death. Useful, but generally available only in major libraries. Gives Prouvé his due and touches on his amazingly brilliant collaborations. No scholarly appendages; some photos.

Prouvé, Jean. *Jean Prouvé: Prefabrication, Structures, and Elements.* Edited by Benedikt Huber and Jean-Claude Steinegger. Translated by Alexander Lieven. New York: Praeger, 1971. One of the few nonencyclopedia treatments of the prefabrication of buildings and of Prouvé's role in the field. Technical terms, but easy to read. Prouvé is dealt with appreciatively and in context. Plates, notes, bibliography, and index. Invaluable considering that most material on Prouvé and his contributions is in difficult-to-get French, English, and Italian architectural journals.

"The Work of Jean Prouvé." *Architectural Design* 33 (1963): 511-525. Complements the few extensive treatments of the architect's work available in English. Solidly professional and laudatory. Published while Prouvé was at the top of his form and attracting international attention and honors. Photos, but few other scholarly appendages.

Clifton K. Yearley

Cross-References

Gaudí Completes the Casa Milá Apartment House in Barcelona (1910), p. 257; German Artists Found the Bauhaus (1919), p. 463; Cranbrook Academy Begins a History of Design Excellence (1925), p. 610; Le Corbusier's Villa Savoye Redefines Architecture (1931), p. 869; Aalto Designs Villa Mairea (1937), p. 1067; Fuller's First Industrial Geodesic Dome Is Erected (1953), p. 1579; Expo 67 Presents Innovative Architectural Concepts (1967), p. 2081.

THE DIARY OF A COUNTRY PRIEST INSPIRES READERS

Category of event: Literature
Time: 1936
Locale: Europe and the United States

*While many people were turning in despair to mass political movements and cha-
rismatic leaders, Georges Bernanos' story of an unprepossessing man who becomes
a vehicle for God's grace suggested that the answer lay elsewhere*

Principal personage:
GEORGES BERNANOS (1888-1948), a French novelist who wrote a powerful story about a young French village priest whose struggles to find
grace in his village provided hope to many readers caught in the despair of the Depression

Summary of Event

George Bernanos' *Journal d'un curé de campagne* (1936; *The Diary of a Country
Priest*), the winner of France's Femina Prize and the Grand Prix of the Académie
Française, became available in English translation in October, 1937. The book had
been a great success in France, the author's native country (though he wrote the
work while living in Spain), but its focus on a Catholic priest's struggles was more
problematic in America. Could a literary work that sought to address the great problems of society through a Roman Catholic cleric's eyes speak to a nation that had,
within the past decade, defeated a Democratic candidate for president largely because of his membership in the Catholic church?

The Catholic press in America celebrated the work as emphatically as the French
had. Bernanos' most valuable praise came from John Kenneth Merton, writing for
the lay Catholic weekly *Commonweal*. Merton characterized the work as a book
"unusually touching and beautiful, [which] despite its exquisite restraint, makes the
reader breathless with intensity." He called some of the characters "beautiful" and
extolled the protagonist's "spirit of heroism that is so perfect as not to be conscious
of itself." *The Diary of a Country Priest* was, in Merton's view, "a remarkable book,
one written with beautiful art, full of a searching and delicate psychology, and revealing a simplicity so crystalline and a courage so humble as to lift what might have
been a sordid tragedy to heroic heights."

What, though, of the American literary world outside the Catholic orbit? Would it
too see the beauty of the work? *The New York Times* trumpeted the publication with
a glowing review on the front page of its book review section, in which Katherine
Woods pronounced the novel to be a work of "deep, subtle and singularly encom-
passing art" likely to "fill a quite definite place in the interest of readers here."
Woods celebrated the work's "greatness as creative art" and called it a "strange and
sad, yet beautiful and triumphant, story." Other publications, too, welcomed the

work with high praise and suggested its import for the American audience.

Yet the simplicity so often cited as the principal source of *The Diary of a Country Priest*'s value, when coupled with the Catholic focus, mitigated against the book's success in the literary market. The book has little action and no excitement. Even John Merton had admitted that the work had "very little" plot "in the ordinary sense." The novel consequently never made it to the best-seller list, and it subsequently fell into relative obscurity. Yet it has remained available in English translation for more than fifty years and has continued to draw praise from those who read it even decades after its initial publication.

What little action the novel contains takes place in an obscure French village. The protagonist is a young, frail, and dying Roman Catholic priest who is largely incapable of inspiring those around him and whose greatest attribute is the ability to absorb lectures from those seemingly more confident, secure, and wise than himself. The book consists of a series of these lectures (and the reflections they inspire) presented as discussions, bracketed between bouts of personal anxiety and small defeats. The plot develops from the reflections these experiences inspire. The work takes place within the individual priest's consciousness as he grapples to comprehend his place and role in the largely unpleasant developments around him.

The priest comes new to his assignment in a small village and worries that the residents neither like nor respect him. His physical and social impairments sap his confidence and impede his efforts to relate to his parishioners; the parish children make fun of his efforts to teach them the faith he sometimes wonders if he still holds. The local merchant seems to take advantage of his impoverished state, and his peculiar diet of bread dipped in wine (necessitated by a growing stomach cancer) causes parishioners to suspect him of alcoholism.

Despite the unrelenting frustration the curate experiences in the town—perhaps because of it—he rises to heroic heights. His earnest ineffectualness and his genuine and seemingly losing battle with despair render him a transcendent hero to whom all who suffer can relate. Though he accomplishes no final feat that might render him "heroic" in the sense that many understand the term, his continued charity throughout his suffering suggests a spiritual triumph.

Impact of Event

Contemporary reviewers located the work's value in its transcendence of the French village setting and in the lessons the book provided for all who struggled in those turbulent times. Georges Bernanos wrote as much about the world as he did about the tiny French village, and the young priest is not so much a denominational manifestation as a representative of each person searching for the good in a society steeped in despair and ugliness. His priest grapples with the very issues that consumed Americans in the late 1930's, questions of social justice and human dignity. Bernanos located much of the cause of these concerns in the very institutions that were to eliminate (or at least ameliorate) them: church and community. The Church sought institutional survival rather than social salvation, and the community blunted and dwarfed its members rather than nurtured them.

If Bernanos seemed cynical about the Church's and community's ability to solve serious social problems, he also suggested that individuals could successfully find solutions through inner, individual, efforts. Though the Church did not always foster virtue and dignity (and often seemed to impede the achievement of those aims), people could find such values in the world about them. The dying priest's last words, spoken in answer to his friend's concern that a priest would not arrive soon enough to provide final absolution, suggested an extrainstitutional route to salvation and dignity. The priest asks if it matters that he will not receive the church's final rite; he answers his own question by noting that "grace is everywhere."

Georges Bernanos, however, came to this conclusion slowly. He was born in the late nineteenth century, when many Frenchmen were divided over the issue of whether they owed their loyalty to the republic or to the monarchy and church. Bernanos grew up strongly in the royal camp and was highly supportive of the Catholic church in its struggle to regain preeminence. He developed this position from his early life experiences, such as his Jesuit education, and bolstered his monarchical bent with political commitments. He joined the reactionary Action Française movement and edited the royalist weekly *L'Avant-Garde de Normandie.* He fought in the French Army during World War I. His views began to change shortly after the war, when he began to question the Catholic church's strong alignment with the wealthy rather than with the poor. He became even more critical of the Church during the Spanish Civil War.

He became disillusioned with his fellow conservative Catholics as he witnessed firsthand Francisco Franco's supporters commit gross violations of human rights in the Spanish Civil War. The more he spoke out about the violations, the more isolated he became from the community in which he had long situated himself. He wrote *The Diary of a Country Priest* in the midst of this profound personal transformation, this disillusionment with the institutions he had so long supported. Evidence of his disillusionment permeates his work and culminates in the young priest's conclusion that grace abounds outside the Church.

Many of these concerns, particularly regarding the French Catholic church, might reasonably be considered more European matters than American. What might explain *The Diary of a Country Priest*'s favorable reception in the American literary world of 1937? Much can be explained by the state of the American social, economic, and cultural scene at the time. Drained by nearly a decade of terrible economic depression, Americans sought solace from their misery. The earlier optimism about the New Deal's ability to move society completely out of the Depression waned by 1937—despite the relative success various programs had achieved. For a short while, such demagogues as Huey Long and Father Coughlin promised to lift the country from its economic malaise, but they too foundered. An assassin felled Long, and with him the promise of his share-the-wealth solutions to the sufferings many Americans endured. Coughlin turned vitriolic in his social criticism, and his increasingly strident and hateful message came to alienate many who had placed with him their own hopes for a solution to their suffering. Cultural historians suggest that Americans had begun to turn inward for relief by 1937, and away from social interpretations of their persistent suffering.

By the latter 1930's, Americans had come to seek personal rather than societal solutions for their problems. *The Diary of a Country Priest* provided the portrait of a young man in much the same state that the Depression had placed many Americans. He was anxious and near despair. If Americans worried about the seeming inability of collective social reform to regenerate society, the French country priest shared their troubling concerns. He too located much of his anxiety in larger social developments that impeded the formation and survival of a just society. Yet he located his solace, his resolution to the problems he identified for himself and his world, in an individual, deeply personal commitment to the struggle for human dignity and grace.

Many American critics could appreciate this struggle and resolution because they too saw the cause of their concerns, and the answer to their uncertainties, to be individual and personal. They too had become cynical about the possibility of societal transformation, about the potential for social justice in the world, and they too saw in the young priest's simplicity and honesty, in his earnest struggle to do right, the dignity Americans sought in their own lives. The young curate's final peace provided hope for Americans frustrated with persistent social and economic dislocation, and in creating such a character, Bernanos provided reason for optimism in a troubled world.

Bibliography

Bernanos, Georges. *The Diary of a Country Priest.* New York: Limited Editions Club, 1986. This English-language version of the novel contains wood engravings by Fritz Eichenberg and an excellent introduction by Robert Coles.

_____. *The Last Essays of Georges Bernanos.* Translated by Joan Ulanov and Barry Ulanov. New York: Greenwood Press, 1968. A collection of six essays that Georges Bernanos wrote roughly a decade after he published *The Diary of a Country Priest* and shortly before his death. The essays cover some of the same issues with which Bernanos grappled in his earlier novel and center on the evils of his time.

Bush, William. *Georges Bernanos.* New York: Twayne, 1969. Surveys Bernanos' artistic vision, summarizes his novels, and provides a brief analysis of each. The most approachable work on Bernanos available in English. Bush organizes his chapters around each of Bernanos' works and provides a brief conclusion at the end. In his chapter on *The Diary of a Country Priest*, he argues that the standard English-language translation mistranslates the priest's final words, and so misses the centrality of Saint Therese of Lisieux to Bernanos' work.

Cooke, John E. *Georges Bernanos: A Study of Christian Commitment.* Amersham, Buckinghamshire, England: Avebury Publishing, 1981. This brief examination of Bernanos' religious life centers on Bernanos' focus on the human struggle for redemption. Cooke suggests that all of Bernanos' work can rightly be understood as the author's attempt to point the modern, corrupted world back toward a spiritual orientation, to the search for grace and societal salvation. Cooke points out Bernanos' conviction that the Middle Ages represented the time when the world had come closest to this ideal, and he suggests that Bernanos sought to prod society back in that direction.

Pells, Richard. *Radical Visions and American Dreams: Culture and Social Thought in the Depression Years.* New York: Harper & Row, 1973. Pells provides a solid one-volume survey of the American cultural scene during the Great Depression and helps set the context for *The Diary of a Country Priest*'s publication in the United States. Though Pells never mentions the novel specifically, his work enables the reader to understand why the novel met with such wide critical praise in America.

Speaight, Robert. *Georges Bernanos: A Study of the Man and the Writer.* London: Collins and Harvill Press, 1973. This is the most comprehensive biography of Bernanos available in English. Focuses on both his literary work and his life, and in this way is very different from the other works cited above. Speaight chronicles Bernanos' early family life, his education, his involvement with Action Française, his religious experiences, his life in Brazil, and his return to Europe in the last years of his life. Because the book focuses on Bernanos' life as well as his work, it best explains his writing in the context of his experiences.

Timothy Kelly

Cross-References

Wittgenstein Emerges as an Important Philosopher (1921), p. 518; Gide's *The Counterfeiters* Questions Moral Absolutes (1925), p. 620; Guthrie's Populist Songs Reflect the Depression-Era United States (1930's), p. 810; Picasso Paints *Guernica* (1937), p. 1062; *The Grapes of Wrath* Portrays Depression-Era America (1939), p. 1138.

LUCE LAUNCHES *LIFE* MAGAZINE

Category of event: Journalism
Time: 1936
Locale: New York, New York

The creation not merely of another American magazine but also of a new genre within the publishing industry precipitated the enormous impact of photography combined with journalism

Principal personages:
HENRY R. LUCE (1898-1967), the creator of *Time* and *Fortune* and editor-in-chief of *Life*
CLARE BOOTHE LUCE (1903-1987), the second wife of Henry Luce, a journalist, playwright, congresswoman, and ambassador and the originator of the *Life* idea
JOHN SHAW BILLINGS (1898-1975), the initial managing editor of *Life*
DANIEL LONGWELL (1899-1968), the first executive editor of *Life*
MARGARET BOURKE-WHITE (1906-1971), a staff photographer and war correspondent for *Life*
ALFRED EISENSTAEDT (1898-   ), a pioneering German photojournalist who joined *Life* in 1936

Summary of Event

Henry Robinson Luce married Clare Boothe Brokaw on November 23, 1935; it was a second marriage for both. The couple returned from a ten-week honeymoon in Cuba in February, 1936, and the announcement of their intent to start a pictorial magazine followed. Henry's biographer, John Kobler, writing in 1968, identified Clare as the source of the idea, and there does survive a pattern for such a magazine she had sketched out three years earlier for Conde Nast, the publisher of *Vanity Fair*, of which she was then editor.

Clare, then thirty-three, had begun her career six years earlier working for *Vogue* magazine and was subsequently to write three relatively successful Broadway plays before involvement with World War II took her back into journalism and thereafter a political role. Henry, not yet forty, had been cofounder with Briton Hadden of Time, Incorporated, and its lead periodical, the successful newsweekly *Time*, from its inception in 1923.

In addition, Luce in February, 1930, had created at the very outset of the Depression a significant monthly magazine for American business called *Fortune*. In March, 1931, he had inaugurated the radio news program *The March of Time*, and in April, 1932, he had acquired and then remodeled into a professional exemplar the periodical *Architectural Forum*.

The name for the new pictorial magazine originally was to be "Dime"—its initial newsstand cost. Over the eight months of frantic preparation, a whole series of alternative working titles were tried, including "Parade," "Scene," "Seen," and "Pictures," while the subtitle remained most descriptive: "The Show-Book of the World."

By midsummer, a mock issue of the magazine had been produced. The decision was made to print the magazine on ten-and-a-half by-fourteen-inch paper, making it somewhat larger than most other magazines of the day; when issues appeared on the newsstands their dimensions allowed them to stand out from the displayed titles competing for the purchaser's attention.

In September, a trial mockup was ready, under the designation "Rehearsal." Throughout the preparatory period, the company had to deal with a large number of unknowns, including locating presses capable of handling the projected print run, equipment permitting quality photographic reproduction on a large scale, and obtaining supplies of coated paper upon which quality images could be sustained.

In describing his intended pictorial magazine, Luce had written that "To see life; to see the world; to eyewitness great events; . . . to see and to take pleasure in seeing; to see and be amazed; to see and be instructed; thus to see, and to be shown, is now the will and new expectancy of half mankind." The obvious title for the unnamed magazine emerged; if "to see life" was the objective, then the medium of the seeing would be called *Life*. Clare Booth Luce had used the very designation in her original sketch for Nast.

Another *Life*, a humor magazine, had existed since 1883, but it was fading rapidly under the impact of the national economic plight and its own inability to keep pace with the times and with the competition of such rivals as *The New Yorker*. The title was purchased for $92,000 in August by Luce and company, and work on the first issue followed immediately. Bearing the date Monday, November 23, 1936, the weekly new *Life* appeared on the newsstands on the preceding Thursday, November 19. A circulation of 250,000 had been guaranteed to potential advertisers, while the initial printing was of 466,000 copies. These sold out within hours of hitting the stands.

Every page of the inaugural issue had some kind of illustration of greater spatial proportion than text, with the exception of page three, which featured an essay entitled "Introduction to This First Issue of *Life*." On the facing page two was a full-page photograph captioned "LIFE BEGINS"—an infant just after birth in the hands of an attending physician.

The first issue's front cover depicted Fort Peck Dam, a Works Progress Administration (WPA) project being built in Montana. The cover photograph was taken by Margaret Bourke-White, whose work also illustrated the lead article on pages nine through seventeen. Color was used in the photographs on eleven of the interior pages, though except for a four-paged article illustrating the paintings of John Steuart Curry of Kansas, all the color was used in advertisements.

Advertising occupied thirty-three whole pages, including three of the covers, plus nine half-pages and three quarter-pages. Advertisements were sold at the rate of $1,500 for a full black-and-white page, $2,250 for color. The magazine itself sold for ten cents; total revenues for the first issue exceeded $110,000 but were insufficient to cover printing costs. Loss of money was a regular venture through many years of publication.

Issues were affectionately known by the staff as the "Big Red." They had a red band at the bottom across the front cover (a feature eliminated with the issue of June 2, 1961). A bold red rectangle with the word "LIFE" in white lettering was set dramatically in the upper-left-hand corner. Only once was this recognition symbol absent: in the April 16, 1937 issue, when it would have interfered with the photo of a rooster's comb. Once, too, the recognition symbol appeared in black—on the November 29, 1963, issue printed after President John F. Kennedy's assasination.

Impact of Event

Henry Luce thought of *Life* as a new kind of magazine. The picture magazine had already appeared in varying degrees. The *Illustrated London News* originated in May, 1842, just after the invention of photography, but was chiefly illustrated by drawings and engravings into the 1920's. *Harper's Weekly* had incorporated Civil War photographs by Mathew Brady, while Boston of the 1880's had *Gleason's Pictorial Drawing Room Companion*. From the beginning of the new century, photography was exploited by major illustrated weeklies in Paris, Leipzig, and Berlin. Luce, though, was aiming for something more—a genre not yet created.

Life was not intended as a war magazine, as its covers made evident. There was much more to see, especially the omnipresent female on at least one of every three covers, with many more inside illustrating fashion and the perennial interest in swimsuits. From its second issue, for sixteen years, *Life* had a regular feature, "Movie of the Week," and thereafter *Life* literally made stars by featuring photos of actors and actresses as well. The magazine's greatest love affair was with Elizabeth Taylor, who appeared on covers a record twelve times.

Yet *Life*'s first decade was dominated by the interactive forces of depression and war. Thus, it became widely known as a war magazine, a development that did not hinder its initial growth. Circulation rose to 5,369,000 copies per week by 1947, the largest circulation of any magazine. Wartime issues beginning October 11, 1943, went overseas without advertising.

Time could be illustrated, but central to its success was its ability to create and use the language of mid-twentieth century America. *Life* instead was intended to provide images of the mid-century world as seen through the eyes of the United States. Regular features of *Life* thus came to spawn other magazines, including its own international editions (from July 22, 1946) and the Spanish language *Life en Español* (from January 5, 1953), as well as *Sports Illustrated* (from August 16, 1954) and *People* (from March 4, 1974). In addition, both as composites from issues and as creations from without, *Life* generated whole series of books—magazine journalism in hard covers.

Life could do essays with photographs, but its best pieces were the arresting illustrations with word captions. On the occasion of the celebration of the 150th anniversary of photography, Lance Morrow noted that photojournalism is not only "the first impression of history" but also, disturbingly, "history's lasting visual impression." Wilson Hicks, in an attempt to define "What Is Photojournalism?," observed that *"Life* had been projected headlong into its own evolutionary state." The magazine was the laboratory wherein the intended artform was accomplished.

Early issues of *Life* show abuses of photographs: cut to eliminate the unwanted or to fit some aesthetic notion of space. Gradually there emerged the awareness that the camera was its own essayist, so that what was actually taken, admittedly with all the selectivity and nonobjectivity of the photographer, was precisely what should appear without further alteration. *Life's* photographers provided on average annually for its fifty-odd issues 350,000 pictures for every 10,000 used, but the editorial section of about two hundred per issue, itself an aesthetic act, held inviolate the image as provided.

Television had already been invented as *Life* emerged, even if Luce identified films and radio as more obvious competitors. Rather than giving the public what it wanted, he wanted to make available "what they must have lest they perish." By perfecting the magazine's craftsmanship, Luce thought his brainchild could compete with its electronic rivals. As late as 1965, George P. Hunt, then *Life's* managing editor, could still observe: "Permanence is what photographs and paintings are. The TV set represents the fleeting moment. You can see the great photos in *Life* forever."

Nevertheless, television was in part destructive of both *Life* and its photojournalistic competitors. *Colliers* and *Woman's Home Companion* both folded in December, 1956; *Saturday Evening Post* was bought out by Time Incorporated and eliminated in February, 1969; *Look* survived until October, 1971. *Life* itself was not far behind.

Between November 23, 1936, and December 29, 1972, 1864 regular weekly issues of *Life* appeared. In addition were special editions, including "Israel's Swift Victory" (1967), "The Kennedys" (1968), and "To the Moon and Back" and "Woodstock" (1970). From 1973 to 1977, *Life* produced only two issues per year, one "special" and a year-end "The Year in Pictures." Thereafter, *Life* resumed as a monthly with occasional special issues, remaining as a survivor of the golden age of photojournalism.

Bibliography

Elson, Robert T. *Time, Inc.: The Intimate History of a Publishing Enterprise, 1923-1941.* Edited by Duncan Norton-Taylor. New York: Atheneum, 1968.
_____. *The World of Time Inc.: The Intimate History of a Publishing Enterprise, Volume Two: 1941-1960.* Edited by Duncan Norton-Taylor. New York: Atheneum, 1973. These volumes and their sequel, Curtis Prendergast's *The World of Time, Inc.: The Intimate History of a Changing Enterprise, Volume Three: 1960-1980* (1986), constitute an official account, with full access to the private papers, of the publishing enterprise. The birth of *Life* is chronicled in volume 1, its success in volume 2. The third volume deals with the magazine's late 1970's revival.
Goldberg, Vicki. *Margaret Bourke-White: A Biography.* New York: Harper, 1986. An informative biography of a principal *Life* photographic contributor.

Henle, Faye. *Au Clare de Luce: Portrait of a Luminous Lady.* New York: S. Daye, 1943. An early biography that has the advantage of emphasizing Clare Booth Luce's own prior editorial success before *Life* was launched.

Hicks, Wilson. *Words and Pictures: An Introduction to Photojournalism.* New York: Harper & Brothers, 1952. By an editor of *Life.* Discusses pictorial journalism; extensively illustrated by examples from *Life.*

Kobler, John. *Luce: His Time, Life, and Fortune.* Garden City, N.Y.: Doubleday, 1968. Written immediately after the death of Luce. Contains valuable information about the creation of the magazines, including the role of Clare Booth Luce's memo on the format and character of *Life.* Bibliography.

The Best of Life. Alexandria, Va.: Time-Life Books, 1973. A selection of the magazine's highlights, compiled after the demise of the weekly version. Captions alongside each selection and picture credits at the end.

Life 50, 1936-1986: The First Fifty Years. Boston: Little, Brown, 1986. An official commemorative, with illustrations of every cover, samples from every year, and brief interpretative essays on each decade. The finest all-around introduction to the magazine and its impact.

Life Goes to the Movies. Alexandria, Va.: Time-Life Books, 1975. Focuses on a social arena that *Life* regularly appreciated and exploited. Stars, studios, and behind-the-scenes aspects of Hollywood are illustrated and put into perspective.

Swanberg, W. A. *Luce and His Empire.* New York: Charles Scribner's Sons, 1972. A more political assessment of Luce and the perspective appearing within his publications. Independent of the official history of the company, and thereby lacking sources of information pertinent especially to *Life.* Thorough index of names. Illustrated with forty-six photographs.

Clyde Curry Smith

Cross-References

The Christian Science Monitor Is Founded (1908), p. 209; Wallace Founds *Reader's Digest* (1922), p. 549; Luce Founds *Time* Magazine (1923), p. 577; *60 Minutes* Becomes the First Televised Newsmagazine (1968), p. 2136; *USA Today* Is Launched (1982), p. 2507.

TUDOR'S *JARDIN AUX LILAS* PREMIERES IN LONDON

Category of event: Dance
Time: January 26, 1936
Locale: London, England

With his Jardin aux lilas, *Antony Tudor created a new form, the psychological ballet, which represented another step forward in the evolution of twentieth century ballet*

Principal personages:
ANTONY TUDOR (WILLIAM COOK, 1908-1987), a British choreographer who enriched ballet by blending it with modern dance and a focus on psychological motivations
MARIE RAMBERT (1888-1982), a founder of London's Ballet Rambert who gave Tudor his early training and opportunities
NORA KAYE (NORA KOREFF, 1920-1987), a great American dramatic ballerina who made her debut in Tudor's *Pillar of Fire*
HUGH LAING (HUGH SKINNER, 1911-1988), the definitive performer of male roles in Tudor ballets
AGNES DE MILLE (1909-   ), the American choreographer who recommended Tudor to Ballet Theatre
RICHARD PLEASANT (1906-1961) and LUCIA CHASE (1897-1986), the founders of Ballet Theatre who first hired Tudor in America

Summary of Event

When Sergei Diaghilev's Ballets Russes broke up in 1929, the company's dancers and choreographers dispersed throughout the West, taking with them the heritage of Diaghilev's bold experiments with contemporary arts and themes. For those who went to England, there was little opportunity for performance; most English ballet was relegated to the music halls. There were, however, two good dance schools in London; one had been formed in 1920 by Marie Rambert, the other in 1926 by Ninette de Valois. Both women had worked with Diaghilev and would found, respectively, Ballet Rambert and the Royal Ballet.

Marie Rambert was interested in following Diaghilev's lead in developing contemporary ballet, and she had an acute eye for talent. In 1930, she presented her Rambert Dancers (later called the Ballet Club) in the first season of English ballet. One of her students who had come to study dance in 1928 helped with lights, stage-managing, refreshments, and anything else that needed doing. He was twenty-two years old; his name was William Cook. Nine years later, he changed his name to Antony Tudor.

After only three years of study, Tudor created his first ballet. According to Rambert, it was not a good piece, but it showed considerable talent. Tudor honed his talents on Rambert's dancers (himself included) for another five years. In 1938, the Ballet

Club presented his first major work, *Jardin aux lilas* (later called *Lilac Garden*).

Jardin aux lilas was unlike anything anyone had seen on the ballet stage. Though working in the idiom of classical ballet, Tudor had transformed the technique itself into a vehicle for exposing the psychological states of his characters.

Jardin aux lilas does not have a plot; rather, it depicts a social situation in which the characters are caught with no means of escape. Set in a lilac garden in Edwardian times, it concerns a young woman, Caroline, who is soon to enter a marriage of convenience to a man she does not love. At a farewell party in the lilac garden, she must say goodbye to the man she does love, and her fiancé must reaffirm his parting from a former mistress. As Edwardian propriety demanded that personal desires be subjugated to the mandates of society, all four main characters are constrained to accept the situation without overtly expressing their true feelings. Yet that first audience saw very clearly the yearning, frustration, and anguish suffered by each.

To accomplish this, Tudor did not use the customary approach to choreography, which was to design steps that would then be danced with appropriate feelings. Instead, he reversed the process and derived the movement from the feelings. He understood that even the posture of a character reveals a psychological state. Hence Caroline stands with her arms straight to her sides, her back stiff, her body charged with the effort of self-control. Tudor used small, everyday gestures to the same effect. Fingers to the temple, tentative reaches, a head turning back over the shoulder all suggested the fragments of thought and feeling that passed through the characters. He used classical steps to express or intensify emotion; no steps were included merely for the sake of dancing.

Tudor's use of the dramatic form also differed from the standard balletic treatment. He chose music (in this case, Ernest Chausson's *Poème for Violin and Orchestra*) that did not have easily identifiable beats or measures but that flowed in long phrases. Tudor choreographed along these sweeping phrases and moved the characters from moment to psychological moment, not from dance to dance. There might be duets, solo passages, and group dances, but these erupted from and receded into the general flow of the ballet.

Unusual uses of time, reminiscent of cinematic effects, also appear in *Jardin aux lilas.* Encounters between Caroline and her lover, between the man she must marry and his mistress, are furtive and fleeting, close-ups, as it were, within the fluid picture. Toward the end of the piece, when Caroline realizes the time is near when she will never see her lover again, she swoons into the arms of the man she must marry, and all action stops while the music sweeps on. As the other characters stay frozen, Caroline alone moves toward her lover, reaching. The reach is somnambulistic and devoid of hope. She then moves backward into the swoon, and all the characters resume action. This short sequence, the turning point of the ballet, is highlighted by the use of these cinematic techniques (freeze-frame, slow-motion, and dream-sequence effects). The cumulative effect of these elements of style was one of austere beauty and poignancy.

Jardin aux lilas was recognized immediately as a masterpiece. Within the next three years, Tudor created three more major works in London. The first of these, *Dark Elegies* (1937), performed to Gustav Mahler's *Kindertotenlieder*, was an expression, in ritual form, of the grief of a village of parents who have lost their children. The piece, though more abstract than *Jardin aux Lilas*, displayed the same potency of feeling beneath its simple, folk-based movements.

Despite his predominant emphasis on the psychological aspects of human difficulty, Tudor had a sense of the comic that came out in the remaining two of his significant London works. *Judgment of Paris* (1938) was a satiric comedy based on the myth of Paris and the Golden Apple. *Gala Performance*, also created in 1938, poked fun at the backstage intrigues of the ballet world and, most particularly, at the pretensions of ballerinas from the three major schools, Russian, Italian, and French.

By 1938, Tudor had left Rambert to form his own company, the London Ballet, for which he did *Judgment of Paris* and *Gala Performance*. In 1939, however, World War II intervened, and the London theaters were closed down. Tudor, though already a recognized master choreographer, had no place to work.

Impact of Event

During the years that Tudor was developing his craft, American choreographer Agnes de Mille was also in London establishing herself as a ballet recital artist. She was in the original cast of *Dark Elegies* and danced the role of Venus in *Judgment of Paris*.

In 1938, de Mille returned to New York. Hearing that the newly formed Ballet Theatre (later American Ballet Theatre) was looking for a choreographer, De Mille urged the company to invite Tudor to America. He arrived in New York in 1939.

In its inaugural season in January, 1940, Ballet Theatre presented his *Jardin aux lilas*, *Dark Elegies*, and *Judgment of Paris*. American audiences and critics alike embraced him as a major new choreographer. Tudor was to spend the remainder of his life primarily in America.

At the time of Tudor's American debut, the new modern dance was gaining rapid ground. Tudor had seen in Europe the works of German expressionists Mary Wigman, Harold Kreutzberg, and Kurt Jooss. He discovered in them the valuable precept that feeling and its gestural expression originate in the torso. Of his mode of working, he said: "We start from the spine and the torso, and we get to the feet later. In ballet school you usually start with the feet." According to American modern dance pioneer Martha Graham, *Dark Elegies* was "the first ballet to invade modern dance."

Tudor's work focused on the experiences of real people rather than on the adventures of the fairy-tale characters, colorful ethnic personalities, or mythic heroes more typical of ballet. Rather than following a narrative about realistic characters, however, he drew portraits of people whose psychological reactions, in combination with their social situations, created the events.

Tudor influenced a whole generation of dancers and choreographers by the way he worked. He was meticulous and would research his subject extensively before beginning a ballet. He derived gesture from the character in the moment, sometimes taking two or three hours to find and work on one movement. This intensive search for the psychological motivation of movement was entirely new to ballet.

Yet Tudor did not necessarily tell his dancers much about the characters or story. Rather, he led them into it by asking questions and by goading them. Indeed, though dancers flocked to his classes and yearned to be in his ballets, they were almost always terrified of being the target of one of his merciless personal barbs. The purpose behind these verbal assaults was to strip away the "ballet persona" that develops early in many young dancers and that often engenders such set reactions to movement that it becomes almost impossible for many dancers to respond to dramatic situations with any spontaneity or truth. There was no doubt that Tudor's ballets brought out unsuspected depths of expression in the dancers who did them.

In 1942, Tudor created what is universally considered to be one of the great ballets of the twentieth century. Set to the music of Arnold Schoenberg's *Verklärte Nacht*, *Pillar of Fire* tells the story of Hagar, a young woman of nineteenth century New England. Facing spinsterhood, Hagar hopes for a match with a friend of the family, but he appears to be more interested in her younger sister. In desperation she gives herself to a roué and is subsequently ostracized by her family and the town. The ballet focuses on the dilemma of those who, like Hagar, have passions that run deeper than social codes and roles can tolerate and who therefore often become outcasts.

In addition to using posture, everyday gesture, and a blend of modern and ballet techniques in *Pillar of Fire*, Tudor also employs two groups of dancers (the "Lovers in Innocence" and the "Lovers in Experience") to underline Hagar's suspension between society's "good" and "bad." The hip-swinging, free-wheeling movements of the Lovers in Experience are in contrast with the softer, more conventional movements of the Lovers in Innocence, which, in turn, contrast with the stiffer movements of the judgmental townspeople.

Tudor worked on *Pillar of Fire* for a solid year. On opening night, the labor was rewarded with thirty curtain calls and, subsequently, the highest critical praise.

On opening night, Hagar was danced by Nora Kaye, who was recognized from then on as a great dramatic ballerina. She was eminently capable of expressing the finest emotional nuances within the difficult, highly stylized movements and was for many years the model for aspiring Tudor dancers. Other original cast members who set a standard for future dramatic dancers were Tudor's principal male interpreter and lifelong companion, Hugh Laing, Tudor himself, and Lucia Chase, who eventually became codirector of Ballet Theatre.

Following *Pillar of Fire*, Tudor created *The Tragedy of Romeo and Juliet* (1943), *Dim Lustre* (1943), and *Undertow* (1945) for Ballet Theatre, *Shadow of the Wind* (1948) for England's Royal Ballet, and in 1975, his last masterwork (for American Ballet Theatre), *The Leaves Are Fading*, an abstract piece with strong lyric undertones.

At a time when English and American ballet were just getting started, Antony Tudor brought to them both distinction and a progressive leap forward in the evolution of ballet. He was the first to achieve a genuine integration of ballet and modern dance and the first to create what has come to be called the psychological ballet. He directly influenced future choreographers of high stature such as Great Britain's Walter Gore and America's Agnes de Mille and Jerome Robbins. His work pulled choreographers away from melodrama and superficial acting and taught dancers to work in depth, to search for the real motivations of movement.

The dramatic ballets of Antony Tudor have been compared to the works of Marcel Proust, Stendhal, and Anton Chekhov for their detailed portraiture of personal inner landscapes. Beginning with *Jardin aux lilas*, Tudor did something no one else thought possible. In the words of dance critic Fernau Hall, "For the first time in the twentieth century a choreographer succeeded in emulating the achievements of good dramatists, novelists and film directors."

Bibliography

Amberg, George. *Ballet: The Emergence of an American Art.* New York: New American Library, 1949. Begins with a background of classical ballet from the nineteenth century through Diaghilev's Ballets Russes and traces the development of ballet in America through the 1940's. A fascinating, exhaustive examination of companies, choreographers, works, dancers, and the evolution of twentieth century American aesthetics as seen in its ballet. Chronology. Repertoire listing of all major American companies of the period. Index.

De Mille, Agnes. *Dance to the Piper.* New York: Little, Brown, 1952. The first volume of De Mille's autobiography. Separate chapters on Marie Rambert, Tudor and Hugh Laing, and Martha Graham. De Mille's brilliant writing makes this a classic of dance biography. Index.

_____. *Speak to Me, Dance with Me.* New York: Little, Brown, 1973. De Mille's letters from her early career years in London. Gives accounts of several trips to the Western United States (including one to work for her uncle, Cecil B. DeMille). Includes her time spent with Tudor, Laing, and Rambert and gives a good sense of the struggle experienced by the independent ballet artists of the 1930's. Interesting "what became of" section of major figures mentioned in the book. Index.

Perlmutter, Donna. *Shadowplay.* New York: Viking, 1991. A complete biography of Tudor that follows his life and career in clear chronological sequence. Detailed descriptions of the creation of Tudor's major ballets, with emphasis on their development as a reflection of Tudor's life and relationships. Bibliography, source notes, choreographic chronology, index.

Rambert, Marie. *Quicksilver.* London: Macmillan, 1972. Rambert's autobiography. Contains interesting accounts of her childhood in Poland (then part of the Russian Empire) and her work with Diaghilev's Ballets Russes, her fostering of Tudor's early career, and the evolution of Ballet Rambert. Factual rather than critical, with many anecdotes of theater and dance greats of the 1920's through 1960's. Index.

Catherine Sim

Cross-References

Duncan Interprets Chopin in Her Russian Debut (1904), p. 113; Pavlova First Performs Her Legendary Solo *The Dying Swan* (1907), p. 187; Diaghilev's Ballets Russes Astounds Paris (1909), p. 241; Fokine's *Les Sylphides* Introduces Abstract Ballet (1909), p. 247; *The Firebird* Premieres in Paris (1910), p. 269; Jooss's Antiwar Dance *The Green Table* Premieres (1932), p. 920.

SHOSTAKOVICH'S *LADY MACBETH OF MTSENSK* IS CONDEMNED

Category of event: Music
Time: January 28, 1936
Locale: Moscow, Union of Soviet Socialist Republics

The condemnation of Dmitri Shostakovich's opera was a landmark in Soviet cultural history, drawing worldwide attention and leading to the oppression of other Soviet artists

Principal personages:
DMITRI SHOSTAKOVICH (1906-1975), the leading Soviet composer of the twentieth century
JOSEPH STALIN (JOSEPH VISSARIONOVICH DZHUGASHVILI, 1879-1953), the general secretary of the Communist Party, absolute ruler of the Soviet Union
NIKOLAI LESKOV (1831-1895), a classic Russian novelist and short-story writer

Summary of Event

In January of 1936, Dmitri Shostakovich was only thirty years old and had already achieved world fame as a leading Soviet composer. At that time, he was in the city of Archangelsk on a concert tour, buoyed by the recent successes of his opera *Lady Macbeth Mtsenskago Uyezda* (*Lady Macbeth of Mtsensk*). On January 28, he went to the railroad station to buy a copy of *Pravda*, the official newspaper of the Soviet Communist Party. He opened the paper and was shocked to read a scathing editorial condemning his opera. It was a turning point in his life and for the future of Soviet culture as a whole.

Shostakovich was born in 1906 in St. Petersburg. When the Bolsheviks seized power in 1917, Shostakovich became a child of the new Soviet state, and his hometown was renamed Leningrad.

As a boy, he exhibited great musical talent and studied at the Leningrad Conservatory. He composed his first symphony at the age of nineteen, and the work was premiered in the West to great acclaim. Shostakovich was the first Soviet composer who came of age after the revolution to become world famous. Symphonies, ballets, film scores, and incidental music followed. His first opera, *The Nose* (1928), was based on a satire of czarist Russia by the novelist Nikolai Gogol.

Shostakovich was an indefatigable worker and versatile composer. By 1929, he had evolved a style that was dazzling, pungent, lyrical, ironic, and haunting—in a word, unique. His musical idols were Ludwig van Beethoven, Modest Mussorgsky, Gustav Mahler, Igor Stravinsky, and innovative Western composers of the 1920's such as Alban Berg.

His fame assured and his individuality seemingly unthreatened, Shostakovich in

1930 began to write a tetralogy of feminist operas about the struggles of Russian women. The tetralogy was modeled on Richard Wagner's *The Ring of the Nibelungs*. The first opera would portray the misery of women under the old regime, the second would present revolutionary women who helped to overthrow the czars, and the third and fourth would celebrate the triumph of the new Soviet heroine of the future.

Only the first opera was to be completed. Shostakovich chose his story of oppressed Russian womanhood from *Lady MacBeth of the Mtsensk District*, a short nineteenth century novel by the Russian classical writer Nikolai Leskov. Shostakovich was also inspired by the operatic models of Georges Bizet's *Carmen* (1875) and Alban Berg's expressionist and atonal opera *Wozzeck* (1925). Both explored important social problems and stormy relationships between men and women.

Leskov's 1868 novel is somewhat reminiscent of Gustave Flaubert's great work *Madame Bovary* of 1857 in its exploration of an intelligent, frustrated woman in a narrow provincial society. Katerina Izmailova is the wife of a boring merchant in a small, provincial Russian town of the 1840's. Stifled by her existence, she takes a young lover, Sergei, poisons her father-in-law after he discovers her unfaithfulness, strangles her husband with the assistance of Sergei, and is sentenced to penal servitude in Siberia along with her lover. When Sergei becomes unfaithful to Katerina in Siberia, Katerina kills his new mistress and herself, and the story ends.

Shostakovich was captivated and inspired by this theme. He composed his opera from 1930 to 1932 and dedicated it to his future wife, Nina Varzar, with whom he had a stormy romance during that period. Shostakovich wrote a lengthy commentary on the opera in which he spelled out his intentions. He intended the drama to be a "tragic satire," prompting some to liken his musical style to the content of the profound novels of Fyodor Dostoevski retold by the comic actor Charlie Chaplin. He also strove to create a Marxist opera in which he would portray Katerina as a victim of a rotten bourgeois society that has corrupted her, leading to her self-destruction and the destruction of others.

Shostakovich played a key role in writing the libretto. He departed from Leskov's story in four major respects. First, the opera was much more a satire on the middle-class, patriarchal society of nineteenth century Russia than the novel had been. Second, Shostakovich incorporated a new episode, a pointed satire on police corruption and arbitrary behavior, into the third act. Third, Katerina was treated sympathetically as a heroic victim of circumstance, despite her adulterous and violent behavior. Finally, the inhuman conditions of penal servitude in Siberia were vividly depicted.

The music and the orchestra were given special prominence to sustain the storyline, and the music flowed without interruption. In the manner of the work of expressionist composers, the music indulged in violent contrasts between lyricism, dissonance, and unusual effects to produce violent contrasts, heighten emotions, and create effects of irony, crudity, and realism. Katerina alone was given lyrical solos to heighten her individuality and her tragic plight. The music also daringly attempted to describe the erotic behavior of the principal characters.

Lady Macbeth of Mtsensk received its premiere on January 22, 1934, in Leningrad, and was produced later that year in Moscow. It was a resounding success, receiving eighty-three performances in Leningrad and ninety-seven in Moscow in just two seasons. Soviet writers hailed it as a great triumph of Soviet culture and a piercing satire of middle-class society. By 1935, it was introduced to the major cities of Europe and was premiered in Cleveland and New York. On the whole, Western critics were favorable, though there was some division of opinion. Some called it a masterpiece of true social criticism and dramatic intensity, while others were put off by its violence, unusual musical effects, and erotic themes.

The Soviet political and cultural scene, however, was changing rapidly. The relatively free, experimental period of the 1920's in culture and the economy was coming to an abrupt end. From 1929 to 1933, the Soviet Union experienced a "second revolution from above" that took the form of forced collectivization of agriculture, rapid industrialization, and the use of state-sponsored terror and forced labor to ensure obedience and conformity. By 1932, the official doctrine of "Socialist Realism" imposed drab, optimistic formulas in art and literature, while newly organized writers' and composers' unions regimented the arts through the supremacy of Communist bureaucrats.

By 1936, Joseph Stalin had become the absolute dictator of the Soviet Union, personally intervening in all state-supervised areas of Soviet life and imposing his views and his will. When he visited the Bolshoi Theater in Moscow in January of 1936 and heard Shostakovich's *Lady Macbeth of Mtsensk*, the fate of Soviet music, and of Soviet culture as a whole, was sealed.

Impact of Event

Stalin left the Bolshoi Theater in a rage, offended by the dissonance, stark realism, eroticism, and tragic theme of the opera. In addition, he was upset by the satirical attack on the police, which he interpreted as an affront to himself. His control of the police was a vital source of his immense power and a weapon of the terror he was unleashing against Soviet society.

The now-famous vehement editorial in *Pravda* followed the next day, on January 28. The long article was entitled "Chaos Instead of Music." It condemned Shostakovich as a bourgeois "formalist" and the opera as filled with "an intentionally ungainly, muddled flood of sounds . . . [that] drown, escape, and drown once more in crashing, gnashing, and screeching." The success of the opera in the West was attributed to its appeal to the depraved tastes of the bourgeoisie. The article warned Shostakovich that things "could end very badly." A week later, a second editorial in *Pravda* condemned Shostakovich's 1935 ballet *The Limpid Stream*. Nevertheless, the first editorial gave Shostakovich an opportunity to redeem himself: *Pravda* recognized his great talent and his ability to express strong and direct emotions in music.

The article was unsigned, meaning that it reflected the views of the highest officials in the party. Some scholars think that much of the article was written by Stalin himself.

Shostakovich was shattered. He was certain that he would be arrested, for this was a time when arrests and executions were commonplace. He kept a suitcase at the ready that contained warm underwear and a sturdy pair of shoes. He could not sleep. This frightening episode cast a shadow over the rest of his life. His anxiety was increased by his friendships with other persecuted avant-garde cultural figures.

Shostakovich became shunned. His works were no longer performed, and his friends would cross to the other side of the street to avoid meeting him. Still, he was allowed to continue teaching. He discreetly withdrew his completed Fourth Symphony and started working on a Fifth Symphony that would rehabilitate himself, a work so successful that when it premiered in November of 1937 it received a forty-minute ovation.

Why was Shostakovich not arrested or executed, as were so many other great Soviet cultural figures? First, he was well known in the West as a product of the revolution and a great Soviet artist. Ironically, the West saw him as a committed Communist, while his Communist critics attacked him as a bourgeois formalist. Nevertheless, it could be argued that his notoriety made him even more vulnerable.

Second, Shostakovich had written three very popular film scores prior to 1934. Stalin loved films as a form of relaxation and appreciated the potential for propaganda and self-glorification that the medium had to offer. Finally, Stalin might have used Shostakovich as an example of an artist who would recant, a model for others. Subsequently, Stalin heaped both rewards and humiliations on the beleaguered composer.

The major significance of the condemnation of *Lady Macbeth of Mtsensk* lay in the powerful warning it sent to all Soviet cultural figures to abandon innovation and to toe the new line of Socialist Realism. The government also seized on *Lady Macbeth of Mtsenk* to mechanize and regiment Soviet cultural life. Shostakovich thus became a test case and a living example of what could happen to a modernist, experimental artist. The condemnation of Shostakovich was followed by a flood of directives controlling every area of cultural life.

The attack on Shostakovich increased the use of two favorite Soviet code words, "formalism" and "Socialist Realism." "Formalism" denoted abstraction, symbolism, and experimentation. Stalin liked opera as well as film. After attending *Lady Macbeth of Mtsensk*, he formulated certain guidelines for opera to be followed, guidelines that illuminated the meaning of "Socialist Realism." Opera, said Stalin, should be optimistic in content, should be filled with simple folk melodies, and should glorify the Soviet system and even the Russian past.

The impact of the condemnation of Shostakovich on the composer's style is still a matter of debate. Some Western critics have argued that his innovative, dashing style of the 1920's was ruined by the incident and that he retreated into stilted formulas and mannerisms. Until the death of Stalin, Soviet critics argued that Shostakovich's style had matured into serious and disciplined art, though he continued to be taken to task from time to time. Shostakovich's posthumously published memoirs, however, make it apparent that he became a kind of secret dissident, eliminating the blatant themes of modernism but using tragic and satirical themes in a critical musical language, at the same time continuing to write film scores and popular works to placate the regime.

In 1958, during the more liberal period of de-Stalinization, *Lady MacBeth of Mtsensk* was revised; the new version was performed in 1963. Shostakovich retitled the opera *Katerina Izmailova* and slightly revised the score and libretto. This time the somewhat changed conditions in both the Soviet Union and the West enabled the opera to be judged more from a musical and dramatic standpoint than an ideological one, and critics hailed it as the greatest Russian opera since Peter Ilich Tchaikovsky's *Pikovaya Dama* of 1890. The verdict of 1936 was thus reversed, and, in this instance, art outlived tyranny.

Bibliography

Leskov, Nikolai. *Lady MacBeth of Mtsensk District.* In *Six Great Russian Short Novels*, edited by Randall Jarrell. Garden City, N.Y.: Doubleday, 1970. Useful edition of the short novel upon which Shostakovich's opera was based, with a fine introduction by Jarrell. Necessary reading for an understanding of the opera.

MacDonald, Ian. *The New Shostakovich.* Boston: Northeastern University Press, 1990. The best book on Shostakovich's life and work. Clarifies misconceptions about the composer in the West. Argues that Shostakovich was losing faith in Communism at the time he wrote *Lady Macbeth of Mtsensk* and afterward adopted strategies to evade censorship while at the same time composing great music to memorialize the sufferings of the Soviet people. Good photographs and an excellent bibliography.

Shostakovich, Dmitri, and A. Preis. *Lady Macbeth of Mtsensk: Or, Katerina Izmailova.* Translated by Edward Downe. New York: G. Schirmer, 1983. Clear, attractive translation of the English libretto that captures the essence of the spicy Russian original.

Schwarz, Boris. *Music and Musical Life in Soviet Russia, 1917-1970.* London: Barrie and Jenkins, 1972. Excellent survey of the period, with fine sections on the episode of the condemnation of *Lady Macbeth of Mtsensk.* Valuable insights into the political and social conditions of the period that affected the music of Shostakovich.

Volkov, Solomon, ed. *Testimony: The Memoirs of Dmitri Shostakovich.* Translated by Antonina W. Bouis. New York: Harper & Row, 1979. Perhaps the most valuable source on the life and work of Shostakovich. Volkov was a friend of Shostakovich and pieced together their many conversations, mostly from 1970-1974. Shostakovich emerges in these memoirs as a secret dissident, outraged by the sufferings caused by the Soviet regime. Posits the interesting theory that Shostakovich was in the tradition of the Russian *yurodivy*, the artist-saints of Russian history who fought tyranny with their spiritual strength. Excellent photographs included.

Leon Stein

Cross-References

The Soviet Union Bans Abstract Art (1922), p. 544; *The Bedbug* and *The Bathhouse* Exemplify Revolutionary Theater (1929), p. 787; Socialist Realism Is Mandated in Soviet Literature (1932), p. 908; Stalin Restricts Soviet Composers (1932), p. 914; Hitler Organizes an Exhibition Denouncing Modern Art (1937), p. 1083; The Nazis Ban Nolde's Paintings (1941), p. 1217; Blacklisting Seriously Depletes Hollywood's Talent Pool (1947), p. 1340; Zhdanov Denounces "Formalism" in Music (1948), p. 1388.

CARNEGIE PUBLISHES HIS SELF-HELP BEST-SELLER

Category of event: Literature
Time: November, 1936
Locale: New York, New York

Dale Carnegie, a farm boy who struggled through adversity to a career in public speaking, achieved fame with his practical advice for business and personal success

Principal personage:
> DALE CARNEGIE (1888-1955), a failed salesman, actor, and writer who founded institutes for the teaching of public speaking and became famous as a writer of self-help books

Summary of Event

Dale Carnegie was born into a world undergoing painful social and economic change. Farms and small communities, for most, represented a mythic past; the future was in the cities. New York, for example, had a population of 125,000 in 1820, 800,000 by 1860, by 1910, more than five million. Many urban inhabitants were immigrants, of whom some nine million entered the United States in the single decade between 1900 and 1910. Most dreamed of solvency, if not success, but they entered a struggle for mere survival in an increasingly complex industrial world.

Formal education had little to offer. A demand for public education was only gradually met. For example, the United States had fewer than eight hundred high schools in 1878; that figure increased only to 5,500 during the next twenty years. High school education, if achieved at all, generally marked the end of formal schooling; in 1904, approximately 100,000 students were enrolled in colleges or universities that, in any case, were more nearly allied to the traditional European studies of Latin, Greek, and rhetoric than to the needs of a newly industrialized age.

An overwhelming demand existed for adult education, and the demand was met in a number of ways. Most successful was the Chautauqua program, which influenced Carnegie in his youth. Founded in 1874, this summer camp had expanded, by 1883, to include a winter home-study program. In 1888, New York began offering free lectures for working people, resulting in an attendance of seven million within the first fifteen years. That idea spread, as did public libraries (largely funded by millionaire Andrew Carnegie) and mechanics' institutes.

For most Americans, however, the printed word remained the primary source of information. While self-help books had long been popular, most still dealt with manners and morals, offering advice on the use of forks and cures for consumption and rabies. Self-help books for men dealt mostly with the vast generalities of Ralph Waldo Emerson, John Ruskin, or Emile Coué.

Carnegie, like many other Americans, had undergone the experience of the outsider in a system that rejected him. Born in Maryville, Missouri, he was the son of a devout Methodist mother, a schoolteacher before her marriage, and a farmer father who had completed six years of education. (The family name was, until 1916, Carnegey.) Dale Carnegie's father was unsuccessful; his crops were wiped out by flood and his livestock by disease. The father suffered severe and suicidal depression, overwhelmed with health problems, debts, and threats of bank foreclosure on the farm. The son attended a one-room school.

The family moved near Warrensburg so that Dale could live at home and attend the tuition-free college that later became Central Missouri State University. Awkward, self-conscious, and poorly dressed, he was a failure until he trained himself to compete in oratorical and debate contests. Eventually, he began to win, and his success gave him confidence. He left the college in 1908, but he never was graduated, having failed in his studies of Latin.

He became for a time a salesman for the International Correspondence School, after which he eked out a living selling meat in small Dakota towns. In 1911, he went to New York to study at the American Academy of Dramatic Arts. The school, founded in 1886, taught a natural acting style that contrasted with the overstated and stylized acting that dominated much of the nineteenth century stage. Carnegie went on the road with an acting company, but he discovered he was not suited for the stage.

In 1912, he was living in a New York slum and attempting to sell cars. Depression and headaches caused him to give up that job, though, and he dreamed of being a writer. (He was eventually, in 1921, to complete a novel, *The Blizzard*, only to have it rejected by publishers and his literary agent.) Deciding to write and teach public speaking, he applied to teach adult courses at Columbia University and New York University but was rejected. At last, he worked out an agreement to teach at the Young Men's Christian Association (YMCA) at 125th Street in Harlem, which was then primarily white. The YMCA doubted the course would prove attractive and offered to pay him only a percentage of profits, rather than the two dollars per session he had requested. He was soon earning thirty dollars per session. By the outbreak of World War I, he was able to hire instructors and to write tracts to standardize his methods.

By this time, he had rejected the formal oratorical techniques he had studied in college and had developed techniques similar to those he had studied at the Academy of Dramatic Arts. In 1915, with J. Berg Esenwein, he wrote *The Art of Public Speaking*, based on his theories. He followed this with *Public Speaking: A Practical Course for Business Men* (1926), *Little Known Facts About Well Known Men* (1934), and a study of his boyhood hero, *Lincoln the Unknown* (1932).

How to Win Friends and Influence People appealed to a wide audience frightened by economic and urban change and, by 1936, wearied of economic depression. In 1936, only 12.9 percent of high school graduates would enter college, but an urbanized and industrialized society with widespread unemployment demanded more skills than did the community life of the past. By 1936, one family in four was reported to be on relief. Thirty-eight percent of U.S. families (11.7 million families) lived beneath the poverty line, then designated as $1,000 a year. In Europe and the

United States, fascists on the political right and socialists and communists on the left wanted to overturn a seemingly failing system, but the majority of Americans simply wanted to survive and, if possible, thrive. To these, Dale Carnegie offered hope.

Impact of Event

How to Win Friends and Influence People was, Carnegie wrote, the book he wished he could have read two decades earlier. He was modest about the book and its future, hoping it would sell fifteen or twenty thousand copies. Instead, the book was a sensational success. Its effects were, on the one hand, personal and immediate, and, on the other, general and far-ranging.

His personal success was quickly obvious. The book soon began to sell five thousand copies a week. Despite parodies by humorists such as James Thurber and uncompromising condemnation by academics and intellectuals, the book appeared for two years on *The New York Times* best-seller list. By the time Carnegie's widow, Dorothy, revised the book in 1981, more than fifteen million copies had been sold.

The effect of this success on his public-speaking courses was also immediate; enrollment dramatically increased. Carnegie was to have problems with these classes during the late 1930's and World War II, but, by 1992, Dale Carnegie training was offered in every U.S. state and in some sixty other countries. Graduates by then numbered 3.5 million. *Life* magazine named him as one of the one hundred most important Americans of the twentieth century.

Carnegie also revolutionized the genre of self-help literature. Rather than speaking as a specialist, Carnegie addressed his students as a slightly more experienced equal speaking to equals, freely admitting his own mistakes. The roots of his style clearly lie in the Methodist sermons of his youth. His work is heavy with anecdotes about people, both famous and unknown, who have overcome adversity using the techniques Carnegie advocates; he often echoes the rhetoric of a Protestant minister, drawing lessons from the parables and other stories of the Scriptures. Carnegie's tone is informal, conversational, even ungrammatical. His sentences generally are brief, although never condescending, and his words are simple.

If in his style he offered a work consistent with the religious experiences of many, in substance he offered a simple, easily comprehended system that was unlike the heavy-handed philosophizing of earlier self-help literature. His most direct source was American philosopher William James, from whom Carnegie borrowed the idea that emotion follows action, rather than precedes it. Logically, then, the imitation of a mood will produce the desired mood. The emotions he advocated are essentially a secularized version of the biblical Golden Rule: courtesy, sensitivity to others, assertiveness rather than aggression. Understanding the need to motivate others, he advocated a system based on rewards and praise, not punishment. He advocated what would later be called conflict resolution and teamwork to replace the aggressive individualism of the mythic American frontier. Implicit everywhere and frequently explicit was the assumption that financial rewards will follow.

Unlike earlier self-help literature, Carnegie's book was an exhortation to action.

He gives instructions on how to use the book and summarizes his points for easy reference. Theories were kept to a minimum; anecdotal accounts were written so that a reader could imitate the behavior described.

Though condemned by critics and academicians, Carnegie's techniques and style, by the late twentieth century, had spread throughout much business literature as well as self-help literature. In the academically sanctioned *A Passion for Excellence* (1985), for example, authors Tom Peters and Nancy Austin incorporated much of Carnegie's anecdotal approach, gave tips for developing courtesy and sensitivity to others, and echoed Carnegie in their advocacy of motivation based on rewards and praise. Carnegie's influence also is evident in literature produced by entrepreneurs such as Mary Kay Ash, founder of Mary Kay Cosmetics, who in *Mary Kay on People Management* (1984), directly echoed Carnegie with chapters on "Golden Rule Management" and instructions about how to make others feel a sense of self-worth. She, too, urged motivation through rewards. Carnegie's views also are echoed in some New Age literature, such as Marilyn Ferguson's *The Aquarian Conspiracy: Personal and Social Transformation in the 1980s* (1980), in which abilities to motivate, engender self-esteem, and demonstrate sensitivity were defined as essential qualities in leaders of the future.

Stress reduction was the subject of the second best-seller produced by Carnegie as a result of his initial success. *How to Stop Worrying and Start Living* (1948) is Carnegie's best and perhaps most influential book. *How to Win Friends and Influence People* was written on the assumption that behavior modification was relatively simple; imitate a feeling, and the feeling will come. In his preface to his next book, however, Carnegie observed that the process turned out to be more complex because of the intervention of emotional blocks, chief among them anxiety or worry, which would later, as he described them, come to be called "stress." At the heart of these blocks, he noted, were unfocused fears about the future, humorlessness and self-importance, depression, inability to deal with criticism and life's inevitable adversities, and inability to accept oneself.

While Carnegie had no access to statistics indicating a relationship between stress and disease, he inferred this relationship from popular psychiatric literature and from personal observation of his father's depression and of his own tension-related headaches while he was living in New York slums. He found many historical anecdotes to show his readers that, if they were suffering, they were not alone. The book ends with thirty-one stories by those who have overcome stress, ranging from relatively unknown businessmen to singing cowboy Gene Autry, baseball star Connie Mack, and boxing champion Jack Dempsey. In effect, Carnegie had produced the first modern work on stress management. Again, he had offered his readers hope with the promise that at least some of their fate was within their control. By the 1990's, six million copies of *How to Stop Worrying and Start Living* had been sold, and its influence had been felt in the writings of such self-help leaders as Norman Vincent Peale and Robert Schuller.

Bibliography

Carnegie, Dale. *How to Develop Self-Confidence and Influence People by Public Speaking.* New York: Simon & Schuster, 1956. An adaptation of *Public Speaking and Influencing Men in Business* (1926), itself an adaptation of *Public Speaking: A Practical Course for Business Men* (1926). Includes chapters on memory development, preparation, and vocabulary development. More a formal textbook than a book of practical hints.

_____. *How to Stop Worrying and Start Living.* New York: Simon & Schuster, 1948. Revised by Dorothy Carnegie for new copyright in 1984.

_____. *How to Win Friends and Influence People.* New York: Simon & Schuster, 1936. The edition currently available was revised by Dorothy Carnegie in 1981.

_____. *The Quick and Easy Way to Effective Speaking.* New York: Simon & Schuster, 1962. Based on *Public Speaking and Influencing Men in Business* (see above), this is a basic skills volume compiled by Dorothy Carnegie from work in progress at the time of her husband's death. It contains practical advice, designed for oral expression but useful, also, for written communication.

Kasson, John F. *Rudeness and Civility: Manners in Nineteenth-Century Urban America.* New York: Hill & Wang, 1990. Gives passing mention to Carnegie and treats his work with contempt as showing the middle classes how to achieve a spurious gentility. This study contains much valuable material about the self-help tradition and the emergence of urbanization and industrialization, but it too facilely categorizes readers of self-help literature and ignores economic motivations.

Kemp, Giles, and Edward Claflin. *Dale Carnegie: The Man Who Influenced Millions.* New York: St. Martin's Press, 1989. Well written, but the authors have compensated for a scarcity of biographical material by fleshing the book out with accounts of Carnegie's training sessions. The writers have pulled together materials from various prefaces, newspaper reports, and reviews, but have obviously had no access to privileged materials.

Meyer, Donald. *The Positive Thinkers: Popular Religious Psychology from Mary Baker Eddy to Norman Vincent Peale and Ronald Reagan.* Rev. ed. Middletown, Conn.: Wesleyan University Press, 1988. This scholarly and difficult work is a primary source as a survey of self-help writers. The scope of the survey causes Meyer to lump together many dissimilar writers, and his distaste for his subject leads to superficial readings of many texts, including Carnegie's.

Betty Richardson

Cross-References

William James's *Pragmatism* Is Published (1907), p. 171; Wittgenstein Emerges as an Important Philosopher (1921), p. 518; The Book-of-the-Month Club and the Literary Guild Are Founded (1926), p. 686; Sartre's *Being and Nothingness* Expresses Existential Philosophy (1943), p. 1262; The Great Books Foundation Is Established (1947), p. 1351.

DISNEY RELEASES *SNOW WHITE AND THE SEVEN DWARFS*

Category of event: Motion pictures
Time: 1937
Locale: The United States

Snow White and the Seven Dwarfs *became a milestone in cinema history as the first full-length animated feature film*

Principal personages:
WALT DISNEY (1901-1966), the producer and creator of the cartoon legend Mickey Mouse and the genius behind the idea of full-length animated films
FRANK THOMAS (1912-   ),
ERIC LARSON (1933-1988),
WARD KIMBALL (1914-   ),
WOLFGANG REITHERMAN (1909-1985),
MILT KAHL (1909-1987), and
LES CLARK (1907-1979), the principal animators of *Snow White and the Seven Dwarfs*

Summary of Event

By 1937, Walt Disney was well known by filmmakers and audiences across the country. His animated hero, Mickey Mouse, was a nationally recognized figure and had been enormously popular since *Steamboat Willie* was released with sound in 1928. Disney's 1933 cartoon version of *The Three Little Pigs* often received larger marquee billing than the feature films at the theaters where it played. Disney's *Silly Symphony* series had successfully wedded classical music to the use of color animation, and one entry in the series, *Flowers and Trees*, had won several film awards.

Yet Walt Disney, far from being content with his position as a leading producer of short animation, had a grander design in mind. One warm evening in 1934, Disney called his animators together on a soundstage at the studio. He told them the story that would become *Snow White and the Seven Dwarfs*, acting out principal parts complete with voice intonations and facial gestures. He created suspense, filled in details, and even provided jokes and sight gags. At the end of the story, when Snow White was awakened from her deadly sleep by Prince Charming and carried away to his castle, many of the hard-boiled animators were in tears. Disney then told them that he planned to make a feature film of the story—not an eight-minute short—as complete and detailed as the story they had just heard.

Financing was a problem from the outset. Despite Disney's successes with short cartoon features, few lenders were willing to risk the half-million dollars that Disney originally projected as the cost of a feature film. The Depression was still stifling the

American economy, and no one was sure that Disney could find audiences of adults as well as children who would pay to watch a feature-length cartoon. As production costs skyrocketed toward the $1,488,000 that the finished *Snow White* cost, Hollywood insiders dubbed the project "Disney's Folly." Desperate for financing to complete the film, Disney was forced to show the incomplete film to his banker. He watched, horrified, as the banker remained grim and unmoved throughout the film. At the film's end, though, the banker turned to Disney and said, "Walt, that film is going to make you a hatful of money." It did.

Technically, the film was an incredibly complex project. Although actual animation did not begin until 1936, story work had been proceeding on an almost daily basis since 1934. It is estimated that more than one million drawings were made during the production of the film. Hollywood knew that a big project was afoot when Disney sent out a call for three hundred artists—a staggering number for a single film, but short of the real total needed. In fact, more than 750 artists worked on the film, including 32 animators, 102 assistants, 107 "inbetweeners" (who filled in bits of action between the animator's drawings), 20 layout artists, 25 background artists, 65 special-effects animators, and 158 inkers and painters.

Technicolor was still a new process in 1937; most films, live action and animated, were still produced in black and white. Studio chemists and artists mixed more than fifteen hundred shades of paint to determine the best hues for painting characters and backgrounds. This care provided a far more subtle and realistic effect than did the bright primary colors of other animation. To create the most realistic possible drawings, live models were used for several principal characters. The best known was Marge Belcher, who modeled Snow White (she later achieved fame as Marge Champion of the Marge and Gower Champion dance team).

As always in animation, finding the right voices for characters was vital. After auditioning more than 150 women, including actress Deanna Durbin, Disney chose Adriana Caselotti, daughter of a Los Angeles vocal coach, to be Snow White. Harry Stockwell voiced the Prince, and Pinto Colvig, better known as the voice of the Disney character Goofy, did the voices of Sleepy and Grumpy.

Disney, sparked by childhood memories of a 1917 silent-film version of *Snow White*, starring Marguerite Clark, nevertheless returned to the classic Brothers Grimm fairy tale as the basis for his film. Parts of the tale were deleted; the film witch, for example, presents Snow White with only a poison apple rather than with the poison lace and combs of the original. Parts of the tale were expanded, especially the roles of the dwarfs, which are only vaguely sketched in the original. Disney experimented with as many as twenty-four dwarf names and personalities (including such alternatives as Deafy, Awful, and Burpy) before settling on the seven that achieved cinematic immortality. The ending was rendered more traditionally romantic; in the Grimm tale, Snow White awakens when the bearers drop her glass coffin and the apple flies from her throat, but Disney had the Prince awaken Snow White with love's first kiss. *Snow White* had its premiere at the Carthay Circle Theater in Hollywood on December 21, 1937.

Impact of Event

Snow White was an enormous success with audiences, both immediately and over time. The film made $8,500,000 during its first release, an astonishing figure in light of the fact that children in 1937 paid a dime for theater admission. Though surpassed in 1939 by *Gone with the Wind*, *Snow White* held the record for a time as the highest-grossing motion picture ever. Furthermore, the film had several financially successful rereleases, including a special fiftieth anniversary release in 1987.

Snow White was a critical success as well. The *New York Daily News* reported in January, 1938, that "Disney has maintained faith with the Brothers Grimm in transferring the broad outline of the plot of the fairy tale to the screen, but he has drawn on his own delicious sense of humor, and that of his staff, for the delightful details that have been worked into the story." The *New York Herald Tribune* also reported in January, 1938, that Disney had "taken a Grimm fairy tale and brought it to such hauntingly beautiful pictorial realization that fantasy and reality are inextricably mingled in a world of fresh wonder and enchantment."

As a further indication of the acceptance of animation as a serious art form, *Snow White* received an Oscar nomination for best score (for Frank Churchill, Paul Smith, and Leigh Harline) and won a special award for Walt Disney for having produced "a significant screen innovation which has charmed millions and pioneered a great new entertainment field for the motion picture cartoon." The award, presented by Shirley Temple, consisted of one full-size Oscar and seven dwarf Oscars.

The *Snow White* record album was the first "original soundtrack" recording ever released; prior to that time, film music was rerecorded for release on records. Disney's use of music as a significant feature of his films, not just as background, began with *Snow White* and continued through the next half-century with such popular songs as "Zip-a-dee Doo-dah," "The Bare Necessities," and "Under the Sea."

Snow White also began the now-common procedure of backing a motion picture by an extensive merchandising campaign. At the time of the film's release, close to one hundred companies in the United States alone had been licensed to produce *Snow White* merchandise. Disney was a pioneer in the field of relating toys, watches, and clothing to a child's (or adult's) filmgoing experience.

The impact of *Snow White* on both Disney's career and on worldwide filmgoing audiences is hard to overstate. For Disney, the success of *Snow White* meant a financial and critical base from which he could launch new experiments. *Snow White*'s pioneering animation was succeeded by more complex animated features such as *Pinocchio* (1940), *Fantasia* (1940), *Alice in Wonderland* (1951), and *Sleeping Beauty* (1959); by ambitious films that combined live action and animation, such as *Song of the South* (1946) and *Mary Poppins* (1964); by highly successful pioneer work in television, both fantasy and documentary; and finally by the entertainment triumphs of Disneyland and Walt Disney World. As the concrete figures atop the Disney headquarters in Burbank, California, attest, Disney was indeed an empire built not only by Mickey Mouse but by seven dwarfs as well.

With *Snow White*, animation came into its own, not as a back-up for feature films or as a clever device for commercials, but as a medium for capturing fantasy for an international audience of all ages. Walt Disney steadfastly maintained that he did not make films for children but for the child in himself and in all viewers. The sheer personal will and tenacity that propelled him to make *Snow White* were reflected in his comment, "Sheer animated fantasy is still my first and deepest production impulse. The fable is the best storytelling device ever conceived, and the screen is its best medium."

Bibliography

The Complete Story of Walt Disney's Snow White and the Seven Dwarfs. New York: Harry N. Abrams, 1987. Illustrated anniversary edition of the Grimm tale that formed the basis of the Disney film. Good beginning point for reference work.

Finch, Christopher. *The Art of Walt Disney.* Rev. ed. New York: Harry N. Abrams, 1975. A concise edition of Finch's much larger earlier work by the same name. Provides a chapter of information on the making of *Snow White* and places the movie in the larger context of Disney's developing art form. Contains 251 illustrations, including 170 full-color plates.

Hollis, Richard, and Brian Sibley. Snow White and the Seven Dwarfs: *The Making of the Classic Film.* New York: Simon & Schuster, 1987. The best single book on the making of the film. Contains backgrounds, sources, anecdotes, and a wealth of early sketches and film plans.

Schickel, Richard. *The Disney Version.* Rev. ed. Simon & Schuster, 1985. A powerful, provocative analysis. Probably the best biographical study of Disney.

Thomas, Bob. *Disney's Art of Animation: From Mickey Mouse to Beauty and the Beast.* New York: Hyperion, 1991. A panoramic look at the films of Disney, including those made after Walt's death. Excellent chapter on the making of *Snow White*, with technical information made available in layman's language. Illustrated.

Evelyn Romig

Cross-References

Hollywood Enters Its Golden Age (1930's), p. 822; The Classic *The Wizard of Oz* Opens (1939), p. 1109; Disney's *Fantasia* Premieres and Redefines the Boundaries of Animation (1940), p. 1195; ABC Makes a Landmark Deal with Disney (1954), p. 1612; *The Flintstones* Popularizes Prime-Time Cartoons (1960), p. 1840; *The Simpsons* Debuts, Anchoring the Fledgling Fox Network (1990), p. 2652.

DREYFUSS DESIGNS THE BELL "300" TELEPHONE

Category of event: Fashion and design
Time: 1937
Locale: New York, New York

Henry Dreyfuss' design for the Bell "300" telephone—which remained the standard desk telephone from its introduction in 1937 until 1950—was a milestone in the coming of age of industrial design in the United States

Principal personages:

HENRY DREYFUSS (1904-1972), a pioneer of industrial design in the United States who applied to manufacturing the maxim that form should follow function

DORIS MARKS DREYFUSS (1903-1972), one of Dreyfuss' first employees and, after their marriage in 1930, his firm's business manager

NORMAN BEL GEDDES (1893-1958), a theatrical designer turned industrial designer whose 1932 book *Horizons* did much to popularize the style known as "streamlining"

WALTER DORWIN TEAGUE (1883-1960), another pioneer in the professionalization of industrial design in the United States

RAYMOND F. LOEWY (1893-1986), an innovator who became identified in the popular mind as the father of the new profession of industrial design

Summary of Event

Henry Dreyfuss was born on March 2, 1904, in New York City. He was graduated from the Ethical Culture Fine Arts High School in 1922. His father and grandfather had been in the theatrical equipment business, supplying costumes and props. Dreyfuss followed family tradition by becoming an apprentice to stage designer Norman Bel Geddes in the design of the sets for the 1924 Broadway hit *The Miracle*. Starting in 1923, Dreyfuss worked as a designer for the stage productions of the Strand Theater in New York City. His success at the Strand led to similar work for the nationwide RKO-Orpheum chain of vaudeville theaters. "Out of the sheer necessity of producing six new sets weekly for 260 weeks," he recalled in his *Designing for People* (1955), "came an understanding of what people like."

Dreyfuss was first attracted to industrial design in 1927, when an executive of Macy's department store asked him to look into the possibility of redesigning the store's merchandise to boost sales. Dreyfuss, though, turned down the job, because he thought that the changes involved would require too-costly retooling. He concluded that the way to improve the design of a product was to work directly with the product's manufacturer before the manufacturer had made a major investment in machinery and materials. "A fundamental premise was involved in my refusal—one from which I have never retreated," he later explained. "An honest job of design should flow from the inside out, not from the outside in."

In April, 1929, Dreyfuss opened his own independent design office on New York's Fifth Avenue. One of his first employees was Doris Marks, whom he married in 1930. After their marriage, she remained active in the firm as business manager. During the firm's early years when clients were few, Dreyfuss kept afloat financially by designing the sets for such Broadway shows as _The Last Mile_ (1930) and _The Cat and the Fiddle_ (1931). Gradually, though, he built up a following among manufacturers. One of his first commissions was his redesign of the mason jar to occupy less space; Dreyfuss achieved the goal by making the jar square with a rounded top. His "Toperator" washing machine for Sears, Roebuck in 1933 was a runaway sales success. So was his design in 1934 of a refrigerator for General Electric that had its motor unit at the bottom, enclosed in an easy-to-clean cabinet, instead of at the top. Starting in 1930, he worked as a consultant for the Bell Telephone Laboratories to design an improved desk telephone. The result of his collaboration with the Bell engineers, the "300" model—introduced in 1937—confirmed his reputation as a leader in the new field of industrial design. The "300" model remained the standard desk telephone until 1950, when it was replaced by another Dreyfuss model.

Other Dreyfuss designs included the "Big Ben" and "Baby Ben" alarm clocks for Westclox, a vacuum cleaner for Hoover, the Eversharp pen, a Royal typewriter, gas stations for Cities Service, bathroom fixtures for Crane, and farm equipment for John Deere. His influence was strongly felt in magazine publishing via his design of the formats for _McCalls_, _Time_, and _Reader's Digest_. His scale model of the "city of tomorrow" for the interior of the perisphere at the New York World's Fair of 1939-1940 did much to bring his name to popular attention.

Dreyfuss' most publicly visible contributions were in the transportation sphere. The two trains that he planned for the New York Central Railroad—the _Mercury_ (1936) and the even more famous _Twentieth Century Limited_ (1938)—set a new standard for luxurious rail travel. He designed the interiors of the American Export Lines ships SS _Independence_ and SS _Constitution_ along with those of many airplanes. He was proudest, though, of the prosthetic devices he invented for the victims of limb loss during World War II.

By the 1950's, his firm had grown to include two offices (in New York City and South Pasadena, California) headed by six partners, with a staff of fifty specialists and office personnel. Dreyfuss himself divided his time between the two offices. His approach to design called for detailed knowledge of all aspects of the manufacturing and selling of the product. Accordingly, he placed heavy emphasis upon research and teamwork in the design process, and he limited his clients to approximately fifteen at a time.

Impact of Event

Interest in industrial product design first appeared in Europe, climaxing in a 1925 Paris exhibition of designs and decorative arts. Industrial design, though, emerged as a profession first in the United States, where the rise of a consumer culture occurred earlier than in Europe. In the 1920's, demand for mass-market consumer items such as automobiles, sewing machines, refrigerators, radios, and other electric appliances increased enormously, and at the suggestion of their advertising agencies, manufacturers began to give more attention to the appearance of their products. Henry Ford's decision to meet increasing competition by replacing the Model T automobile with the new Model A in 1927 gave other businessmen a high-profile demonstration of the importance of style to sales. The Great Depression further pushed manufacturers into searching for ways to boost sales by making products more attractive and efficient.

The leading philosopher of the emergent profession of industrial design was Dreyfuss' mentor in stage design, Norman Bel Geddes. Geddes' 1932 book *Horizons* did much to popularize what became the dominant American style of the 1930's, streamlining, which emphasized the separation of the outer shell of a product from its internal mechanism. The outer shell typically had a smooth and flowing surface with rounded edges. Streamlining was strongly influenced by research in aerodynamics— the techniques for eliminating the friction of wind resistance to a moving vehicle. Researchers had concluded that the teardrop was the aerodynamically most efficient shape for a moving vehicle. Industrial designers in the 1930's extended the teardrop shape from its use in locomotives and automobiles and began to apply it to stationary objects.

Geddes was a technocratic utopian who envisaged industrial design transforming the world. A similar vision animated Walter Dorwin Teague. Teague had a successful career as an advertising illustrator before he began his second career as an industrial designer by creating (around 1930) several cameras for Eastman Kodak. He would count among his clients such other corporate giants as Ford, Texaco, and DuPont. Teague and Dreyfuss took the initiative in promoting organization of a professional association for industrial designers; they in turn brought in Raymond F. Loewy to constitute the founding triumvirate responsible for the establishment in 1944 of the Society of Industrial Designers.

Loewy came to personify for the lay public the new profession. Loewy—who had been born in Paris in 1893—launched his own independent design firm in New York City the same year that Dreyfuss opened his office. He would go on to become a household name with such designs as the Gestetner stencil duplicating machine (1929); the remodeled Coldspot refrigerator for Sears, Roebuck (1934); the interior of the Pennsylvania Railroad's *Broadway Limited* train (1938); the Chrysler Motors Building at the New York World's Fair of 1939-1940; the red-and-white package for Lucky Strike cigarettes (1941); the Greyhound Scenicruiser bus (1954); and the Studebaker Champion (1947), Starliner (1953), and Avanti (1962) automobiles.

Dreyfuss lacked Loewy's personal flamboyance and flair for self-publicity. Brown was his favorite color, not only for his suits but also for his office decor. He shared, however, Loewy's pragmatism. He saw increasing sales for the client as the industrial designer's primary responsibility. He applied to design problems a five-point yardstick: utility and safety, ease of maintenance, cost, sales appeal, and appearance. Although many of his designs reflected the dominant streamline model, he was no rigid devotee of that style. The keystone of his design credo was the maxim that "the most efficient machine is the one that is built around a person."

Thus, Dreyfuss' goal was to achieve maximum simplicity in fitting a product's form to its function. He was wary about moving too far ahead of popular taste. The industrial designer, Dreyfuss commented in his *Designing for People* (1955), "is a businessman as well as a person who makes drawings and models. He is a keen observer of public taste. . . . He has an understanding of merchandising, how things are made, packed, distributed, and displayed. He accepts the responsibility of his position as a liaison linking management, engineering, and the consumer and cooperates with all three."

Dreyfuss was elected president of the Society of Industrial Designers in 1947. He was a consultant in industrial design at the California Institute of Technology and lectured in engineering at the University of California at Los Angeles. He had privately printed a pictorial record of his designs: *Ten Years of Industrial Design, Henry Dreyfuss, 1929-1939* (1939); *A Record of Industrial Designs, 1929 Through 1947* (1947); *Industrial Design—A Progress Report, 1929-1952* (1952); and *Industrial Design—A Pictorial Accounting, 1929-1957* (1957). His *Designing for People* combined autobiographical reminiscences with a summation of his design philosophy. He presented the data he had accumulated about the physical dimensions of the "average" American in *The Measure of Man: Human Factors in Design* (1960).

Bibliography

Bush, Donald J. *The Streamlined Decade.* New York: George Braziller, 1975. An excellent survey, with accompanying extensive illustrations, of the application of streamlining to locomotives, automobiles, ships, airplanes, industrial products, and even buildings during the 1930's.

Dreyfuss, Henry. *Designing for People.* New York: Simon & Schuster, 1955. A handsome volume, all aspects of which (jacket, binding, typography, and page layout) were designed by Dreyfuss himself. The text combines autobiographical reminiscences with a summation of Dreyfuss' design philosophy. "Everything—absolutely everything—I know about industrial design is in these papers," he declared.

_____. *The Measure of Man: Human Factors in Design.* New York: Whitney Library of Design, 1960. A portfolio containing charts summarizing the data that Dreyfuss compiled on the physical dimensions of the "average" American for the guidance of industrial designers.

Meikle, Jeffrey L. *Twentieth Century Limited: Industrial Design in America, 1925-1939.* Philadelphia: Temple University Press, 1979. A detailed and thoroughly researched account of the formative years of the industrial design profession in the United States. The focus is upon the so-called big four of Geddes, Loewy, Teague, and Dreyfuss. Illuminating upon the assumptions, concepts, and visions influencing, and underlying, their design work.

Pulos, Arthur J. *American Design Ethic: A History of Industrial Design.* Cambridge, Mass.: MIT Press, 1983. A pioneering survey of American product design from the colonial period to the 1940's. Approximately the last third of the volume is devoted to the post-1920's period, when industrial design began to emerge as a recognized profession. Lavishly illustrated; includes an extensive bibliography.

_____. *The American Design Adventure, 1940-1975.* Cambridge, Mass.: MIT Press, 1988. Pulos carries on his history of American industrial design from where his first volume left off, with the same first-rate results.

John Braeman

Cross-References

Hoffmann and Moser Found the Wiener Werkstätte (1903), p. 79; Behrens Designs the AEG Turbine Factory (1909), p. 219; Rietveld Designs the Red-Blue Chair (1918), p. 458; German Artists Found the Bauhaus (1919), p. 463; Cranbrook Academy Begins a History of Design Excellence (1925), p. 610; A Paris Exhibition Defines Art Deco (1925), p. 654; Loewy Pioneers American Industrial Design (1929), p. 777.

PICASSO PAINTS *GUERNICA*

Category of event: Art
Time: 1937
Locale: Paris, France

Created for the Paris International Exposition, the painting expresses a great artist's horror at the bombing of the Basque capital Guernica during the Spanish Civil War

Principal personages:
PABLO PICASSO (1881-1973), the most prolific, famous, and versatile artist of the twentieth century
FRANCISCO FRANCO (1892-1975), the Fascist dictator who took power from the Spanish republic in a civil war

Summary of Event

Spanish by birth, Pablo Picasso spent most of his working life in France, in or near Paris. His political sympathies were always on the left (he joined the Communist Party in 1944), though his art did not begin to contain explicit political themes until the beginning of the Spanish Civil War, when a group of right-wing military officers, headed by Francisco Franco, attacked the democratically elected government of Spain. Outgunned by Franco and his allies (the Fascist regimes of Germany and Italy), the Spanish republic waged a losing battle over a three-year period, gradually relinquishing territory to the rebels, who mercilessly bombed the civilian population.

In early 1937, Picasso had written a poem ridiculing Franco, rejecting his rebellion, treating him as a subhuman type, and evoking the violence of war: the screaming of women, children, and animals, of inanimate objects such as beds, chairs, and curtains, and of nature itself—a holocaust of screaming that could be seen and smelled because it permeated everything. Picasso's strongest statement against the assault on the republic, however, came after the bombing on April 26, 1937, of the Basque capital Guernica, where sixteen hundred of seven thousand inhabitants were killed and seventy percent of the town destroyed during an attack by forty-three German bombers and low-flying planes armed with machine guns. Working at a furious rate over the course of a month, the artist produced a monumental canvas (twenty-five feet by eleven feet), fulfilling a commission given to him by the Spanish republic for the Paris International Exhibition. The painting was received not merely as a protest against a horrible act of war but as a symbol of the irrational forces of terror that had been loosed not only on Spain but on humanity as a whole in the twentieth century.

The stark brutality of this enormous painting is emphasized by Picasso's use of shades of black and white against a rectangular background, creating a field of violence, a killing ground. This mythic scene, expressive of the world's cruelty and not solely the product of a particular evil act, seems timeless, universal. The scene is dominated by the fragmented figures of human beings and animals arranged both horizontally and vertically—all with mouths open, screaming: a man tumbling from a burning building, a woman lamenting the dead baby in her arms, a dead soldier, fallen from his horse, his body in pieces. Another woman, dazed by the desolation and chaos, is on one knee, her head thrust upward on a diagonal toward a light another screaming woman holds over the soldier. As in so much of Picasso's painting, human faces and bodies are distorted (heads elongated, eyes, hands, and limbs enlarged), shown frontally and in profile at the same time, and flattened against the picture plane in order to increase the emotional impact of the setting and the conception of a people, a whole nation, suffering.

Several commentators have remarked that images of a horse and a bull are at the heart of the painting, linking it to Picasso's earlier bullfight paintings, which employed symbolic evocations of these animals to suggest the power and mobility the artist found compelling. In *Guernica*, the horse is clearly under attack; the bull, however, stands apparently unharmed and impassive, perhaps as an evocation of the impersonal brutality that attracts certain human beings to the bullfight but also of the terrible force the ritual of the bullfight seeks to master. At least one critic has interpreted the bull as hovering protectively above the woman wailing over her dead child, though the bull may have more to do with presenting death as part of the ritualistic recurrence of events such as the bullfight and war. In this respect, human beings and animals suffer the same fate. By juxtaposing horse and bull, Picasso seems to acknowledge his identification with the victims while frankly confessing that violence is inherent in the makeup of the universe. It is an austere vision and highly abstract, as befits a painting purporting to encompass the core conflict in the nature of the world and the inevitability of death—so often seen in the human and animal skulls Picasso painted and sculpted before *Guernica*.

The light bulb shining at the top center and the tile floor visible at the bottom of the painting suggest Picasso's effort to render the horror of war within the confines of art. This is not a naturalistic painting, in which the artist tries to re-create the look and the feel of the actual setting and event or the perspective of an eyewitness; instead, the painting offers a highly personal and aesthetic reaction to death and destruction, a deliberate distancing of the artist from the historical facts in order to portray the human condition.

The heavy symbolic load of *Guernica* is balanced by the fluidity of Picasso's line, the deftly drawn, flaring nostrils, teeth, and tongue of the horse, the almost equally wide open, concave mouths of the human victims who shout out the vitality of the life that is extinguished. This grim lyricism heightens emotional identification with the lives lost. The expressiveness of the art is at one with the expressiveness of its doomed figures. *Guernica* has been considered one of Picasso's finest paintings since his cubist period because it manages to suffuse the personal symbols and figures of his work with the struggles of a whole people and the fate of twentieth century civilization.

Impact of Event

Until *Guernica*, exactly where Picasso stood on the great issues of his time was not understood. It was supposed that he sympathized with leftist and democratic causes, but his art was not interpreted as having a particularly political orientation, even though many 1930's artists, writers, and musicians had created works that were socially and politically oriented—even directly supportive of political ideologies such as communism and anarchism.

In *Guernica*, Picasso fused his great reputation with the aspirations not only of the Spanish republic but also of all those politically progressive artists and activists who regarded Spain as the testing ground for the defense against Fascism. The prestige he lent to the cause of saving Spain can hardly be exaggerated. He had been previously attacked by certain Communist Party ideologues for finding refuge in what they regarded as a solely personal, idiosyncratic, and decadent art that did not reflect the aspirations of the masses or dignify their struggle. While *Guernica* is hardly an example of Socialist Realism, the kind of art the Communist Party saw as faithfully rendering the everyday as well as the heroic actions of the people, there is a sense of collective humanity in the painting that made it possible for Picasso to earn his place on the left (having been dismissed as a "degenerate" modern artist by the Nazis) while maintaining his standing as the foremost artist of his time. In 1939, the Museum of Modern Art in New York City gave Picasso his largest retrospective to date, calling it "Picasso: Forty Years of His Art." The exhibition included more than three hundred works, including *Guernica*, which had already been shown to great acclaim in London, Chicago, Los Angeles, and San Francisco.

Picasso ensured his standing among radicals by issuing in pamphlet form a series of etchings called *The Dream and Lie of Franco* (1937), later produced as postcards and sold to raise money for the Republican cause. The image of Picasso as an aloof artist alienated from his society gave way to the image of the artist expressing solidarity with the people, thus ratifying the social and political involvements of many of his contemporaries in art throughout the 1930's. On December 18, 1937, Picasso sent a statement of his political commitment to the American Artists' Congress in New York, affirming that the most important values of humanity were at stake in the attack on Spain. From that point on, he would periodically issue political statements, often drafted by his close Communist friends. Picasso would continue his involvement with the Communist Party in the postwar years, attending and designing posters for Party congresses.

Guernica was only one of a series of works that Picasso and other artists created in the years immediately preceding World War II that expressed a sense of foreboding, even of apocalypse. The somber and savage quality of many of his paintings produced during the war period express a personal despair, best evoked in a series of still lifes depicting the skulls of bulls' heads, their flesh flayed and lit by a naked candle flame, that Picasso produced during the Occupation.

Picasso's adamant refusal to leave Paris during the Occupation and his spurning of German offers of fuel to warm his studio made the artist a symbol of resistance. In one often-told story, Picasso is said to have been visited in his studio by a German officer who spotted a photograph of *Guernica* and wanted to know if Picasso had done it. "No," Picasso is supposed to have replied, "you did." In fact, there is some doubt about exactly how uncompromising Picasso's position toward the Germans actually was, but his loyalty to Paris became the stuff of legend, making him into a symbol of freedom and the unvanquished spirit and elevating him into a category all his own.

Throughout the war, the artist continued to create chilling examples of the impact of war on his consciousness. In *Death's Head* (1943), he strips away most of the human features from the face, leaving only the rounded, hollow eyes and jagged slits for the nose and mouth, suggesting the darkness and hollowness of war at a point when the wrenching emotions of *Guernica* have been spent. Similarly, *The Charnel House* (1945) goes beyond *Guernica* in presenting war's aftermath; in the later painting, the earth has become a mortuary, the resting place of the dead, where there is no screaming, where everything has been reduced to a ghastly silence in a world that is just discovering the atrocities of the concentration camps. Instead of the moving figures of *Guernica*, the bodies in *The Charnel House* are tumbled together as in a mass grave, with parts of bodies twisted together or gouging into one another; a frozen gasp of agony is expressed on the face of a woman upended and pressing down on the bodies below her. Humanity itself is rent and mangled in the painting.

Perhaps what is most gruesome about *The Charnel House* is that it is not, like *Guernica*, associated directly with war or with a catastrophic event, for the heap of broken corpses is shown beneath a mundane domestic scene: a white table with an empty jug and an empty saucepan. It is as if the war—not shown on the canvas— has resulted in the bankruptcy of everyday life, which rests upon (or covers up) a mountain of death.

In the long term, Picasso's *Guernica* contributed to a postwar questioning of the foundations of civilization. The Spanish Civil War and World War II were not seen merely as an aberration, a savage interlude between periods of peace, but as the outcome of malevolent strains within civilization itself, a much more frightening vision of the end of things than the insight that first prompted Picasso to paint *Guernica*.

Bibliography

Beardsley, John. *First Impressions: Picasso.* New York: Harry N. Abrams, 1991. A lucid introductory study with a chapter on *Guernica* and a large foldout illustration of the painting. Describes several other works Picasso created during the Spanish Civil War and World War II and situates both paintings and sculptures in their historical context. Color plates and index.

Blunt, Anthony. *Picasso's "Guernica."* New York: Oxford University Press, 1969. Heavily illustrated study (many of the plates are of the forty-five preliminary drawings) with photographs of the painting at various stages of realization. Blunt discusses *Guernica* in the context of Picasso's other work and in terms of European traditions that go back to antiquity. Large foldout of the painting and notes.

Gilot, Françoise. *Matisse and Picasso.* London: Bloomsbury, 1990. Incisive comments on *Guernica* and other works created during the Spanish Civil War and World War II in the light of Picasso's friendship and rivalry with his great contemporary. Having lived with Picasso for several years, and as an artist herself, Gilot provides a unique and sensitive reading of his art and its development. Notes and index.

Hilton, Timothy. *Picasso.* London: Thames and Hudson, 1975. Part of a chapter on *Guernica*, with several illustrations and discussion of preliminary drawings and the artist's related works. Notes the impact of Surrealism on Picasso's poetry and painting and some of the negative American responses to the style, and concludes that *Guernica* is a competent but not a breakthrough work.

Huffington, Arianna Stassinopoulos. *Picasso: Creator and Destroyer.* New York: Simon & Schuster, 1988. Although Huffington provides very little discussion of Picasso's art, she summarizes reactions to it and analyzes the biographical background of his paintings, including *Guernica.* Some aspects of this biography are sensationalized, but it does contain important information drawn from extensive interviews with the artist's friends and associates. Photographs, extensive bibliography, and index.

Sommer, Robin Langley. *Picasso.* New York: Smithmark, 1988. Sumptuous reproductions of Picasso's paintings and drawings, including a huge foldout of *Guernica*, enlargements of the bull and the horse, and a pencil-on-paper sketch and a pencil-and-crayon-on-paper sketch for the painting. Includes a full-page illustration of *The Charnel House* and many other color plates, with accompanying text.

Walther, Ingo E., and Hugh Beyer, trans. *Pablo Picasso, 1881-1973.* Cologne, Germany: Benedikt Taschen, 1986. An introductory study that includes a chapter on Picasso's wartime experience, a two-page layout of *Guernica*, and several black-and-white and color plates of work done during the war, including *The Charnel House.* An informative text, with sidebars quoting the artist on various aspects of his work and his attitude toward art. Detailed, illustrated chronology of the life and work and an extensive bibliography.

Carl Rollyson

Cross-References

The Salon d'Automne Rejects Braque's Cubist Works (1908), p. 204; Apollinaire Defines Cubism in *The Cubist Painters* (1913), p. 337; The Soviet Union Bans Abstract Art (1922), p. 544; New York's Museum of Modern Art Is Founded (1929), p. 782; Rivera's Rockefeller Center Mural Is Destroyed (1934), p. 957; García Lorca's *Poet in New York* Is Published (1940), p. 1179.

AALTO DESIGNS VILLA MAIREA

Category of event: Architecture
Time: 1937-1938
Locale: Noormarkku, Finland

Aalto's design of Villa Mairea, a masterpiece, confirmed him as one of the world's leading architects and helped to revolutionize residential architecture

Principal personages:
ALVAR AALTO (1898-1976), a distinguished twentieth century architect
AINO MARIO AALTO (1894-1949), an architect-designer and Alvar's first wife
ERIK GUNNAR ASPLUND (1885-1940), a Swedish architect and Alvar's friend
LE CORBUSIER (CHARLES-ÉDOUARD JEANNERET, 1887-1965), an early influence on Aalto
WALTER GROPIUS (1883-1969), a founder of modern architecture and an influence on Aalto
FRANK LLOYD WRIGHT (1867-1959), a distinguished architect and a humanistic influence on Aalto and Villa Mairea

Summary of Event

Alvar Aalto's design and construction of Villa Mairea in Noormarkku, Finland, in 1937 and 1938 produced one of the masterpieces of modern domestic architecture. Among architects and architectural critics, the structure has been accorded rank with Ludwig Mies van der Rohes' Tugendhat House (1930), Le Corbusier's Villa Savoye (1931), and Frank Lloyd Wright's Fallingwater (1936) as a twentieth century landmark. Like many other impressive art works, Villa Mairea also represented a fruitful symbiosis between wealthy, intellectually progressive clients and an inspired architect, the evolution of whose own maturing work required opportunity, empathy, and experimental freedom.

Aalto's patrons and clients were millionaires Henry and Maire Gullichsen. Maire Ahlström Gullichsen was heiress to Finland's Ahlström fortune, wealth that had been earned over three generations in lumber, pulp mills, paper products, and furniture. Upon his marriage to Maire, Henry Gullichsen became chairman of the board of the Ahlström business, while Maire, a painter by profession as well as a successful executive, collaborated with Alvar Aalto and his designer-architect wife, Aino, in manufacturing and marketing the Aaltos' unique wood and plywood furniture. Both Gullichsens were patrons of the arts and, like the Aaltos, were also social and political liberals who looked forward to contributing to fuller lives for workers and employers alike.

By 1937, Aalto had been a practicing architect for fifteen years. Until then, both his writings about his architectural philosophy and his works clearly indicated the influence of the earlier works of Walter Gropius, Le Corbusier, and several of their disciples, including Aalto's Swedish friend and colleague Sven Markelius (Jonsson). Aalto's early works and writings thus showed his adherence to a strict rationalist or functionalist style known as modern architecture or the International Style. Thus Aalto, like all functionalists, rejected the older architectural criteria of aestheticism and decorativeness. Instead, he believed that a building should reflect only its specific needs. Just as an engineer would design a machine for a definite purpose rather than with an artistic end in mind, the rationalist architect, too, treated each of his structures as a discrete product of social, technical, psychological, and economic organization, with himself as a presumptive social administrator. The creation of beauty, of course, was not ignored, but it was a secondary consideration in the design of functionalist architecture.

Aalto's earlier designs and structures, therefore, display the characteristically spartan, boxlike, elementary geometric forms that Le Corbusier, himself a painter as well as author and architect, derived from purist and cubist painting. There was ample evidence of this bent in four of Aalto's most important commissions before 1937: the *Turun-Sanomat* newspaper building (1928-1929), the Paimio Tuberculosis Sanatorium (1930-1933), the Viipuri Municipal Library (1933-1935), and the Helsinki Savoy Restaurant (1937). The modernist style is also reflected in his (and Aino's) splendidly distinctive functional furniture, which by the mid-1930's had gained international acclaim.

By the late 1930's, however, Aalto's perspectives were changing. There were several explanations for this. To begin with, after the departure of Eliel Saarinen for America, Aalto aspired to replace him as Finland's dominant national architect. Then, too, during the 1930's, with the broadening of his influential professional contacts in Europe and America, he shed much of his remaining provincialism. Morever, the freedom vouchsafed him by the Gullichsens to design their vacation home in Noormarkku allowed him to synthesize all that was best in his previous designs.

Aalto sited Villa Mairea in the West Finnish hills among pine forests on an Ahlström family estate that contained domestic architecture representative of three generations of one of Finland's leading families. The villa was intended to serve as a vacation home for the Gullichsens and their children, as an art studio for Maire, and as a business and entertainment center—or, as need be, a retreat—for both husband and wife. Aalto was to design everything: building, interior decor and furnishings, swimming pool, and sauna.

Completed, the villa established a great sense of privacy yet satisfied all of the Gullichsens' practical and aesthetic requirements. The building was a U-shaped, open structure that nevertheless was subtly divided into living and service areas. Thus, although the ground-floor living spaces were flowing and continuous, they could be broken up for the display or enjoyment of the family's collected art by means of easily movable partitions (in which art works were also stored), and dining facilities were separate. The ample living room was divided between a private Finnish hearth and, by way of contrast, a substantial, well-planted solarium with large picture windows. Far left of the main entrance was a superstructure that served as Maire Gullichsen's studio, which on the second floor gave way to another living room and bedrooms with boldly projecting windows. To the rear, visible directly through back windows of the main living room, ran a covered portico that ended in a right angle containing a sauna—almost Japanese in its motifs—and a kidney-shaped swimming pool. The home's rough "U" was closed by forest.

Aalto's inimitable detailing marked both exterior and interior. Outside, there were venetian blinds, exposed vertical board and batten, columns bound by willow withes, and a natural turf-and-grass roof for the sauna. The inside featured pole-space dividers, living-room pillars protected by leather wrappings, slatted wood ceilings of Finnish birch, distinctive ventilation through tens of thousands of hand-bored holes in the living-room ceiling, daringly ingenious staircases, and, throughout, specially designed Aalto furniture. Villa Mairea, as critic Göran Schildt summarized, embodied "the vernacular tradition, the organic overall conception of Art Nouveau, Neo-Classical humanism, rational Functionalism, Japanese feeling for texture and Aalto's personal susceptibility to the complex interaction of natural forces."

Impact of Event

The completed Villa Mairea marked Aalto's maturation. His background and character, blended through experience with his work, modified, romanticized, and humanized his earlier rationalist ideology and functionalist architecture. Born in 1898, Aalto spent formative years in a rural, heavily forested Finland that, until 1917, was a western province of Imperial Russia untouched by extensive industrialization and urbanization. Even its major resources and their related industries—timber, wood and paper products, mining, and water power—required only small, isolated rural communities. The forces and mythologies of nature were part of his environment, as they were for his father, a surveyor, and his grandfather, a forester. Respect for nature, terrain, and environment, qualities that began manifesting themselves in Aalto's designs of the Paimio Sanatorium, the Viipuri Library, and the Finnish Pavilion (at the 1937 Paris Exposition), became even more striking after completion of Villa Mairea.

By the late 1930's, Aalto was taking full advantage of his clients' natural environments and designing structures that afforded them the most humane living and working conditions. The Sunila Sulphate Mill, completed in 1939, thus rises out of its granitic terrain faced by a warm, rough Finnish brick, its horizontal lines softened by a slight arch over the central structure and accented by a tall smokestack. Nearby employees' and executive housing, initially a small, cellular community that Aalto planned around a communal laundry and steam bath—later expanded to include larger civic and community centers—has been kept to human proportions by using the broken granite moraine to divide dwellings into modest clusters. Furthermore, at Aalto's insistence, few of the houses are identical; in line with the evolution of Finland's ancient village housing, provisions were made for each home to expand as family needs changed. Aalto carefully discriminated between the need for standardized production of construction materials and standardized housing.

Aalto's concern with placing humans more properly in their natural surroundings by the use of rugged, natural materials became even more apparent in his design of the Finnish Pavilion for the 1939 New York World's Fair. A proud nationalist aware of his country's need for good relations with the United States, he built the pavilion of Finnish woods, the interior highlighted by an undulating wooden display wall reminiscent of the northern lights. The pavilion was a warm, inviting structure adjacent to the American exhibition and, clearly, was a romantic alternative to the International Style. Aalto's new rationalism had accomplished much the same effect in his stepped multiple housing project at Kauttua, where varied residential structures marched up a hillside as in an Italian hill town and where Aalto's use of vertical poles and metal railings, covered with vines, repeated themes from the surrounding trees and forests.

With the reconstruction required in 1940 after the end of the Russo-Finnish War— one immense consequence of which was the loss of Karelia, Finland's most populous province, and the forced resettlement of a huge population—Aalto even more imaginatively spoke to his desire to clarify relations between man and nature in his design of the cellular housing project of Rovaniemi. More impressive still was his plan for the Finnish Technical Institute at Otaniemi, on the outskirts of Helsinki, where terrain almost entirely dictated the character of the structure. Thereafter, just as Aalto had drawn some inspiration from Frank Lloyd Wright's Fallingwater house in Pennsylvania, so too his own future work was characterized increasingly by his departures from literal rationalism toward a more personal, more humane, architectural expression. The evolution of his style is visible in his later works, such as his design of the Baker House (1946-1949) at the Massachusetts Institute of Technology, where Aalto taught part-time from 1945 to 1951.

Aalto definitively signaled his presence at Villa Mairea. He was soon viewed as Finland's national architect and as an international figure of the front rank—some thought the greatest architect alive. He had reversed the formulas of Gropius and Le Corbusier; his mature view was that nature, not the machine, was the architect's most important model. His humane perspective in America alone won him the allegiance of young architects such as Hugh Stebbins, Charles Warren Callister, and Ralph Rapson. Aalto mastered the use of his origins and its vernacular, building within the whole fabric of his environment yet bending modern materials to achieve his purposes. A warm, modest man, he lacked Le Corbusier's capacity for stridency and self-advertisement and the urge to monumentality found in some others. He was a brilliant innovator, exquisitely sensitive to his local traditions and conditions and yet able to draw upon all of architecture's major styles for the benefit of humankind.

Bibliography

Aalto, Alvar. *Alvar Aalto.* Edited by Karl Fleig. Zurich: Les Éditions d'Architecture

Artemis, 1970. Splendid text and photos of Aalto's major works. Parallel texts in German, French, and English recite detailed descriptions of Aalto structures, designs, and furnishings. Hundreds of photos and plans, but no other reader aids. Worth careful perusal.

Donnelly, Marion C. *Architecture in the Scandinavian Countries.* Cambridge, Mass.: MIT Press, 1992. Important in placing Aalto in the specific vernaculars of Scandinavia. An authoritative, easily read survey. Many excellent photos and annotated texts. Appendices, chapter notes, fine up-to-date bibliography, and an excellent index.

Giedion, Siegfried. *Space, Time, and Architecture.* 5th rev. ed. Cambridge, Mass.: Harvard University Press, 1967. A recognized classic and a handmaiden to most architects' recapitulation of their own professional history. Should be read in its entirety, but Giedion early understood the importance of Aalto's outlook and work and thus included a full chapter on him before he was widely known. Some illustrative matter, notes and bibliography, as well as an index. Outstanding, whether or not one shares the author's critical pronouncements.

Gutheim, Frederick. *Alvar Aalto.* New York: George Braziller, 1960. Five brief, sketchy, and superficial chapters that suffice only for an introduction to Aalto. Should be supplemented with the work of Fleig, Pearson, or Schildt for any real understanding of the man or his works. Many good photos, plans, a chronology of works, brief select bibliography, and an adequate index.

Pearson, Paul David. *Alvar Aalto and the International Style.* New York: Whitney Library of Design, 1978. Authoritative and appreciative. Organization is chronological, and the text is easily read and detailed. A fine one-volume review of Aalto's origins, career, achievements, and philosophies. Prominence is accorded to Villa Mairea. Scores of excellent photos and plans, good chapter notes, useful bibliography—particularly for article materials—and a solid triple-columned index. Must reading for laymen and experts alike.

Schildt, Göran. *Alvar Aalto: The Decisive Years.* New York: Rizzoli, 1986. Enjoyable and indispensable. Matchless for intimate, personal perspectives on Aalto's mature years. Schildt was Aalto's favorite critic, and he does a brilliant job of summarizing Aalto's and other functionalists' ideas about a technological utopia. Also discusses changes in Aalto's rationalist beliefs. Contains much material on Villa Mairea. Scores of excellent photos, including personal ones, and plans. Includes a detailed list of Aalto's works from 1928 to 1939 along with drawings and thumbnail descriptions. No notes, bibliography, or index. Outstanding.

Clifton K. Yearley

Cross-References

Hoffmann Designs the Palais Stoclet (1905), p. 124; Gaudí Completes the Casa Milá Apartment House in Barcelona (1910), p. 257; German Artists Found the Bauaus (1919), p. 463; Cranbrook Academy Begins a History of Design Excellence (1925),

p. 610; Le Corbusier's Villa Savoye Redefines Architecture (1931), p. 869; Wright Founds the Taliesin Fellowship (1932), p. 902; Le Corbusier Designs and Builds Chandigarh (1951), p. 1503; Fuller's First Industrial Geodesic Dome Is Erected (1953), p. 1579; Saarinen Designs Kennedy Airport's TWA Terminal (1956), p. 1716; Kahn Blends Architecture and Urban Planning in Dacca (1962), p. 1919.

RENOIR MARKS THE HIGH POINT
OF PREWAR FILMMAKING

Category of event: Motion pictures
Time: 1937-1939
Locale: Paris, France

With such socially conscious films as The Grand Illusion *and* The Rules of the
Game, *Jean Renoir established himself as one of the world's premier directors*

Principal personages:
> JEAN RENOIR (1894-1979), an acclaimed director considered by many the
> world's greatest
> CHARLES SPAAK (1903-1975), a screenwriter who collaborated with Re-
> noir
> PIERRE FRESNAY (1897-1975), an actor who played the role of de Boeldieu
> in *The Grand Illusion*
> ERICH VON STROHEIM (1885-1957), a director of many motion pictures
> and an actor who played the role of von Rauffenstein in *The Grand
> Illusion*
> MARCEL DALIO (1900-1983), an actor who played the roles of Rosenthal
> in *The Grand Illusion* and Robert de la Chesnaye in *The Rules of the
> Game*
> JEAN BACHELET (1894-   ), a photographer who worked with Renoir
> on many films

Summary of Event

When it premiered on June 4, 1937, at the Marivaux Cinema in Paris, Jean Renoir's film *La Grande Illusion* (*The Grand Illusion*) marked the culmination of Renoir's career as a French motion-picture director who explored social themes, expressed sympathy for workers, and criticized establishment capitalism. Renoir's films before 1937 included *Le Crime de M. Lange* (1936; *The Crime of Monsieur Lange*), about a worker who saves a company and then kills the boss. Earlier, Renoir showed interest in the naturalistic tales of Émile Zola and Maxim Gorky, with a silent film, *Nana*, in 1926 and a talking film, *Les Bas-fonds* (*The Lower Depths*), in 1936. He made *La Vie est à nous* (*The People of France*), blatantly proletarian propaganda, in 1936, but it did not have a public screening in France until 1969.

The Grand Illusion is a continuation of Renoir's preoccupation with working peoples' struggles against social and political tyranny. Set during World War I, the film sets forth a view of the future that makes heroes of an unlikely team, the mechanic Maréchal and the rich Jew Rosenthal. While a plea for peace, it is not altogether an antiwar film, because its heroes escape captivity to continue their struggle against their common enemies, the old order of European aristocracy and the German army.

La Règle du jeu (*The Rules of the Game*), released in a cut print in 1939, was hooted by its first audiences, nearly lost when its original negative was destroyed during Allied bombing raids during World War II, and finally restored to something near its original length in 1956. Despite the film's stormy beginning, its reputation grew tremendously over the decades until it became one of the world's most critically acclaimed achievements in motion pictures. In the film, Renoir examines again the relationships of workers and owners, servants and masters, with a dashing hero who is killed by a jealous husband, a wealthy aesthete of Jewish ancestry who is married to a moralistic Austrian, and two complementary poachers—one a failed artist and the other a failed servant.

Both motion pictures were achievements of a distinctive style that has been praised as realistic and democratic. Deep-focus shots were made of scenes in which several events occurred simultaneously, allowing spectators to observe a variety of movements, characters, and complications in a single field of vision. Subjects intermingle, as war and captivity bring together men of contrasting social backgrounds in *The Grand Illusion*, and love throws together men and women of varying social classes in *The Rules of the Game*. Both narratives follow similar patterns: from prison enclosure to pastoral liberation in *The Grand Illusion*; from sophisticated urban hypocrisy to pastoral farce in *The Rules of the Game*. The director casts a cold eye on decaying values, but he also exposes a sympathetic understanding of the trials through which people pass as their values are tested and found wanting.

The Grand Illusion explores the ironies of a war in which the officers of the opposing armies may have more in common with one another than they have with the men who serve under their commands. Von Rauffenstein is a gentleman with training and tastes shared by de Boeldieu; when together, they often speak English, which is not understood by the commoners, as the language of the aristocracy. Von Rauffenstein is the commandant of a gloomy and massive castle used as a prison for French, English, and Russian prisoners of war. He is not happy to be a policeman, but he has little choice, since he is crippled and scarred from battle. Von Rauffenstein is forced, by his code of honor, to shoot de Boeldieu when the French officer helps his men to escape the German prison.

Maréchal and Rosenthal make their escape and nearly die of hunger and exhaustion, but they finally reach an idyllic, though not completely safe, haven in the farm home of a German widow, Elsa, and her little girl. The French soldiers are warmly received by this family of the enemy, and they celebrate Christmas together. Eventually, the Frenchmen continue their escape, despite Maréchal's love for Elsa, and they succeed in crossing the border into Switzerland before a German patrol spots them. Several borders are crossed in the film's symbolic use of realistic material, including the sexual borders that disappear when the prisoners dress as women to present a musical entertainment and, of course, the social and racial borders that are dissolved when the laborer allies himself with the Jewish bourgeoisie.

When de Boeldieu dies, von Rauffenstein cuts the blossom of his geranium, and by this gesture enhances the symbolic richness of the film. Of such details *The Rules of the Game* is full, such as a car wreck, a rabbit and bird hunt on a country estate, and a musical entertainment that concludes in a dance of death. The social texture of life in this motion picture is richly complicated, but moving across the boundaries of class distinctions are two profoundly interesting characters—the game poacher Marceau and the failed artist Octave, played by Renoir himself. The film complicates human relationships through the game of love, but it also analyzes the rules governing the game of civilization.

Impact of Event

The Grand Illusion won several prizes for Renoir, including one in Venice in 1937 for best artistic production and one in New York in 1938 for best foreign film. Most interesting, however, is the vote by an international jury at the Brussels World's Fair in 1958 that ranked the film fifth among the best films of all time. *The Rules of the Game* has earned similar respect, having been chosen as the third greatest film ever made by an international poll of film critics in 1962. The latter film also earned the dubious honor of being hissed by its first audiences in Paris, banned by Nazis and Fascists, but praised by President Franklin Roosevelt.

As a political statement, *The Grand Illusion* seemed to challenge militarist solutions to personal and social problems; indeed, some believed the film was highly pacifistic. Such an interpretation, however, has to take into account the sympathetic treatment of the soldiers as men doing their duties, sacrificing personal comforts, and devoting themselves to patriotism. In this respect, then, *The Grand Illusion* is romantic. Certainly, when de Boeldieu diverts German attention to assist the escapes of Maréchal and Rosenthal, de Boeldieu is performing a very romantic act of self-sacrifice.

To describe de Boeldieu's self-sacrifice as a theatrical role in the grand manner would not be an exaggeration. Renoir frequently used the device of theater or musical performance as a visual metaphor within his films. This technique of self-reflection and self-commentary would be taken up with equal sophistication by younger directors, such as François Truffaut and Federico Fellini. Truffaut, certainly, and Fellini perhaps were both students of Renoir's film style, against which they increasingly defined themselves.

It may seem odd to say that the self-reflective technique of theatricality within a motion picture is in a realistic style. The realism, though, is in the ostentatious claim by art to mirror reality, by drama to show an audience to itself, and by art to abstract the timeless from the temporal. Renoir's theatrical metaphors perform these functions. The soldiers' show in drag, followed by de Boeldieu's grand operatic gestures of self-sacrifice (which he carefully directs and stages for maximum effect), enclosed by von Rauffenstein's stiffly disciplined show of power—these reveal a confidence that play and art reveal essential truths and at the same time can be instruments for individual freedom and personal integrity. Soldiers dressed as women are men expressing their sexual and romantic desires. Grand gestures of sacrifice focus on tragic heroes, allowing romantic ones to escape. Discipline without purpose becomes an iron prison of the spirit.

Mechanical motions, from phonographs to crippled soldiers, occur in counterpoint to organic development in *The Grand Illusion* (ironically presented in von Rauffenstein's cutting the geranium blossom, as well as in the contrast between the massive prison and the idyllic farm). Similar counterpoint occurs in *The Rules of the Game*, but discipline is a source of integrity in that film, in which social order preserves individual identity from the anarchy represented by a thief (Marceau, a rabbit poacher) and an aviator (Jurieux, a solo flier). Although the film's protagonist, Chesnaye, seems to arrange and explain events, he is able to do so largely because of the animating spirit of the artist Octave. The fact that Renoir played this part is surely a reason the film is so intriguingly successful as a self-reflective experience of art. Octave is nearly a victim of misunderstanding, but he is also a figure of animality (symbolized by his wearing of a bear costume), which unites people in an organic way. Octave is a complement to Chesnaye. Their relationship is a warm advance on the destructive one that marked the pairs in *The Grand Illusion*.

Still, audiences did not like what they saw in *The Rules of the Game*, perhaps because it told them they were decadent without direction, careless about the value of life. The film ends with Chesnaye excusing a murder and turning back into his lighted chateau after Octave has wearily moved into the darkness of the opposite direction. The ending could leave an audience feeling dislocated, torn apart at the center, as form separates from substance, discipline from vitality. This joyless conclusion irritated the Nazis and Fascists condemned by the movie. Others, such as President Roosevelt, saw something different.

Perhaps the most lasting impact of *The Rules of the Game* is in its portrayal of the triumph of the will to be, to endure, even when the game seems about to end and the rules are shown to be vulnerable to passion and to chance. Chesnaye, like a master of ceremonies, turns away from his audience at the end, and Octave moves into the audience as he moves into the darkness. (Renoir, like Chesnaye, turned away from his European audience and moved, like Octave, into an American one when he migrated to the United States during the war and later became an American citizen.) There is an affirmative consequence from these opposing movements, as the spirit of life disappears into the audience itself, where it can rejuvenate as it hibernates through the long, dark spiritual winter that is expected to follow (and did, in the war years). Such a residue of feeling, a calm beneath the passion spent, is more lasting because it is more realistic for living beings, moving through organic rhythms of light and dark, vigor and rest. Here is the major impact of the film, and of others directed by Renoir: entertainments end, ironies soften, and artists disappear through their art into their audiences.

Bibliography

Durgnat, Raymond. *Jean Renoir*. Berkeley: University of California Press, 1974. A masterful survey of Renoir's life and work, with analyses of Renoir's films in chronological order. Durgnat presents Renoir as a storyteller with a mind to share. Contains a bibliography, an index, and many photographs, both stills from the films and views of Renoir at home and at work.

Ellis, Jack C. "Golden Age of French Cinema, 1935-1939." In *A History of Film.* 3d ed. Englewood Cliffs, N.J.: Prentice-Hall, 1990. Sees Renoir's career as peaking in the era when films by Jacques Feyder, Marcel Pagnol, and Marcel Carné drew upon a rich literary, theatrical, and painting tradition. Political turmoil, with escapist tendencies, was reflected in their movies. Includes stills, a list of major films, and a bibliography.

Faulkner, Christopher. *The Social Cinema of Jean Renoir.* Princeton, N.J.: Princeton University Press, 1986. A demanding study of the origins of Renoir's themes in political activity of the 1930's. Faulkner employs techniques of ethnography to analyze many of Renoir's films, including *The Grand Illusion* and *The Rules of the Game.* Contains a bibliography and index.

Leprohon, Pierre. *Jean Renoir.* Translated by Brigid Elson. New York: Crown, 1971. Presents Renoir as a painter's son and a craftsman who matured during the 1930's with three masterworks. The American Renoir is sketched as struggling to please Hollywood but eager to return to his sources. Contains excerpts of interviews, screenplays, essays, anecdotes, filmography, bibliography, and index.

Mast, Gerald. "France Between the Wars." In *A Short History of the Movies.* 3d ed. Indianapolis, Ind.: Bobbs-Merrill, 1981. French experimental film of the 1920's prepared for the triumphant films of the 1930's. Analyzes *The Crime of Monsieur Lange, The Grand Illusion*, and *The Rules of the Game.* Surveys René Clair, Jean Vigo, Jacques Feyder, Marcel Carné, and Jacques Prévert. Contains an index and a valuable bibliography/filmography.

Pechter, William S. "Radical Freedom: Aspects of Jean Renoir." In *Twenty-Four Times a Second: Films and Film-Makers.* New York: Harper & Row, 1971. Pechter sees a continuity of theme over thirty years of Renoir's work. Failure to resolve conflicts between individual freedom and social commitments results in sadness.

Thompson, Kristin. "An Aesthetic of Discrepancy: *The Rules of the Game.*" In *Breaking the Glass Armor: Neoformalist Film Analysis.* Princeton, N.J.: Princeton University Press, 1988. A difficult essay, forming a long chapter in a book pursuing a technique of formalist analysis. Asking what constitutes the film's realism, Thompson shows the causes in discrepancies between classical and contrary narrative structures.

Richard D. McGhee

Cross-References

The Birth of a Nation Popularizes New Film Techniques (1915), p. 402; Von Stroheim Films His Silent Masterpiece *Greed* (1924), p. 593; *All Quiet on the Western Front* Stresses the Futility of War (1929), p. 767; Welles's *Citizen Kane* Breaks with Traditional Filmmaking (1941), p. 1200; The Italian New Wave Gains Worldwide Acclaim (1942), p. 1228; The French New Wave Ushers in a New Era of Cinema (1956), p. 1710.

BERG'S *LULU* OPENS IN ZURICH

Category of event: Music
Time: June 2, 1937
Locale: Zurich, Switzerland

Alban Berg's Lulu, *written in a personalized version of the twelve-tone compositional style, premiered in Zurich in truncated form; the completed version would not premiere until 1979*

> *Principal personages:*
> ALBAN BERG (1885-1935), the Austrian composer of two operatic masterworks, *Wozzeck* and *Lulu*
> HELENE BERG (?-1976), the composer's wife and widow, who prevented the performance of the complete score of *Lulu* during her lifetime
> FRANK WEDEKIND (1864-1918), the German playwright whose plays inspired Berg to write his final opera

Summary of Event

The performance history of the opera *Lulu* is one of the most complicated in musical history. It took three quarters of a century between the opera's conception and its world premiere in the definitive form intended by its composer, Alban Berg, before an audience could comfortably say it had seen the "real" *Lulu*. The tortuous stage history of *Lulu* involves the composer's premature death, a world war, a succession of provocative but inadequate productions, a good deal of scholarly bickering, and even a ghost.

As a young man, Alban Berg was deeply impressed by a May, 1905, performance of Frank Wedekind's play *Die Büsche der Pandora* (1904; *Pandora's Box*, 1918). Wedekind himself had been inspired by reports of the gruesome murders of Jack the Ripper in London and wrote a play on the topic. To avoid almost certain difficulties with the German censor, he published only the first three acts of the play as *Erdgeist* (1895; *Earth Spirit*, 1914), and eventually the remaining portions of the play were published as *Pandora's Box*. Like Freud before him, Wedekind discovered that German and Austrian audiences at the turn of the century were not willing to tolerate his radical views. What made the work so shocking was its implicit call for complete female sexual freedom and its depiction of human sexuality as an endlessly disruptive force. One prominent scholar has called Wedekind's plays "sex tragedies *par excellence*, a ferocious battle in the Nietzschean sense between the sexes and ultimately a conflict between spirit (man) and flesh (woman)."

When Berg died on Christmas Eve, 1935, he had completed the short score for the entire opera, but not the full orchestral score. Erwin Stein had prepared the complete piano-vocal score (the reduction of the full score for voice parts and piano), but the engraving by Berg's publisher, Universal Editions, was halted by the onset of World

War II and never completed. Although he was not Jewish, Berg was denounced by the German press for sharing the "decadence" of the Arnold Schoenberg circle of composers.

For the opera's world premiere in Zurich, Switzerland, on June 2, 1937, at which Nuri Hadzic sang the role of Lulu and Robert Denzler conducted, the musicians had full access only to the first two acts of the piece. In place of the crucial third act, the musicians made use of fragments from Berg's previously published *Lulu Symphony*, which was a sort of advertisement for the opera-in-progress. (The *Lulu Symphony* had premiered in Berlin in November, 1934.) The woefully truncated third act, used until 1979, consisted of twelve minutes of music, ending with the murder of Lulu and her companion, the Countess Geschwitz, by Jack the Ripper. The use of fragments of the *Lulu Symphony* was a stage director's attempt to round out the action and had not been sanctioned by Berg.

The first concert performance of *Lulu* after the interruption of World War II occurred in Berg's native Vienna on March 16, 1949, and the first postwar stage production took place at Essen, Germany, on March 7, 1953, still with the truncated, improvised third act. This was the version that served for the production of the Hamburg State Opera, a version that was widely influential during the 1960's, for the American premiere, in Santa Fe, New Mexico, on August 7, 1963 (sung in English), and the Metropolitan Opera's premiere, on March 18, 1977 (in German).

What had become of Berg's third act? Why did it take forty-three years between the composer's death and its premiere? The answer lies with a misguidedly loyal widow. Helene Berg was determined to prevent the completion of her late husband's final opera. A spiritualist, she claimed to be in constant contact with the ghost of her husband, who, she said, urged her to prevent any attempts to complete the score, and she preserved the Bergs' residence in the way that it stood on the day of Alban's death. She also claimed to have been told by Berg's friends, the composers Schoenberg, Anton von Webern, and Alexander von Zemlinsky, that the opera was "unfinishable." Although her word was accepted as fact for many years, the few critics who gained access to the manuscript materials reported that the score was basically complete and could easily be performed; it remains puzzling why Universal Editions collaborated with the widow's obstinacy.

Not until Helene Berg's death in 1976 did the publisher relent and allow wider access to the manuscript. The Austrian scholar Friedrich Cerha was chosen to examine and complete the orchestral score, and the Paris Opera was chosen to offer the world premiere on February 24, 1979, with the soprano Teresa Stratas in the title role and Pierre Boulez conducting; the production staged was by Patrice Chereau. Despite some complaints about Chereau's direction, the production was widely celebrated as a success, and it confirmed the integrity and vision of Berg's total conception.

Impact of Event

For his first opera, *Wozzeck*, which premiered in 1925, Alban Berg reordered the scenes of Georg Büchner's tragedy *Woyzeck* (1836); when he began to compose *Lulu* in 1929, Berg had to cut an enormous amount of material, shorten the dialogue, and combine the two Lulu plays of Wedekind into one. The surprise is that Berg was able to compress Wedekind's vast and philosophically meaningful materials into seven long operatic scenes that critics generally regard as more coherent and dramatically effective than the Lulu plays. Although *Wozzeck* remains one of the monuments of twentieth century music, Berg's goals for *Lulu* were even greater. Critic George Perle has argued that "between *Wozzeck* and *Lulu* Berg's musical language was transformed."

As a student and disciple of the German composer Arnold Schoenberg, Berg was a proponent of Schoenberg's twelve-tone compositional theory, known as serialism. Schoenberg's theory challenged the traditional use of tonality in Western music by advocating the complete equality of twelve tones in the musical scale. The basic melodic strategy of the opera would be dictated by Berg's choice of tone row (a nonrepeating series of the twelve tones of the scale) to depict the character of Lulu. Berg's devotion to Schoenberg's ideal, though, was tempered by his own lyrical and melodic gifts. Although expressionism as an artistic style, whether in music or painting, is often accused of exaggerating the horrific and grotesque, Berg's musical expressionism shows a preference for the lyrical and romantic, resulting in the often-repeated critical putdown that Berg is the "twelve-tone Puccini."

Having made the basic decision that character would determine the musical structure, Berg then made the even more provocative decision that the tone row associated with Lulu (the twelve notes of the scale, used in equal measure) would determine the entire musical action of the opera. All the other characters in the opera are either lovers, victims, or attempted manipulators of Lulu. In her key Act II aria, usually called "Lied der Lulu," Lulu asserts her innocence, depicting herself as a natural woman who cannot help being universally desired.

Among the victims of Lulu are Doctor Goll, who succumbs to a heart attack; a painter, who slits his throat in a fit of jealousy; and Doctor Schon, the most important male figure in the opera, who is shot by Lulu with the very pistol with which he demands that Lulu kill herself. In the descending half of the opera, Lulu finds that even as a prostitute her charms are less and less in demand. By selling her sexual favors, she has repudiated her claim to be free and has set the pattern for her ultimate victimization when both she and her lesbian admirer, the Countess Geschwitz, are stabbed by Jack the Ripper. Lulu's death scream ("Todesschrei") and Geschwitz's subsequent tender death song ("Lulu, my angel") bring the opera to its conclusion.

That scream, like its famous visual counterpart, Edvard Munch's painting "The Cry," is practically the signature of the expressionist style, and the cry of Lulu, like the opera to which she lends her name, provides vivid articulation of the desire and suffering of mankind in the twentieth century. As Douglas Jarman notes in his study of Berg's music, Act III of *Lulu* is largely recapitulatory, bringing Lulu from her amoral innocence of the first act to her final degradation and death at the hands of

Jack the Ripper. Jarman's thesis, that Berg's obsession with symmetry in his com-position reflects his pessimistic assessment of life (with characters who are trapped in a cycle of ascent invariably followed by descent and death), perhaps offers a hint at the true motivation of Helene Berg: By preventing the release of Act III, she could keep hidden the bleak pessimism of Berg's vision of life. The complete version of the opera perhaps reveals Berg's indebtedness to one of his philosophical heroes, Friedrich Nietzsche. According to Nietzsche's theory of "eternal return," mankind is doomed to enact endless repetitions of the events of life; in this light, the actions of Lulu, her lovers, and her victims are irrelevant. All one can do, argued Nietzsche, is affirm life, for all its pain and problems; and the affirmation of life, finally, is what *Lulu* glowingly provides. The opera has increasingly been recognized as one of the towering artistic masterpieces of the century, and even as serialism has declined in prestige, popular appreciation of *Lulu* has continued to grow.

Bibliography

Carner, Mosco. *Alban Berg: The Man and the Work.* London: Duckworth, 1975. Solid musical and dramatic study, with Freudian hints, by the most prominent student of Giacomo Puccini. The dissimilar composers, near-contemporaries, shared only the determination to depict sexual neuroses on the operatic stage.

Jarman, Douglas. *The Music of Alban Berg.* London: Faber, 1979. Argues that Berg's music reflects his deeply pessimistic, Schopenhauerian view of life.

Perle, George. *Lulu.* Vol. 2 in *The Operas of Alban Berg.* Berkeley: University of California Press, 1985. An exhaustive study of Berg's two operas, by the Ameri-can composer and musicologist who argued tirelessly for the release of the third act of *Lulu.*

_____. *Serial Composition and Atonality.* 2d ed. Berkeley: University of California Press, 1969. The best treatment of twelve-tone technique, a topic that, however, is likely to remain chillingly forbidding to the layman.

Reich, Willi. *Alban Berg.* Reprint. New York: Vienna House, 1974. A useful intro-ductory study of the life and works of Berg, by a Viennese friend.

Rosen, Charles. *Arnold Schoenberg.* New York: Viking Press, 1975. A lucid and sympathetic introduction to the seminal figure in musical expressionism and seri-alism.

Schmidgall, Gary. *Literature as Opera.* New York: Oxford University Press, 1977. A provocative study of the literary sources of great operas. Claims that the difficult playwrights Büchner and Wedekind find their ideal musical interpreter in Berg; Berg's style is marked by "rootlessness and flexibility, extreme distortion and nervous tension."

Ulrich, Homer, and Paul A. Pisk. *A History of Music and Musical Style.* New York: Harcourt Brace Jovanovich, 1963. Written at the height of serialist phase among American academic composers; a relatively painless introduction.

Byron Nelson

Cross-References

Schoenberg Breaks with Tonality (1908), p. 193; Webern's *Six Pieces for Large Orchestra* Premieres in Vienna (1913), p. 367; *The Rite of Spring* Stuns Audiences (1913), p. 373; Schoenberg Develops His Twelve-Tone System (1921), p. 528; Berg's *Wozzeck* Premieres in Berlin (1925), p. 680.

GREAT EVENTS
FROM
HISTORY II

CHRONOLOGICAL LIST OF EVENTS

VOLUME I

VOLUME II

VOLUME III

VOLUME IV